P9-AGA-258

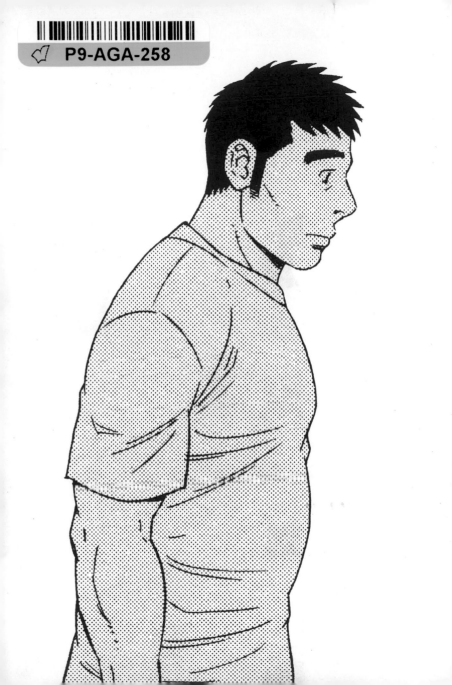

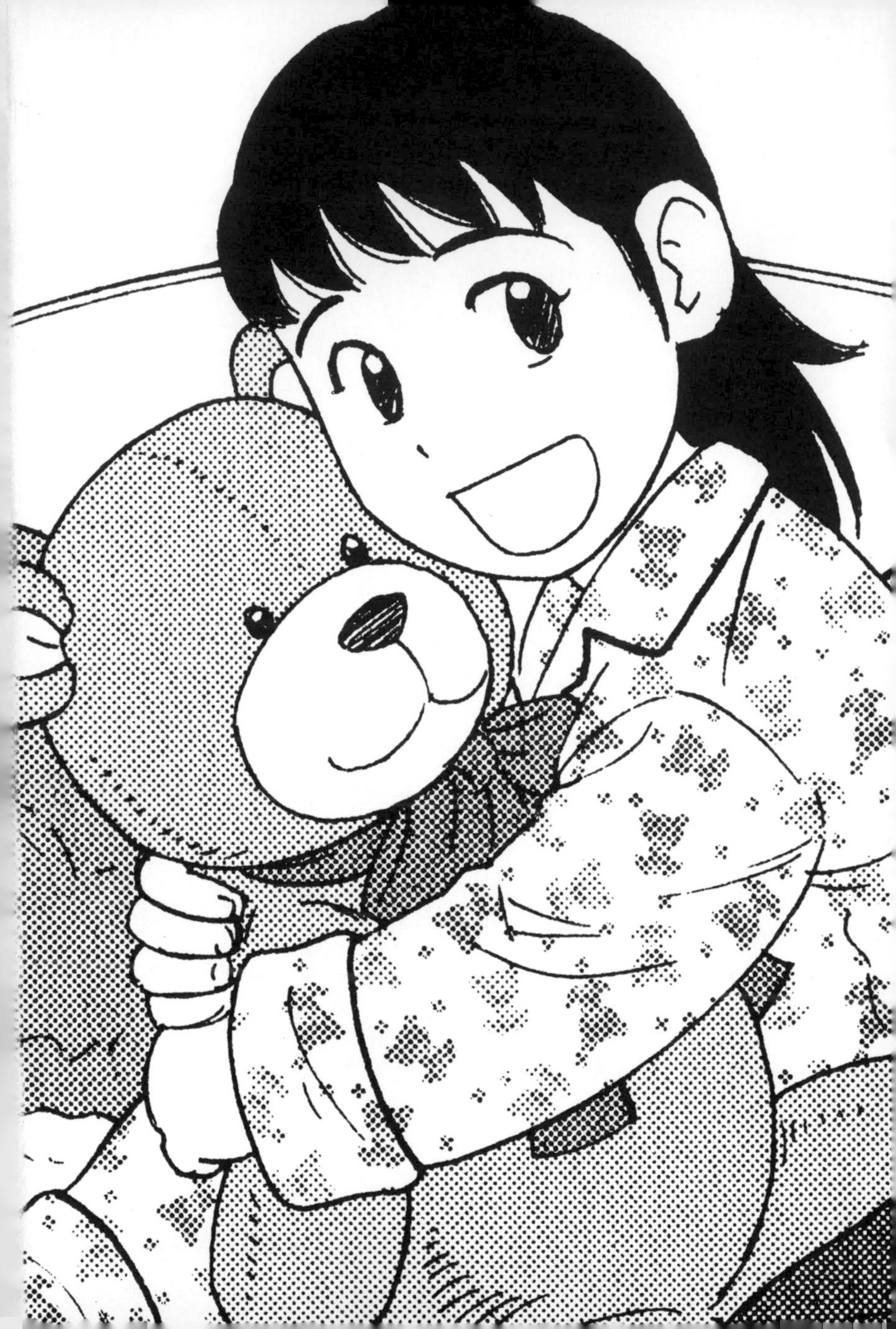

MY BROTHER'S HUSBAND

VOLUME 2

GENGOROH TAGAME

TRANSLATED FROM THE JAPANESE BY ANNE ISHII

PANTHEON BOOKS, NEW YORK

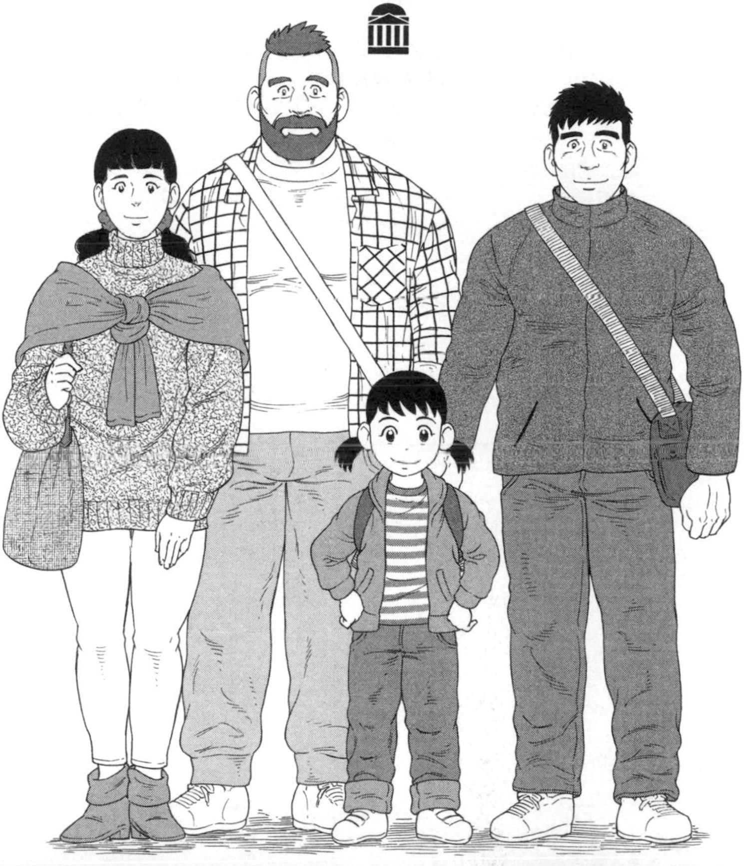

THIS IS A WORK OF FICTION. NAMES, CHARACTERS, PLACES, AND INCIDENTS EITHER ARE
THE PRODUCT OF THE AUTHOR'S IMAGINATION OR ARE USED FICTITIOUSLY. ANY RESEMBLANCE
TO ACTUAL PERSONS, LIVING OR DEAD, EVENTS, OR LOCALES IS ENTIRELY COINCIDENTAL.

TRANSLATION COPYRIGHT © 2018 BY ANNE ISHII

ALL RIGHTS RESERVED. PUBLISHED IN THE UNITED STATES BY PANTHEON BOOKS, A DIVISION
OF PENGUIN RANDOM HOUSE LLC, NEW YORK, AND DISTRIBUTED IN CANADA BY RANDOM HOUSE
OF CANADA, A DIVISION OF PENGUIN RANDOM HOUSE CANADA LIMITED, TORONTO. ORIGINALLY
PUBLISHED IN JAPAN AS *OTŌTO NO OTTO* BY FUTABASHA PUBLISHERS LTD., TOKYO, IN 2016.
COPYRIGHT © 2016 BY GENGOROH TAGAME. ALL RIGHTS RESERVED. THIS ENGLISH-LANGUAGE
EDITION PUBLISHED BY ARRANGEMENT WITH FUTABASHA PUBLISHERS LTD., TOKYO.

PANTHEON BOOKS AND COLOPHON ARE REGISTERED TRADEMARKS OF
PENGUIN RANDOM HOUSE LLC.

LIBRARY OF CONGRESS CATALOGING-IN-PUBLICATION DATA
NAMES: TAGAME, GENGOROH, [DATE] AUTHOR, ARTIST. ISHII, ANNE, TRANSLATOR.
TITLE: MY BROTHER'S HUSBAND / GENGOROH TAGAME ; TRANSLATED BY ANNE ISHII.
OTHER TITLES: OTOUTO NO OTTO. ENGLISH.
DESCRIPTION: FIRST AMERICAN EDITION. NEW YORK : PANTHEON, 2018.
IDENTIFIERS: LCCN 2016047082 (PRINT). LCCN 2016050241 (EBOOK).
ISBN 9781101871539 (V. 2 : HARDCOVER). ISBN 9781101871546 (EBOOK).
SUBJECTS: LCSH: GAY MEN--JAPAN--COMIC BOOKS, STRIPS, ETC. GRAPHIC NOVELS.
BISAC: FICTION/FAMILY LIFE. COMICS & GRAPHIC NOVELS/LITERARY.
COMICS & GRAPHIC NOVELS/MANGA/GAY & LESBIAN.
CLASSIFICATION: LCC PN6790.J33 T255613 2017 (PRINT).
LCC PN6790.J33 (EBOOK). DDC 741.5/952--DC23
LC RECORD AVAILABLE AT LCCN.LOC.GOV/2016047082

WWW.PANTHEONBOOKS.COM

JACKET AND CASE ILLUSTRATION BY GENGOROH TAGAME
JACKET AND CASE DESIGN BY CHIP KIDD
PRODUCTION ASSISTANCE BY JOHN KURAMOTO

PRINTED IN THE UNITED STATES OF AMERICA
FIRST AMERICAN EDITION

9 8 7 6 5 4 3 2 1

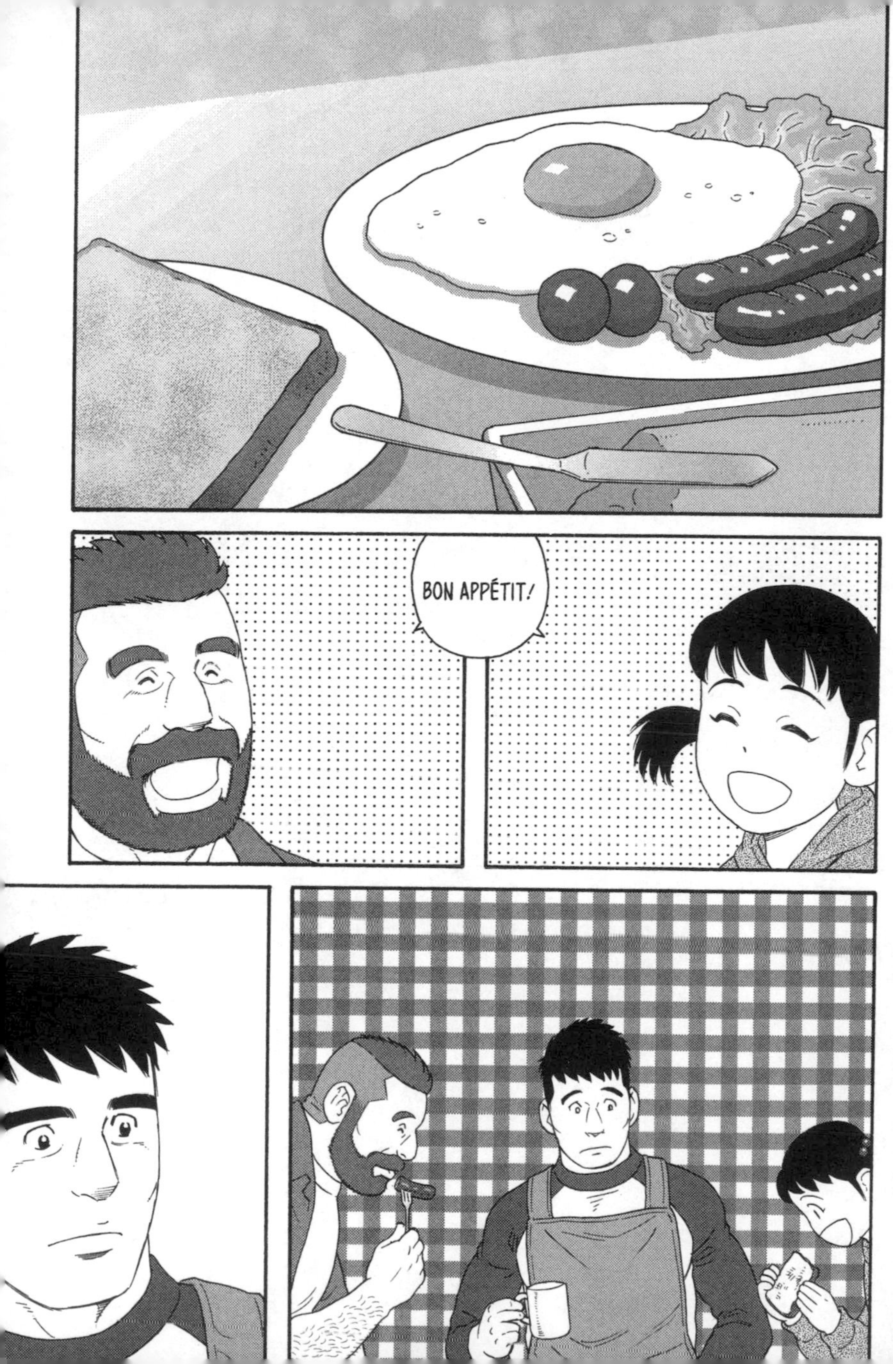
BON APPÉTIT!

CHAPTER FIFTEEN

WORRIED

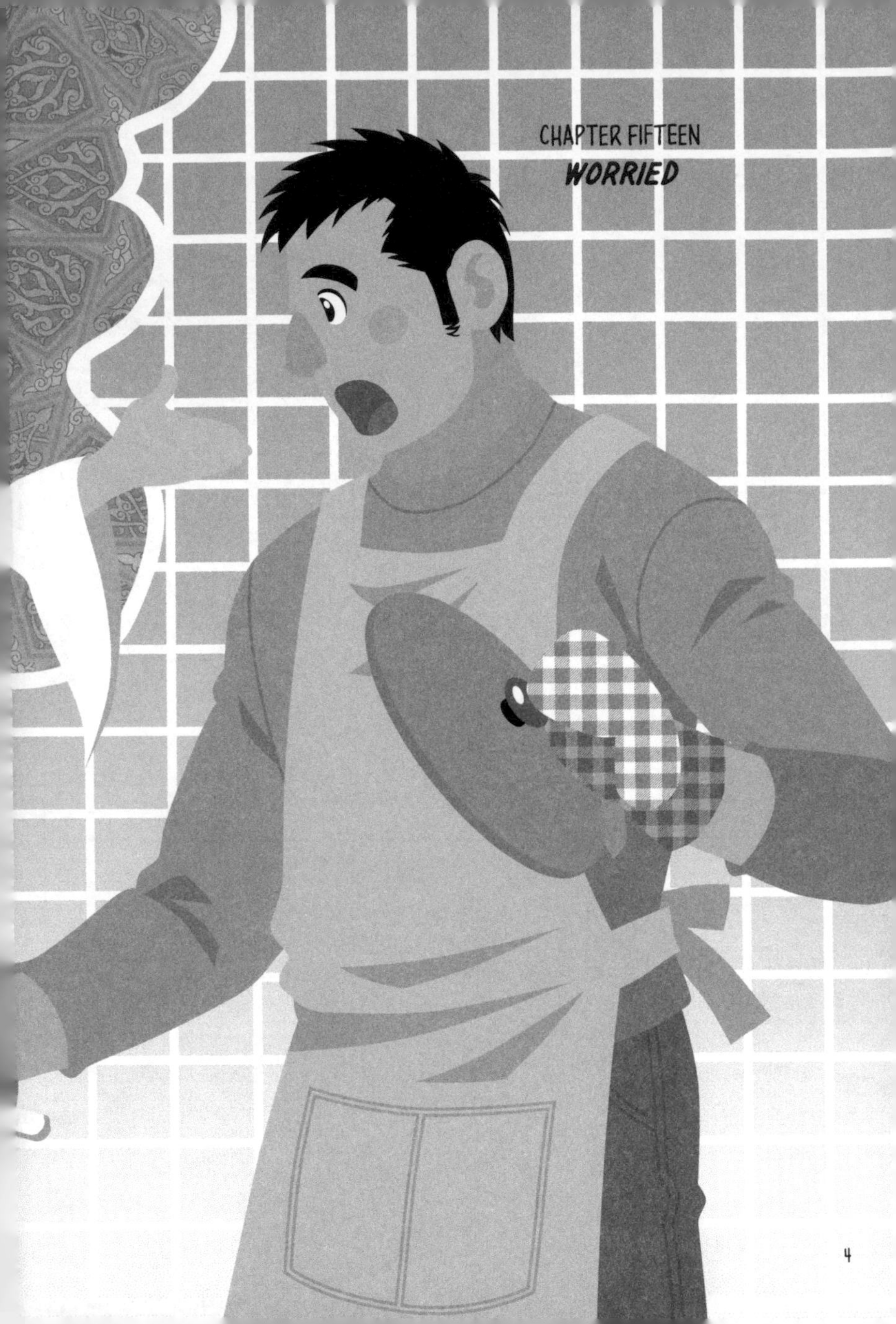

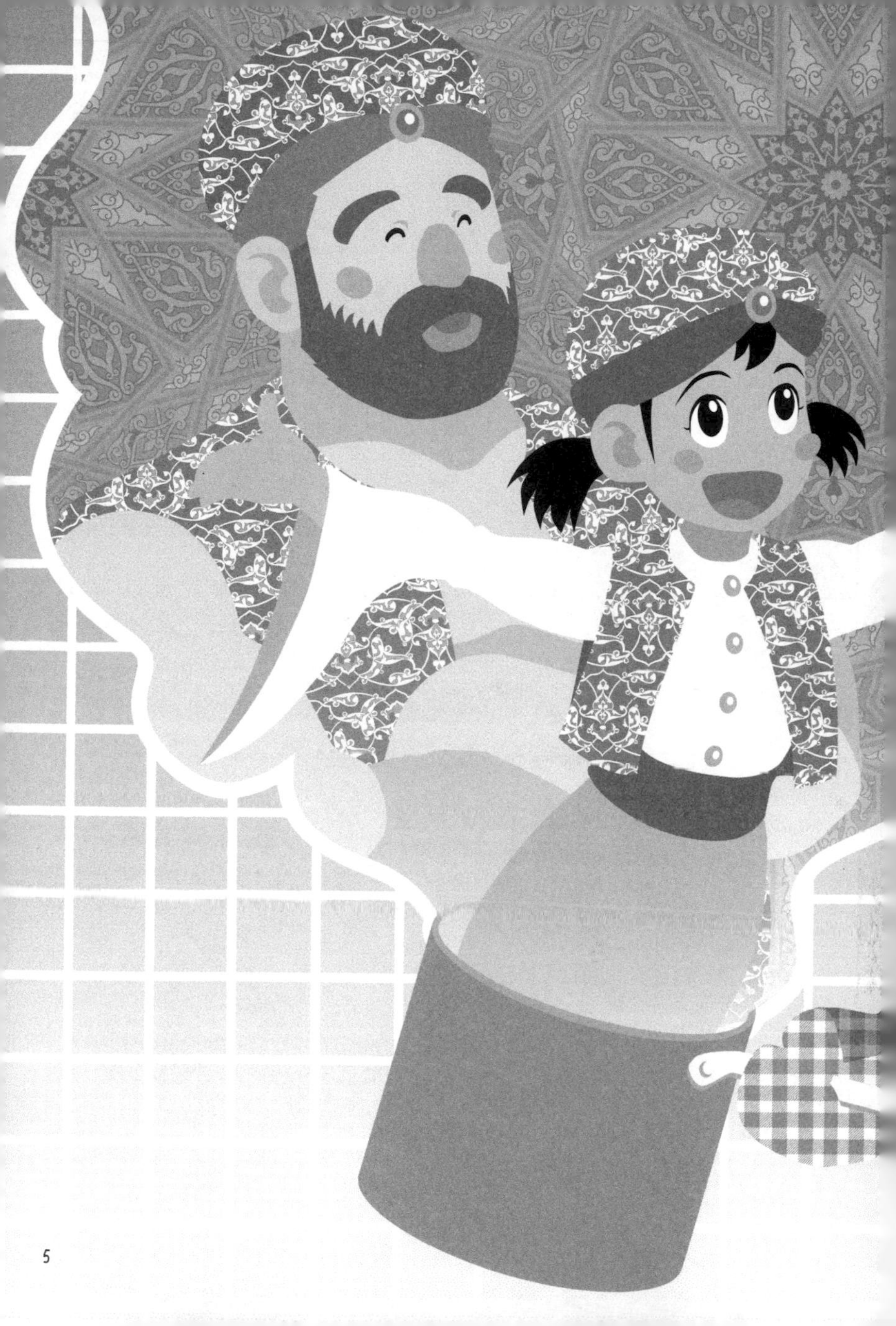

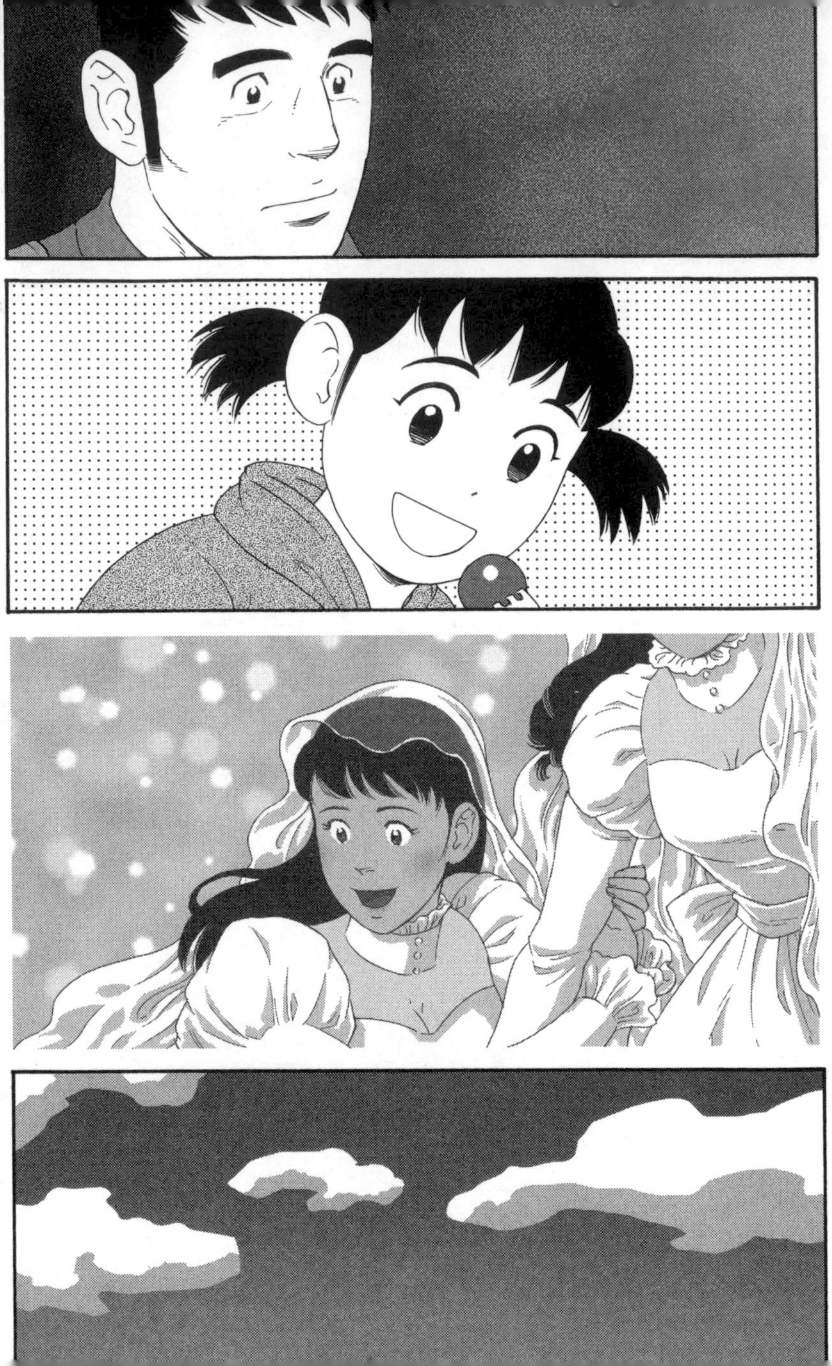

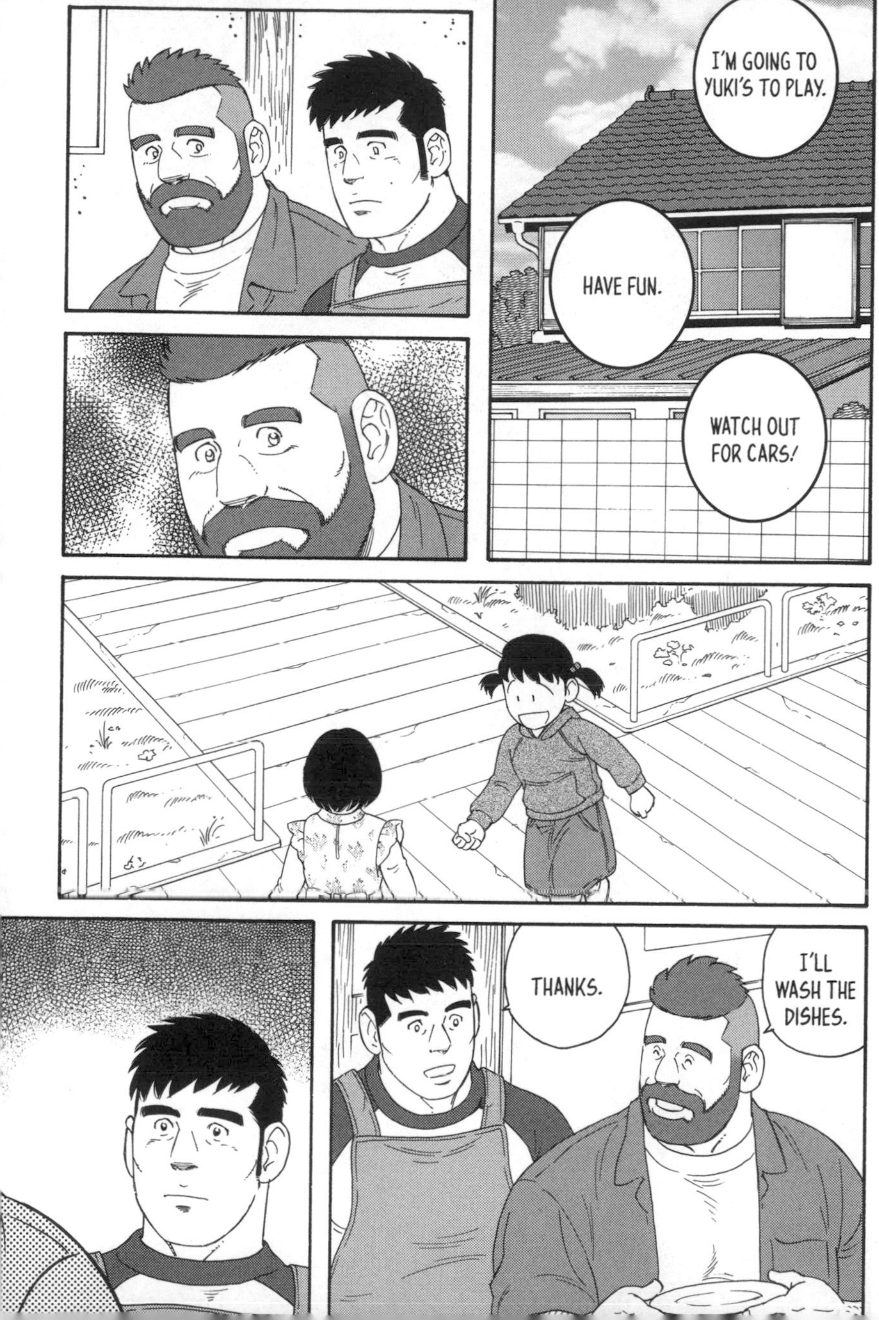
I'M GOING TO YUKI'S TO PLAY.
HAVE FUN.
WATCH OUT FOR CARS!
I'LL WASH THE DISHES.
THANKS.

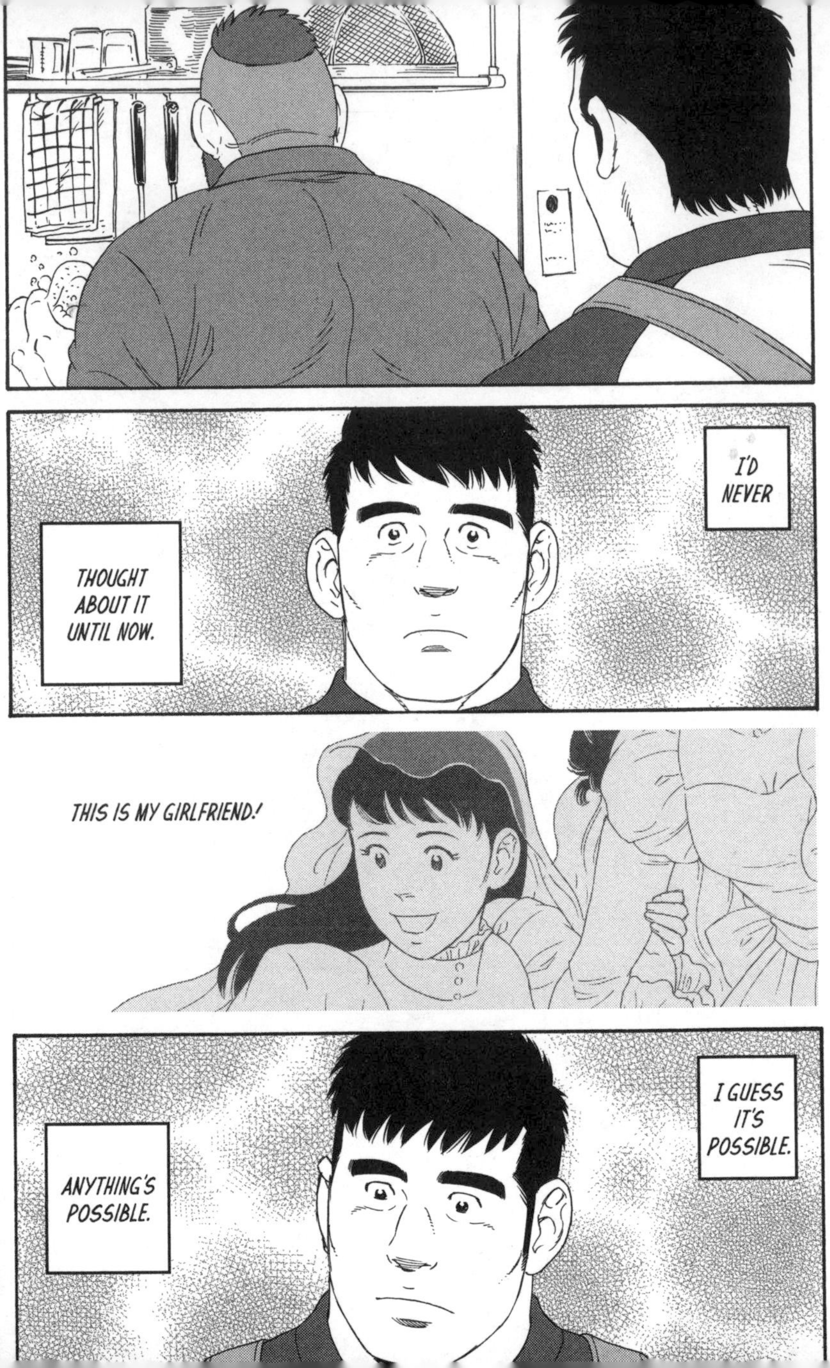
I'D NEVER
THOUGHT ABOUT IT UNTIL NOW.
THIS IS MY GIRLFRIEND!
I GUESS IT'S POSSIBLE.
ANYTHING'S POSSIBLE.

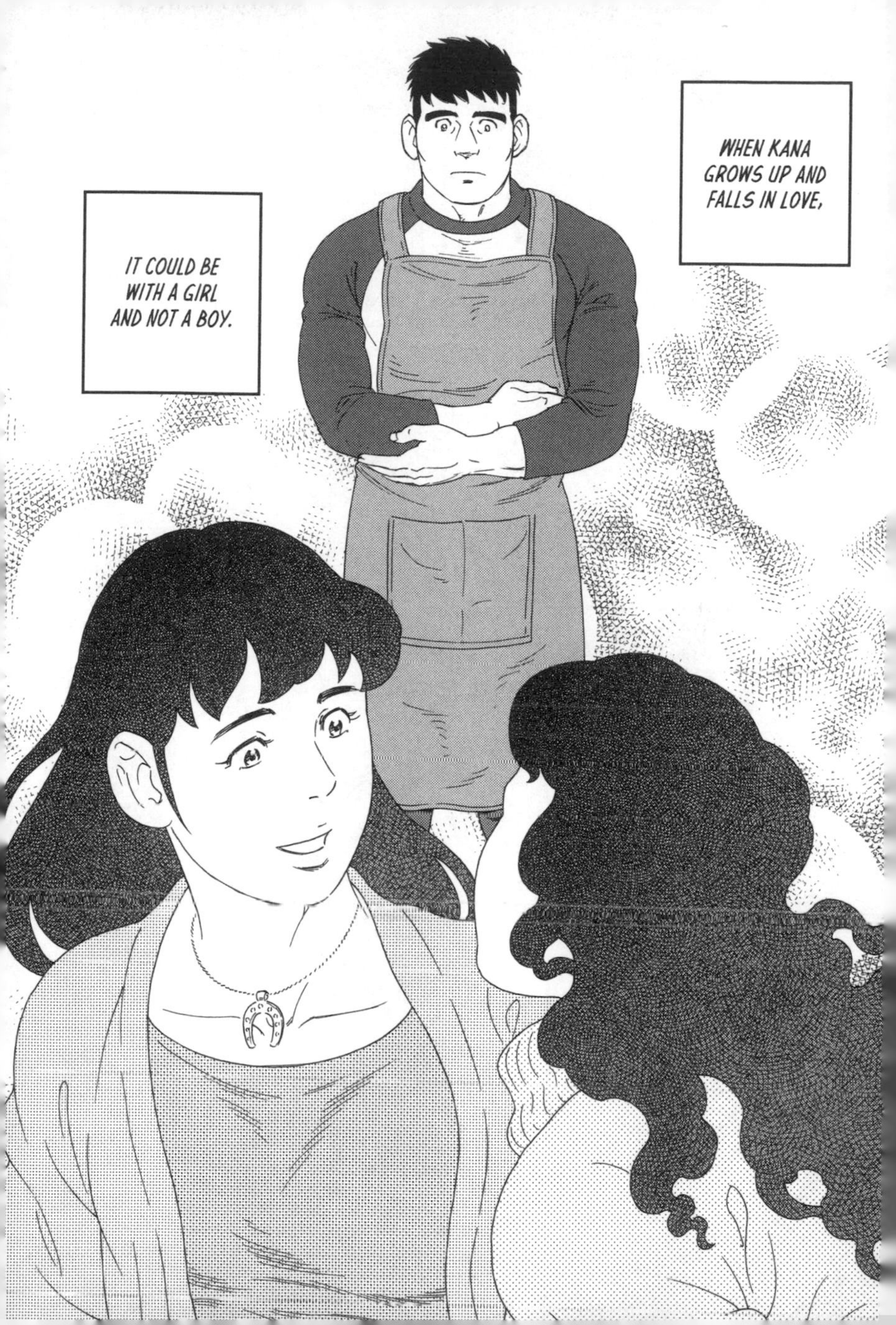
WHEN KANA GROWS UP AND FALLS IN LOVE,
IT COULD BE WITH A GIRL AND NOT A BOY.

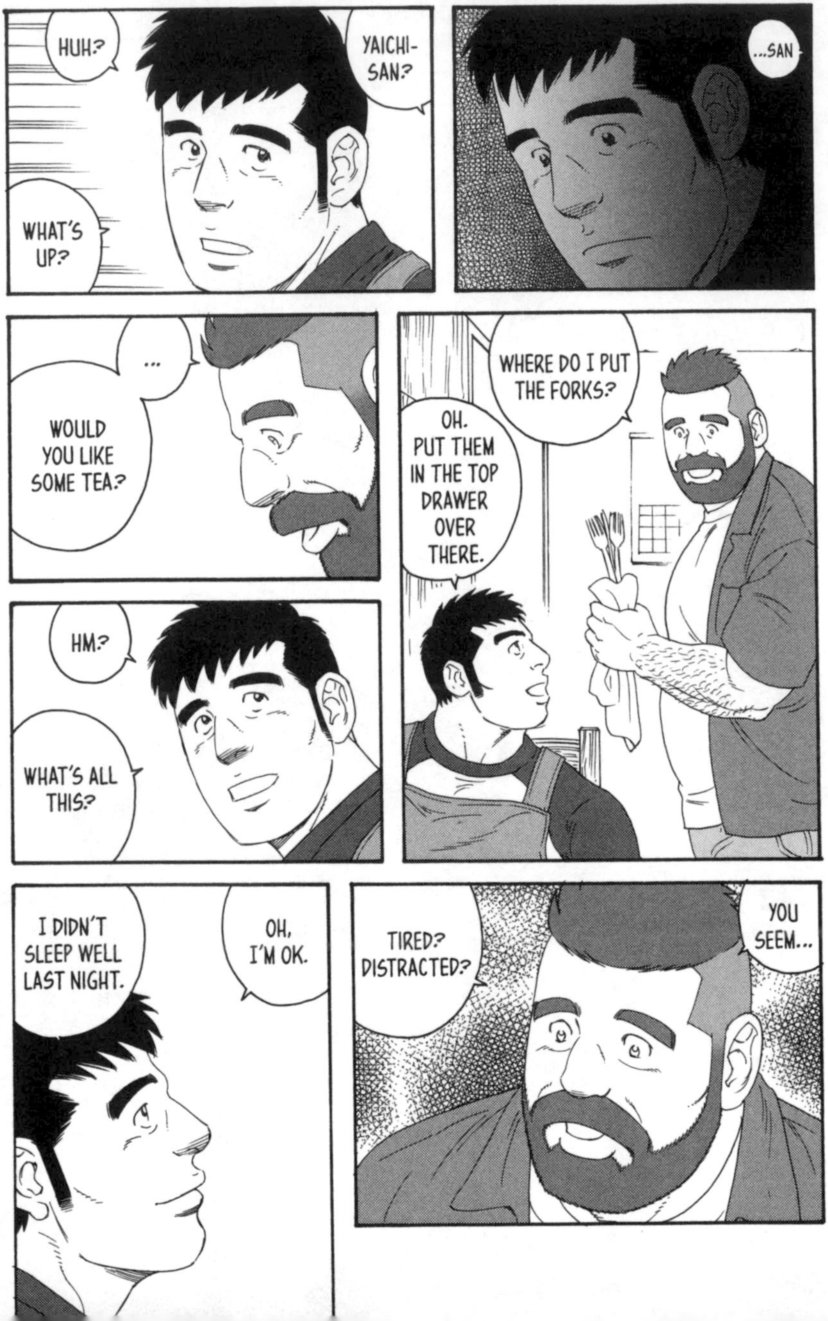
...SAN
YAICHI-SAN?
HUH?
WHAT'S UP?
WHERE DO I PUT THE FORKS?
OH. PUT THEM IN THE TOP DRAWER OVER THERE.
...
WOULD YOU LIKE SOME TEA?
HM?
WHAT'S ALL THIS?
YOU SEEM...
TIRED? DISTRACTED?
OH, I'M OK.
I DIDN'T SLEEP WELL LAST NIGHT.

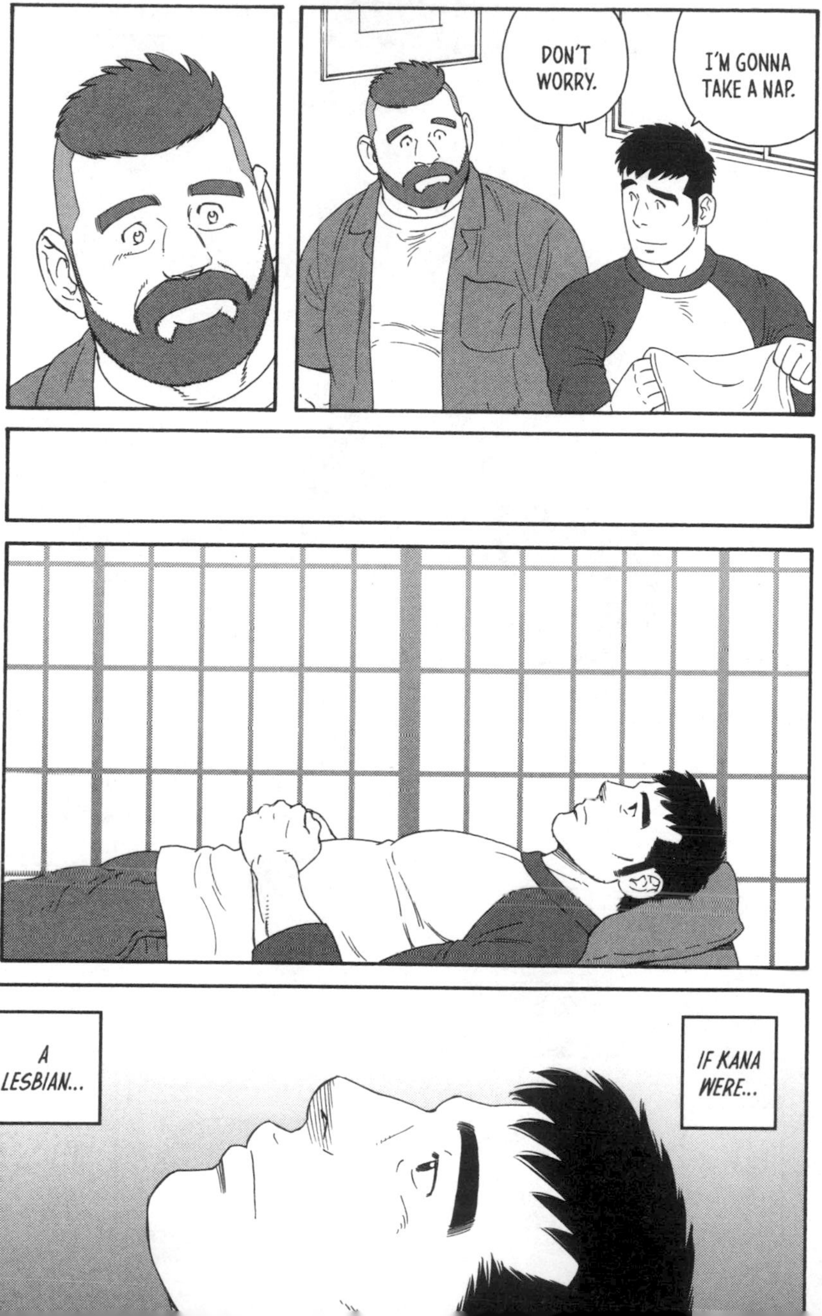
I'M GONNA TAKE A NAP.
DON'T WORRY.
IF KANA WERE...
A LESBIAN...

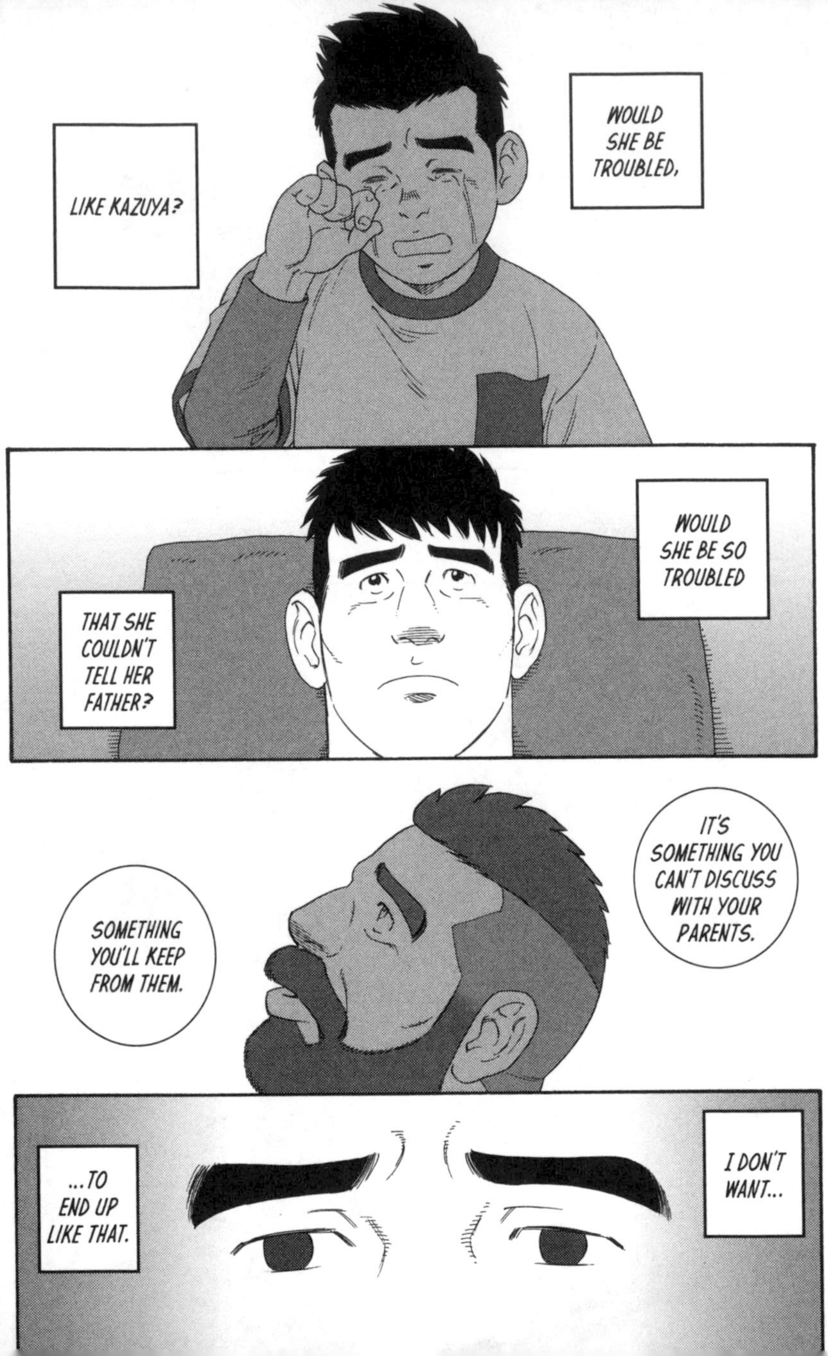
WOULD SHE BE TROUBLED,
LIKE KAZUYA?
WOULD SHE BE SO TROUBLED
THAT SHE COULDN'T TELL HER FATHER?
IT'S SOMETHING YOU CAN'T DISCUSS WITH YOUR PARENTS.
SOMETHING YOU'LL KEEP FROM THEM.
I DON'T WANT...
...TO END UP LIKE THAT.

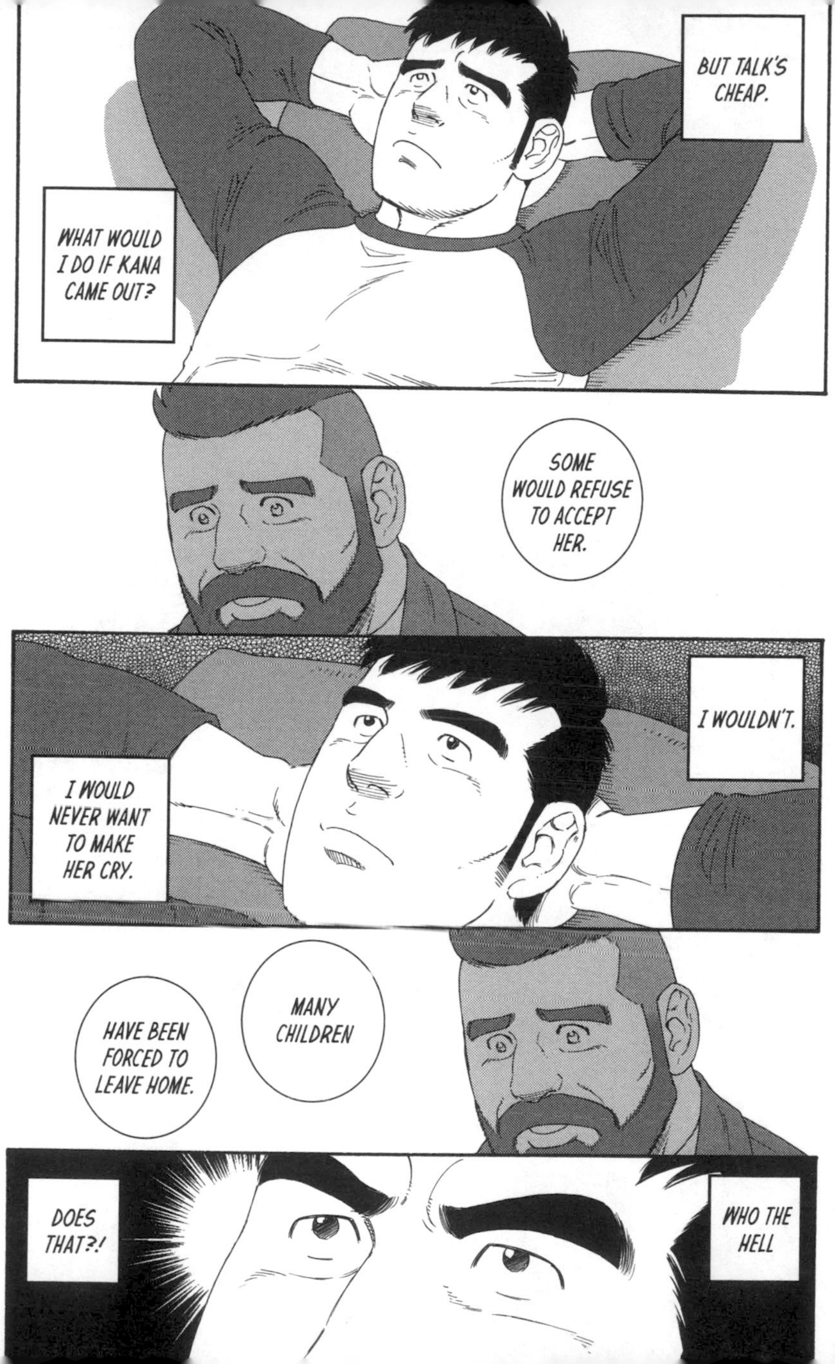
BUT TALK'S CHEAP.
WHAT WOULD I DO IF KANA CAME OUT?
SOME WOULD REFUSE TO ACCEPT HER.
I WOULDN'T.
I WOULD NEVER WANT TO MAKE HER CRY.
MANY CHILDREN
HAVE BEEN FORCED TO LEAVE HOME.
WHO THE HELL
DOES THAT?!

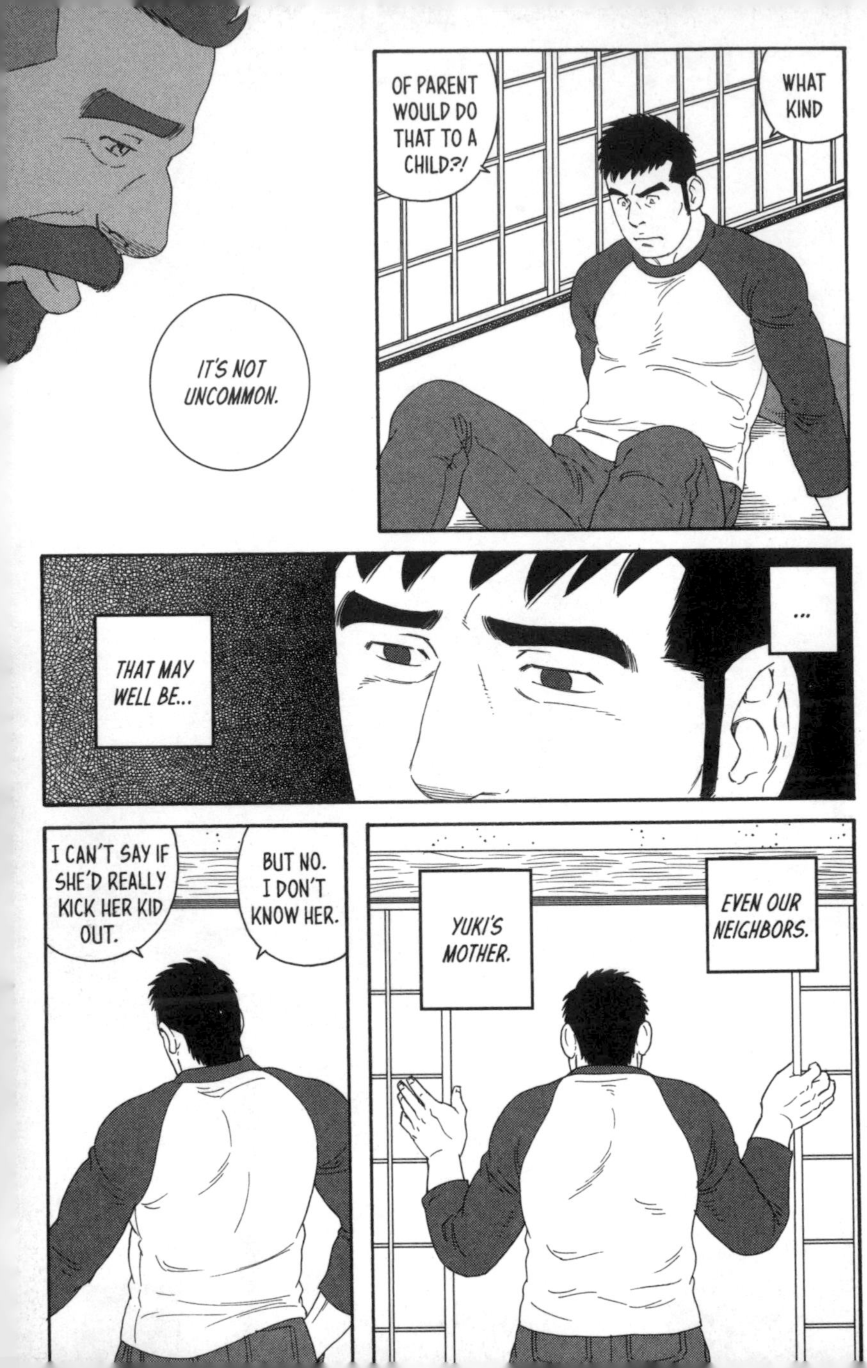
WHAT KIND
OF PARENT WOULD DO THAT TO A CHILD?!
IT'S NOT UNCOMMON.
...
THAT MAY WELL BE...
EVEN OUR NEIGHBORS.
YUKI'S MOTHER.
BUT NO. I DON'T KNOW HER.
I CAN'T SAY IF SHE'D REALLY KICK HER KID OUT.

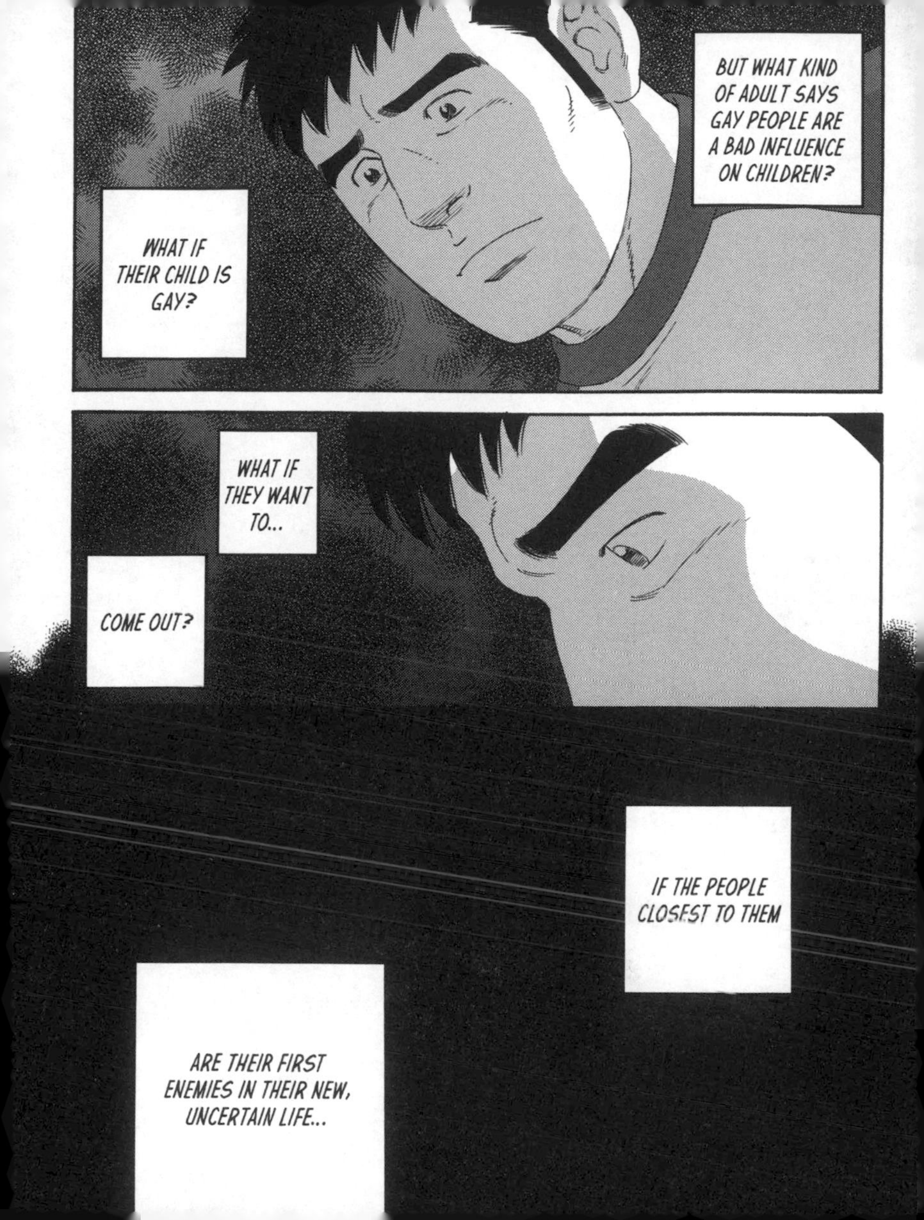
BUT WHAT KIND OF ADULT SAYS GAY PEOPLE ARE A BAD INFLUENCE ON CHILDREN?
WHAT IF THEIR CHILD IS GAY?
WHAT IF THEY WANT TO...
COME OUT?
IF THE PEOPLE CLOSEST TO THEM
ARE THEIR FIRST ENEMIES IN THEIR NEW, UNCERTAIN LIFE...

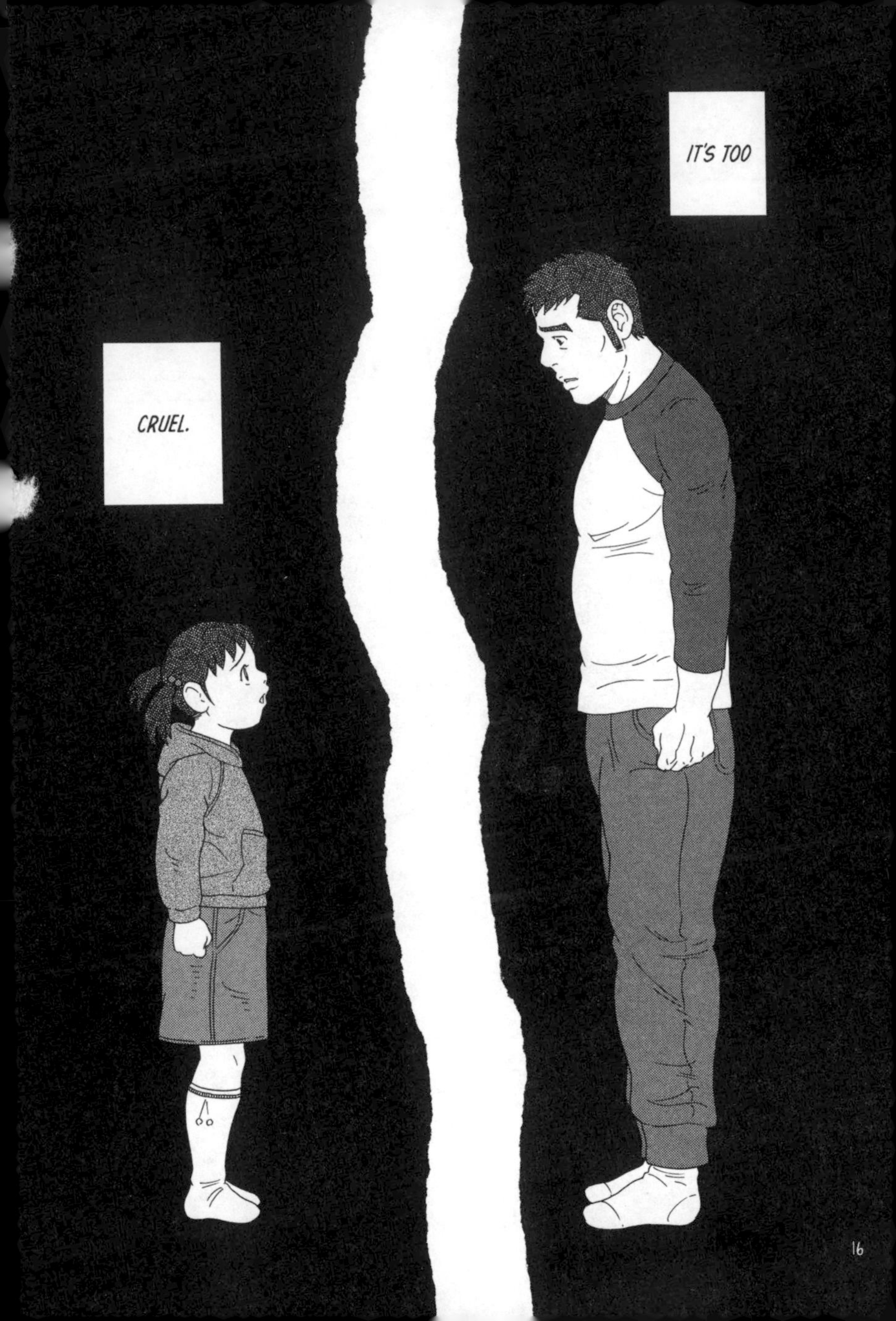
IT'S TOO
CRUEL.

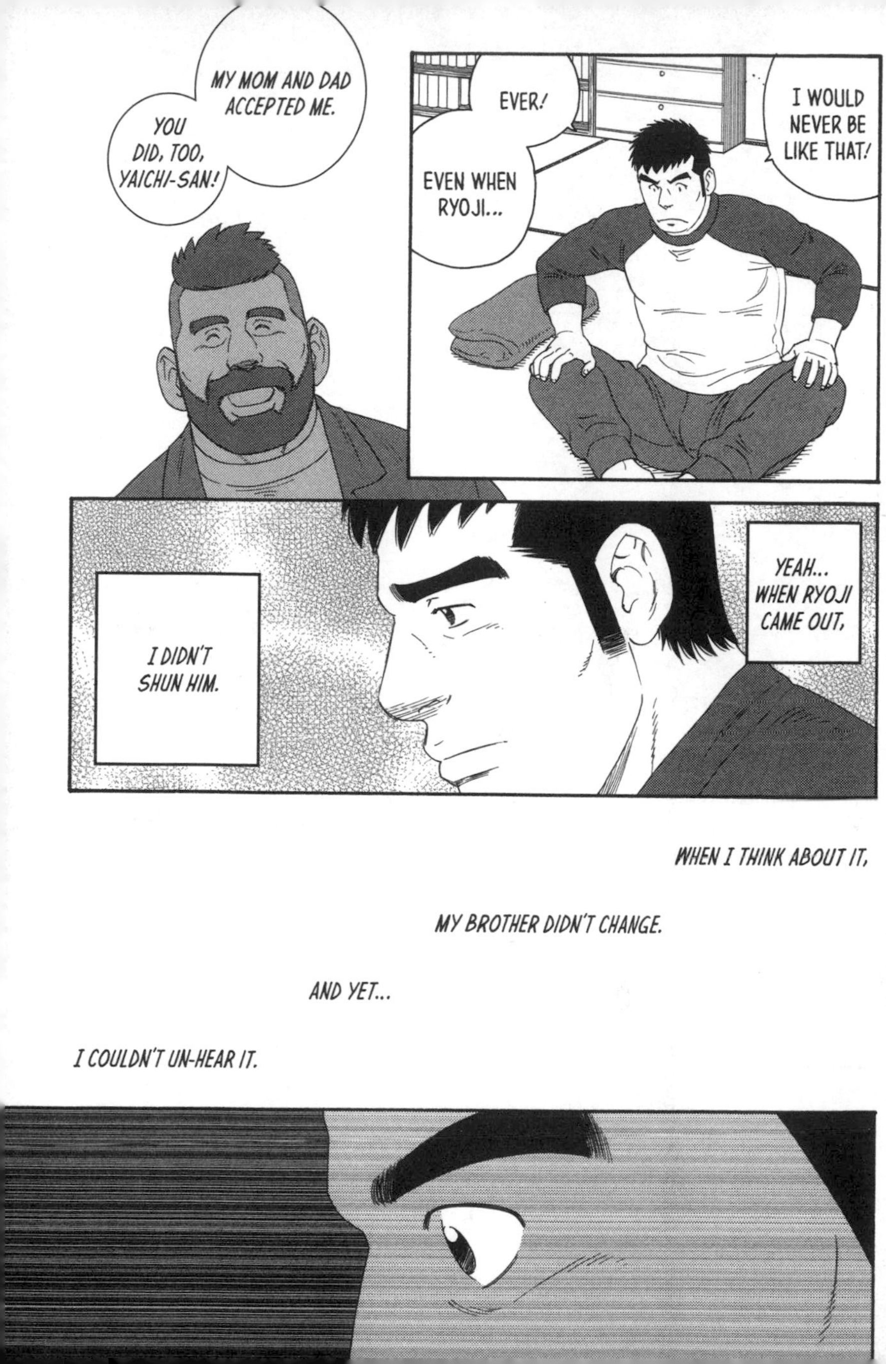
I WOULD NEVER BE LIKE THAT!
EVER!
EVEN WHEN RYOJI...
MY MOM AND DAD ACCEPTED ME.
YOU DID, TOO, YAICHI-SAN!
YEAH... WHEN RYOJI CAME OUT,
I DIDN'T SHUN HIM.
WHEN I THINK ABOUT IT,
MY BROTHER DIDN'T CHANGE.
AND YET...
I COULDN'T UN-HEAR IT.

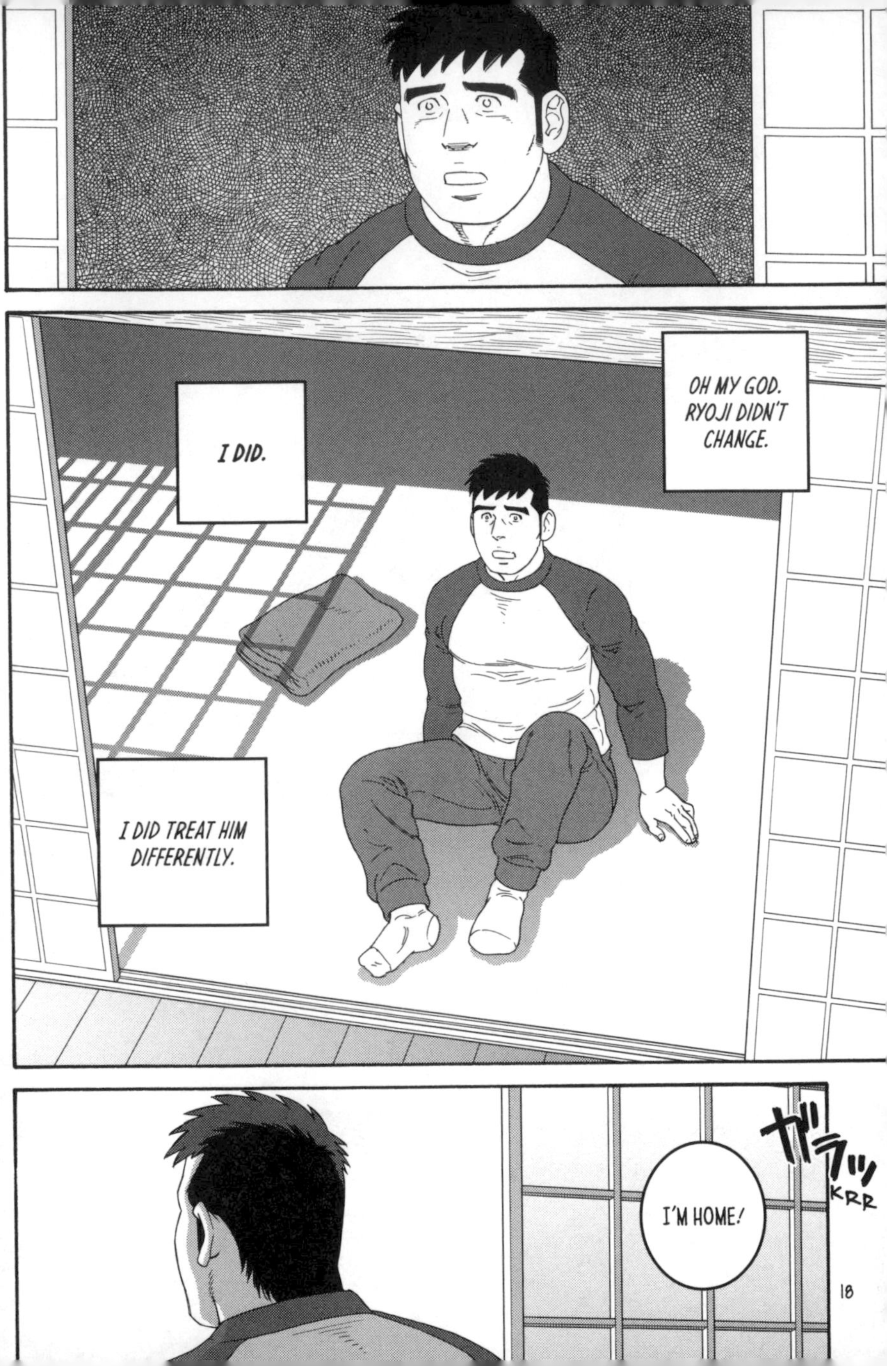
OH MY GOD. RYOJI DIDN'T CHANGE.
I DID.
I DID TREAT HIM DIFFERENTLY.
ガラッ
KRR
I'M HOME!

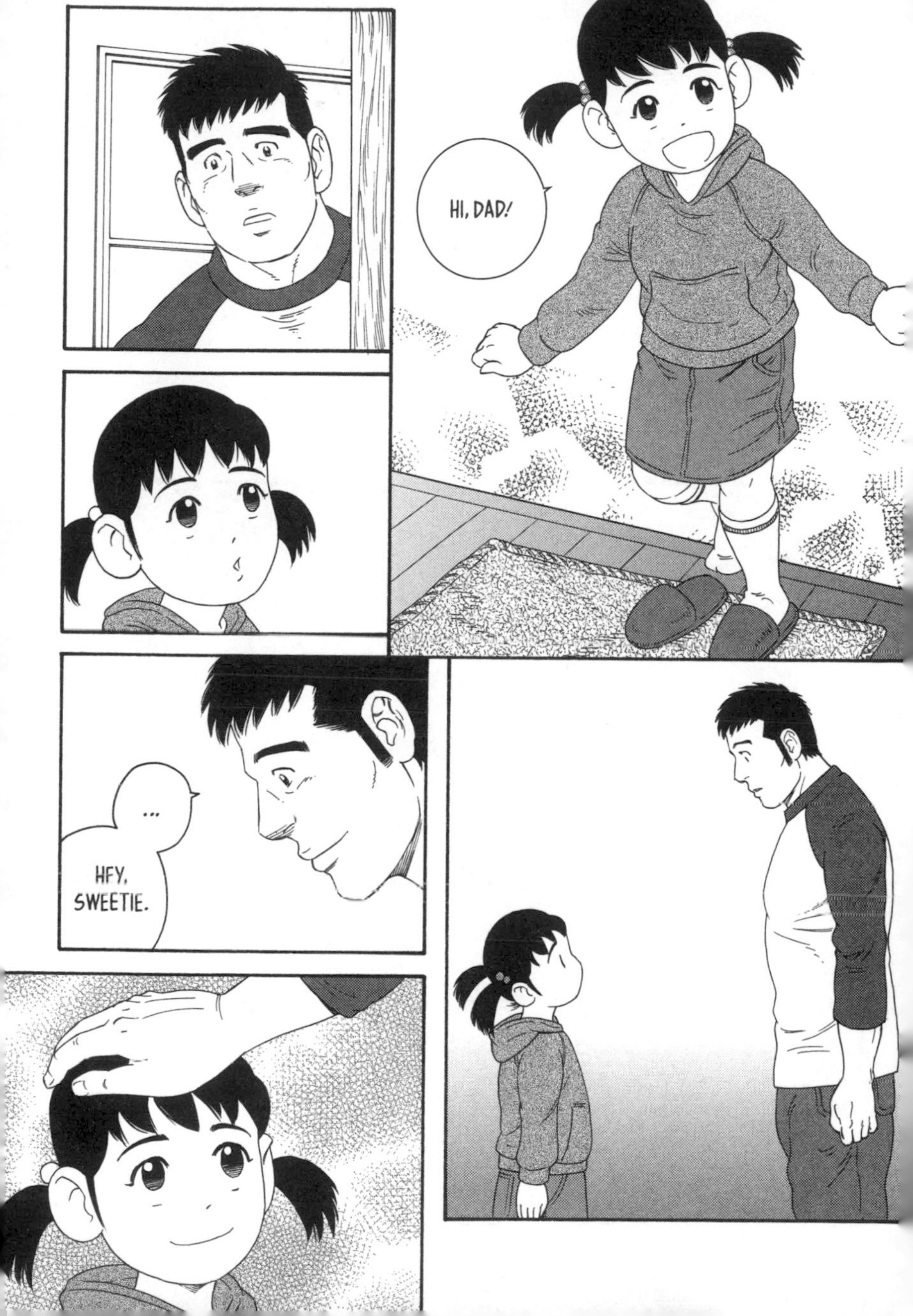
HI, DAD!
...
HEY, SWEETIE.

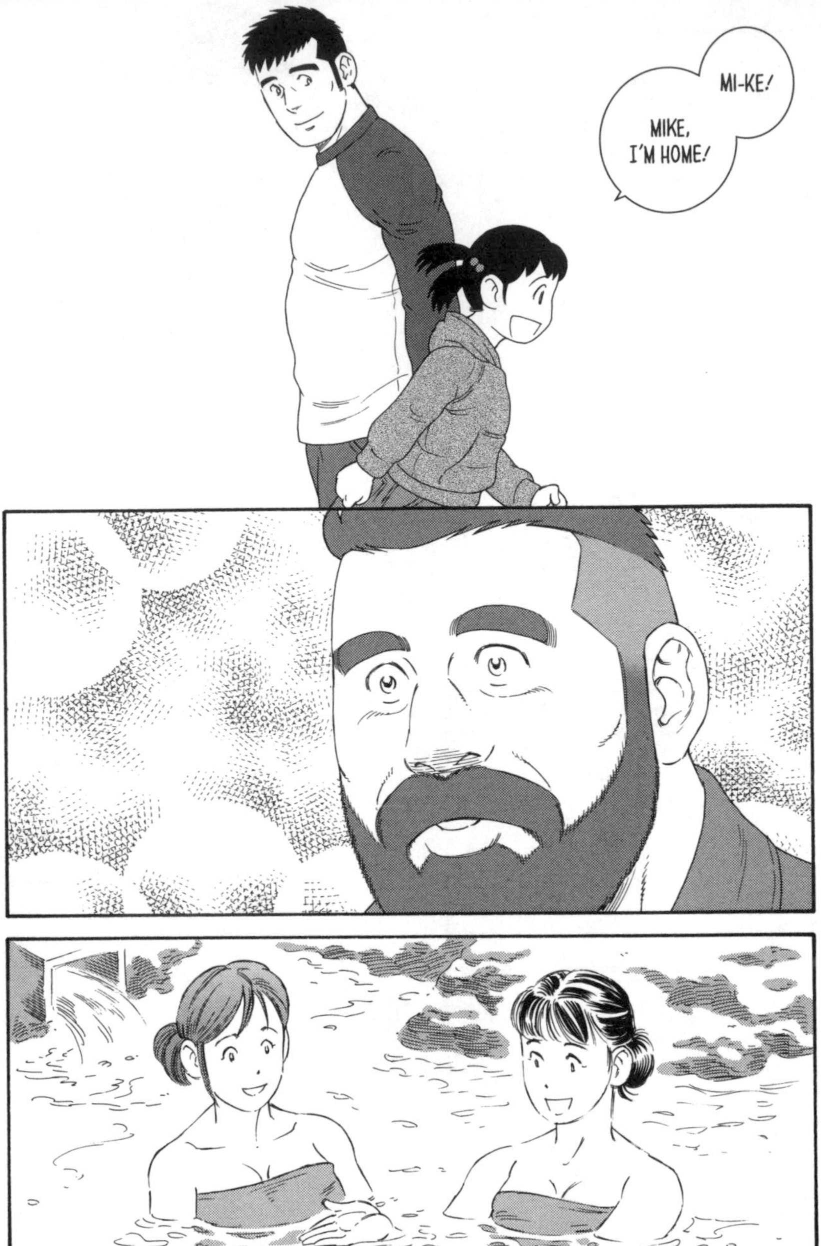
MI-KE!
MIKE, I'M HOME!

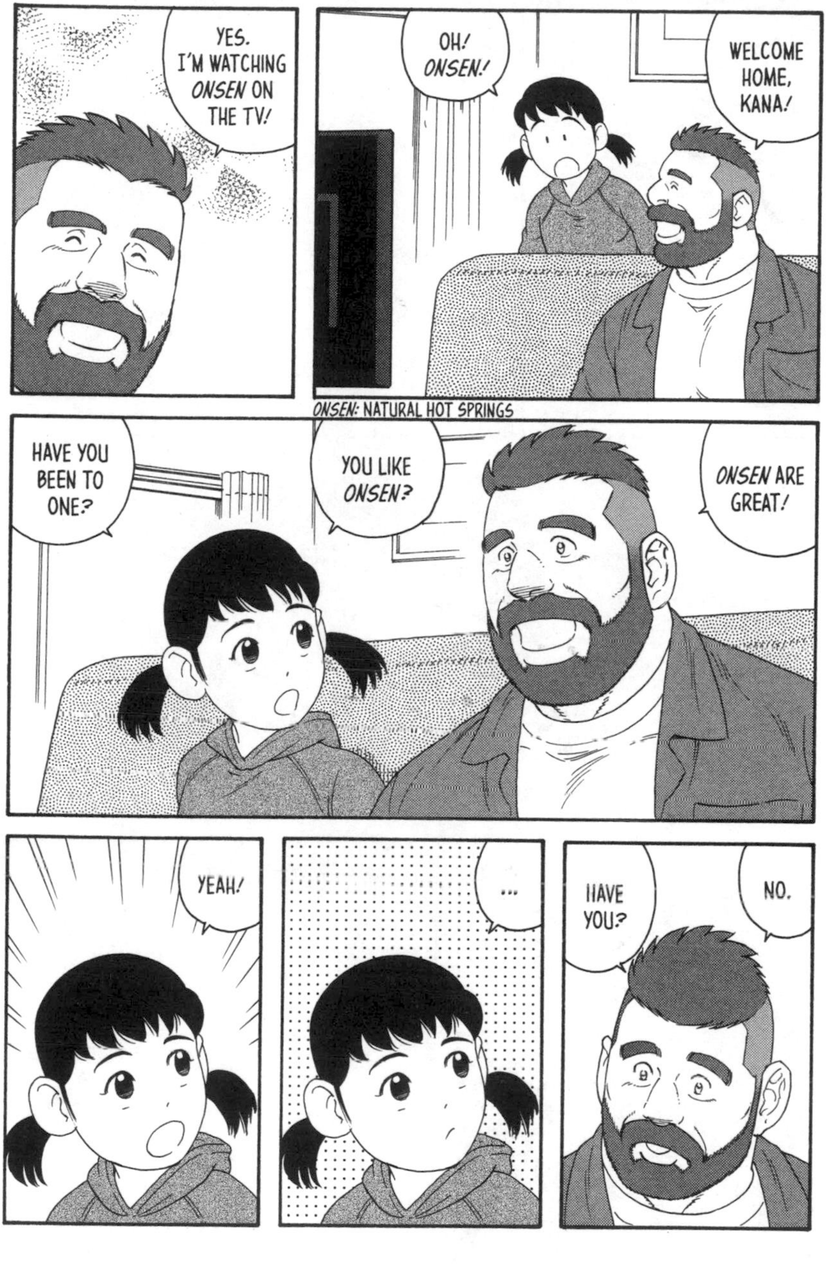
WELCOME HOME, KANA!
OH! *ONSEN!*
YES. I'M WATCHING *ONSEN* ON THE TV!
ONSEN: NATURAL HOT SPRINGS
ONSEN ARE GREAT!
YOU LIKE *ONSEN?*
HAVE YOU BEEN TO ONE?
NO.
HAVE YOU?
...
YEAH!

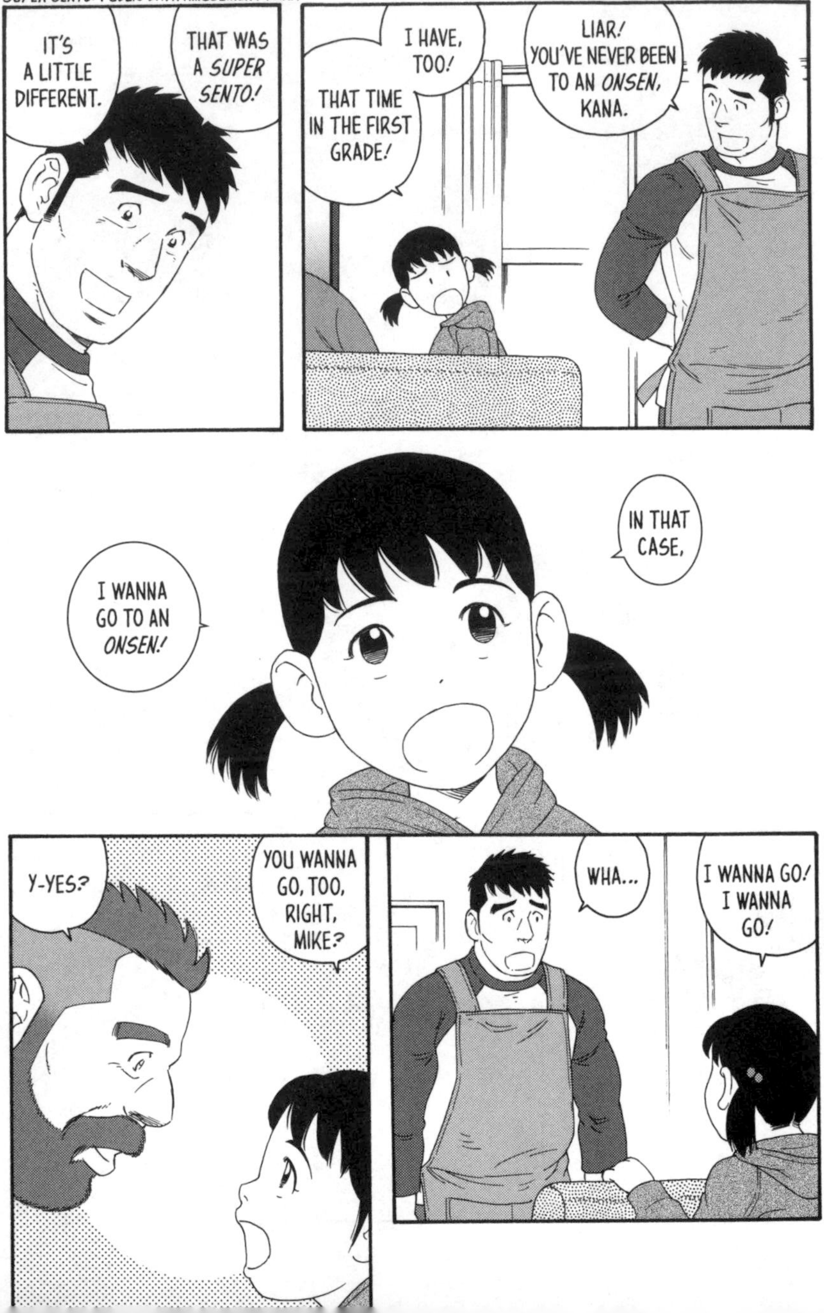
LIAR! YOU'VE NEVER BEEN TO AN *ONSEN,* KANA.
I HAVE, TOO!
THAT TIME IN THE FIRST GRADE!
THAT WAS A *SUPER SENTO!*
IT'S A LITTLE DIFFERENT.
IN THAT CASE,
I WANNA GO TO AN *ONSEN!*
I WANNA GO! I WANNA GO!
WHA...
YOU WANNA GO, TOO, RIGHT, MIKE?
Y-YES?

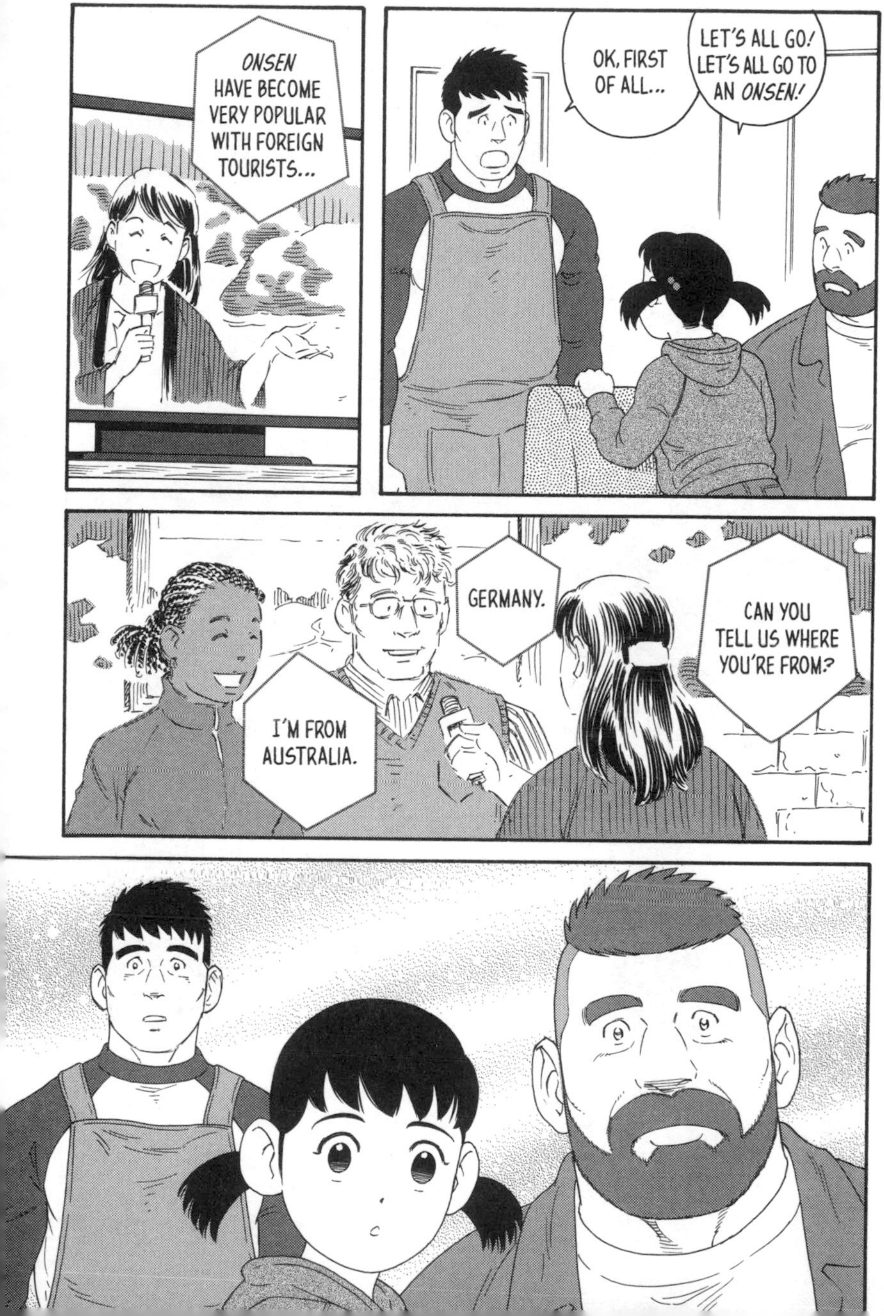
LET'S ALL GO! LET'S ALL GO TO AN *ONSEN!*
OK, FIRST OF ALL...
ONSEN HAVE BECOME VERY POPULAR WITH FOREIGN TOURISTS...
CAN YOU TELL US WHERE YOU'RE FROM?
GERMANY.
I'M FROM AUSTRALIA.

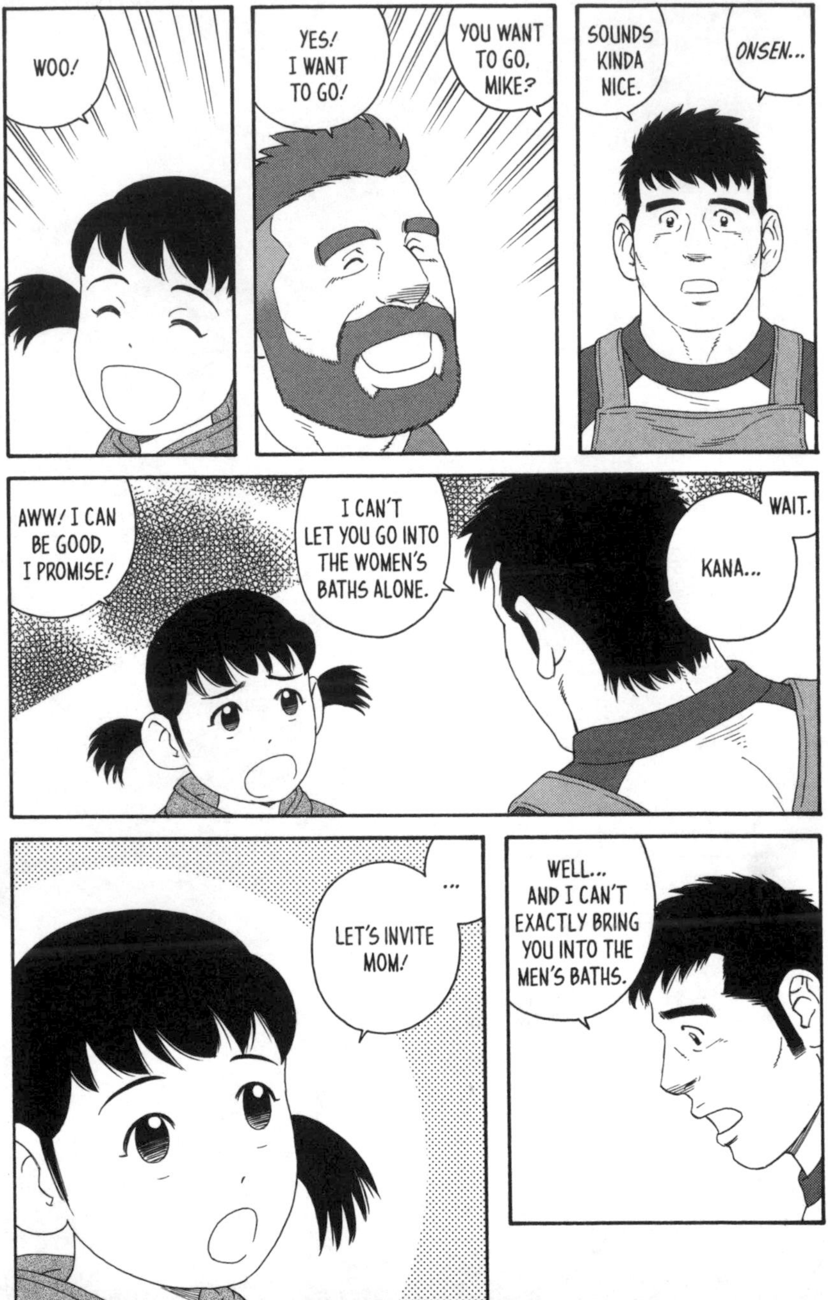
ONSEN...
SOUNDS KINDA NICE.
YOU WANT TO GO, MIKE?
YES! I WANT TO GO!
WOO!
WAIT.
KANA...
I CAN'T LET YOU GO INTO THE WOMEN'S BATHS ALONE.
AWW! I CAN BE GOOD, I PROMISE!
WELL... AND I CAN'T EXACTLY BRING YOU INTO THE MEN'S BATHS.
...
LET'S INVITE MOM!

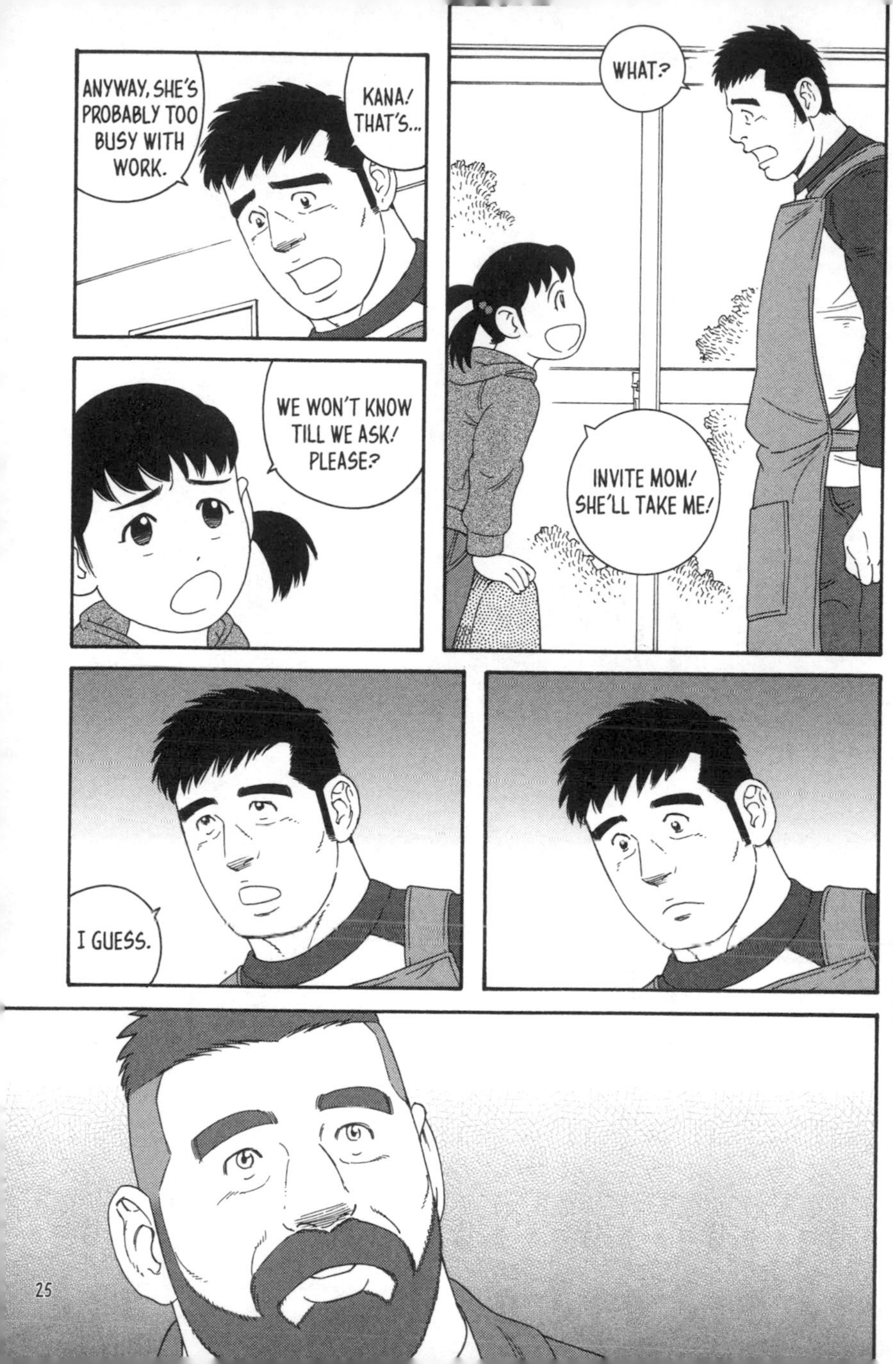
WHAT?
INVITE MOM! SHE'LL TAKE ME!
KANA! THAT'S...
ANYWAY, SHE'S PROBABLY TOO BUSY WITH WORK.
WE WON'T KNOW TILL WE ASK! PLEASE?
I GUESS.

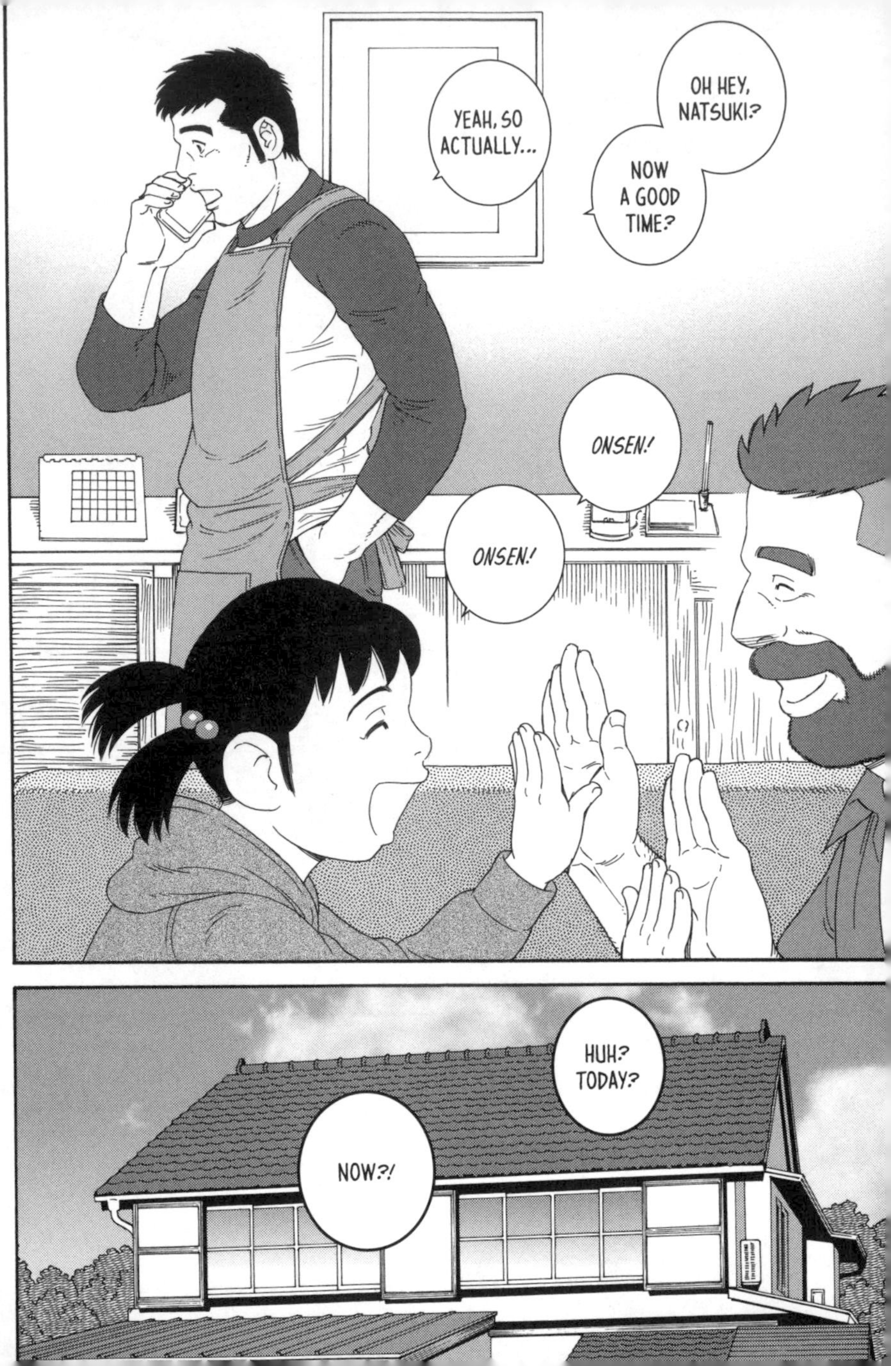
OH HEY, NATSUKI?
NOW A GOOD TIME?
YEAH, SO ACTUALLY...
ONSEN!
ONSEN!
HUH? TODAY?
NOW?!

CHAPTER SIXTEEN
ONSEN

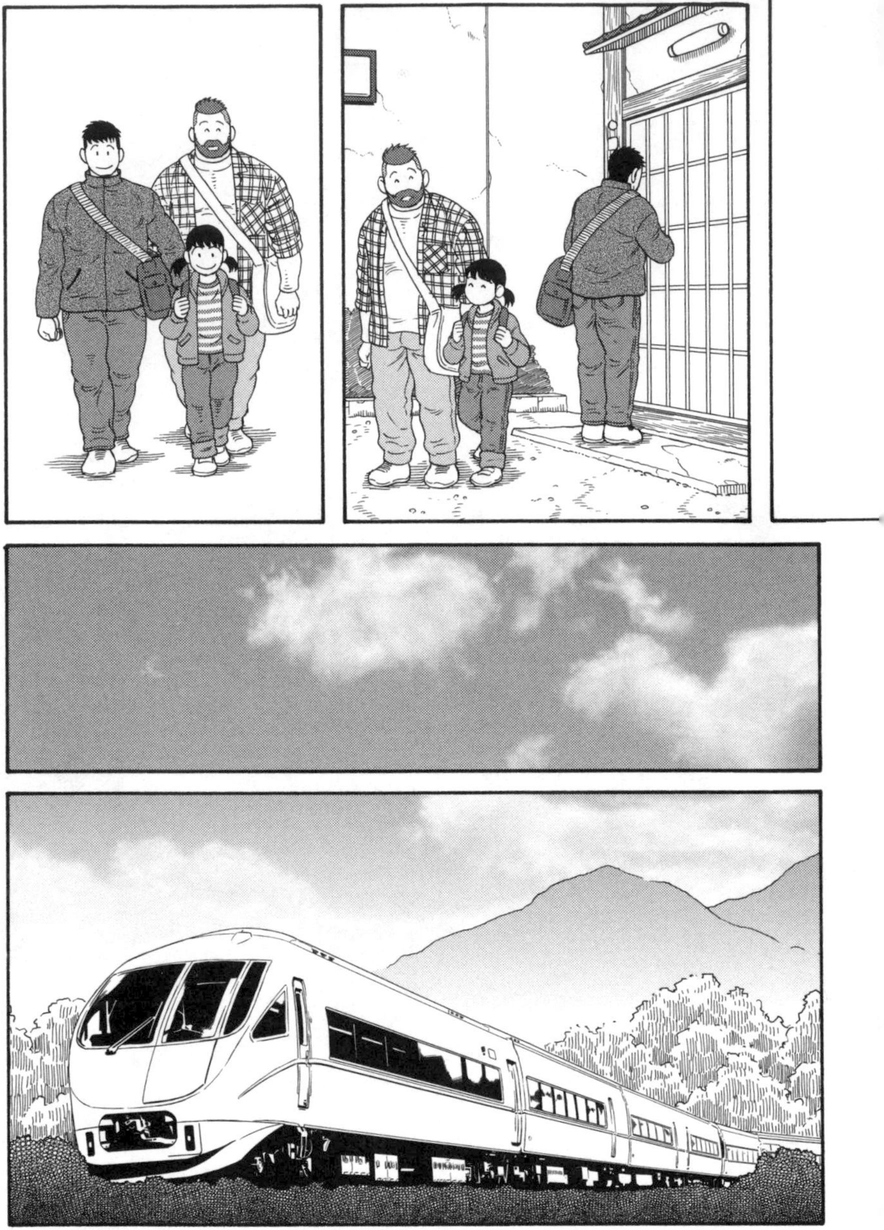

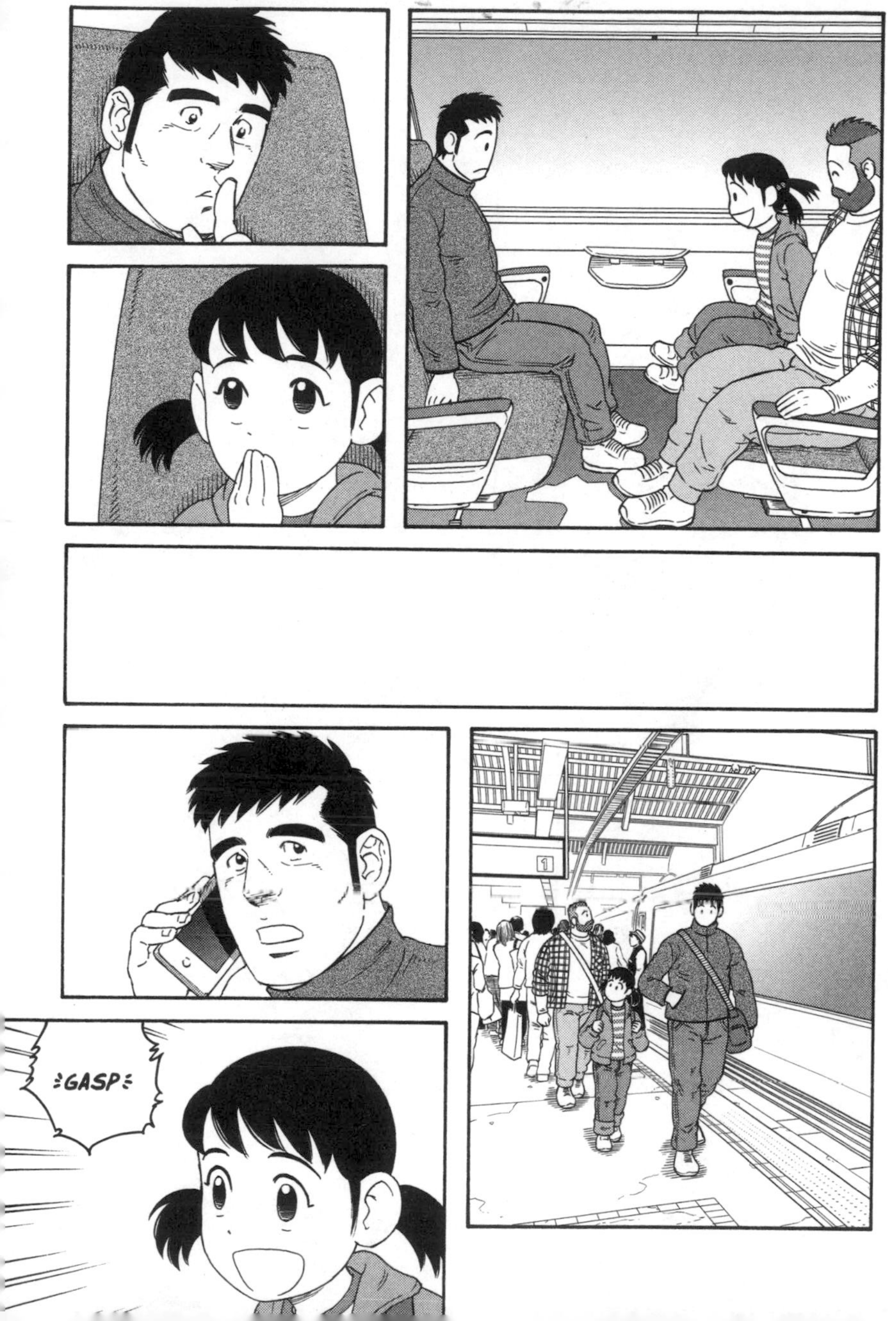
GASP

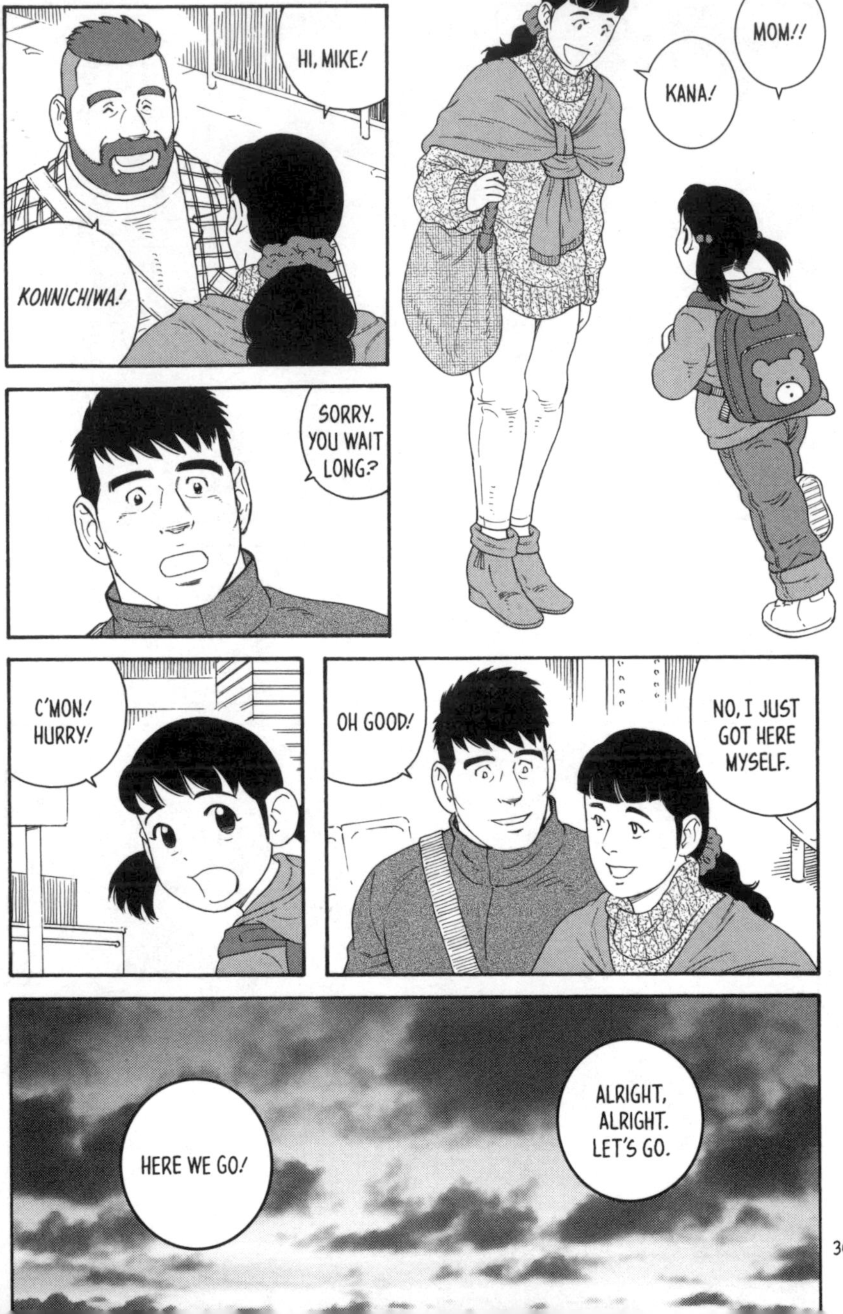
MOM!!
KANA!
HI, MIKE!
KONNICHIWA!
SORRY. YOU WAIT LONG?
NO, I JUST GOT HERE MYSELF.
OH GOOD!
C'MON! HURRY!
ALRIGHT, ALRIGHT. LET'S GO.
HERE WE GO!

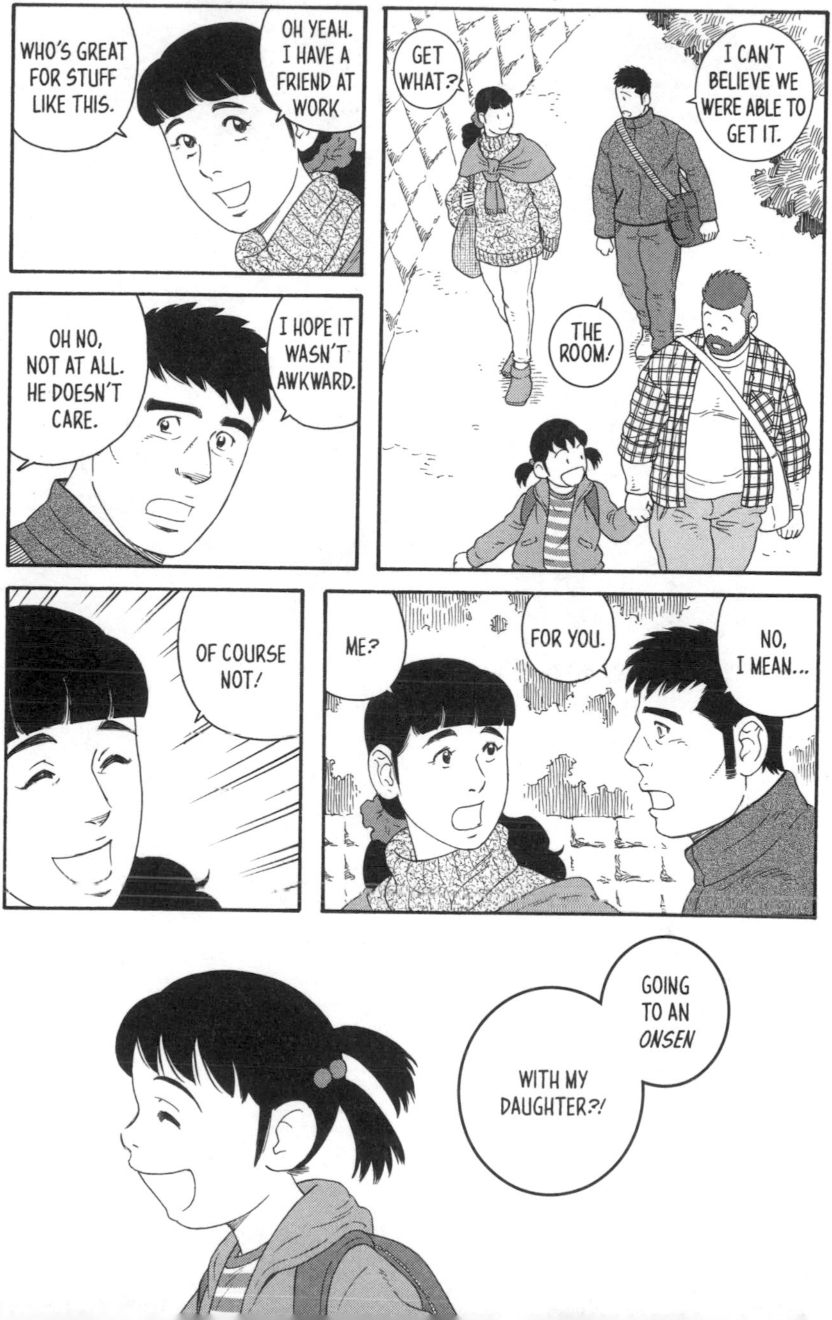
I CAN'T BELIEVE WE WERE ABLE TO GET IT.
GET WHAT?
THE ROOM!
OH YEAH. I HAVE A FRIEND AT WORK
WHO'S GREAT FOR STUFF LIKE THIS.
I HOPE IT WASN'T AWKWARD.
OH NO, NOT AT ALL. HE DOESN'T CARE.
NO, I MEAN...
FOR YOU.
ME?
OF COURSE NOT!
GOING TO AN *ONSEN*
WITH MY DAUGHTER?!

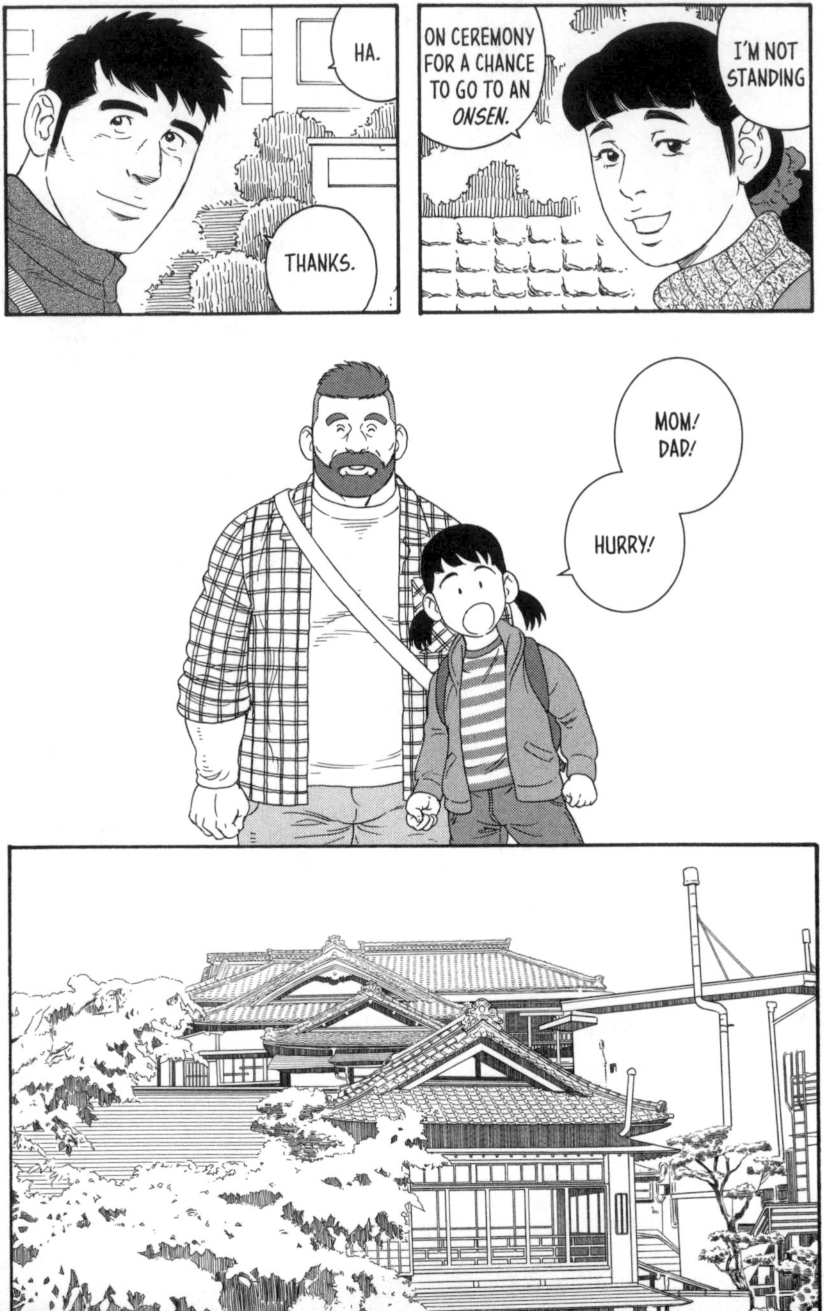
I'M NOT STANDING
ON CEREMONY FOR A CHANCE TO GO TO AN *ONSEN.*
HA.
THANKS.
MOM! DAD!
HURRY!

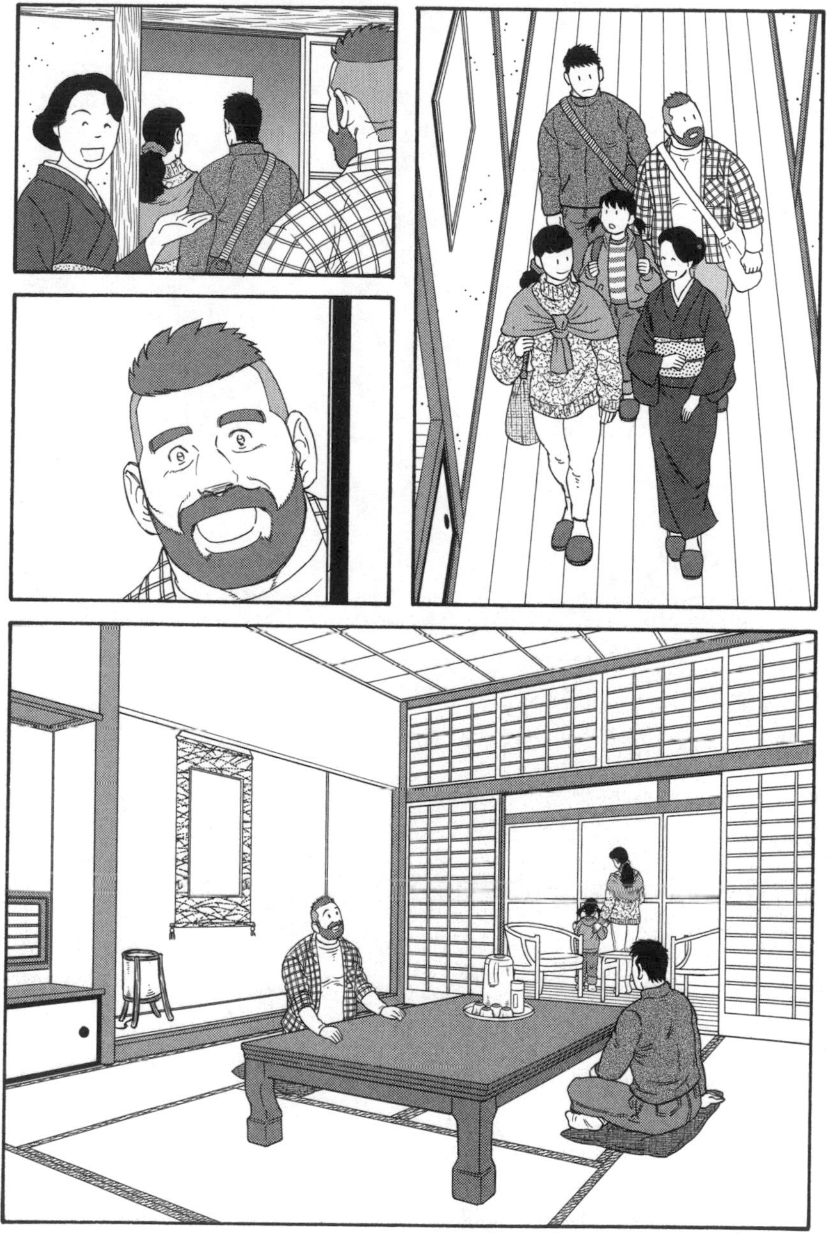

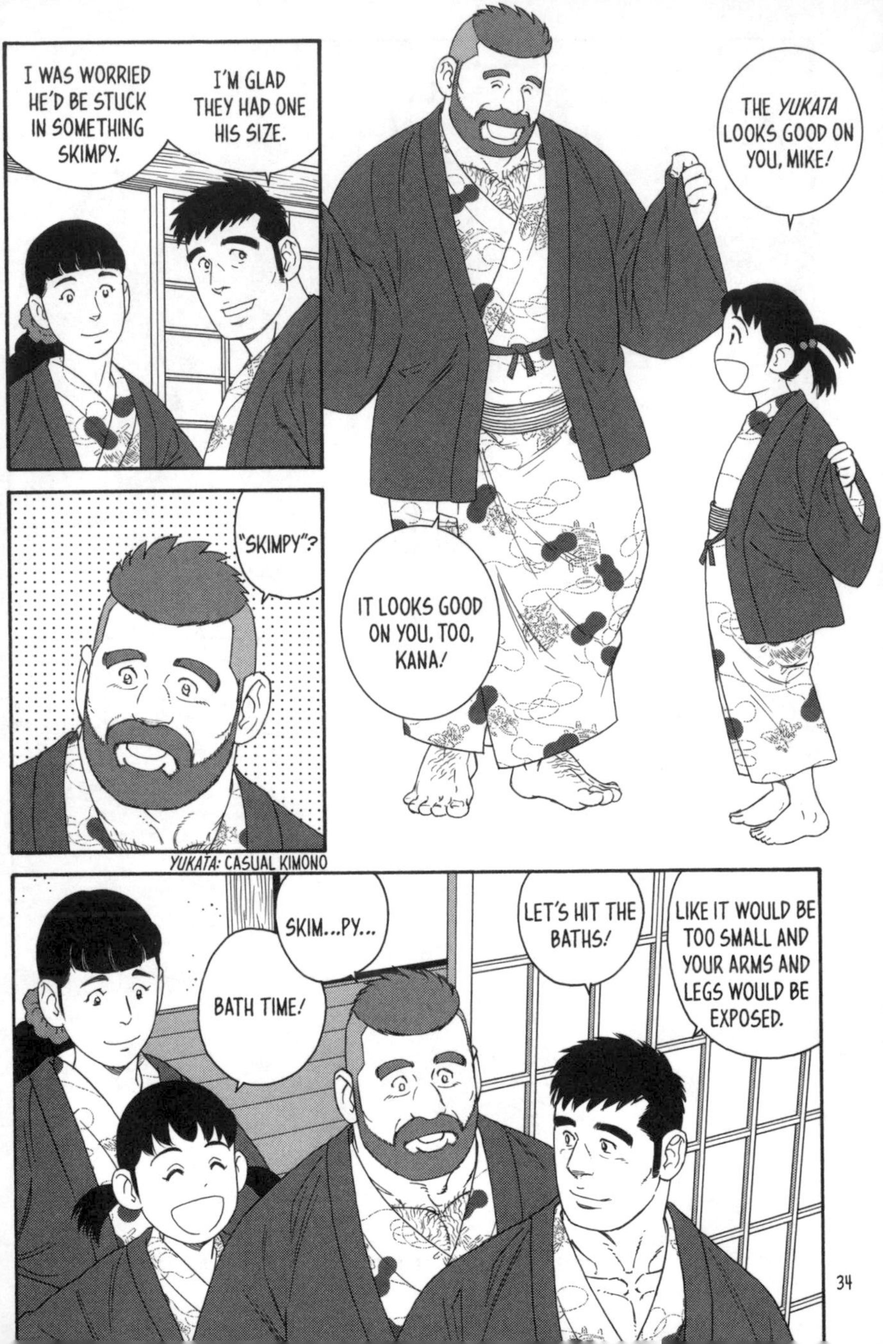
THE *YUKATA* LOOKS GOOD ON YOU, MIKE!
IT LOOKS GOOD ON YOU, TOO, KANA!
I'M GLAD THEY HAD ONE HIS SIZE.
I WAS WORRIED HE'D BE STUCK IN SOMETHING SKIMPY.
"SKIMPY"?
LIKE IT WOULD BE TOO SMALL AND YOUR ARMS AND LEGS WOULD BE EXPOSED.
LET'S HIT THE BATHS!
SKIM...PY...
BATH TIME!

YUKATA: CASUAL KIMONO

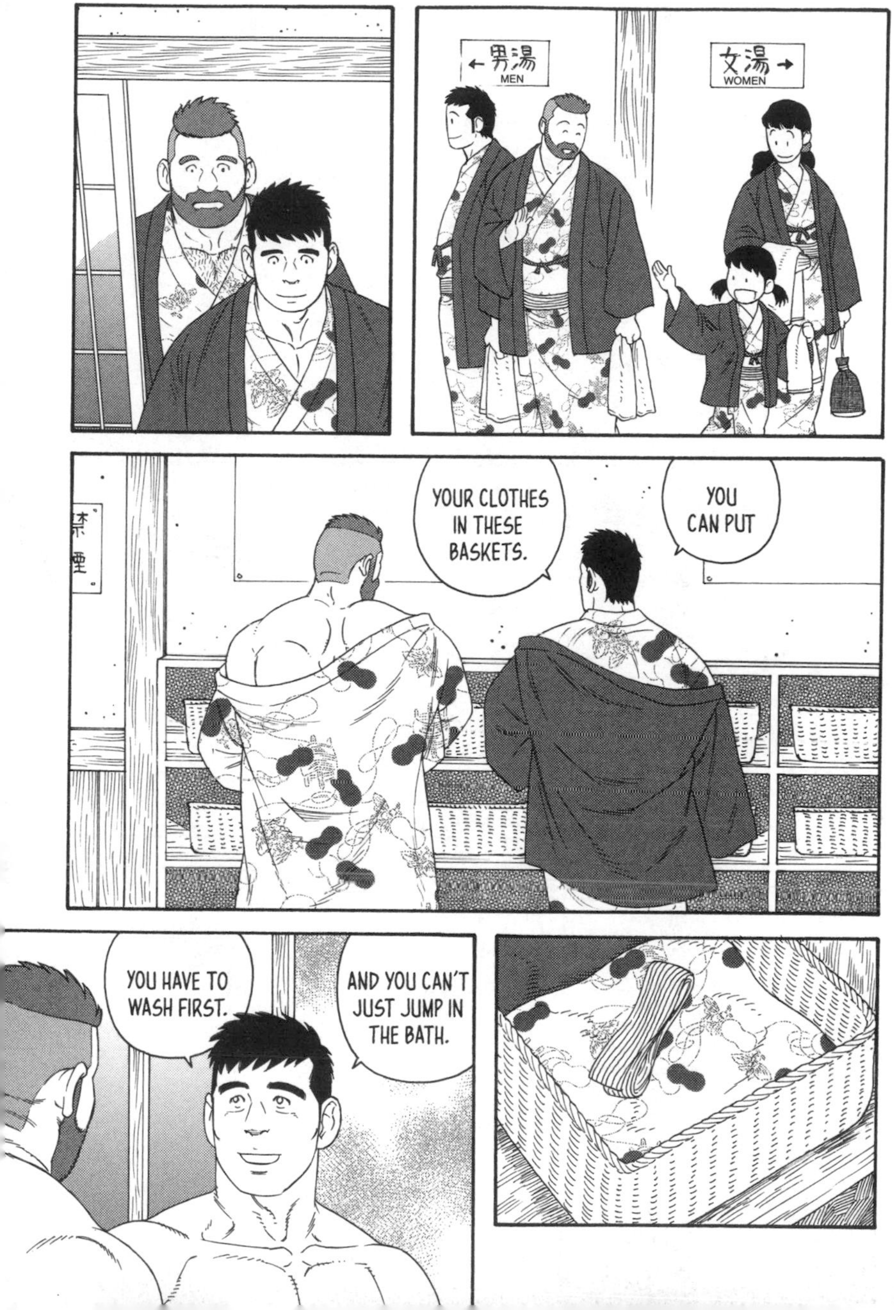

女湯 →
WOMEN
← 男湯
MEN
YOU CAN PUT
YOUR CLOTHES IN THESE BASKETS.
禁煙
AND YOU CAN'T JUST JUMP IN THE BATH.
YOU HAVE TO WASH FIRST.

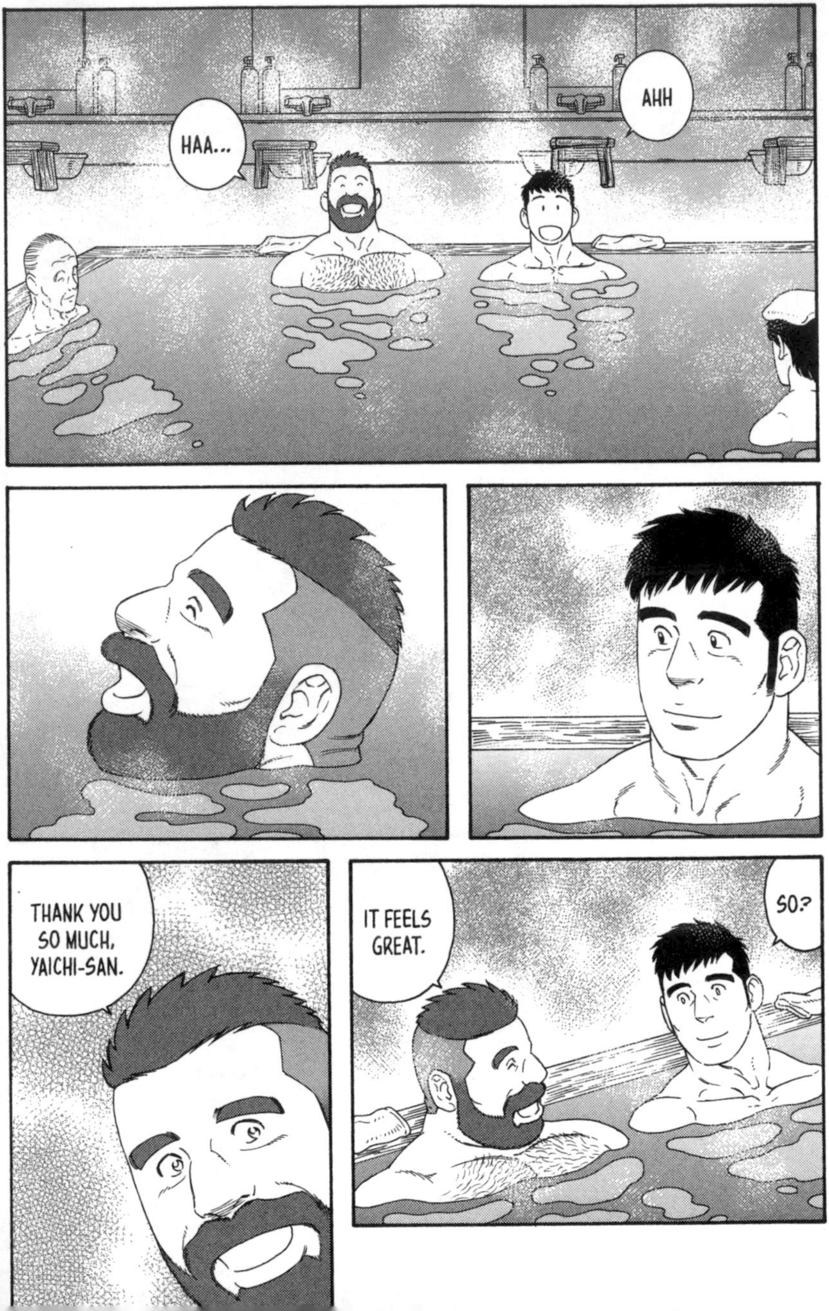
AHH
HAA...
SO?
IT FEELS GREAT.
THANK YOU SO MUCH, YAICHI-SAN.

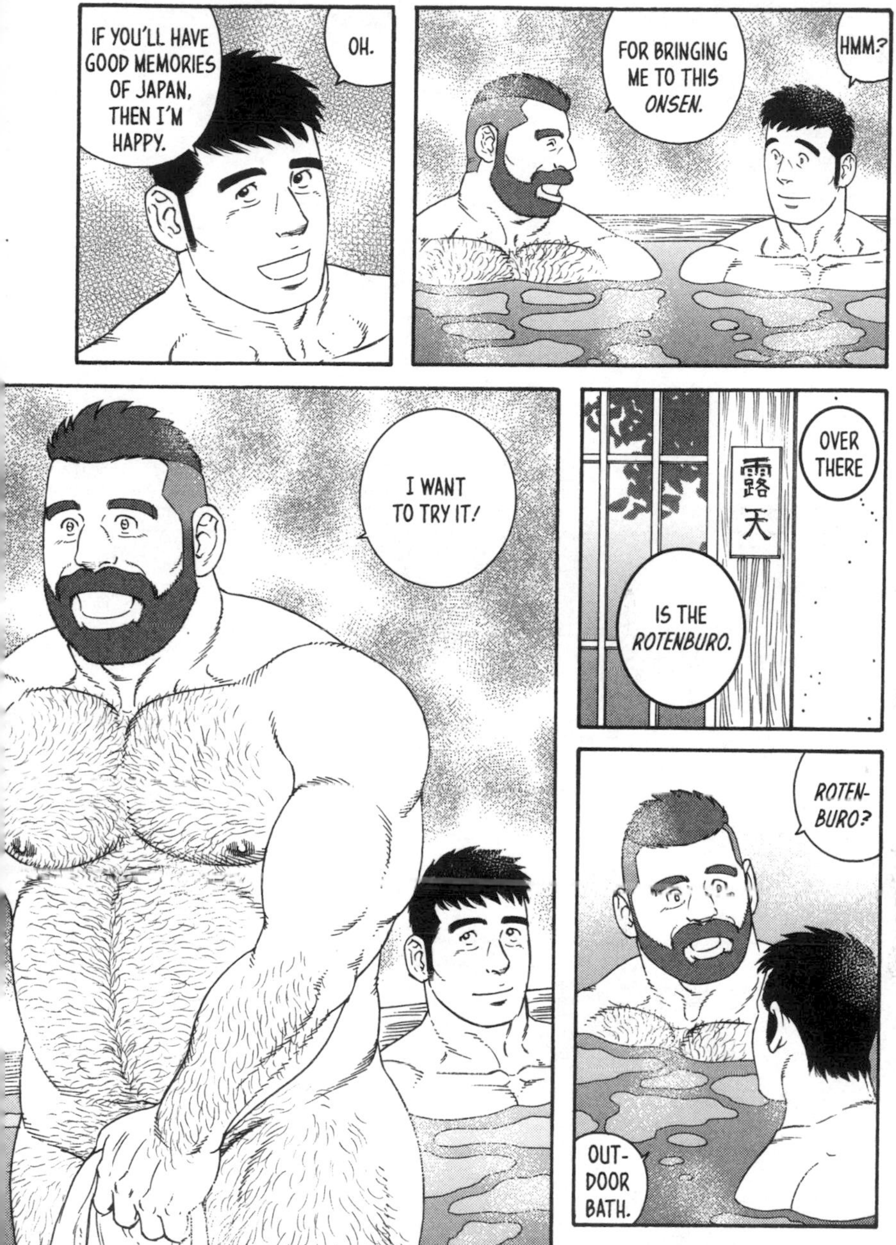
HMM?
FOR BRINGING ME TO THIS *ONSEN*.
OH.
IF YOU'LL HAVE GOOD MEMORIES OF JAPAN, THEN I'M HAPPY.
OVER THERE
露天
IS THE *ROTENBURO*.
ROTEN-BURO?
OUT-DOOR BATH.
I WANT TO TRY IT!

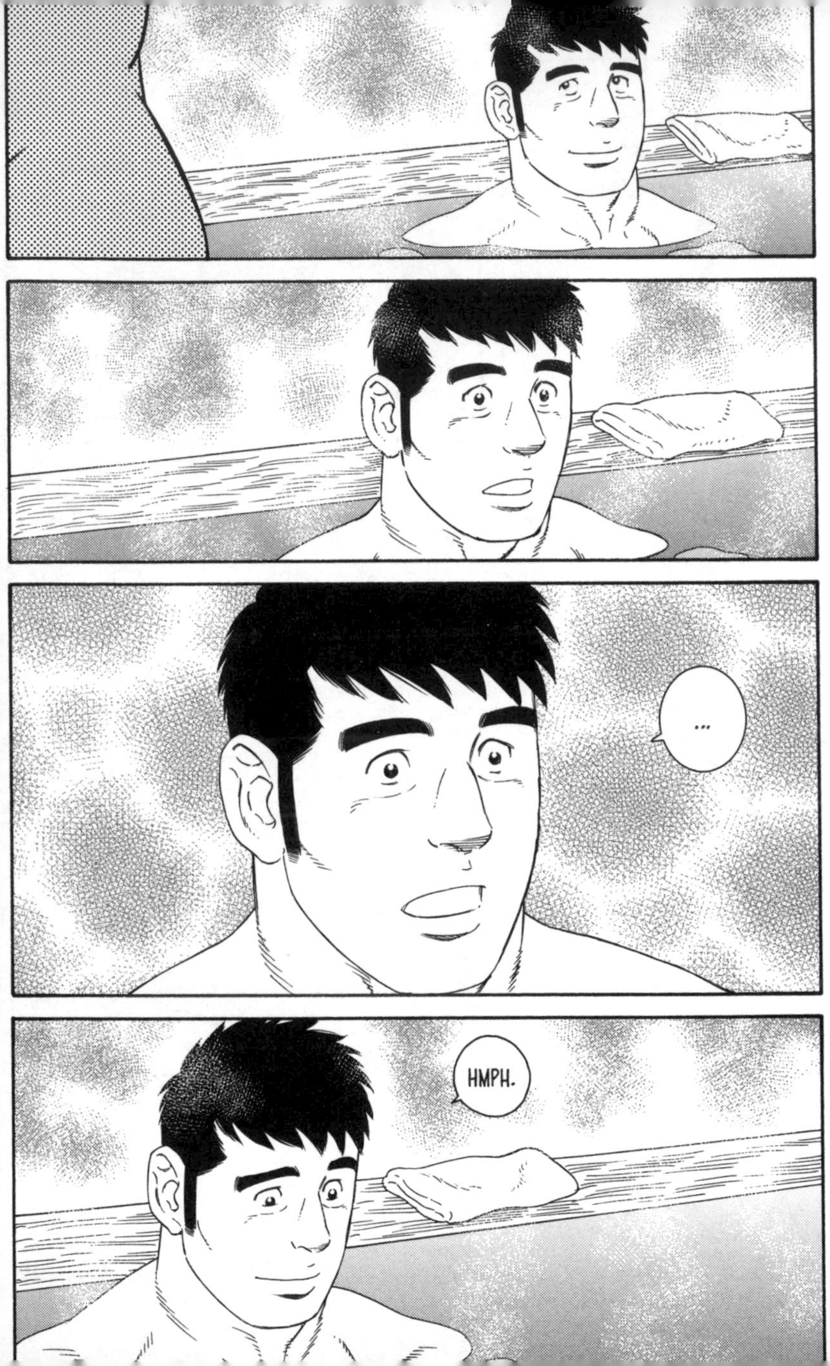
...
HMPH.

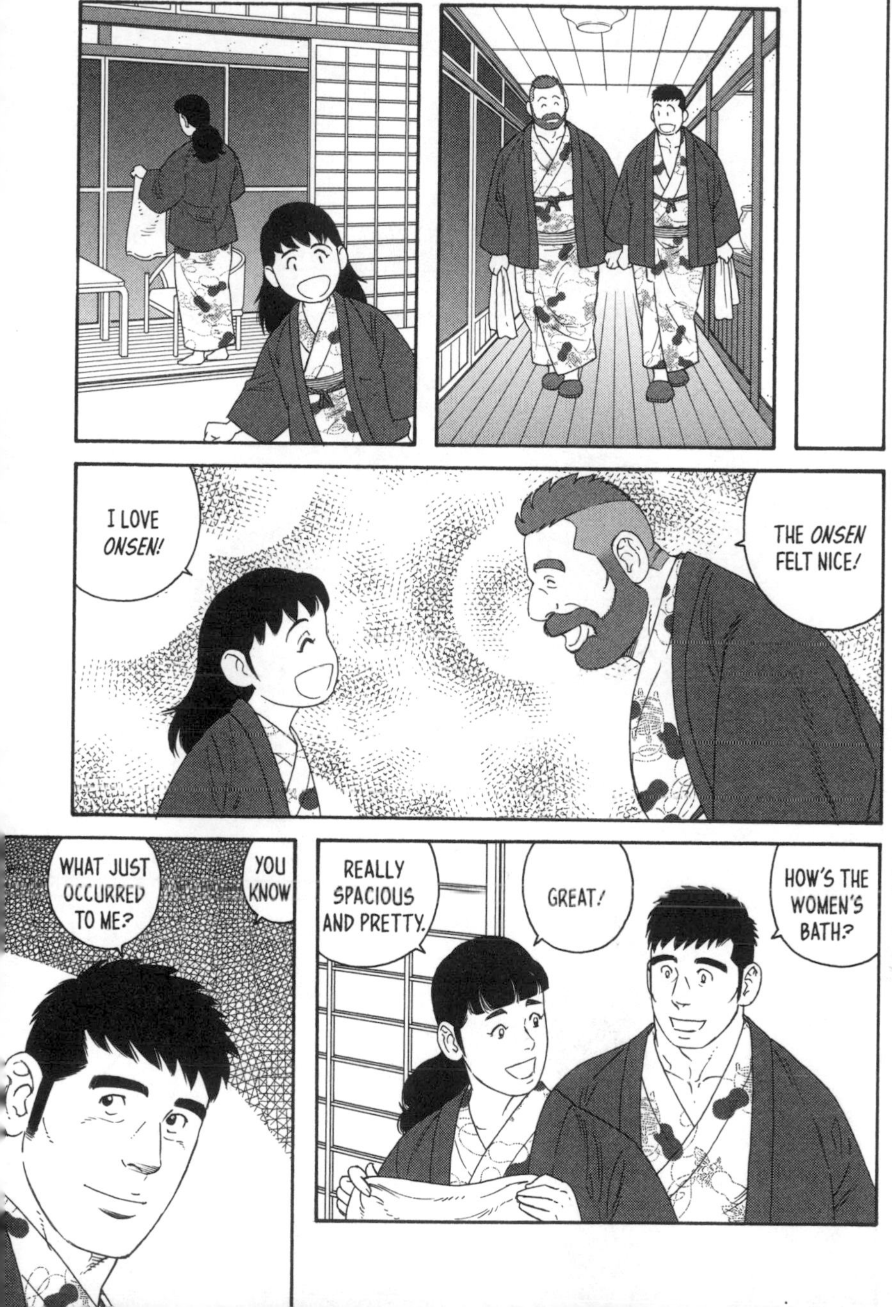
THE *ONSEN* FELT NICE!
I LOVE *ONSEN*!
HOW'S THE WOMEN'S BATH?
GREAT!
REALLY SPACIOUS AND PRETTY.
YOU KNOW
WHAT JUST OCCURRED TO ME?

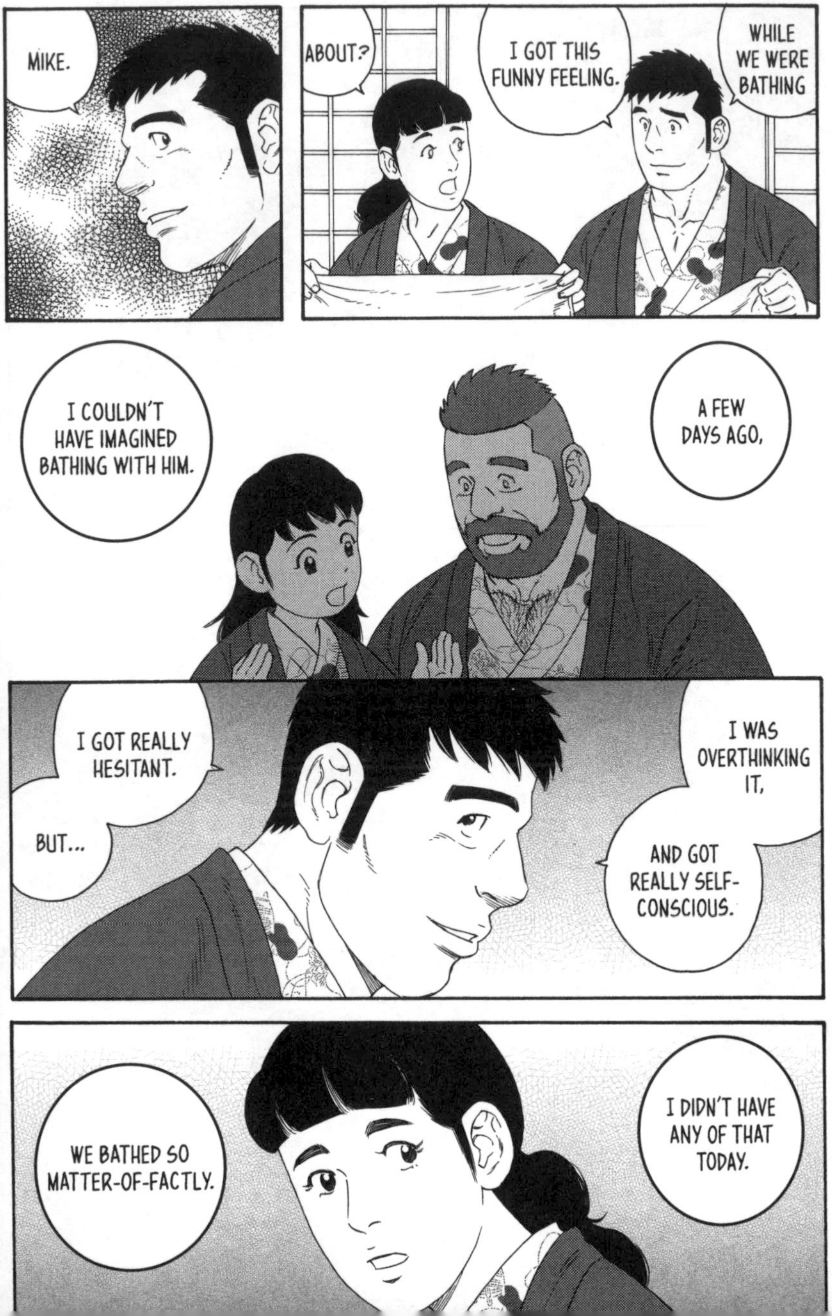
WHILE WE WERE BATHING
I GOT THIS FUNNY FEELING.
ABOUT?
MIKE.
A FEW DAYS AGO,
I COULDN'T HAVE IMAGINED BATHING WITH HIM.
I WAS OVERTHINKING IT,
AND GOT REALLY SELF-CONSCIOUS.
I GOT REALLY HESITANT.
BUT...
I DIDN'T HAVE ANY OF THAT TODAY.
WE BATHED SO MATTER-OF-FACTLY.

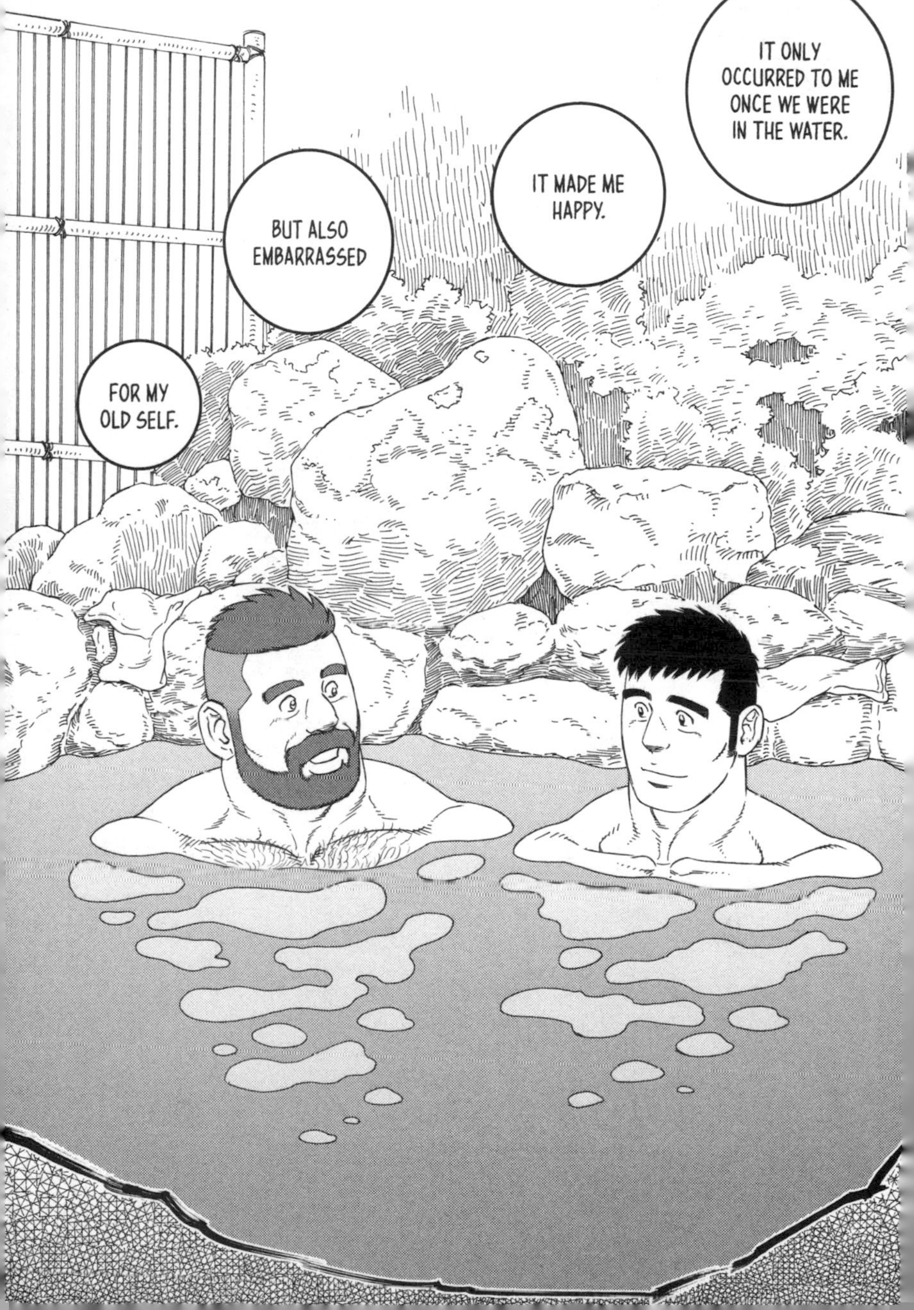
IT ONLY OCCURRED TO ME ONCE WE WERE IN THE WATER.
IT MADE ME HAPPY.
BUT ALSO EMBARRASSED
FOR MY OLD SELF.

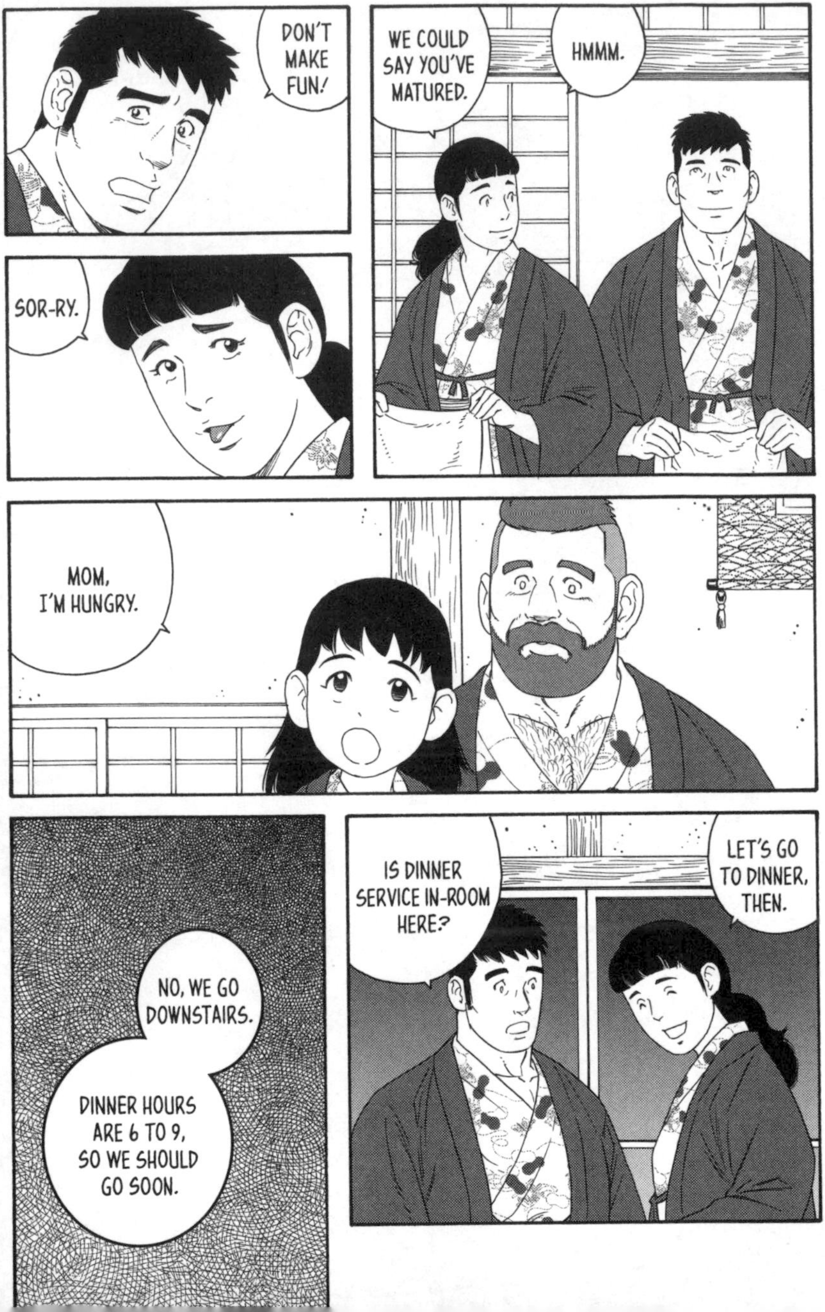
HMMM.
WE COULD SAY YOU'VE MATURED.
DON'T MAKE FUN!
SOR-RY.
MOM, I'M HUNGRY.
LET'S GO TO DINNER, THEN.
IS DINNER SERVICE IN-ROOM HERE?
NO, WE GO DOWNSTAIRS.
DINNER HOURS ARE 6 TO 9, SO WE SHOULD GO SOON.

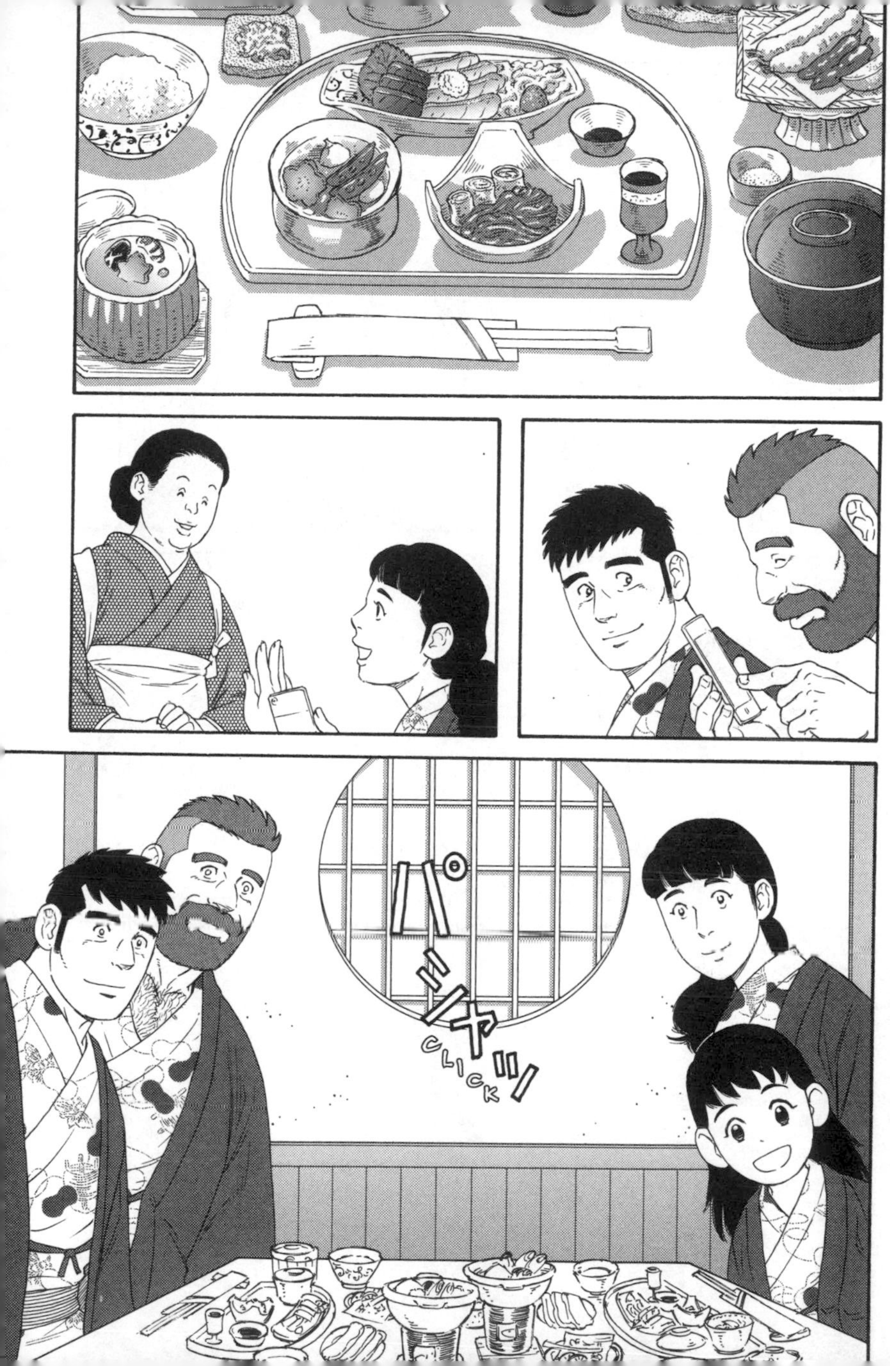
パシャ!!
CLICK

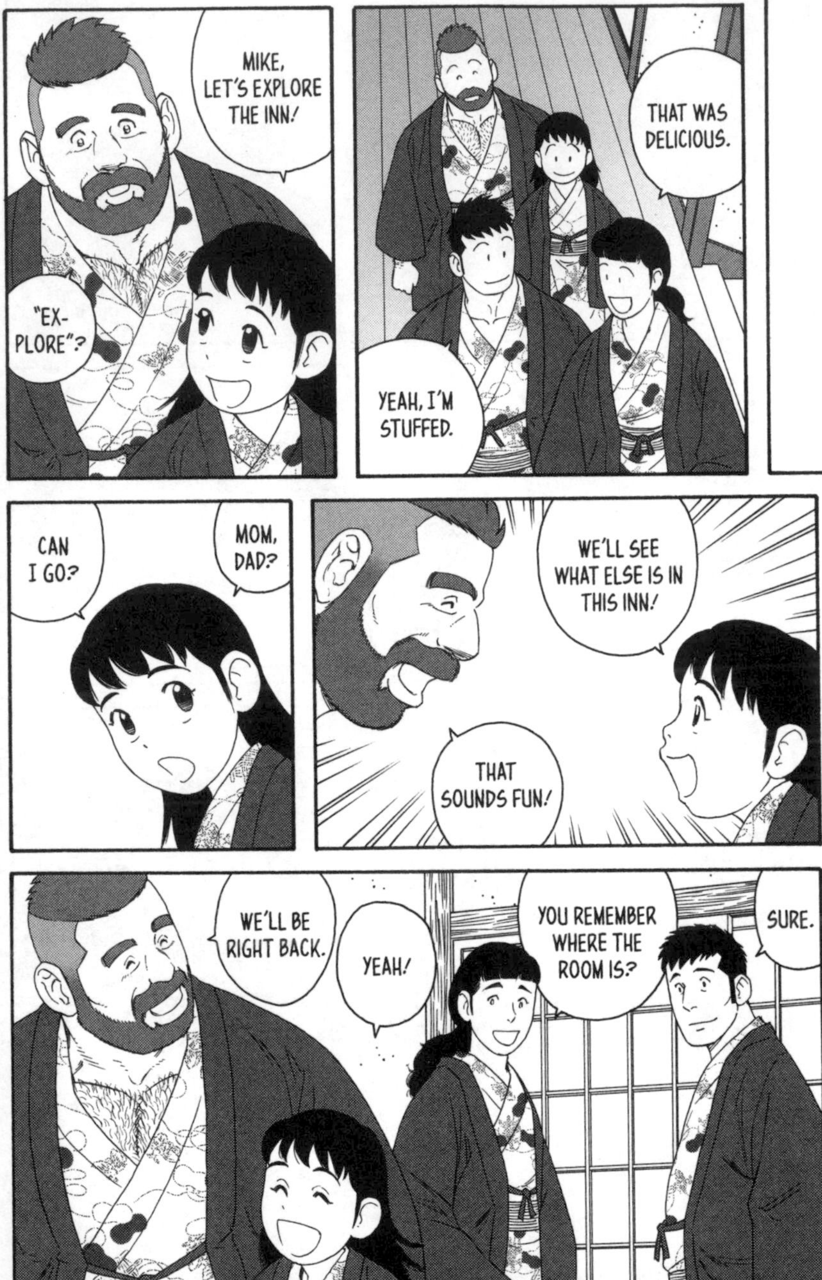
THAT WAS DELICIOUS.
YEAH, I'M STUFFED.
MIKE, LET'S EXPLORE THE INN!
"EX-PLORE"?
WE'LL SEE WHAT ELSE IS IN THIS INN!
THAT SOUNDS FUN!
MOM, DAD?
CAN I GO?
SURE.
YOU REMEMBER WHERE THE ROOM IS?
YEAH!
WE'LL BE RIGHT BACK.

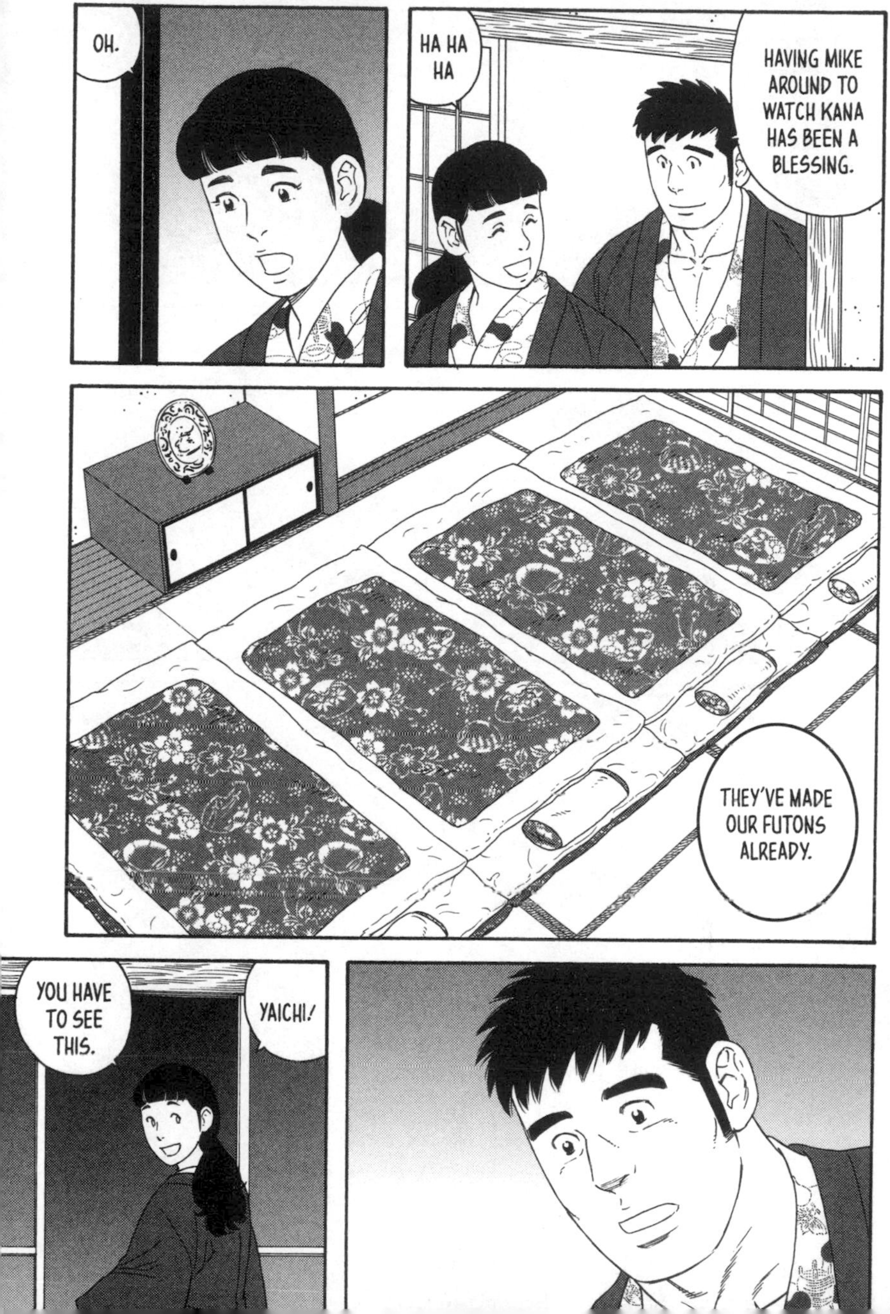
HAVING MIKE AROUND TO WATCH KANA HAS BEEN A BLESSING.
HA HA HA
OH.
THEY'VE MADE OUR FUTONS ALREADY.
YAICHI!
YOU HAVE TO SEE THIS.

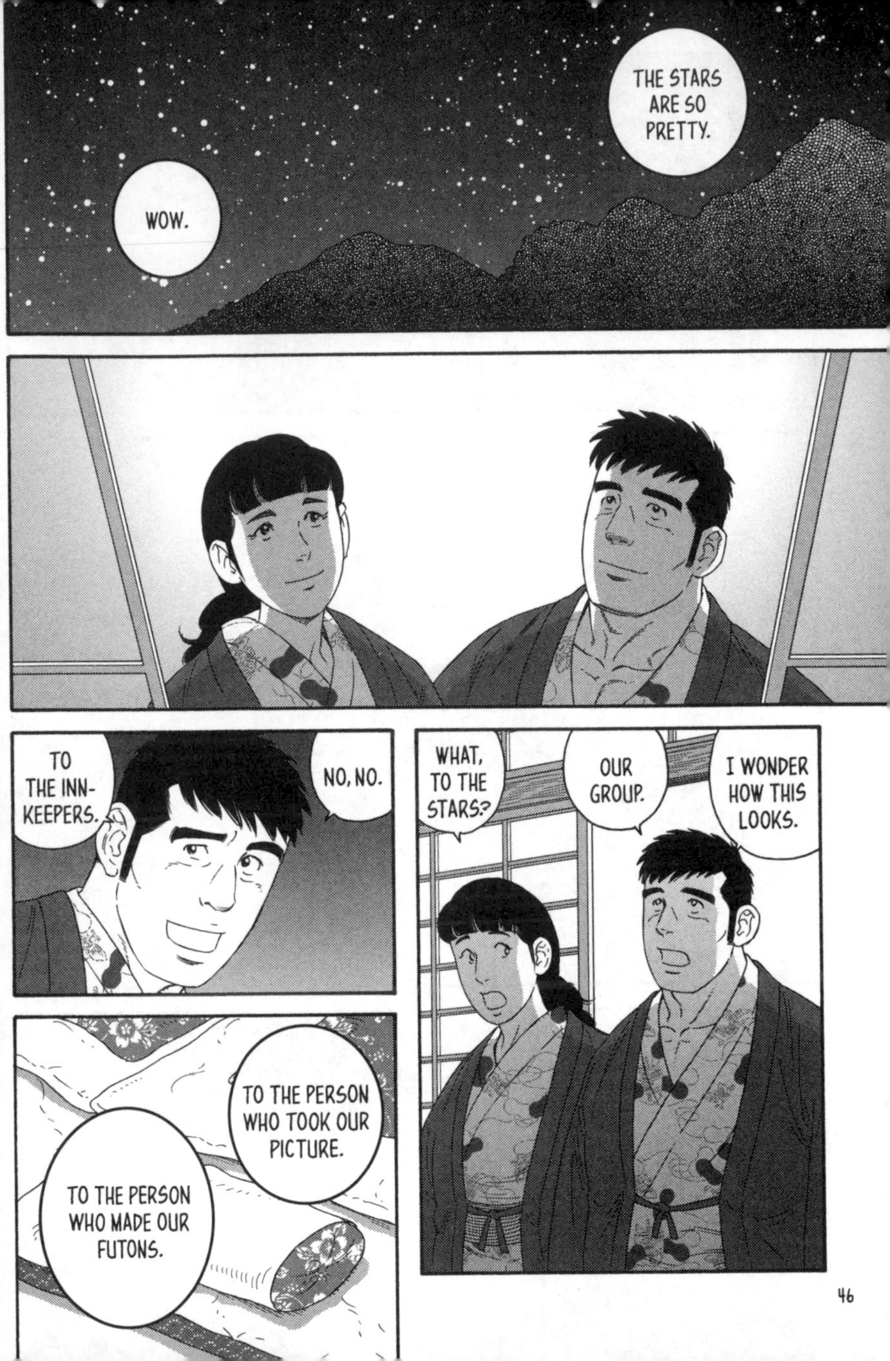

THE STARS ARE SO PRETTY.
WOW.
I WONDER HOW THIS LOOKS.
OUR GROUP.
WHAT, TO THE STARS?
NO, NO.
TO THE INN-KEEPERS.
TO THE PERSON WHO TOOK OUR PICTURE.
TO THE PERSON WHO MADE OUR FUTONS.

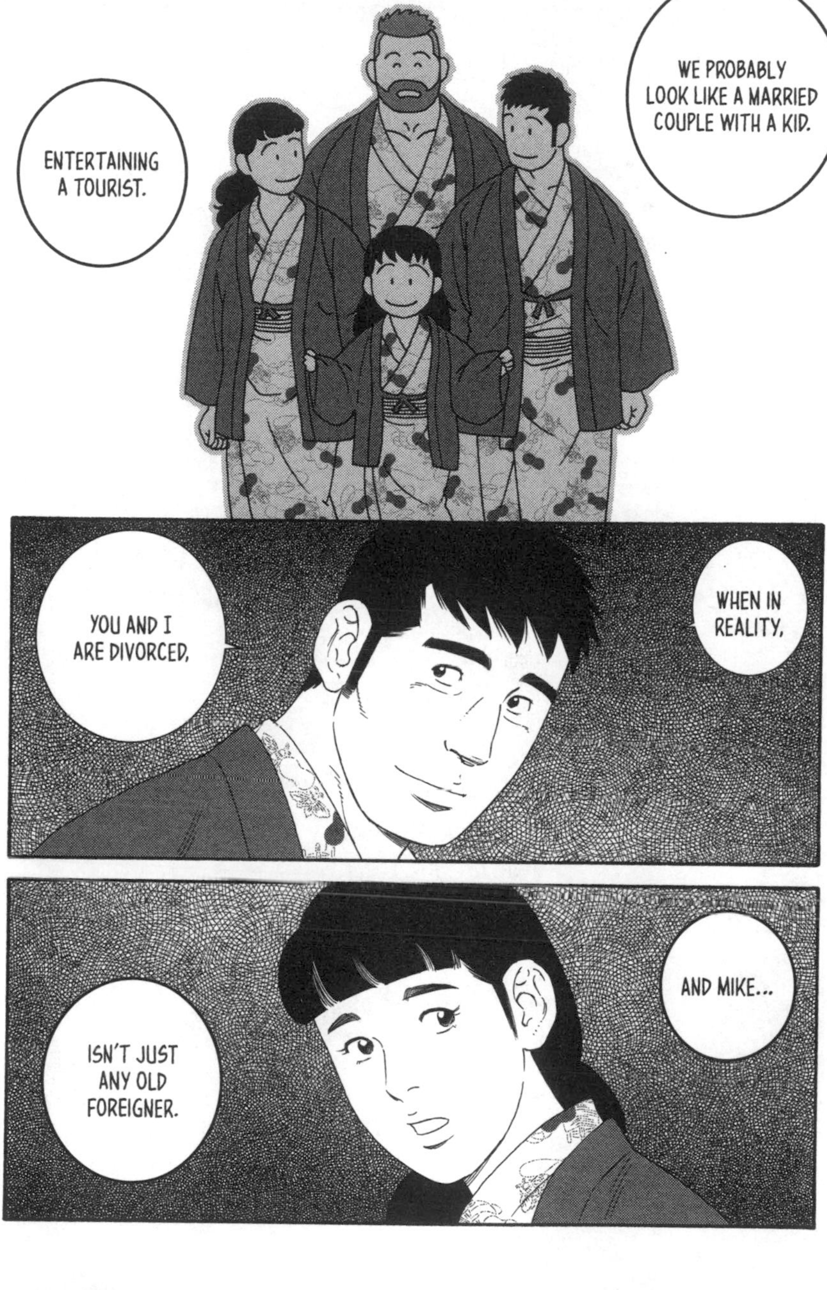
WE PROBABLY LOOK LIKE A MARRIED COUPLE WITH A KID.
ENTERTAINING A TOURIST.
WHEN IN REALITY,
YOU AND I ARE DIVORCED,
AND MIKE...
ISN'T JUST ANY OLD FOREIGNER.

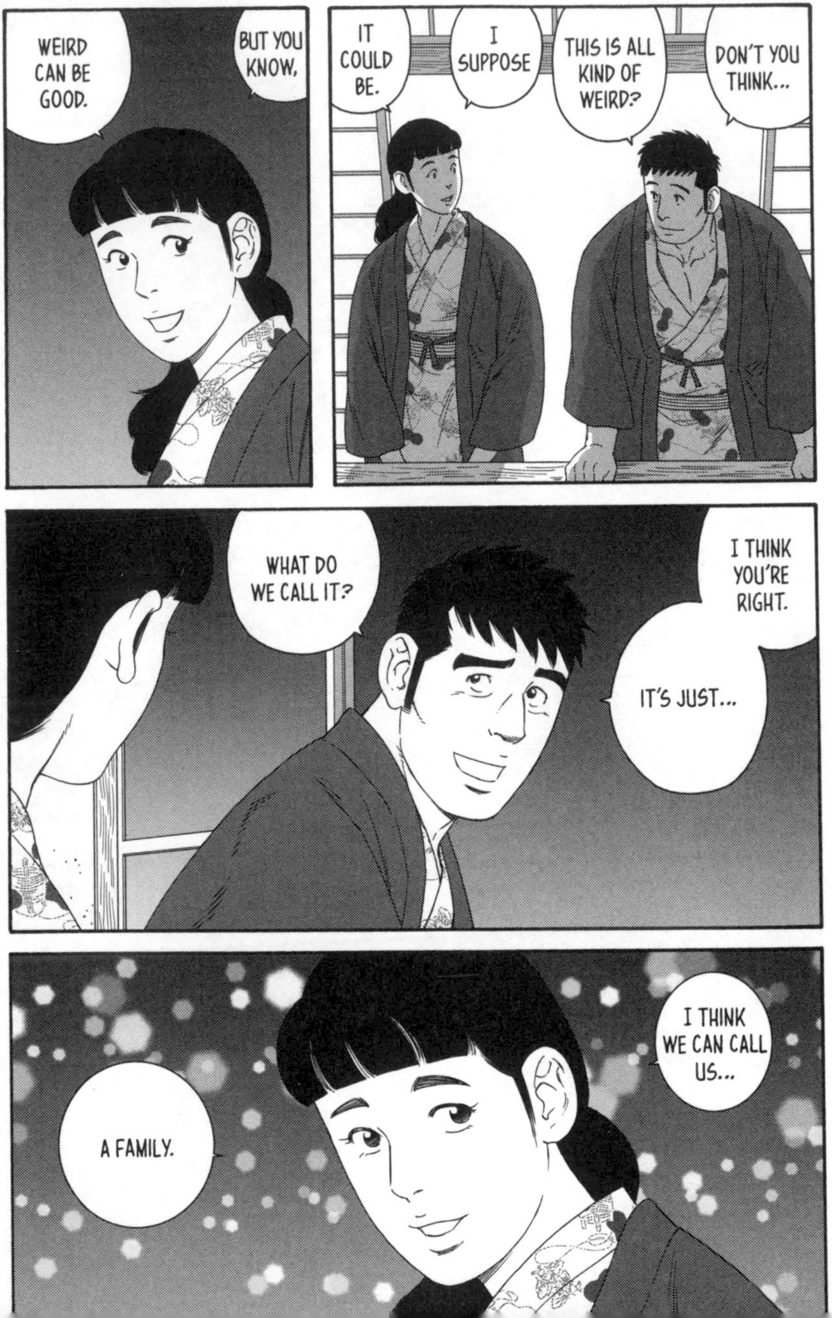
DON'T YOU THINK...
THIS IS ALL KIND OF WEIRD?
I SUPPOSE
IT COULD BE.
BUT YOU KNOW,
WEIRD CAN BE GOOD.
I THINK YOU'RE RIGHT.
IT'S JUST...
WHAT DO WE CALL IT?
I THINK WE CAN CALL US...
A FAMILY.

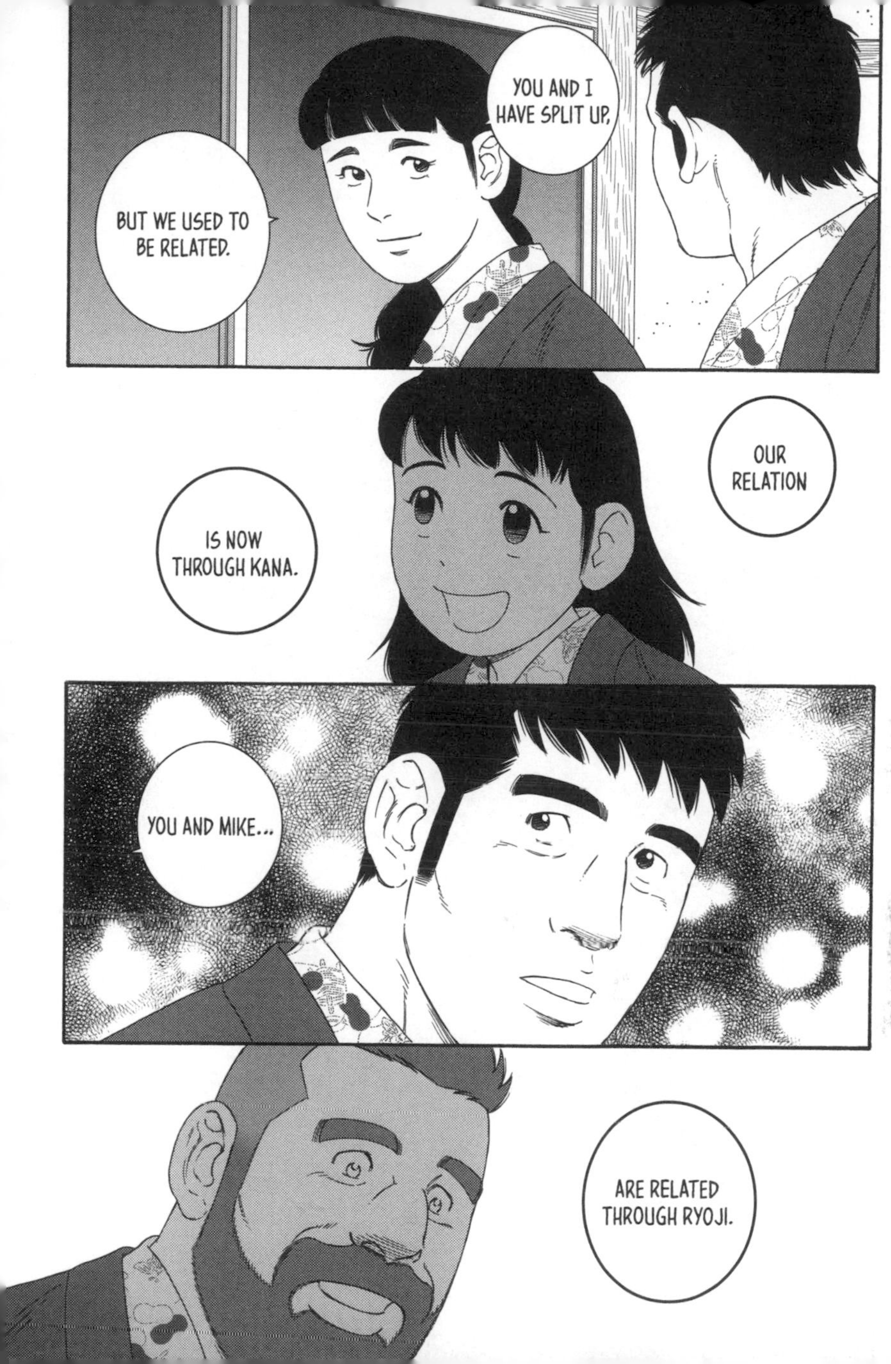
YOU AND I HAVE SPLIT UP,
BUT WE USED TO BE RELATED.
OUR RELATION
IS NOW THROUGH KANA.
YOU AND MIKE...
ARE RELATED THROUGH RYOJI.

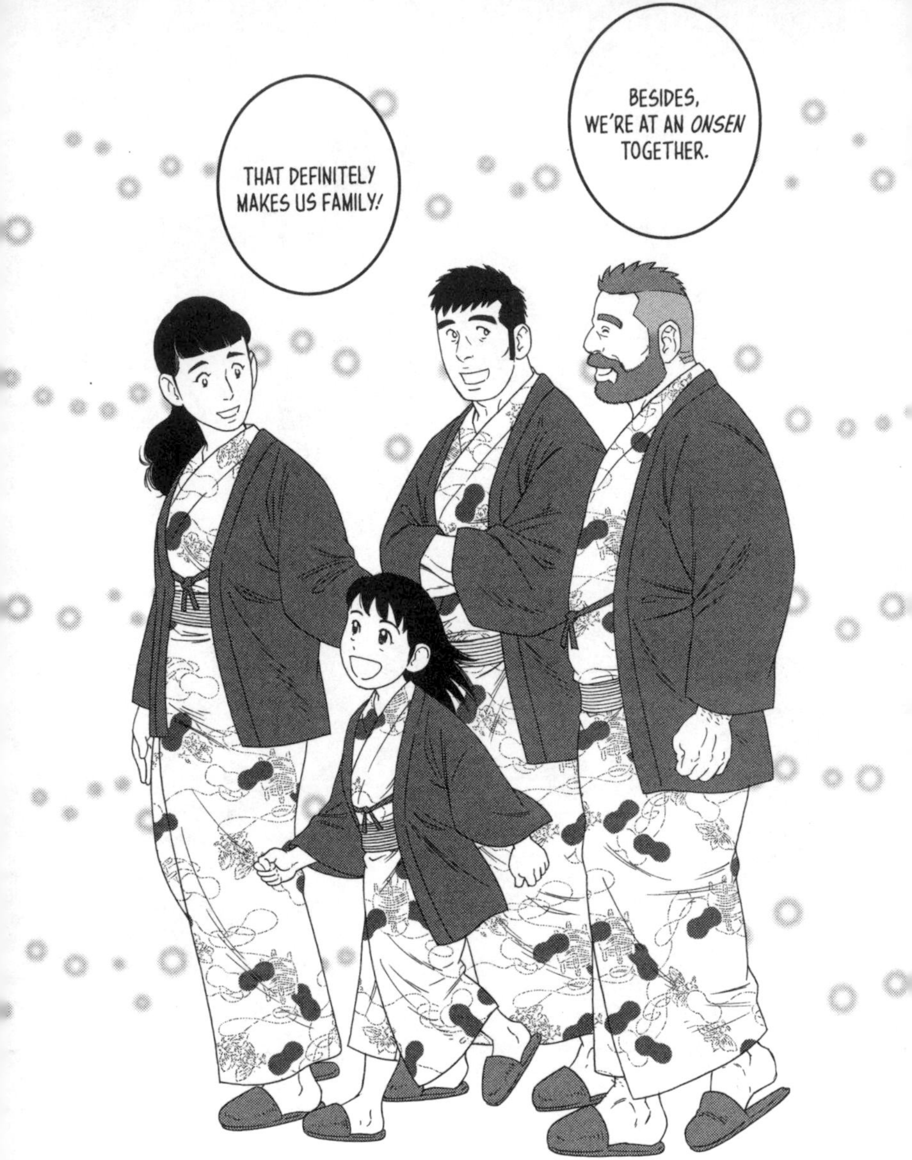
BESIDES, WE'RE AT AN ONSEN TOGETHER.
THAT DEFINITELY MAKES US FAMILY!

CHAPTER SEVENTEEN

WASABI ICE CREAM

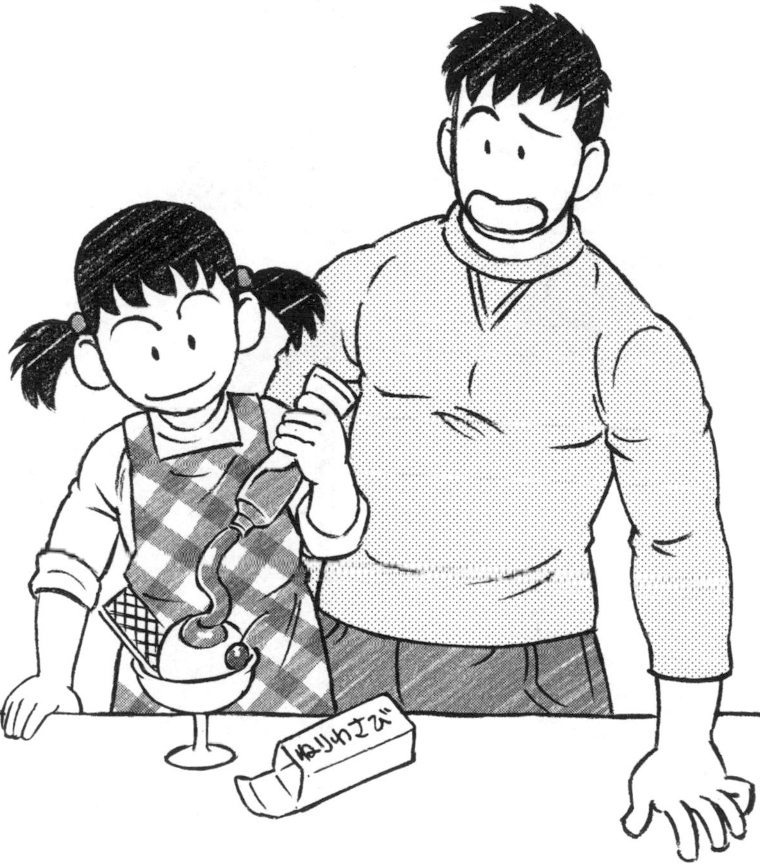
ねりわさび

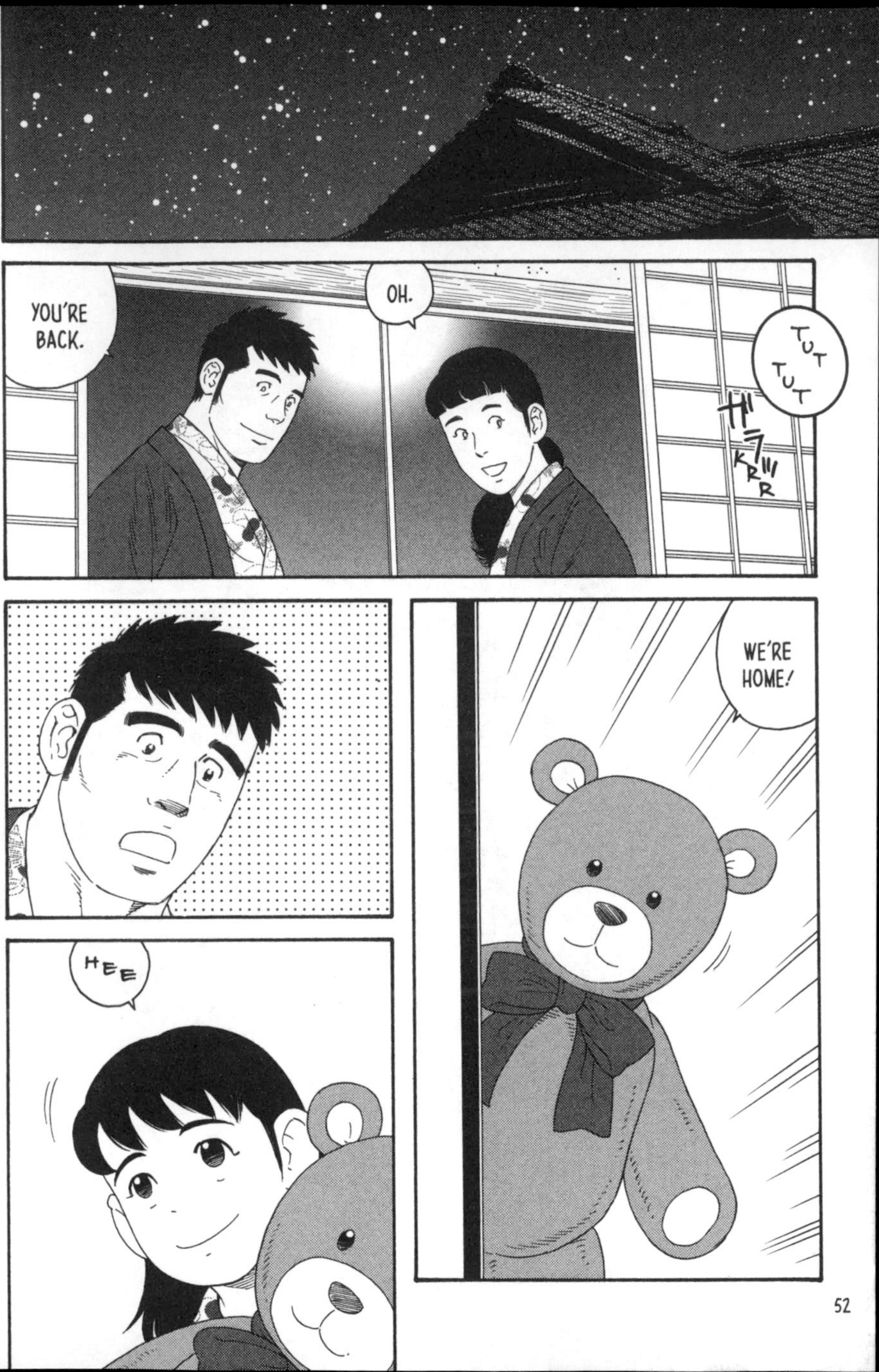
TUT TUT
KRR
OH.
YOU'RE BACK.
WE'RE HOME!
HEE

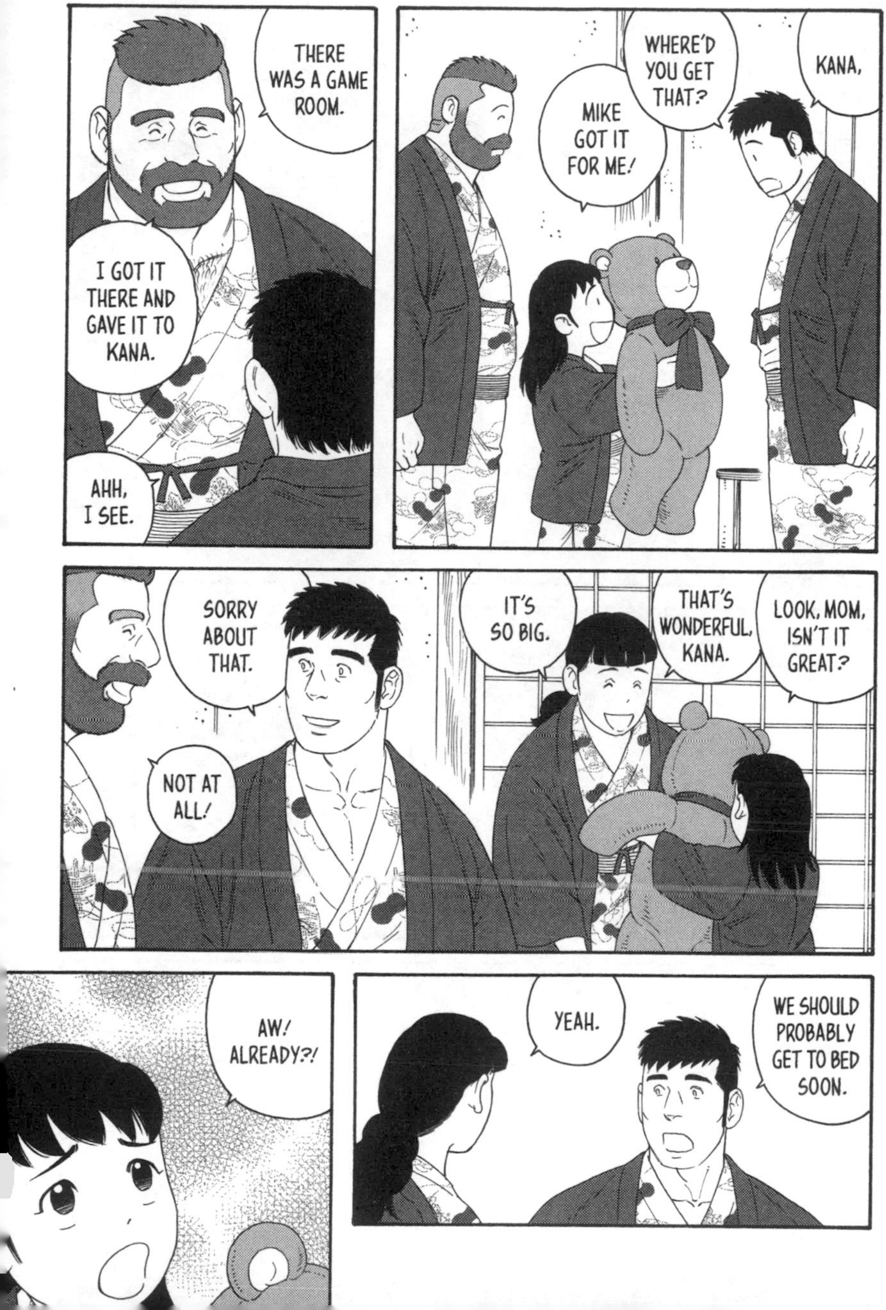
KANA,
WHERE'D YOU GET THAT?
MIKE GOT IT FOR ME!
THERE WAS A GAME ROOM.
I GOT IT THERE AND GAVE IT TO KANA.
AHH, I SEE.
LOOK, MOM, ISN'T IT GREAT?
THAT'S WONDERFUL, KANA.
IT'S SO BIG.
SORRY ABOUT THAT.
NOT AT ALL!
WE SHOULD PROBABLY GET TO BED SOON.
YEAH.
AW! ALREADY?!

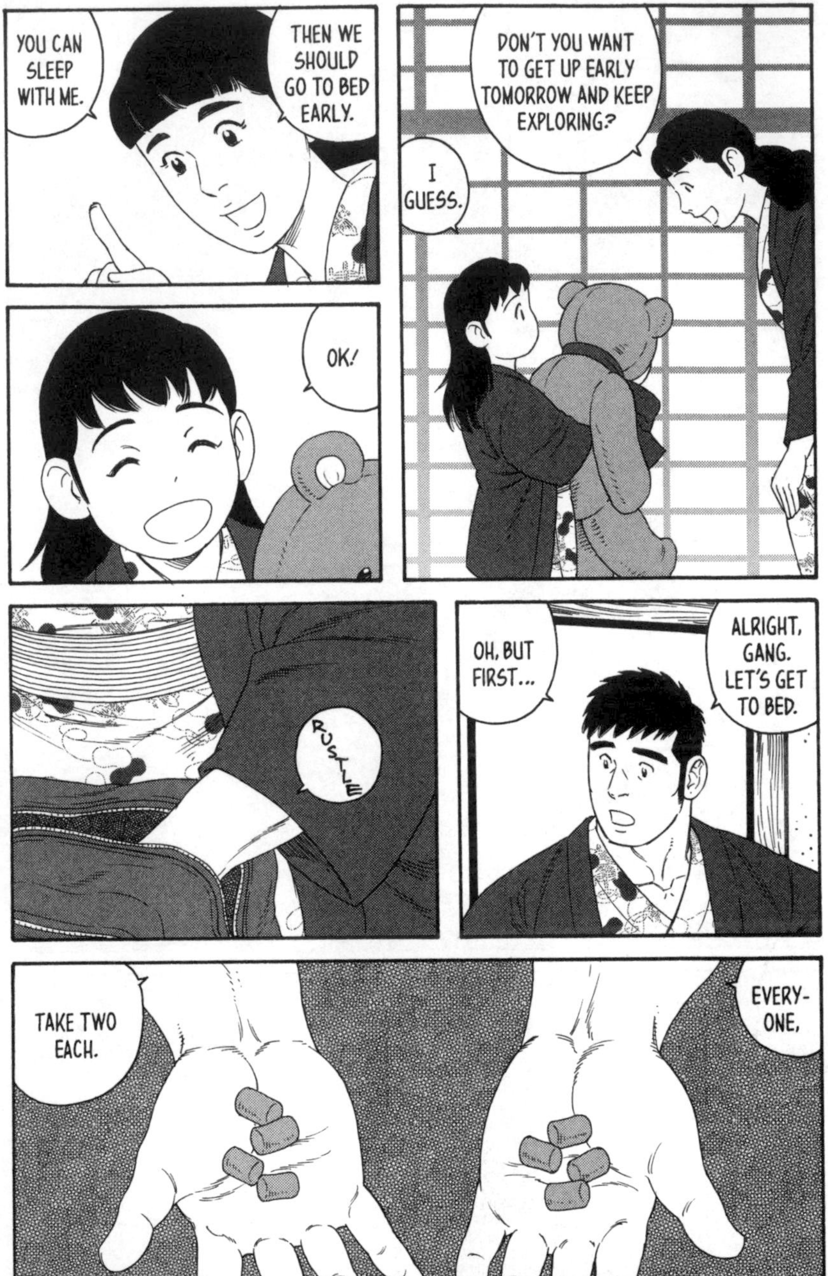
DON'T YOU WANT TO GET UP EARLY TOMORROW AND KEEP EXPLORING?
I GUESS.
THEN WE SHOULD GO TO BED EARLY.
YOU CAN SLEEP WITH ME.
OK!
ALRIGHT, GANG. LET'S GET TO BED.
OH, BUT FIRST...
RUSTLE
EVERY-ONE,
TAKE TWO EACH.

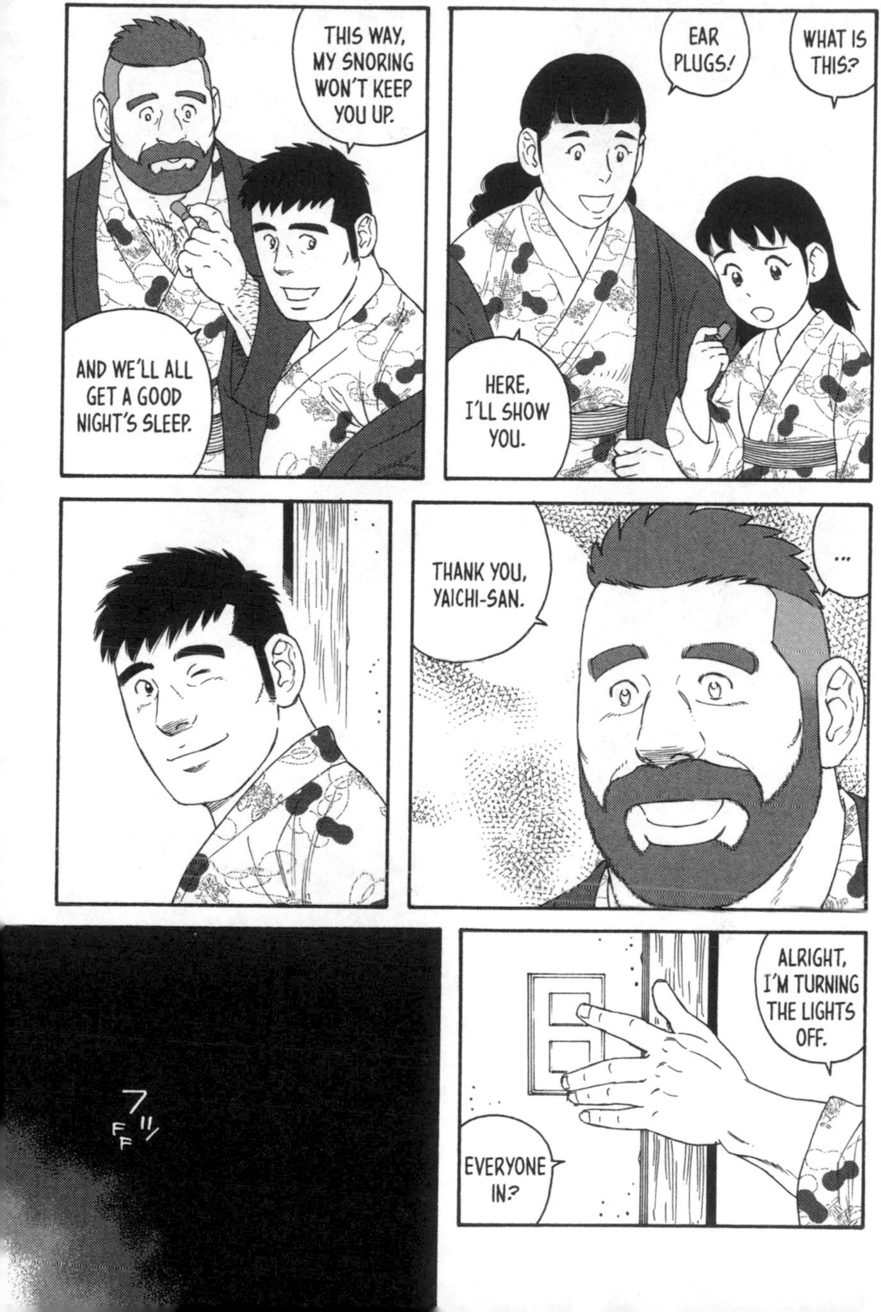
WHAT IS THIS?
EAR PLUGS!
HERE, I'LL SHOW YOU.
THIS WAY, MY SNORING WON'T KEEP YOU UP.
AND WE'LL ALL GET A GOOD NIGHT'S SLEEP.
...
THANK YOU, YAICHI-SAN.
ALRIGHT, I'M TURNING THE LIGHTS OFF.
EVERYONE IN?
FF

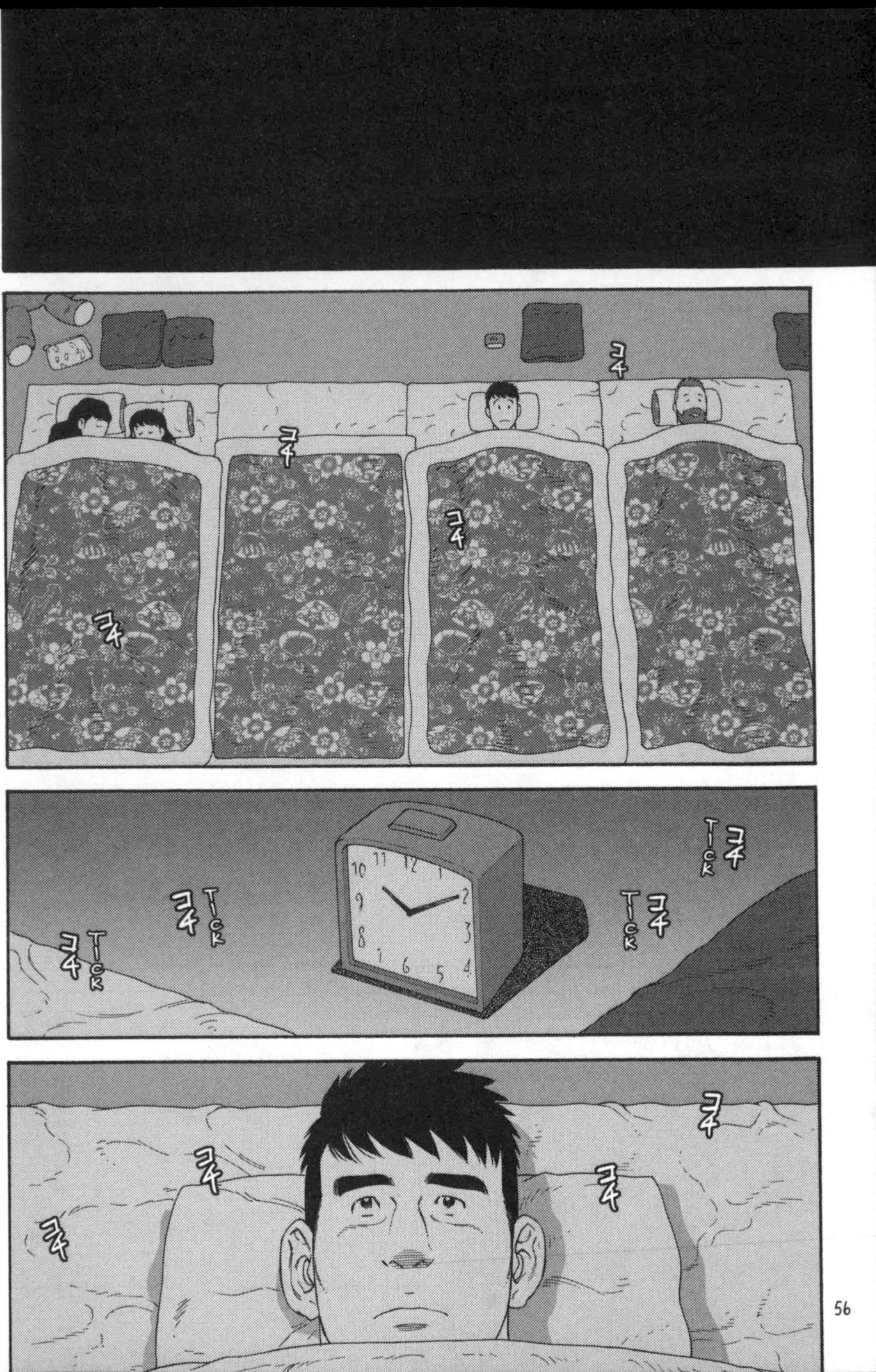
コチ
コチ
コチ
コチ
コチ TICK
コチ TICK
コチ TICK
コチ TICK
コチ
コチ
コチ
コチ

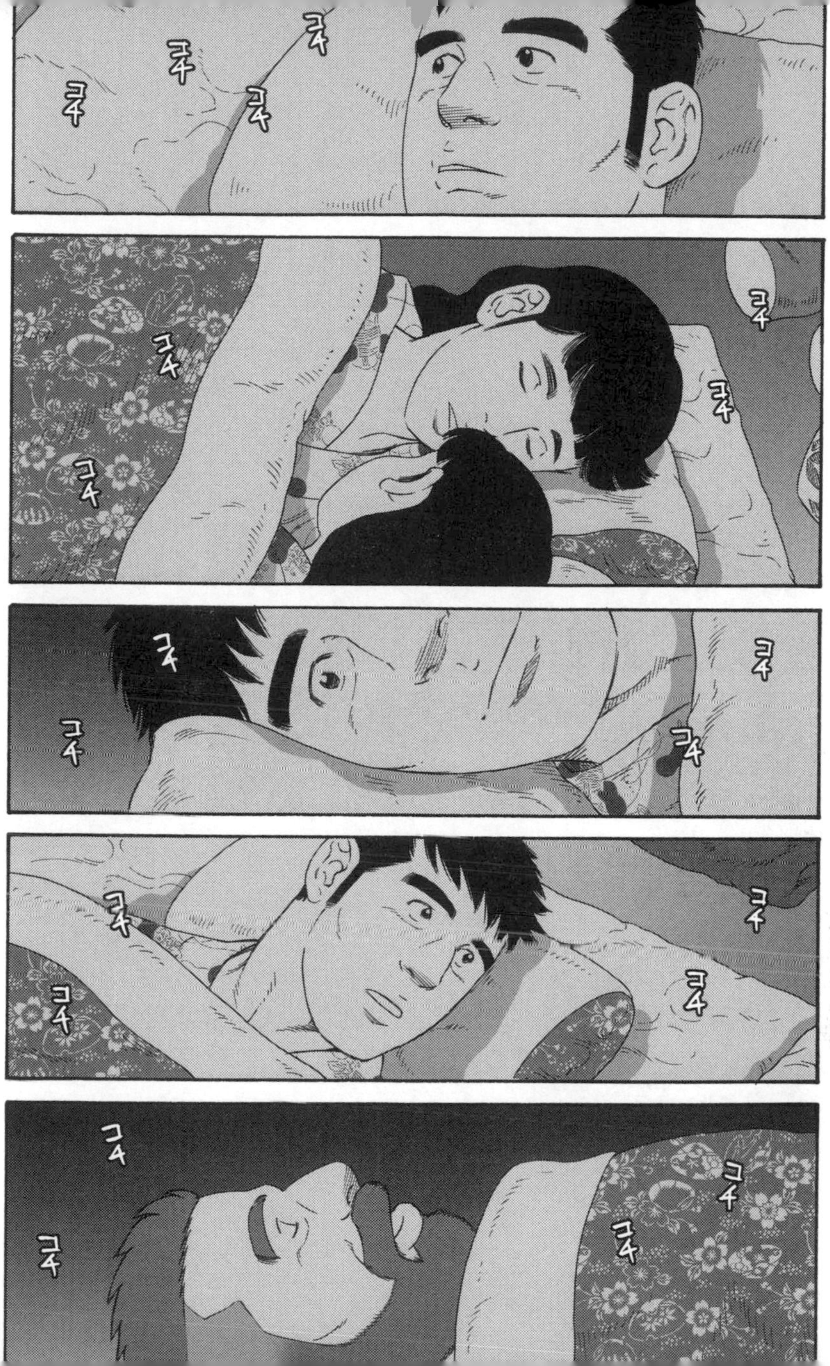
コキ
コキ
コキ
コキ
コキ
コキ
コキ
コキ
コキ
コキ
コキ
コキ
コキ
コキ
コキ
コキ
コキ
コキ
コキ
コキ

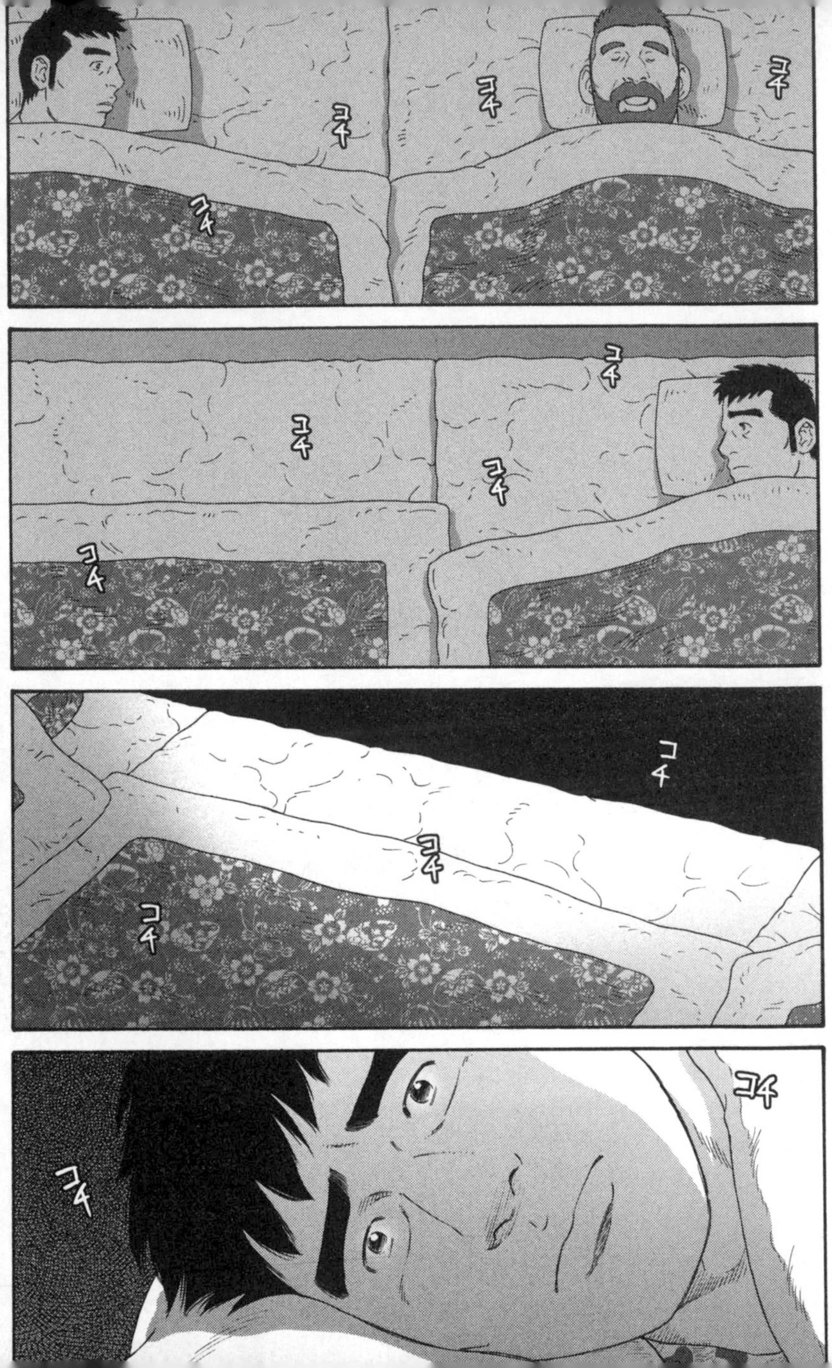
コチ
コチ
コチ
コチ
コチ
コチ
コチ
コチ
コチ
コチ
コチ
コチ
コチ
コチ

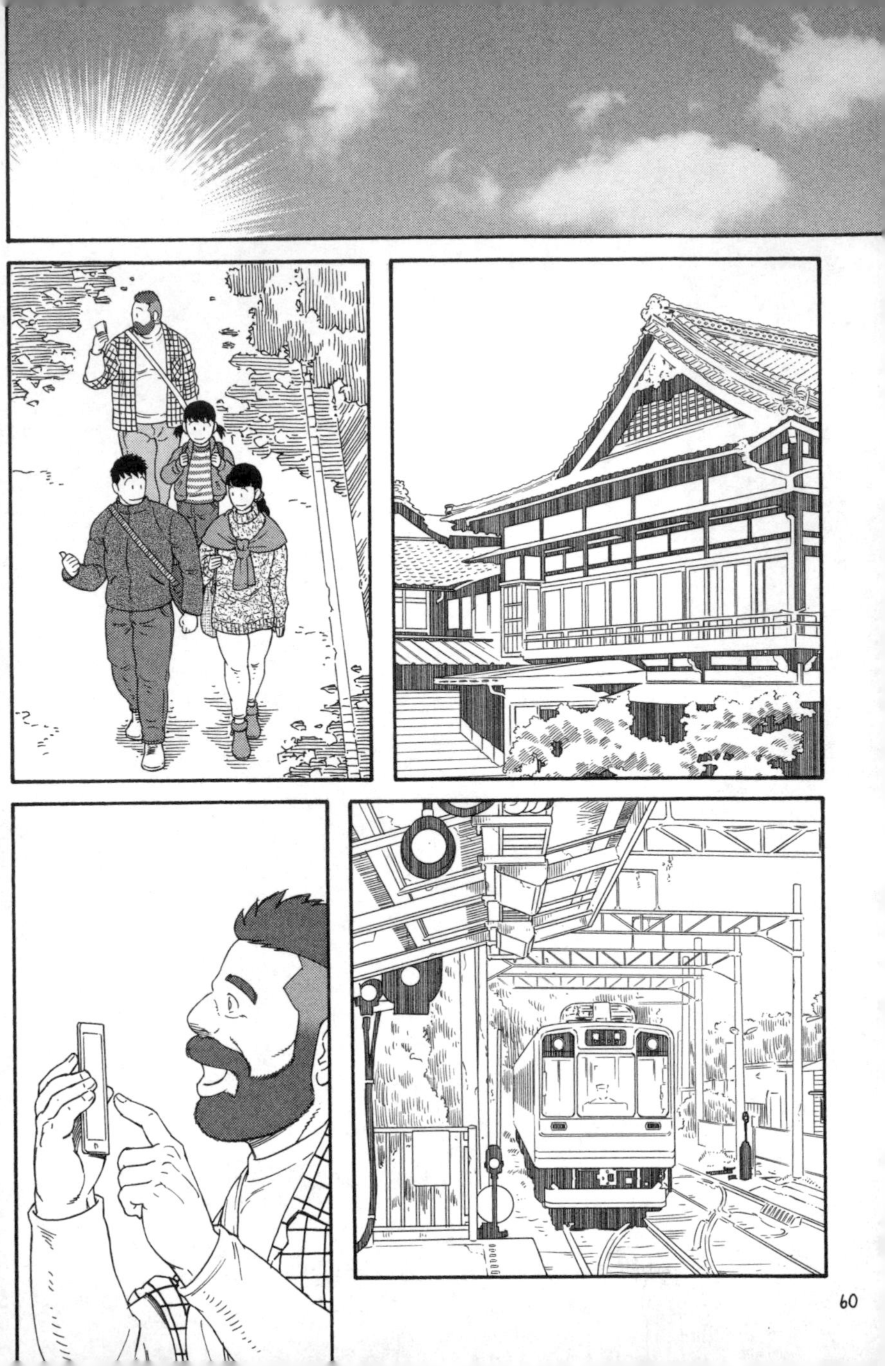

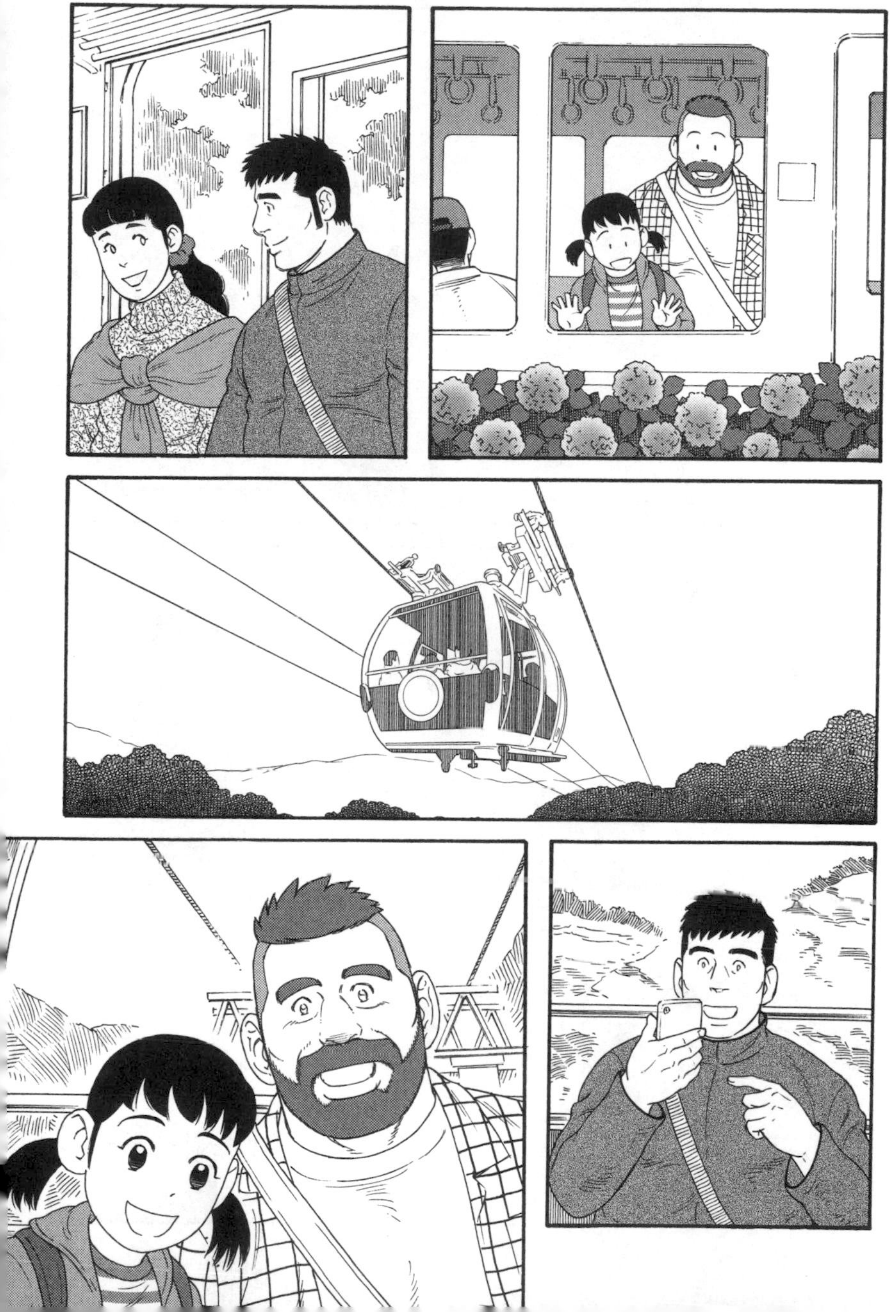

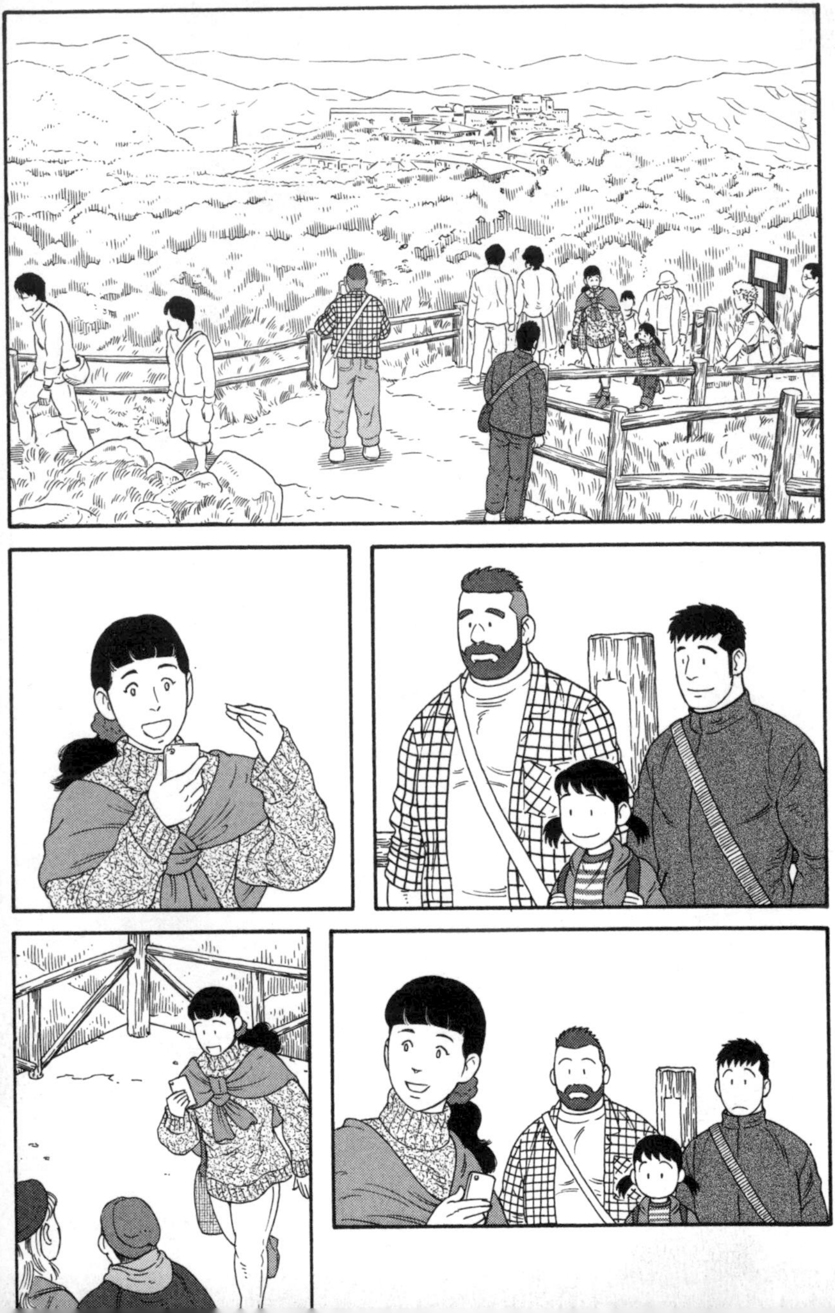

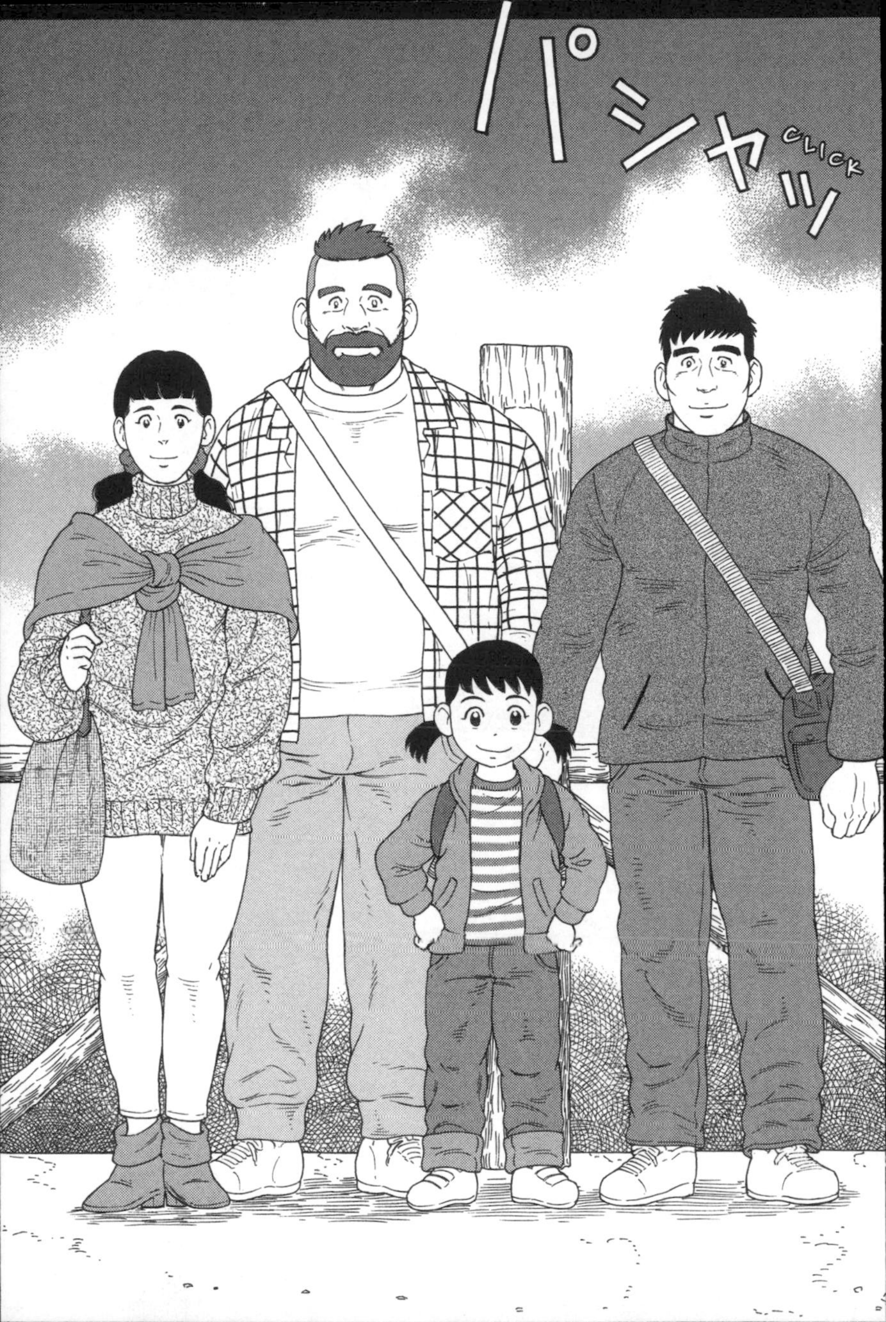
パシャッ
CLICK

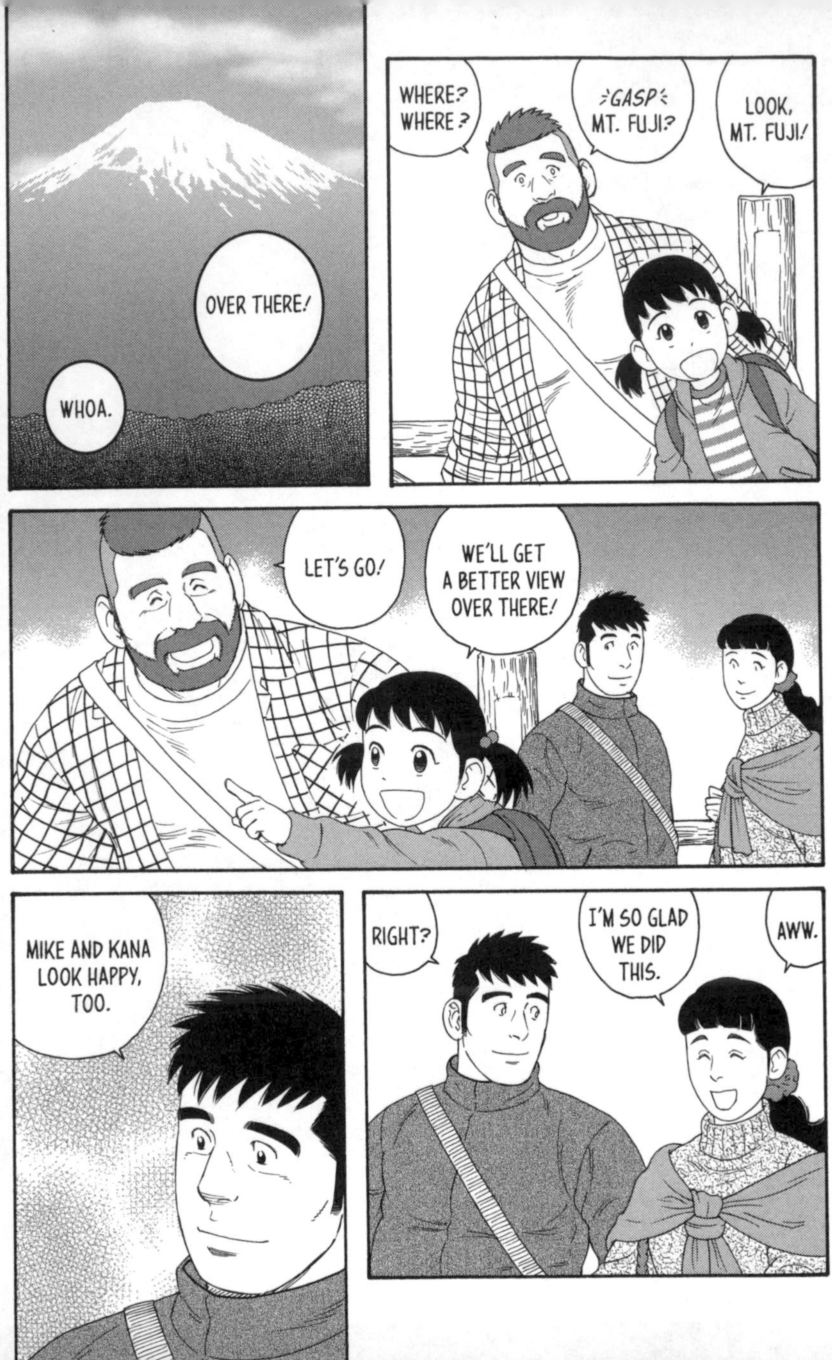
LOOK, MT. FUJI!
⸗GASP⸗ MT. FUJI?
WHERE? WHERE?
OVER THERE!
WHOA.
WE'LL GET A BETTER VIEW OVER THERE!
LET'S GO!
AWW.
I'M SO GLAD WE DID THIS.
RIGHT?
MIKE AND KANA LOOK HAPPY, TOO.

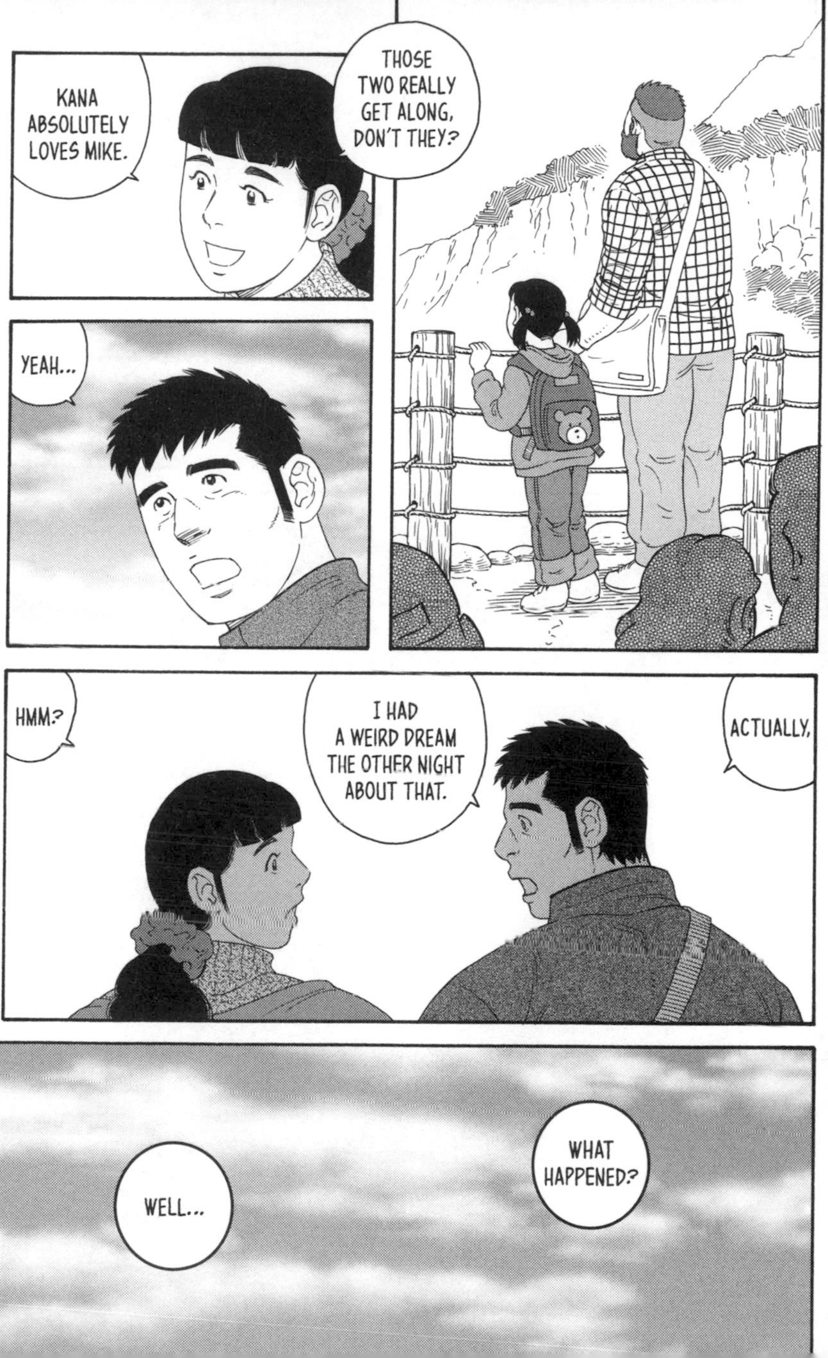
THOSE TWO REALLY GET ALONG, DON'T THEY?
KANA ABSOLUTELY LOVES MIKE.
YEAH...
ACTUALLY,
I HAD A WEIRD DREAM THE OTHER NIGHT ABOUT THAT.
HMM?
WHAT HAPPENED?
WELL...

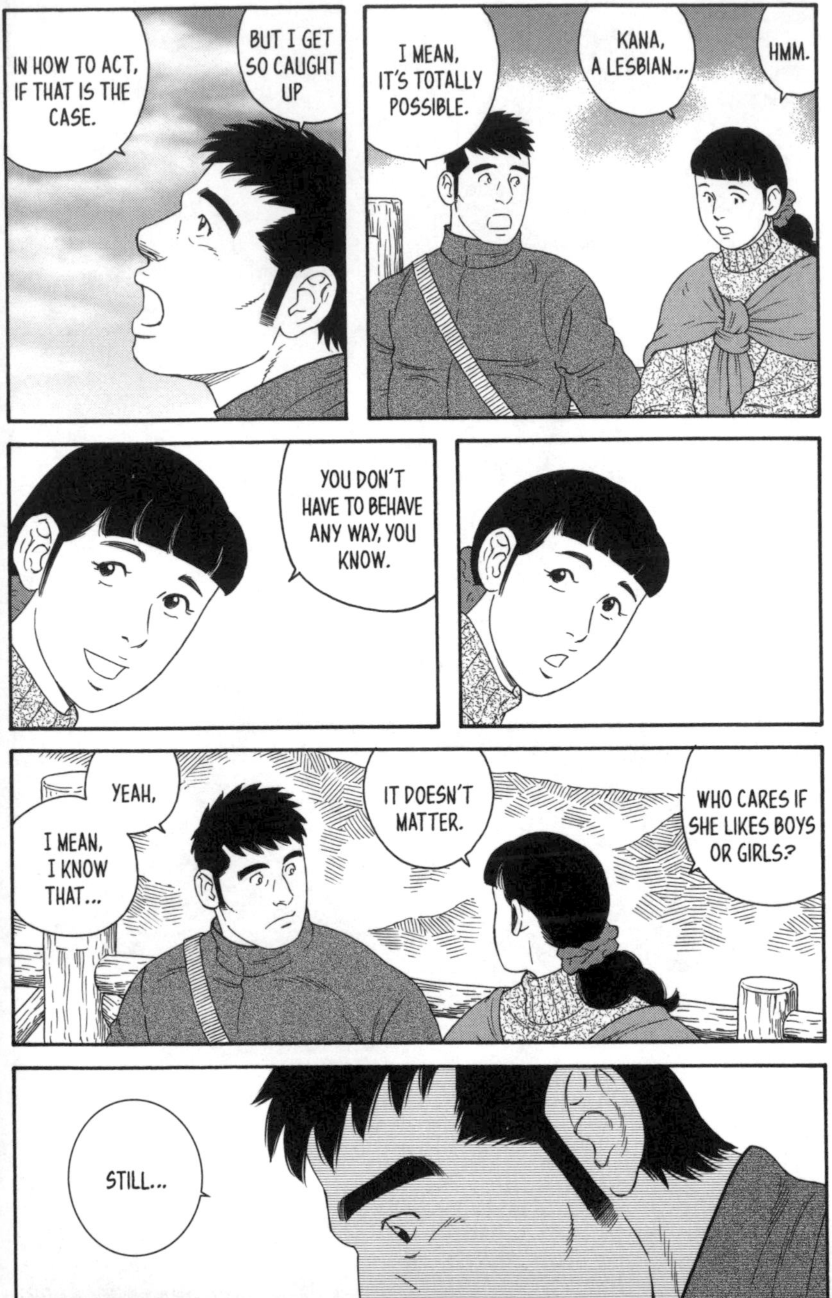
HMM.
KANA, A LESBIAN...
I MEAN, IT'S TOTALLY POSSIBLE.
BUT I GET SO CAUGHT UP
IN HOW TO ACT, IF THAT IS THE CASE.
YOU DON'T HAVE TO BEHAVE ANY WAY, YOU KNOW.
WHO CARES IF SHE LIKES BOYS OR GIRLS?
IT DOESN'T MATTER.
YEAH,
I MEAN, I KNOW THAT...
STILL...

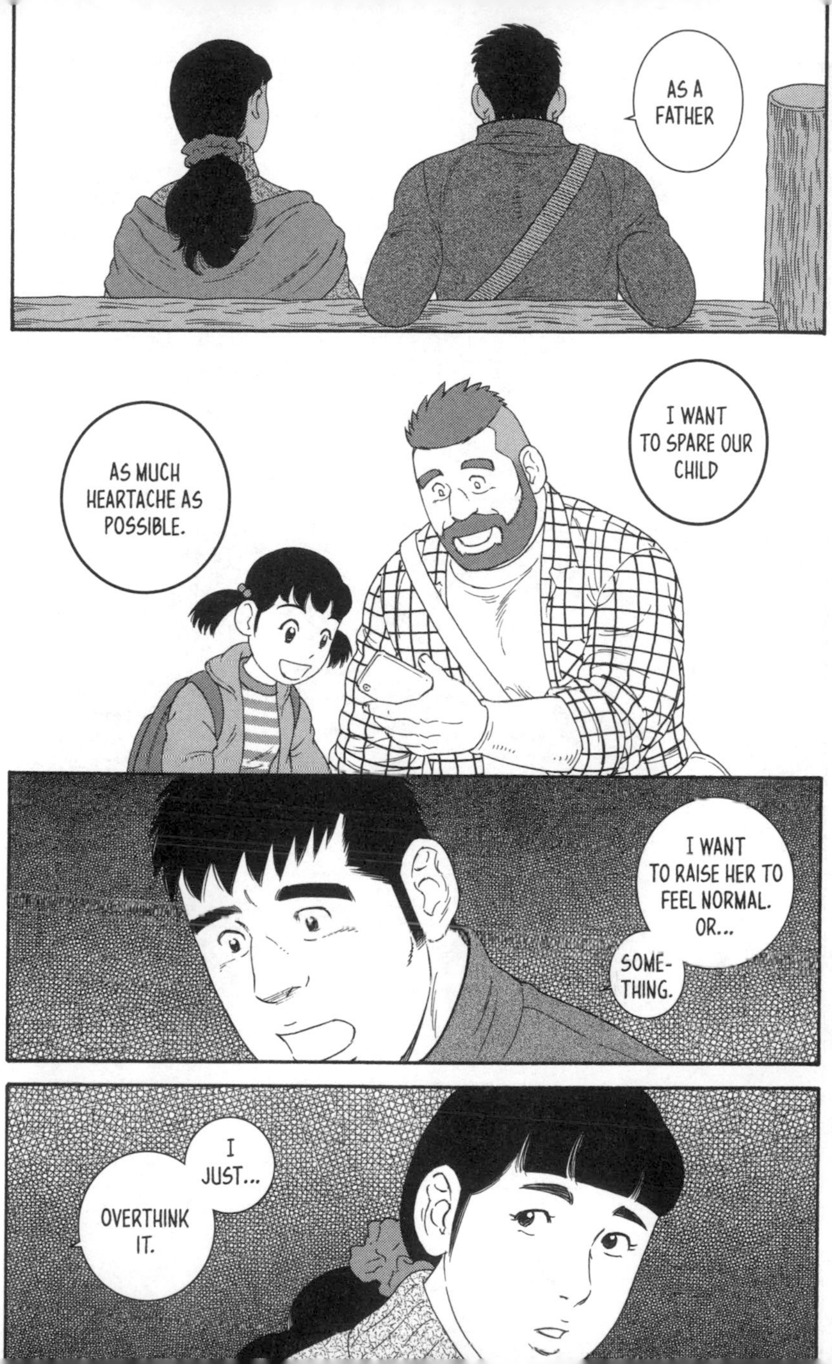
AS A FATHER
I WANT TO SPARE OUR CHILD
AS MUCH HEARTACHE AS POSSIBLE.
I WANT TO RAISE HER TO FEEL NORMAL. OR...
SOME-THING.
I JUST...
OVERTHINK IT.

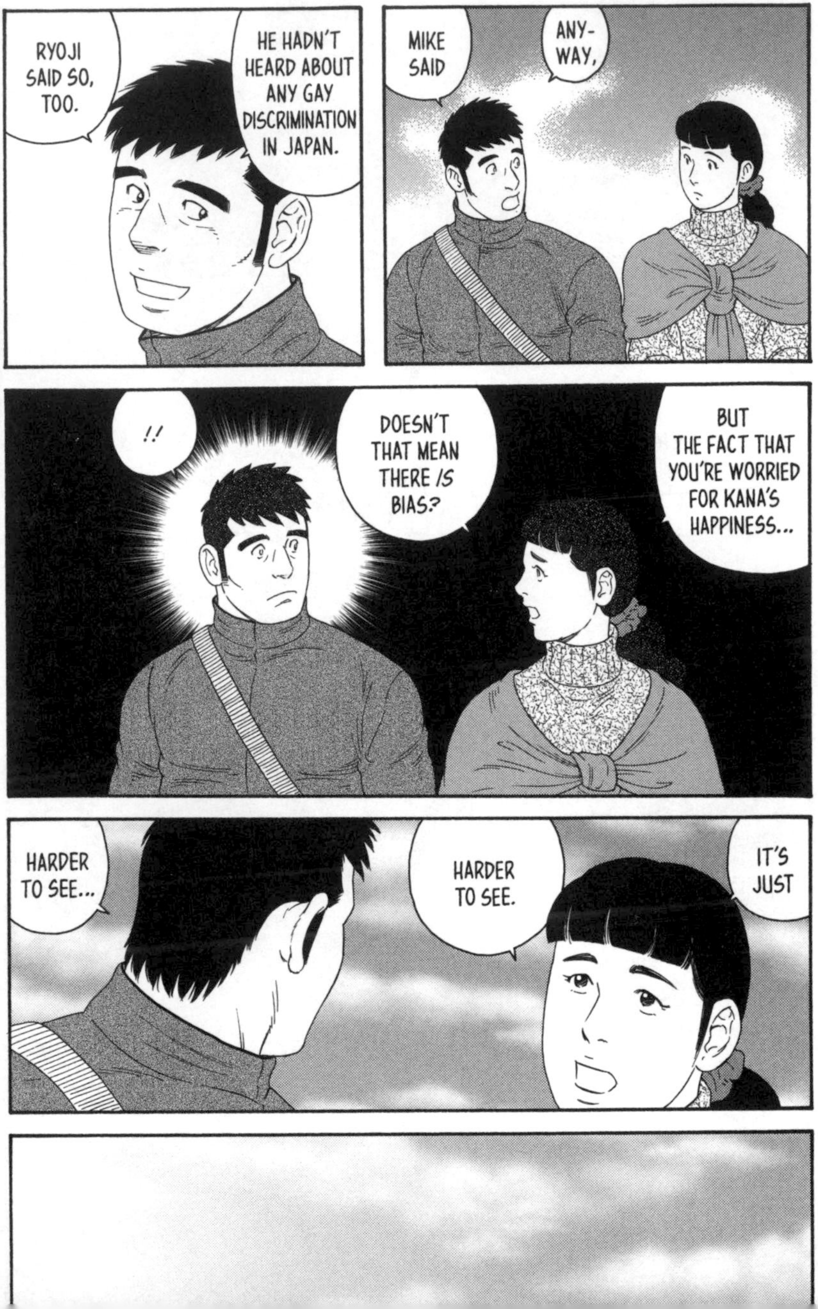
ANY-WAY,
MIKE SAID
HE HADN'T HEARD ABOUT ANY GAY DISCRIMINATION IN JAPAN.
RYOJI SAID SO, TOO.
BUT THE FACT THAT YOU'RE WORRIED FOR KANA'S HAPPINESS...
DOESN'T THAT MEAN THERE *IS* BIAS?
!!
IT'S JUST
HARDER TO SEE.
HARDER TO SEE...

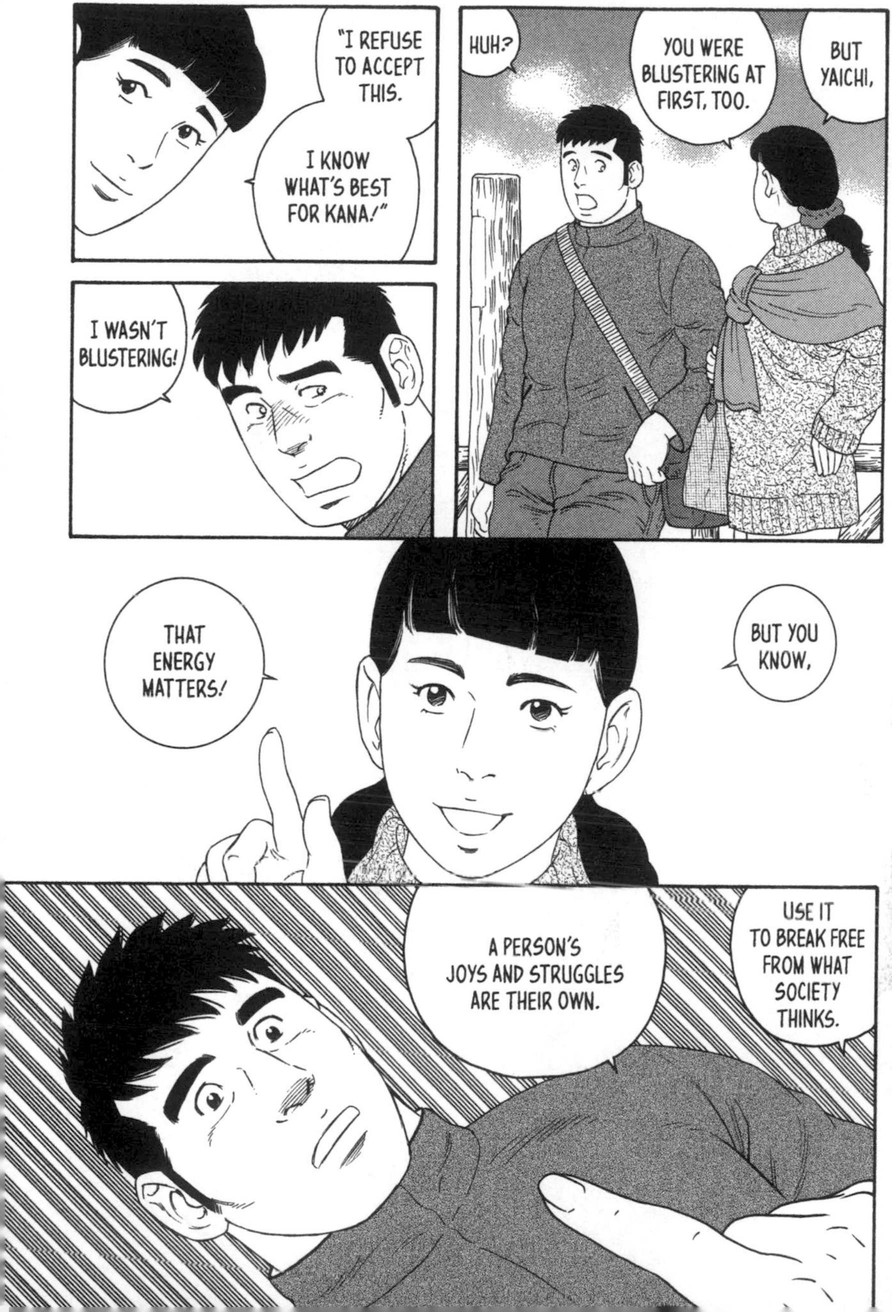
BUT YAICHI,
YOU WERE BLUSTERING AT FIRST, TOO.
HUH?
"I REFUSE TO ACCEPT THIS.
I KNOW WHAT'S BEST FOR KANA!"
I WASN'T BLUSTERING!
BUT YOU KNOW,
THAT ENERGY MATTERS!
USE IT TO BREAK FREE FROM WHAT SOCIETY THINKS.
A PERSON'S JOYS AND STRUGGLES ARE THEIR OWN.

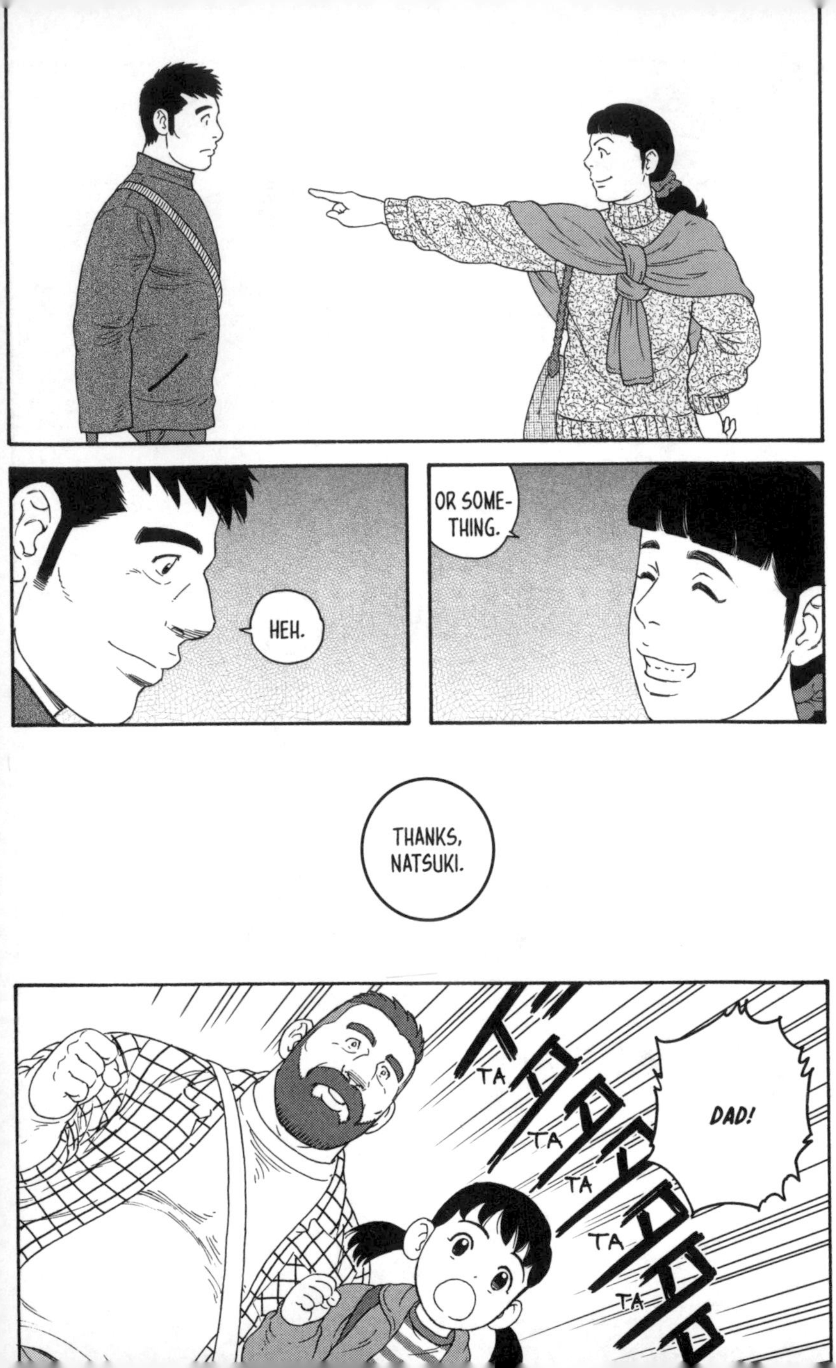
OR SOME-
THING.
HEH.
THANKS, NATSUKI.
DAD!
TA
TA
TA
TA
TA

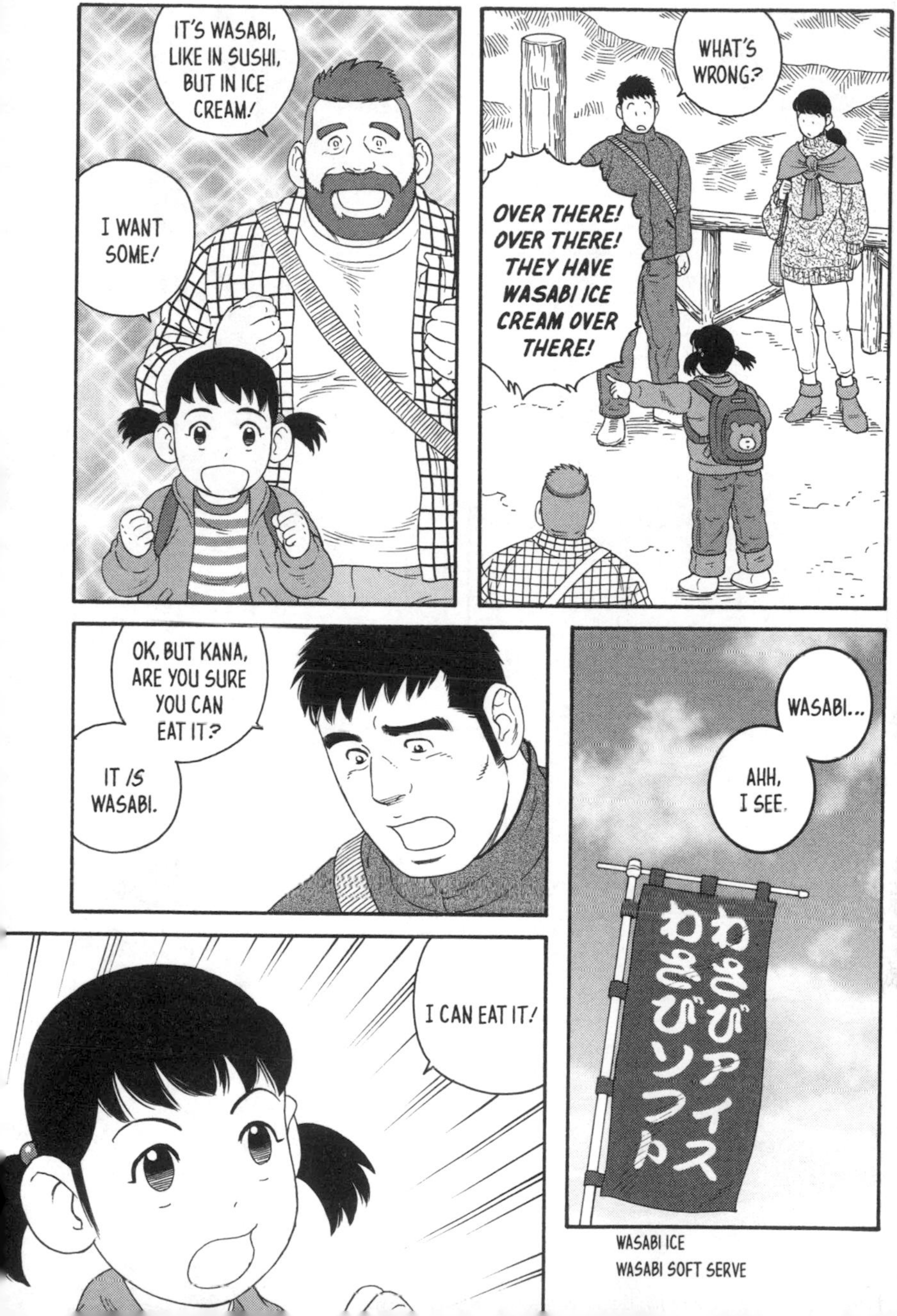
WHAT'S WRONG?
OVER THERE! OVER THERE! THEY HAVE WASABI ICE CREAM OVER THERE!
IT'S WASABI, LIKE IN SUSHI, BUT IN ICE CREAM!
I WANT SOME!
WASABI...
AHH, I SEE.
わさびアイス
わさびソフト
OK, BUT KANA, ARE YOU SURE YOU CAN EAT IT?
IT IS WASABI.
I CAN EAT IT!
WASABI ICE
WASABI SOFT SERVE

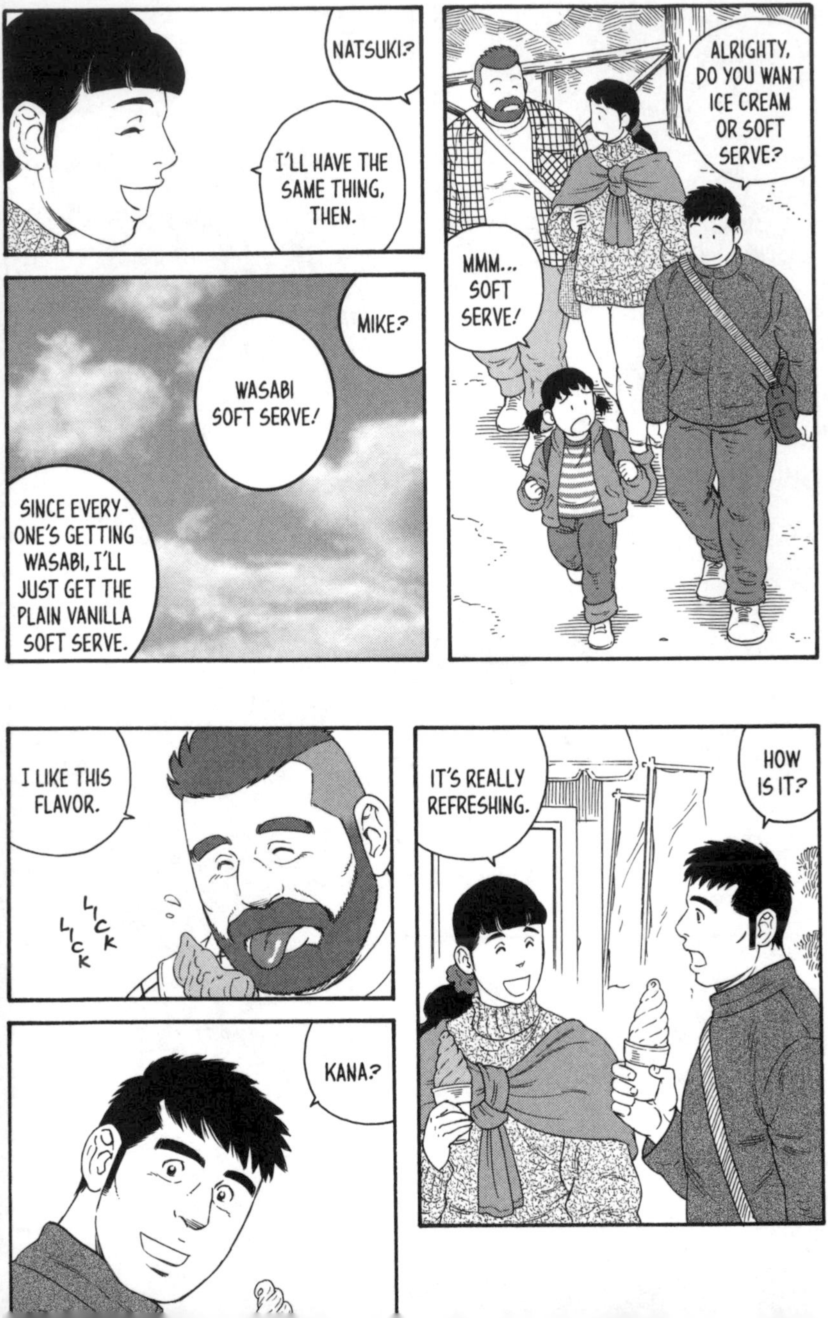
ALRIGHTY, DO YOU WANT ICE CREAM OR SOFT SERVE?
MMM... SOFT SERVE!
NATSUKI?
I'LL HAVE THE SAME THING, THEN.
MIKE?
WASABI SOFT SERVE!
SINCE EVERY-ONE'S GETTING WASABI, I'LL JUST GET THE PLAIN VANILLA SOFT SERVE.
HOW IS IT?
IT'S REALLY REFRESHING.
I LIKE THIS FLAVOR.
LICK LICK
KANA?

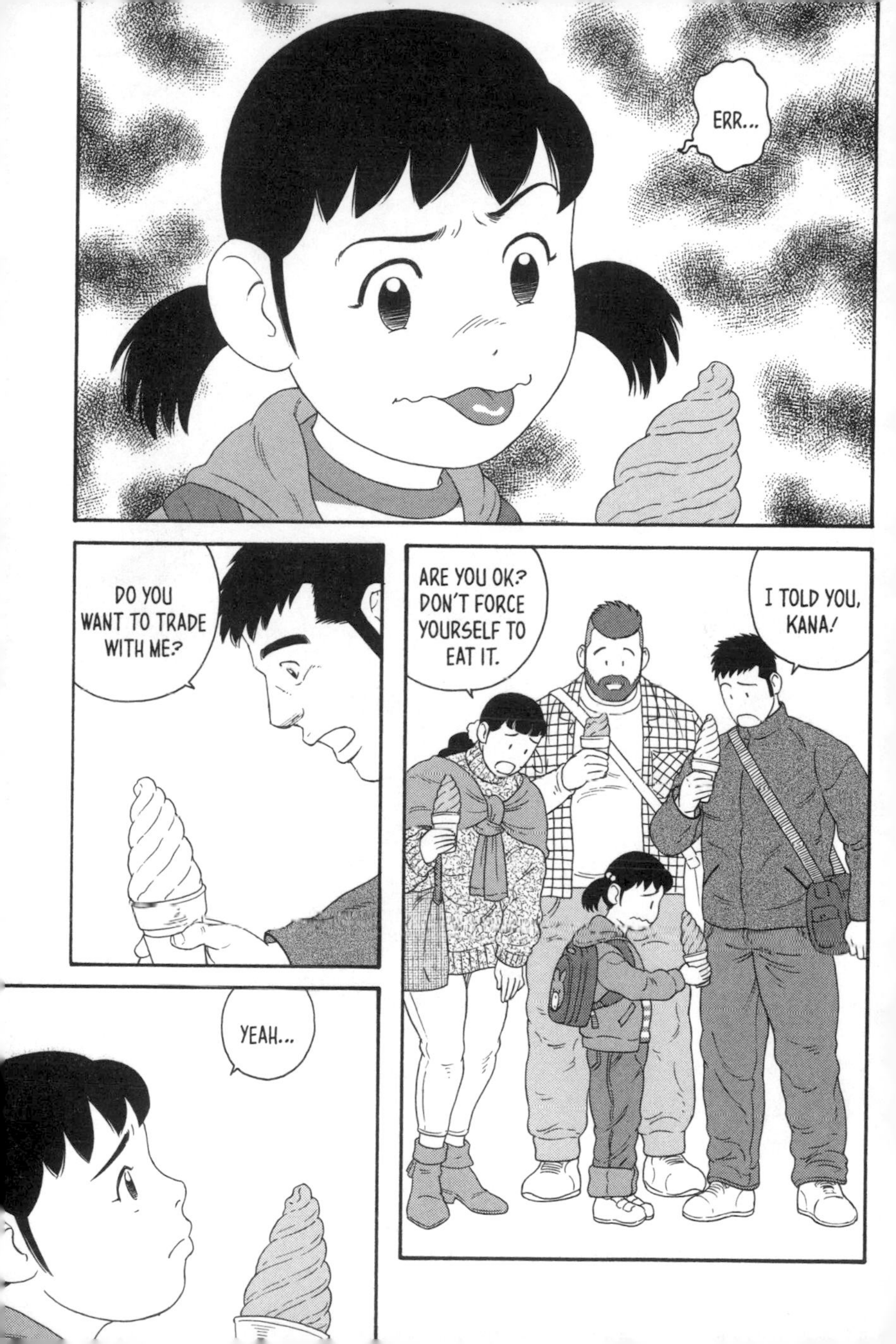
ERR...
I TOLD YOU, KANA!
ARE YOU OK? DON'T FORCE YOURSELF TO EAT IT.
DO YOU WANT TO TRADE WITH ME?
YEAH...

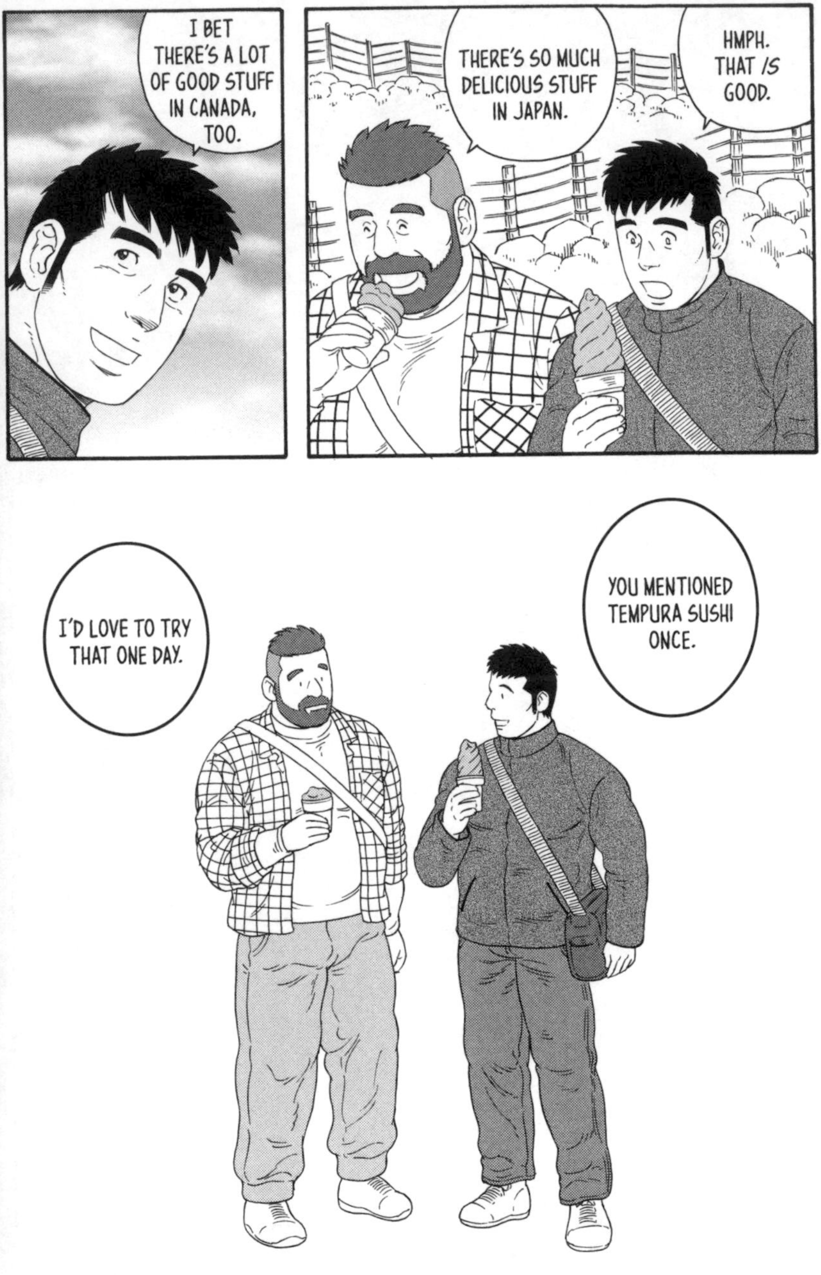
HMPH. THAT *IS* GOOD.
THERE'S SO MUCH DELICIOUS STUFF IN JAPAN.
I BET THERE'S A LOT OF GOOD STUFF IN CANADA, TOO.
YOU MENTIONED TEMPURA SUSHI ONCE.
I'D LOVE TO TRY THAT ONE DAY.

CHAPTER EIGHTEEN

DECISIONS

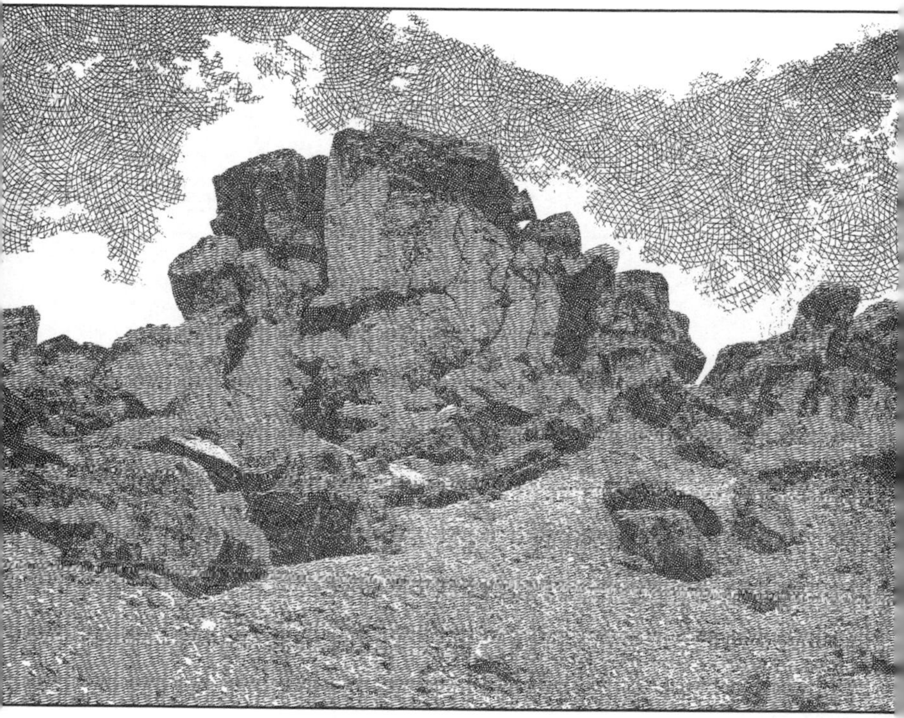

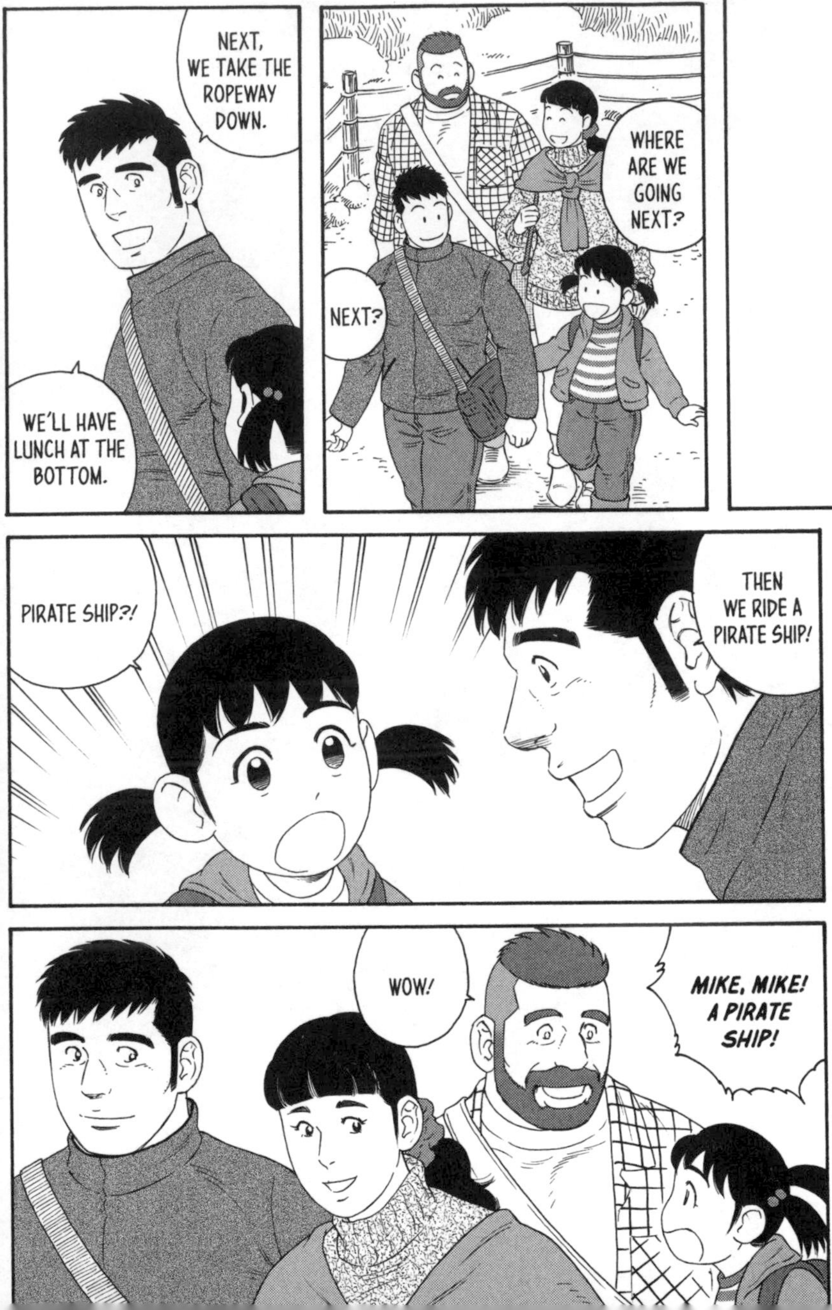
WHERE ARE WE GOING NEXT?
NEXT?
NEXT, WE TAKE THE ROPEWAY DOWN.
WE'LL HAVE LUNCH AT THE BOTTOM.
THEN WE RIDE A PIRATE SHIP!
PIRATE SHIP?!
MIKE, MIKE! A PIRATE SHIP!
WOW!

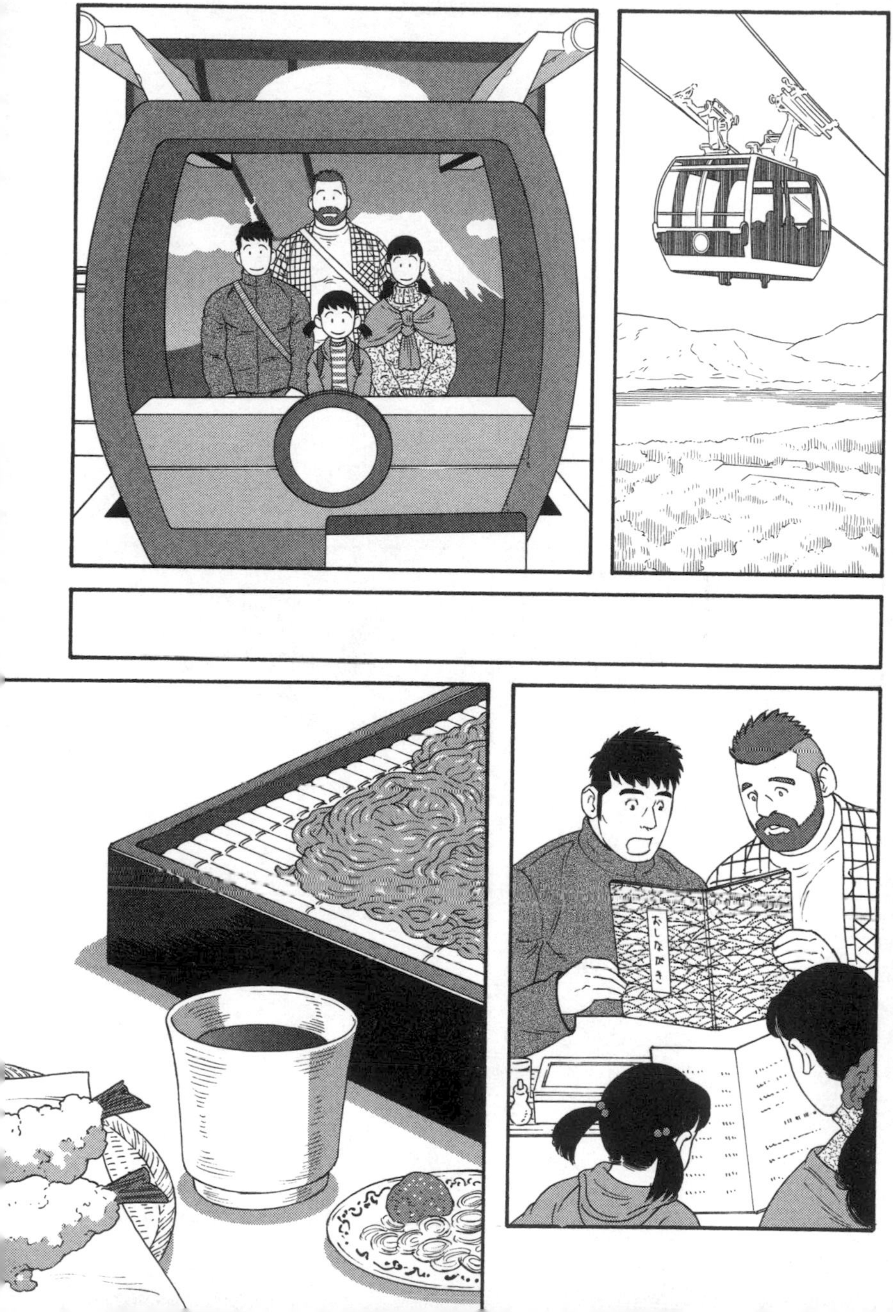
おしながき

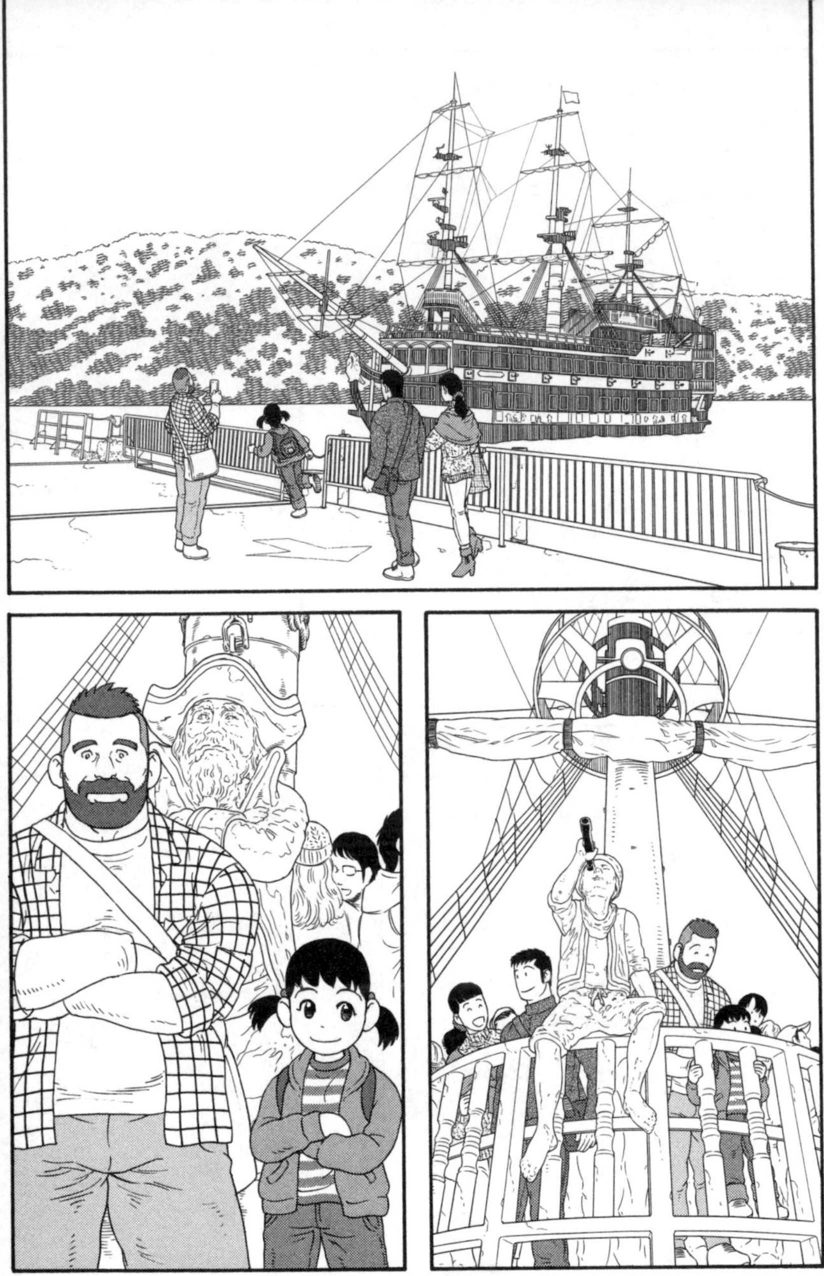

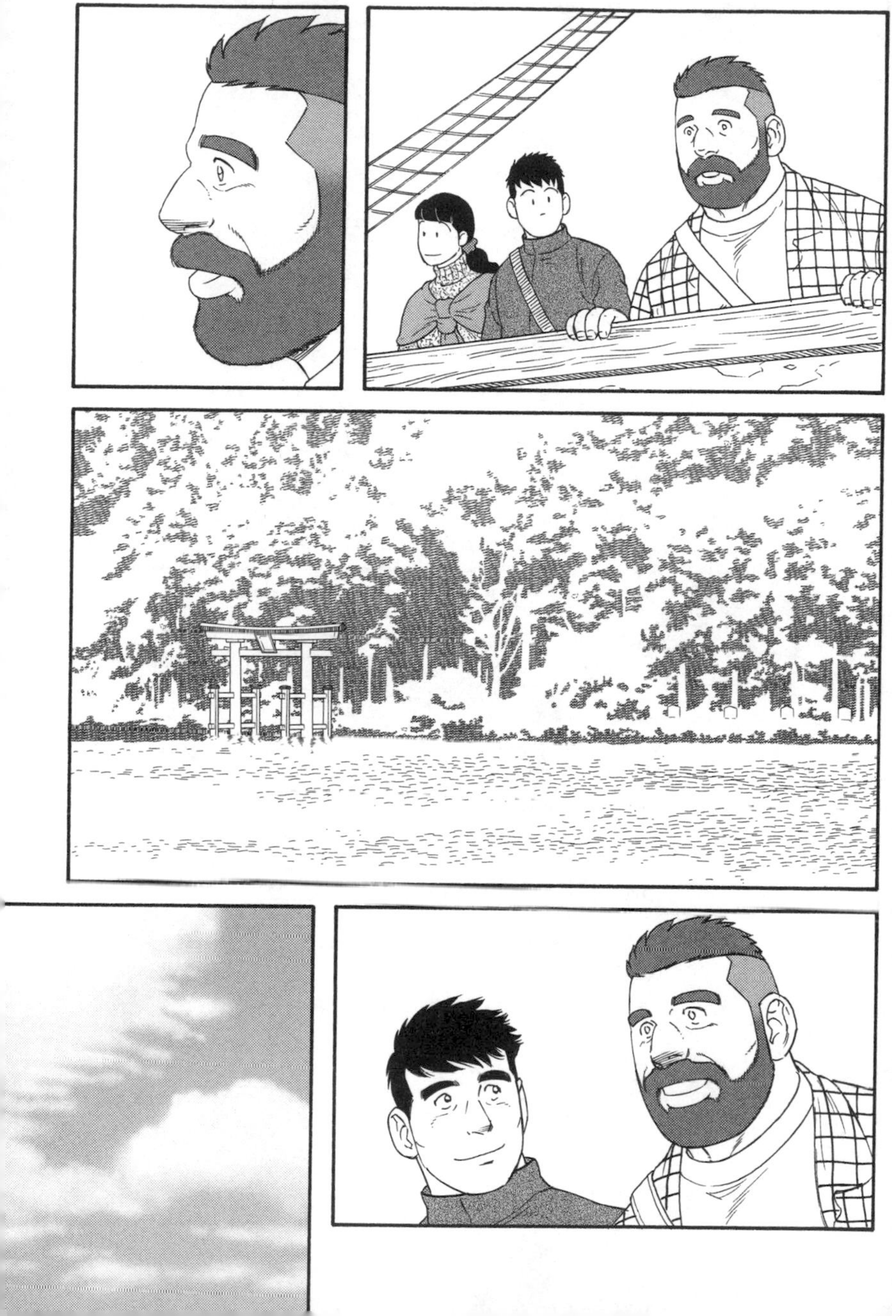

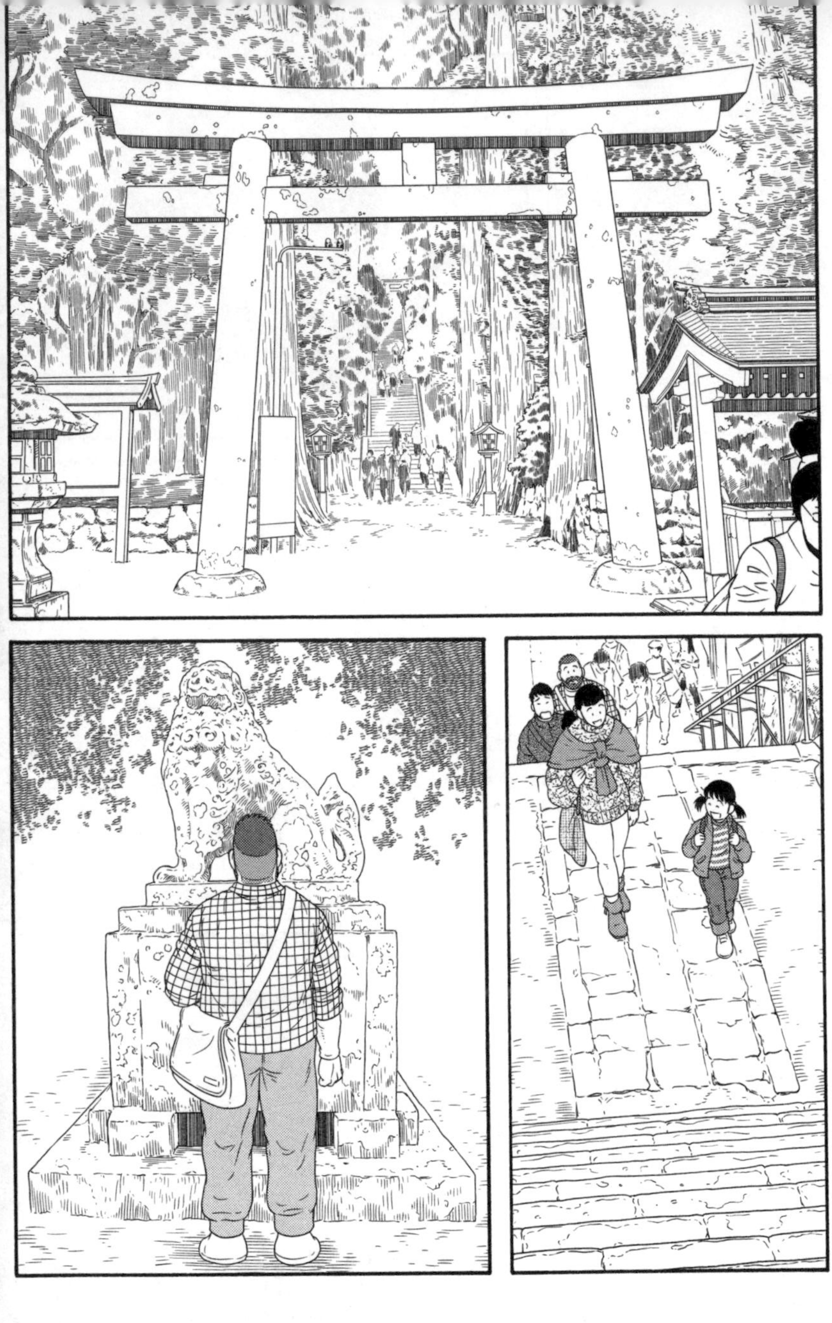

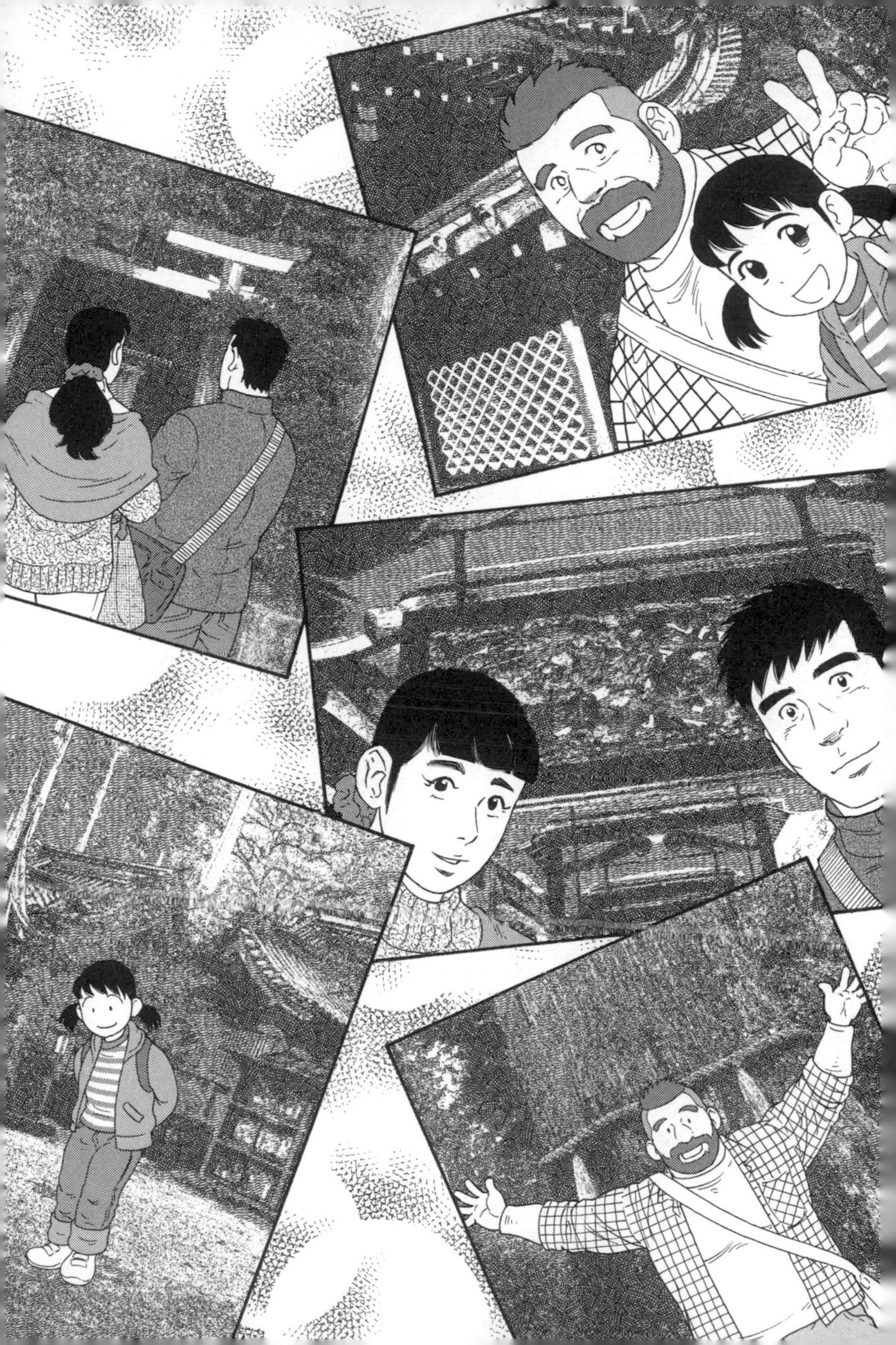

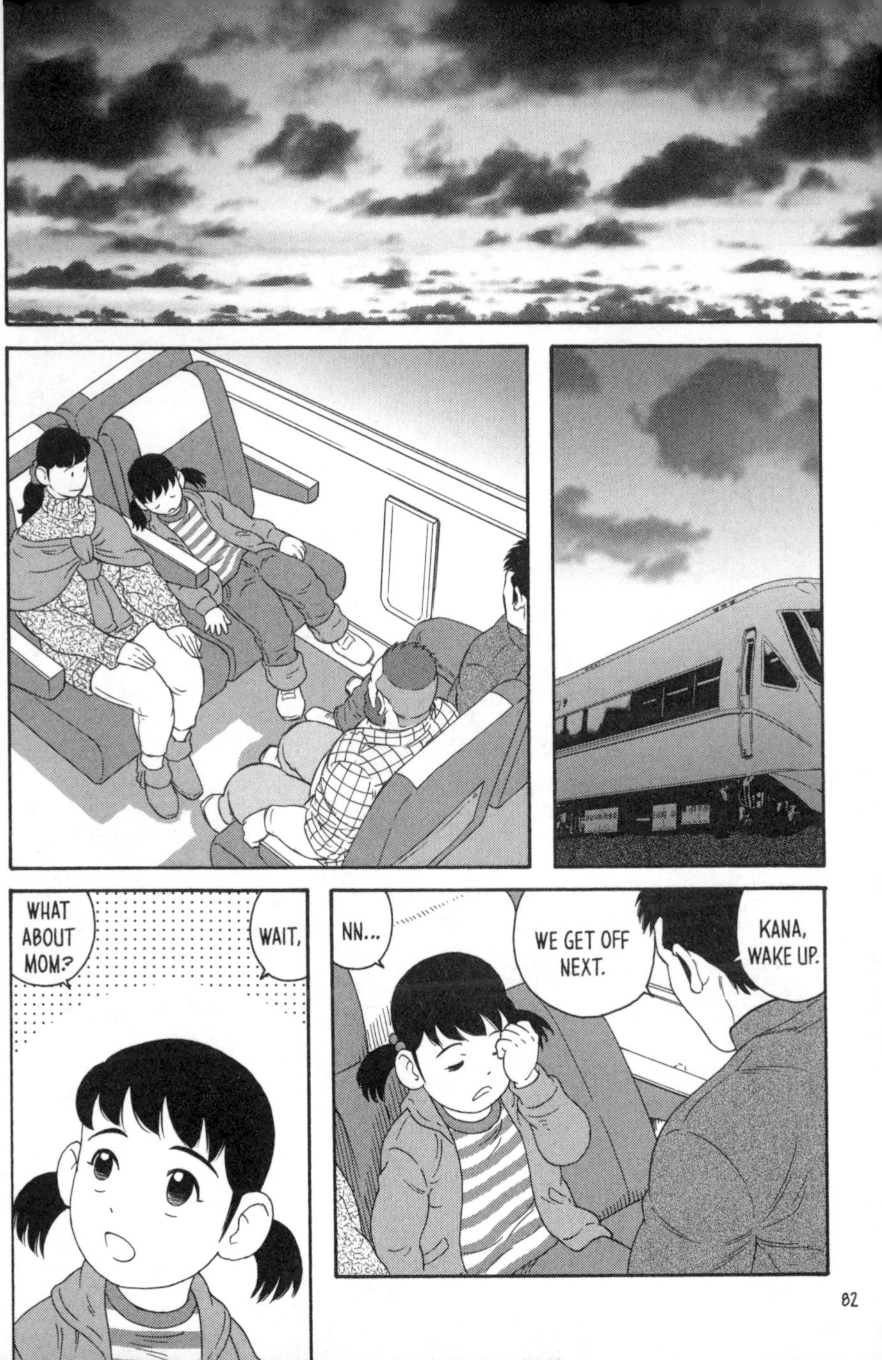
KANA, WAKE UP.
WE GET OFF NEXT.
NN...
WAIT,
WHAT ABOUT MOM?

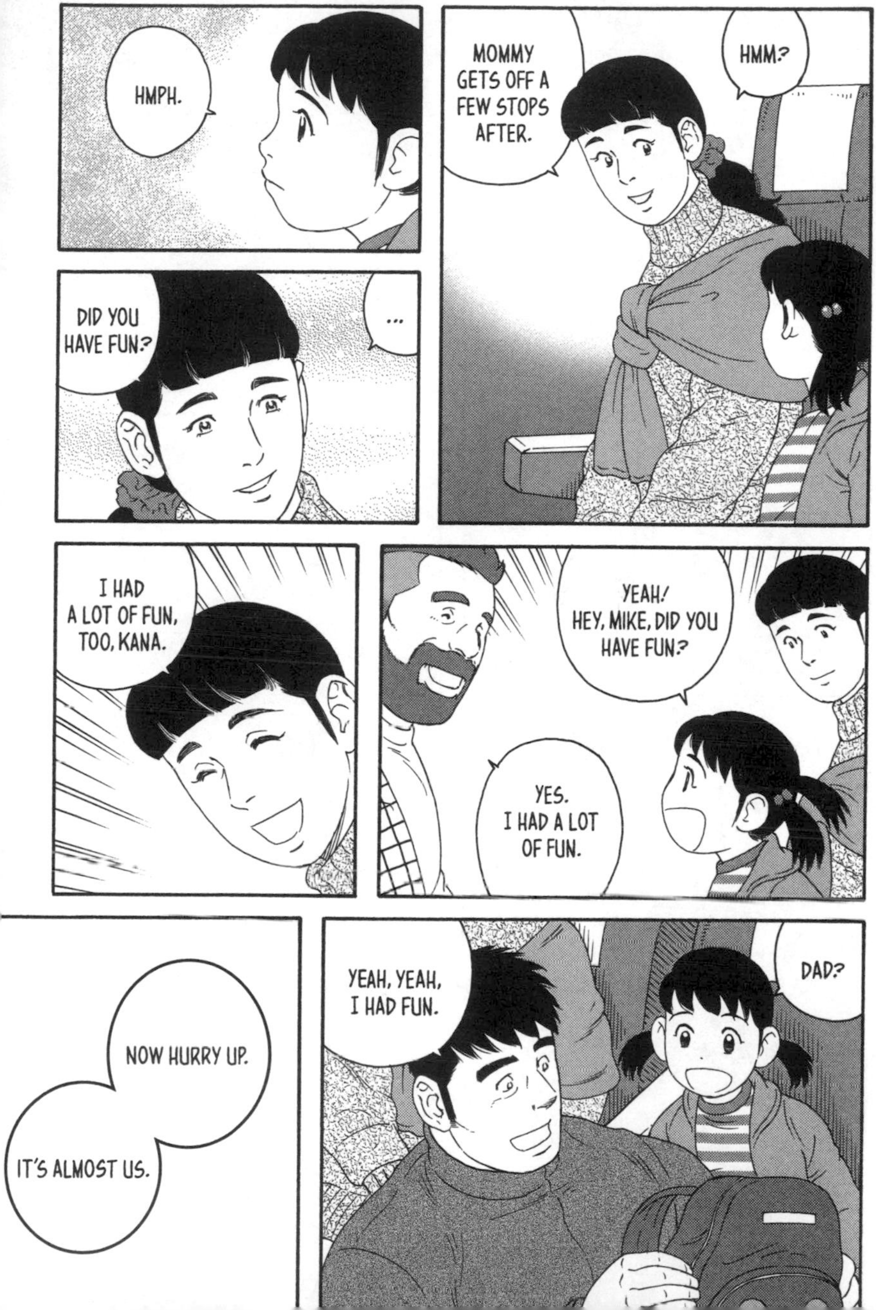
MOMMY GETS OFF A FEW STOPS AFTER.
HMM?
HMPH.
DID YOU HAVE FUN?
...
YEAH! HEY, MIKE, DID YOU HAVE FUN?
YES. I HAD A LOT OF FUN.
I HAD A LOT OF FUN, TOO, KANA.
DAD?
YEAH, YEAH, I HAD FUN.
NOW HURRY UP.
IT'S ALMOST US.

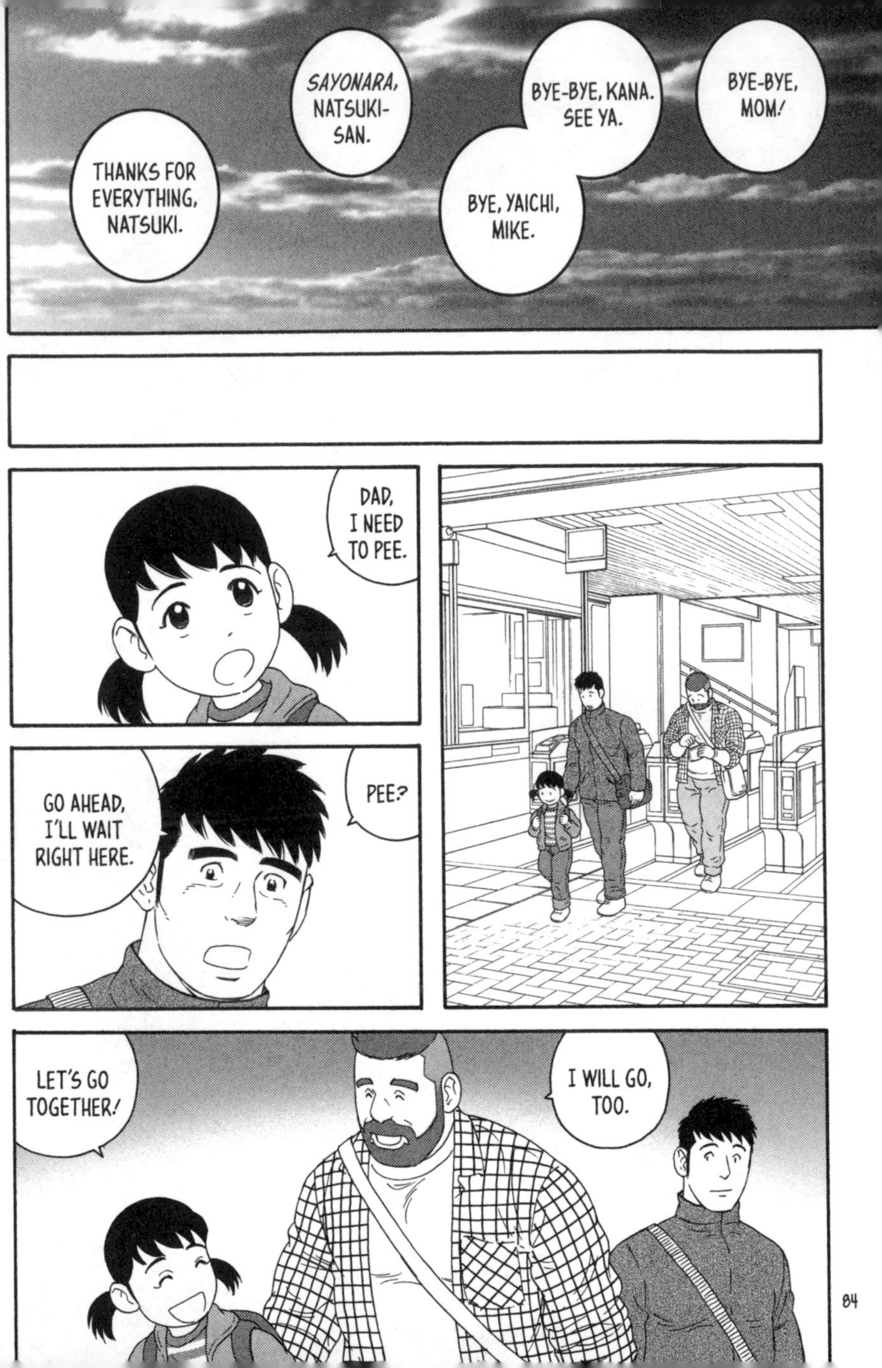
BYE-BYE, MOM!
BYE-BYE, KANA. SEE YA.
BYE, YAICHI, MIKE.
SAYONARA, NATSUKI-SAN.
THANKS FOR EVERYTHING, NATSUKI.
DAD, I NEED TO PEE.
PEE?
GO AHEAD, I'LL WAIT RIGHT HERE.
I WILL GO, TOO.
LET'S GO TOGETHER!

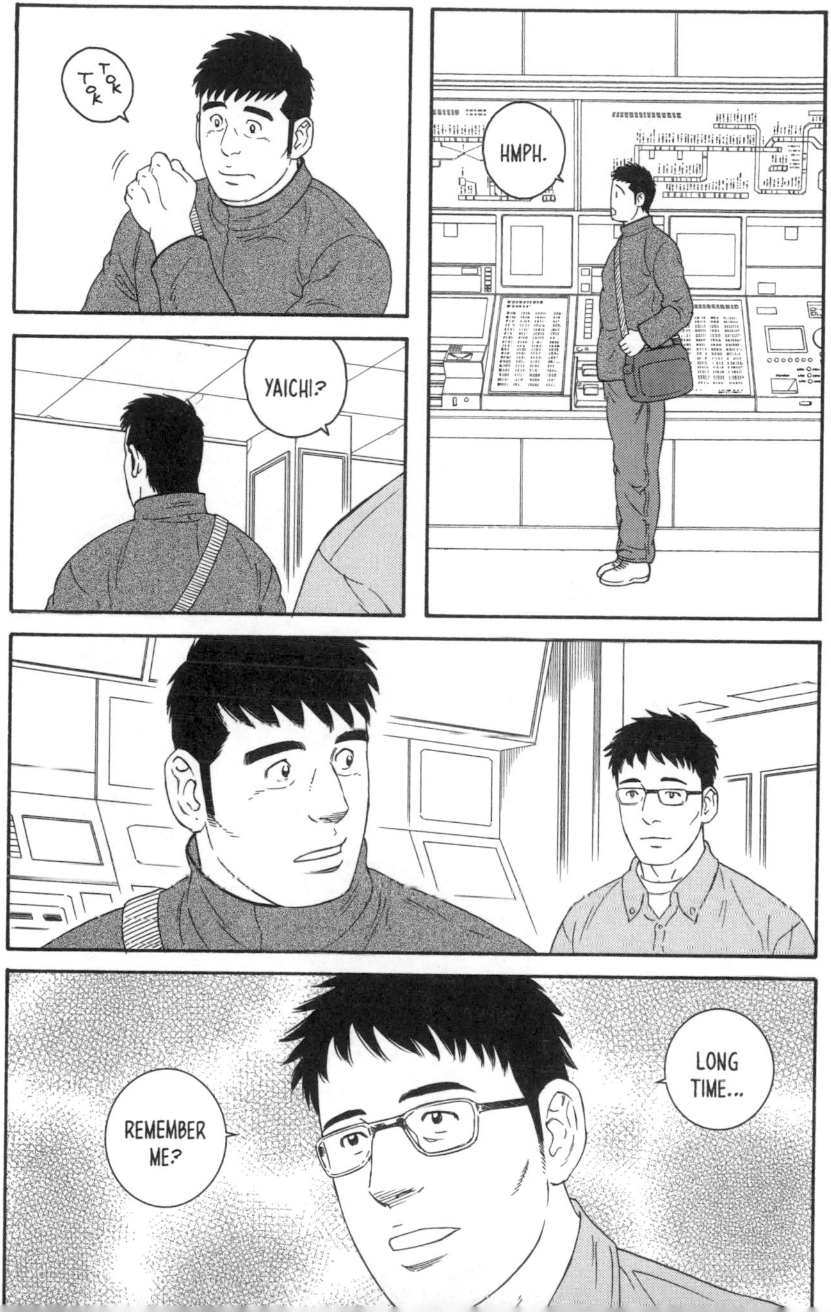
HMPH.
TOK TOK
YAICHI?
LONG TIME...
REMEMBER ME?

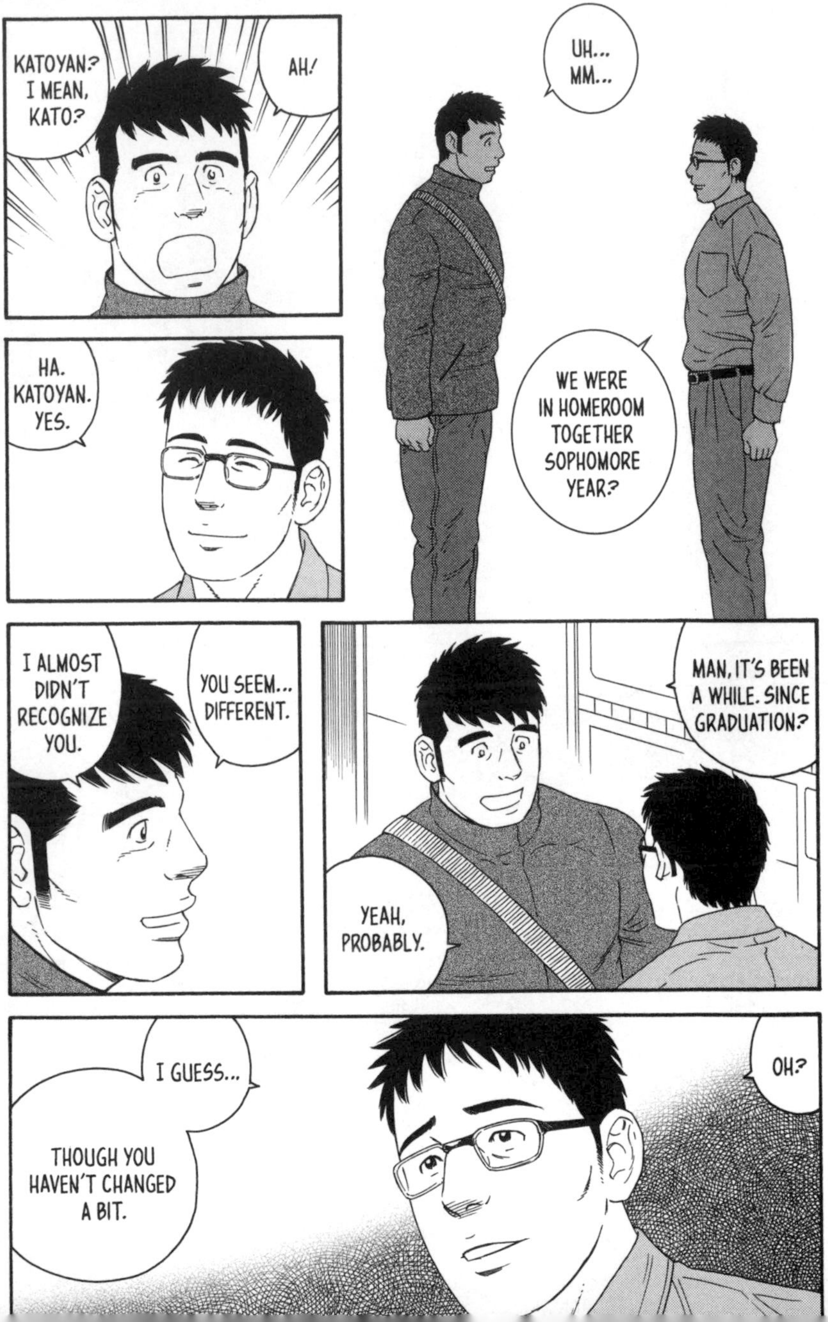
UH... MM...
WE WERE IN HOMEROOM TOGETHER SOPHOMORE YEAR?
AH!
KATOYAN? I MEAN, KATO?
HA. KATOYAN. YES.
MAN, IT'S BEEN A WHILE. SINCE GRADUATION?
YEAH, PROBABLY.
YOU SEEM... DIFFERENT.
I ALMOST DIDN'T RECOGNIZE YOU.
OH?
I GUESS...
THOUGH YOU HAVEN'T CHANGED A BIT.

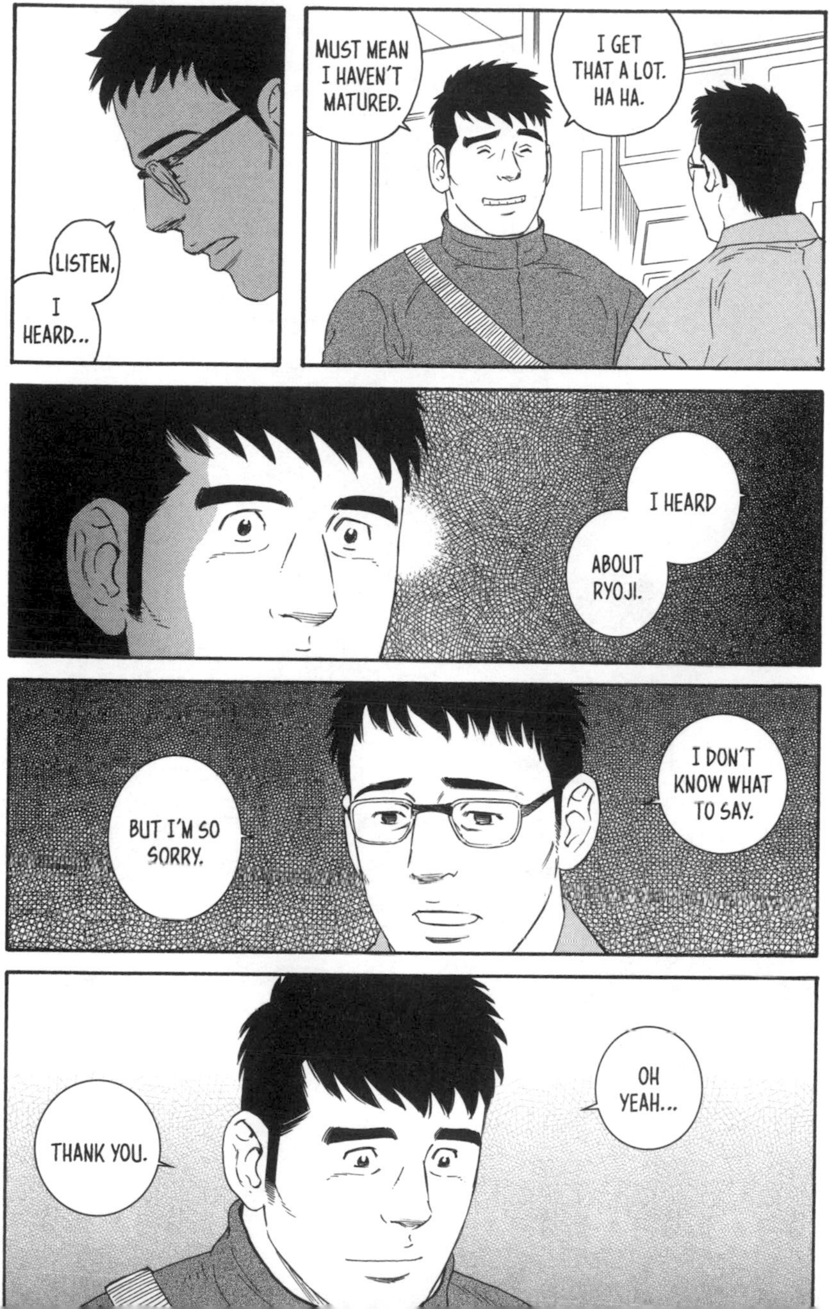
I GET THAT A LOT. HA HA.
MUST MEAN I HAVEN'T MATURED.
LISTEN,
I HEARD...
I HEARD
ABOUT RYOJI.
I DON'T KNOW WHAT TO SAY.
BUT I'M SO SORRY.
OH YEAH...
THANK YOU.

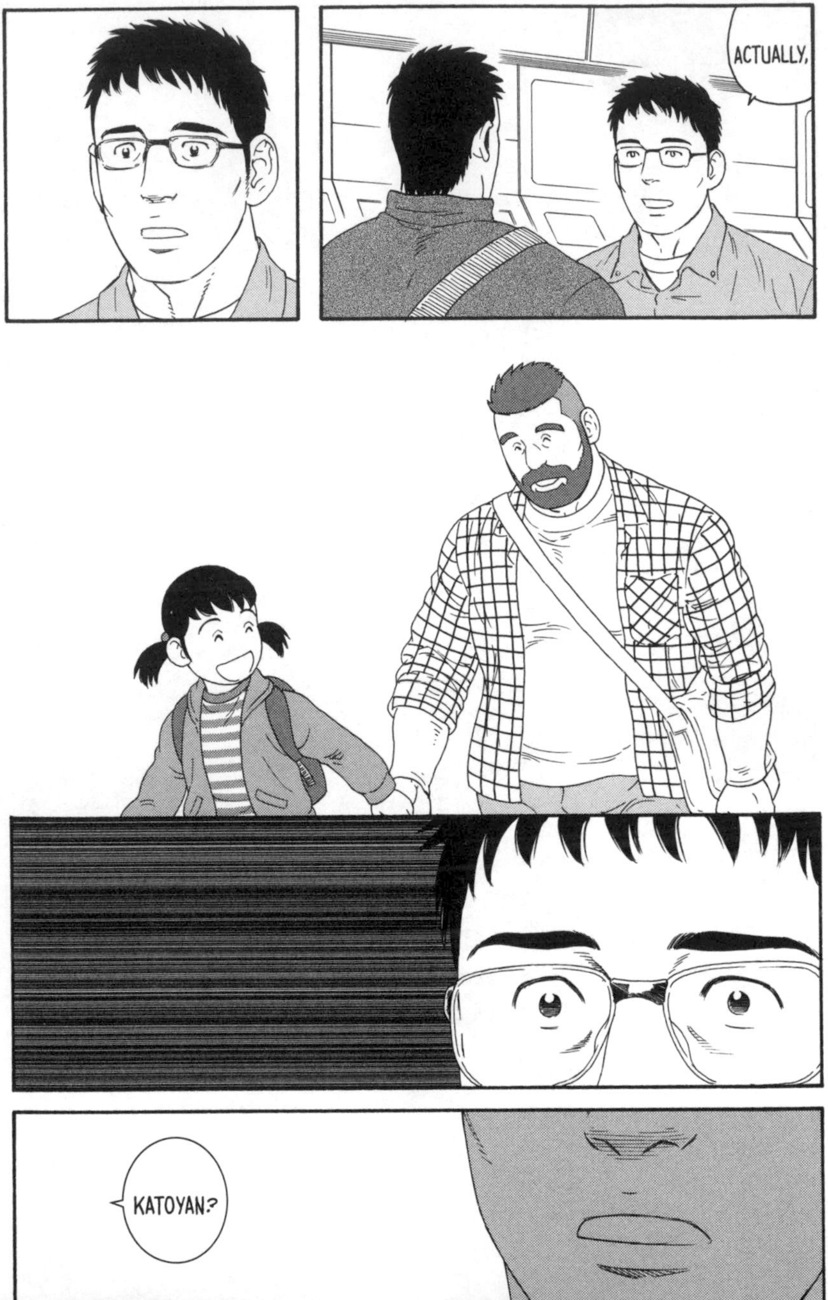
ACTUALLY,
KATOYAN?

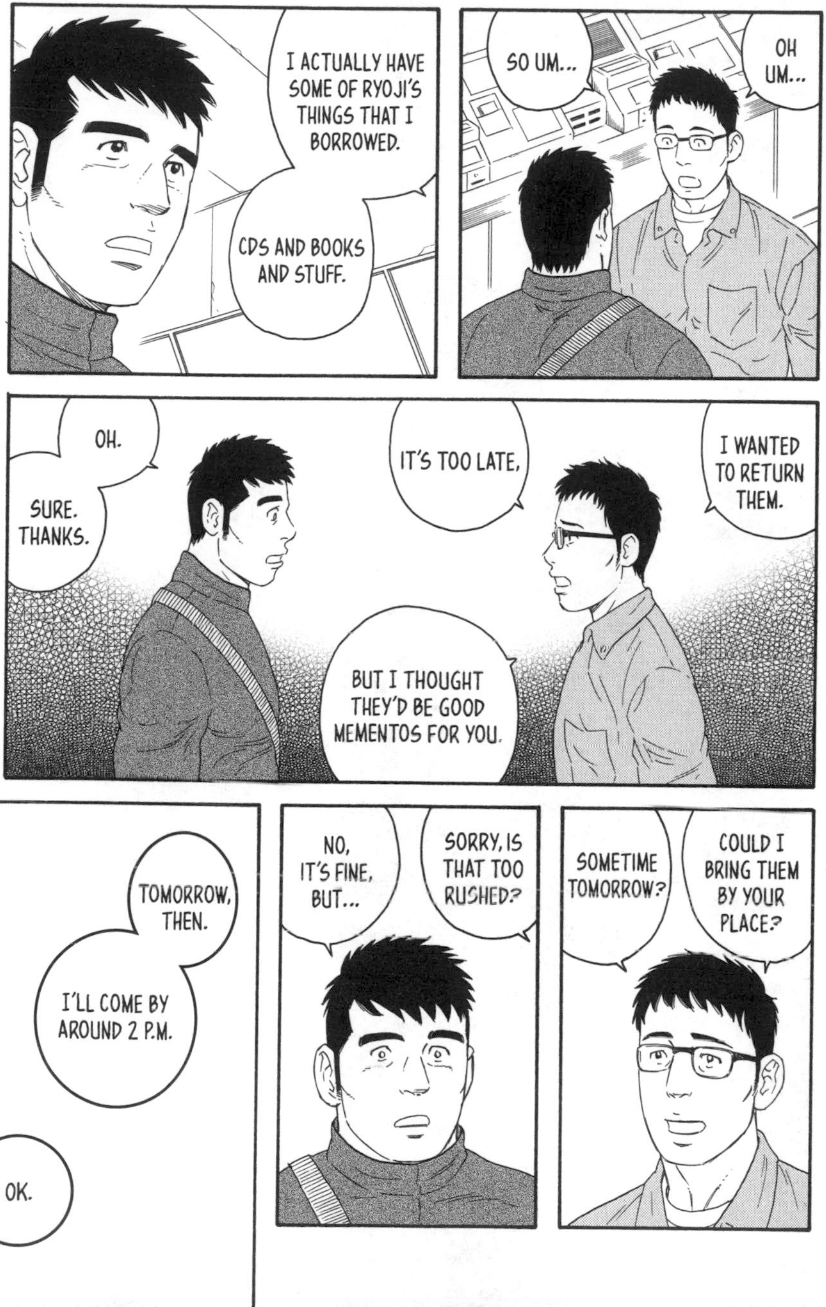
OH UM...
SO UM...
I ACTUALLY HAVE SOME OF RYOJI'S THINGS THAT I BORROWED.
CDS AND BOOKS AND STUFF.
I WANTED TO RETURN THEM.
IT'S TOO LATE,
BUT I THOUGHT THEY'D BE GOOD MEMENTOS FOR YOU.
OH.
SURE. THANKS.
COULD I BRING THEM BY YOUR PLACE?
SOMETIME TOMORROW?
SORRY, IS THAT TOO RUSHED?
NO, IT'S FINE, BUT...
TOMORROW, THEN.
I'LL COME BY AROUND 2 P.M.
OK.

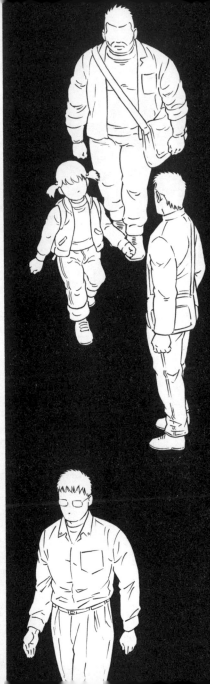

SURE, KATOYAN.

SEE YOU TOMORROW!

DADDY, I'M ALL DONE!

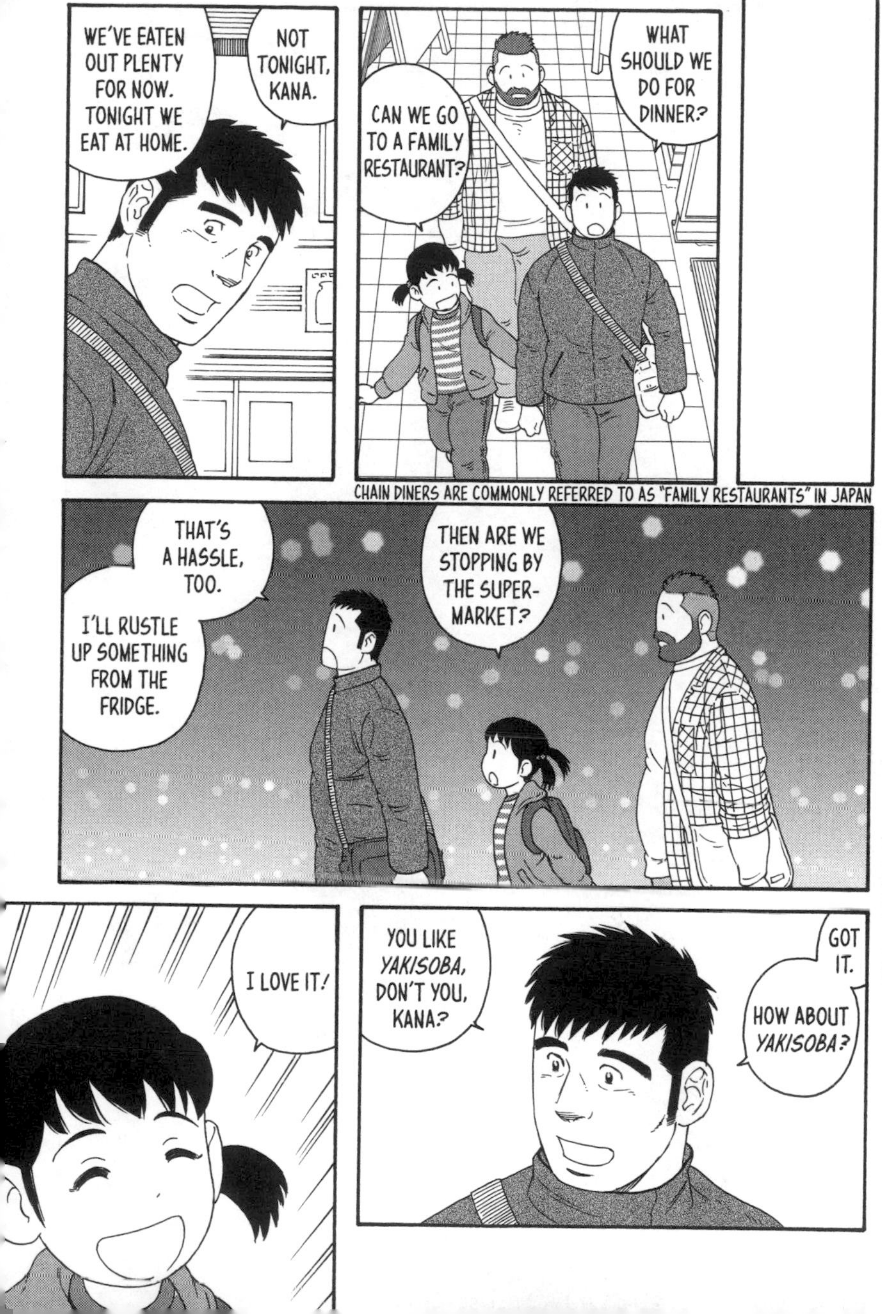
WHAT SHOULD WE DO FOR DINNER?
CAN WE GO TO A FAMILY RESTAURANT?
NOT TONIGHT, KANA.
WE'VE EATEN OUT PLENTY FOR NOW. TONIGHT WE EAT AT HOME.
CHAIN DINERS ARE COMMONLY REFERRED TO AS "FAMILY RESTAURANTS" IN JAPAN
THEN ARE WE STOPPING BY THE SUPER-MARKET?
THAT'S A HASSLE, TOO.
I'LL RUSTLE UP SOMETHING FROM THE FRIDGE.
GOT IT.
HOW ABOUT *YAKISOBA*?
YOU LIKE *YAKISOBA*, DON'T YOU, KANA?
I LOVE IT!

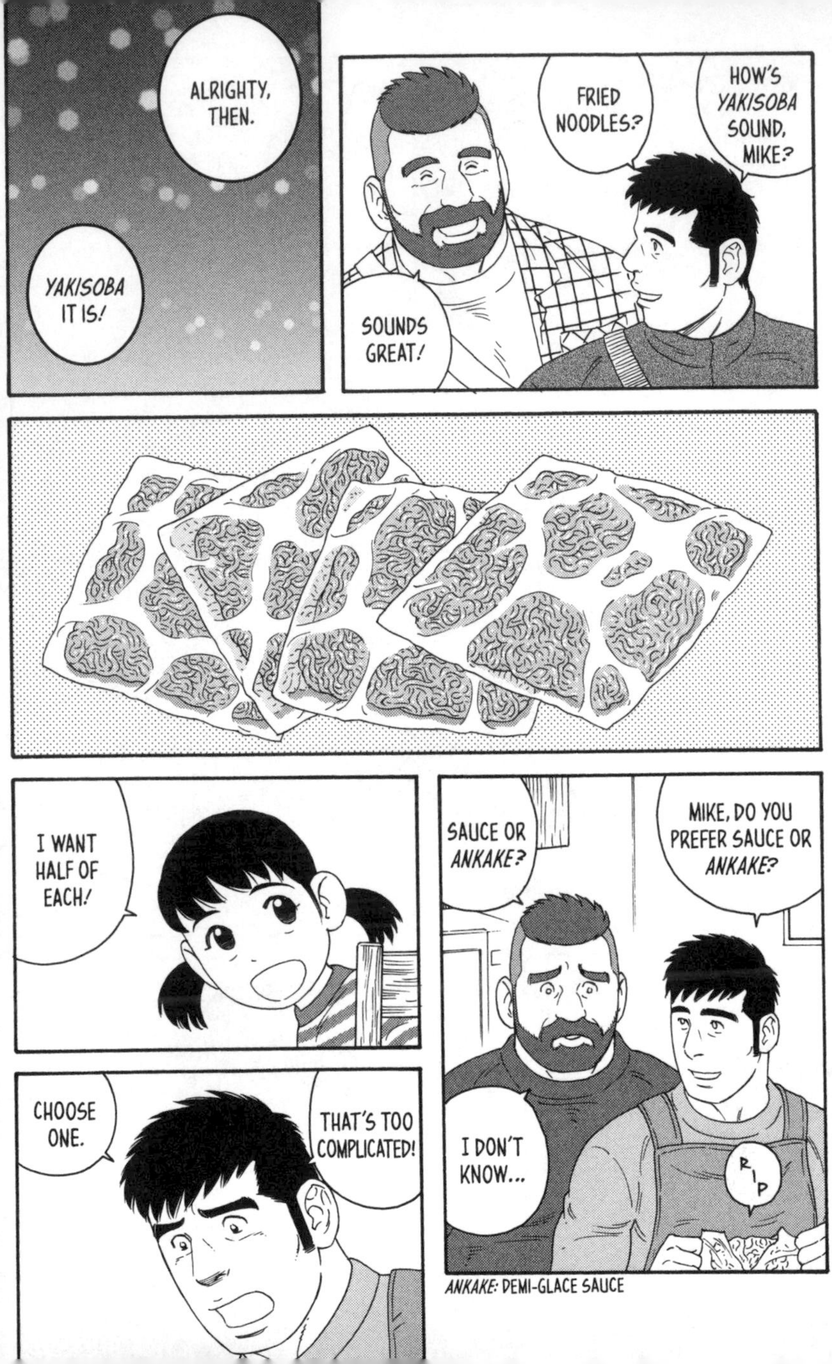
HOW'S *YAKISOBA* SOUND, MIKE?
FRIED NOODLES?
SOUNDS GREAT!
ALRIGHTY, THEN.
YAKISOBA IT IS!
MIKE, DO YOU PREFER SAUCE OR *ANKAKE*?
SAUCE OR *ANKAKE*?
RIP
I DON'T KNOW...
I WANT HALF OF EACH!
THAT'S TOO COMPLICATED!
CHOOSE ONE.

ANKAKE: DEMI-GLACE SAUCE

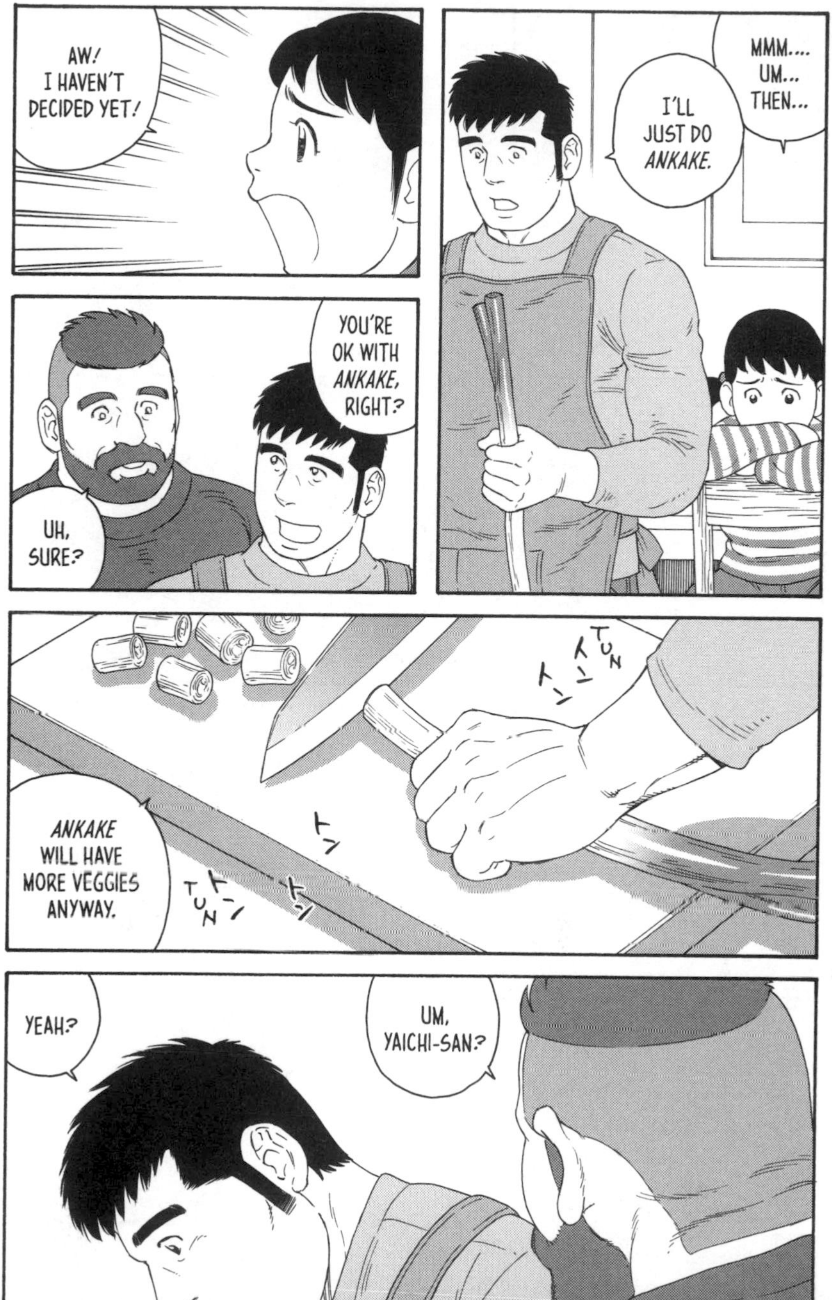
MMM.... UM... THEN...
I'LL JUST DO *ANKAKE.*
AW! I HAVEN'T DECIDED YET!
YOU'RE OK WITH *ANKAKE,* RIGHT?
UH, SURE?
TUN
ANKAKE WILL HAVE MORE VEGGIES ANYWAY.
TUN
UM, YAICHI-SAN?
YEAH?

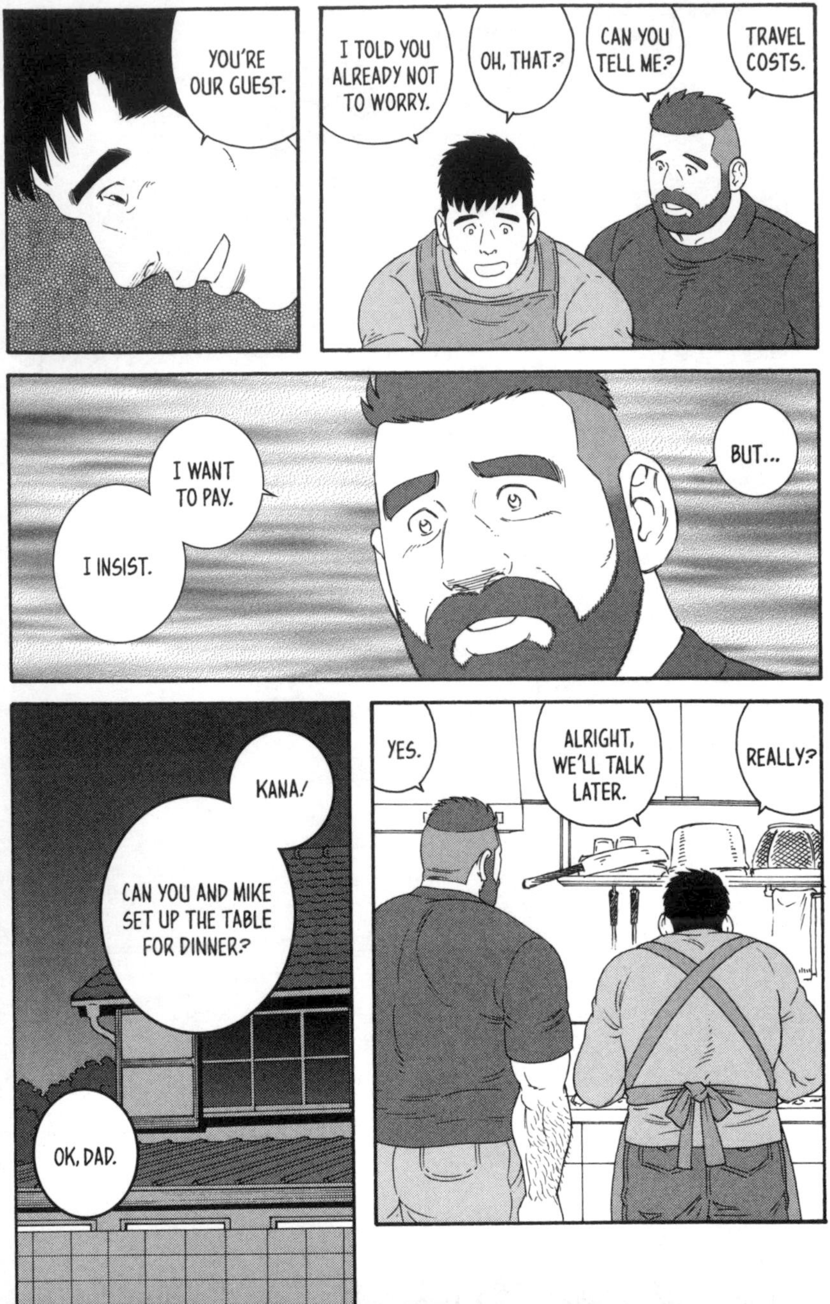
TRAVEL COSTS.
CAN YOU TELL ME?
OH, THAT?
I TOLD YOU ALREADY NOT TO WORRY.
YOU'RE OUR GUEST.
BUT...
I WANT TO PAY.
I INSIST.
REALLY?
ALRIGHT, WE'LL TALK LATER.
YES.
KANA!
CAN YOU AND MIKE SET UP THE TABLE FOR DINNER?
OK, DAD.

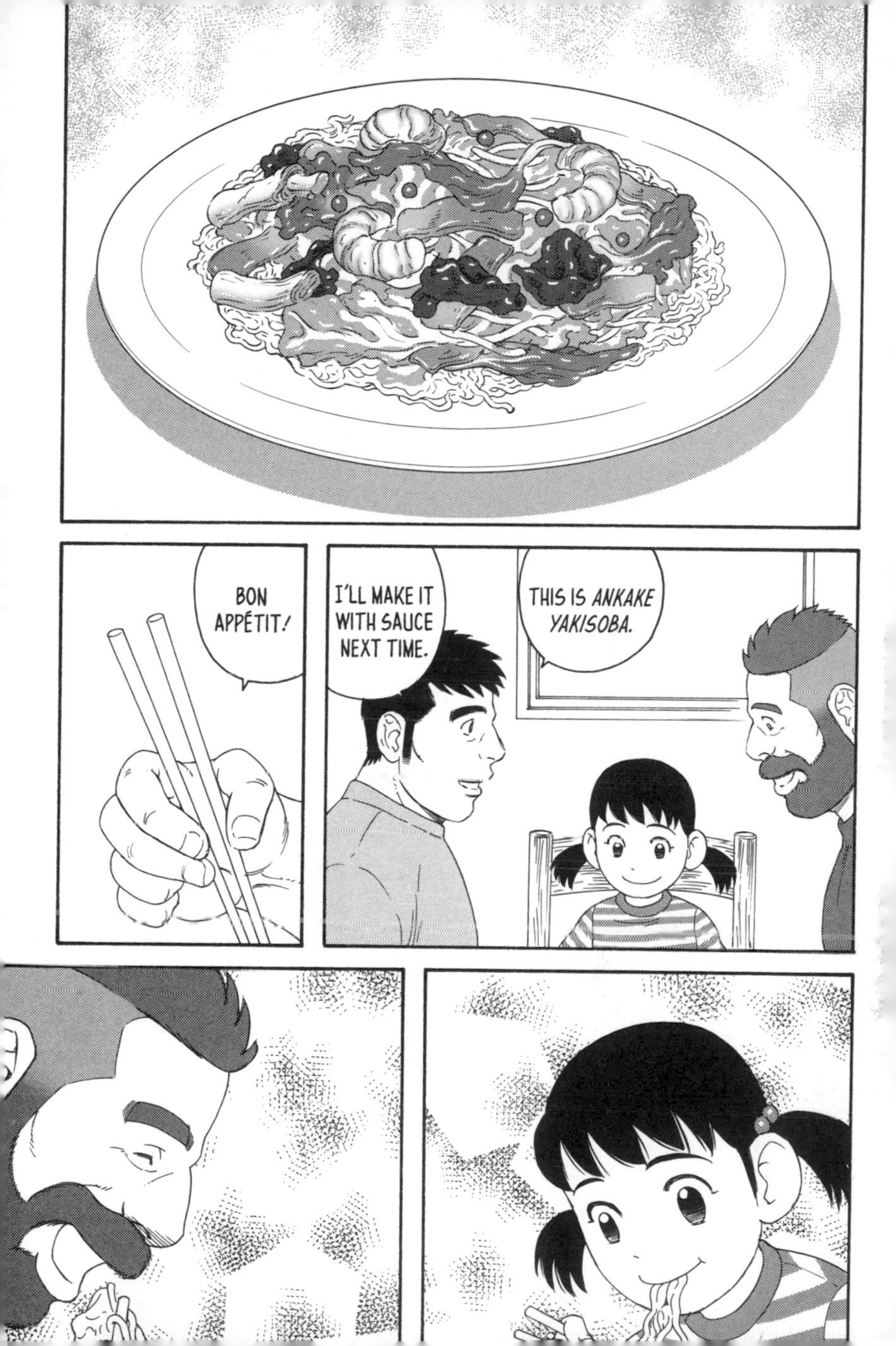
THIS IS *ANKAKE YAKISOBA.*
I'LL MAKE IT WITH SAUCE NEXT TIME.
BON APPÉTIT!

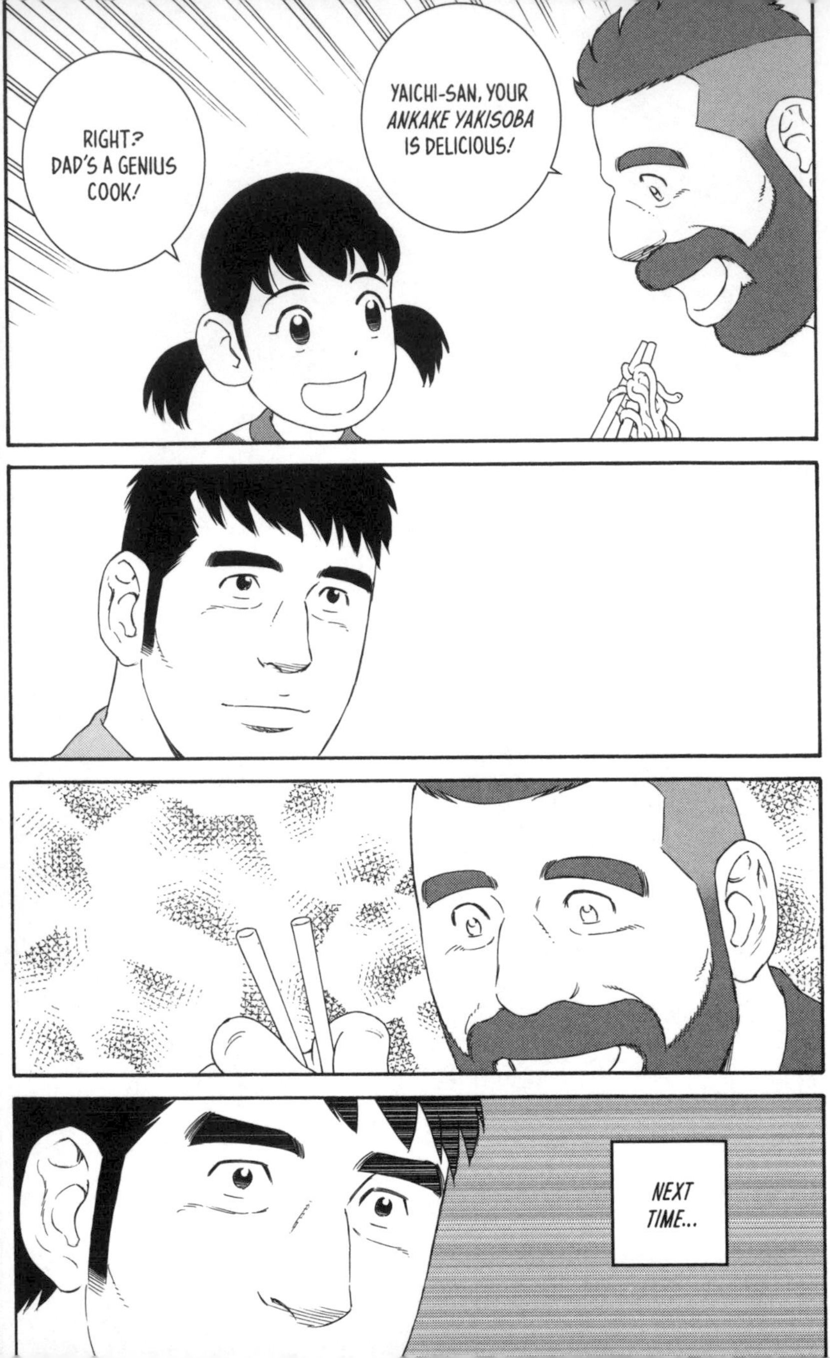
YAICHI-SAN, YOUR *ANKAKE YAKISOBA* IS DELICIOUS!
RIGHT? DAD'S A GENIUS COOK!
NEXT TIME...

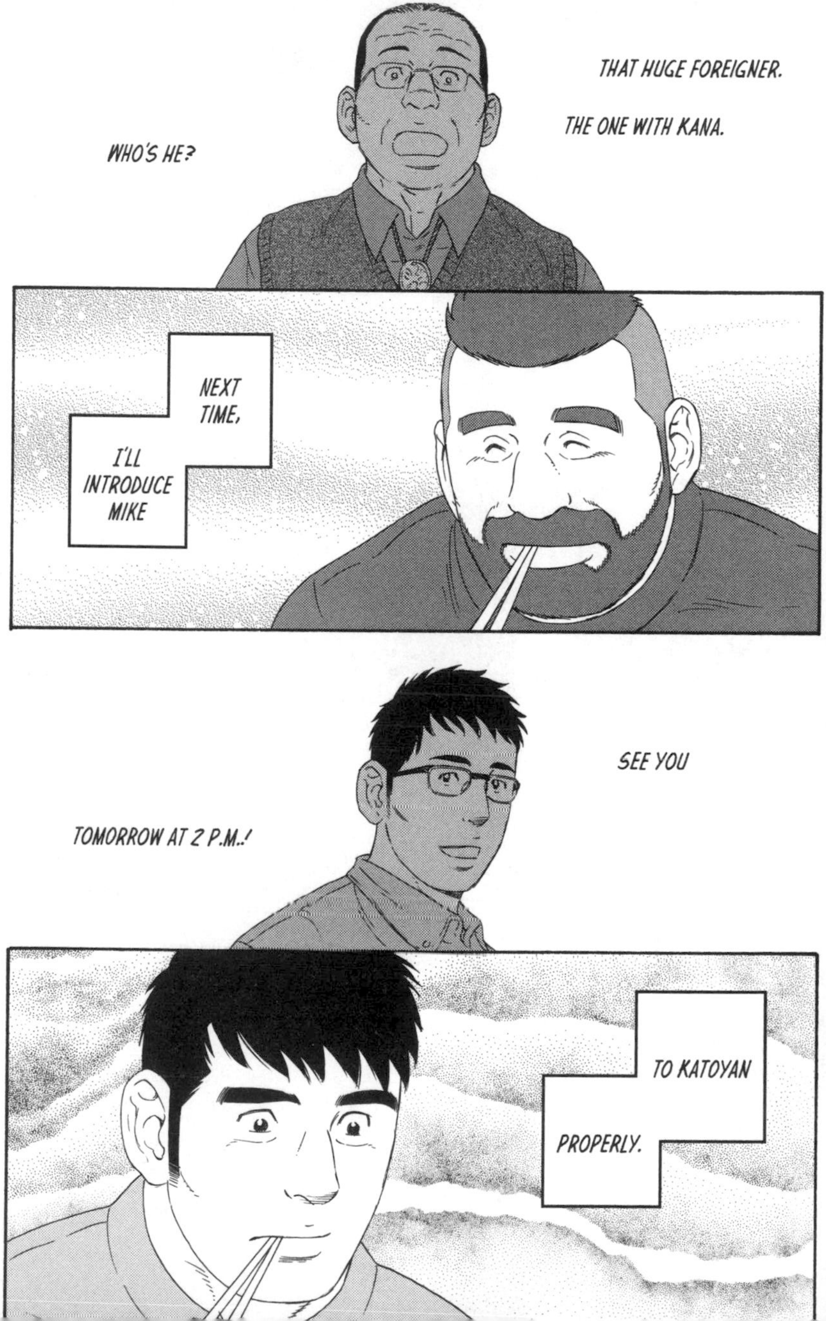
THAT HUGE FOREIGNER.
THE ONE WITH KANA.
WHO'S HE?
NEXT TIME,
I'LL INTRODUCE MIKE
SEE YOU
TOMORROW AT 2 P.M.!
TO KATOYAN
PROPERLY.

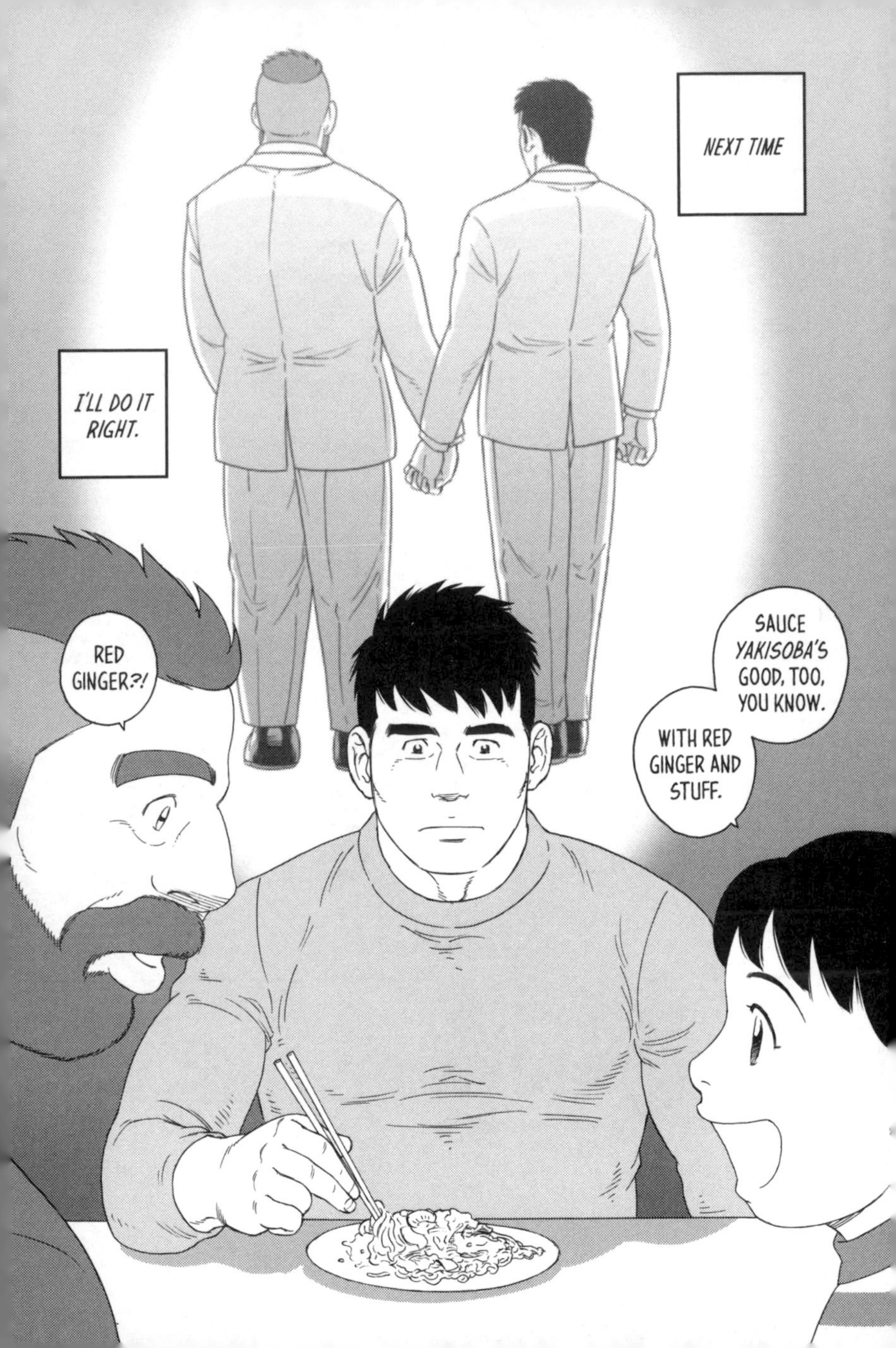
NEXT TIME
I'LL DO IT RIGHT.
SAUCE *YAKISOBA'S* GOOD, TOO, YOU KNOW.
WITH RED GINGER AND STUFF.
RED GINGER?!

ASSORTED BAKED SWEETS

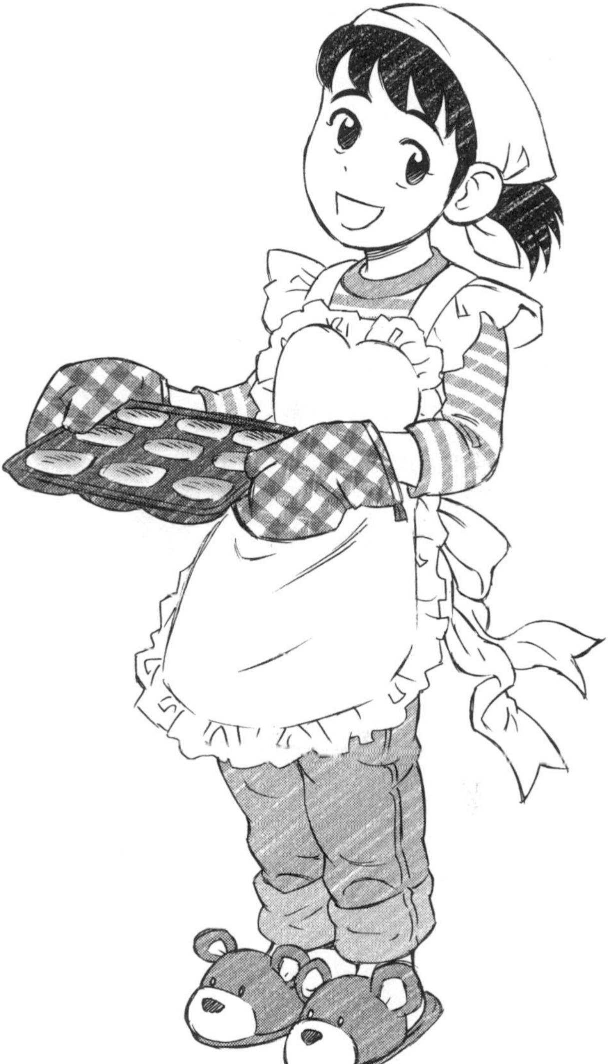

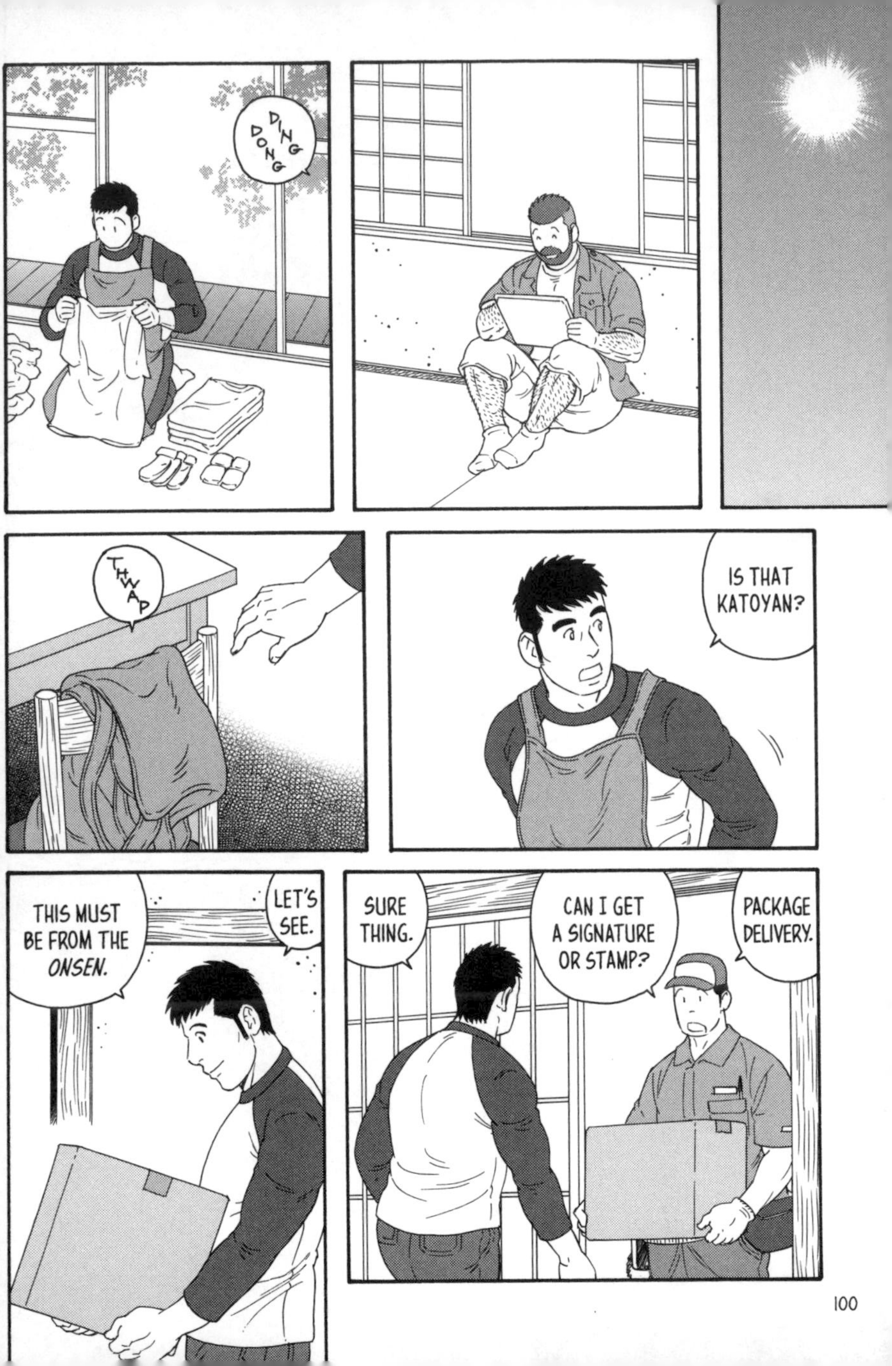
DING DONG
IS THAT KATOYAN?
THWAP
PACKAGE DELIVERY.
CAN I GET A SIGNATURE OR STAMP?
SURE THING.
LET'S SEE.
THIS MUST BE FROM THE *ONSEN.*

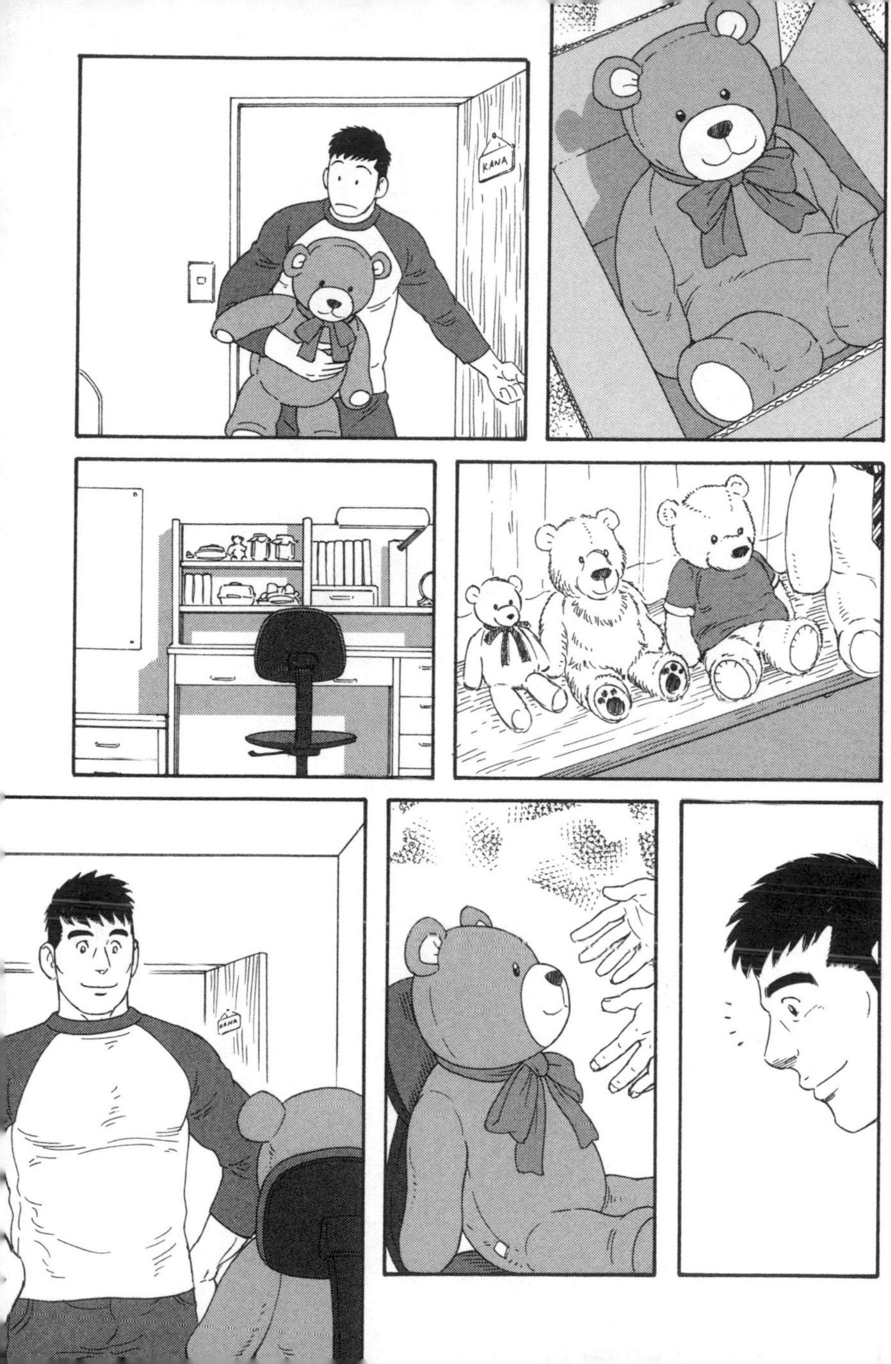
KANA
KANA

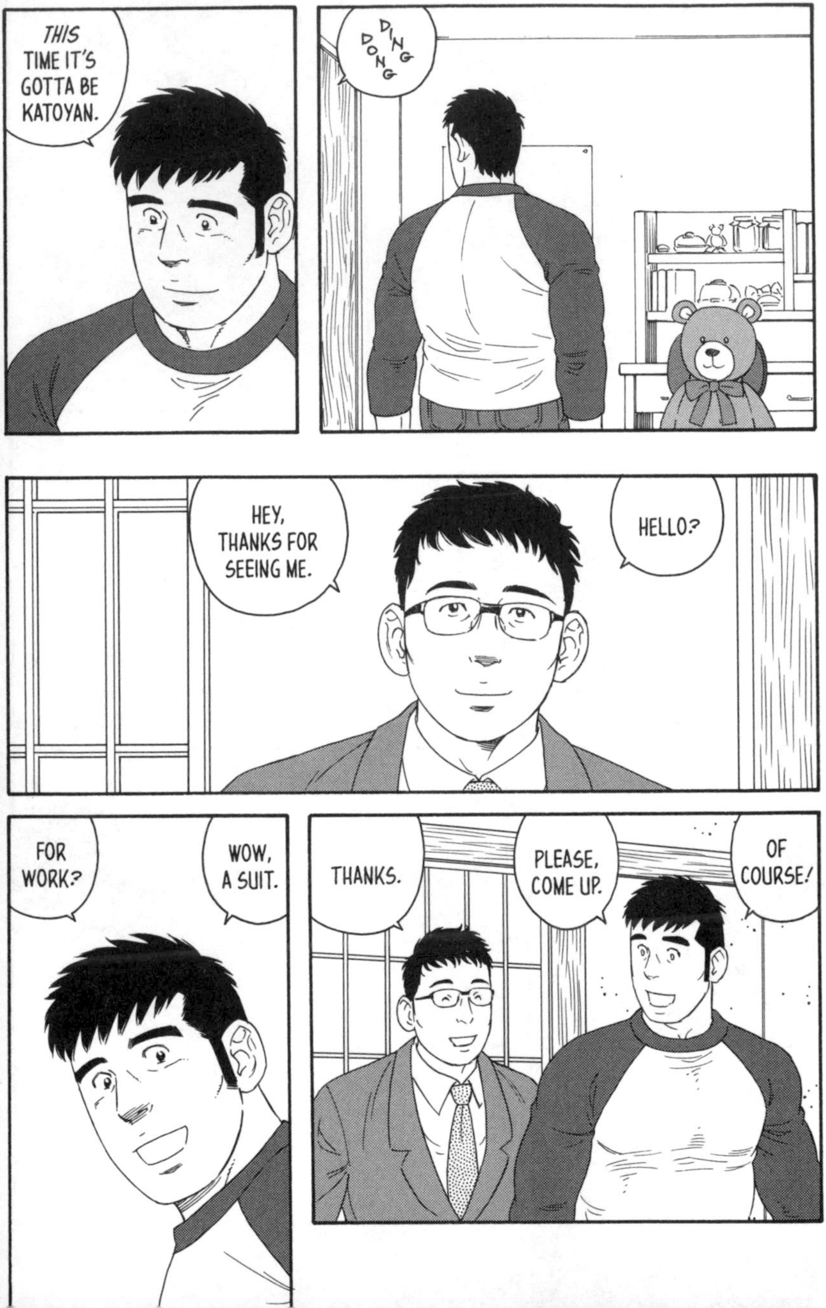
DING DONG
THIS TIME IT'S GOTTA BE KATOYAN.
HELLO?
HEY, THANKS FOR SEEING ME.
OF COURSE!
PLEASE, COME UP.
THANKS.
WOW, A SUIT.
FOR WORK?

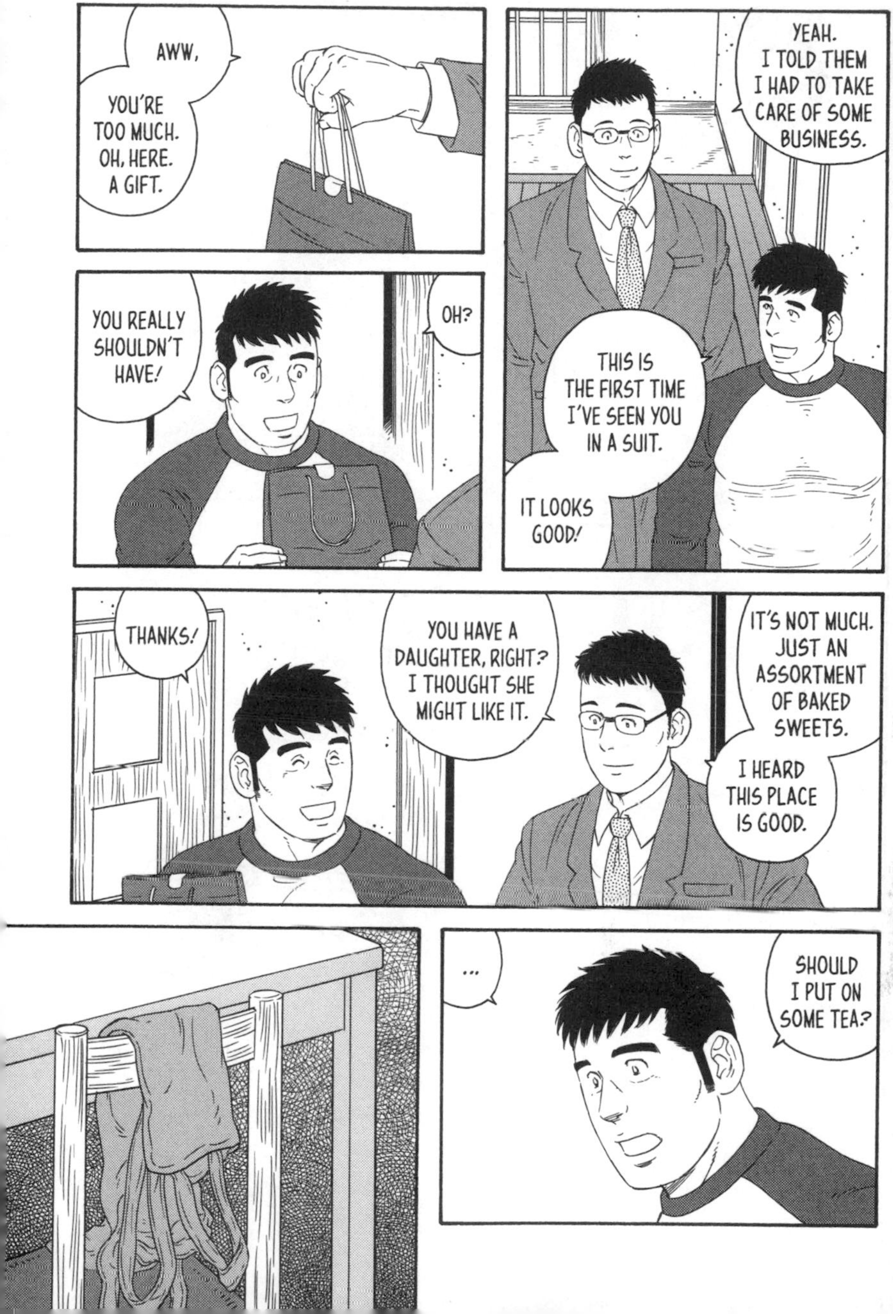
YEAH. I TOLD THEM I HAD TO TAKE CARE OF SOME BUSINESS.
THIS IS THE FIRST TIME I'VE SEEN YOU IN A SUIT.
IT LOOKS GOOD!
AWW,
YOU'RE TOO MUCH. OH, HERE. A GIFT.
OH?
YOU REALLY SHOULDN'T HAVE!
IT'S NOT MUCH. JUST AN ASSORTMENT OF BAKED SWEETS.
I HEARD THIS PLACE IS GOOD.
YOU HAVE A DAUGHTER, RIGHT? I THOUGHT SHE MIGHT LIKE IT.
THANKS!
SHOULD I PUT ON SOME TEA?
...

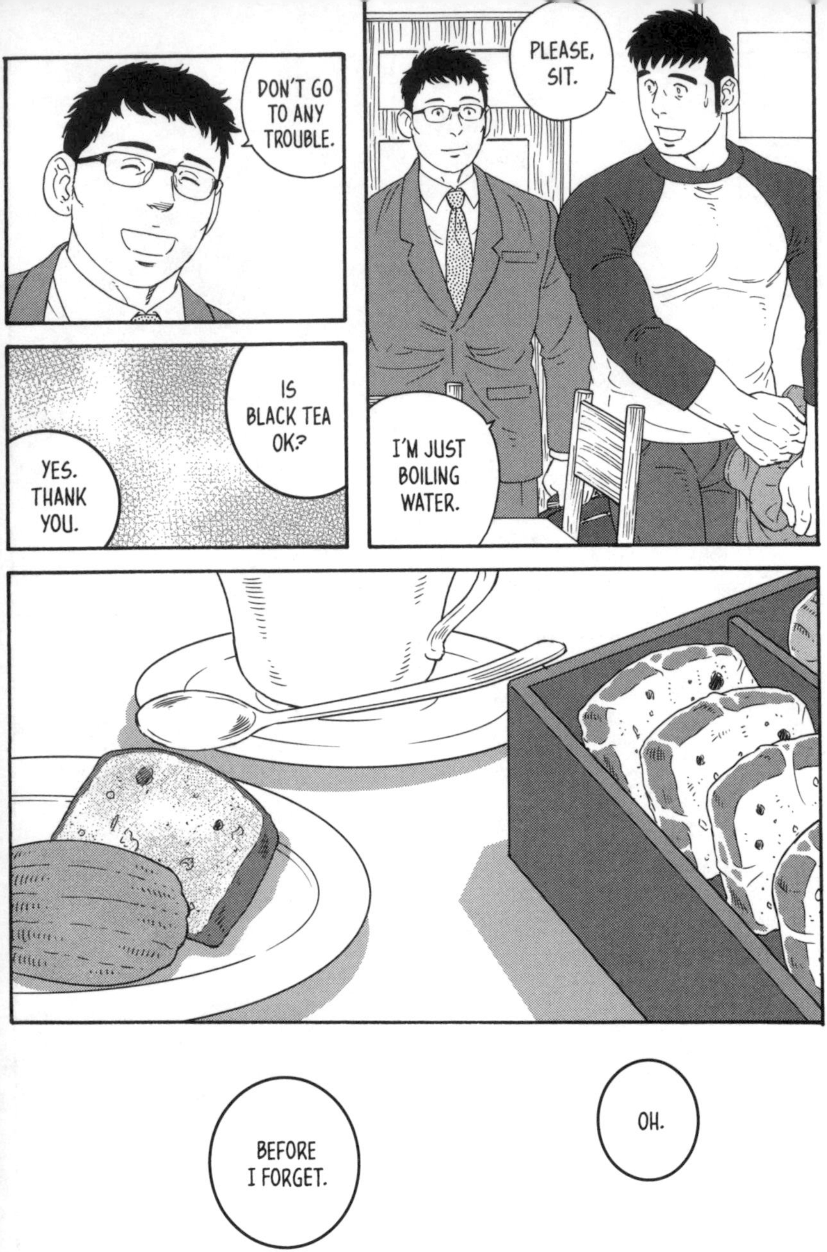
PLEASE, SIT.
I'M JUST BOILING WATER.
DON'T GO TO ANY TROUBLE.
IS BLACK TEA OK?
YES. THANK YOU.
OH.
BEFORE I FORGET.

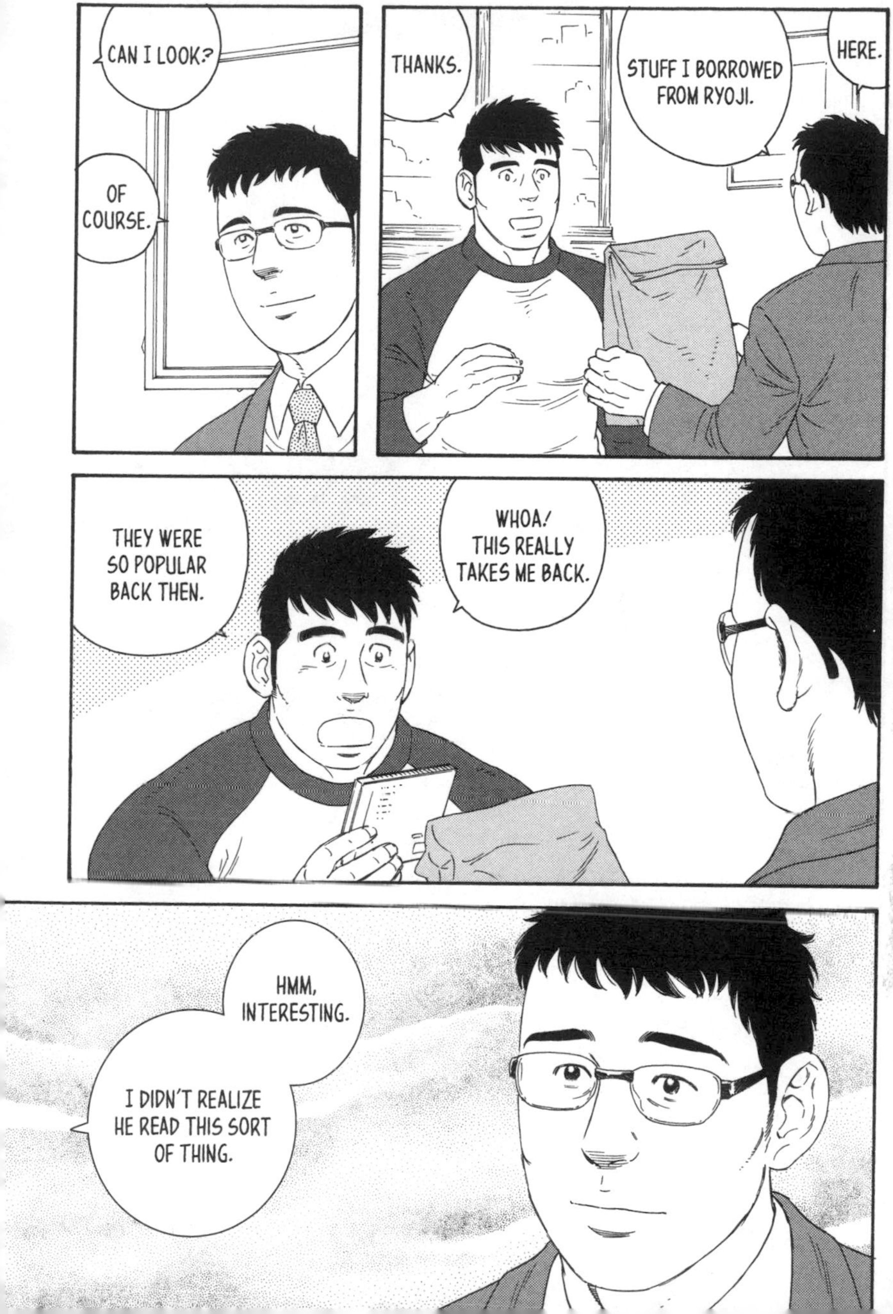
HERE.
STUFF I BORROWED FROM RYOJI.
THANKS.
CAN I LOOK?
OF COURSE.
WHOA! THIS REALLY TAKES ME BACK.
THEY WERE SO POPULAR BACK THEN.
HMM, INTERESTING.
I DIDN'T REALIZE HE READ THIS SORT OF THING.

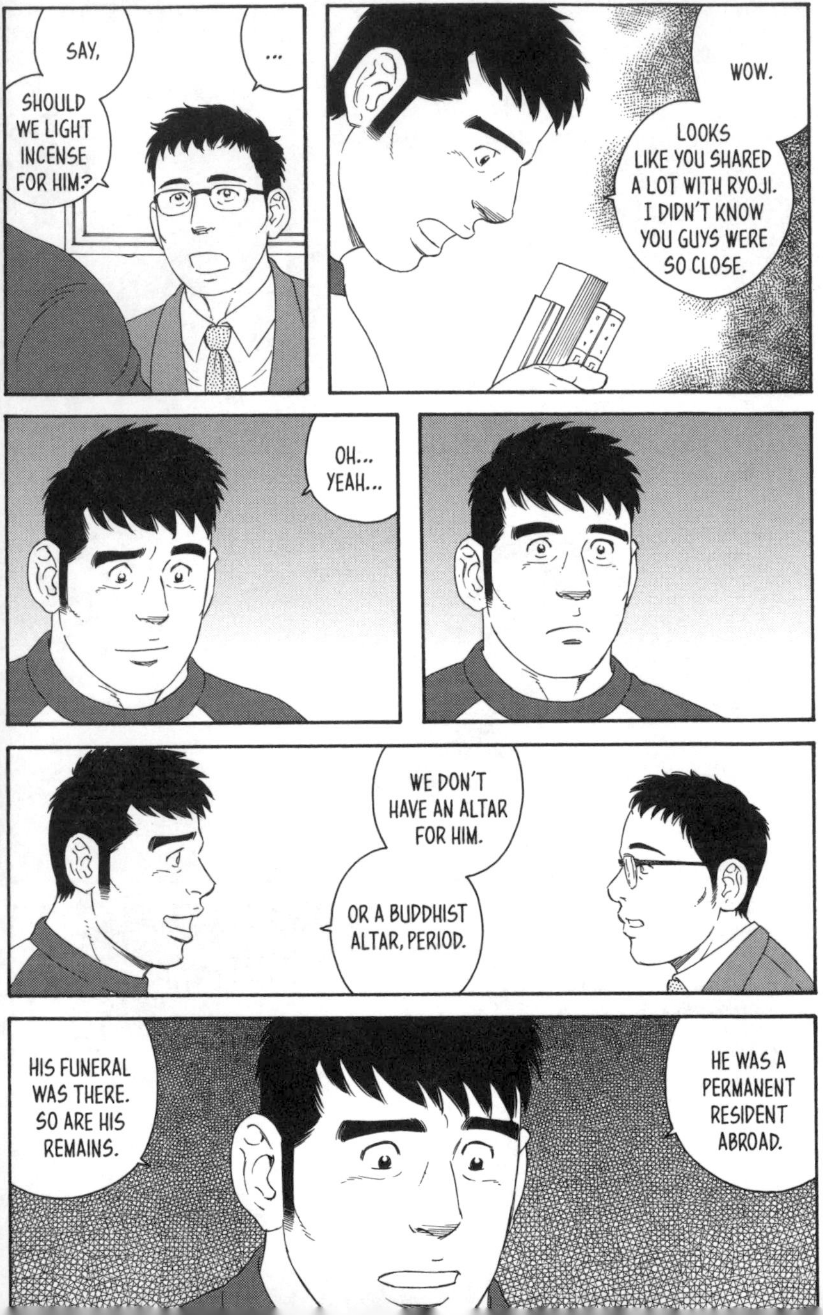
WOW.
LOOKS LIKE YOU SHARED A LOT WITH RYOJI. I DIDN'T KNOW YOU GUYS WERE SO CLOSE.
...
SAY,
SHOULD WE LIGHT INCENSE FOR HIM?
OH... YEAH...
WE DON'T HAVE AN ALTAR FOR HIM.
OR A BUDDHIST ALTAR, PERIOD.
HE WAS A PERMANENT RESIDENT ABROAD.
HIS FUNERAL WAS THERE. SO ARE HIS REMAINS.

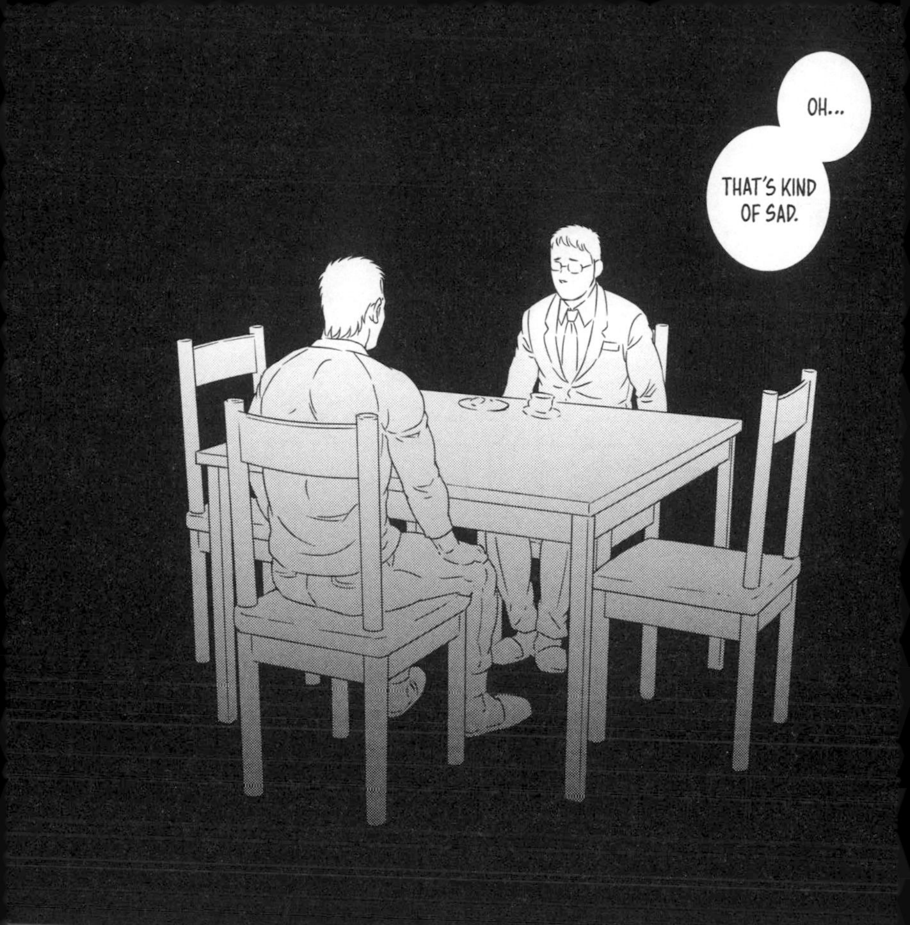
OH...
THAT'S KIND OF SAD.

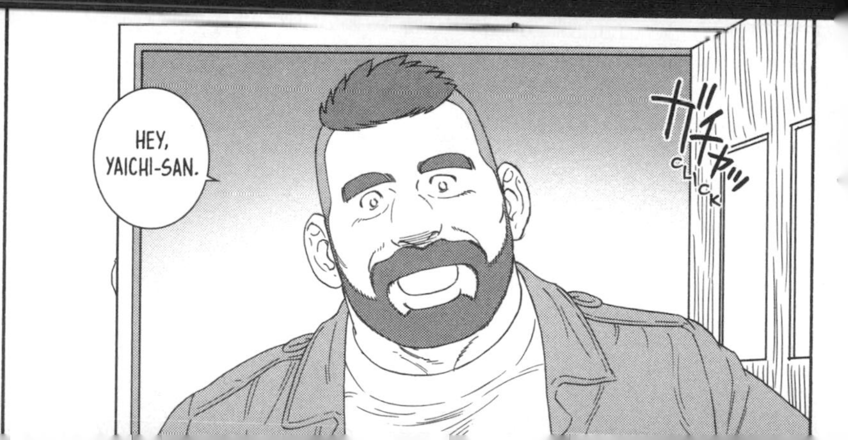
ガチャッ
CLICK
HEY, YAICHI-SAN.

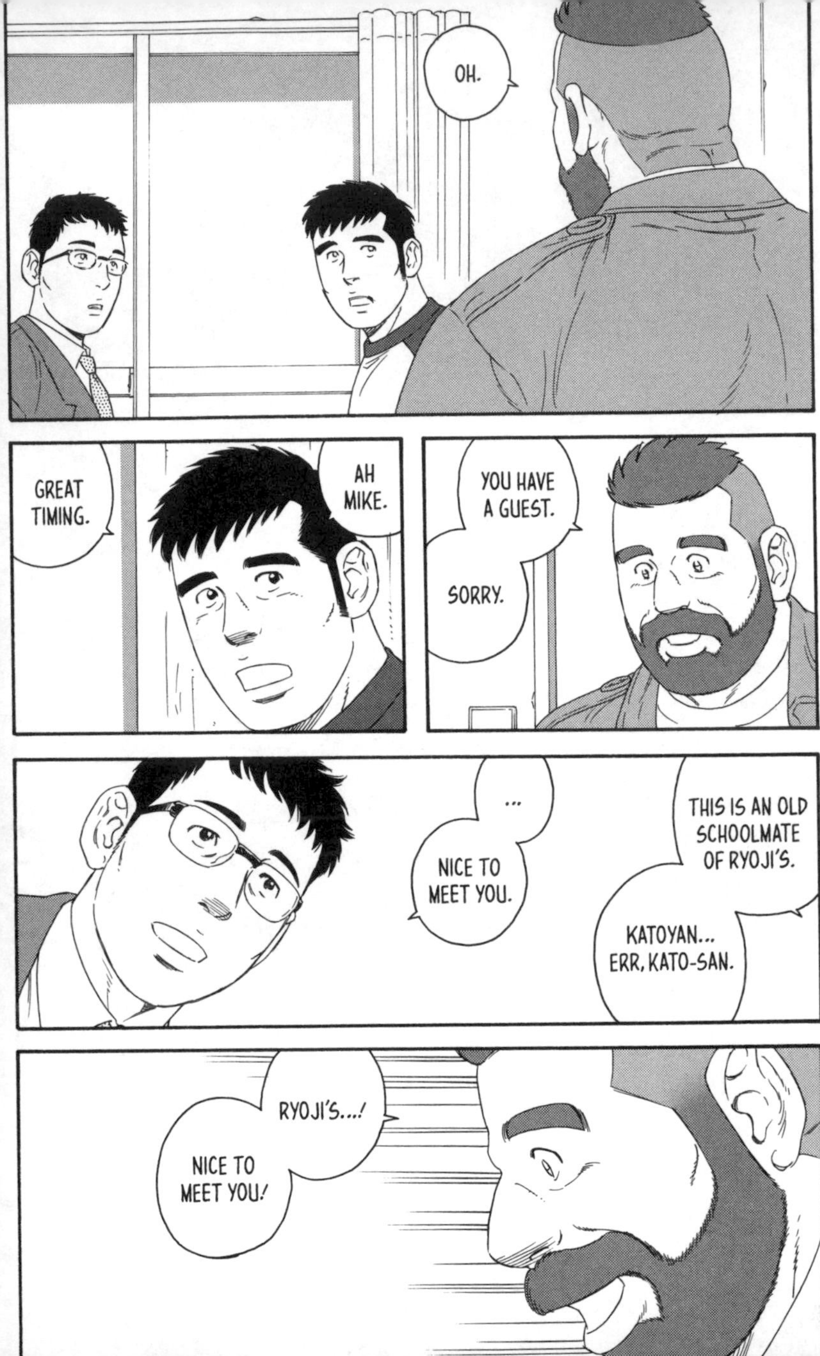
OH.
YOU HAVE A GUEST.
SORRY.
AH MIKE.
GREAT TIMING.
THIS IS AN OLD SCHOOLMATE OF RYOJI'S.
KATOYAN... ERR, KATO-SAN.
...
NICE TO MEET YOU.
RYOJI'S...!
NICE TO MEET YOU!

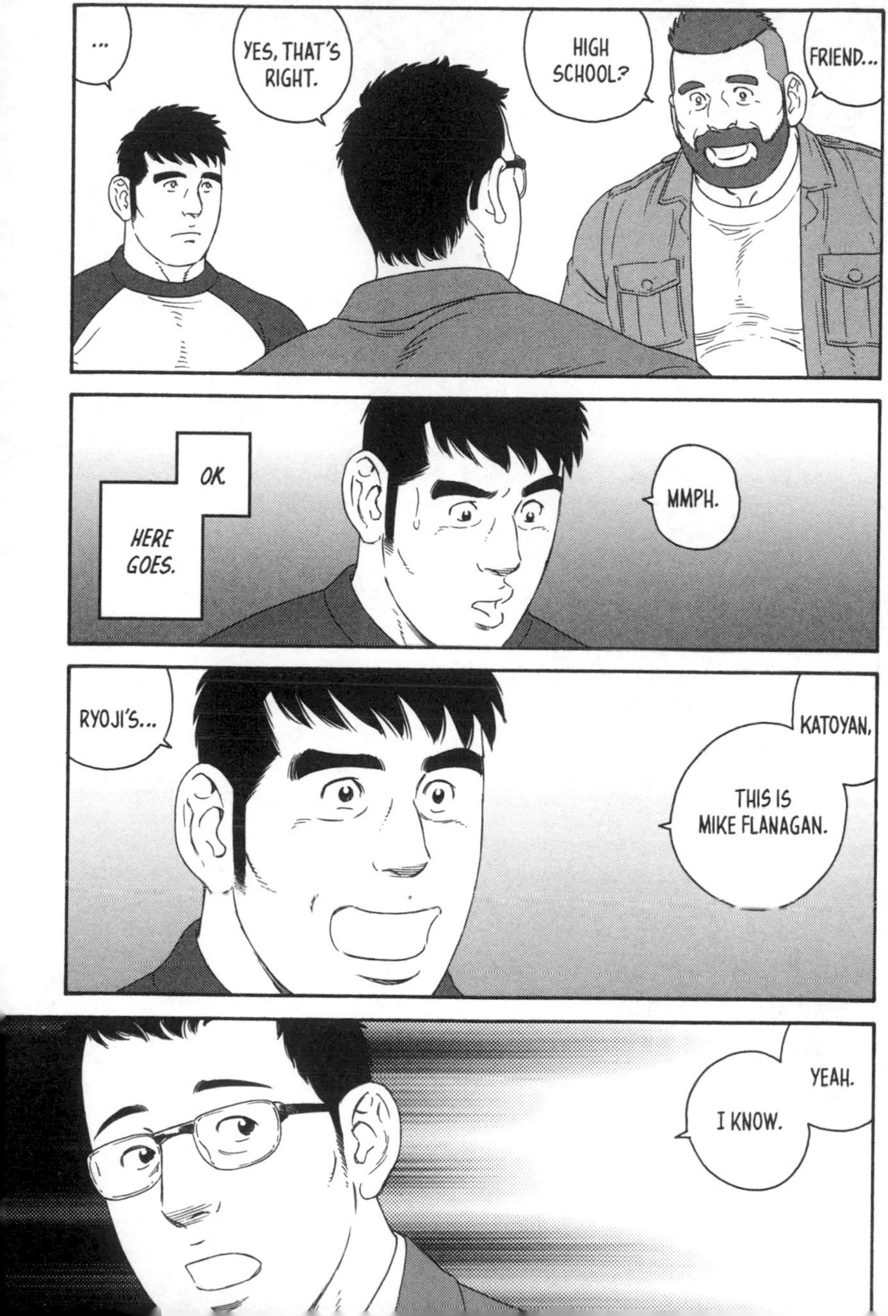
FRIEND...
HIGH SCHOOL?
YES, THAT'S RIGHT.
...
MMPH.
OK.
HERE GOES.
KATOYAN,
THIS IS MIKE FLANAGAN.
RYOJI'S...
YEAH.
I KNOW.

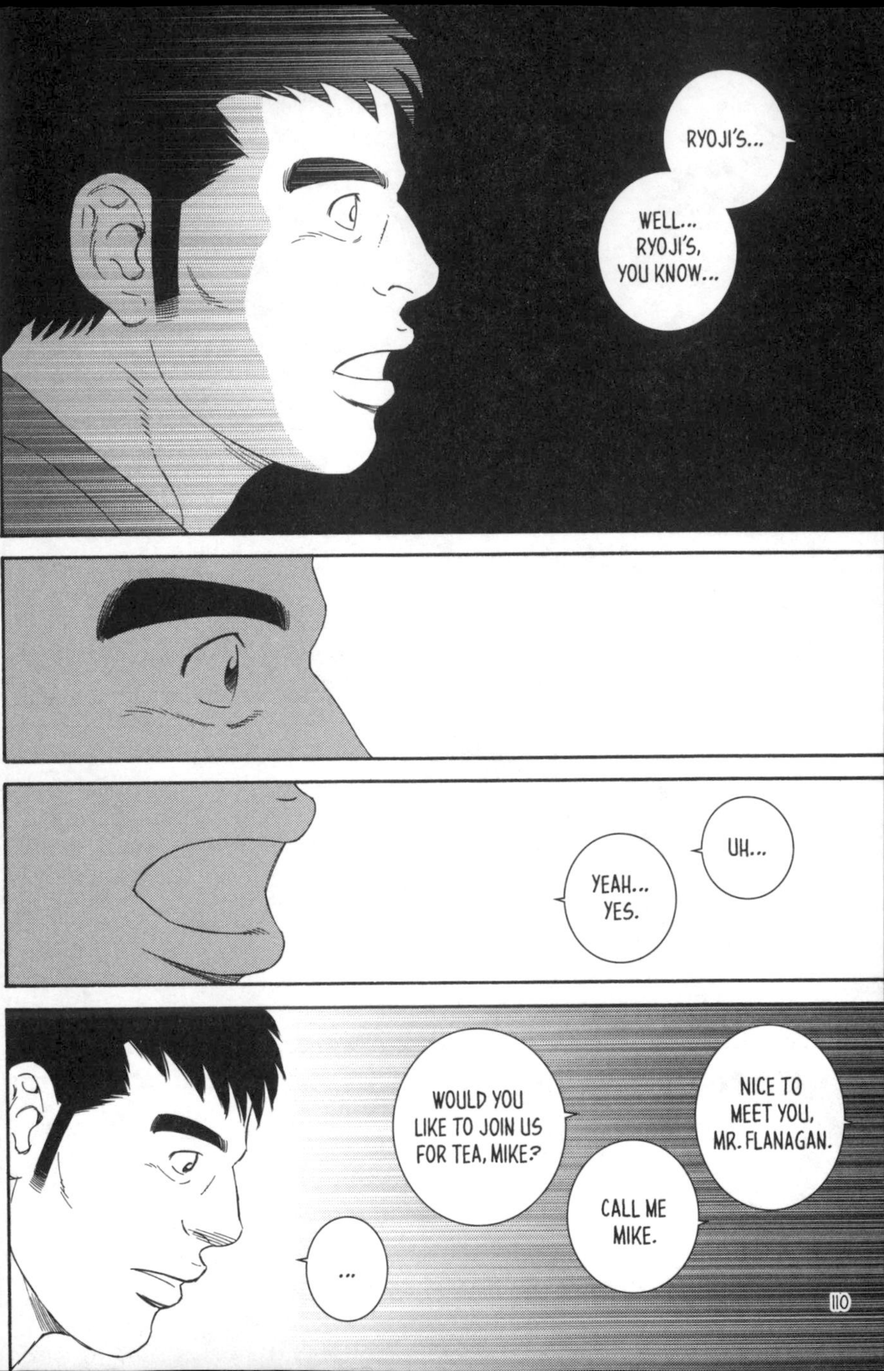
RYOJI'S...
WELL... RYOJI'S, YOU KNOW...
UH...
YEAH... YES.
NICE TO MEET YOU, MR. FLANAGAN.
CALL ME MIKE.
WOULD YOU LIKE TO JOIN US FOR TEA, MIKE?
...

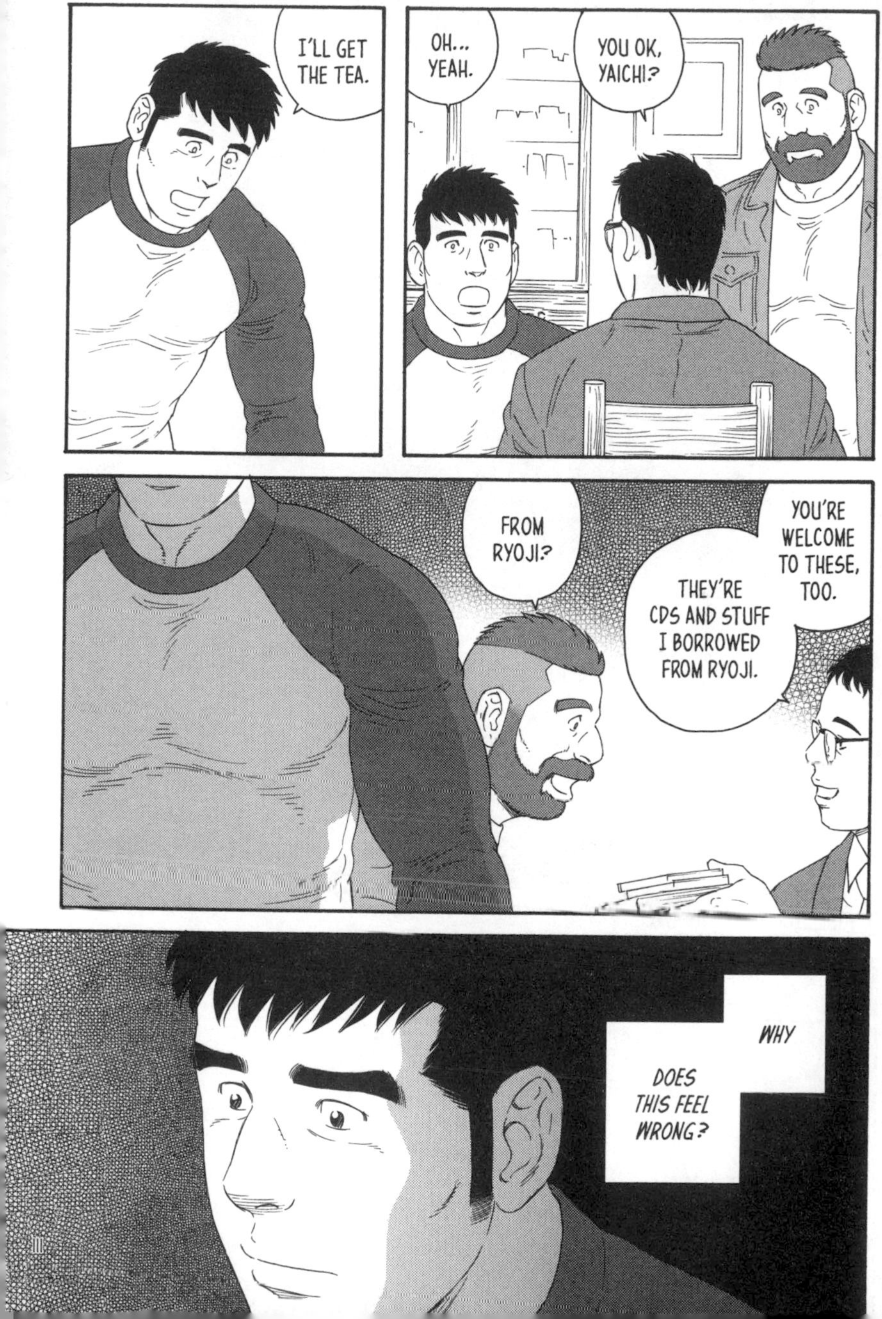
YOU OK, YAICHI?
OH... YEAH.
I'LL GET THE TEA.
YOU'RE WELCOME TO THESE, TOO.
THEY'RE CDS AND STUFF I BORROWED FROM RYOJI.
FROM RYOJI?
WHY
DOES THIS FEEL WRONG?

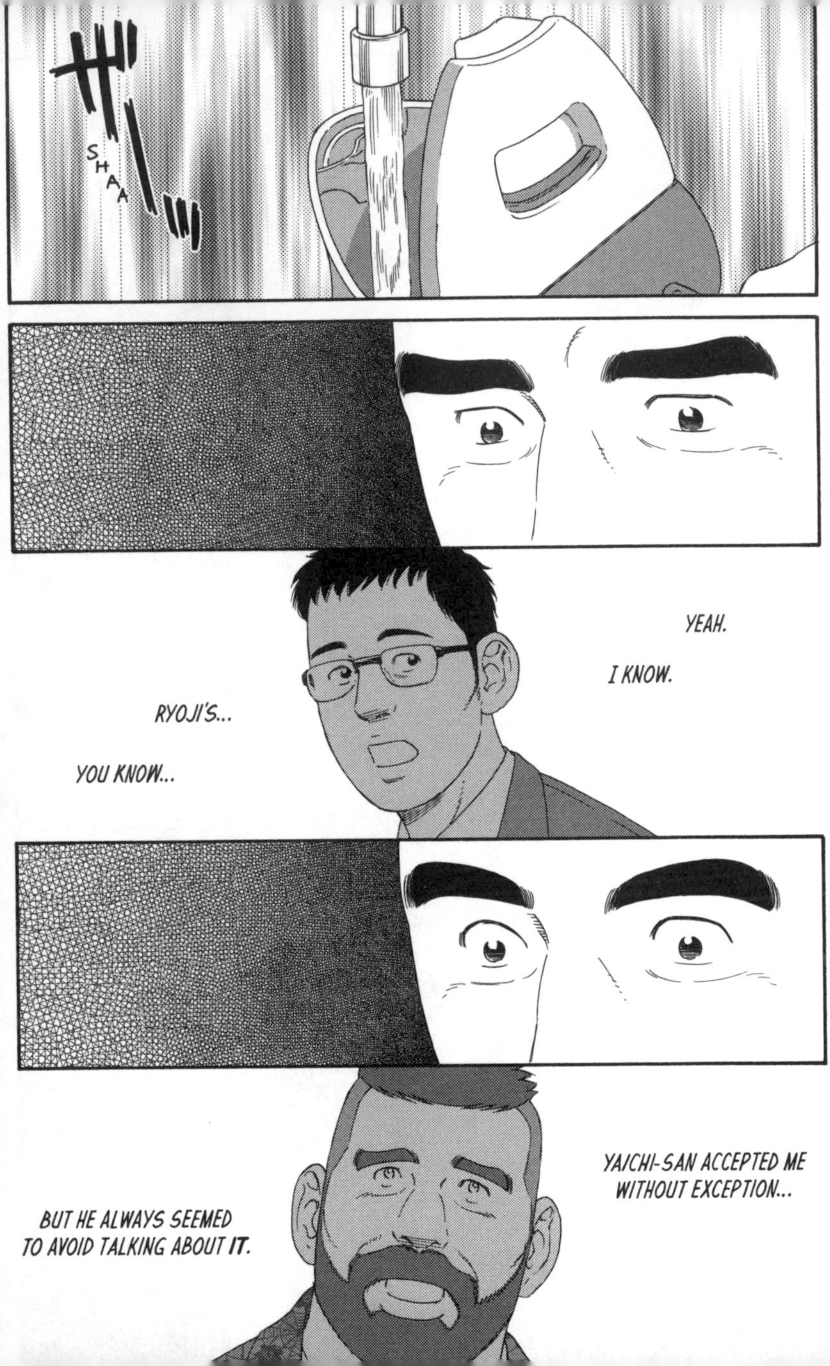
SHAAA
YEAH.
I KNOW.
RYOJI'S...
YOU KNOW...
YAICHI-SAN ACCEPTED ME WITHOUT EXCEPTION...
BUT HE ALWAYS SEEMED TO AVOID TALKING ABOUT **IT**.

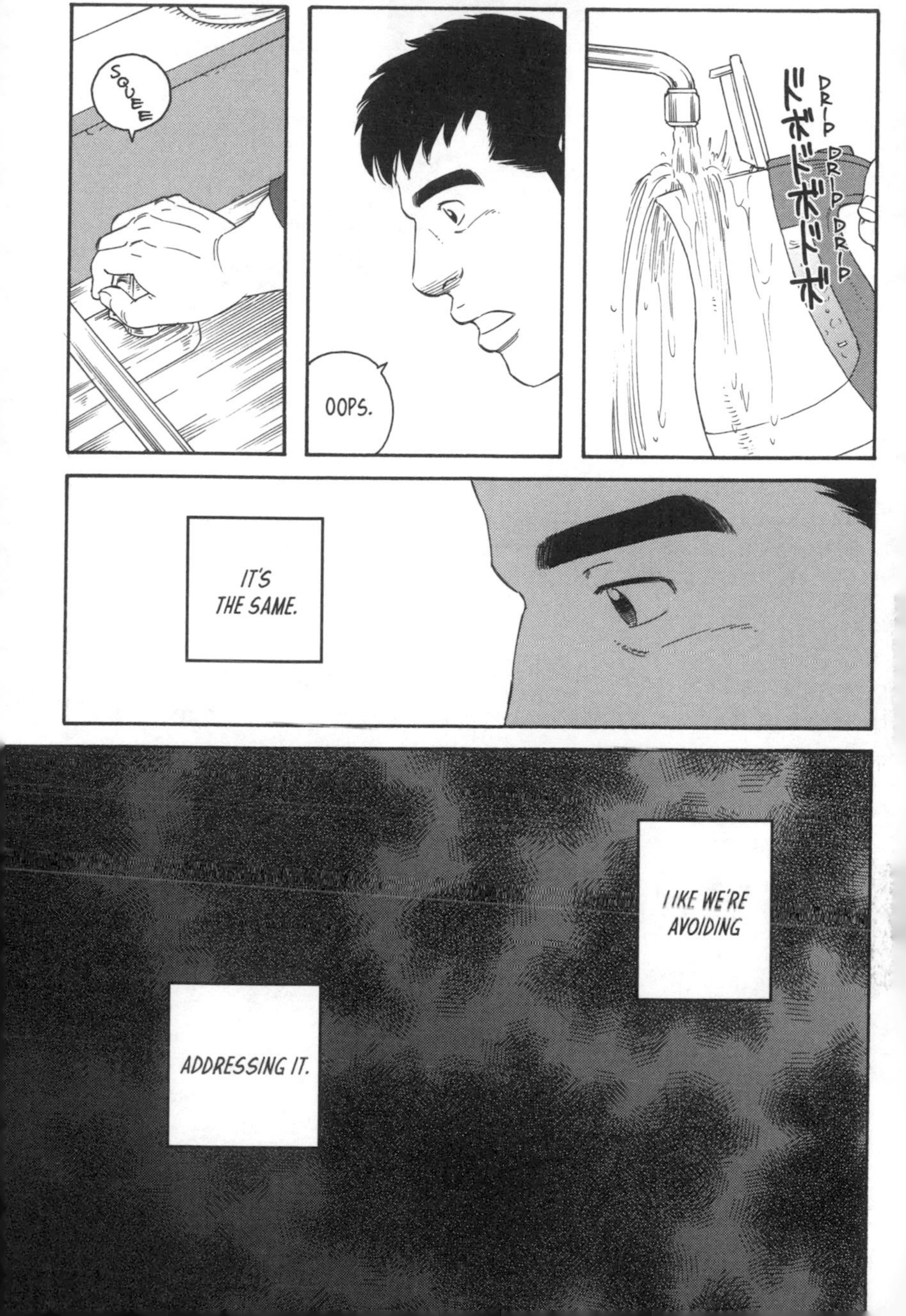
DRIP DRIP DRIP
ドボドボドボ
OOPS.
SQUEE
IT'S THE SAME.
LIKE WE'RE AVOIDING
ADDRESSING IT.

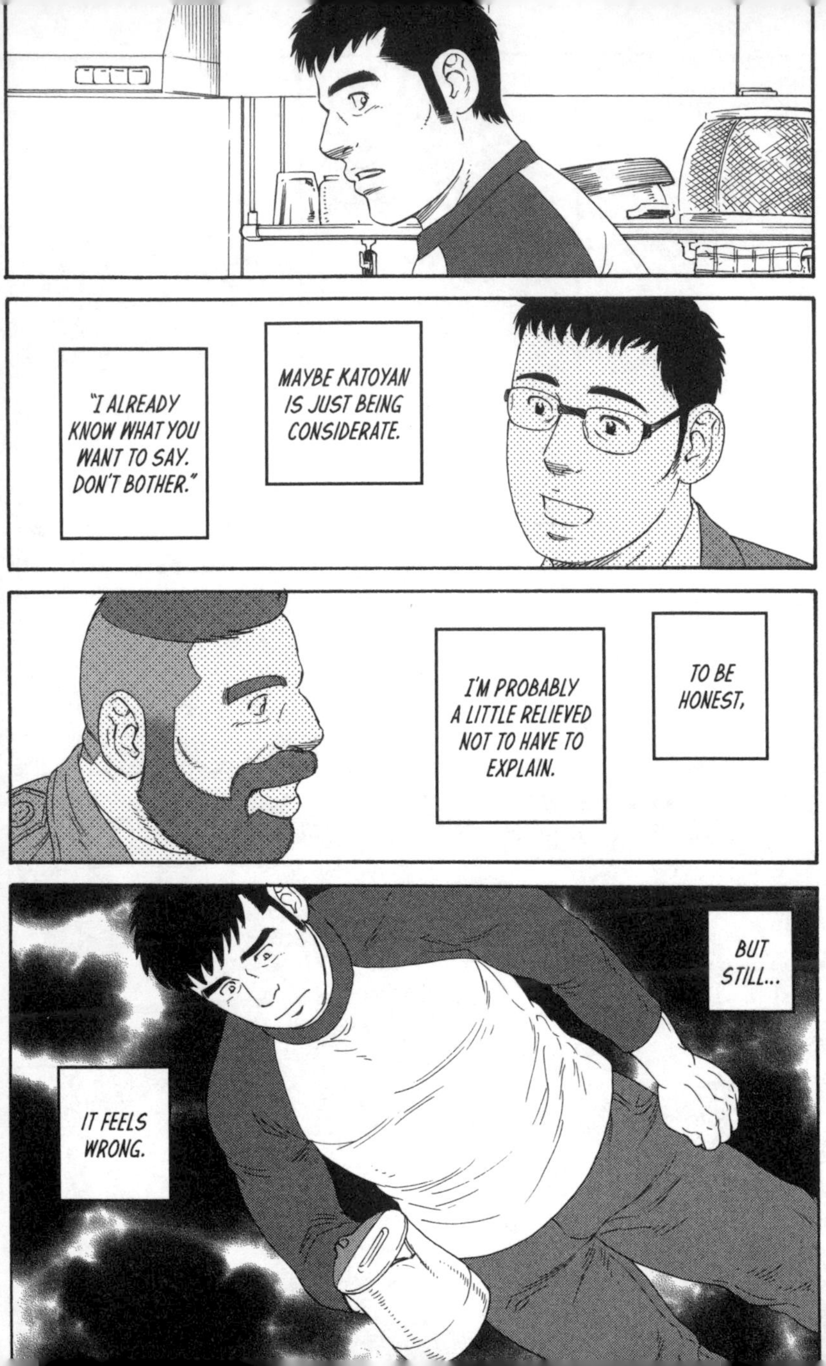
MAYBE KATOYAN IS JUST BEING CONSIDERATE.
"I ALREADY KNOW WHAT YOU WANT TO SAY. DON'T BOTHER."
TO BE HONEST,
I'M PROBABLY A LITTLE RELIEVED NOT TO HAVE TO EXPLAIN.
BUT STILL...
IT FEELS WRONG.

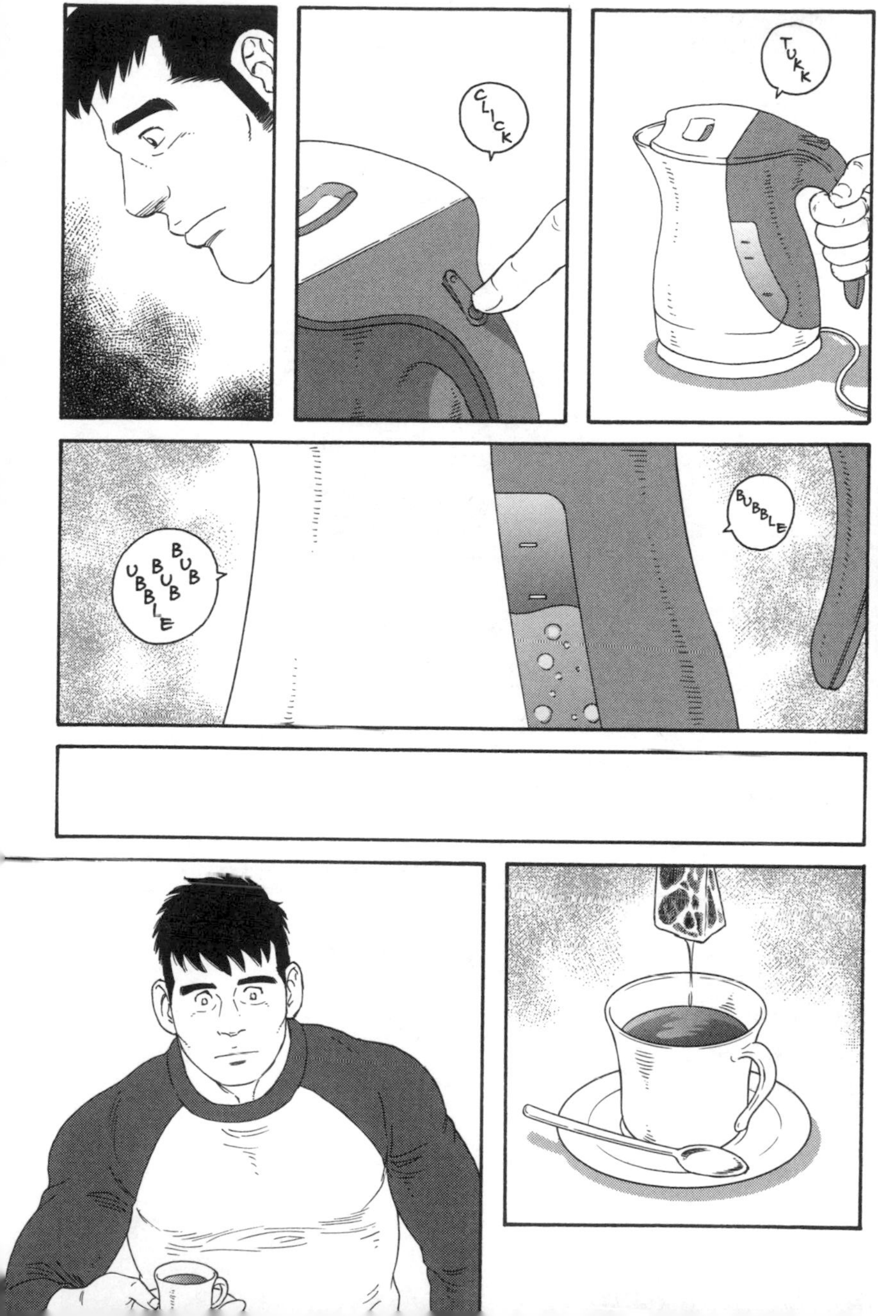
TUKK
CLICK
BUBBLE
BUBBUBUBBLE

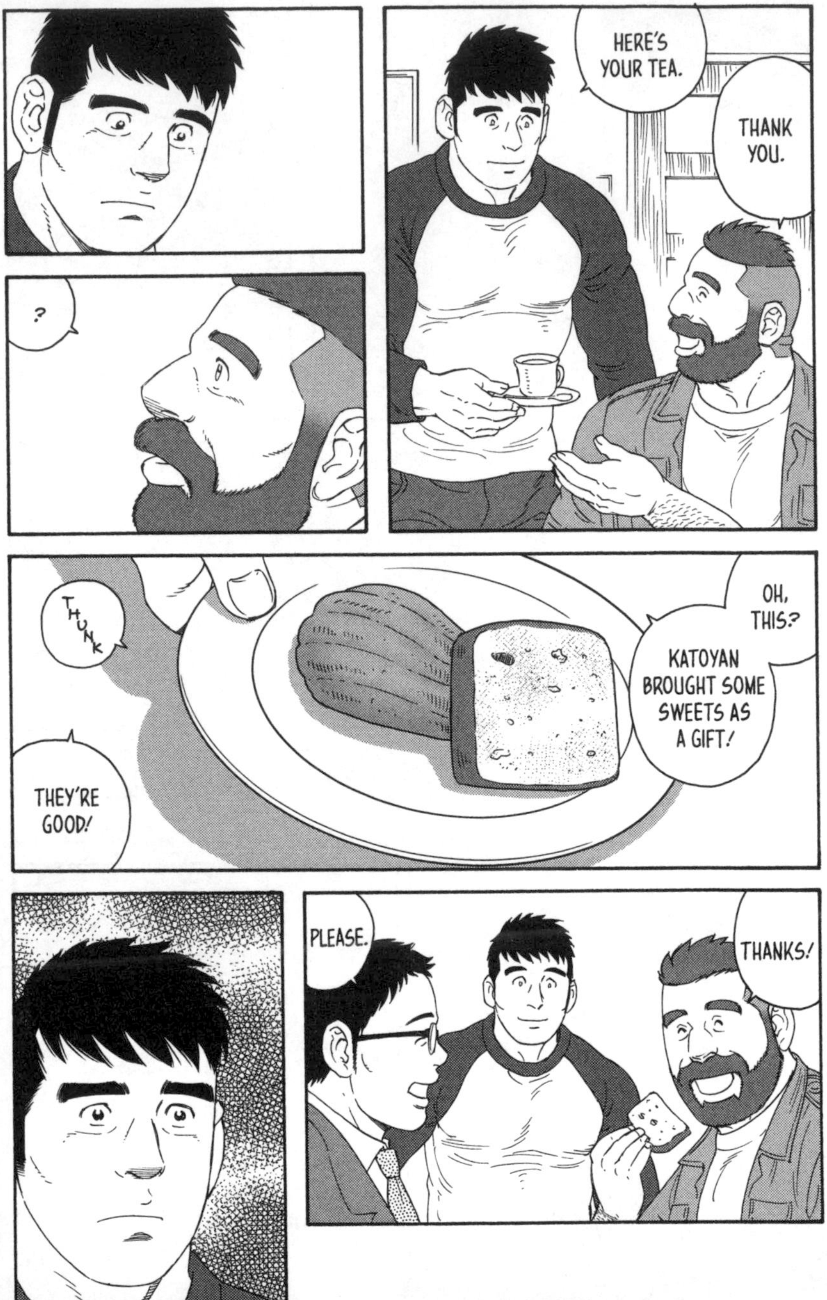
HERE'S YOUR TEA.
THANK YOU.
?
OH, THIS?
KATOYAN BROUGHT SOME SWEETS AS A GIFT!
THUNK
THEY'RE GOOD!
THANKS!
PLEASE.

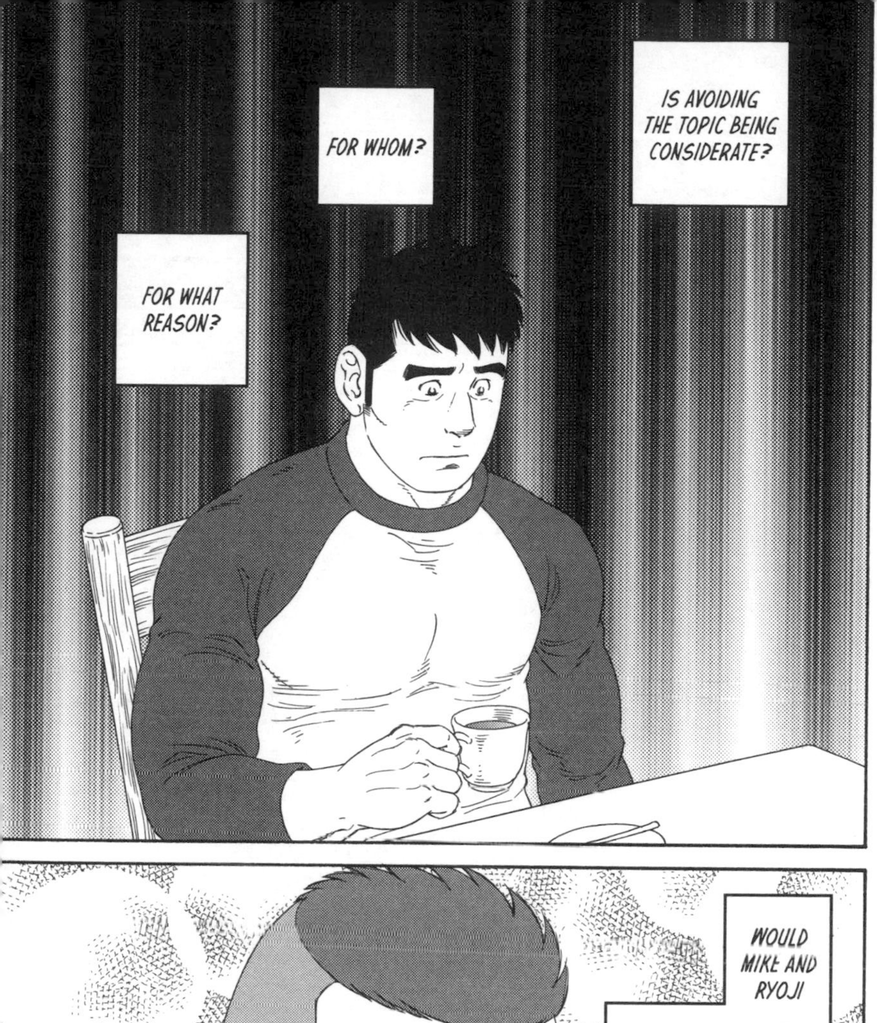
IS AVOIDING THE TOPIC BEING CONSIDERATE?
FOR WHOM?
FOR WHAT REASON?
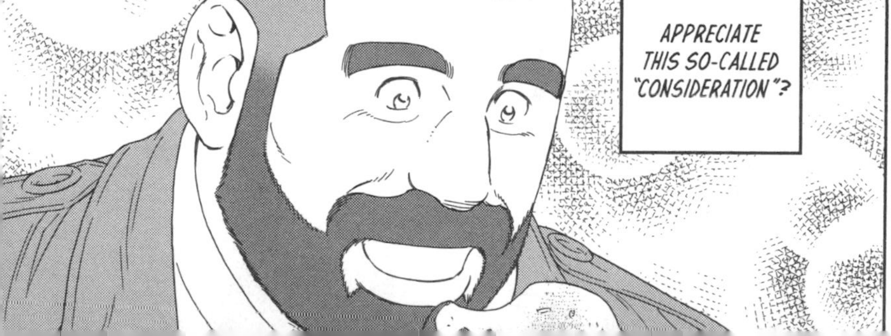
WOULD MIKE AND RYOJI
APPRECIATE THIS SO-CALLED "CONSIDERATION"?

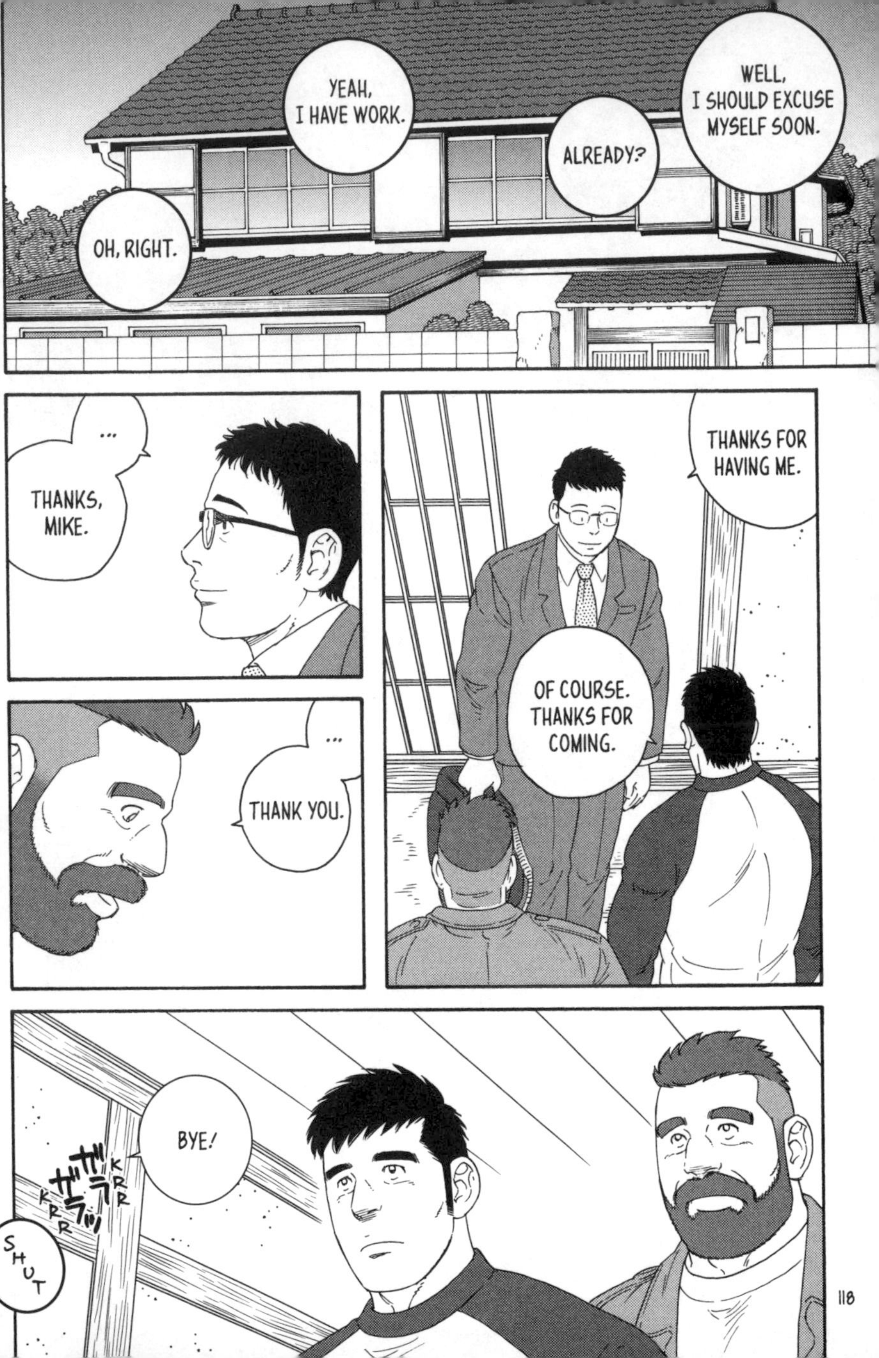
WELL, I SHOULD EXCUSE MYSELF SOON.
ALREADY?
YEAH, I HAVE WORK.
OH, RIGHT.
THANKS FOR HAVING ME.
OF COURSE. THANKS FOR COMING.
...
THANKS, MIKE.
...
THANK YOU.
BYE!
ガラッ KRR
ガラッ KRR
SHUT

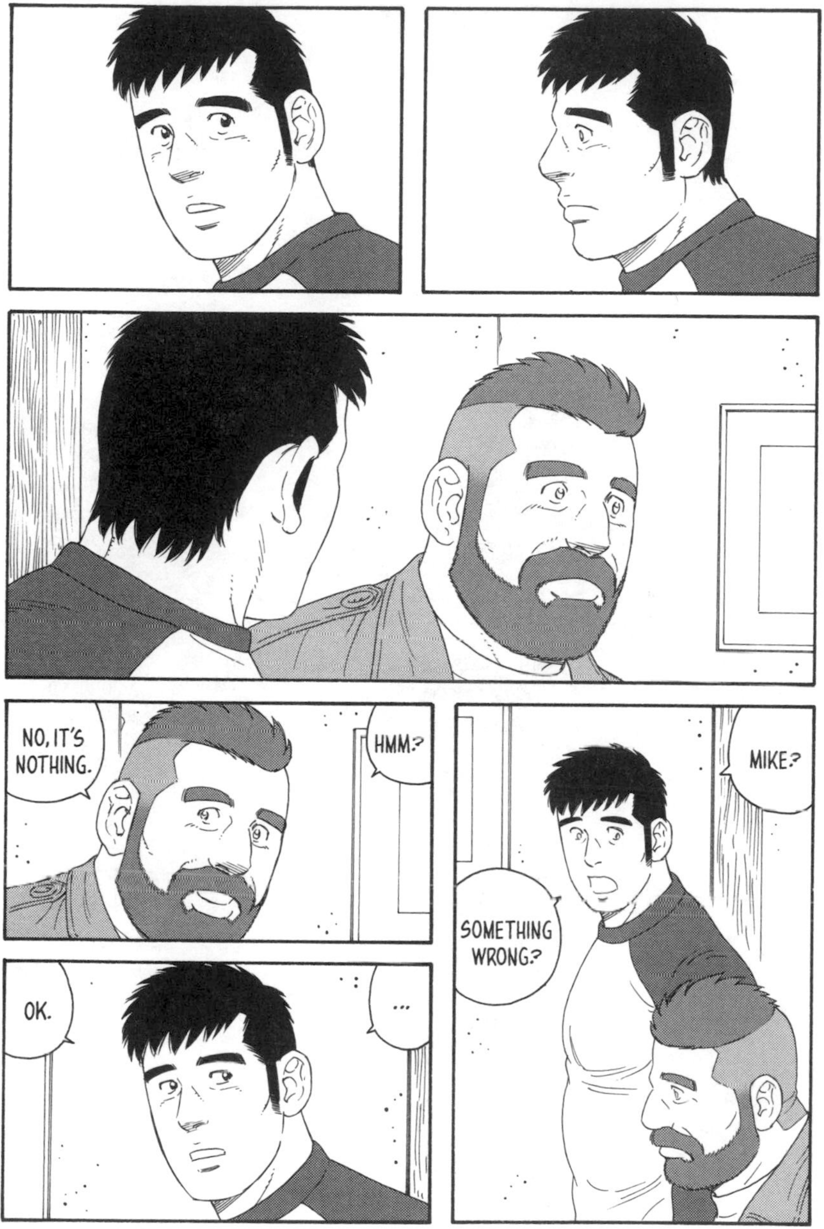
MIKE?
SOMETHING WRONG?
HMM?
NO, IT'S NOTHING.
...
OK.

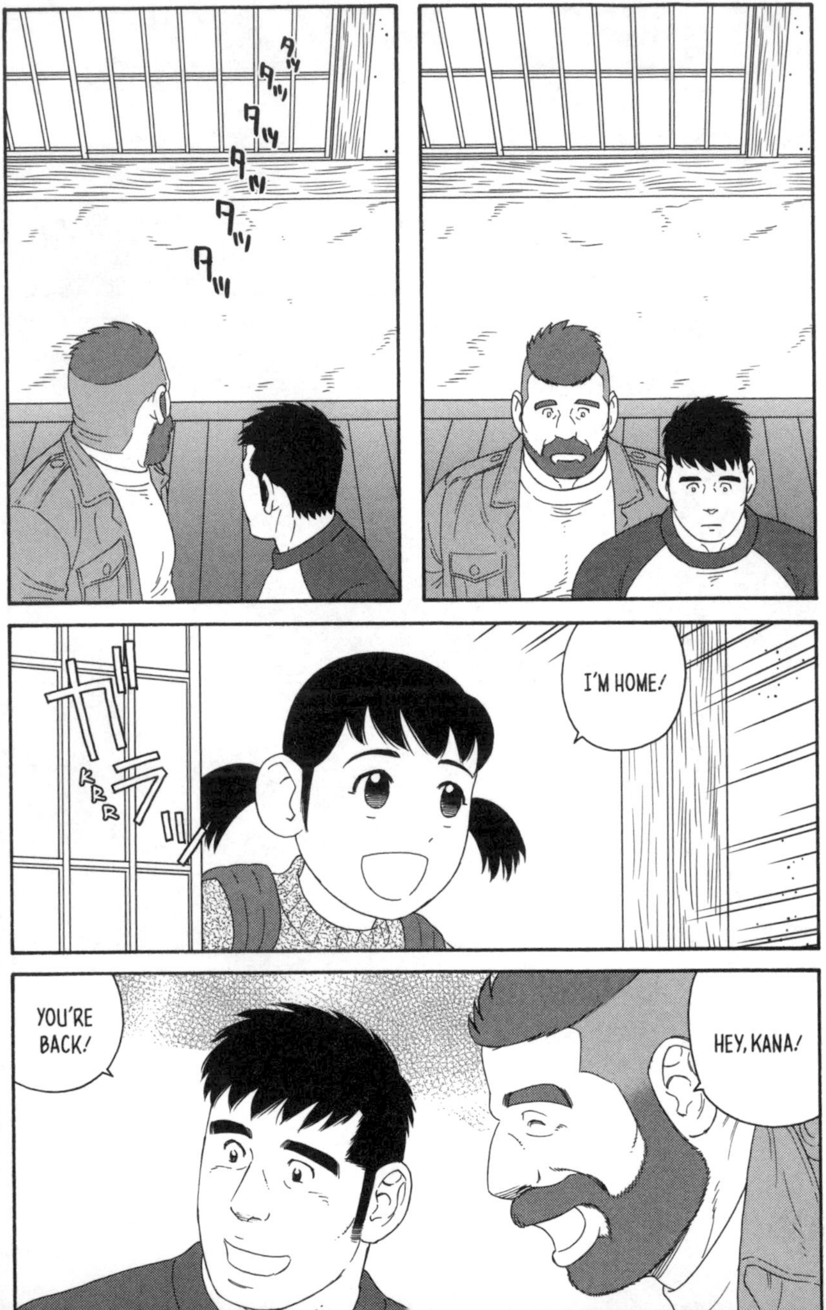
タッ
タッ
タッ
タッ
タッ
タッ
タッ
I'M HOME!
ガラッ
KRR
HEY, KANA!
YOU'RE BACK!

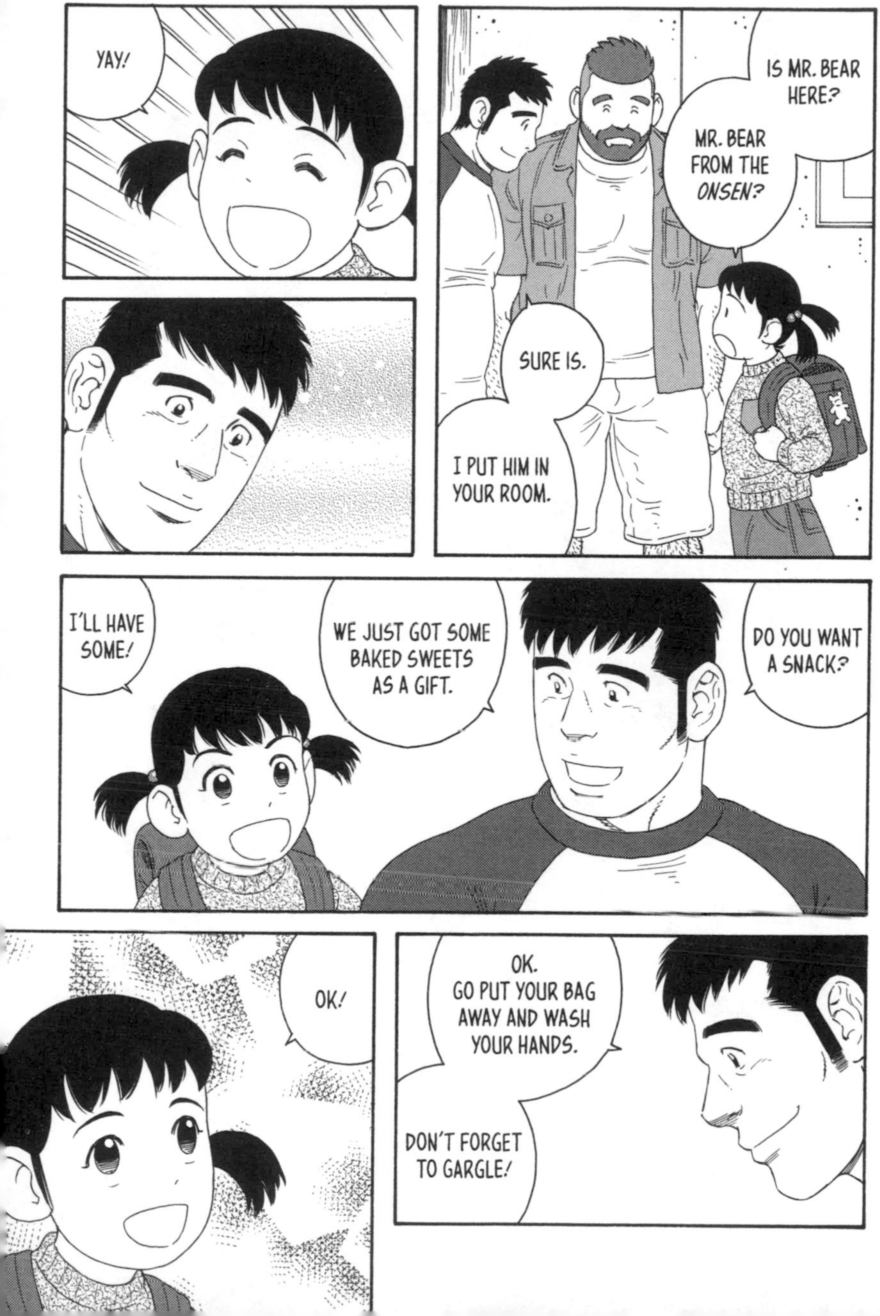
IS MR. BEAR HERE?
MR. BEAR FROM THE *ONSEN*?
SURE IS.
I PUT HIM IN YOUR ROOM.
YAY!
DO YOU WANT A SNACK?
WE JUST GOT SOME BAKED SWEETS AS A GIFT.
I'LL HAVE SOME!
OK. GO PUT YOUR BAG AWAY AND WASH YOUR HANDS.
DON'T FORGET TO GARGLE!
OK!

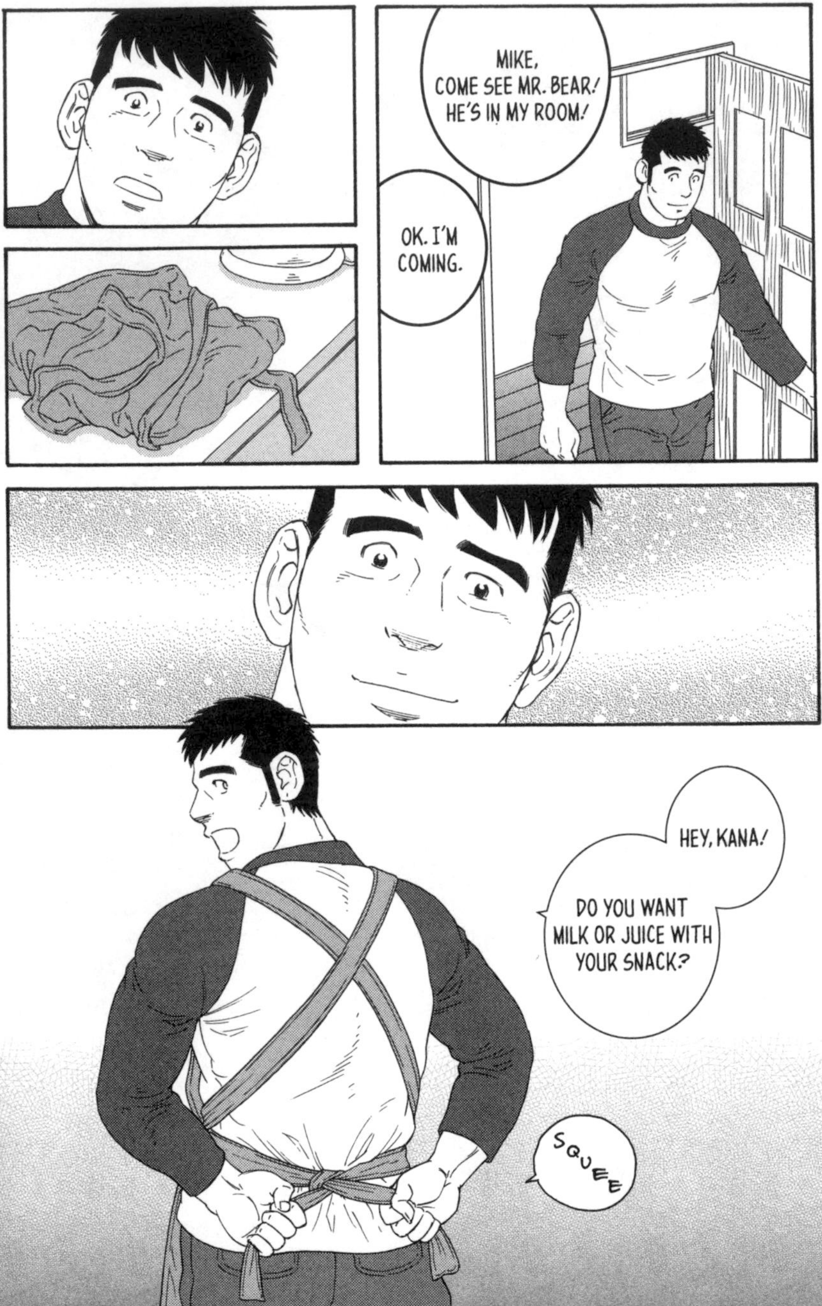
MIKE, COME SEE MR. BEAR! HE'S IN MY ROOM!
OK. I'M COMING.
HEY, KANA!
DO YOU WANT MILK OR JUICE WITH YOUR SNACK?
SQUEE

CHAPTER TWENTY

SECRETS

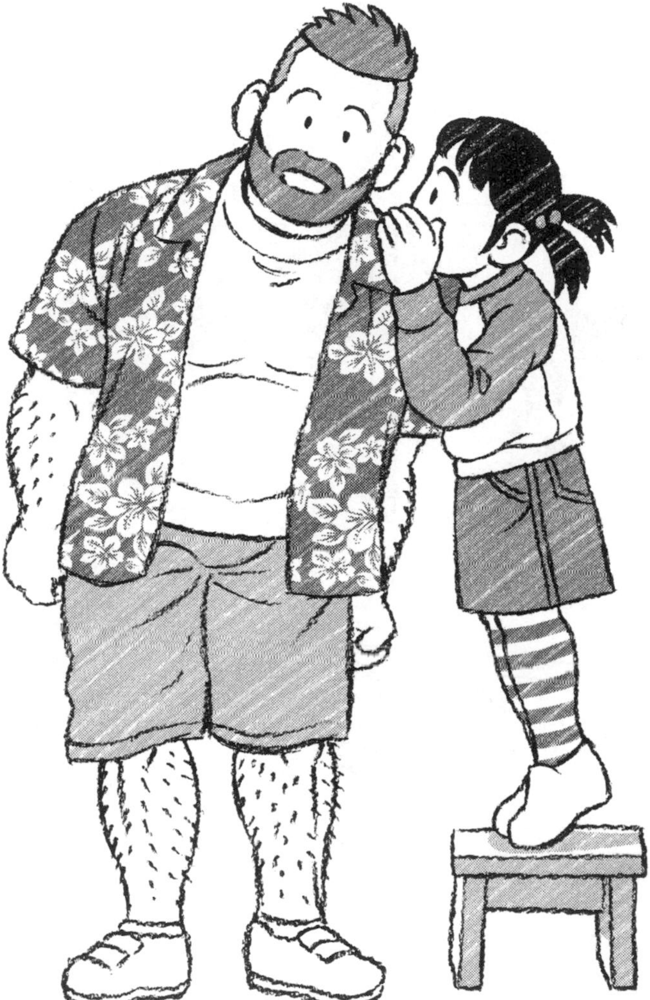

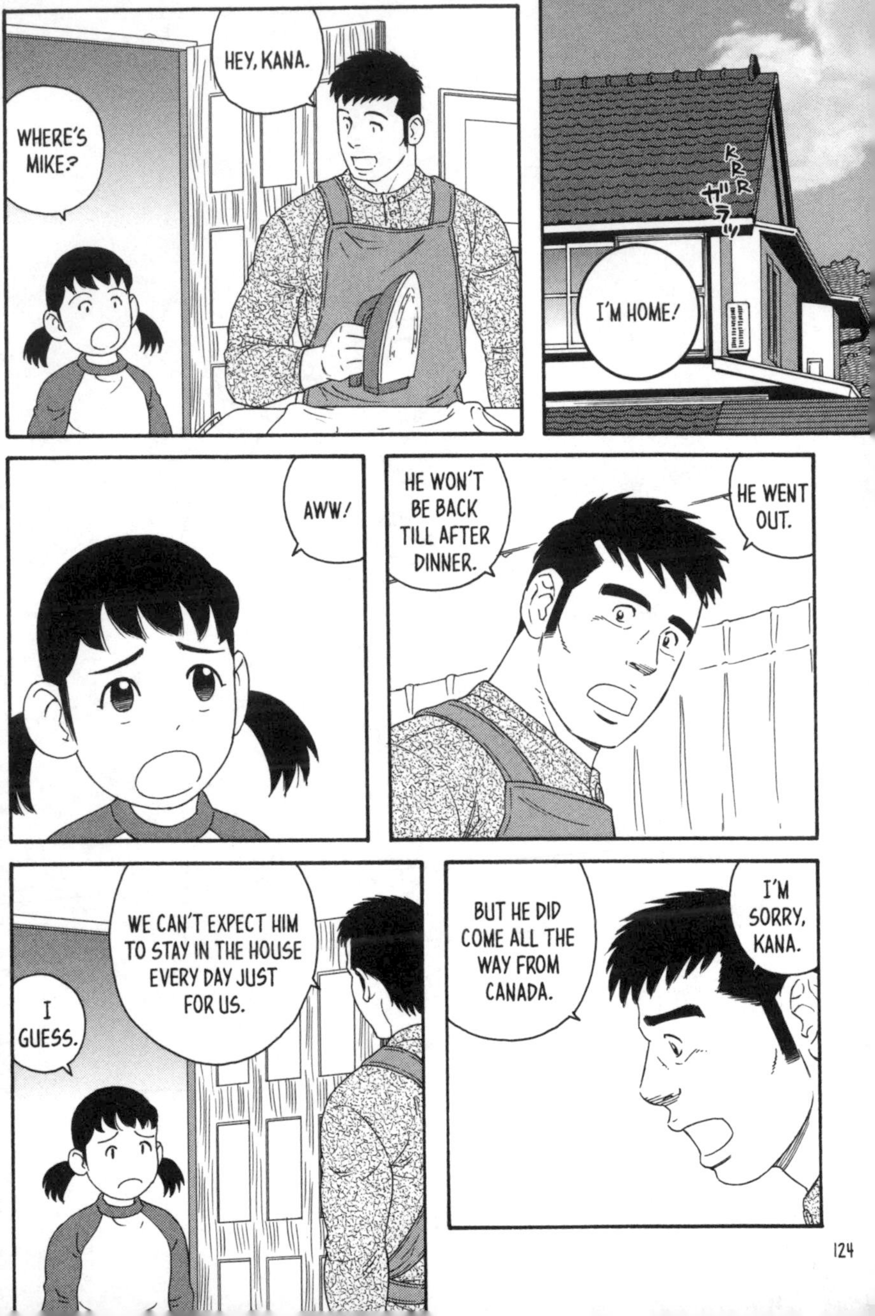
KRR
ガラッ
I'M HOME!
HEY, KANA.
WHERE'S MIKE?
HE WENT OUT.
HE WON'T BE BACK TILL AFTER DINNER.
AWW!
I'M SORRY, KANA.
BUT HE DID COME ALL THE WAY FROM CANADA.
WE CAN'T EXPECT HIM TO STAY IN THE HOUSE EVERY DAY JUST FOR US.
I GUESS.

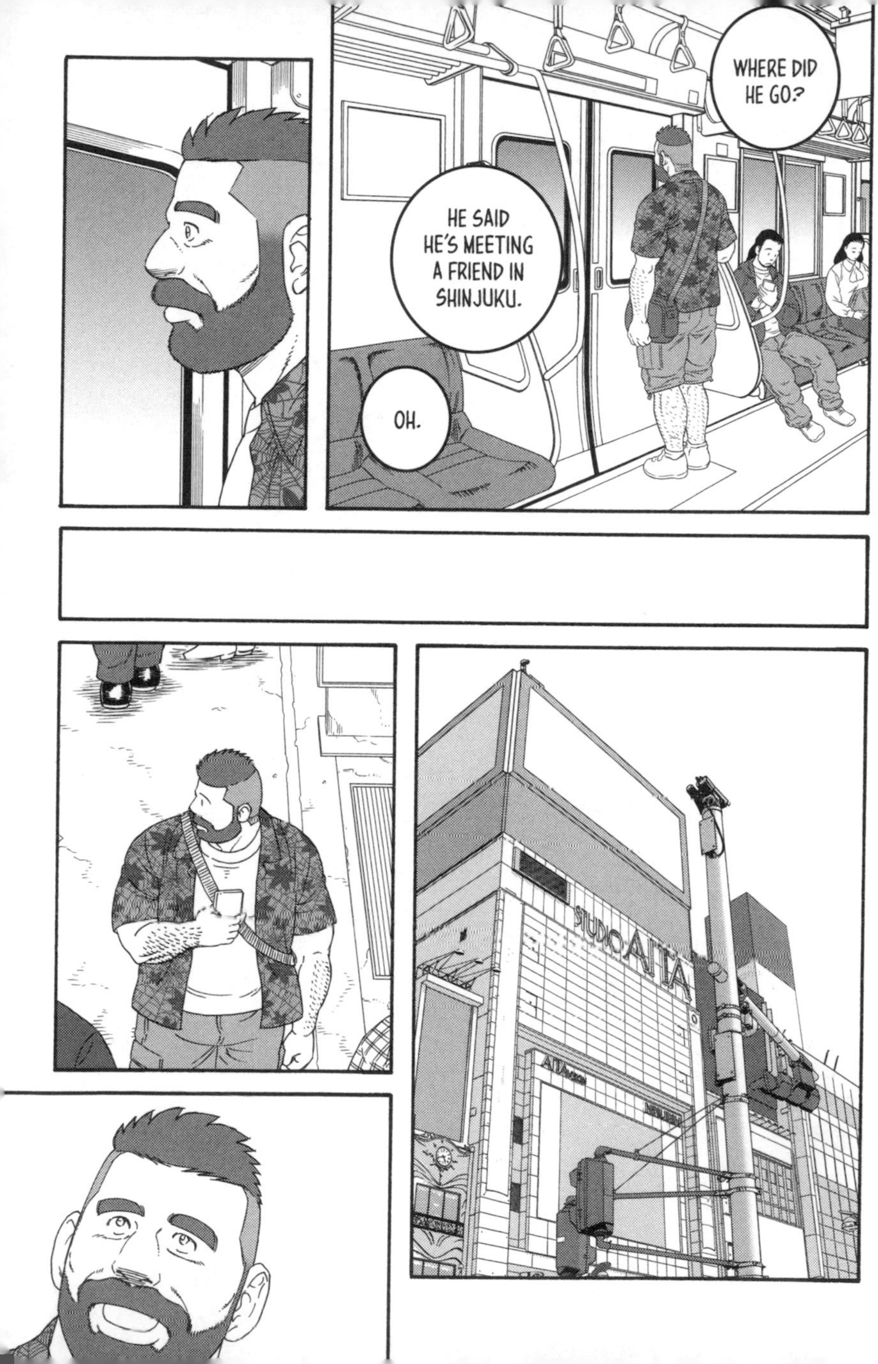
WHERE DID HE GO?
HE SAID HE'S MEETING A FRIEND IN SHINJUKU.
OH.

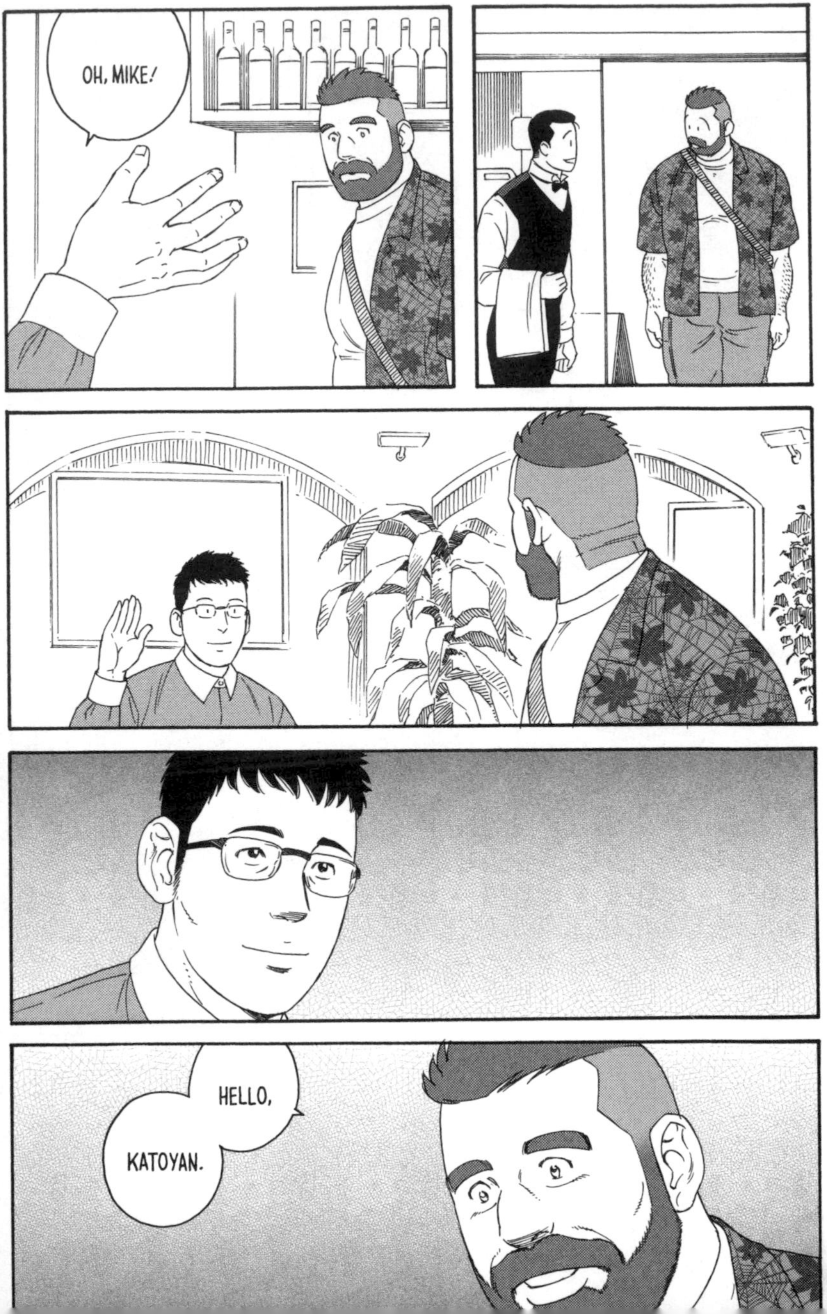
OH, MIKE!
HELLO,
KATOYAN.

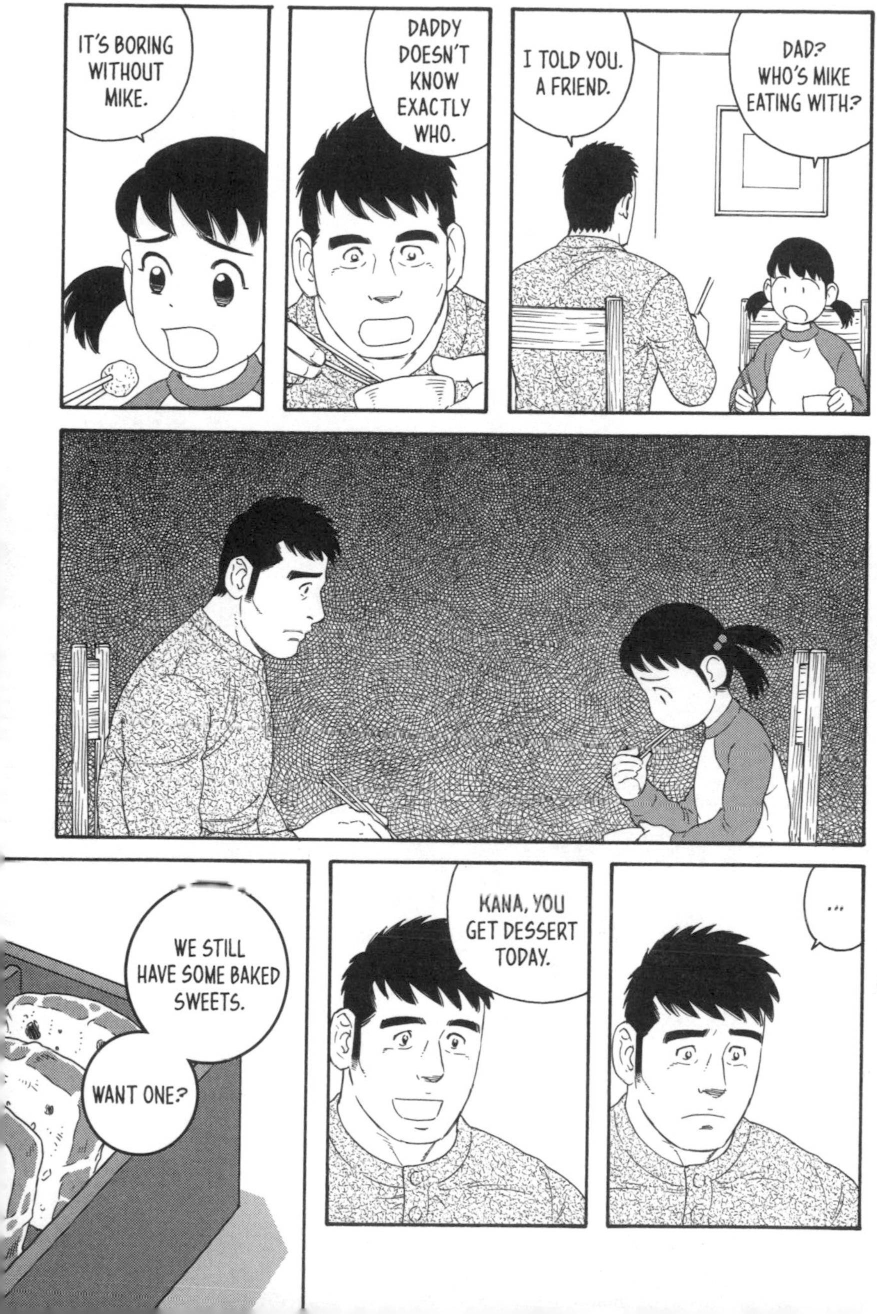
DAD? WHO'S MIKE EATING WITH?
I TOLD YOU. A FRIEND.
DADDY DOESN'T KNOW EXACTLY WHO.
IT'S BORING WITHOUT MIKE.
...
KANA, YOU GET DESSERT TODAY.
WE STILL HAVE SOME BAKED SWEETS.
WANT ONE?

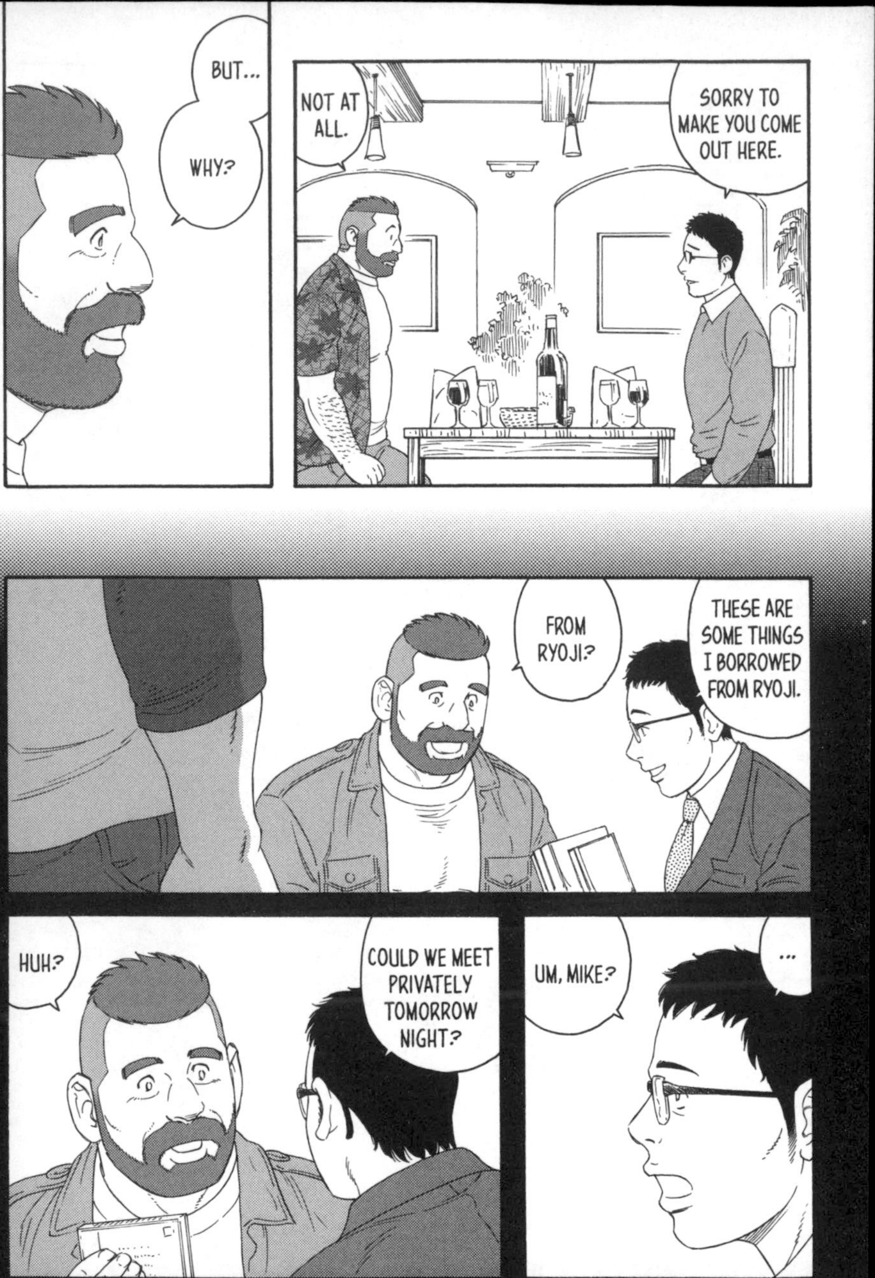
SORRY TO MAKE YOU COME OUT HERE.
NOT AT ALL.
BUT...
WHY?
THESE ARE SOME THINGS I BORROWED FROM RYOJI.
FROM RYOJI?
...
UM, MIKE?
COULD WE MEET PRIVATELY TOMORROW NIGHT?
HUH?

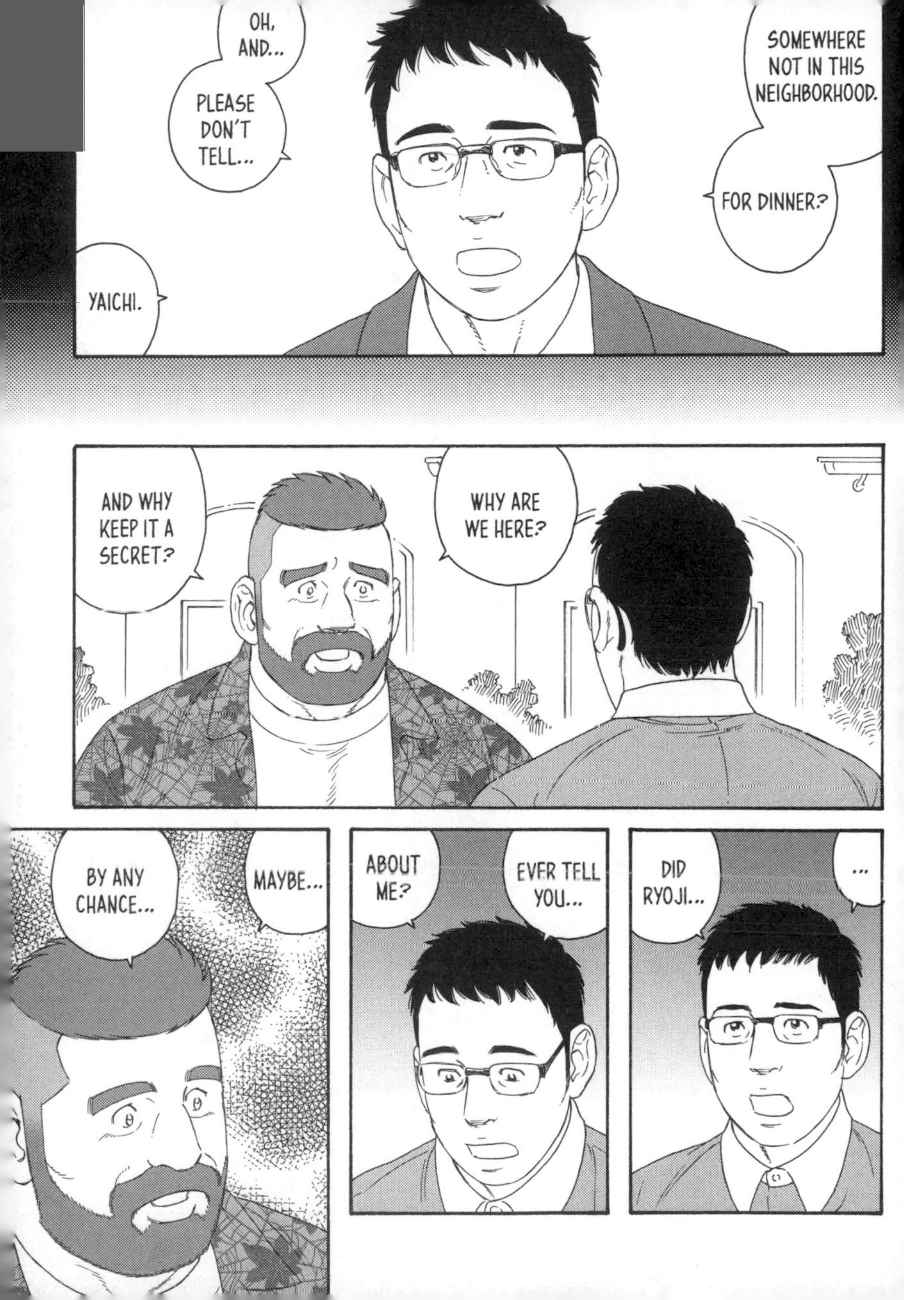
SOMEWHERE NOT IN THIS NEIGHBORHOOD.
FOR DINNER?
OH, AND...
PLEASE DON'T TELL...
YAICHI.
WHY ARE WE HERE?
AND WHY KEEP IT A SECRET?
...
DID RYOJI...
EVER TELL YOU...
ABOUT ME?
MAYBE...
BY ANY CHANCE...

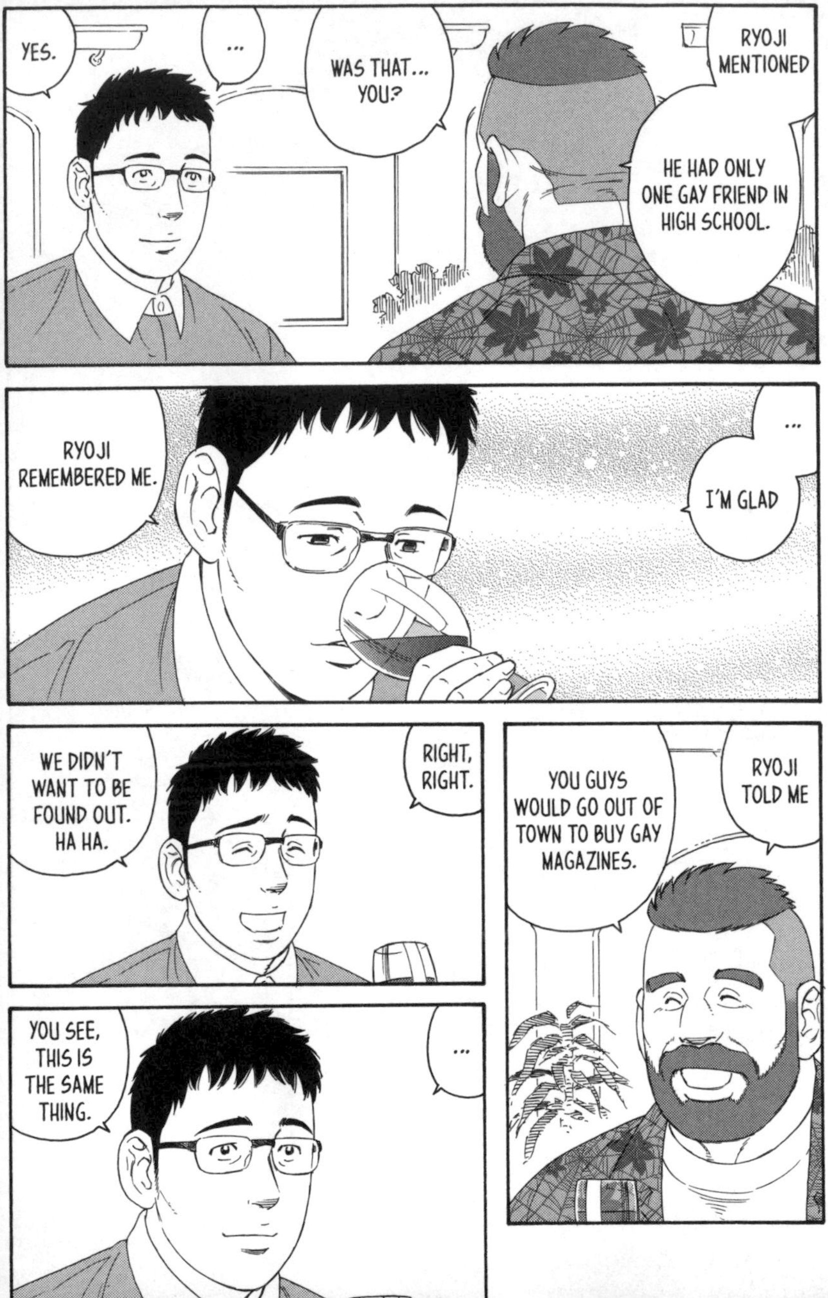
RYOJI MENTIONED
HE HAD ONLY ONE GAY FRIEND IN HIGH SCHOOL.
WAS THAT... YOU?
...
YES.
...
I'M GLAD
RYOJI REMEMBERED ME.
RYOJI TOLD ME
YOU GUYS WOULD GO OUT OF TOWN TO BUY GAY MAGAZINES.
RIGHT, RIGHT.
WE DIDN'T WANT TO BE FOUND OUT. HA HA.
...
YOU SEE, THIS IS THE SAME THING.

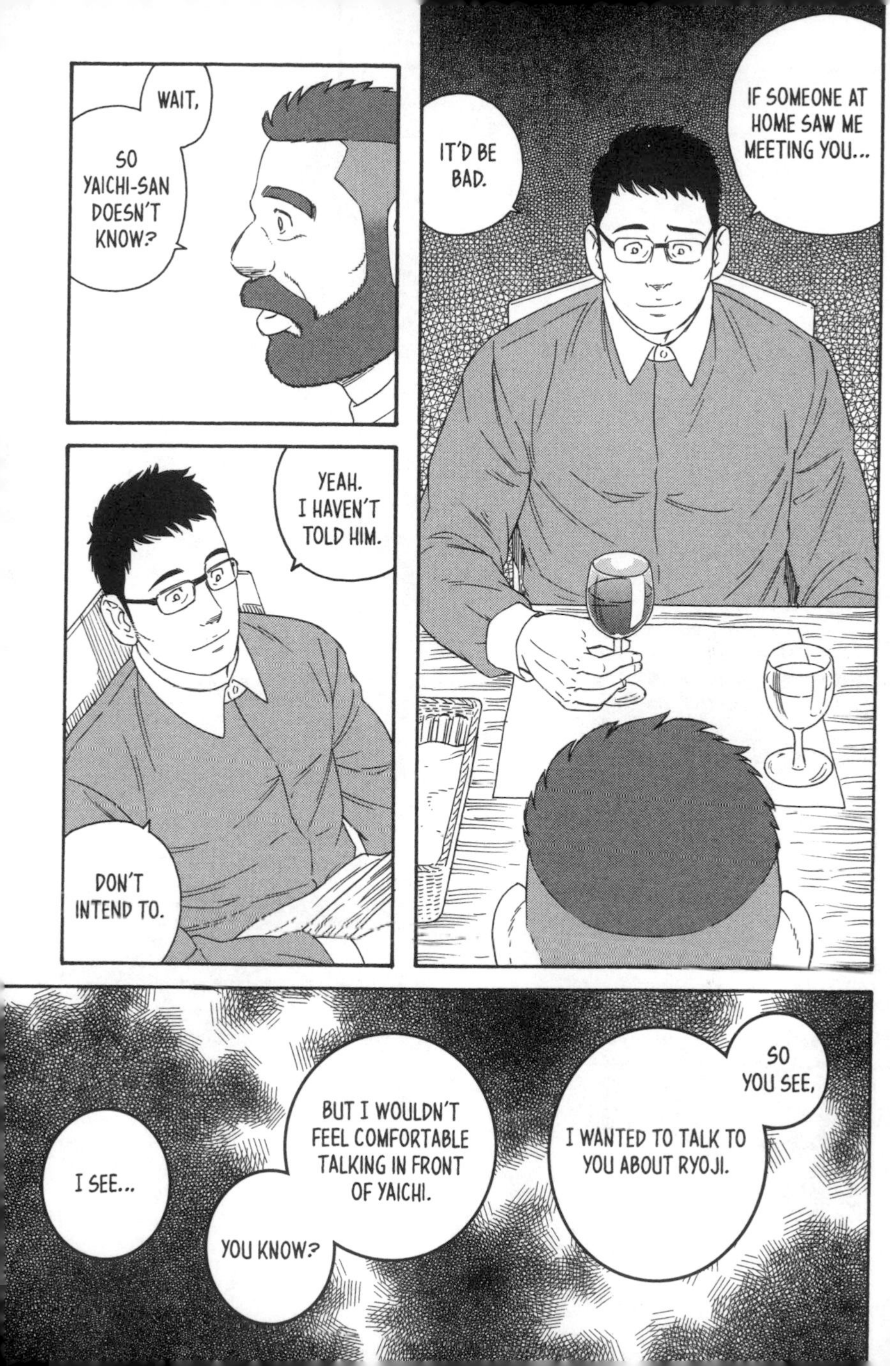
IF SOMEONE AT HOME SAW ME MEETING YOU...
IT'D BE BAD.
WAIT,
SO YAICHI-SAN DOESN'T KNOW?
YEAH. I HAVEN'T TOLD HIM.
DON'T INTEND TO.
SO YOU SEE,
I WANTED TO TALK TO YOU ABOUT RYOJI.
BUT I WOULDN'T FEEL COMFORTABLE TALKING IN FRONT OF YAICHI.
YOU KNOW?
I SEE...

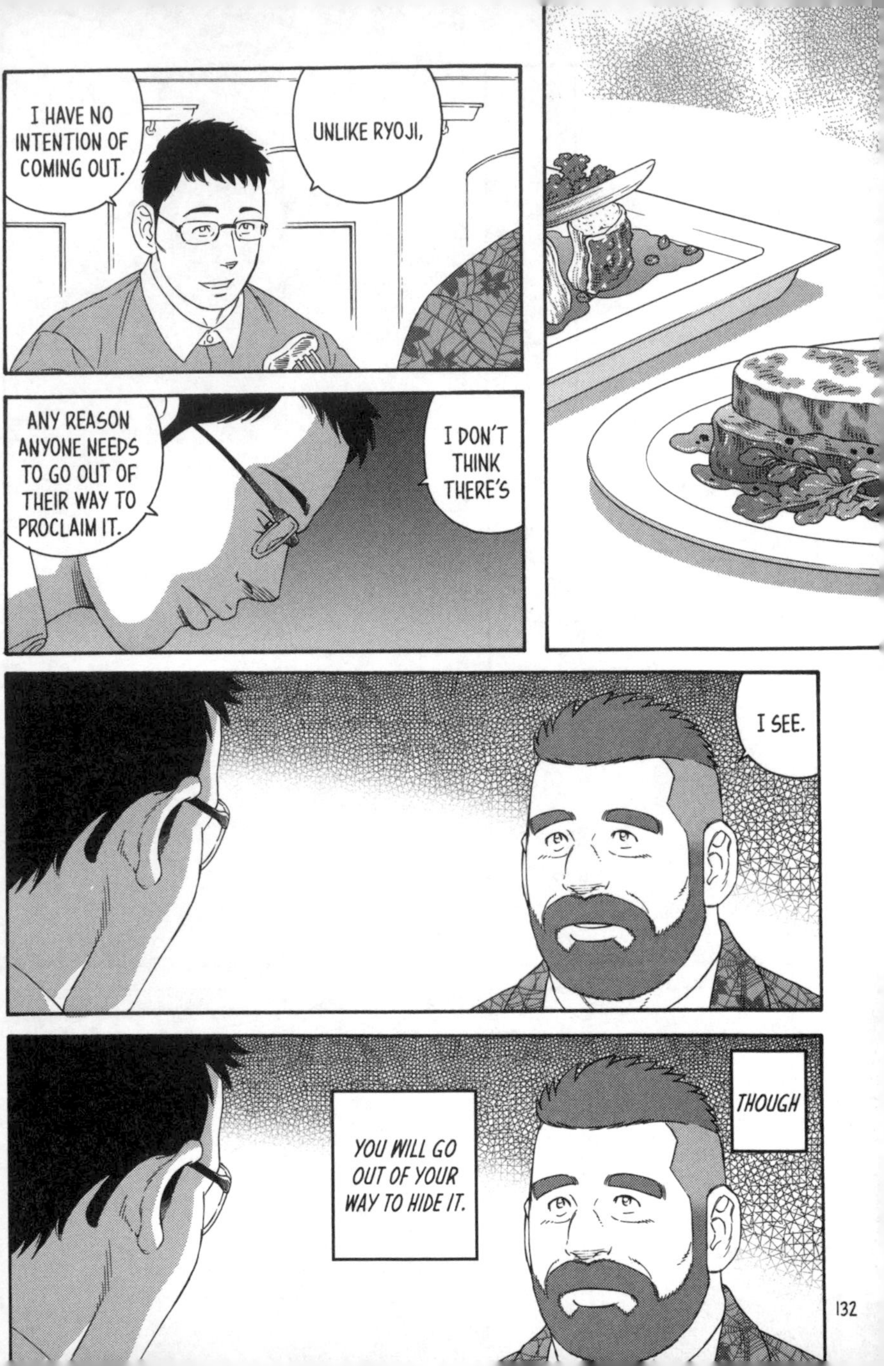
UNLIKE RYOJI,
I HAVE NO INTENTION OF COMING OUT.
I DON'T THINK THERE'S
ANY REASON ANYONE NEEDS TO GO OUT OF THEIR WAY TO PROCLAIM IT.
I SEE.
THOUGH
YOU WILL GO OUT OF YOUR WAY TO HIDE IT.

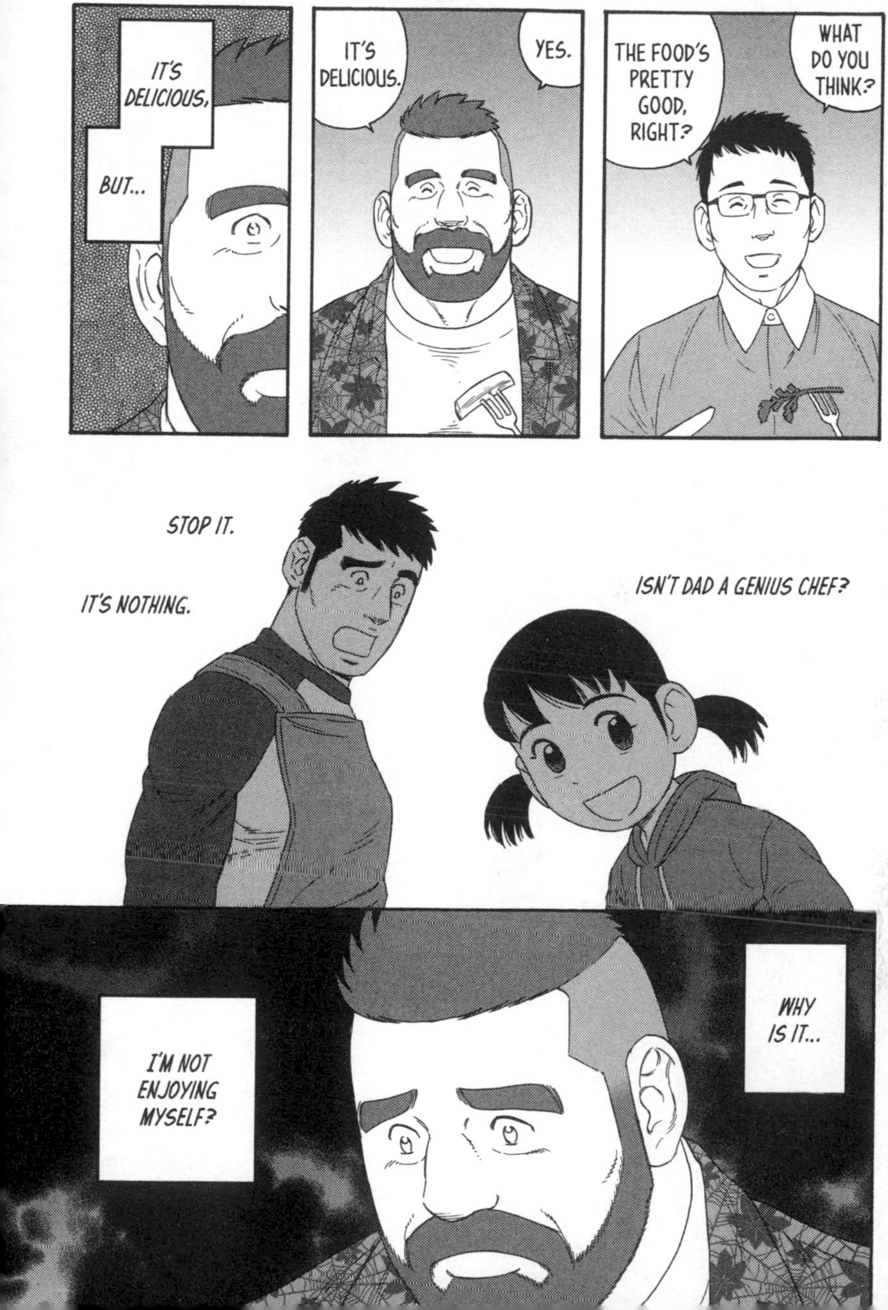
WHAT DO YOU THINK?
THE FOOD'S PRETTY GOOD, RIGHT?
YES.
IT'S DELICIOUS.
IT'S DELICIOUS,
BUT...
ISN'T DAD A GENIUS CHEF?
STOP IT.
IT'S NOTHING.
WHY IS IT...
I'M NOT ENJOYING MYSELF?

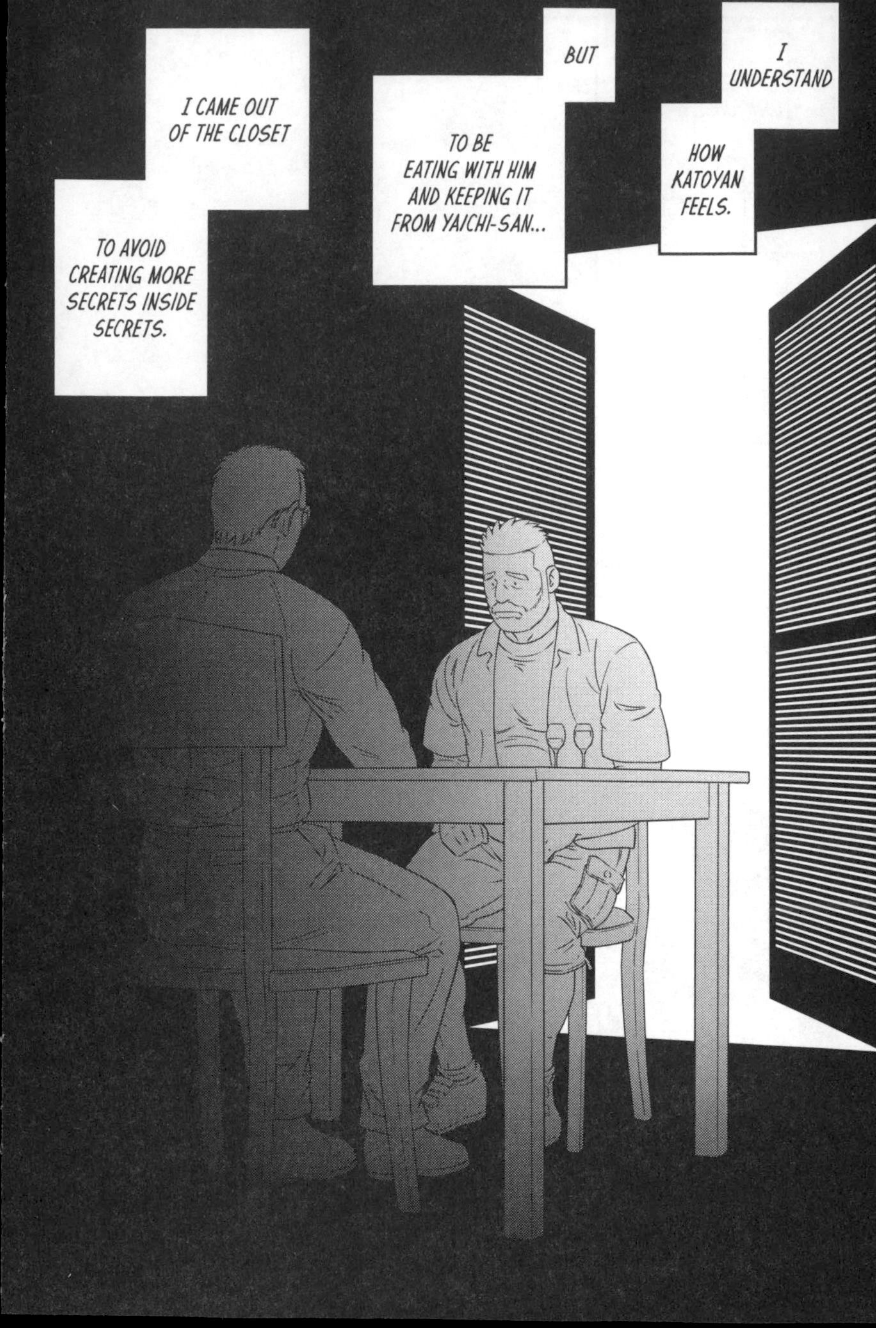
I UNDERSTAND
HOW KATOYAN FEELS.
BUT
TO BE EATING WITH HIM AND KEEPING IT FROM YAICHI-SAN...
I CAME OUT OF THE CLOSET
TO AVOID CREATING MORE SECRETS INSIDE SECRETS.

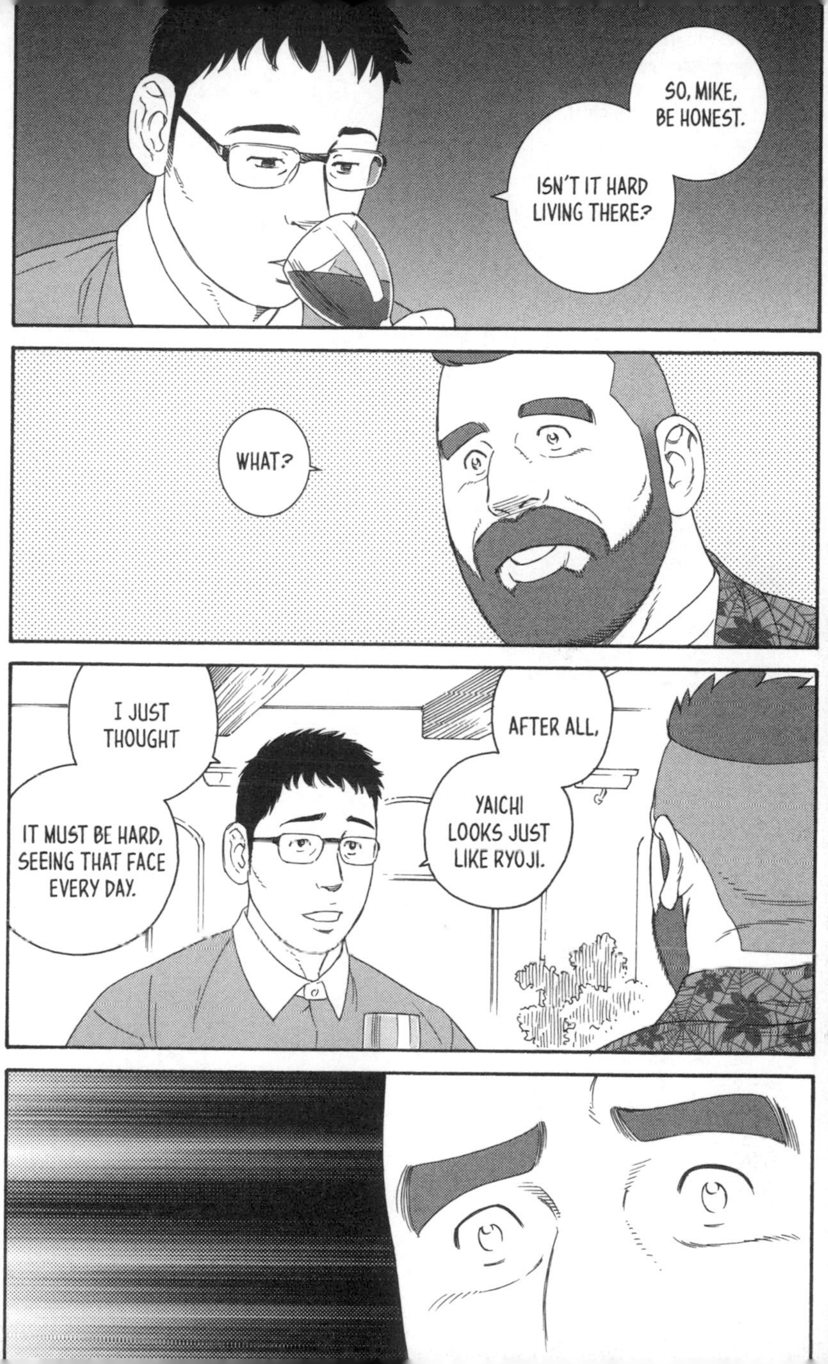
SO, MIKE, BE HONEST.
ISN'T IT HARD LIVING THERE?
WHAT?
AFTER ALL,
YAICHI LOOKS JUST LIKE RYOJI.
I JUST THOUGHT
IT MUST BE HARD, SEEING THAT FACE EVERY DAY.

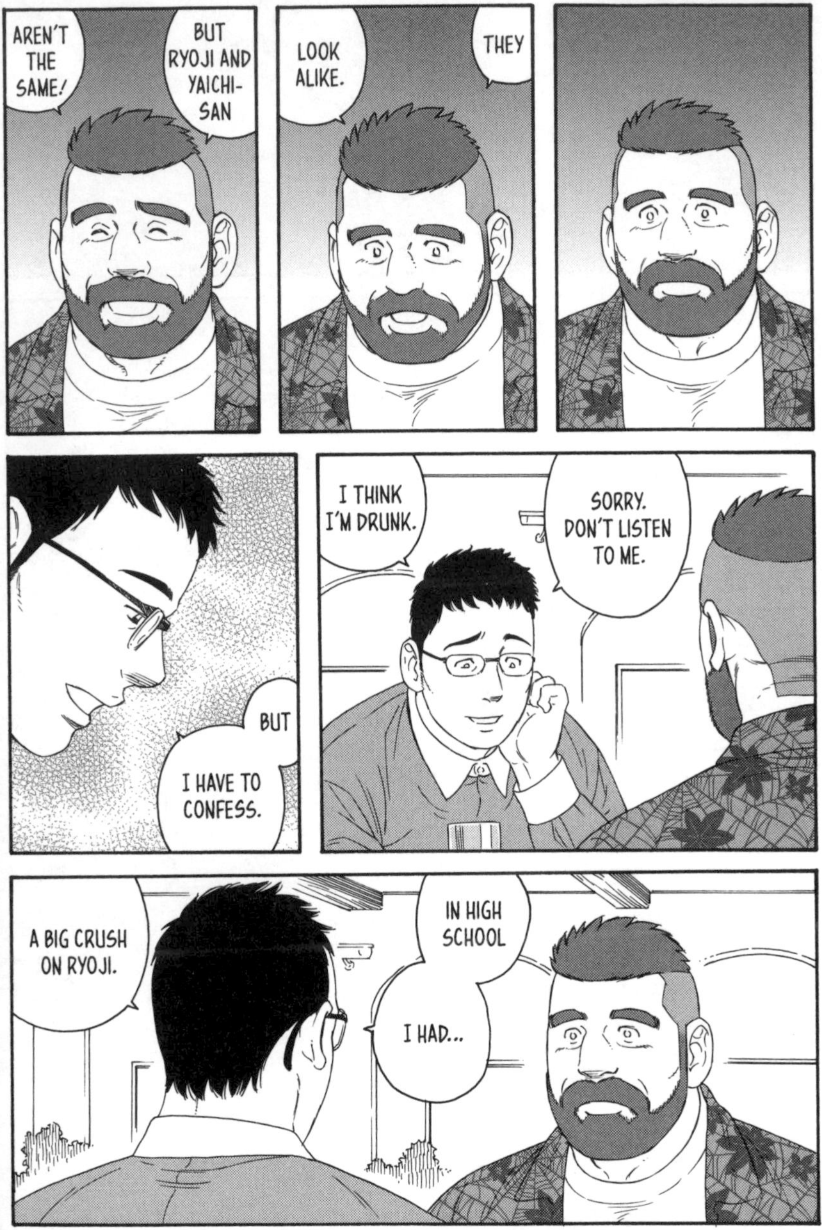
THEY
LOOK ALIKE.
BUT RYOJI AND YAICHI-SAN
AREN'T THE SAME!
SORRY. DON'T LISTEN TO ME.
I THINK I'M DRUNK.
BUT
I HAVE TO CONFESS.
IN HIGH SCHOOL
I HAD...
A BIG CRUSH ON RYOJI.

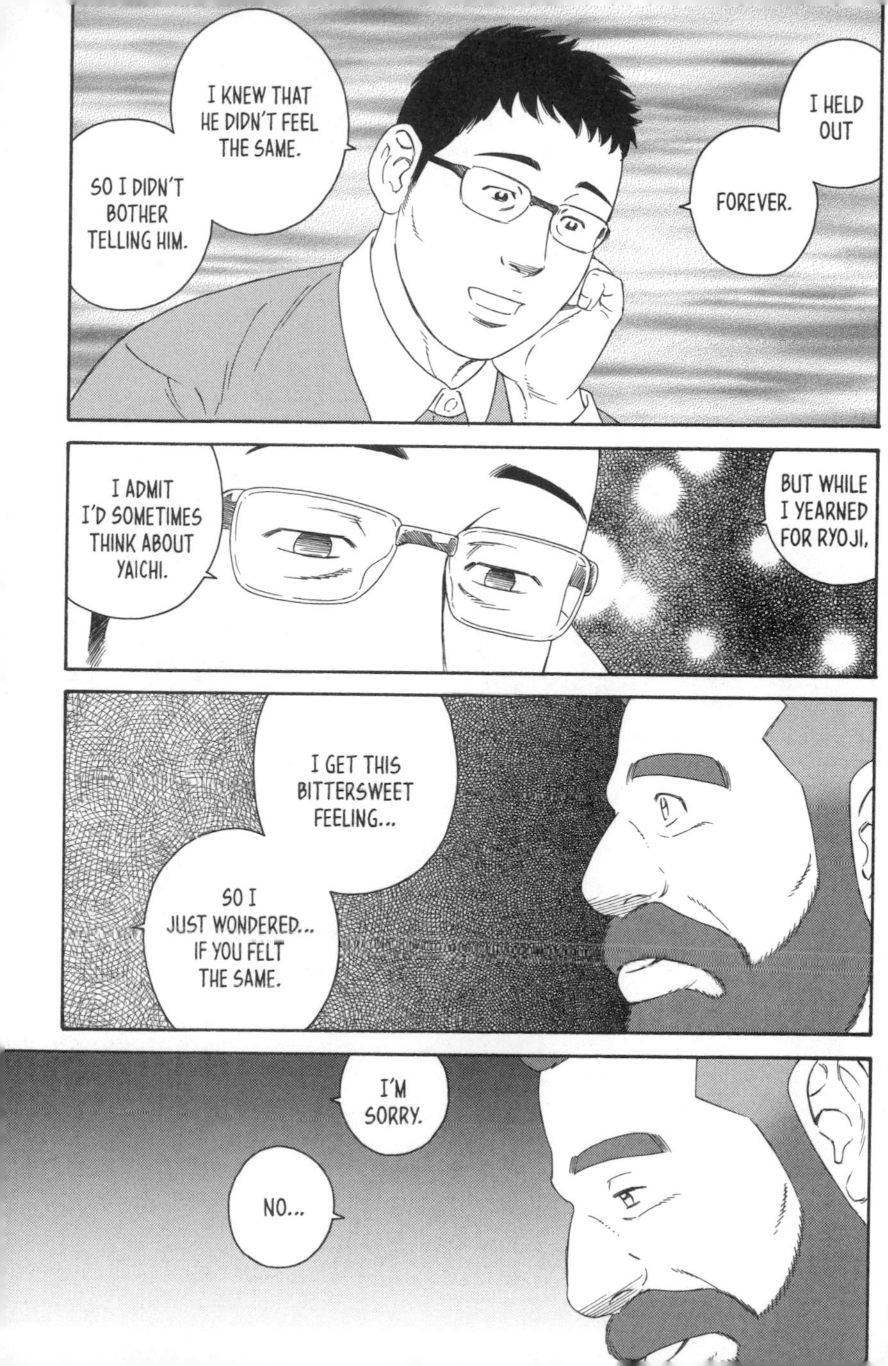
I HELD OUT
FOREVER.
I KNEW THAT HE DIDN'T FEEL THE SAME.
SO I DIDN'T BOTHER TELLING HIM.
BUT WHILE I YEARNED FOR RYOJI,
I ADMIT I'D SOMETIMES THINK ABOUT YAICHI.
I GET THIS BITTERSWEET FEELING...
SO I JUST WONDERED... IF YOU FELT THE SAME.
I'M SORRY.
NO...

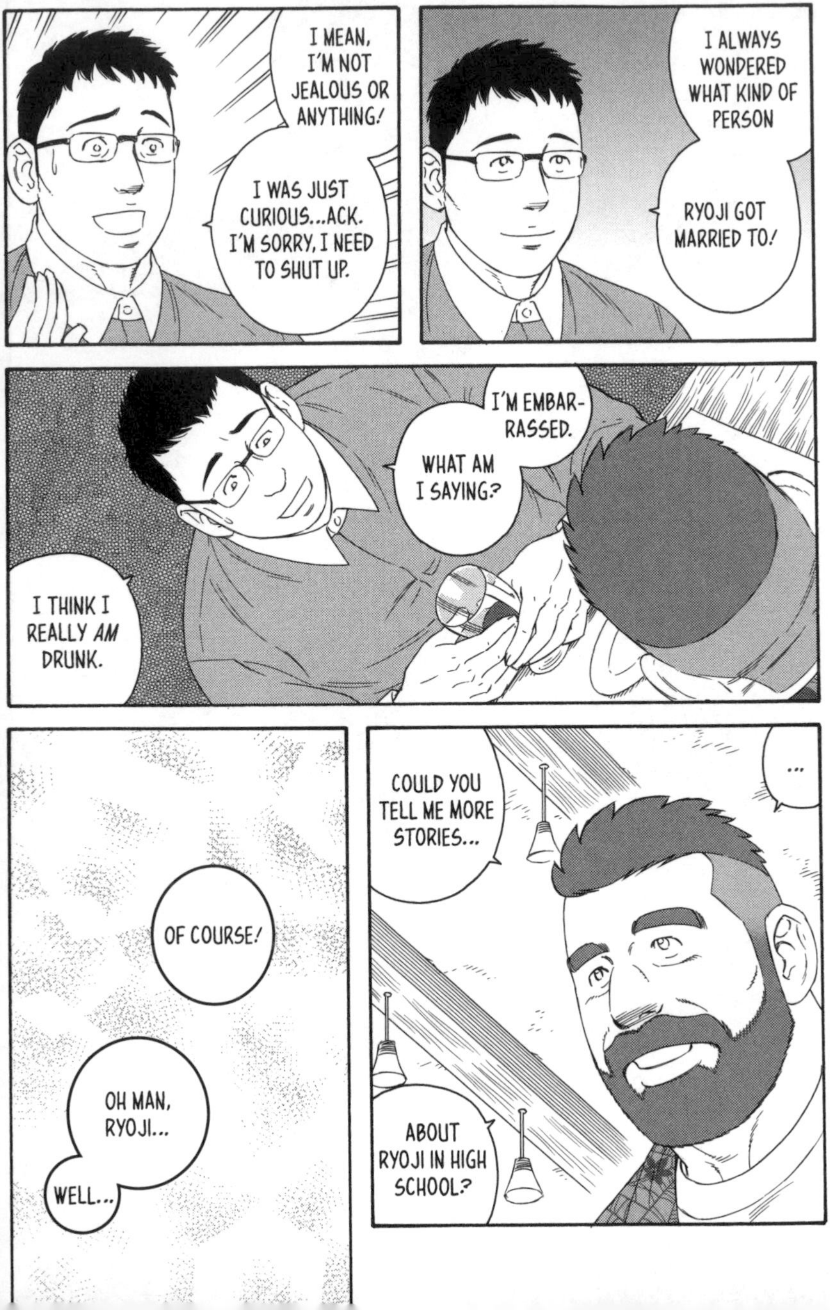
I ALWAYS WONDERED WHAT KIND OF PERSON
RYOJI GOT MARRIED TO!
I MEAN, I'M NOT JEALOUS OR ANYTHING!
I WAS JUST CURIOUS...ACK. I'M SORRY, I NEED TO SHUT UP.
I'M EMBARRASSED.
WHAT AM I SAYING?
I THINK I REALLY *AM* DRUNK.
...
COULD YOU TELL ME MORE STORIES...
ABOUT RYOJI IN HIGH SCHOOL?
OF COURSE!
OH MAN, RYOJI...
WELL...

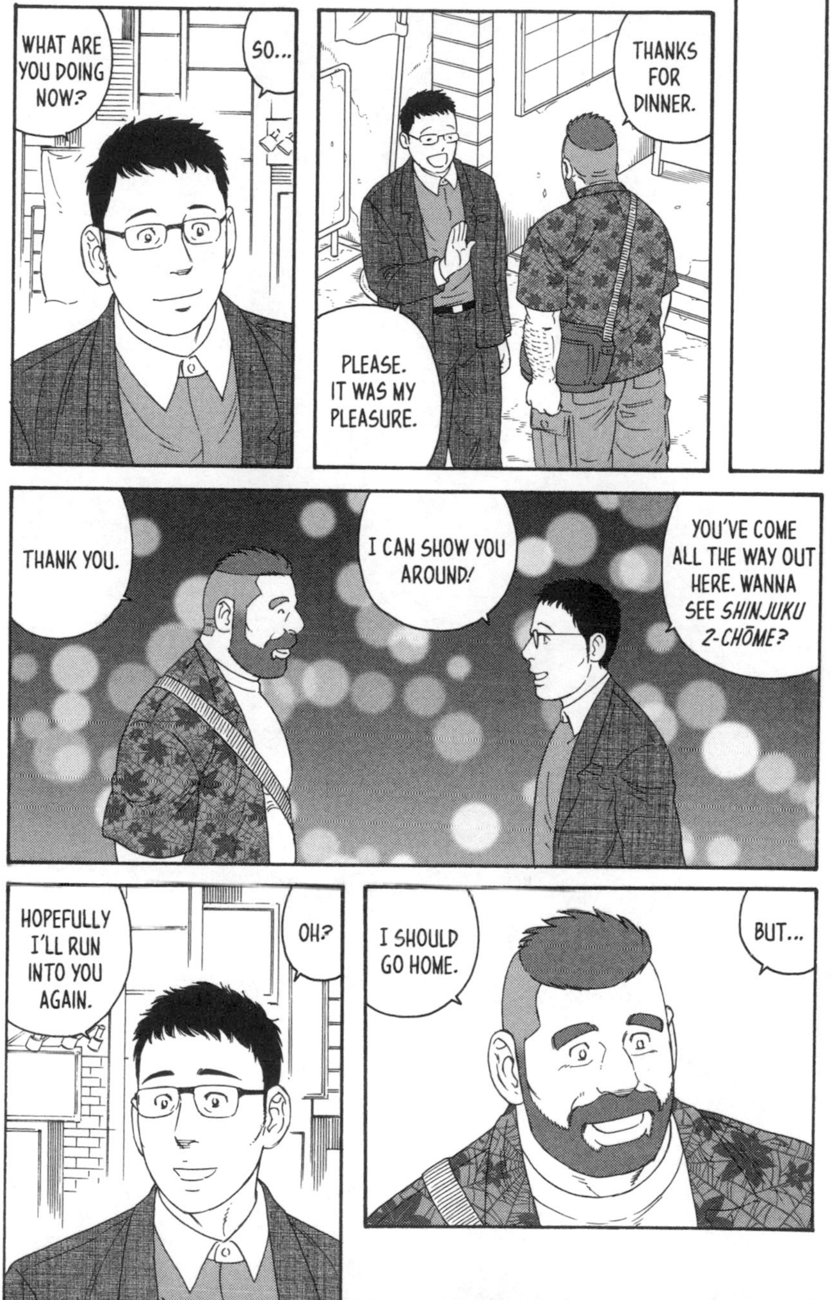
THANKS FOR DINNER.
PLEASE. IT WAS MY PLEASURE.
SO...
WHAT ARE YOU DOING NOW?
YOU'VE COME ALL THE WAY OUT HERE. WANNA SEE *SHINJUKU 2-CHŌME?*
I CAN SHOW YOU AROUND!
THANK YOU.
BUT...
I SHOULD GO HOME.
OH?
HOPEFULLY I'LL RUN INTO YOU AGAIN.

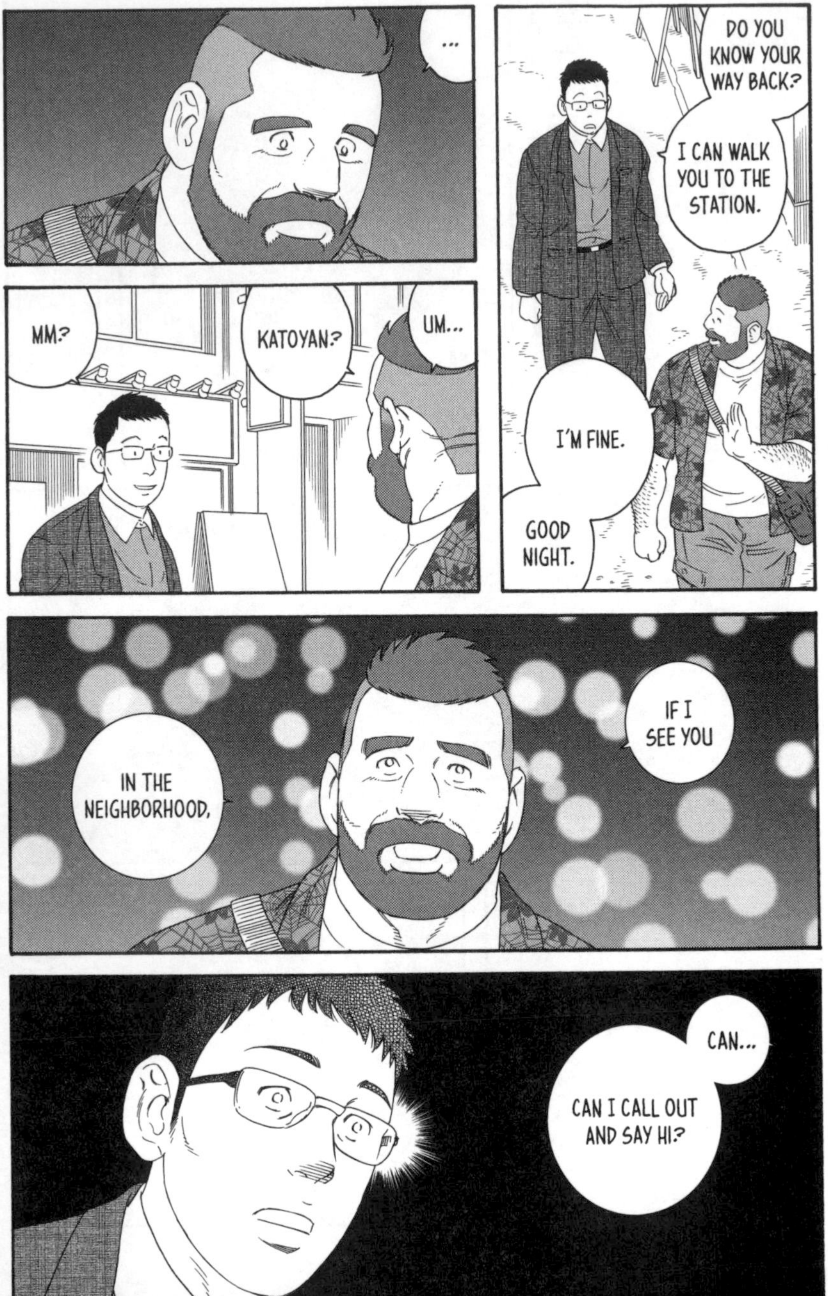
DO YOU KNOW YOUR WAY BACK?
I CAN WALK YOU TO THE STATION.
I'M FINE.
GOOD NIGHT.
...
UM...
KATOYAN?
MM?
IF I SEE YOU
IN THE NEIGHBORHOOD,
CAN...
CAN I CALL OUT AND SAY HI?

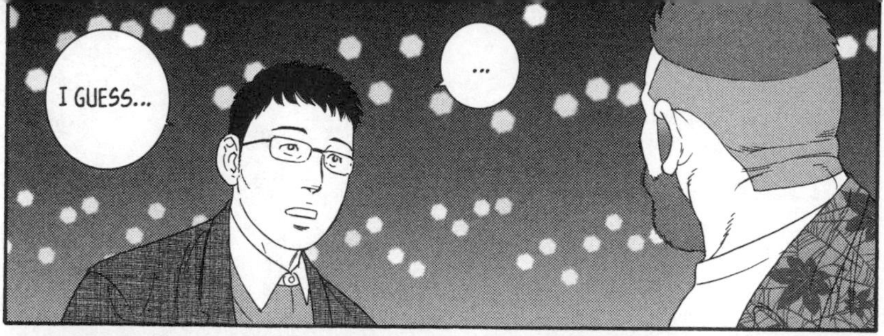
...
I GUESS...

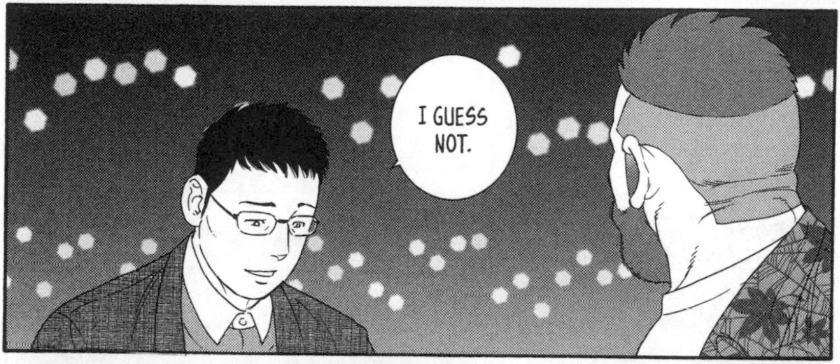
I GUESS NOT.

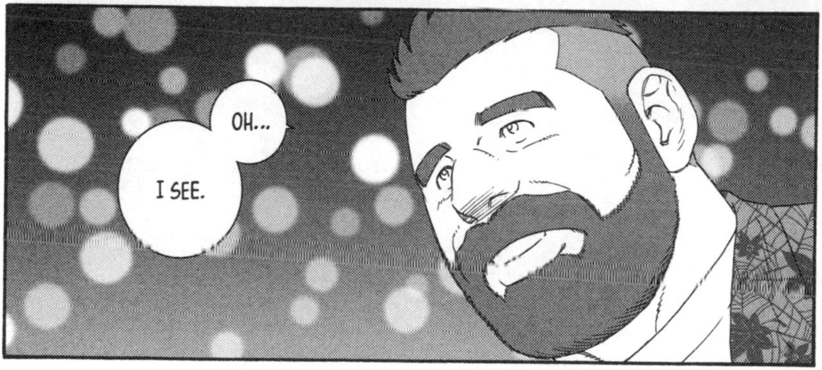
OH...
I SEE.

GOOD NIGHT, KATOYAN.

GOOD NIGHT.

SEE YOU.

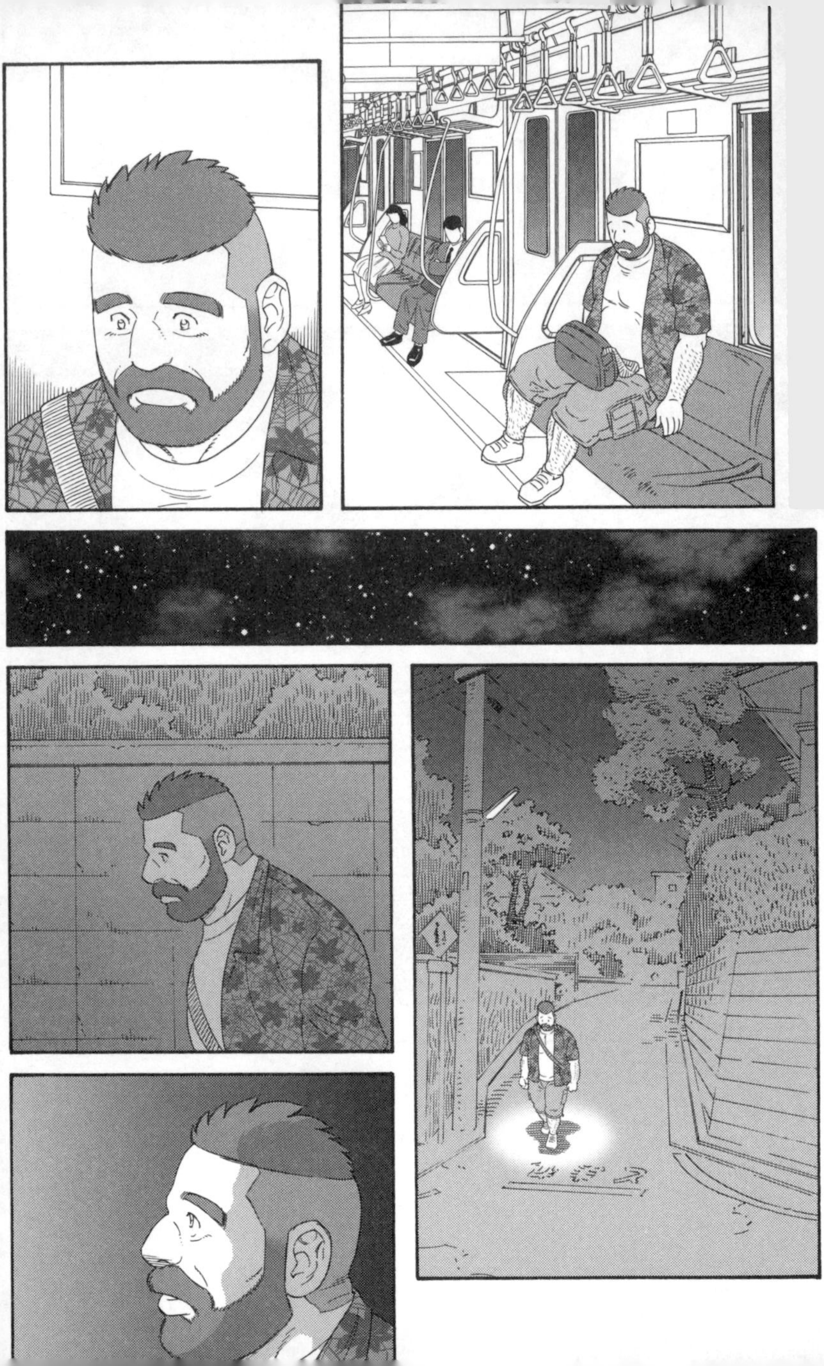

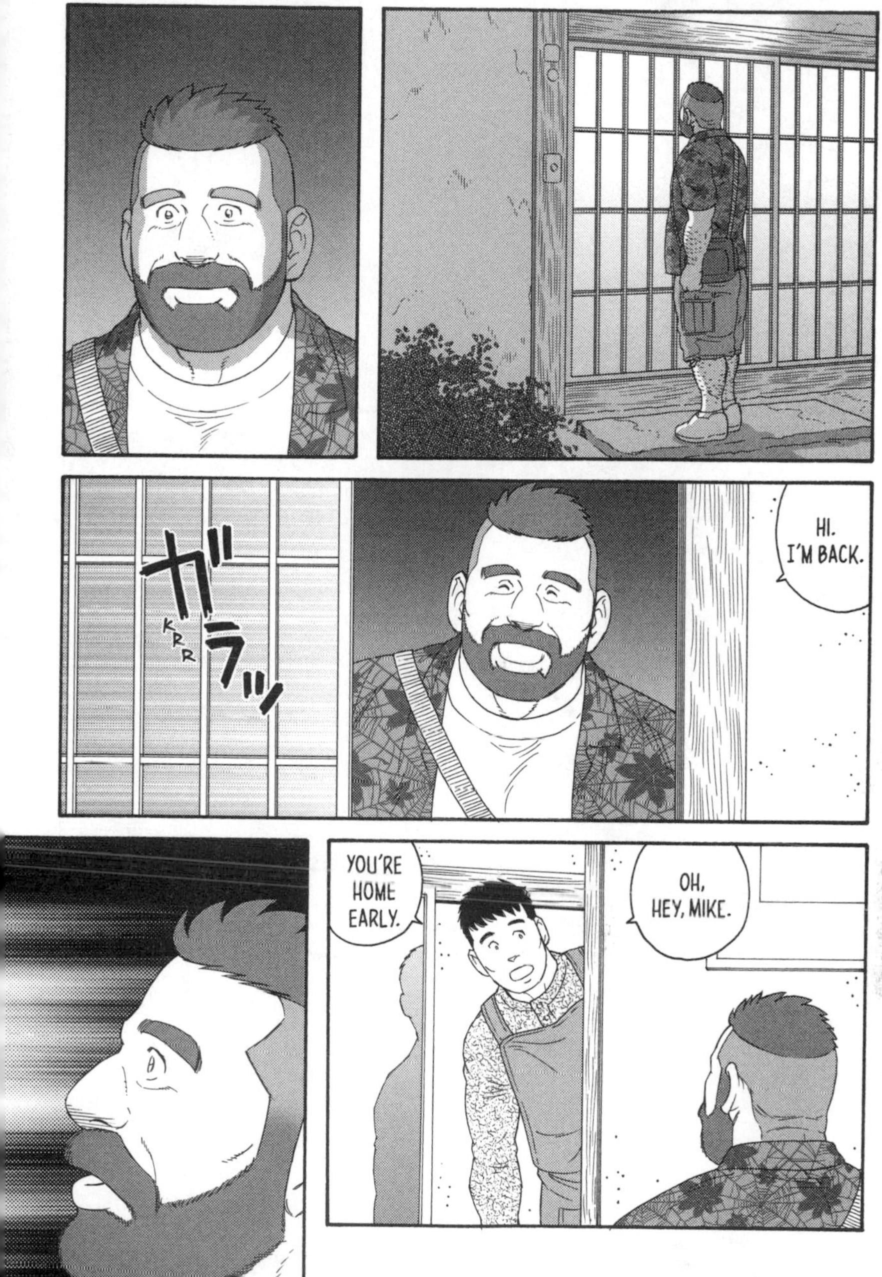
HI. I'M BACK.
ガラッ
KRR
OH, HEY, MIKE.
YOU'RE HOME EARLY.

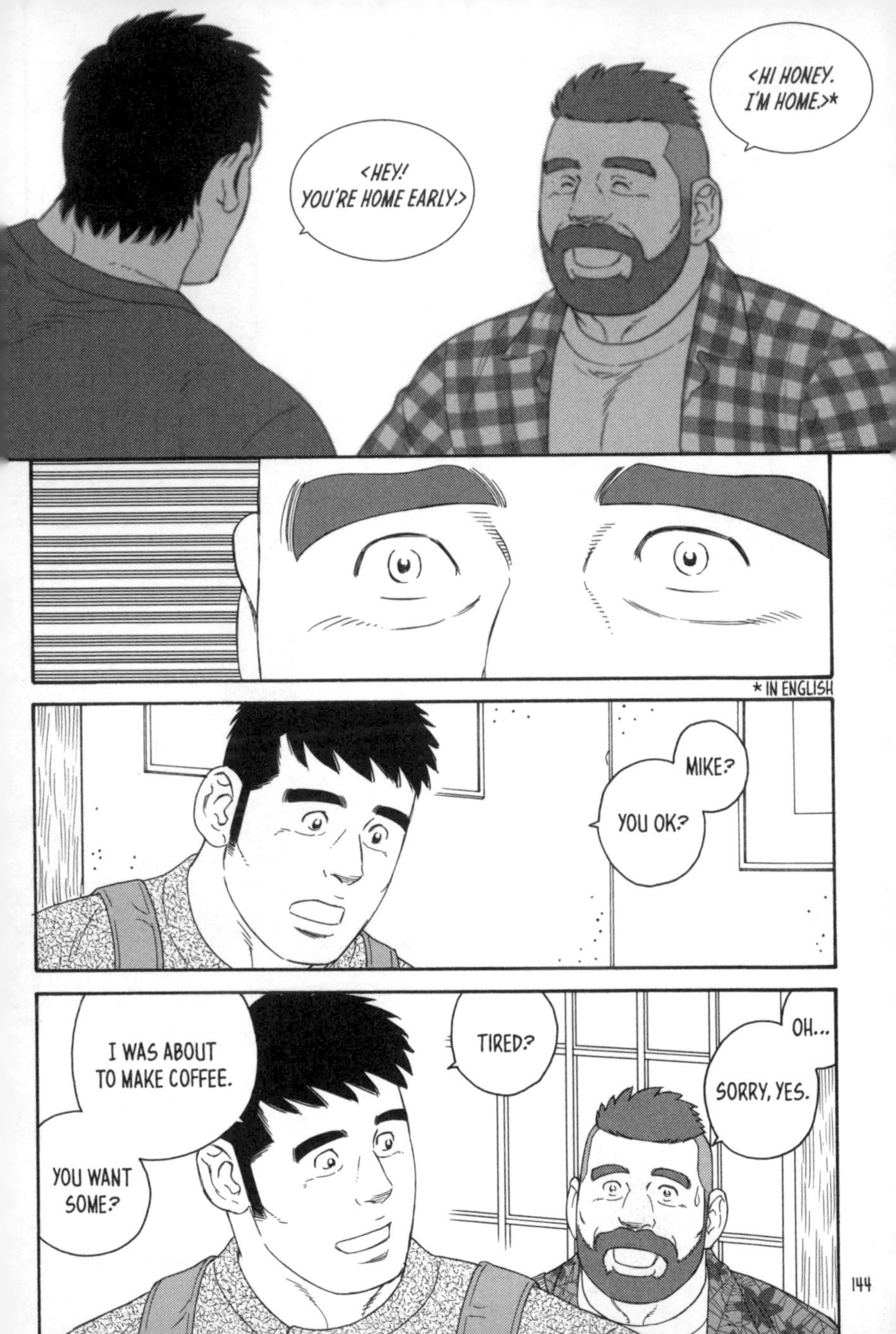
<HI HONEY. I'M HOME.>*
<HEY! YOU'RE HOME EARLY.>
MIKE?
YOU OK?
OH...
SORRY, YES.
TIRED?
I WAS ABOUT TO MAKE COFFEE.
YOU WANT SOME?

* IN ENGLISH

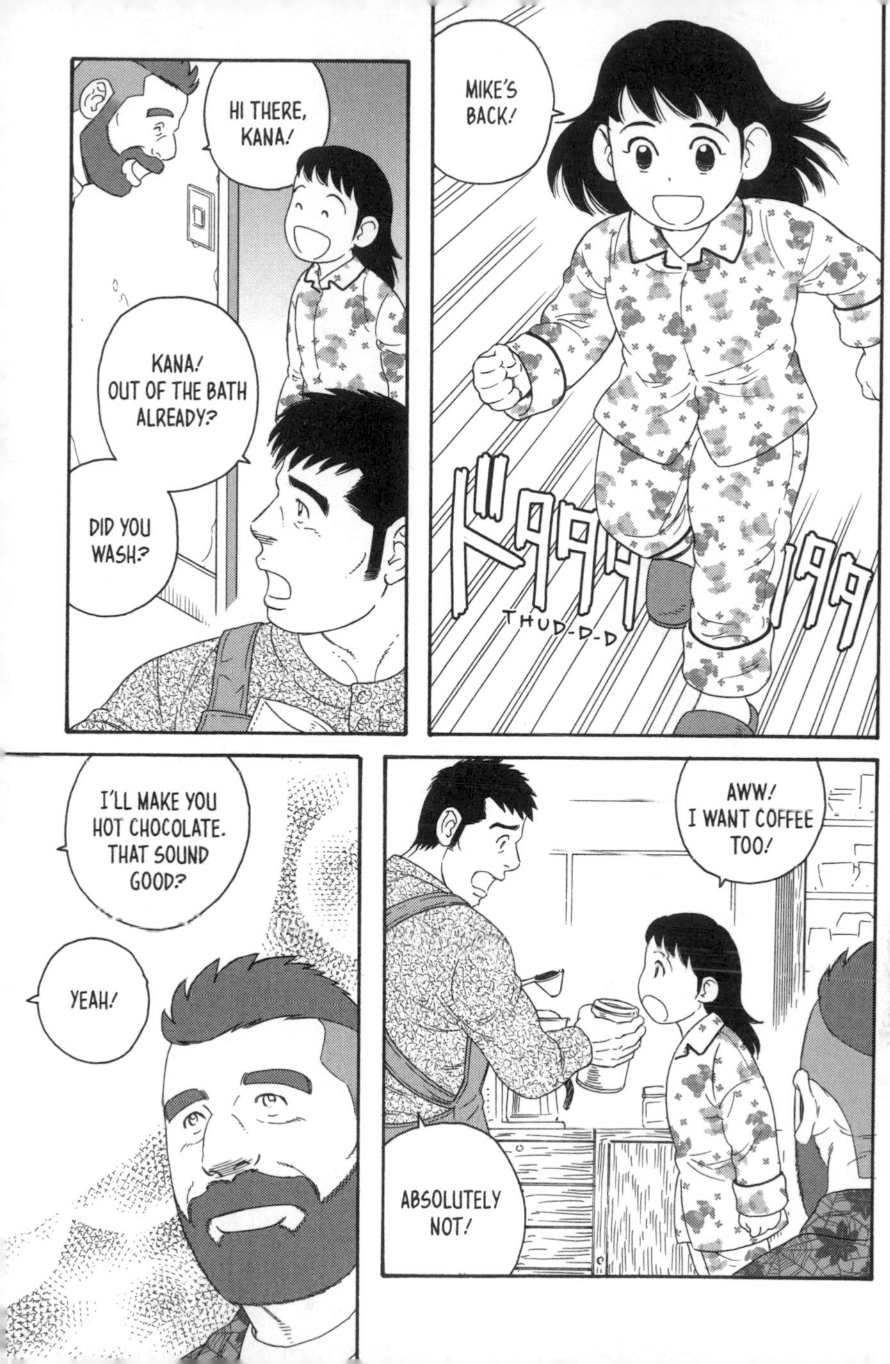

MIKE'S BACK!
THUD-D-D
HI THERE, KANA!
KANA! OUT OF THE BATH ALREADY?
DID YOU WASH?
AWW! I WANT COFFEE TOO!
ABSOLUTELY NOT!
I'LL MAKE YOU HOT CHOCOLATE. THAT SOUND GOOD?
YEAH!

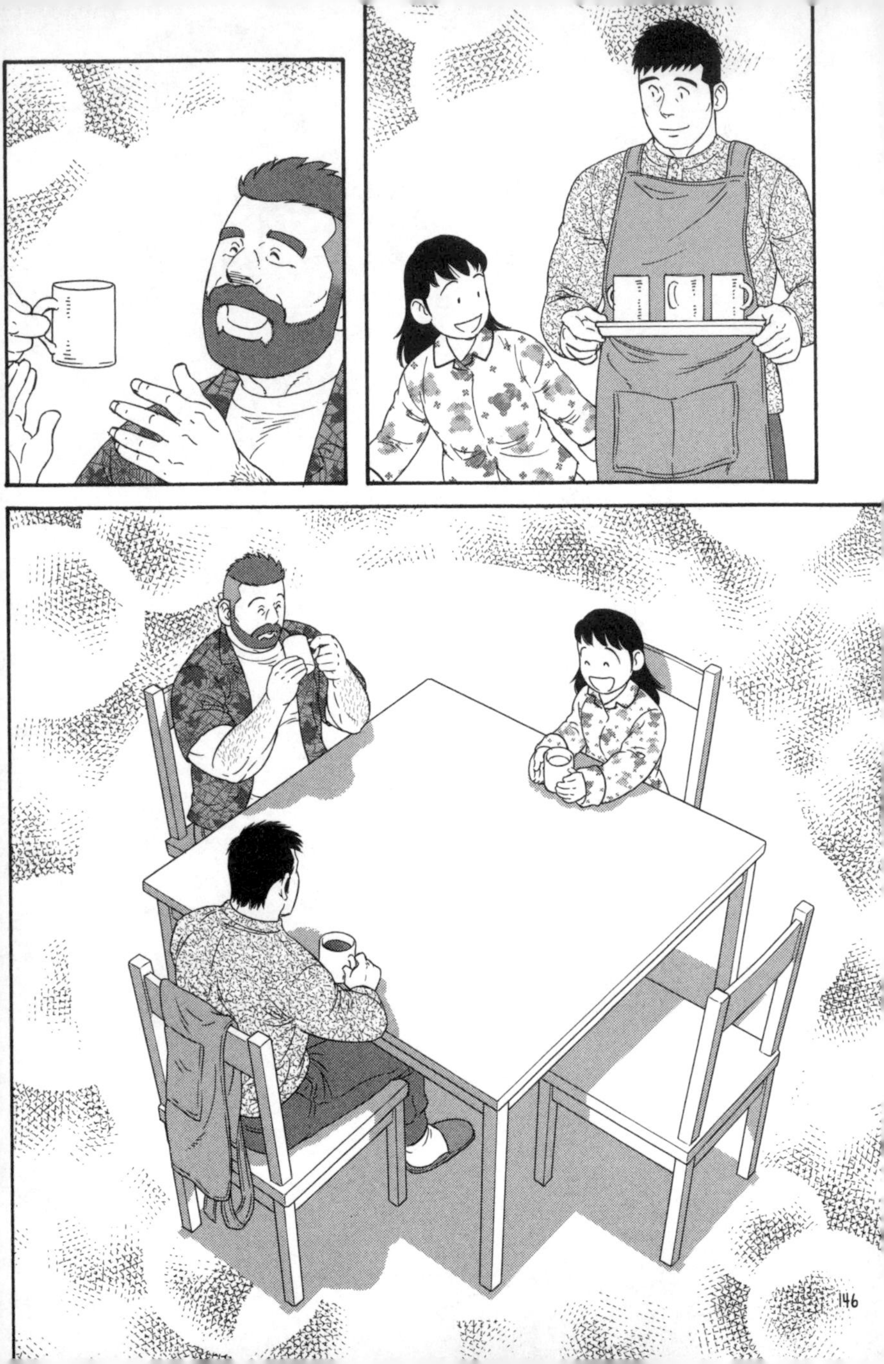

CHAPTER TWENTY-ONE

FORGOTTEN ITEMS

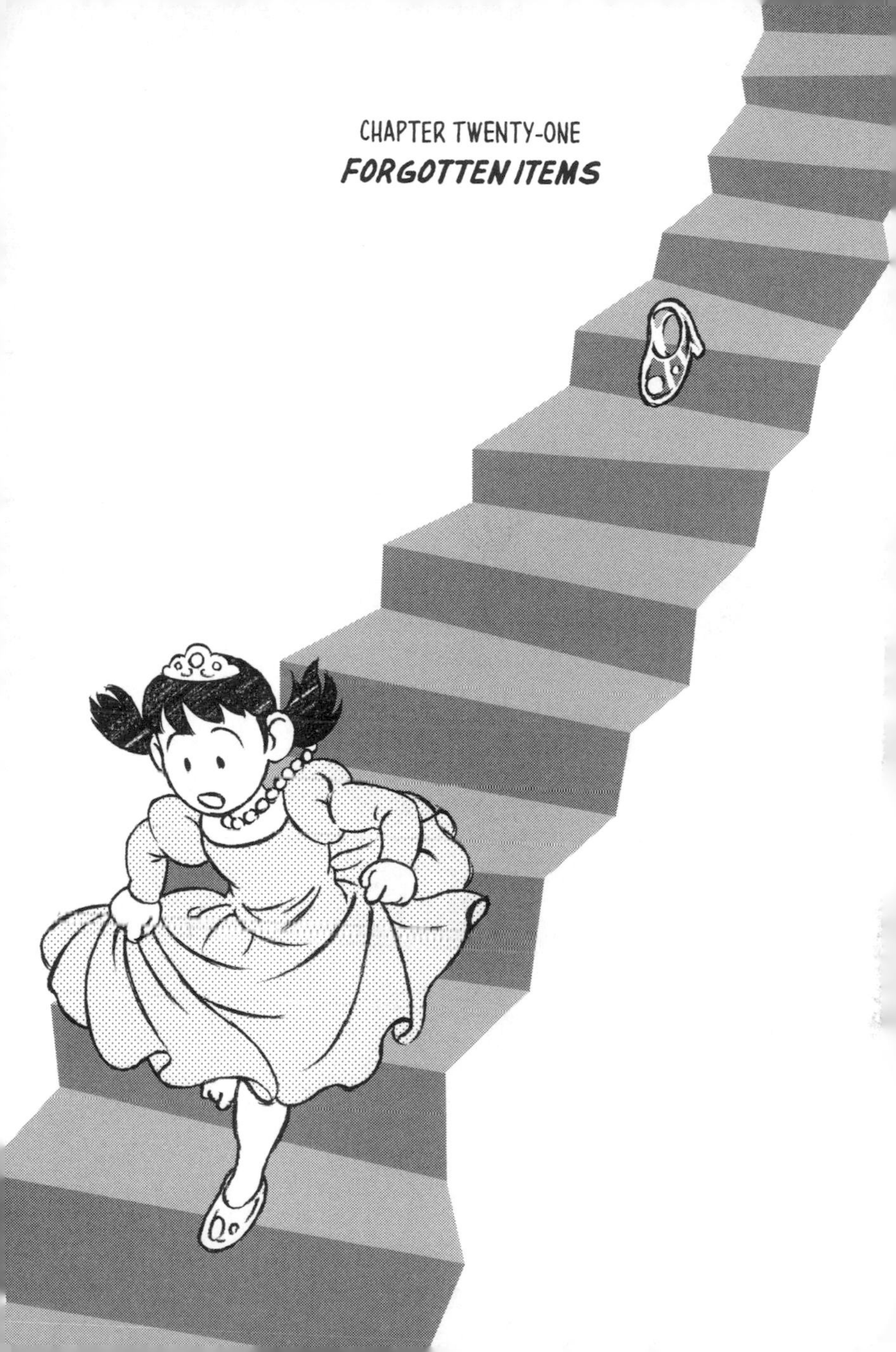

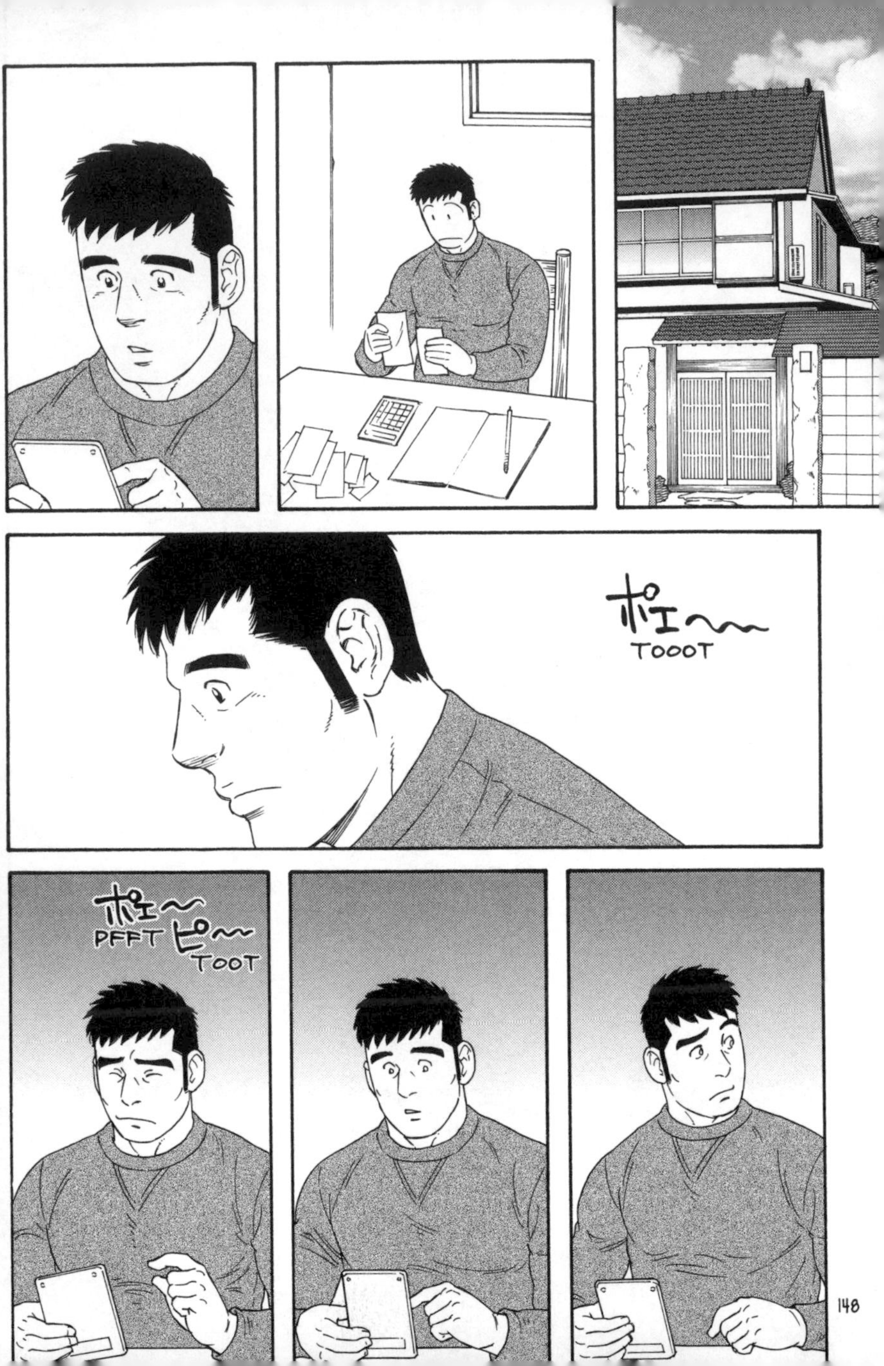
ポエ〜〜
TOOOT
ポェ〜
PFFT
ピ〜
TOOT

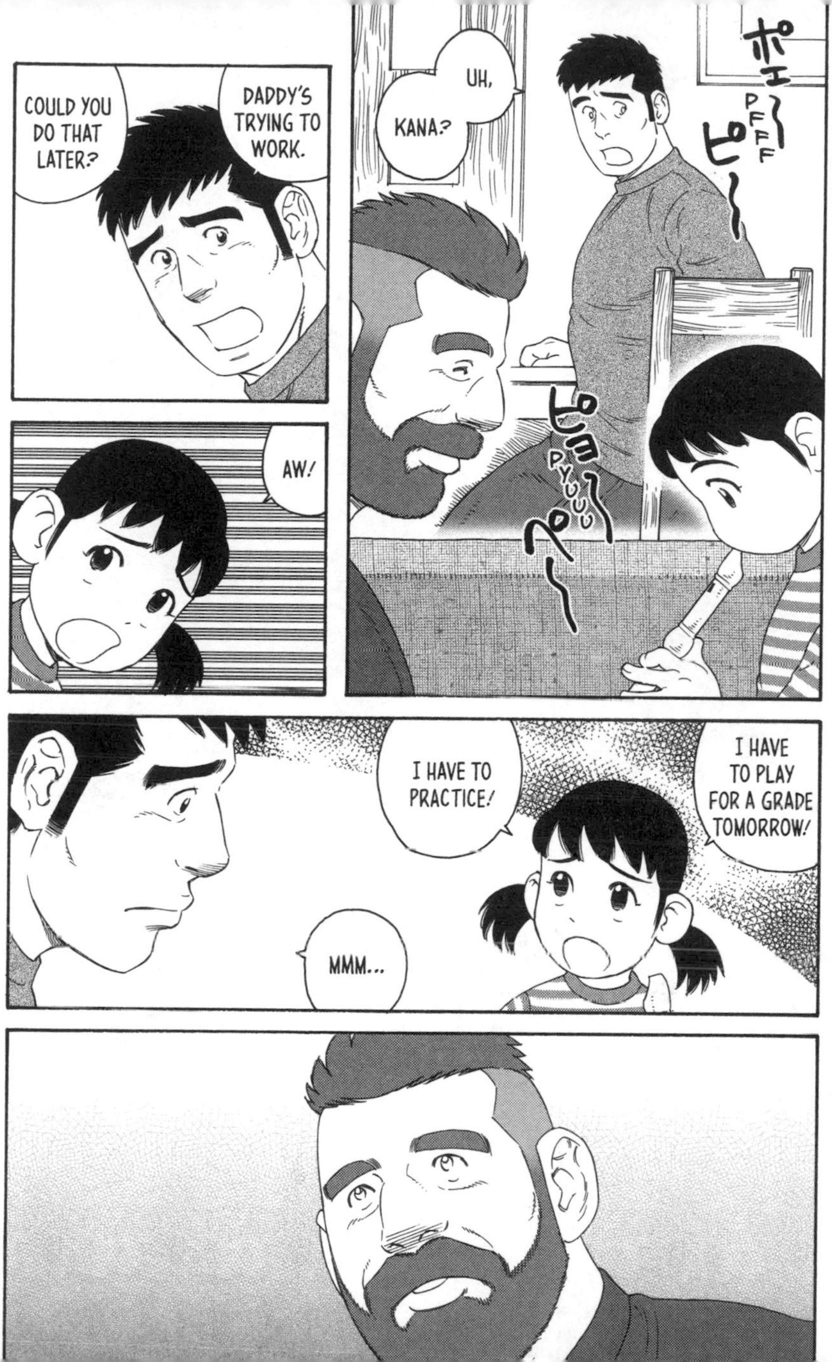

ポエ〜ピ〜
PFFF
UH,
KANA?
ピョ〜ペ〜
PYUUU
DADDY'S TRYING TO WORK.
COULD YOU DO THAT LATER?
AW!
I HAVE TO PLAY FOR A GRADE TOMORROW!
I HAVE TO PRACTICE!
MMM...

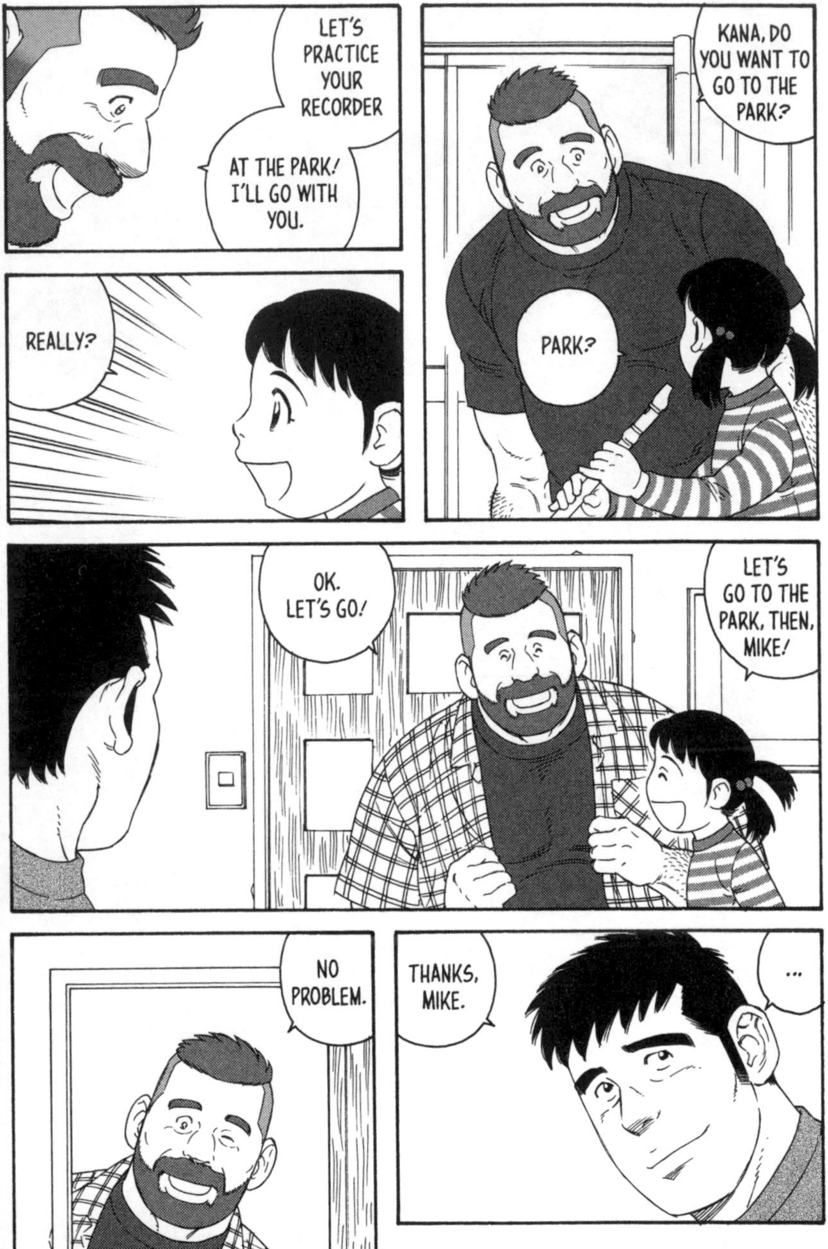
KANA, DO YOU WANT TO GO TO THE PARK?
PARK?
LET'S PRACTICE YOUR RECORDER
AT THE PARK! I'LL GO WITH YOU.
REALLY?
LET'S GO TO THE PARK, THEN, MIKE!
OK. LET'S GO!
...
THANKS, MIKE.
NO PROBLEM.

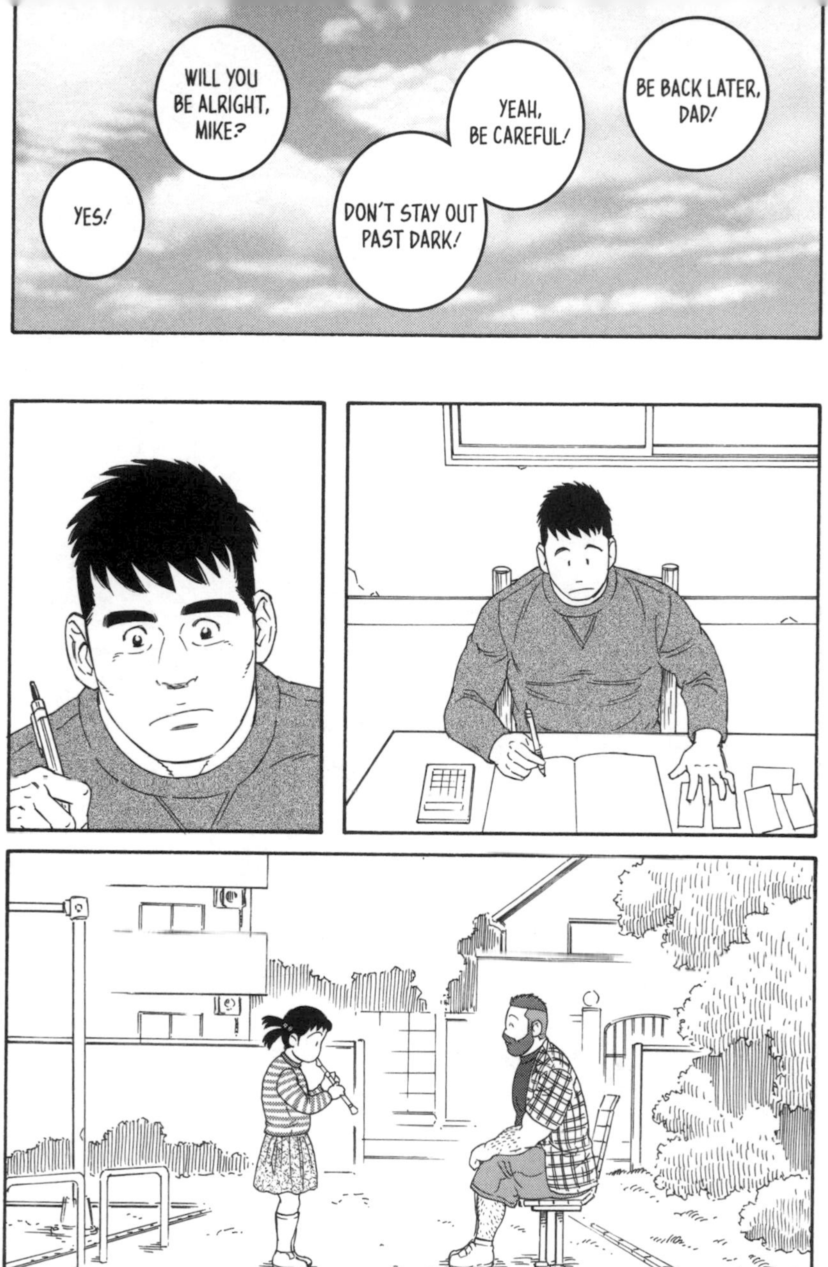
BE BACK LATER, DAD!
YEAH, BE CAREFUL!
DON'T STAY OUT PAST DARK!
WILL YOU BE ALRIGHT, MIKE?
YES!

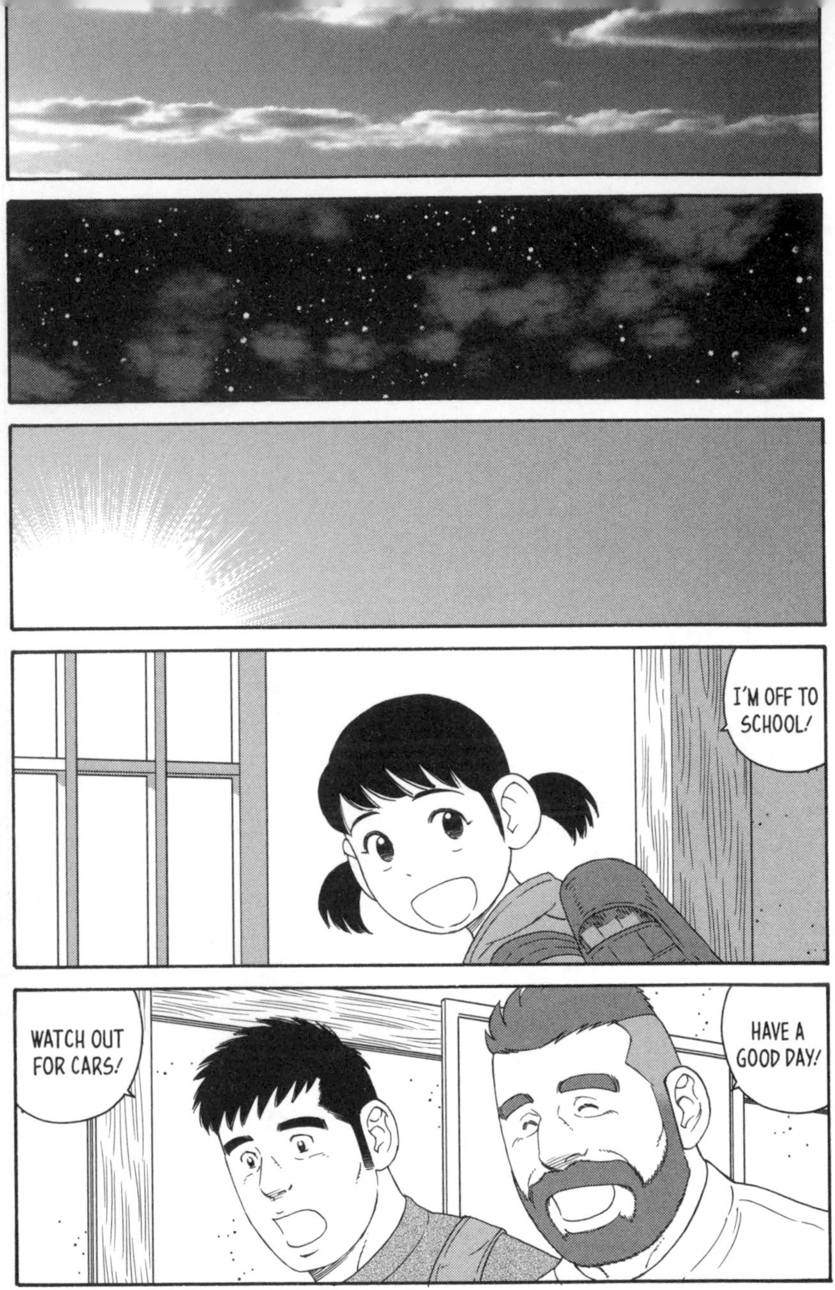
I'M OFF TO SCHOOL!
HAVE A GOOD DAY!
WATCH OUT FOR CARS!

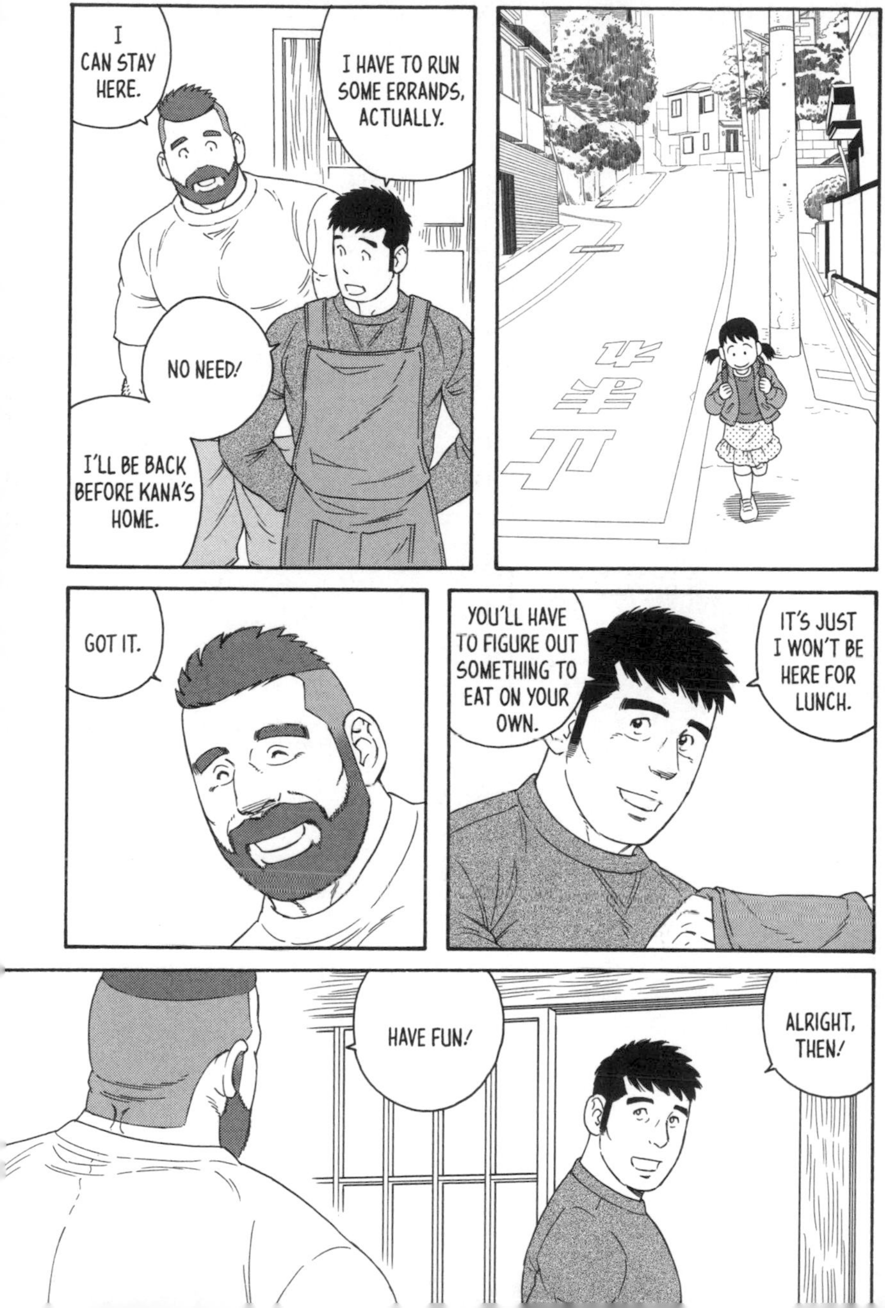
I HAVE TO RUN SOME ERRANDS, ACTUALLY.
I CAN STAY HERE.
NO NEED!
I'LL BE BACK BEFORE KANA'S HOME.
IT'S JUST I WON'T BE HERE FOR LUNCH.
YOU'LL HAVE TO FIGURE OUT SOMETHING TO EAT ON YOUR OWN.
GOT IT.
ALRIGHT, THEN!
HAVE FUN!

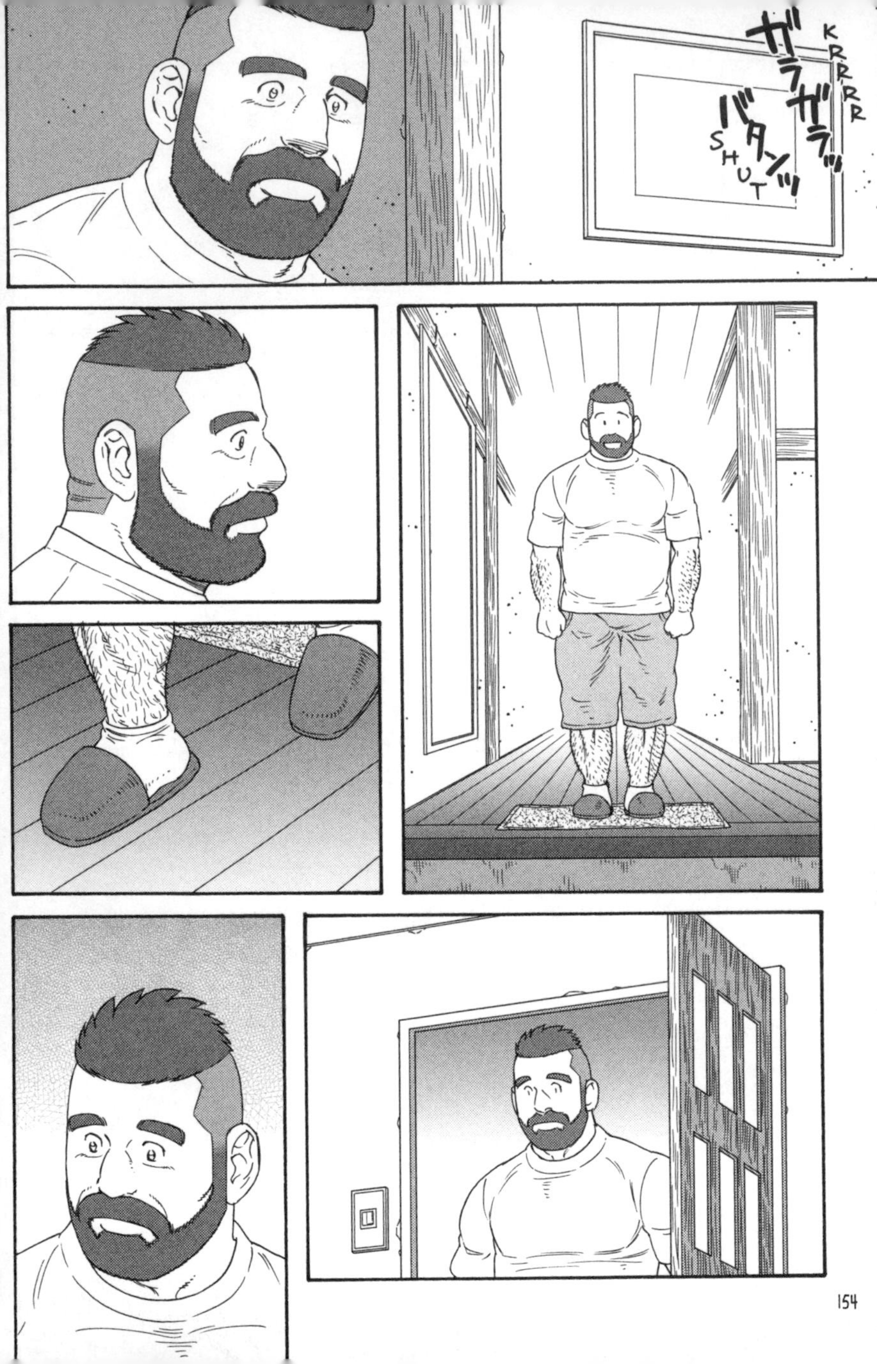
ガラガラッ
KRRRRR
バタンッ
SHUT

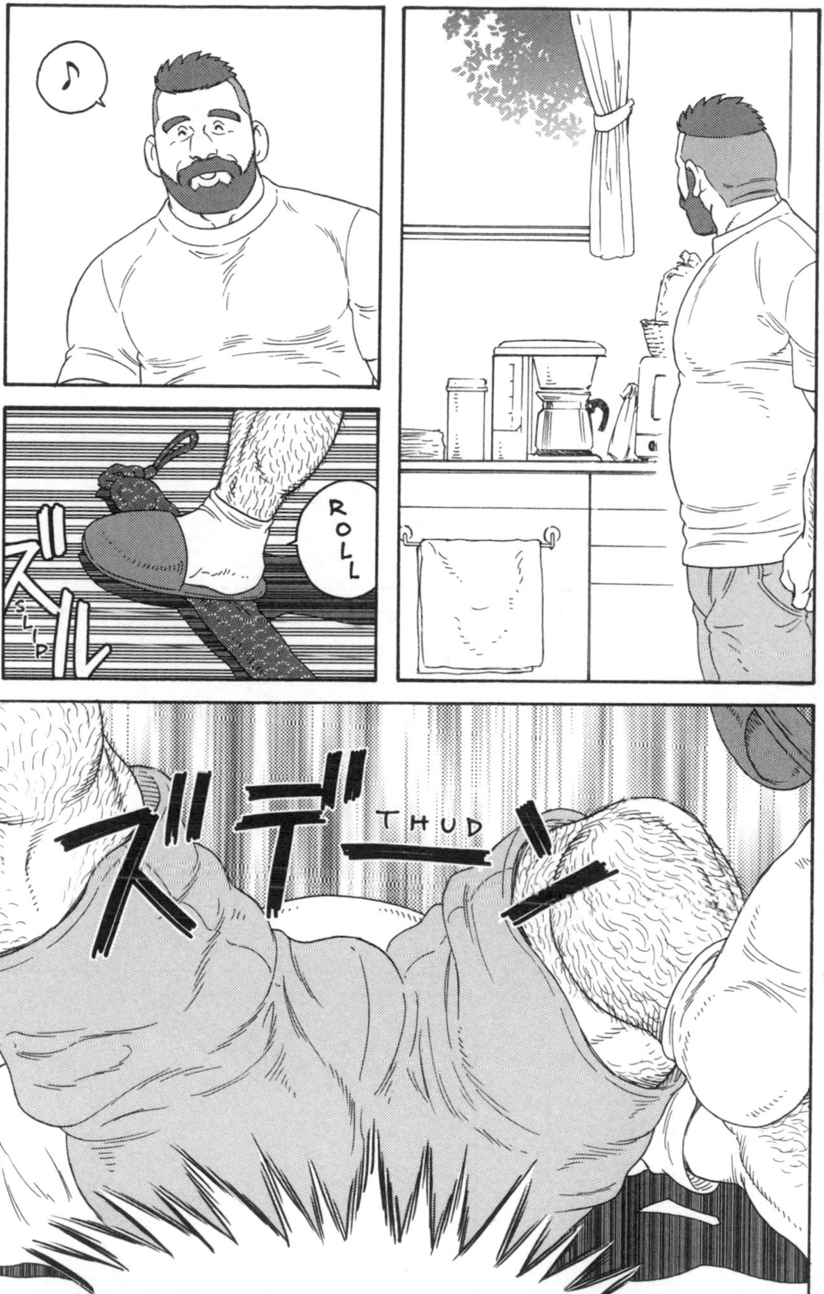
♪
ROLL
ズル
SLIP
ズデー
THUD

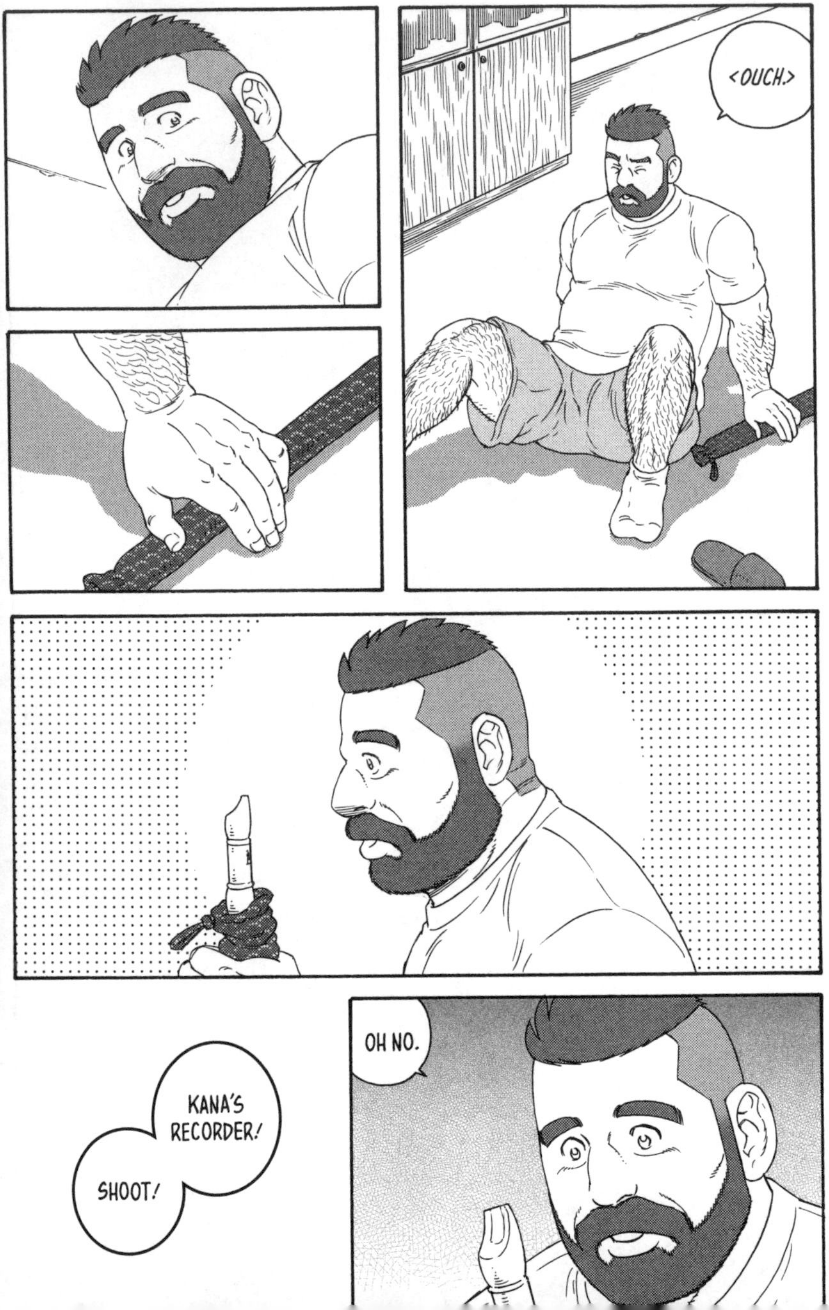
<OUCH.>
OH NO.
KANA'S RECORDER!
SHOOT!

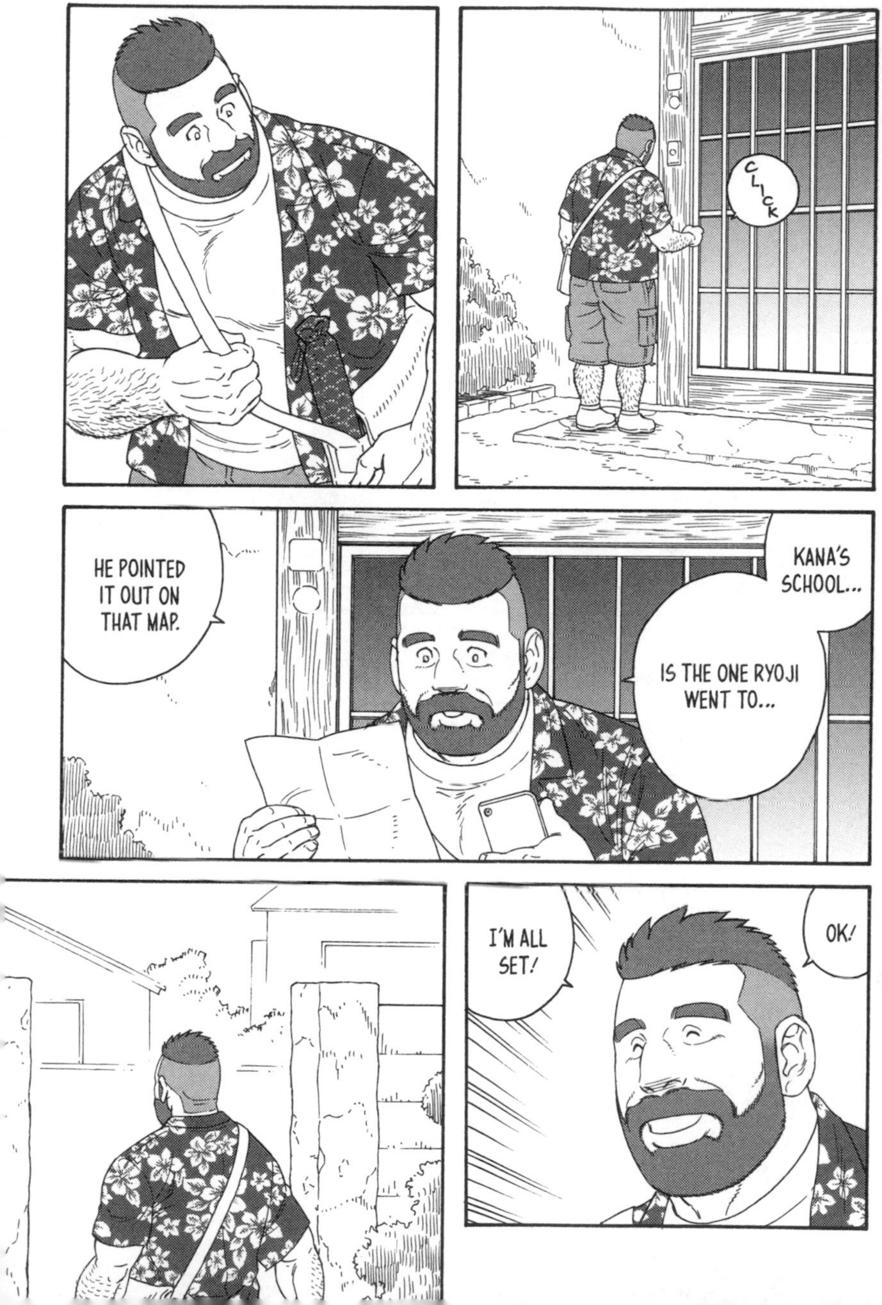
CLICK
KANA'S SCHOOL...
IS THE ONE RYOJI WENT TO...
HE POINTED IT OUT ON THAT MAP.
OK!
I'M ALL SET!

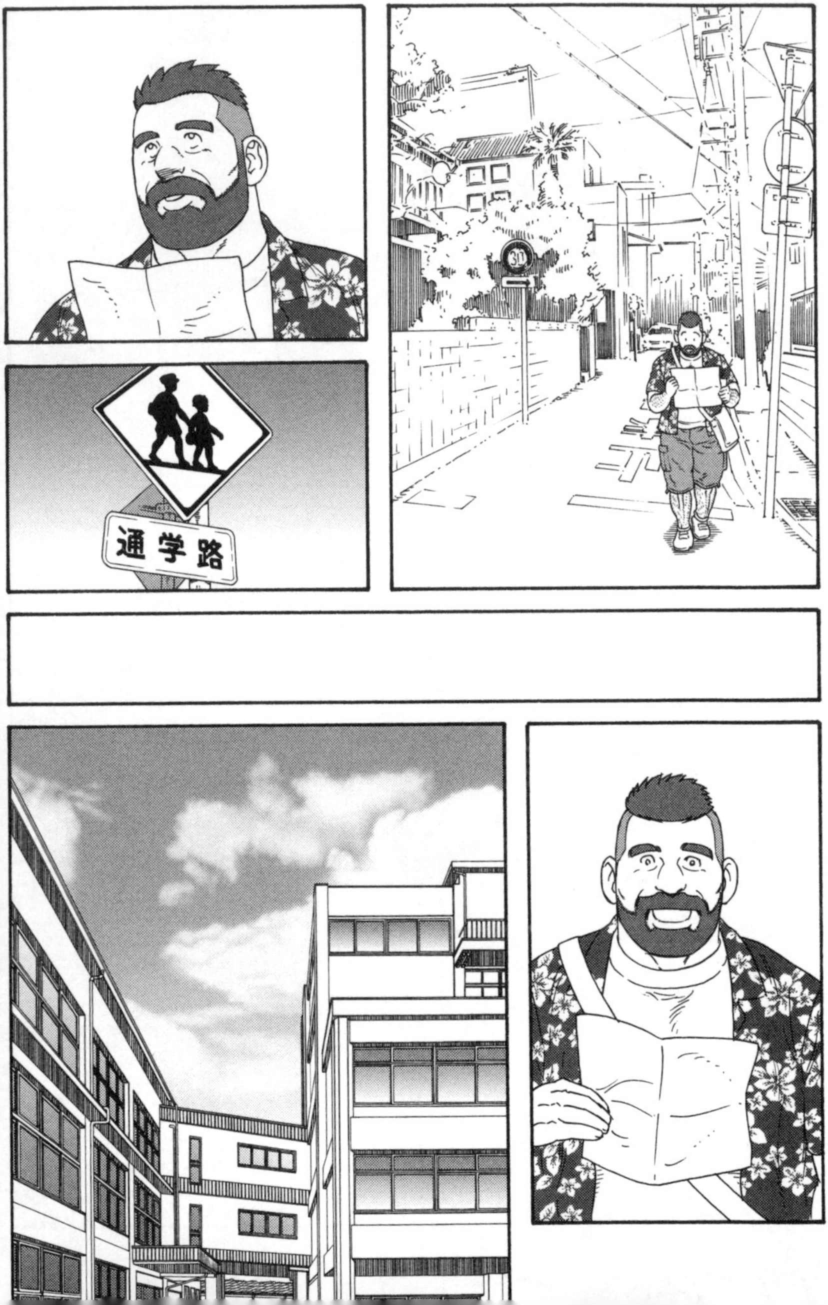
30
通学路

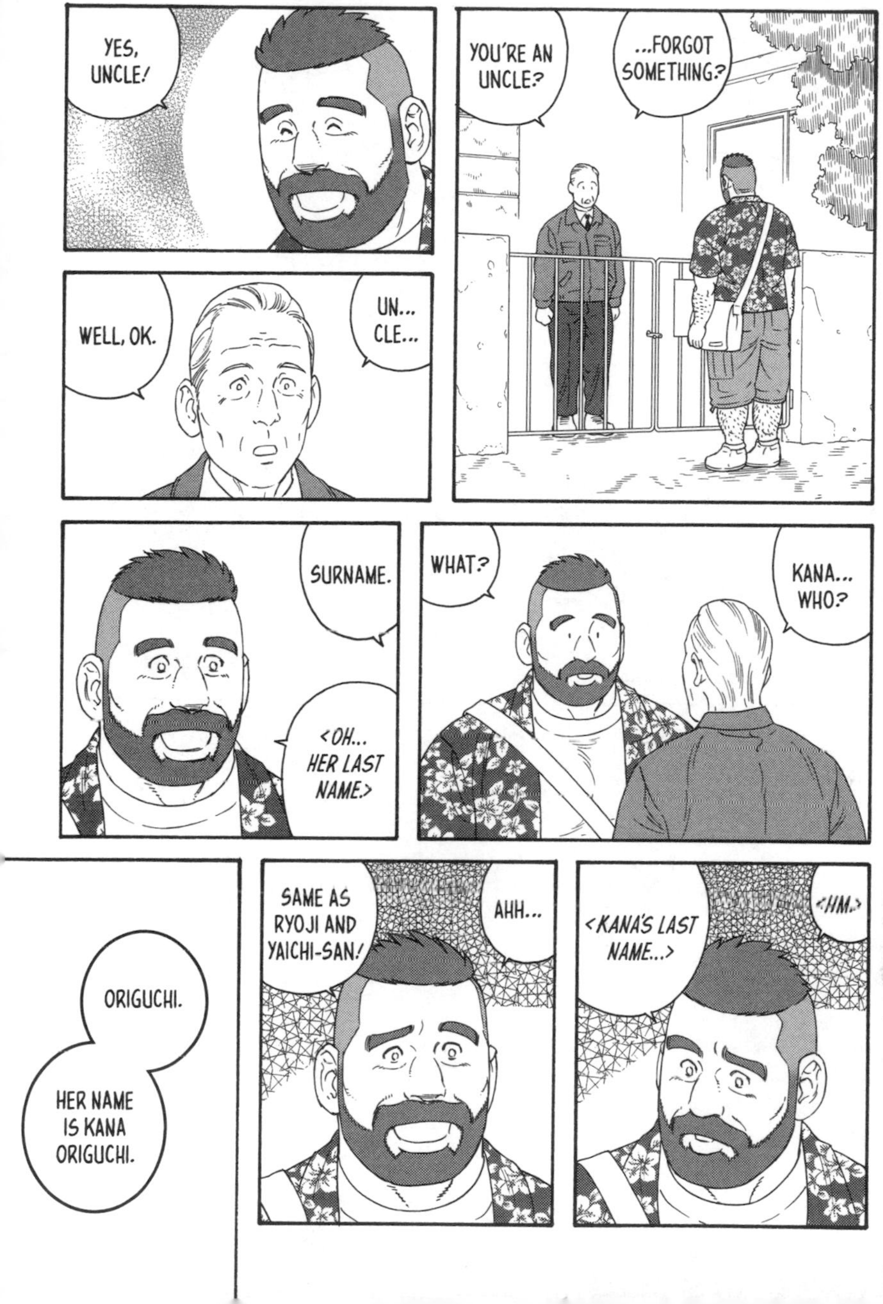
...FORGOT SOMETHING?
YOU'RE AN UNCLE?
YES, UNCLE!
UN... CLE...
WELL, OK.
KANA... WHO?
WHAT?
SURNAME.
<OH... HER LAST NAME.>
<HM.>
<KANA'S LAST NAME...>
AHH...
SAME AS RYOJI AND YAICHI-SAN!
ORIGUCHI.
HER NAME IS KANA ORIGUCHI.

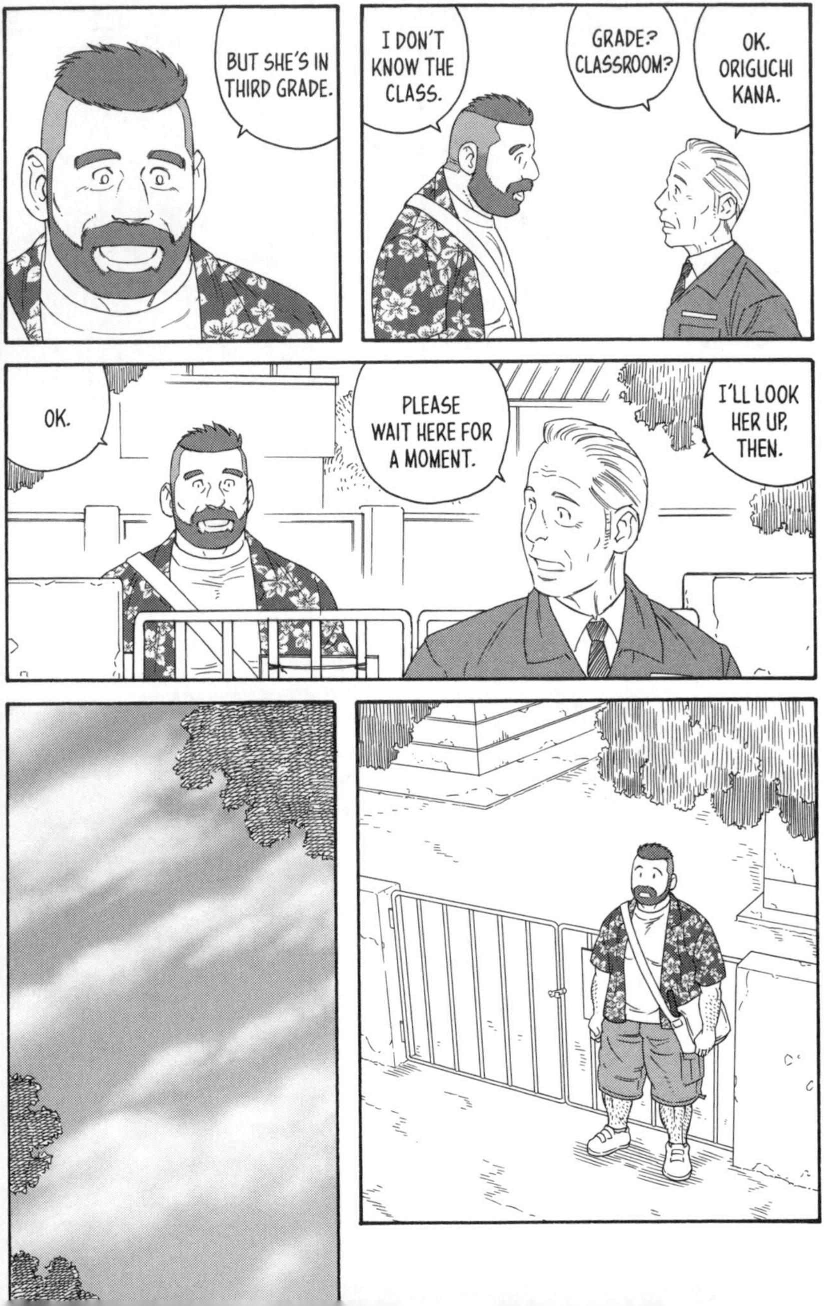
OK. ORIGUCHI KANA.
GRADE? CLASSROOM?
I DON'T KNOW THE CLASS.
BUT SHE'S IN THIRD GRADE.
I'LL LOOK HER UP, THEN.
PLEASE WAIT HERE FOR A MOMENT.
OK.

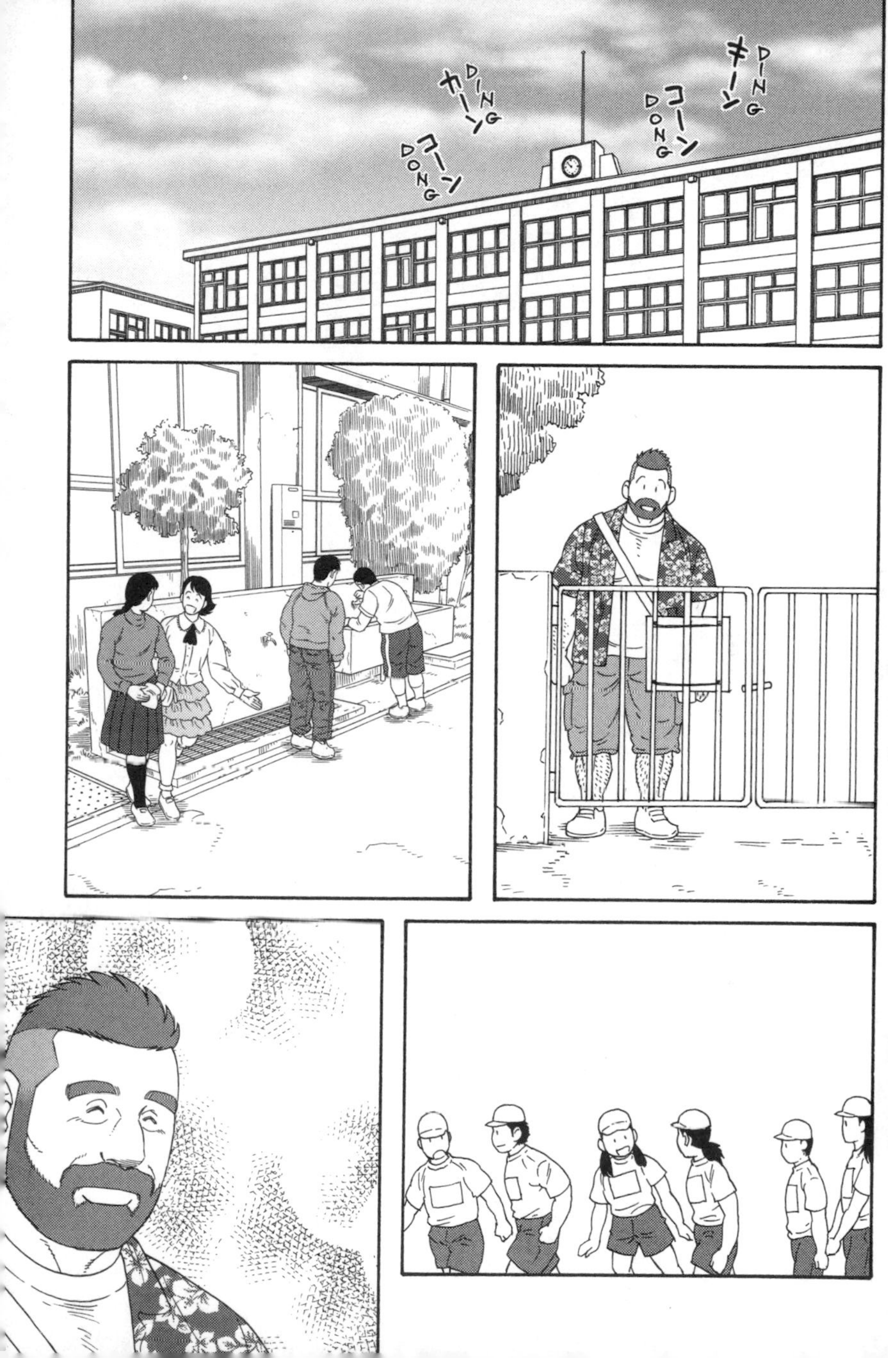
キーン DING
コーン DONG
カーン DING
コーン DONG

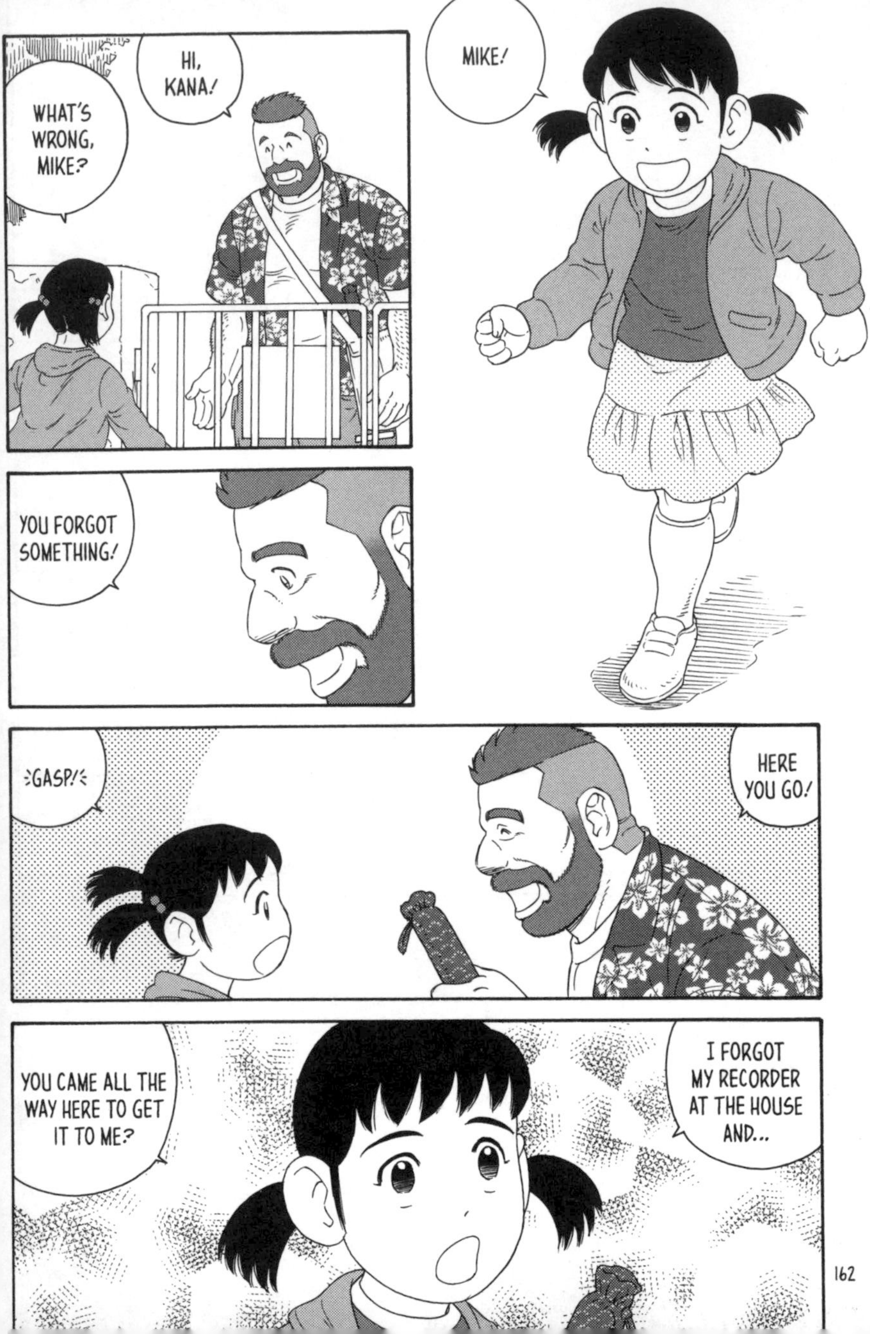
MIKE!
HI, KANA!
WHAT'S WRONG, MIKE?
YOU FORGOT SOMETHING!
HERE YOU GO!
GASP!
I FORGOT MY RECORDER AT THE HOUSE AND...
YOU CAME ALL THE WAY HERE TO GET IT TO ME?

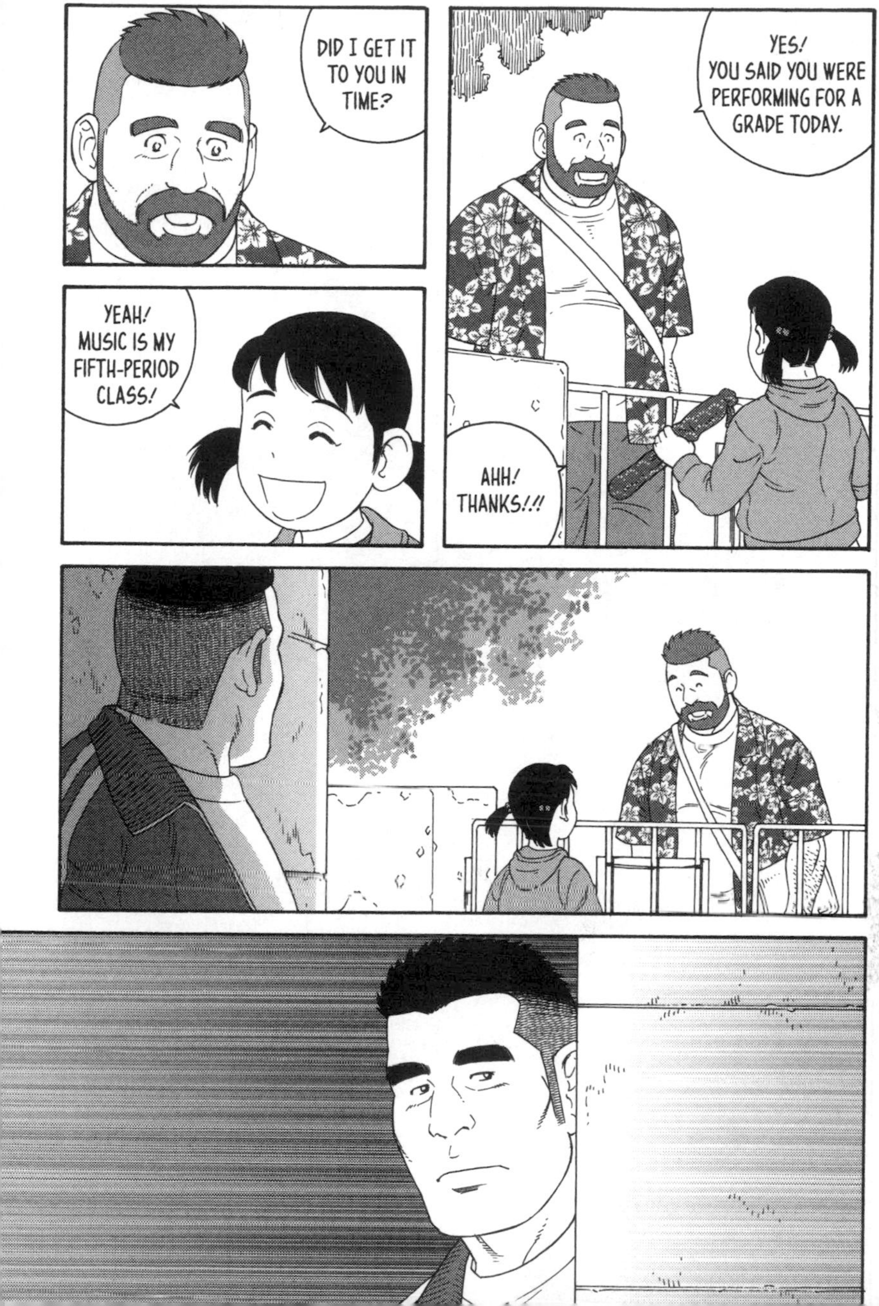
YES!
YOU SAID YOU WERE PERFORMING FOR A GRADE TODAY.
AHH! THANKS!!!
DID I GET IT TO YOU IN TIME?
YEAH! MUSIC IS MY FIFTH-PERIOD CLASS!

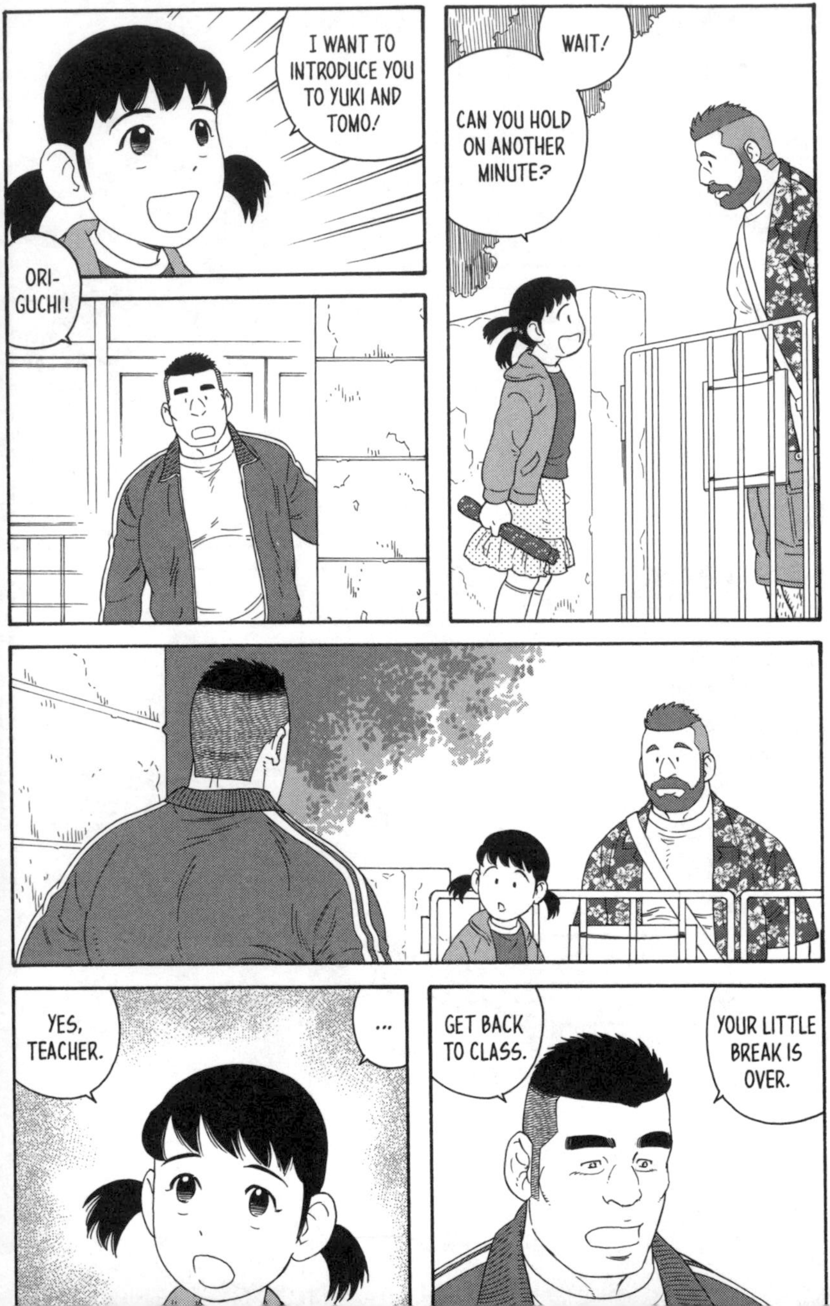
WAIT!
CAN YOU HOLD ON ANOTHER MINUTE?
I WANT TO INTRODUCE YOU TO YUKI AND TOMO!
ORI-GUCHI!
YOUR LITTLE BREAK IS OVER.
GET BACK TO CLASS.
...
YES, TEACHER.

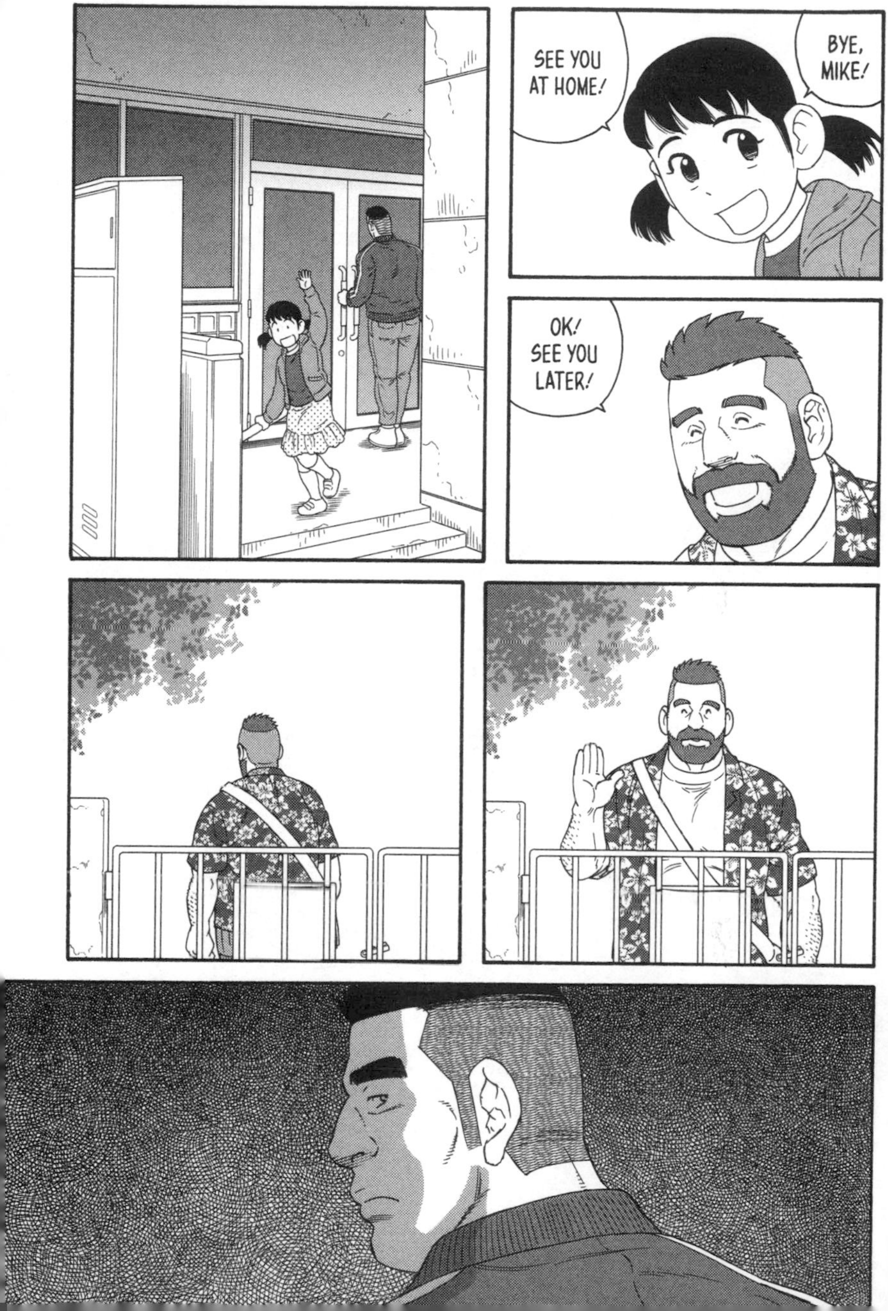
BYE, MIKE!
SEE YOU AT HOME!
OK! SEE YOU LATER!

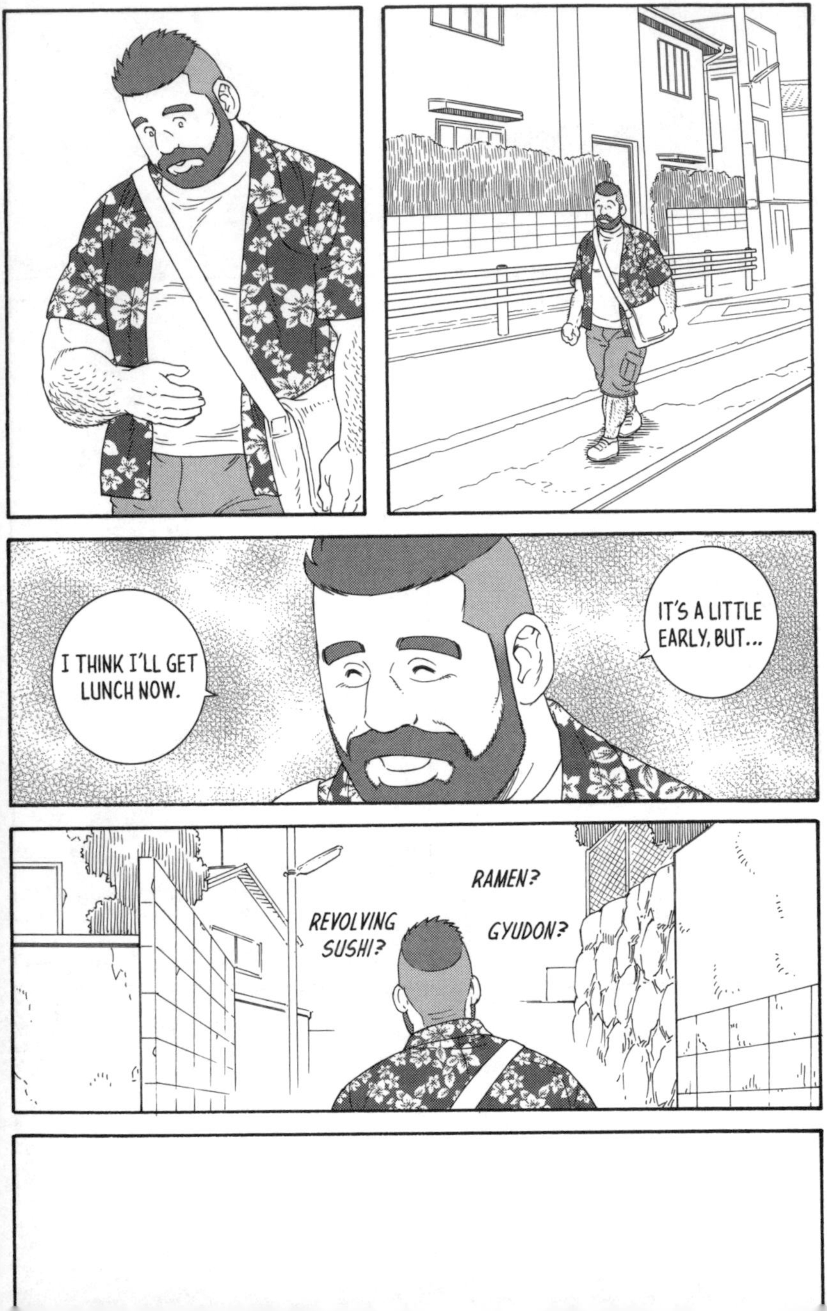
IT'S A LITTLE EARLY, BUT...
I THINK I'LL GET LUNCH NOW.
RAMEN?
GYUDON?
REVOLVING SUSHI?

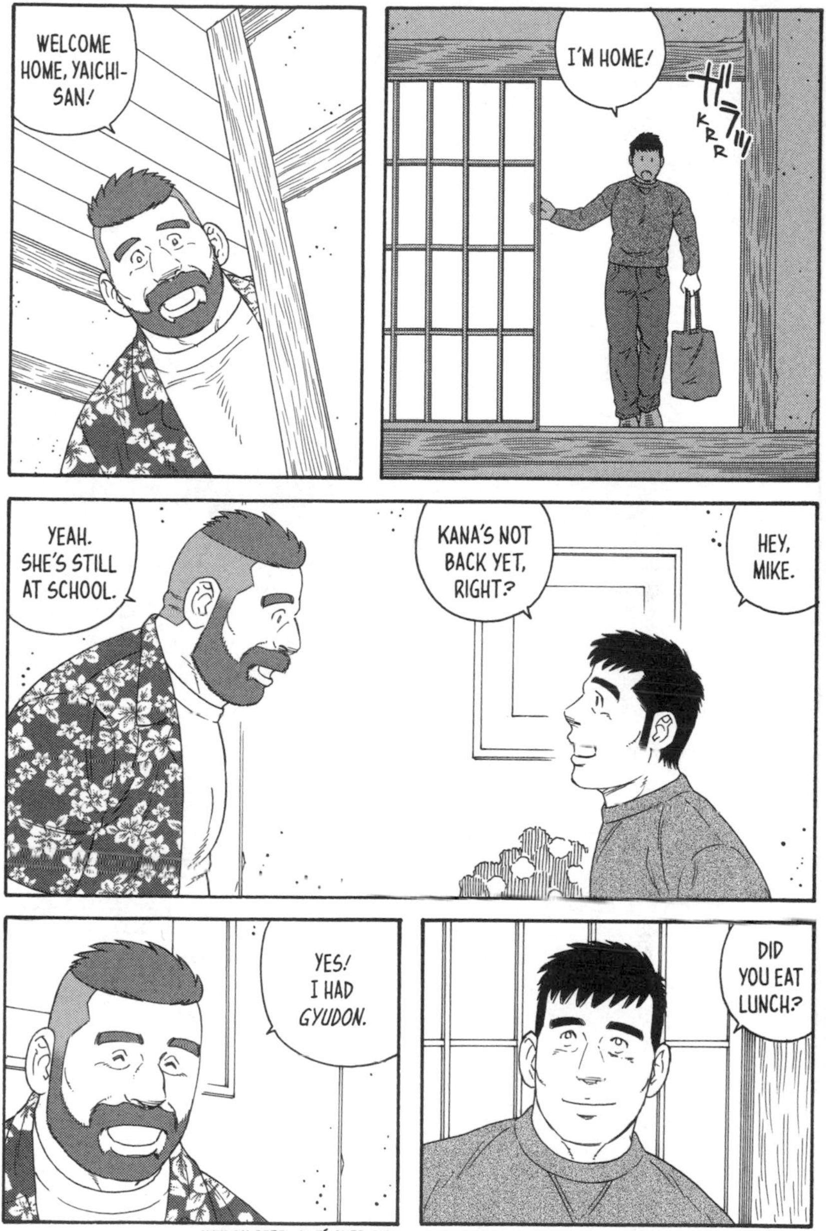
I'M HOME!
ガラッ
KRRR
WELCOME HOME, YAICHI-SAN!
HEY, MIKE.
KANA'S NOT BACK YET, RIGHT?
YEAH. SHE'S STILL AT SCHOOL.
DID YOU EAT LUNCH?
YES! I HAD *GYUDON.*

GYUDON: BEEF SAUTÉ OVER RICE

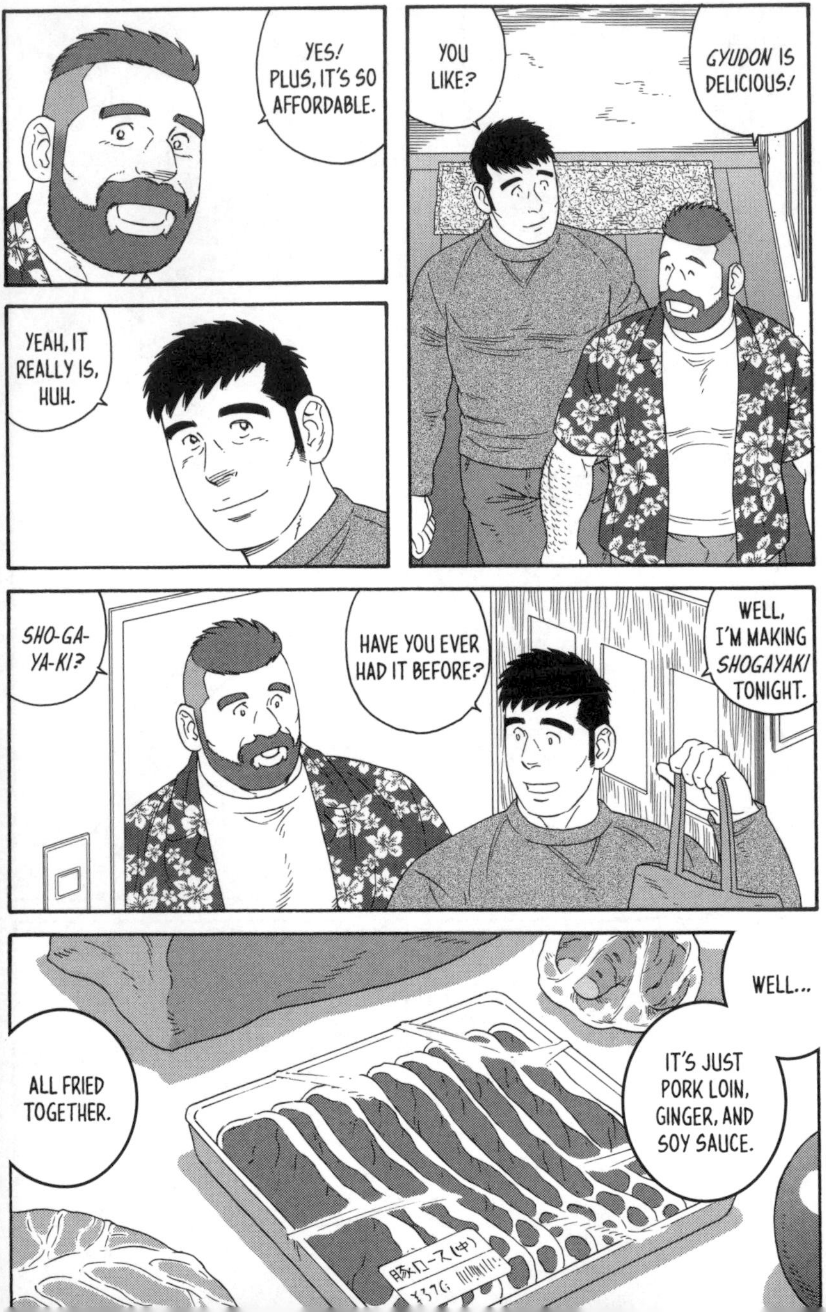
GYUDON IS DELICIOUS!
YOU LIKE?
YES! PLUS, IT'S SO AFFORDABLE.
YEAH, IT REALLY IS, HUH.
WELL, I'M MAKING SHOGAYAKI TONIGHT.
HAVE YOU EVER HAD IT BEFORE?
SHO-GA-YA-KI?
WELL...
IT'S JUST PORK LOIN, GINGER, AND SOY SAUCE.
ALL FRIED TOGETHER.
豚ロース(中)

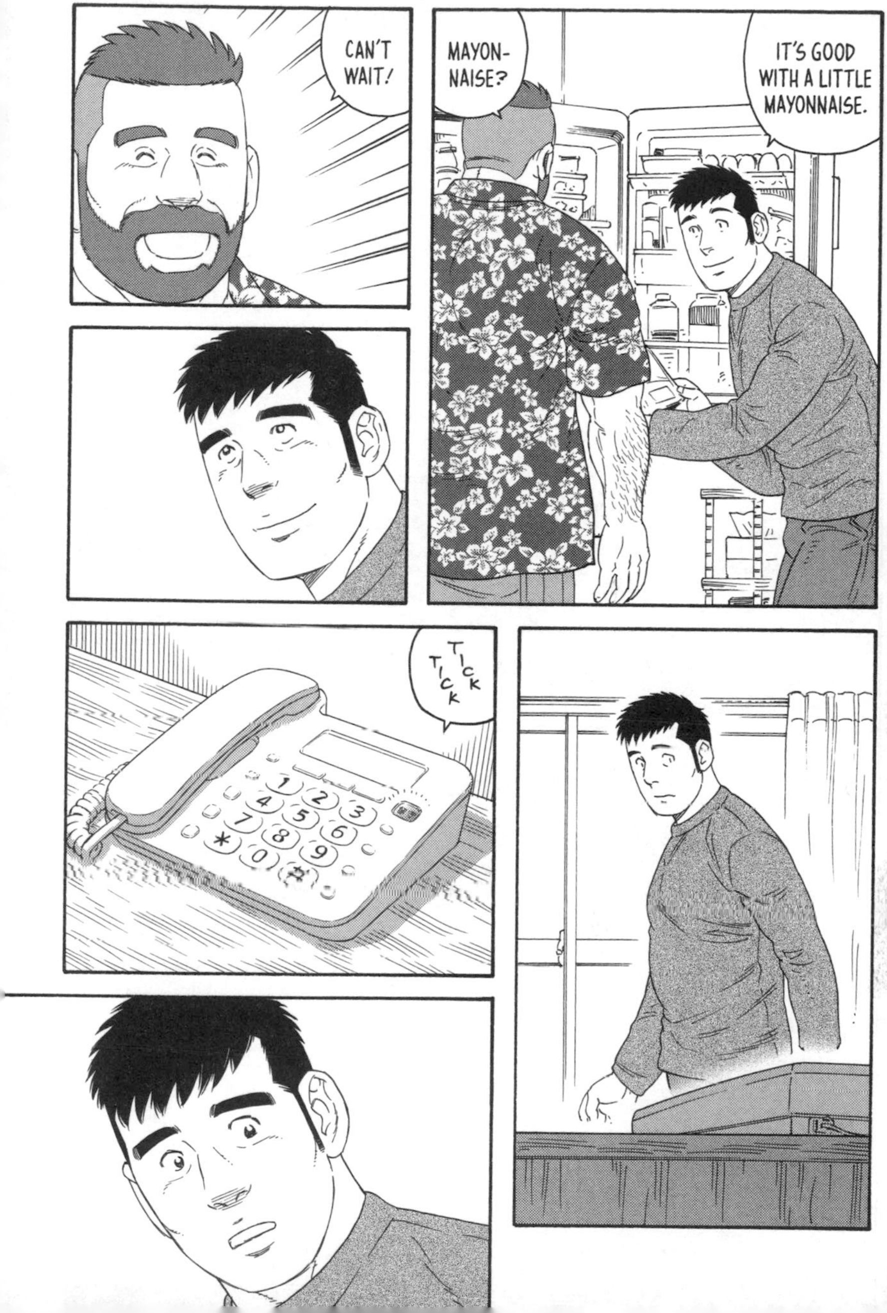
IT'S GOOD WITH A LITTLE MAYONNAISE.
MAYON-NAISE?
CAN'T WAIT!
TICK TICK

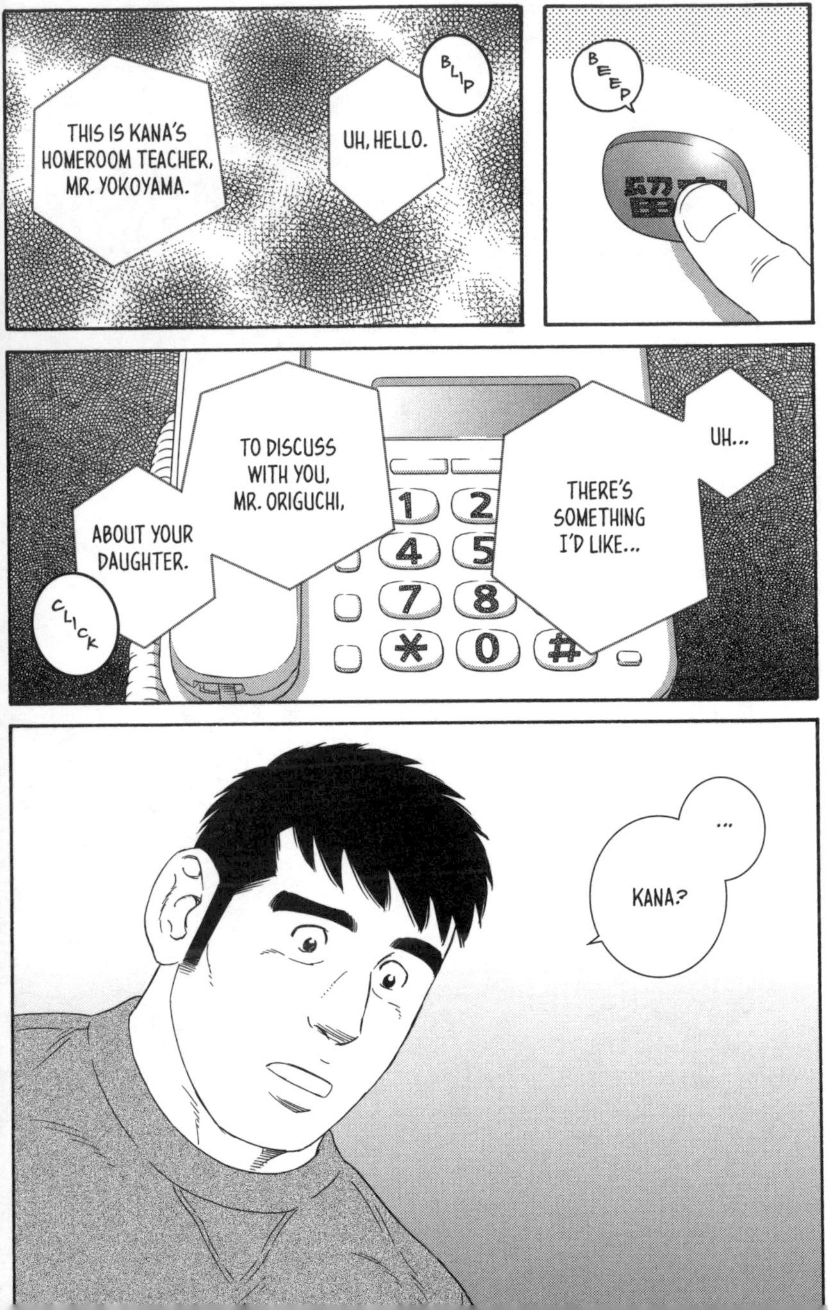
BEEP
BLIP
UH, HELLO.
THIS IS KANA'S HOMEROOM TEACHER, MR. YOKOYAMA.
UH...
THERE'S SOMETHING I'D LIKE...
TO DISCUSS WITH YOU, MR. ORIGUCHI,
ABOUT YOUR DAUGHTER.
CLICK
...
KANA?

CHAPTER TWENTY-TWO

INTRODUCTIONS

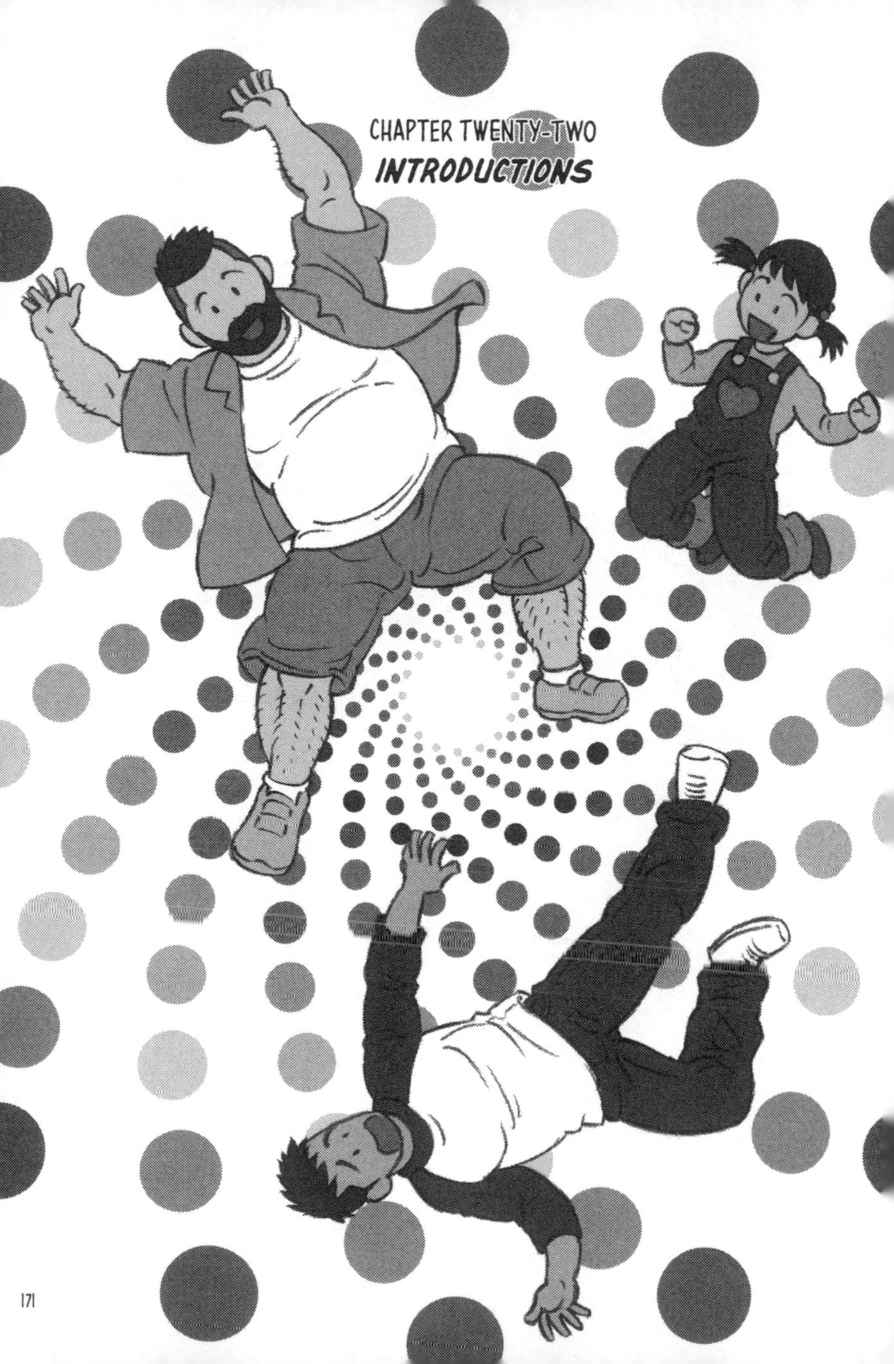

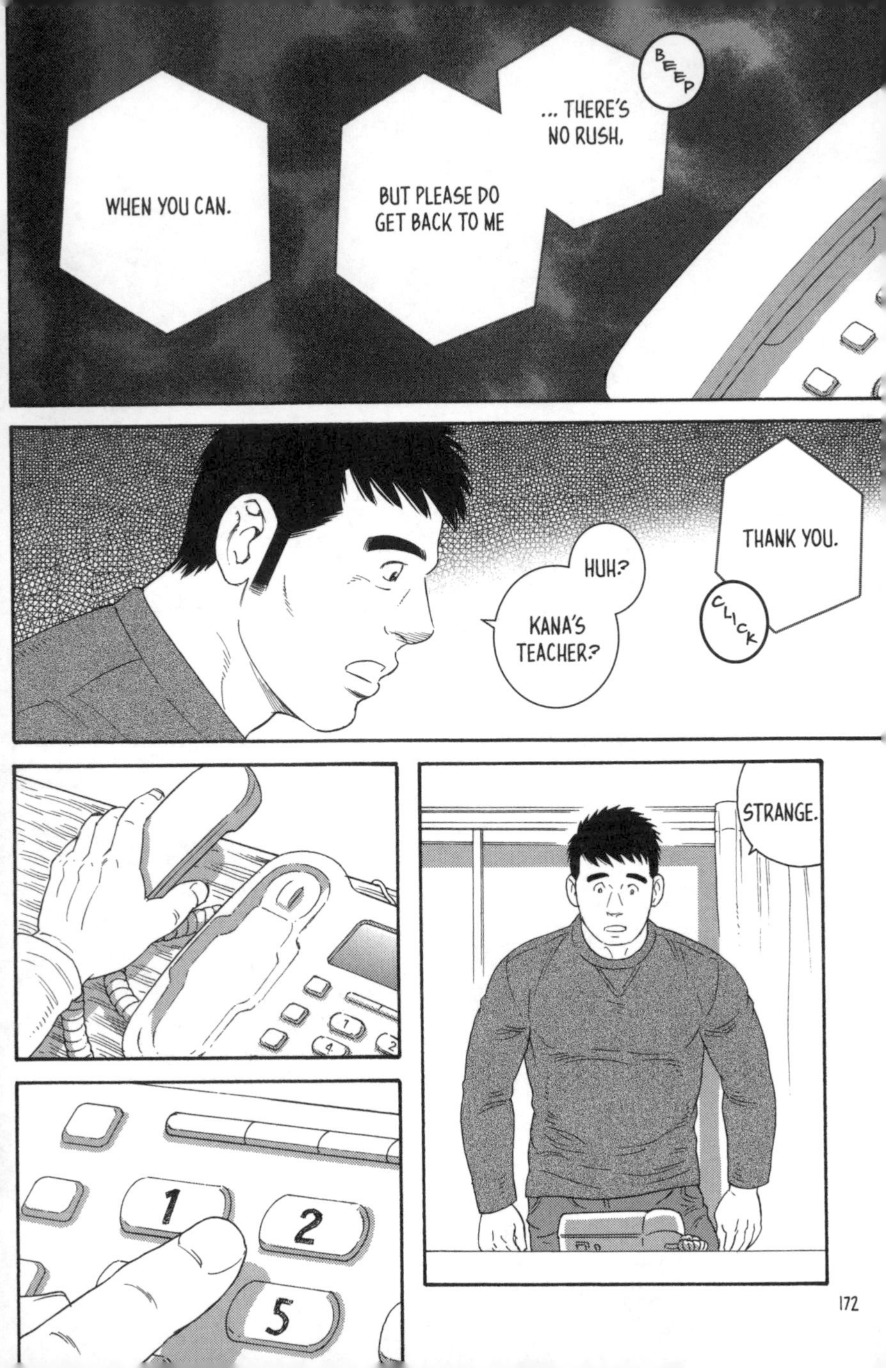
BEEP
... THERE'S NO RUSH,
BUT PLEASE DO GET BACK TO ME
WHEN YOU CAN.
THANK YOU.
CLICK
HUH?
KANA'S TEACHER?
STRANGE.

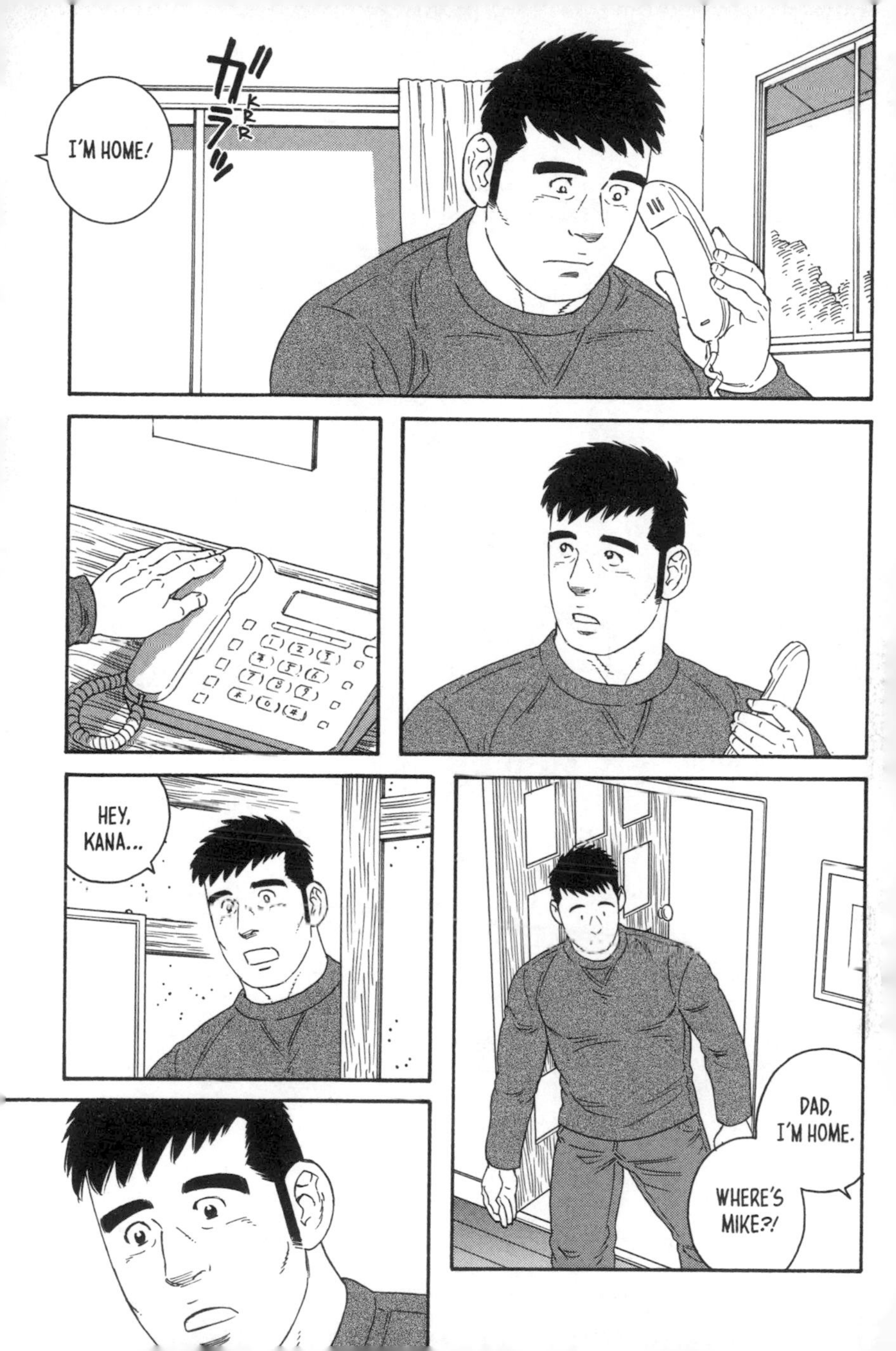
ガラッ
KRR
I'M HOME!
DAD, I'M HOME.
WHERE'S MIKE?!
HEY, KANA...

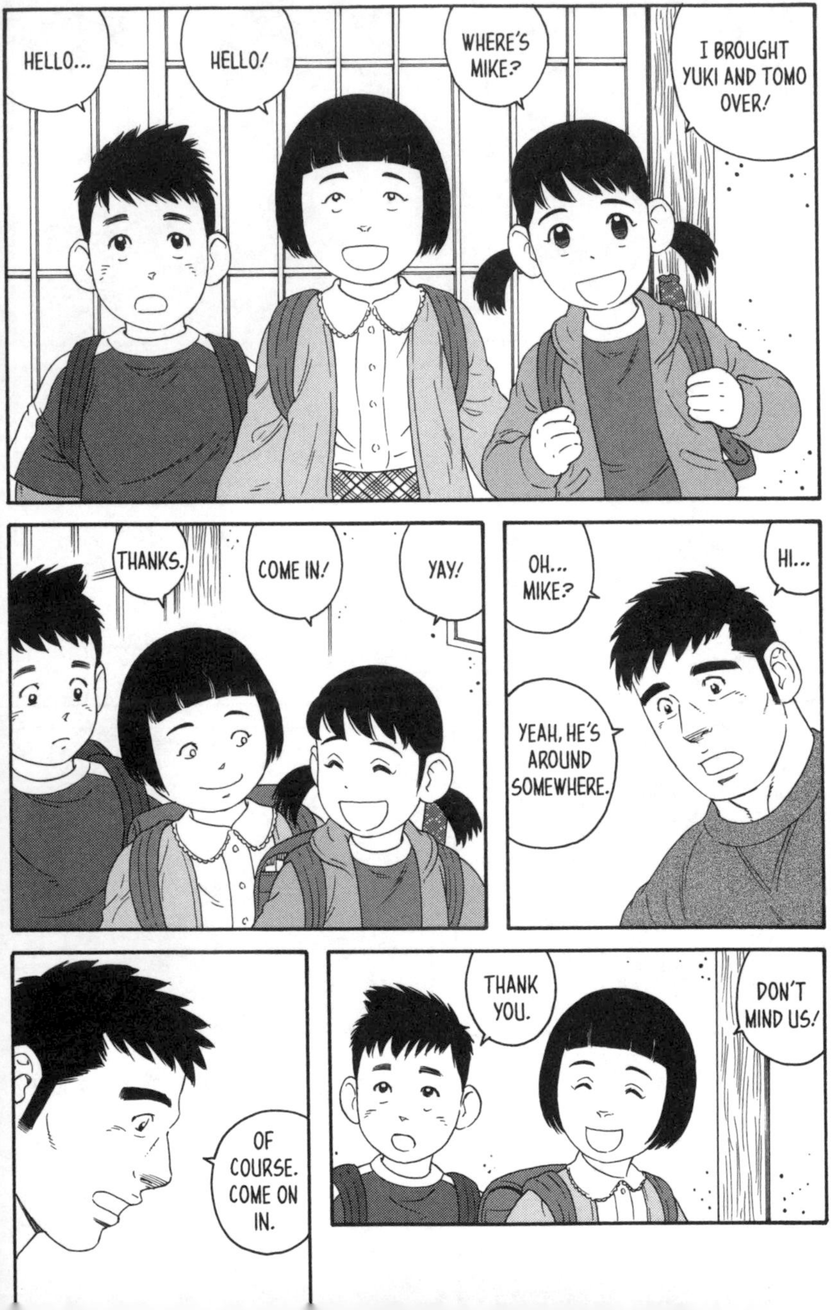
I BROUGHT YUKI AND TOMO OVER!
WHERE'S MIKE?
HELLO!
HELLO...
HI...
OH... MIKE?
YEAH, HE'S AROUND SOMEWHERE.
YAY!
COME IN!
THANKS.
DON'T MIND US!
THANK YOU.
OF COURSE. COME ON IN.

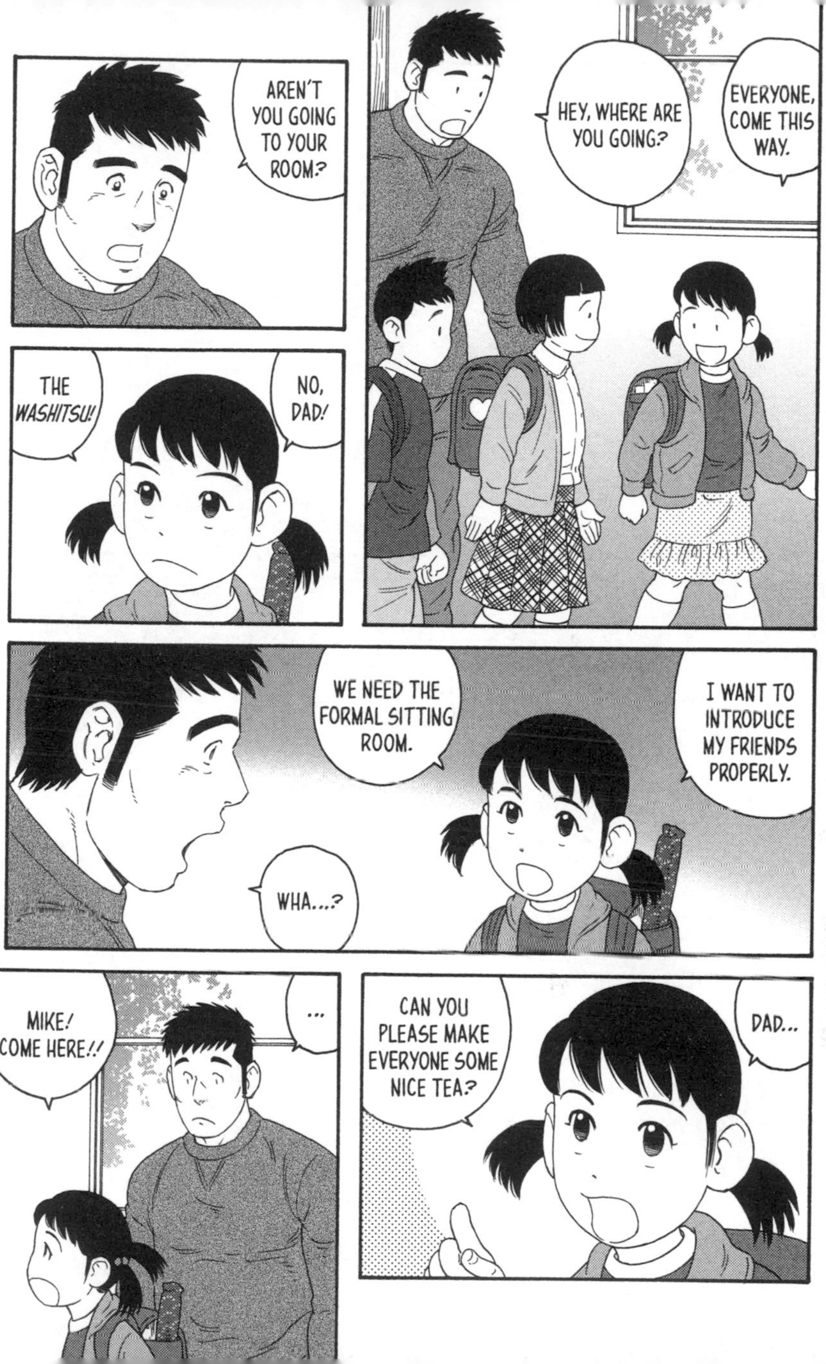
EVERYONE, COME THIS WAY.
HEY, WHERE ARE YOU GOING?
AREN'T YOU GOING TO YOUR ROOM?
NO, DAD!
THE *WASHITSU!*
I WANT TO INTRODUCE MY FRIENDS PROPERLY.
WE NEED THE FORMAL SITTING ROOM.
WHA...?
DAD...
CAN YOU PLEASE MAKE EVERYONE SOME NICE TEA?
...
MIKE! COME HERE!!

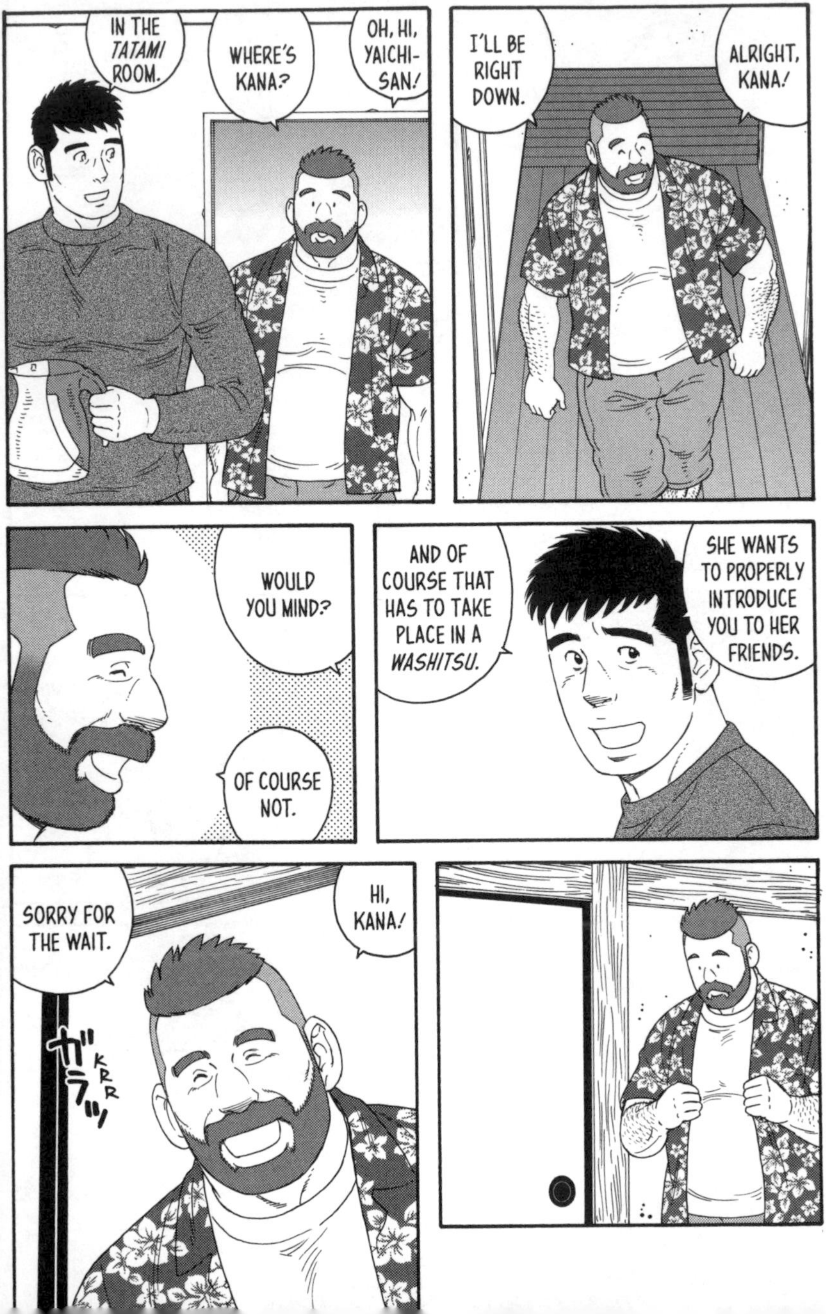
ALRIGHT, KANA!
I'LL BE RIGHT DOWN.
OH, HI, YAICHI-SAN!
WHERE'S KANA?
IN THE *TATAMI* ROOM.
SHE WANTS TO PROPERLY INTRODUCE YOU TO HER FRIENDS.
AND OF COURSE THAT HAS TO TAKE PLACE IN A *WASHITSU*.
WOULD YOU MIND?
OF COURSE NOT.
HI, KANA!
SORRY FOR THE WAIT.
ガラッ
KRR

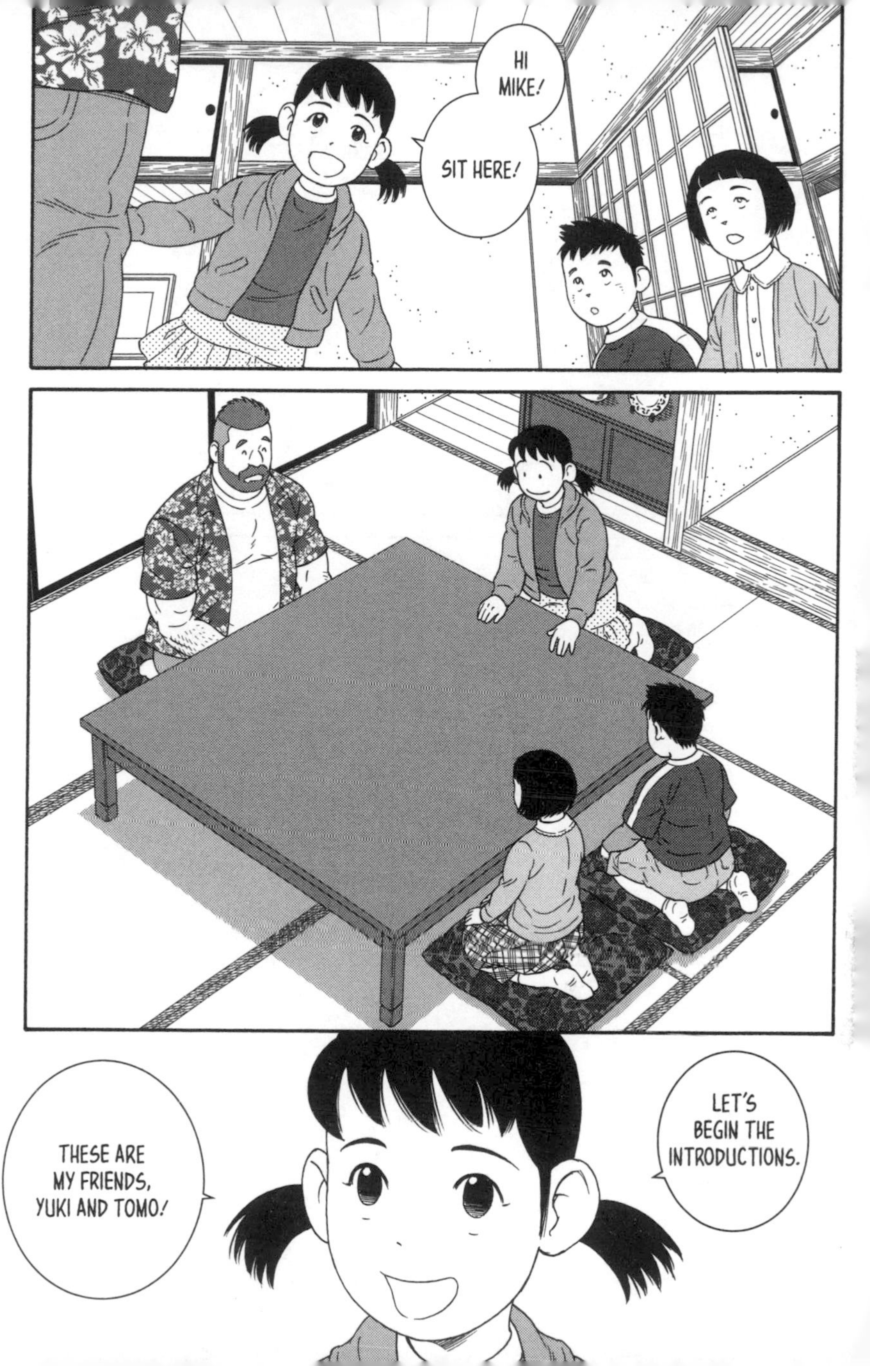
HI MIKE!
SIT HERE!
LET'S BEGIN THE INTRODUCTIONS.
THESE ARE MY FRIENDS, YUKI AND TOMO!

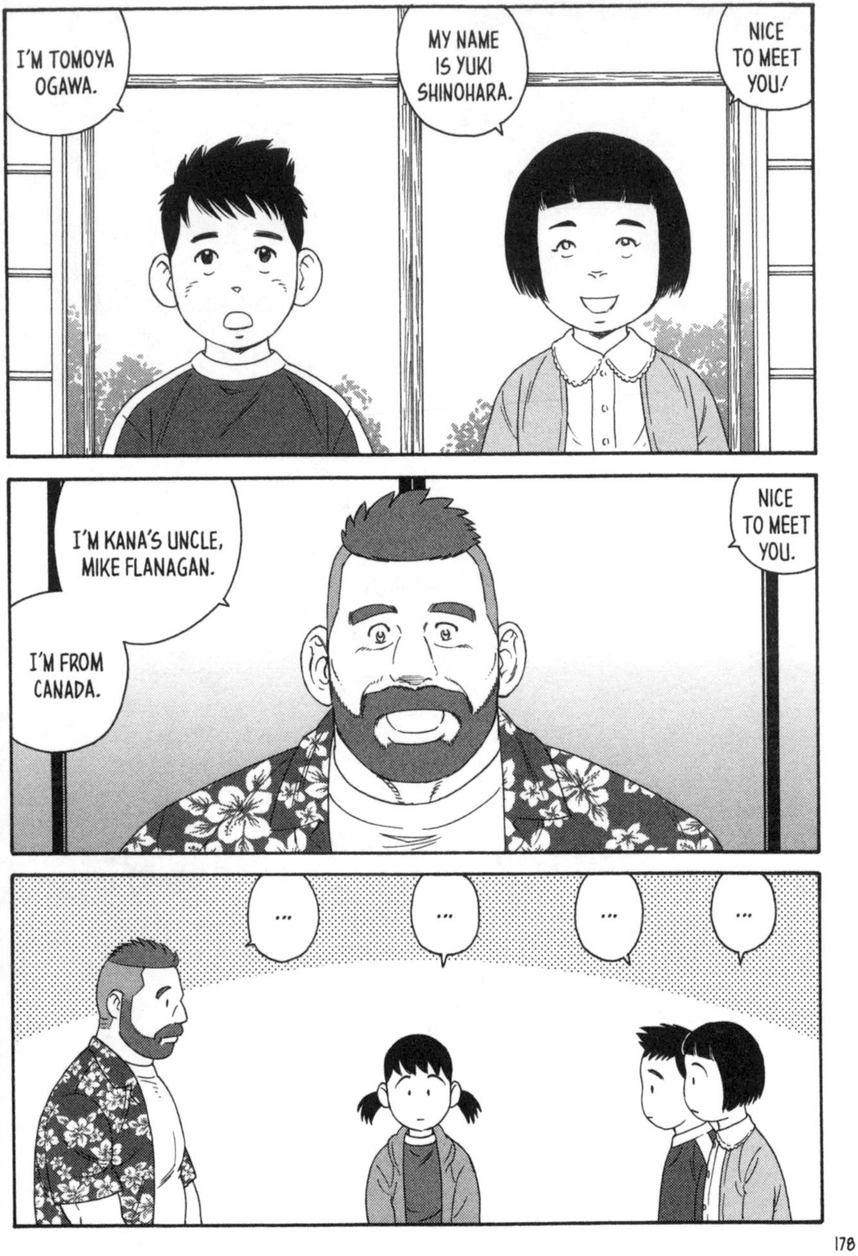
NICE TO MEET YOU!
MY NAME IS YUKI SHINOHARA.
I'M TOMOYA OGAWA.
NICE TO MEET YOU.
I'M KANA'S UNCLE, MIKE FLANAGAN.
I'M FROM CANADA.
...
...
...
...

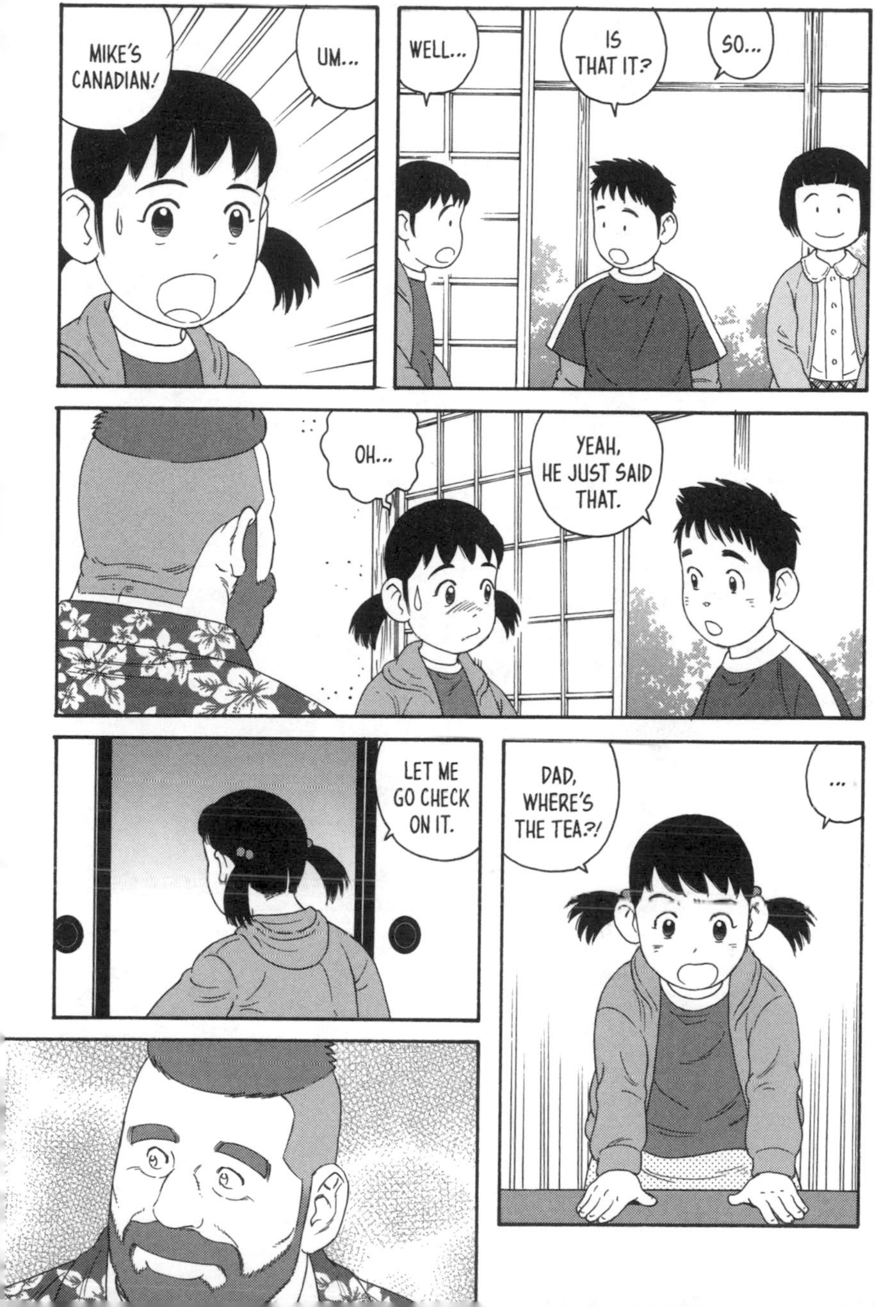
SO...
IS THAT IT?
WELL...
UM...
MIKE'S CANADIAN!
YEAH, HE JUST SAID THAT.
OH...
...
DAD, WHERE'S THE TEA?!
LET ME GO CHECK ON IT.

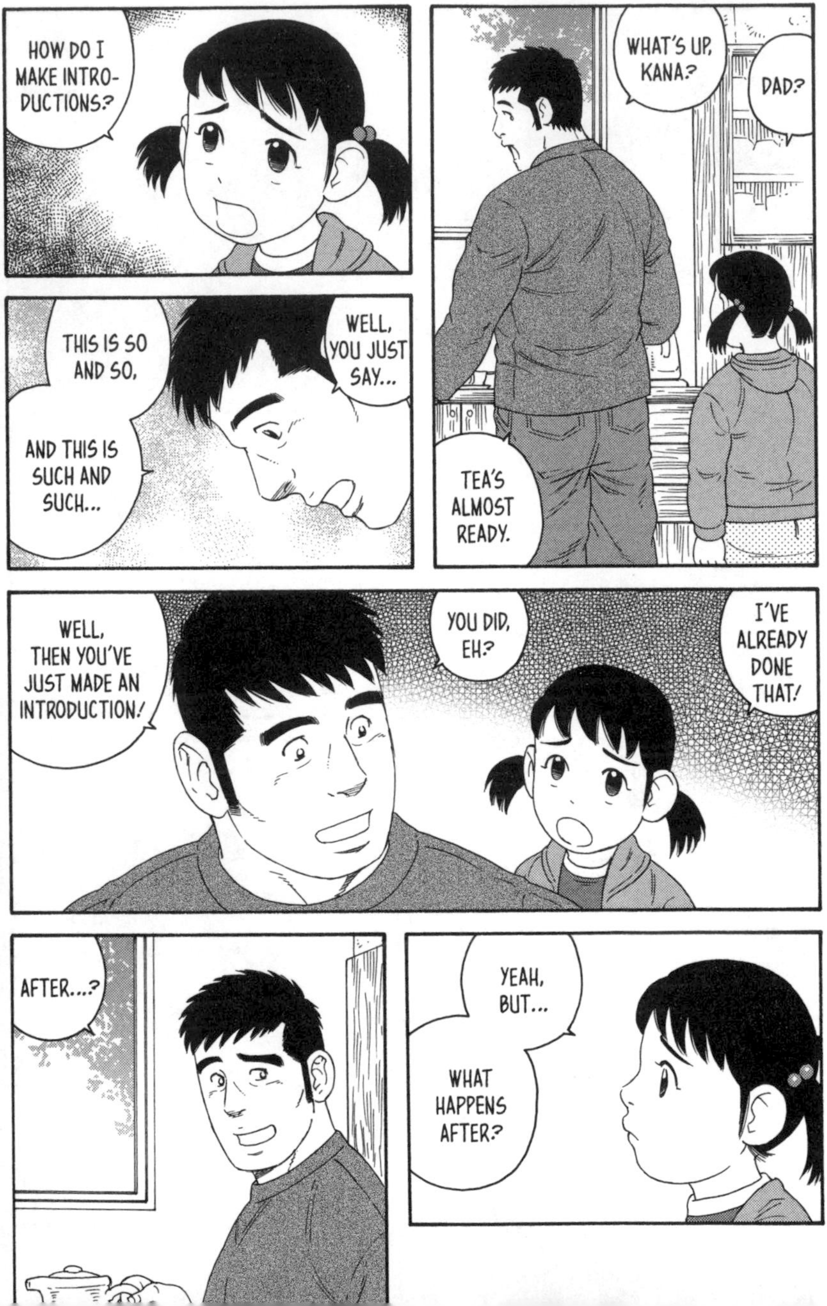
DAD?
WHAT'S UP, KANA?
TEA'S ALMOST READY.
HOW DO I MAKE INTRO-DUCTIONS?
WELL, YOU JUST SAY...
THIS IS SO AND SO,
AND THIS IS SUCH AND SUCH...
I'VE ALREADY DONE THAT!
YOU DID, EH?
WELL, THEN YOU'VE JUST MADE AN INTRODUCTION!
YEAH, BUT...
WHAT HAPPENS AFTER?
AFTER...?

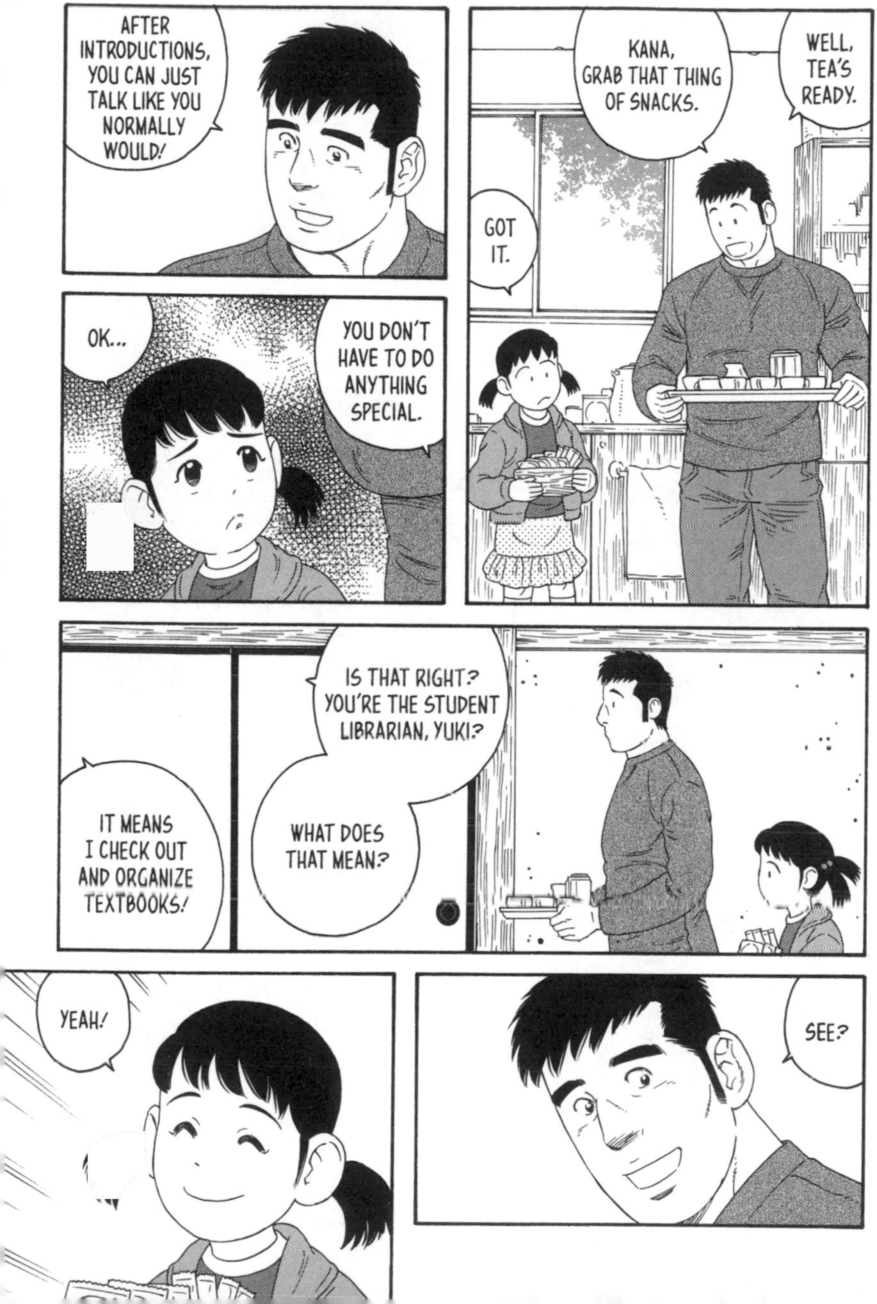
WELL, TEA'S READY.
KANA, GRAB THAT THING OF SNACKS.
GOT IT.
AFTER INTRODUCTIONS, YOU CAN JUST TALK LIKE YOU NORMALLY WOULD!
YOU DON'T HAVE TO DO ANYTHING SPECIAL.
OK...
IS THAT RIGHT? YOU'RE THE STUDENT LIBRARIAN, YUKI?
WHAT DOES THAT MEAN?
IT MEANS I CHECK OUT AND ORGANIZE TEXTBOOKS!
SEE?
YEAH!

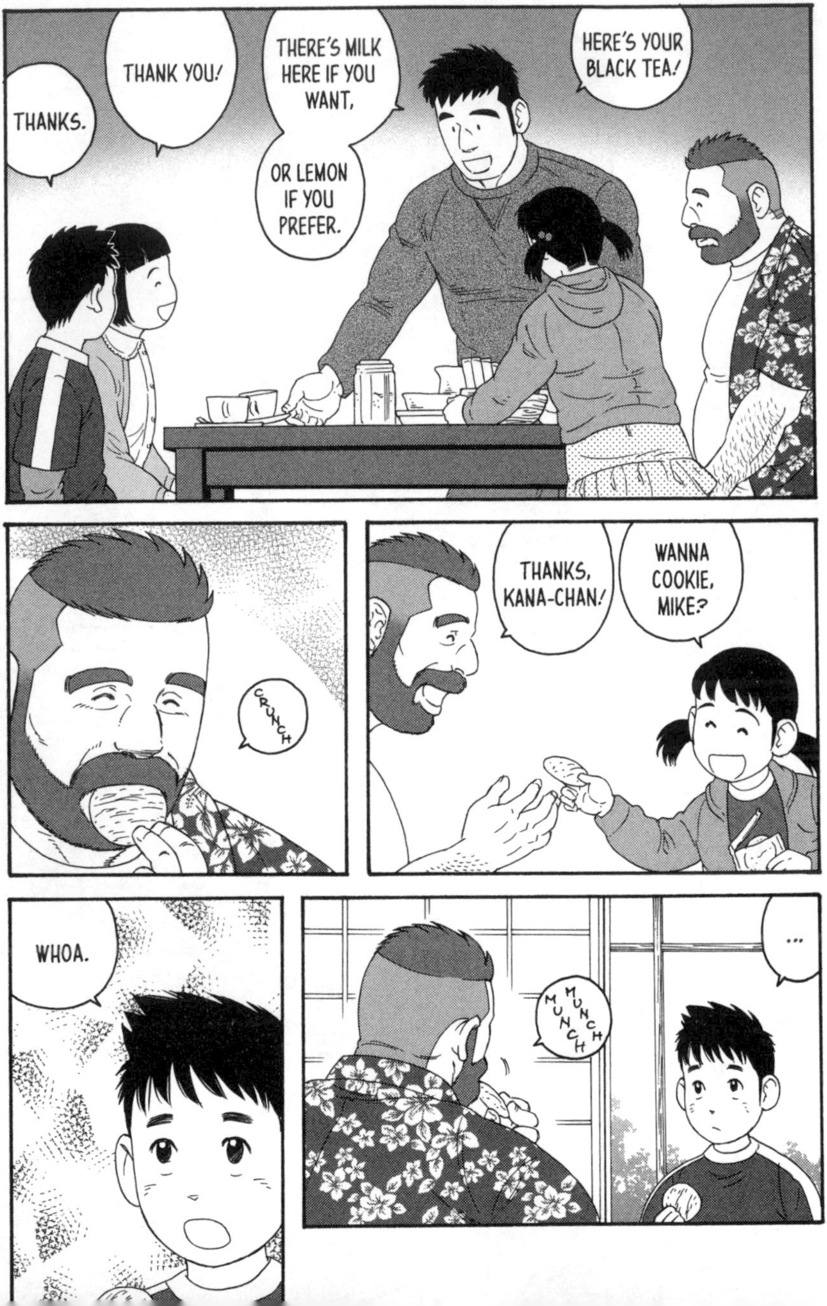
HERE'S YOUR BLACK TEA!
THERE'S MILK HERE IF YOU WANT,
OR LEMON IF YOU PREFER.
THANK YOU!
THANKS.
WANNA COOKIE, MIKE?
THANKS, KANA-CHAN!
CRUNCH
...
MUNCH MUNCH
WHOA.

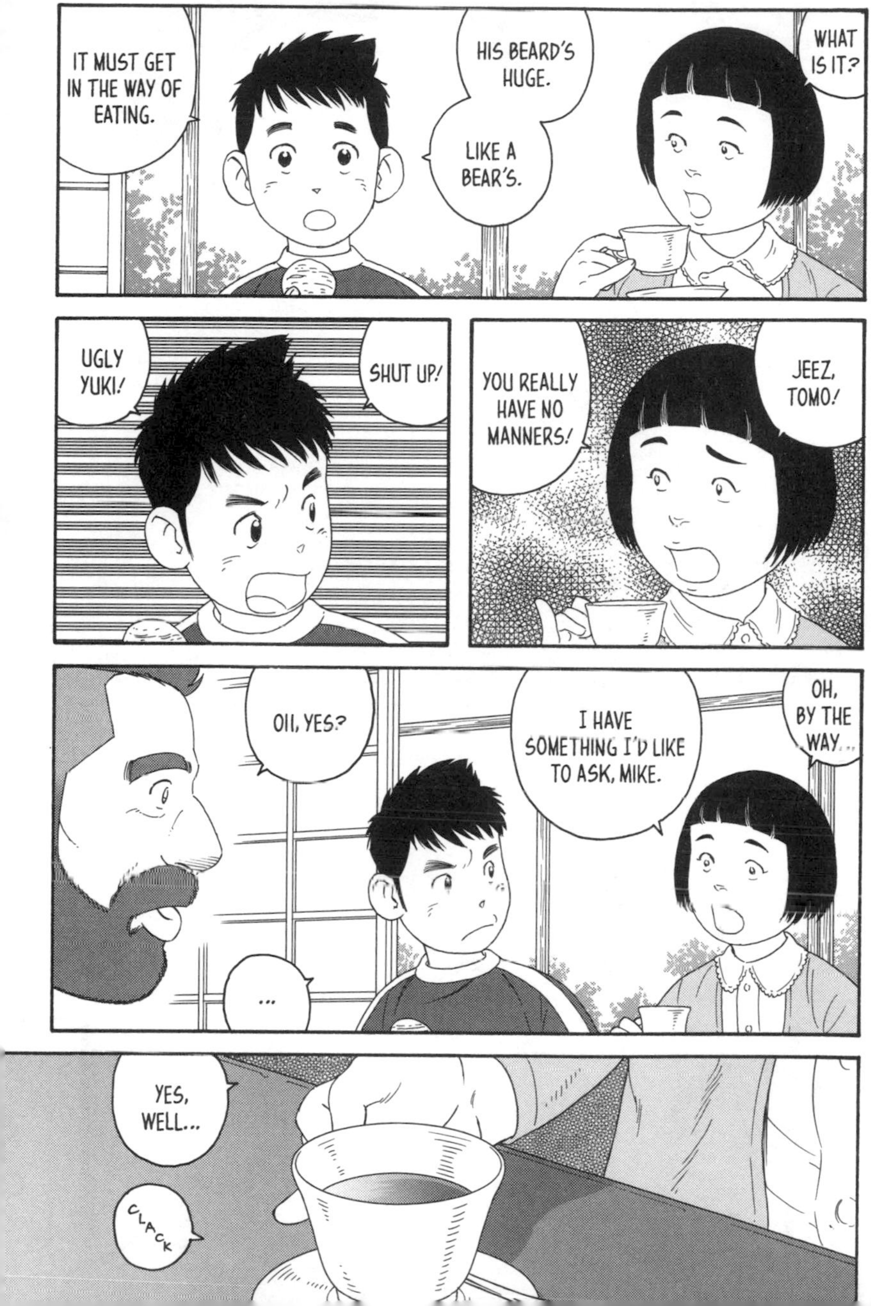
WHAT IS IT?
HIS BEARD'S HUGE.
LIKE A BEAR'S.
IT MUST GET IN THE WAY OF EATING.
JEEZ, TOMO!
YOU REALLY HAVE NO MANNERS!
SHUT UP!
UGLY YUKI!
OH, BY THE WAY...
I HAVE SOMETHING I'D LIKE TO ASK, MIKE.
OII, YES?
...
YES, WELL...
CLACK

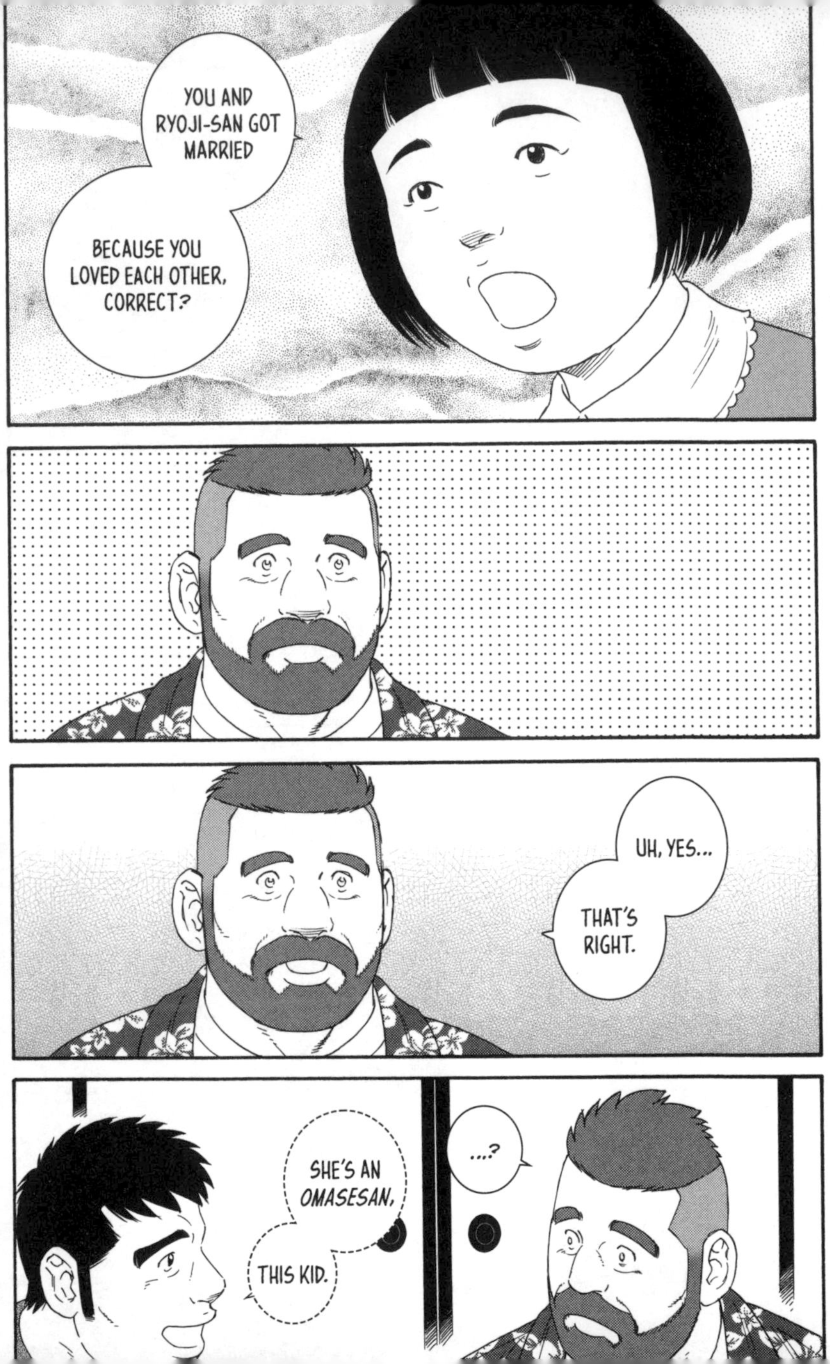
YOU AND RYOJI-SAN GOT MARRIED
BECAUSE YOU LOVED EACH OTHER, CORRECT?
UH, YES...
THAT'S RIGHT.
...?
SHE'S AN *OMASESAN*,
THIS KID.

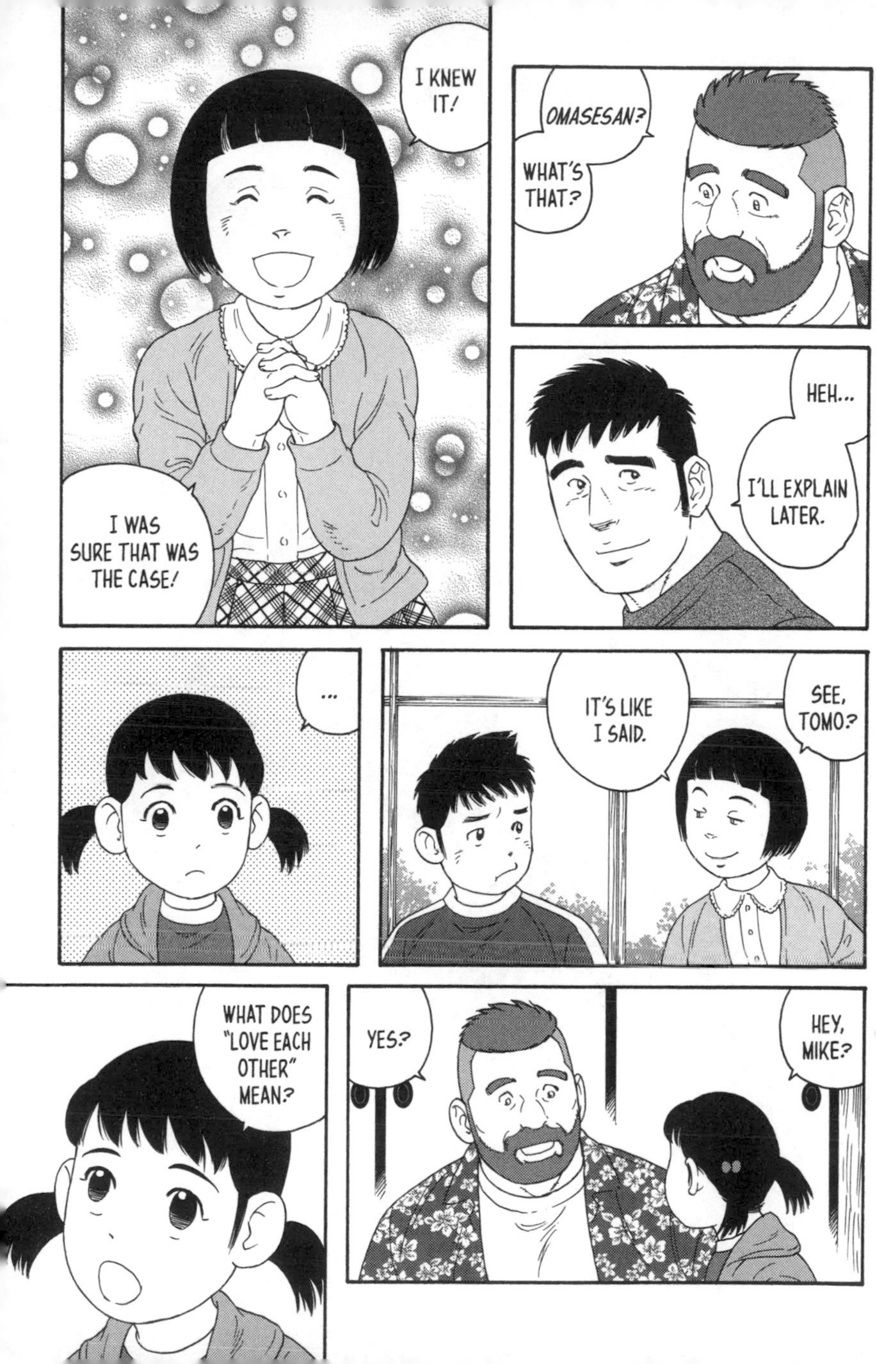
OMASESAN?
WHAT'S THAT?
HEH...
I'LL EXPLAIN LATER.
I KNEW IT!
I WAS SURE THAT WAS THE CASE!
SEE, TOMO?
IT'S LIKE I SAID.
...
HEY, MIKE?
YES?
WHAT DOES "LOVE EACH OTHER" MEAN?

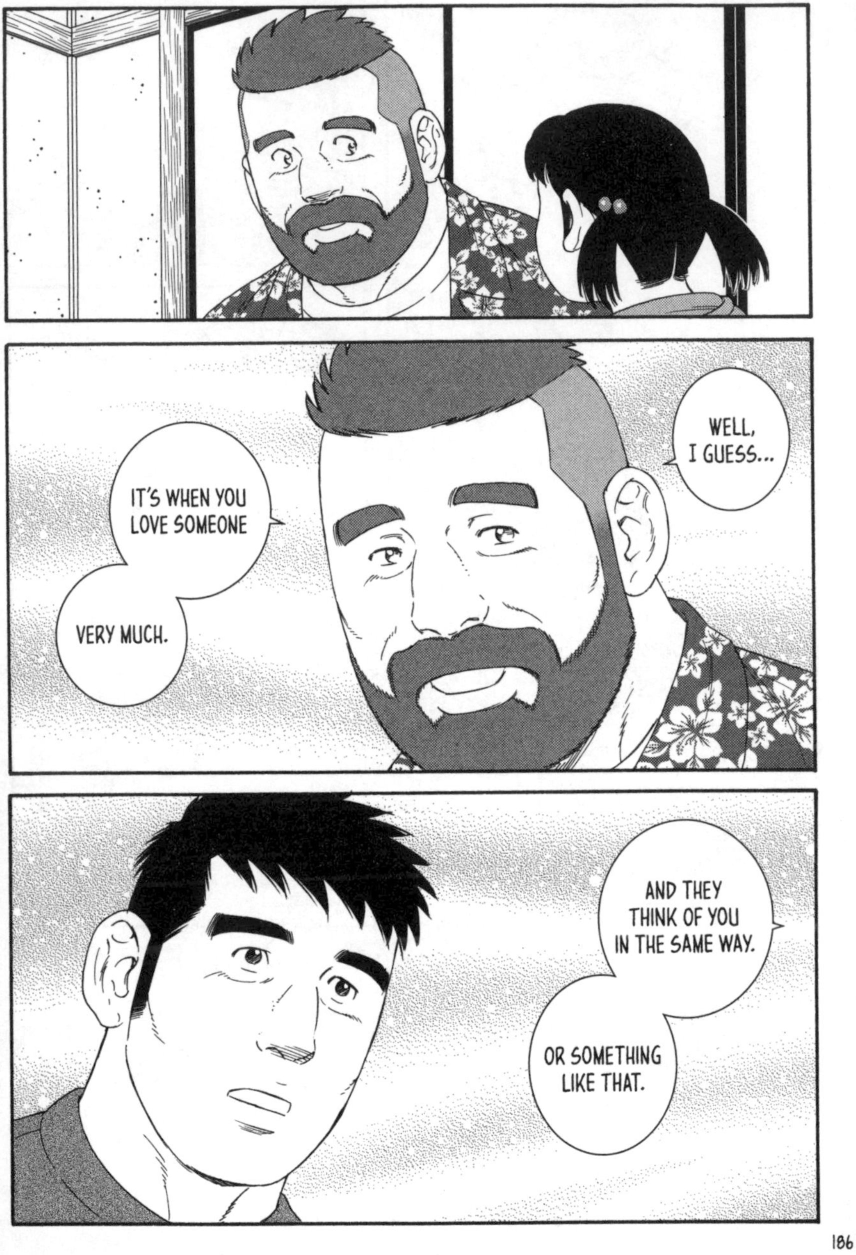
WELL, I GUESS...
IT'S WHEN YOU LOVE SOMEONE
VERY MUCH.
AND THEY THINK OF YOU IN THE SAME WAY.
OR SOMETHING LIKE THAT.

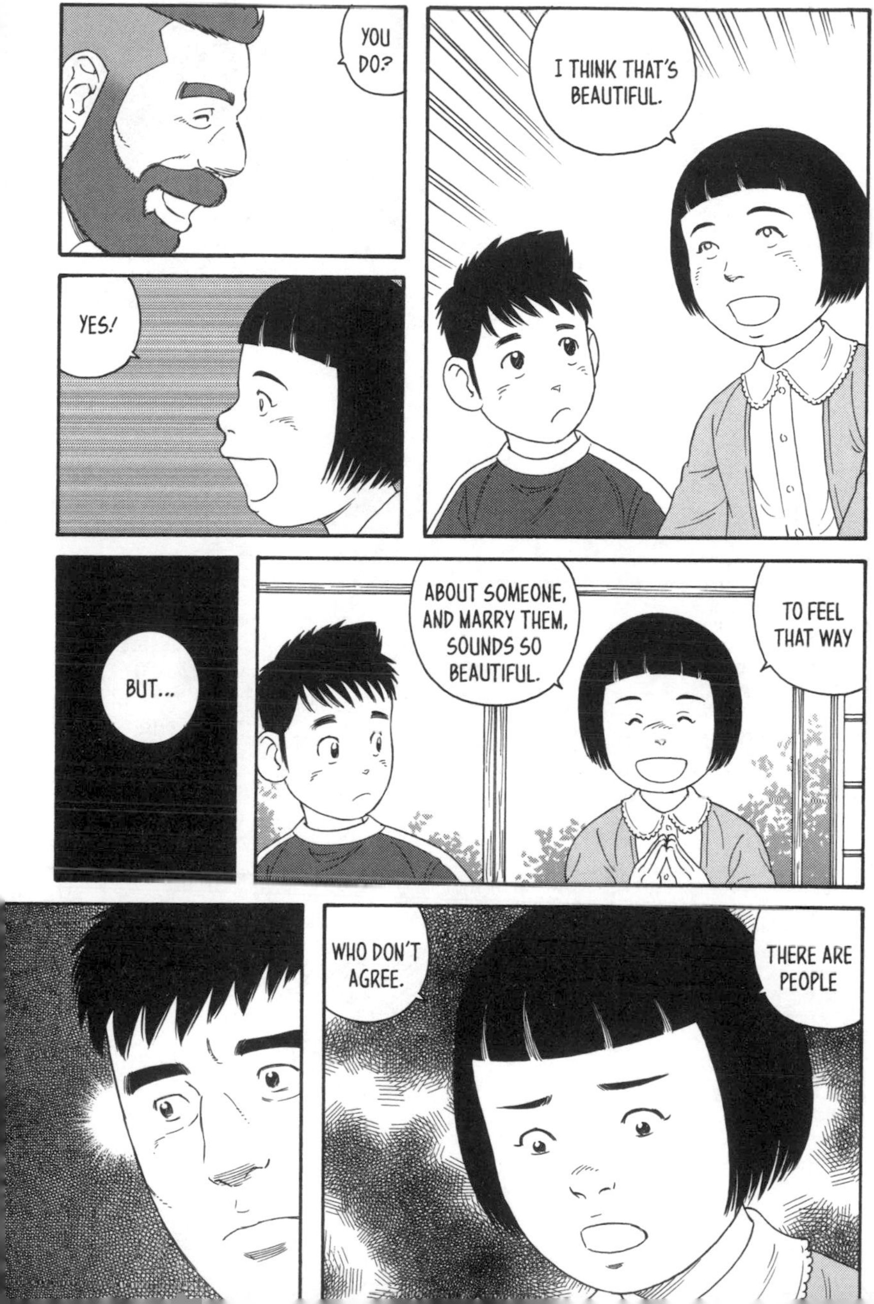
I THINK THAT'S BEAUTIFUL.
YOU DO?
YES!
TO FEEL THAT WAY
ABOUT SOMEONE, AND MARRY THEM, SOUNDS SO BEAUTIFUL.
BUT...
THERE ARE PEOPLE
WHO DON'T AGREE.

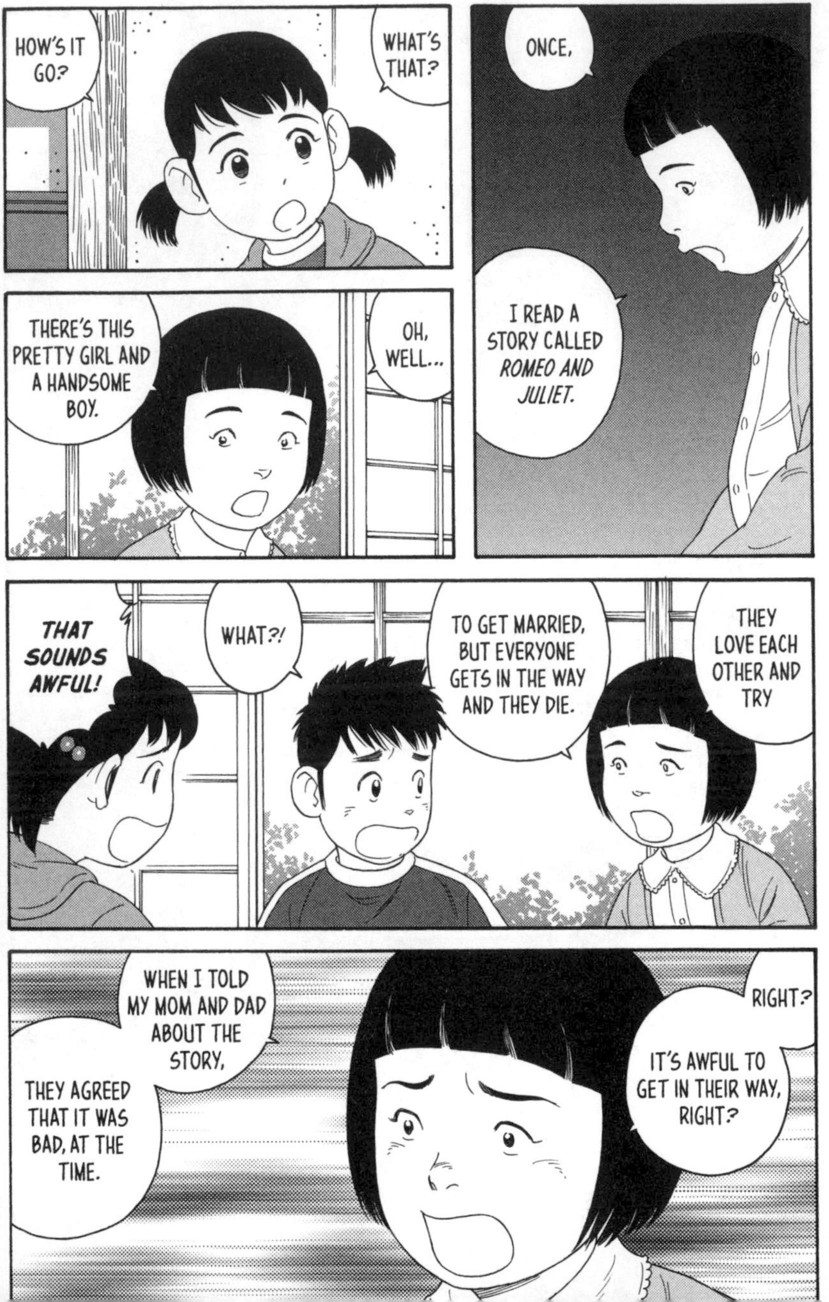
ONCE,
I READ A STORY CALLED *ROMEO AND JULIET.*
WHAT'S THAT?
HOW'S IT GO?
OH, WELL...
THERE'S THIS PRETTY GIRL AND A HANDSOME BOY.
THEY LOVE EACH OTHER AND TRY
TO GET MARRIED, BUT EVERYONE GETS IN THE WAY AND THEY DIE.
WHAT?!
THAT SOUNDS AWFUL!
RIGHT?
IT'S AWFUL TO GET IN THEIR WAY, RIGHT?
WHEN I TOLD MY MOM AND DAD ABOUT THE STORY,
THEY AGREED THAT IT WAS BAD, AT THE TIME.

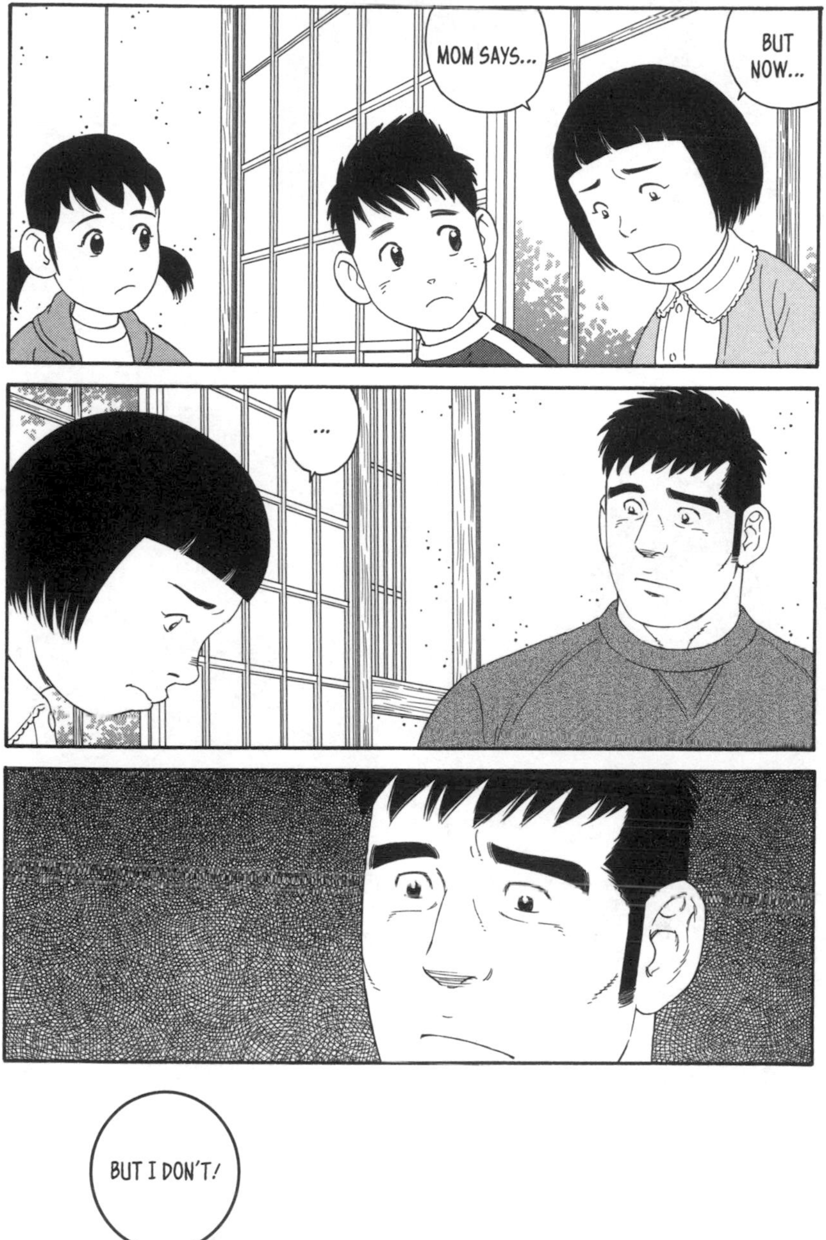
BUT NOW...
MOM SAYS...
...
BUT I DON'T!

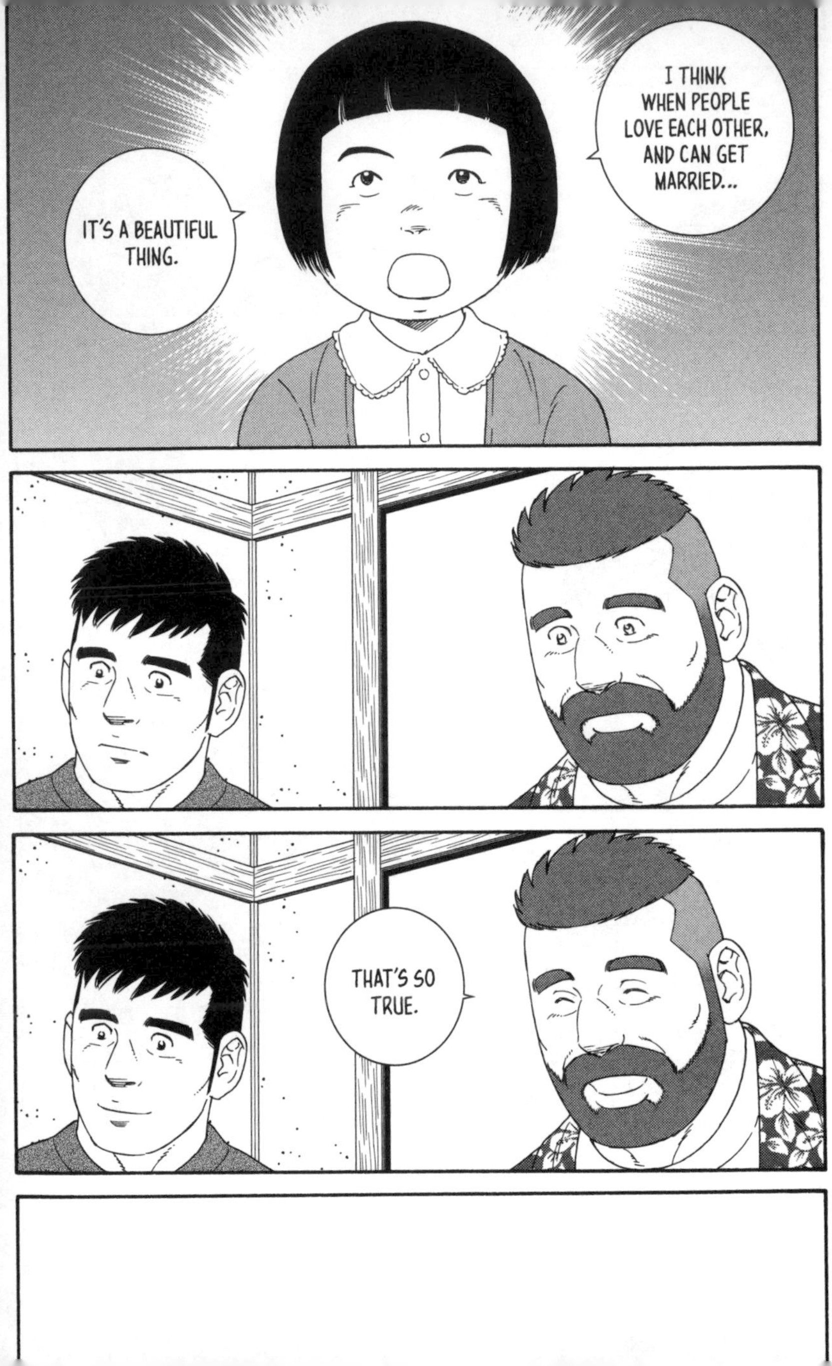
I THINK WHEN PEOPLE LOVE EACH OTHER, AND CAN GET MARRIED...
IT'S A BEAUTIFUL THING.
THAT'S SO TRUE.

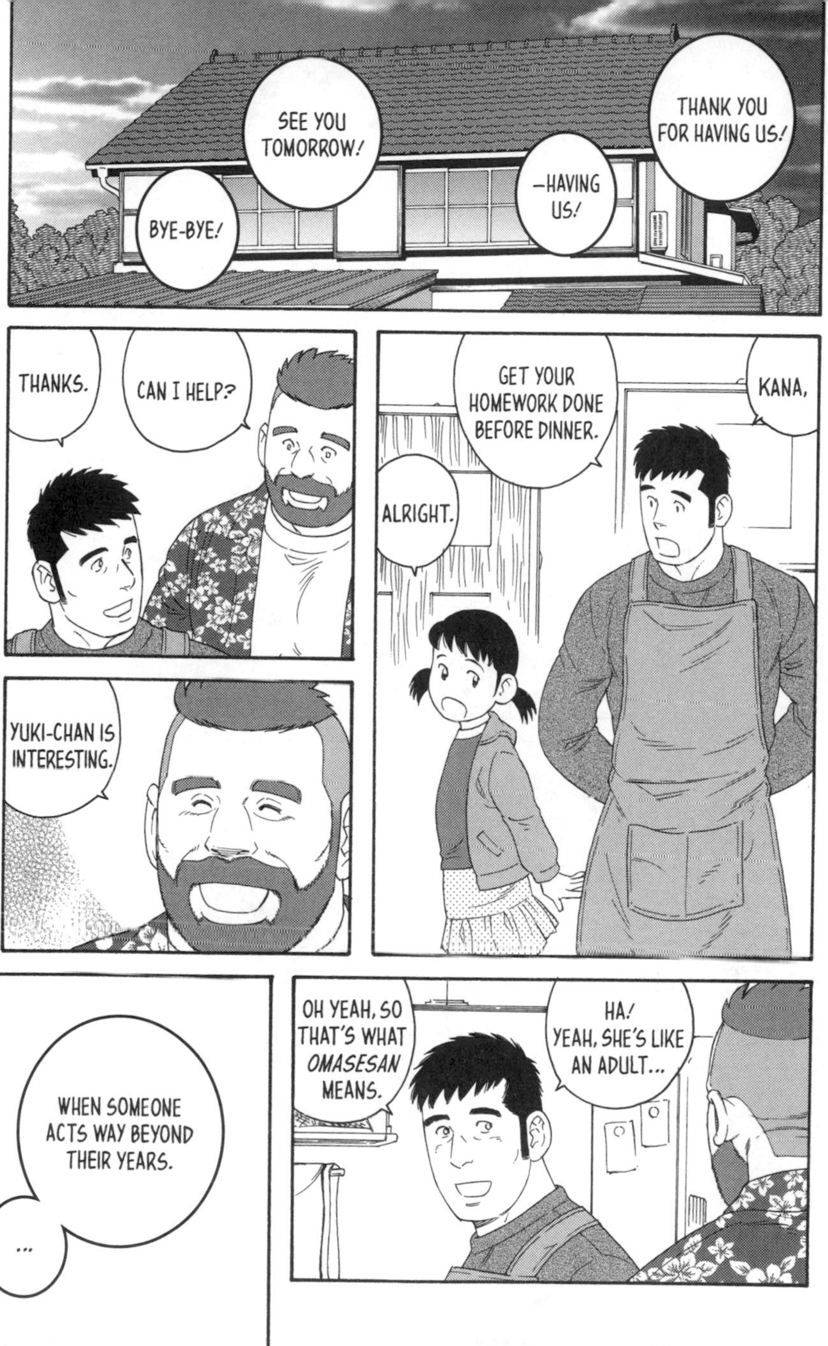
THANK YOU FOR HAVING US!
—HAVING US!
SEE YOU TOMORROW!
BYE-BYE!
KANA,
GET YOUR HOMEWORK DONE BEFORE DINNER.
ALRIGHT.
CAN I HELP?
THANKS.
YUKI-CHAN IS INTERESTING.
HA! YEAH, SHE'S LIKE AN ADULT...
OH YEAH, SO THAT'S WHAT *OMASESAN* MEANS.
WHEN SOMEONE ACTS WAY BEYOND THEIR YEARS.
...

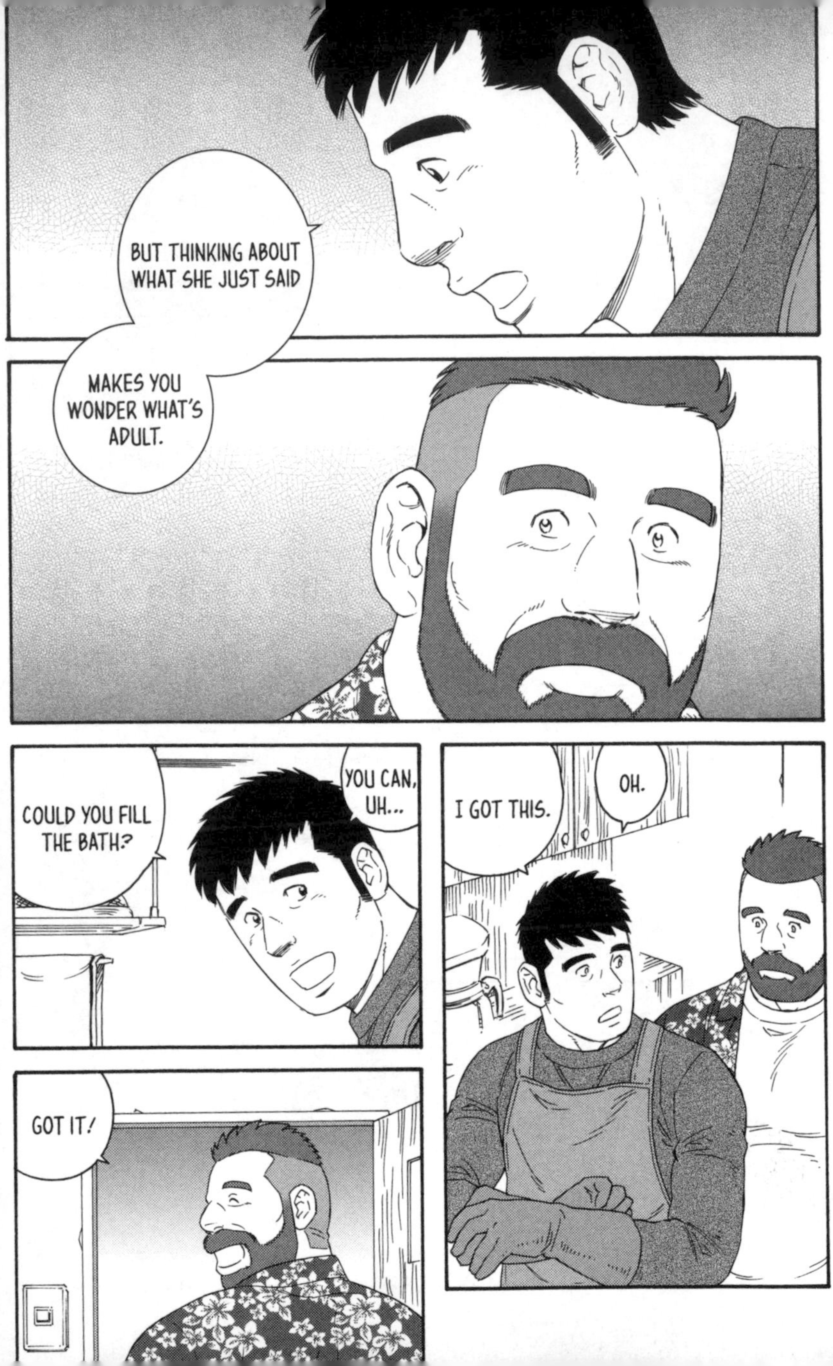
BUT THINKING ABOUT WHAT SHE JUST SAID
MAKES YOU WONDER WHAT'S ADULT.
OH.
I GOT THIS.
YOU CAN, UH...
COULD YOU FILL THE BATH?
GOT IT!

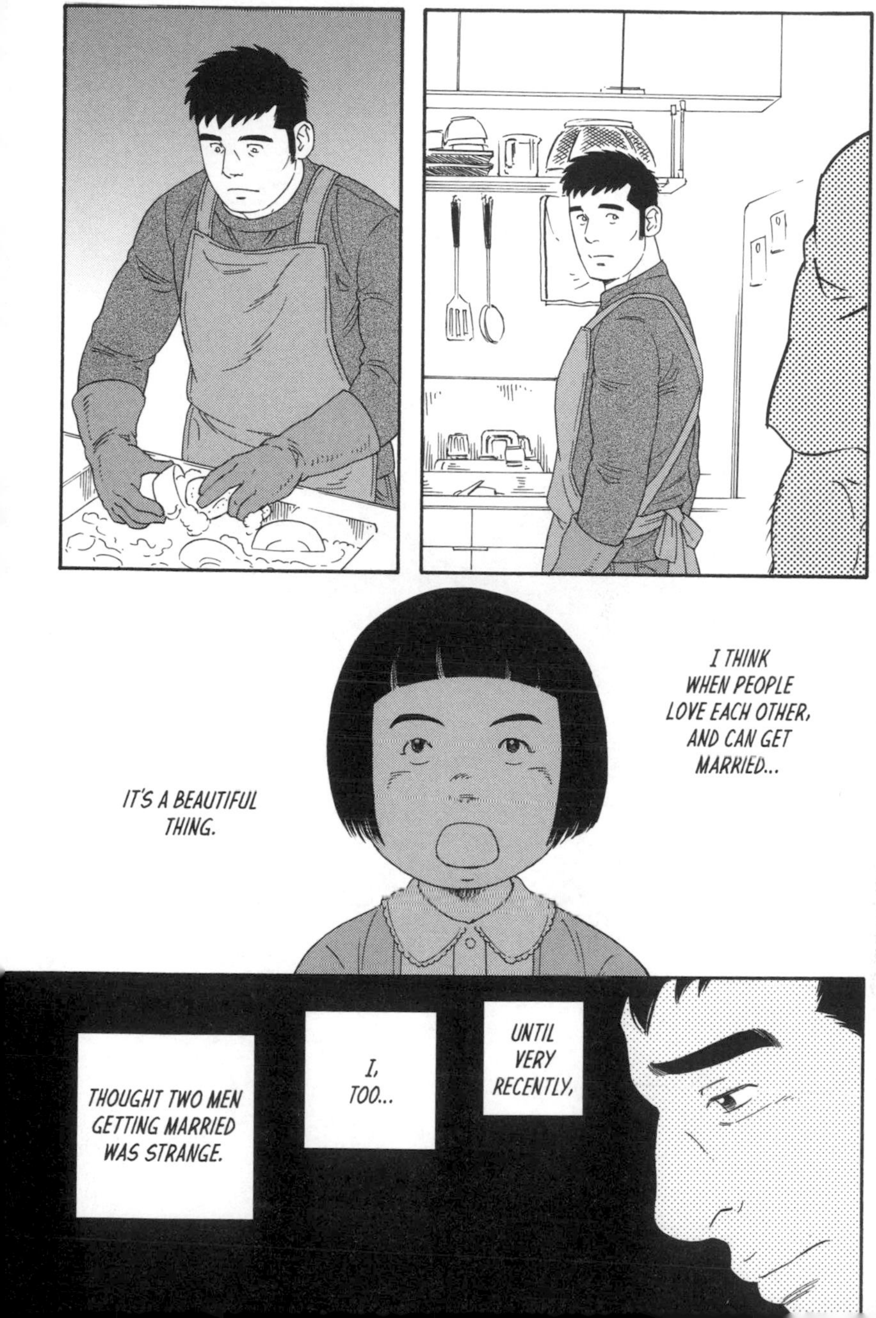
I THINK WHEN PEOPLE LOVE EACH OTHER, AND CAN GET MARRIED...
IT'S A BEAUTIFUL THING.
UNTIL VERY RECENTLY,
I, TOO...
THOUGHT TWO MEN GETTING MARRIED WAS STRANGE.

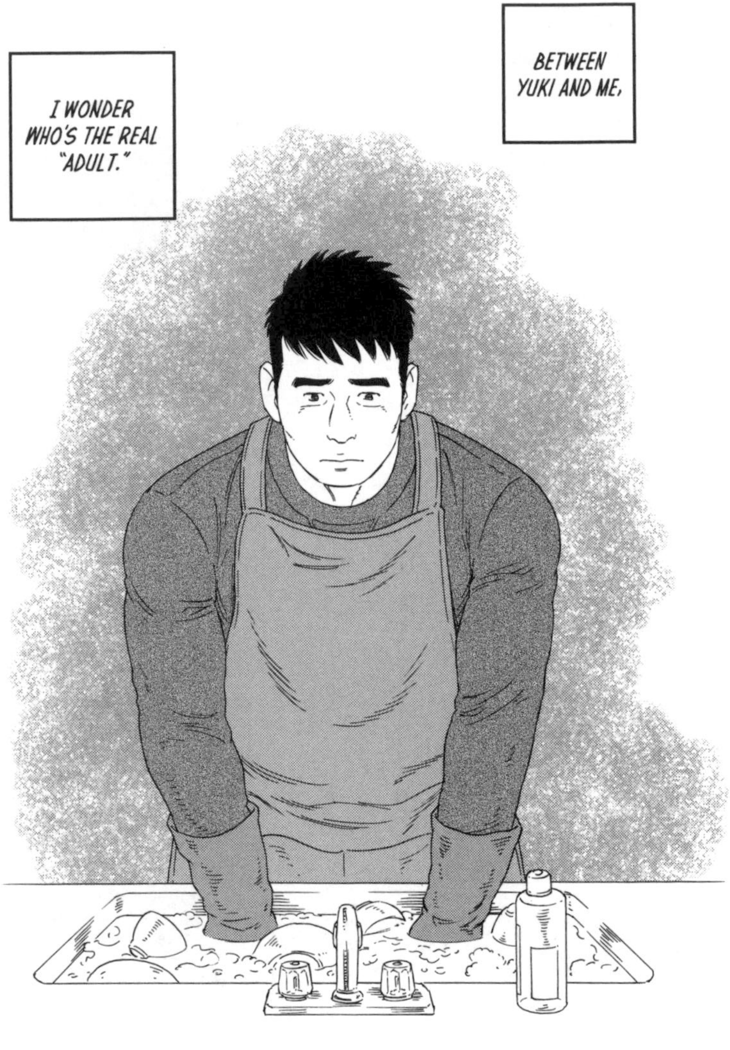
BETWEEN YUKI AND ME,
I WONDER WHO'S THE REAL "ADULT."

CHAPTER TWENTY-THREE

DAY TO DAY

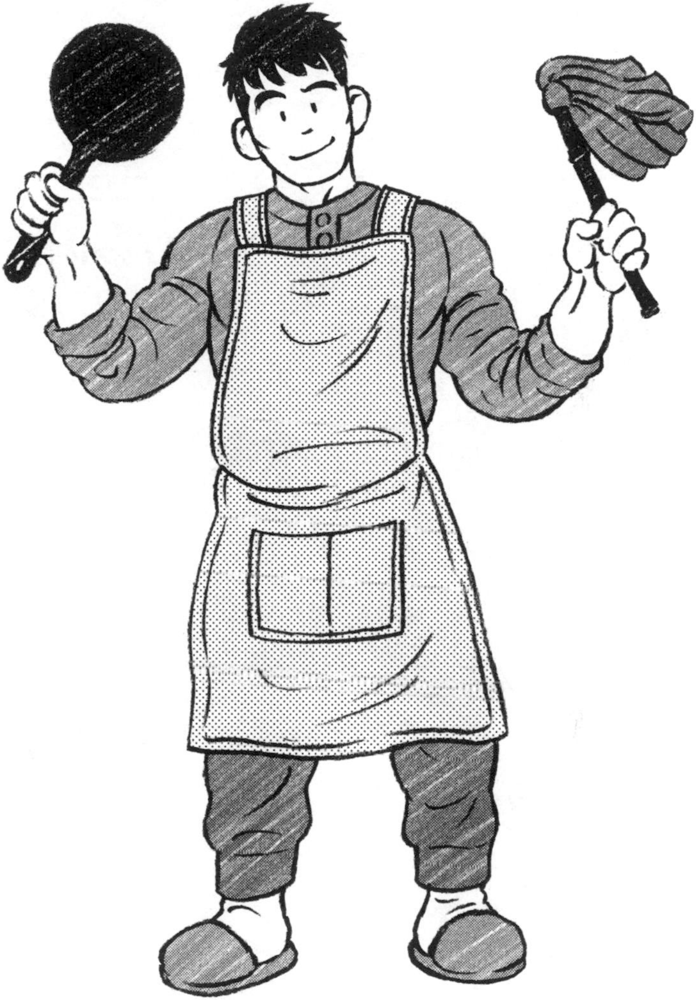

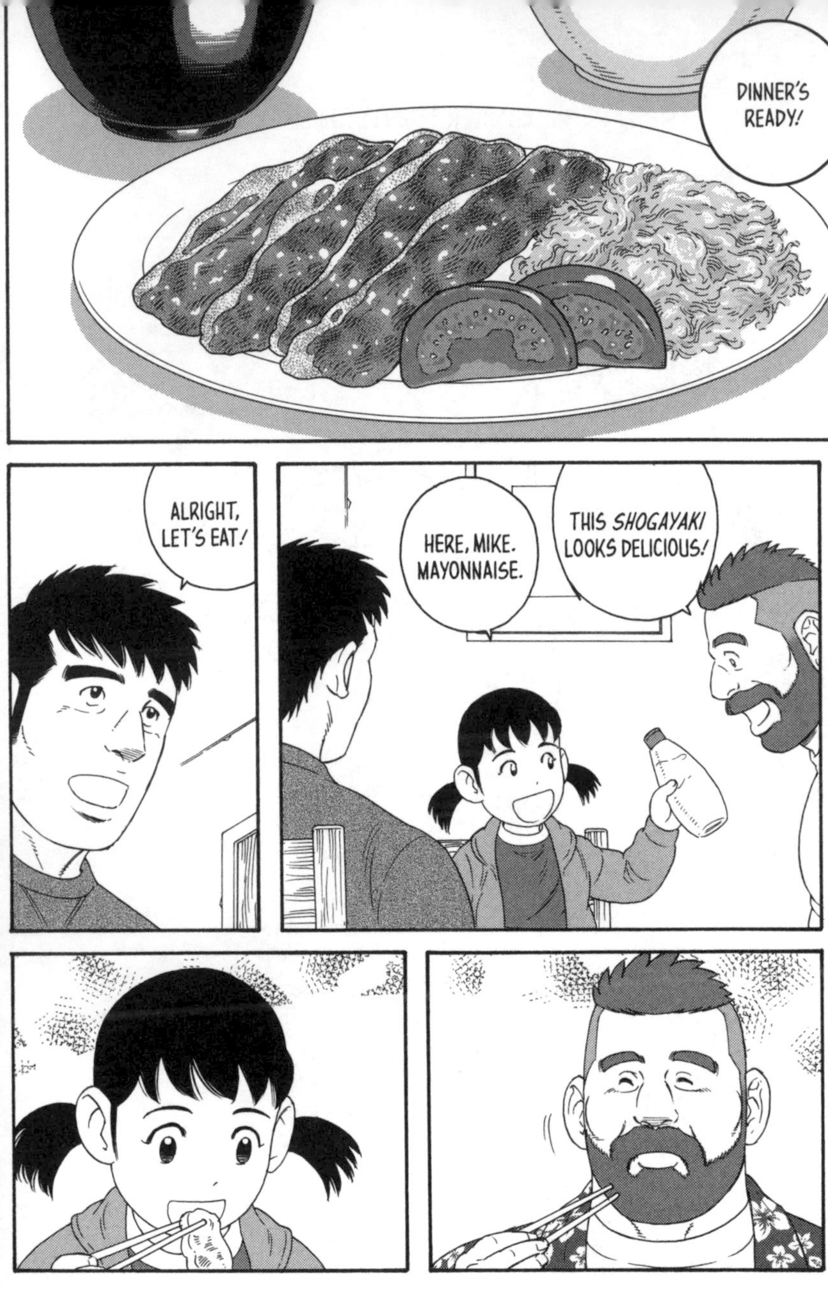
DINNER'S READY!
THIS *SHOGAYAKI* LOOKS DELICIOUS!
HERE, MIKE. MAYONNAISE.
ALRIGHT, LET'S EAT!

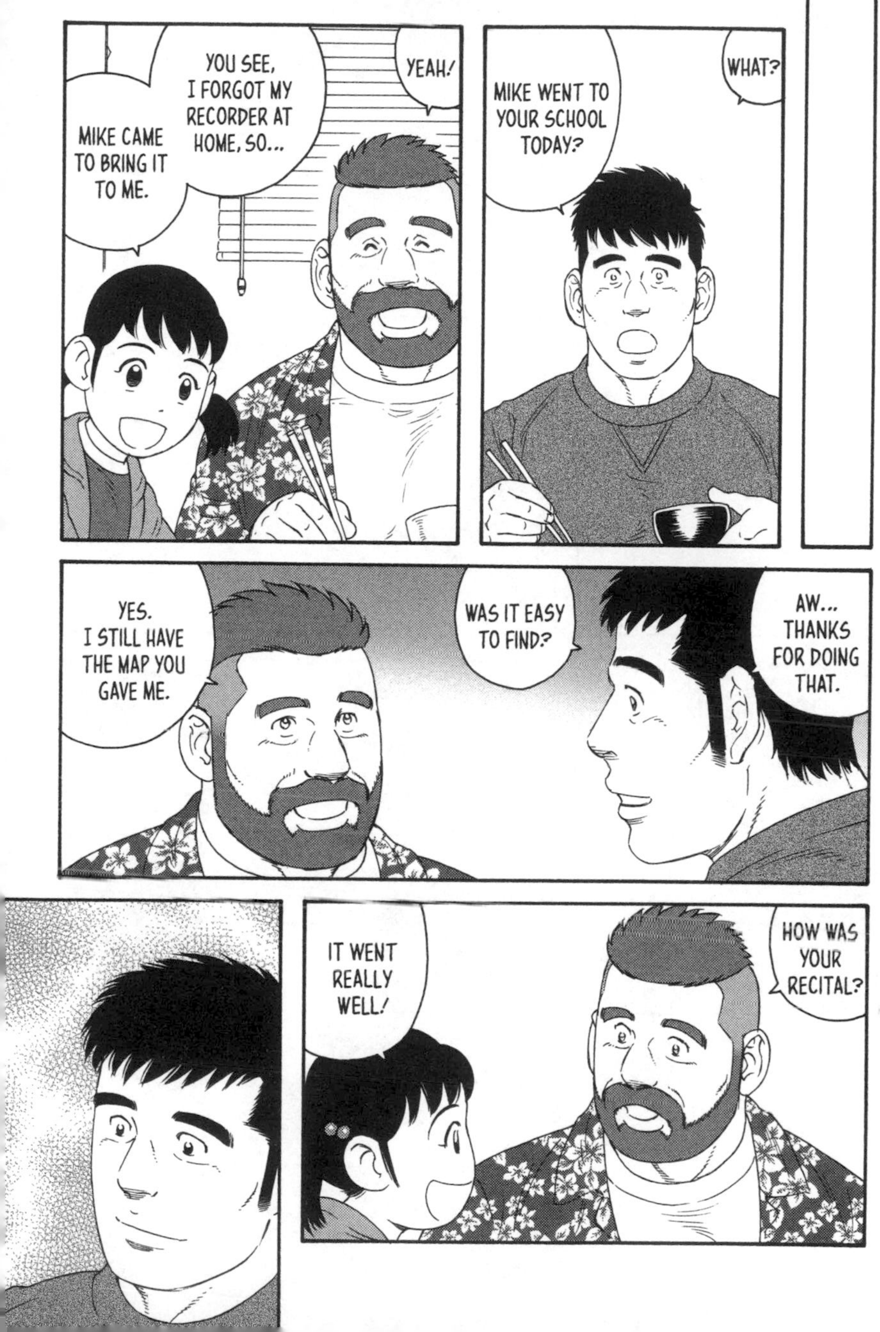
WHAT?
MIKE WENT TO YOUR SCHOOL TODAY?
YEAH!
YOU SEE, I FORGOT MY RECORDER AT HOME, SO...
MIKE CAME TO BRING IT TO ME.
AW... THANKS FOR DOING THAT.
WAS IT EASY TO FIND?
YES. I STILL HAVE THE MAP YOU GAVE ME.
HOW WAS YOUR RECITAL?
IT WENT REALLY WELL!

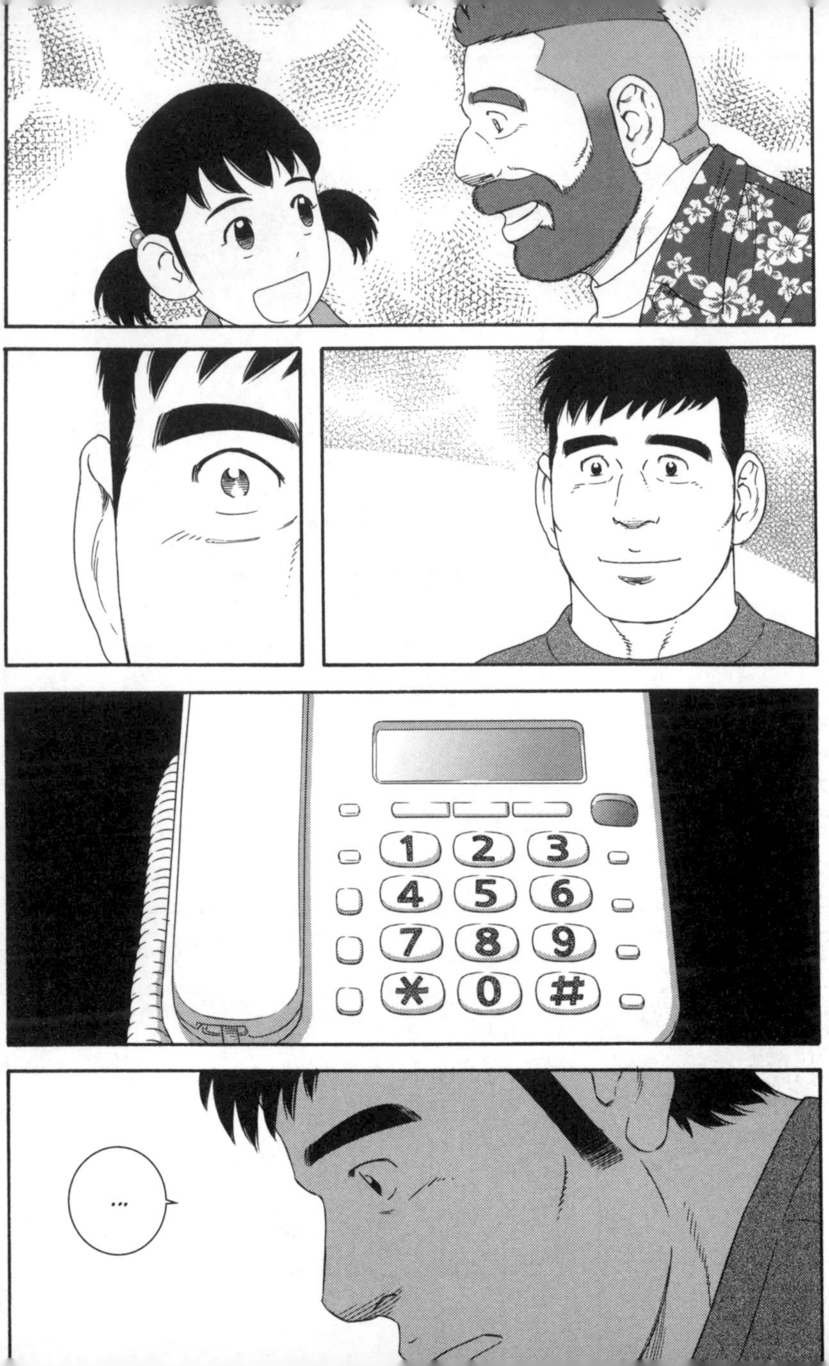
...

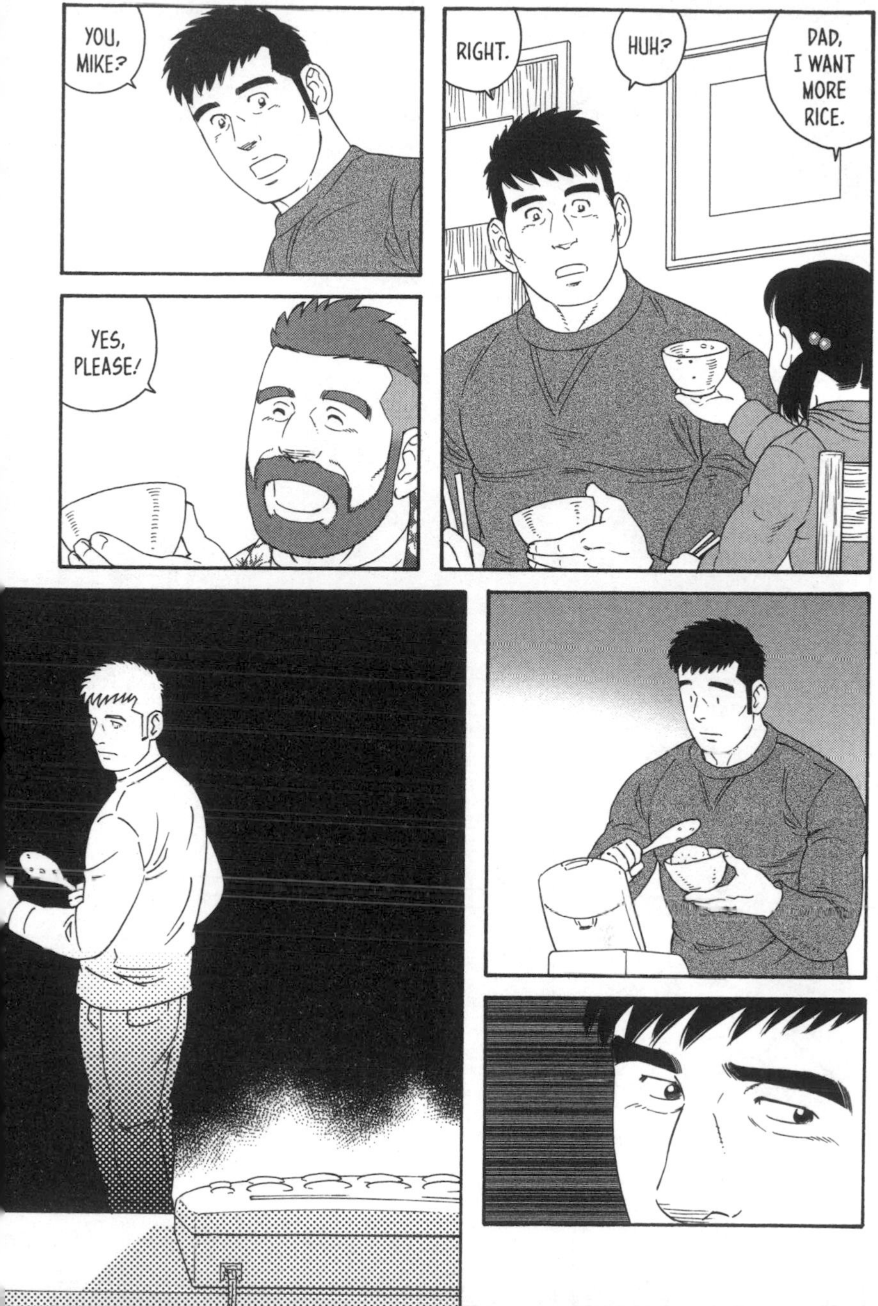
DAD, I WANT MORE RICE.
HUH?
RIGHT.
YOU, MIKE?
YES, PLEASE!

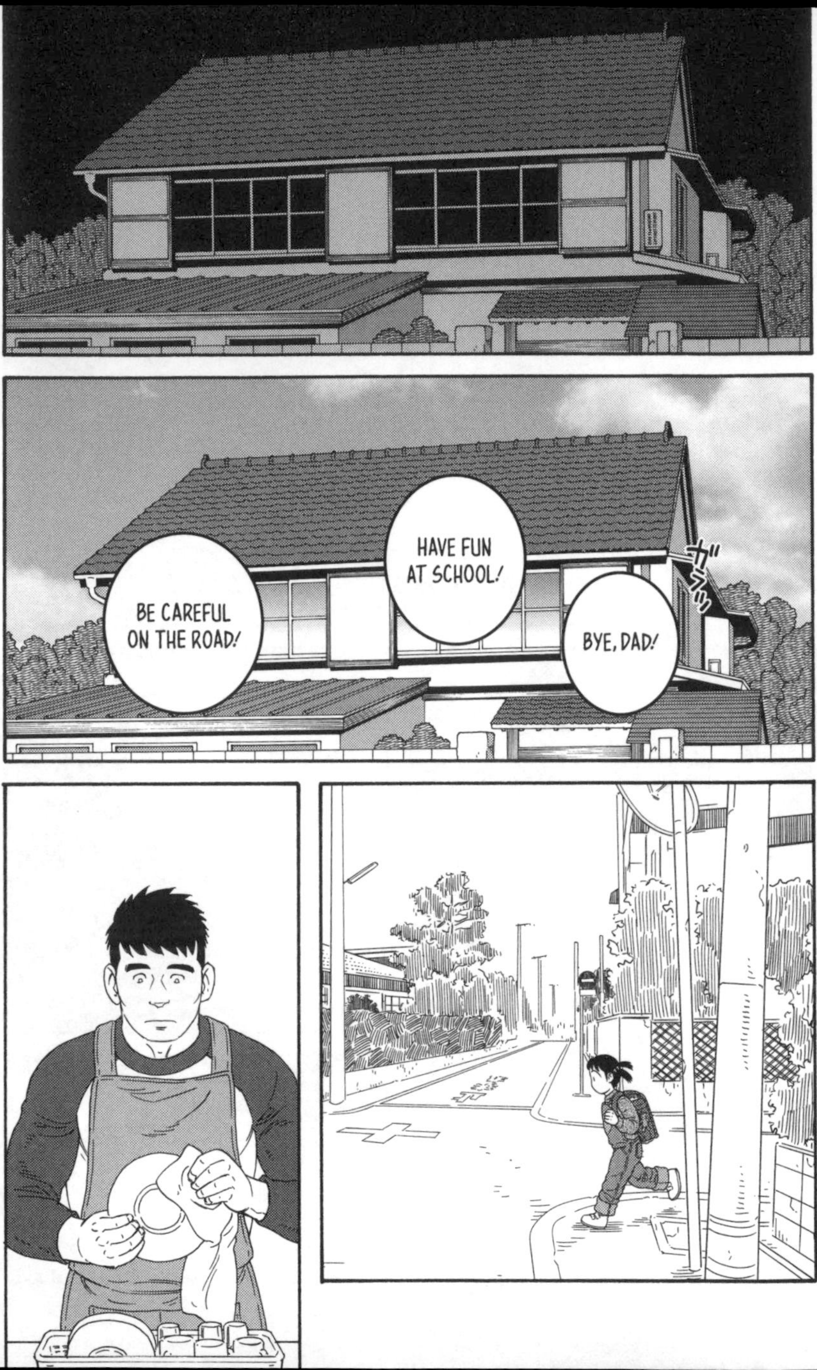
ガラッ
BYE, DAD!
HAVE FUN AT SCHOOL!
BE CAREFUL ON THE ROAD!

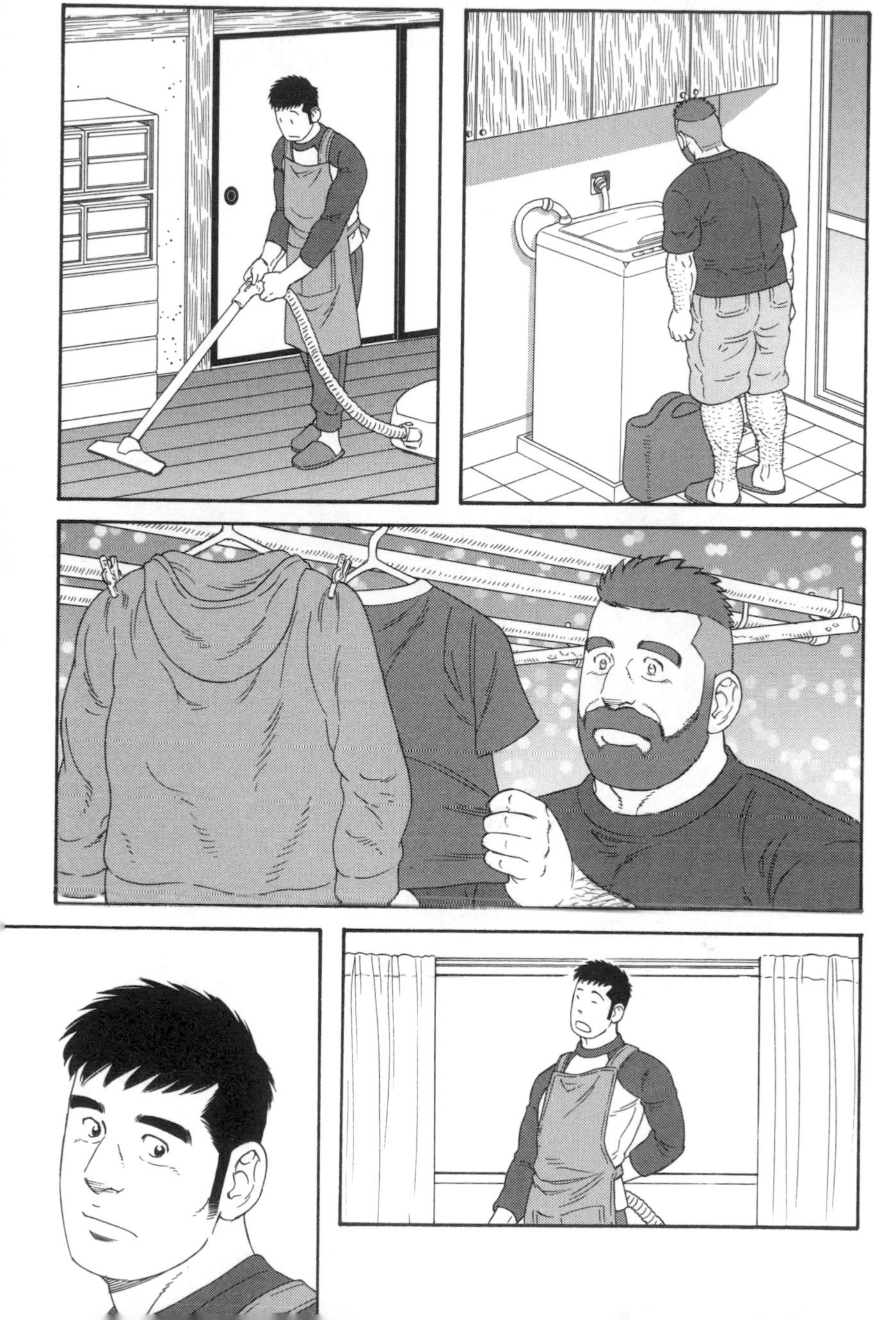

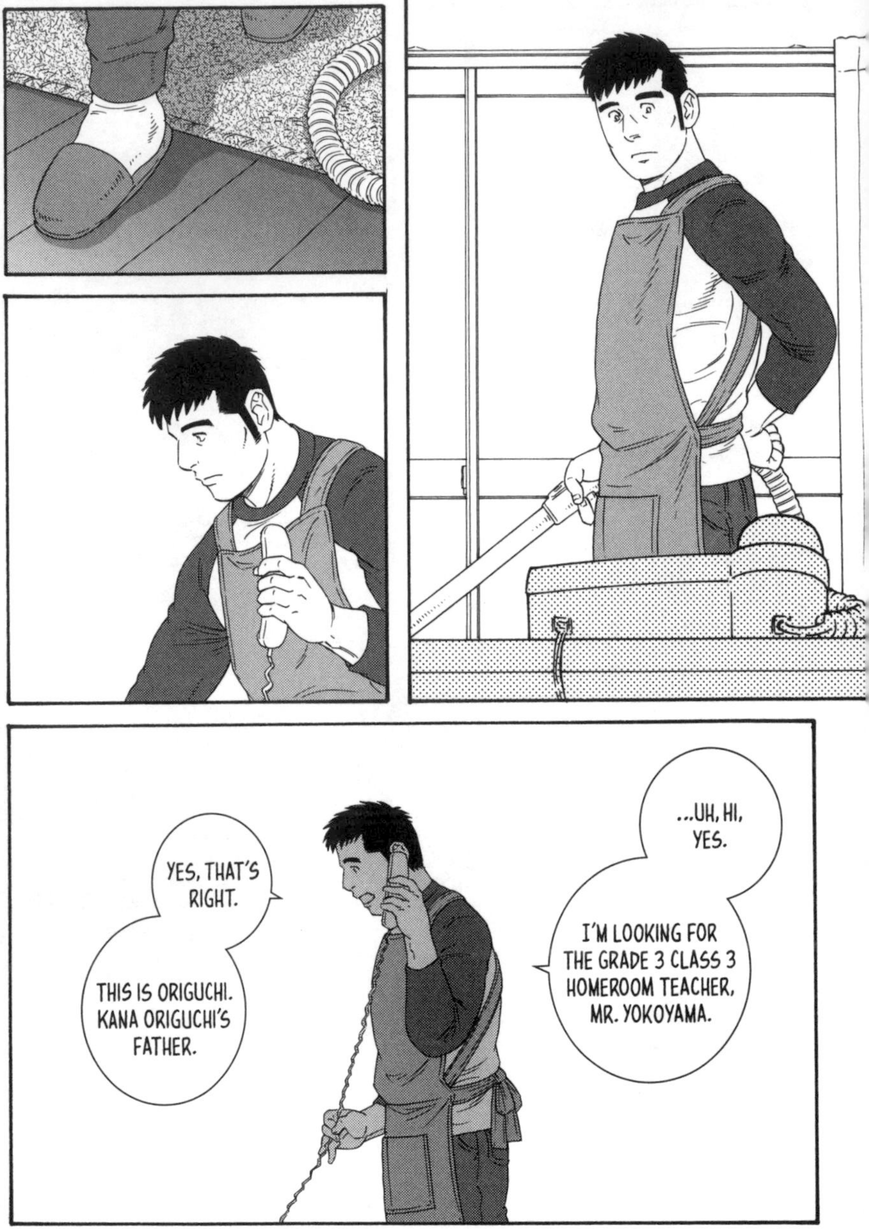
...UH, HI, YES.
I'M LOOKING FOR THE GRADE 3 CLASS 3 HOMEROOM TEACHER, MR. YOKOYAMA.
YES, THAT'S RIGHT.
THIS IS ORIGUCHI. KANA ORIGUCHI'S FATHER.

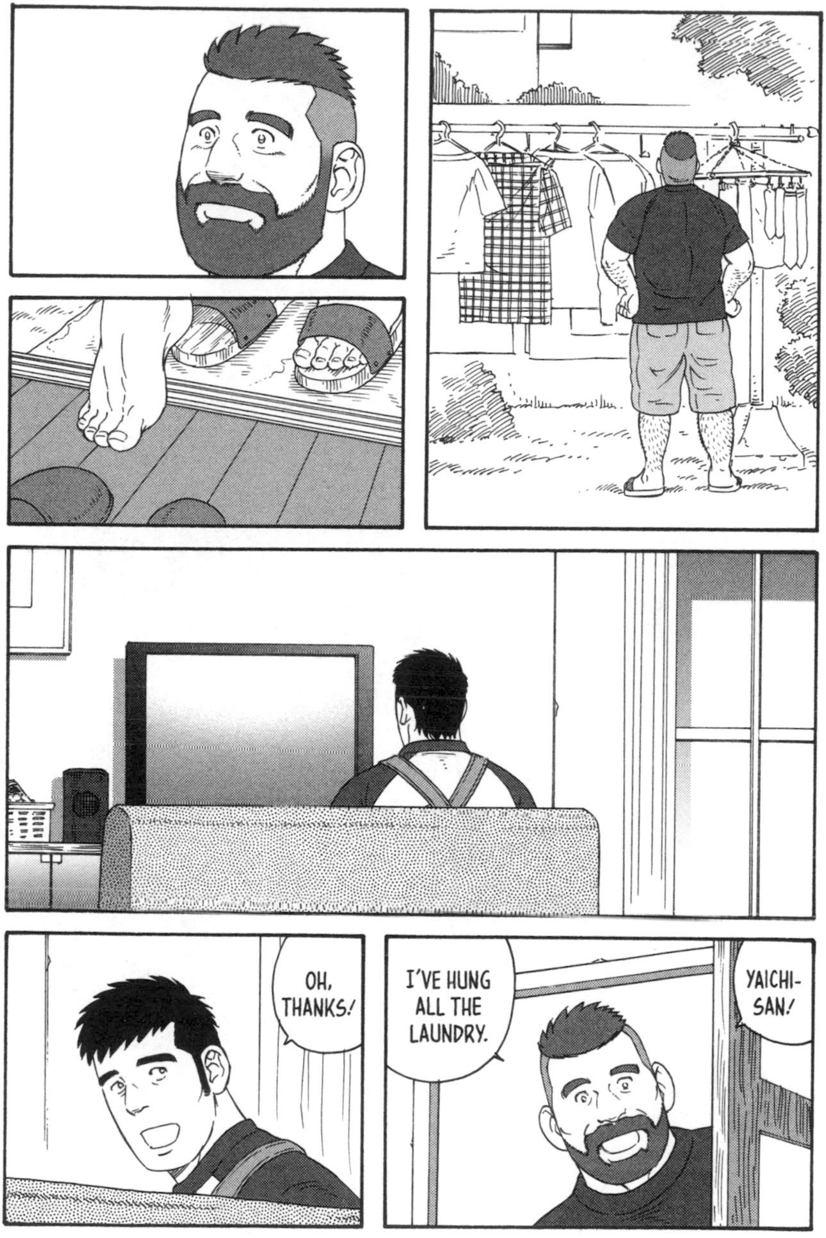
YAICHI-SAN!
I'VE HUNG ALL THE LAUNDRY.
OH, THANKS!

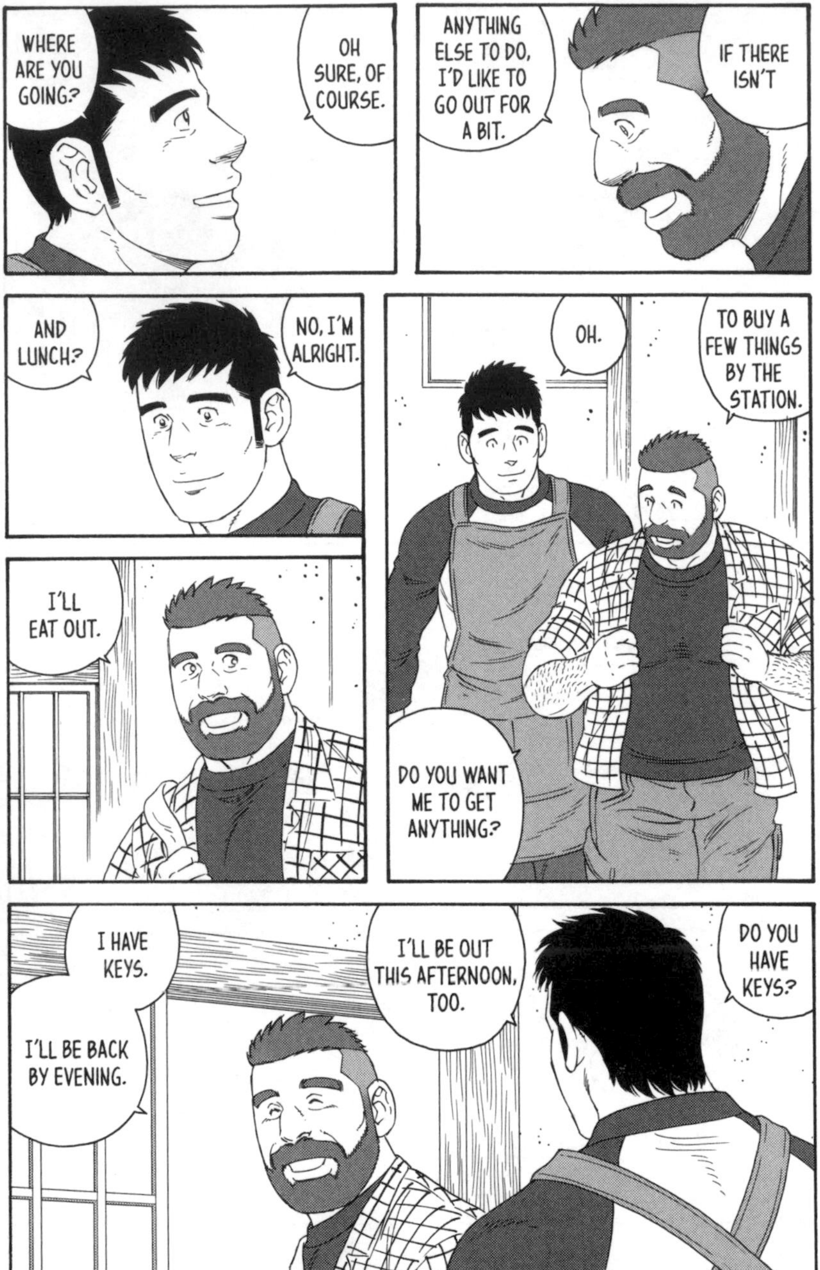
IF THERE ISN'T
ANYTHING ELSE TO DO, I'D LIKE TO GO OUT FOR A BIT.
OH SURE, OF COURSE.
WHERE ARE YOU GOING?
TO BUY A FEW THINGS BY THE STATION.
OH.
DO YOU WANT ME TO GET ANYTHING?
NO, I'M ALRIGHT.
AND LUNCH?
I'LL EAT OUT.
DO YOU HAVE KEYS?
I'LL BE OUT THIS AFTERNOON, TOO.
I HAVE KEYS.
I'LL BE BACK BY EVENING.

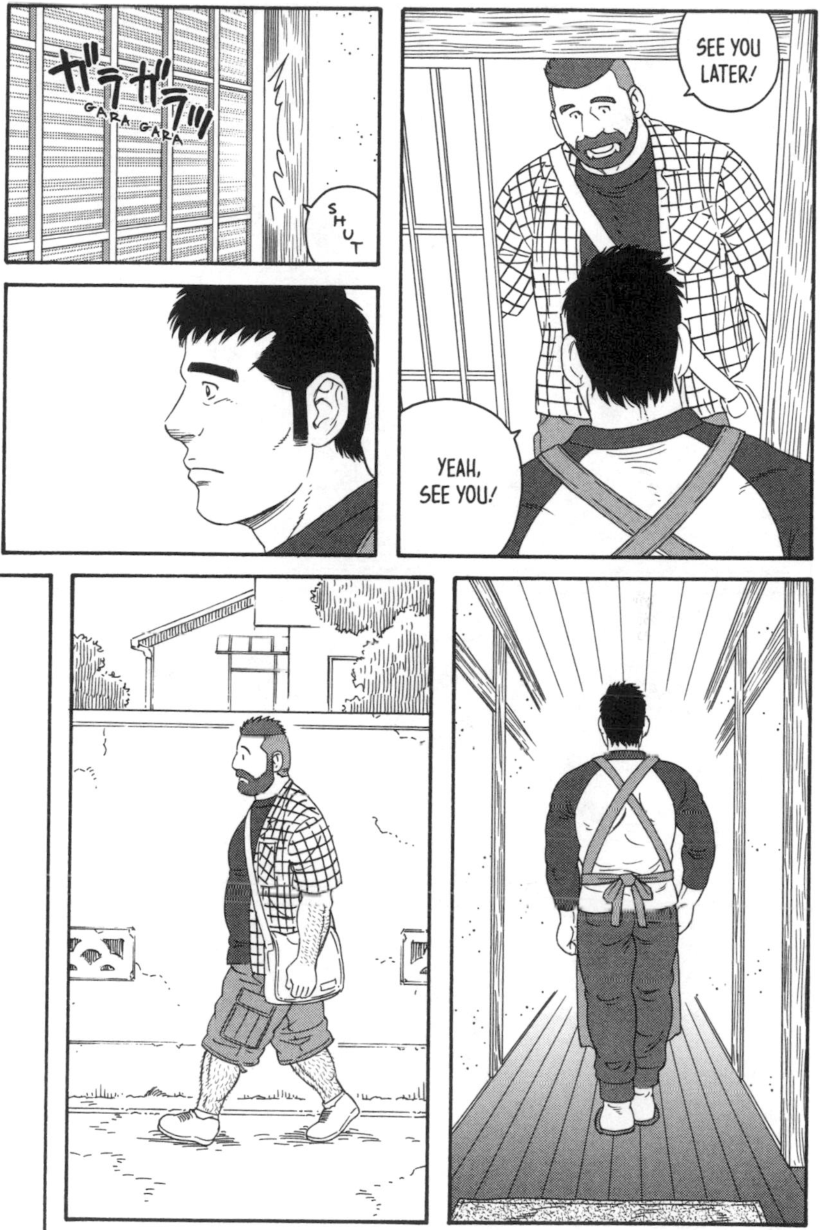
SEE YOU LATER!
YEAH, SEE YOU!
ガラガラッ
GARA GARA
SHUT

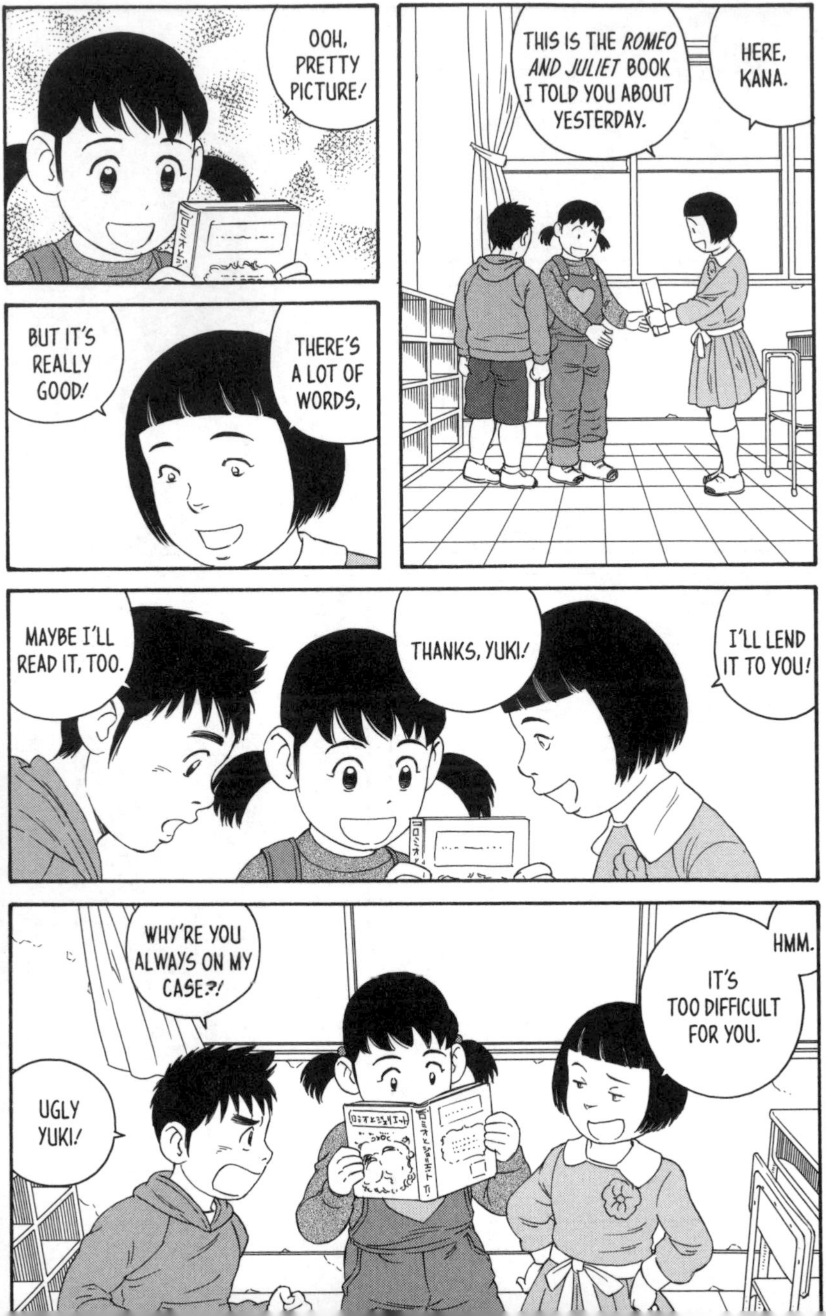
HERE, KANA.
THIS IS THE *ROMEO AND JULIET* BOOK I TOLD YOU ABOUT YESTERDAY.
OOH, PRETTY PICTURE!
THERE'S A LOT OF WORDS,
BUT IT'S REALLY GOOD!
I'LL LEND IT TO YOU!
THANKS, YUKI!
MAYBE I'LL READ IT, TOO.
HMM.
IT'S TOO DIFFICULT FOR YOU.
WHY'RE YOU ALWAYS ON MY CASE?!
UGLY YUKI!

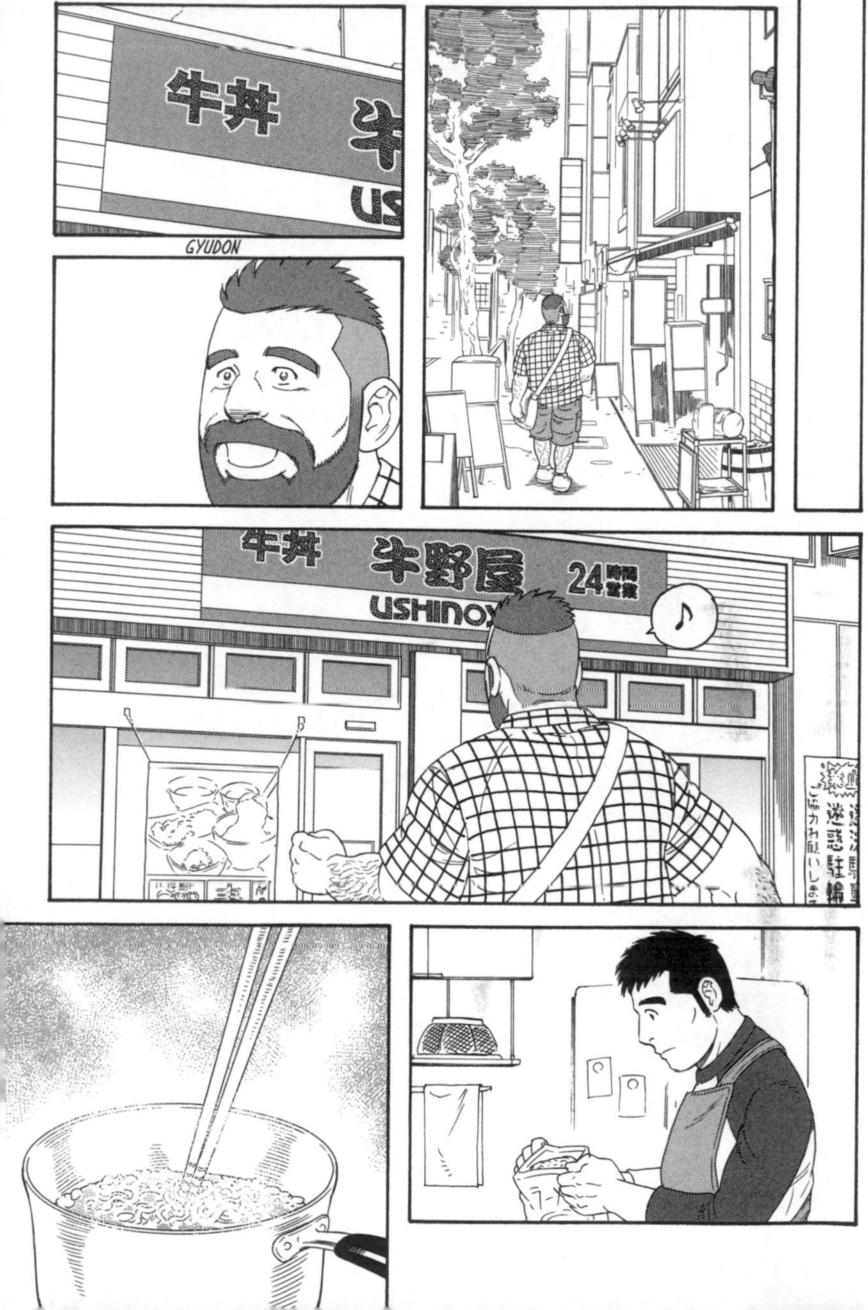

牛丼 牛
US
GYUDON
牛丼 牛野屋 24時間営業
USHINOY
♪

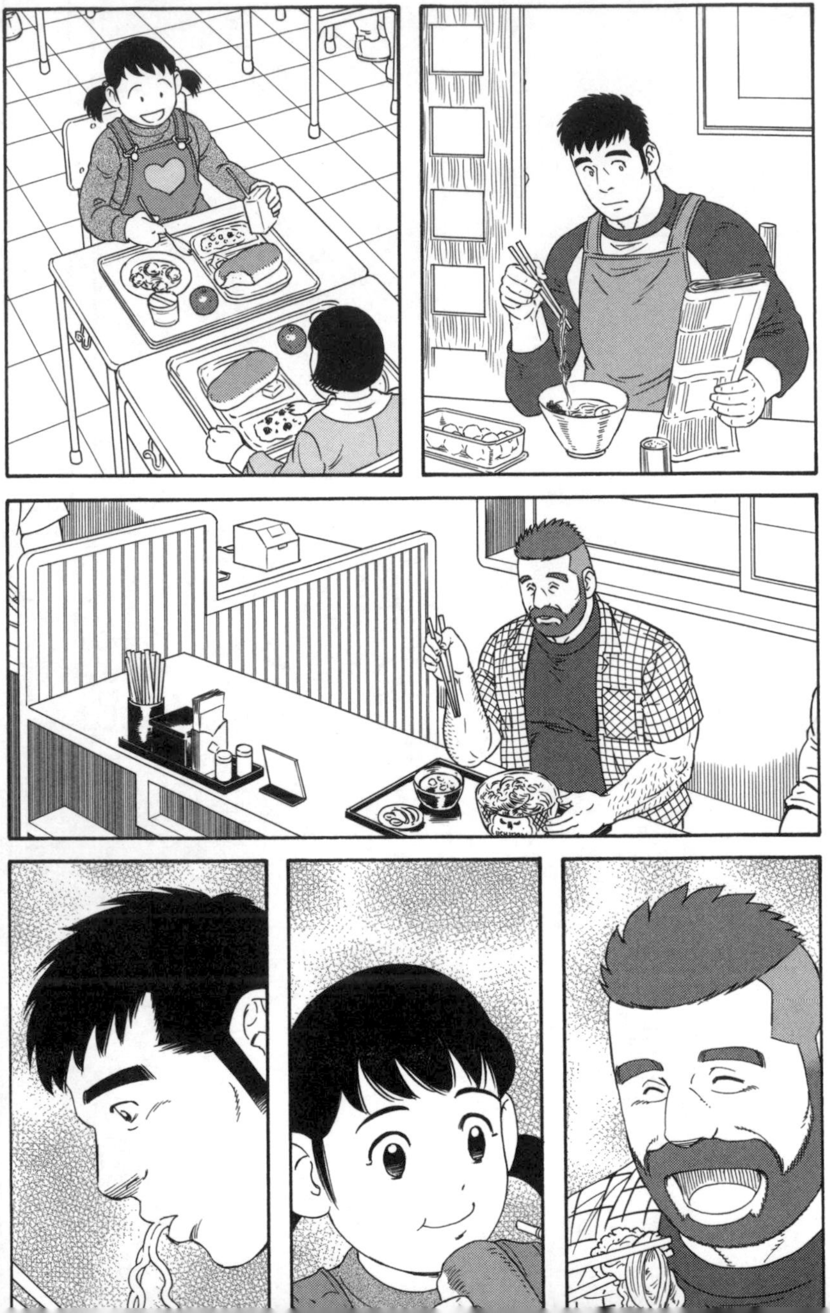

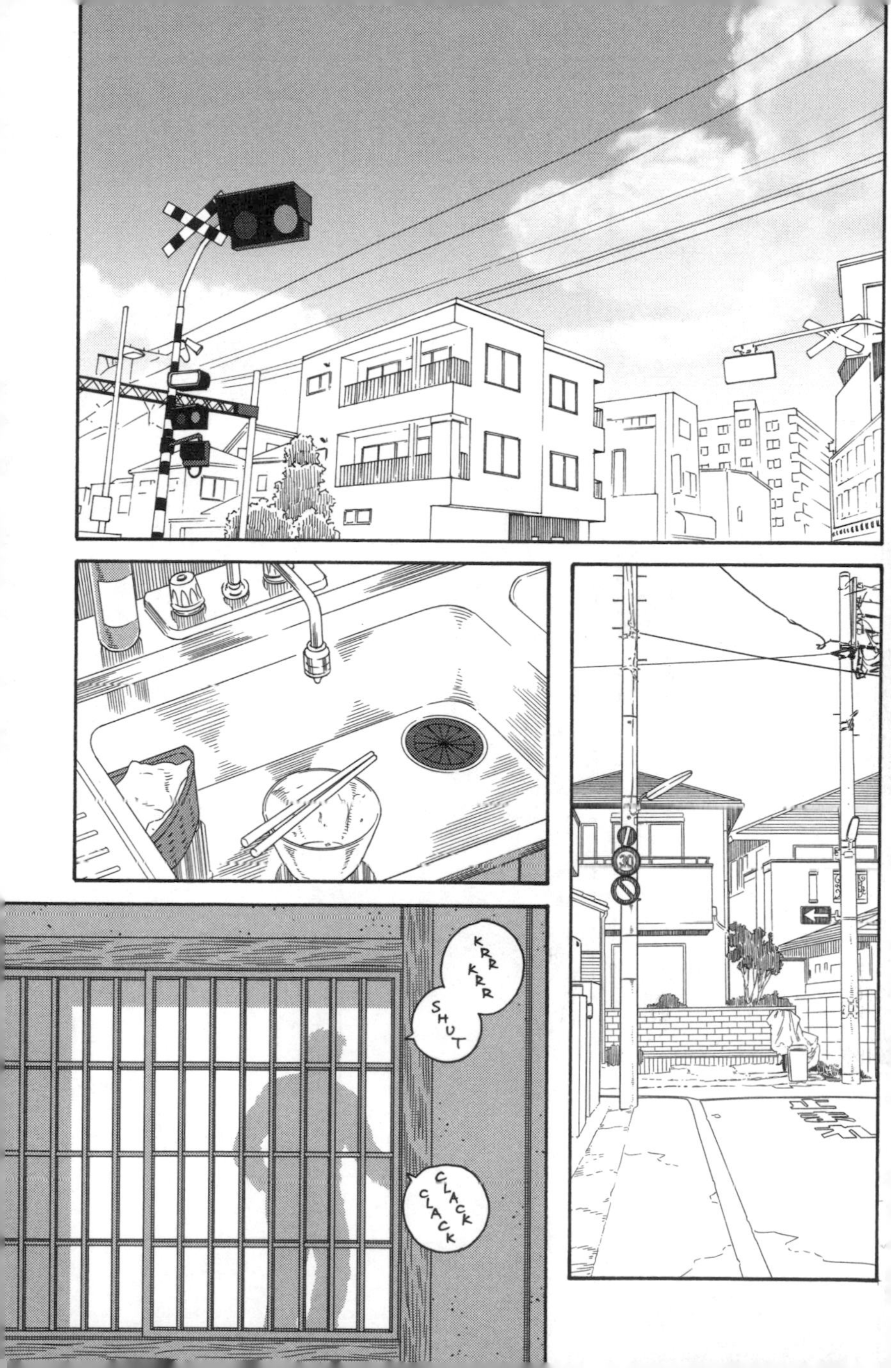
30
KRR KRR
SHUT
CLACK CLACK

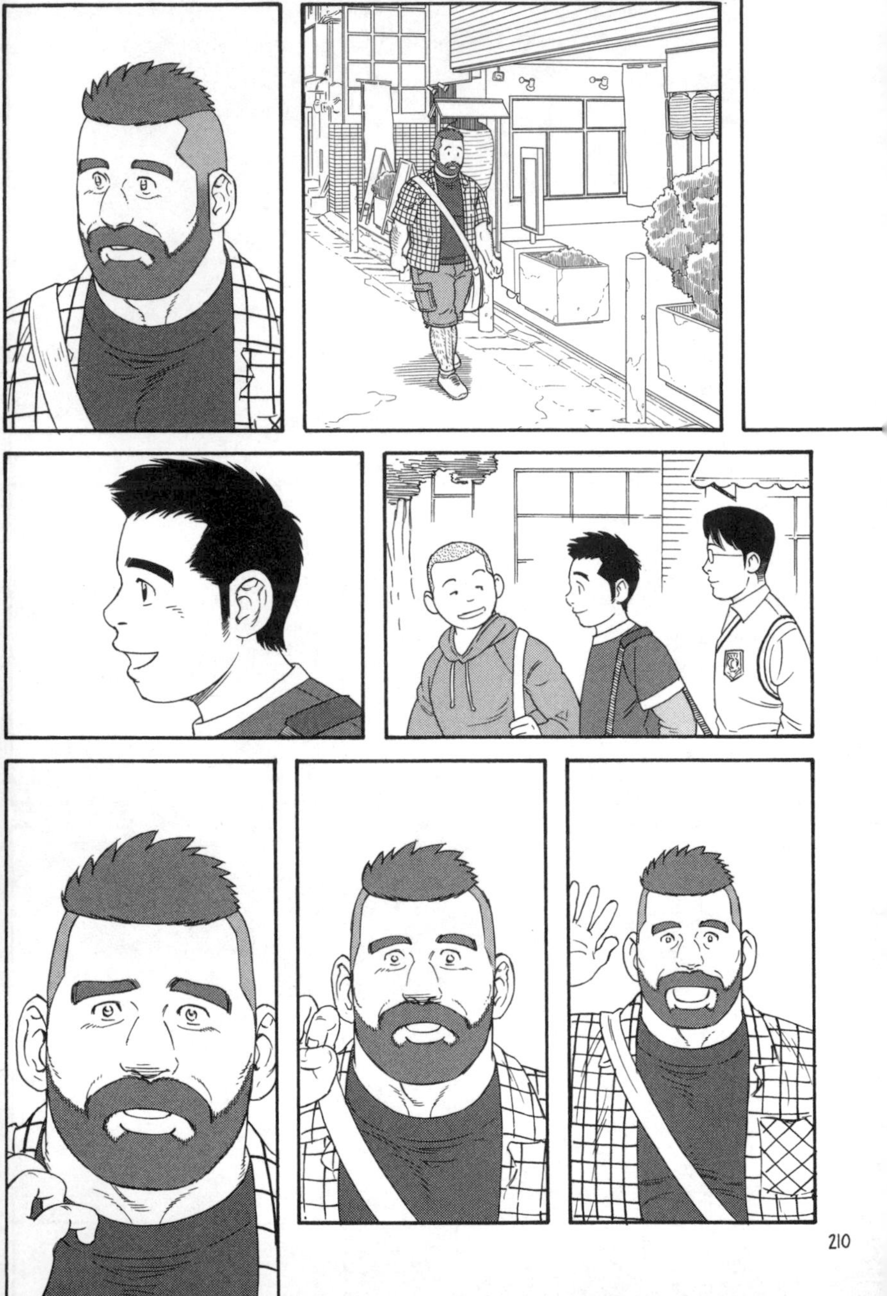

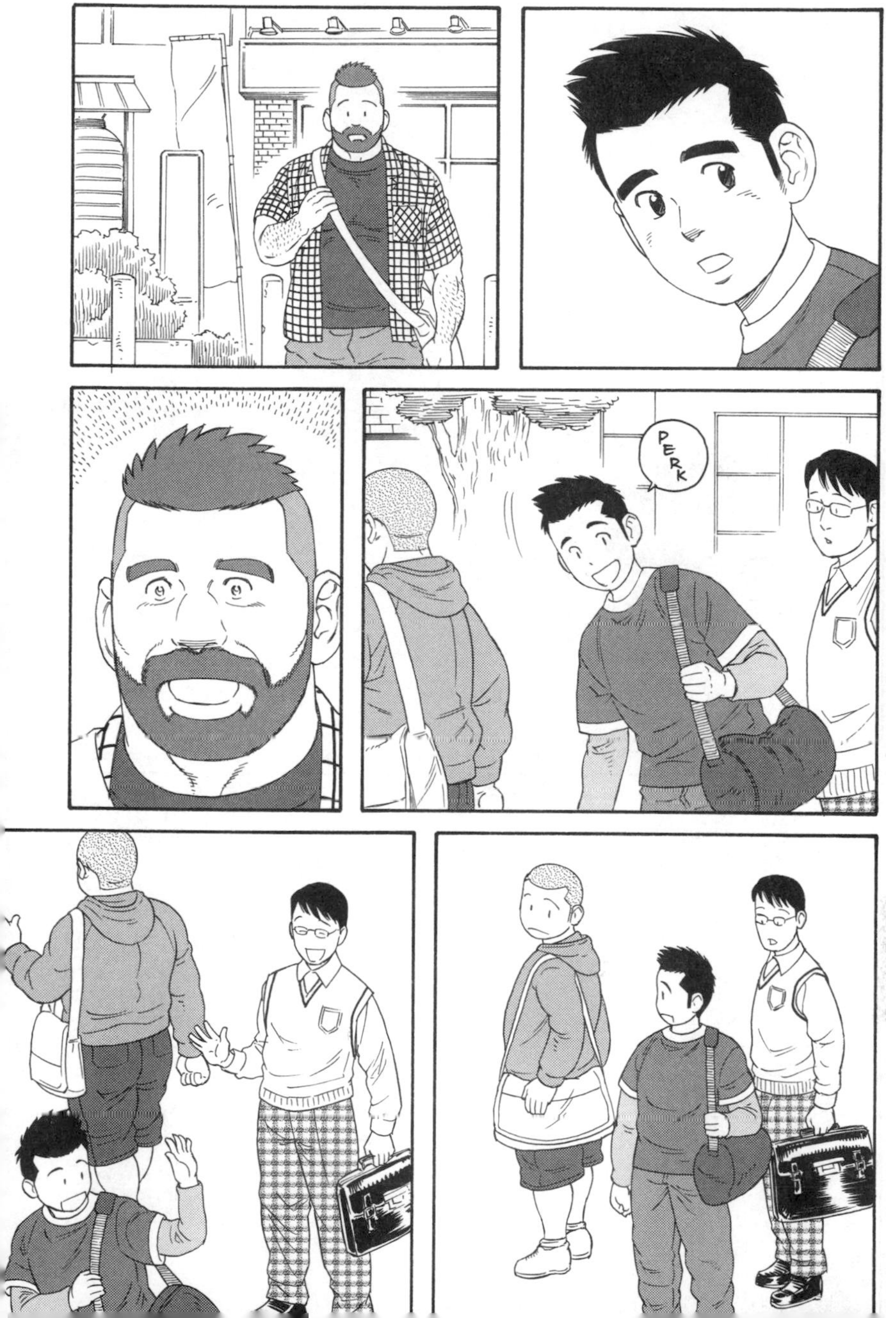
PERK

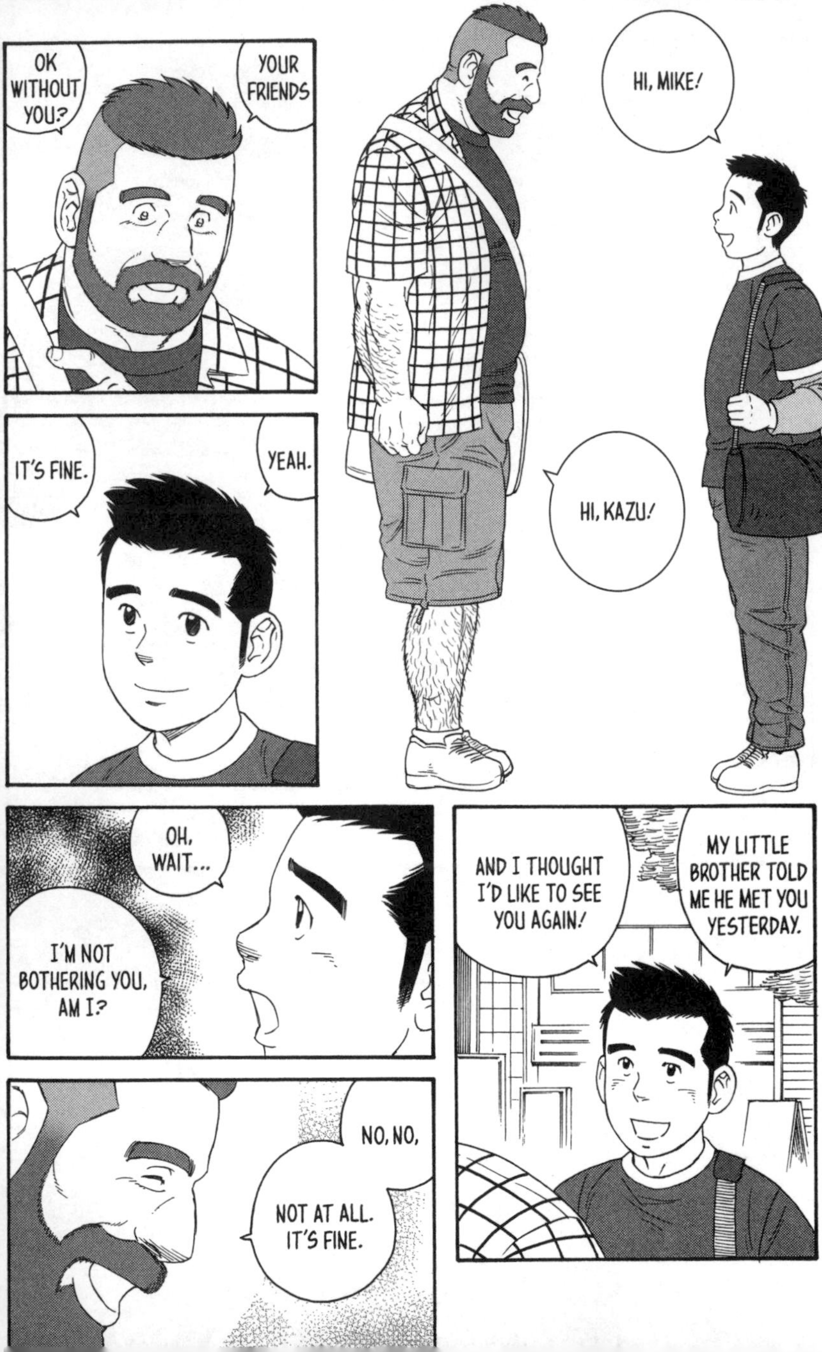
HI, MIKE!
HI, KAZU!
YOUR FRIENDS
OK WITHOUT YOU?
YEAH.
IT'S FINE.
MY LITTLE BROTHER TOLD ME HE MET YOU YESTERDAY.
AND I THOUGHT I'D LIKE TO SEE YOU AGAIN!
OH, WAIT...
I'M NOT BOTHERING YOU, AM I?
NO, NO,
NOT AT ALL. IT'S FINE.

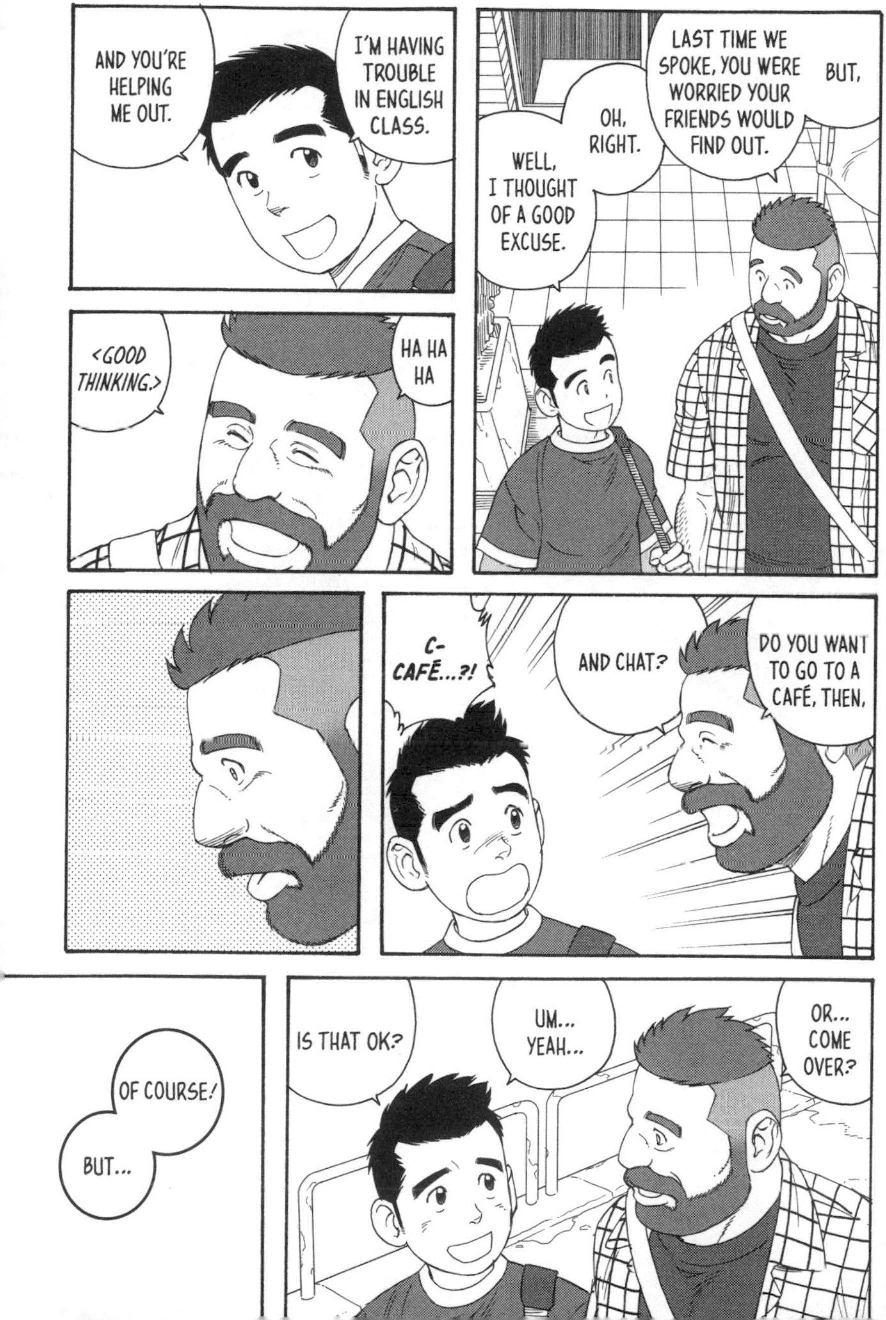
BUT,
LAST TIME WE SPOKE, YOU WERE WORRIED YOUR FRIENDS WOULD FIND OUT.
OH, RIGHT.
WELL, I THOUGHT OF A GOOD EXCUSE.
I'M HAVING TROUBLE IN ENGLISH CLASS.
AND YOU'RE HELPING ME OUT.
HA HA HA
<GOOD THINKING.>
DO YOU WANT TO GO TO A CAFÉ, THEN,
AND CHAT?
C-CAFÉ...?!
OR... COME OVER?
UM... YEAH...
IS THAT OK?
OF COURSE!
BUT...

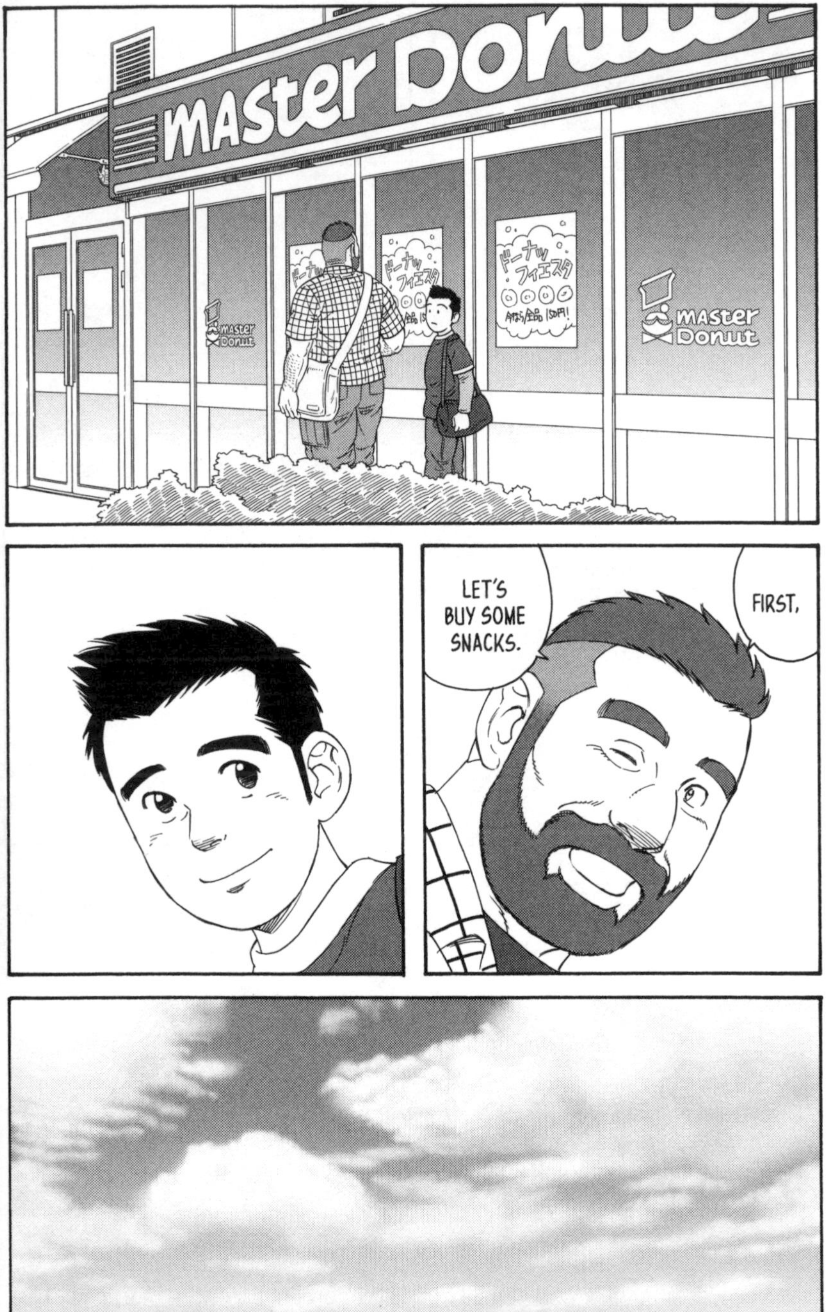
master Donut
ドーナツ フィエスタ
今なら全品150円!
master Donut
FIRST,
LET'S BUY SOME SNACKS.

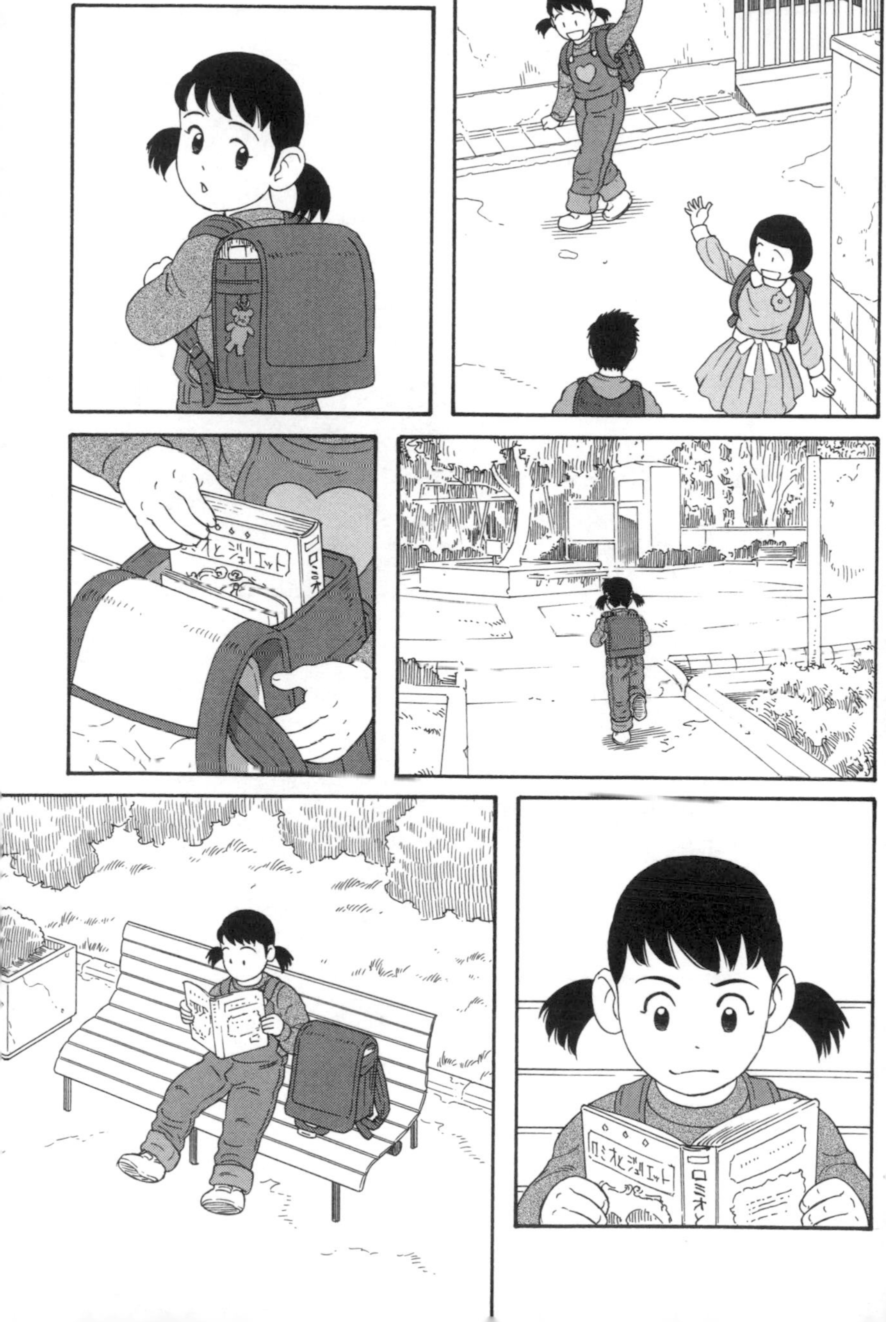
ロミオとジュリエット

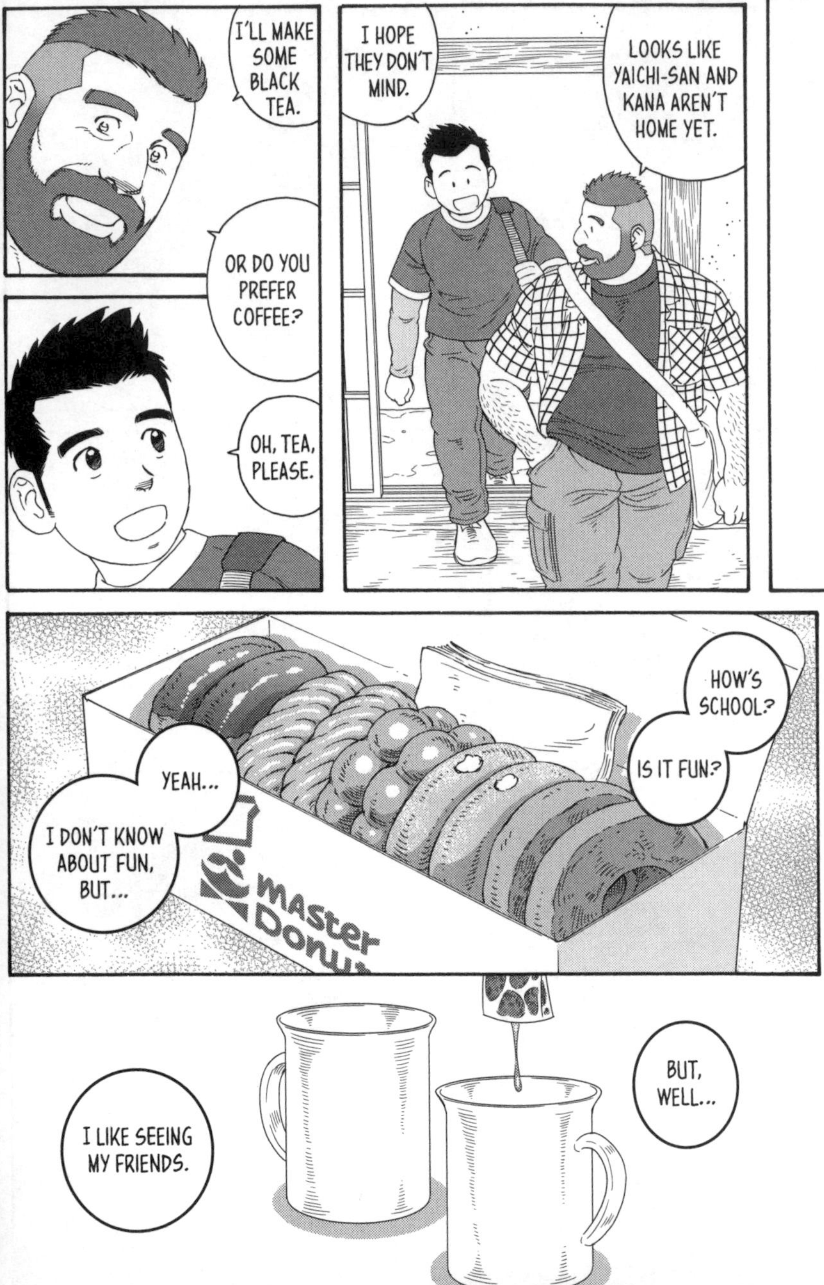
LOOKS LIKE YAICHI-SAN AND KANA AREN'T HOME YET.
I HOPE THEY DON'T MIND.
I'LL MAKE SOME BLACK TEA.
OR DO YOU PREFER COFFEE?
OH, TEA, PLEASE.
HOW'S SCHOOL?
IS IT FUN?
YEAH...
I DON'T KNOW ABOUT FUN, BUT...
master Donut
BUT, WELL...
I LIKE SEEING MY FRIENDS.

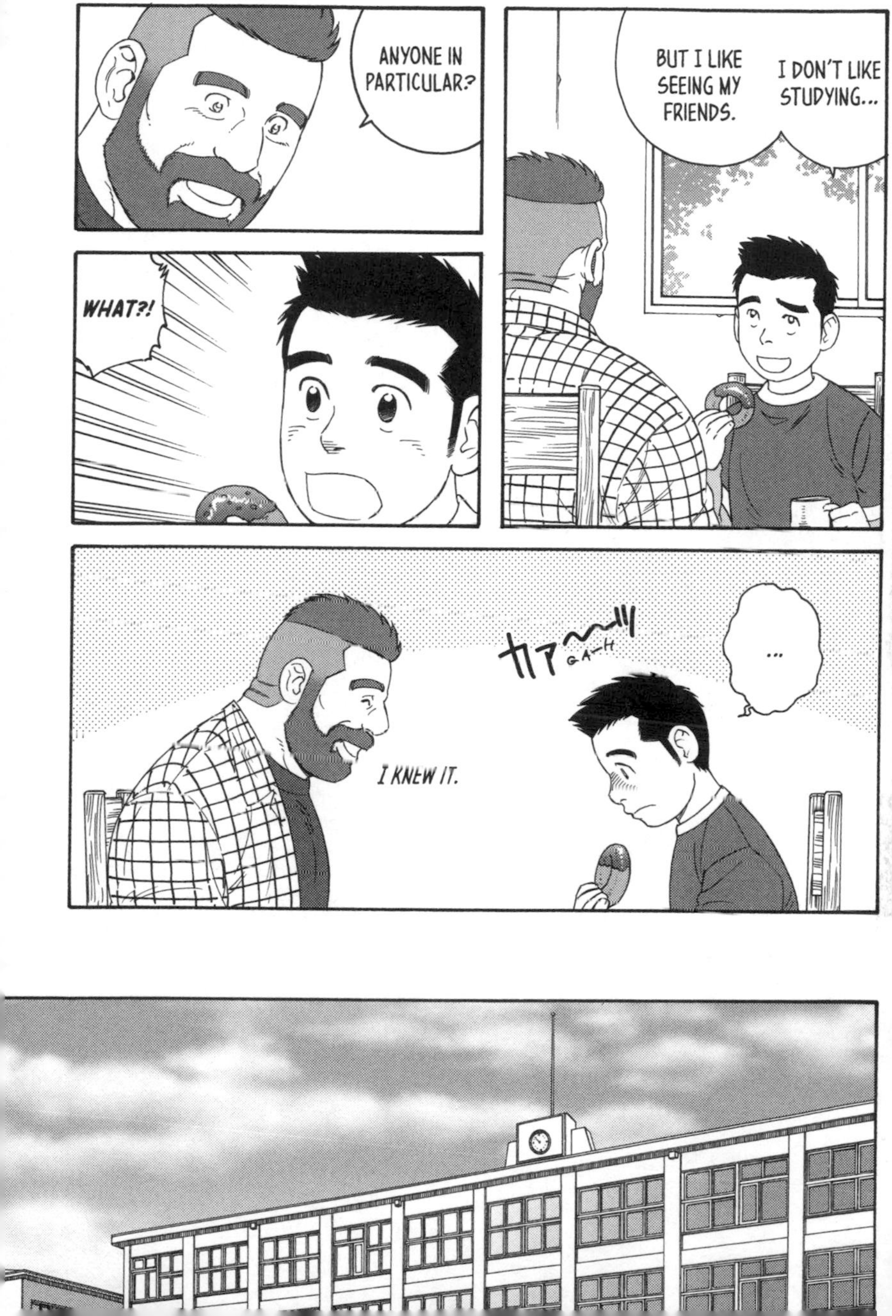
I DON'T LIKE STUDYING...
BUT I LIKE SEEING MY FRIENDS.
ANYONE IN PARTICULAR?
WHAT?!
...
カァ〜ッ
GA-H
I KNEW IT.

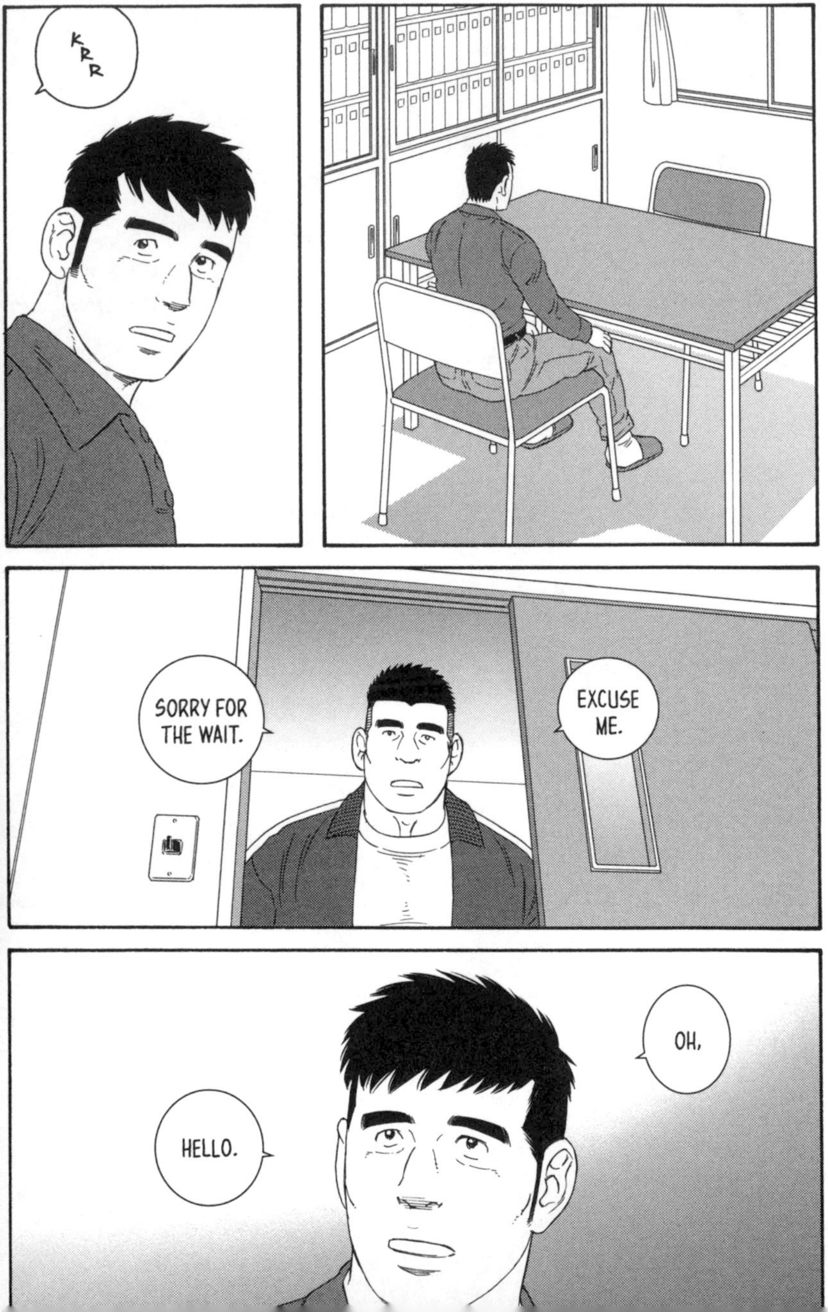
KRR
EXCUSE ME.
SORRY FOR THE WAIT.
OH,
HELLO.

CHAPTER TWENTY-FOUR

MEATBALL HOT POT

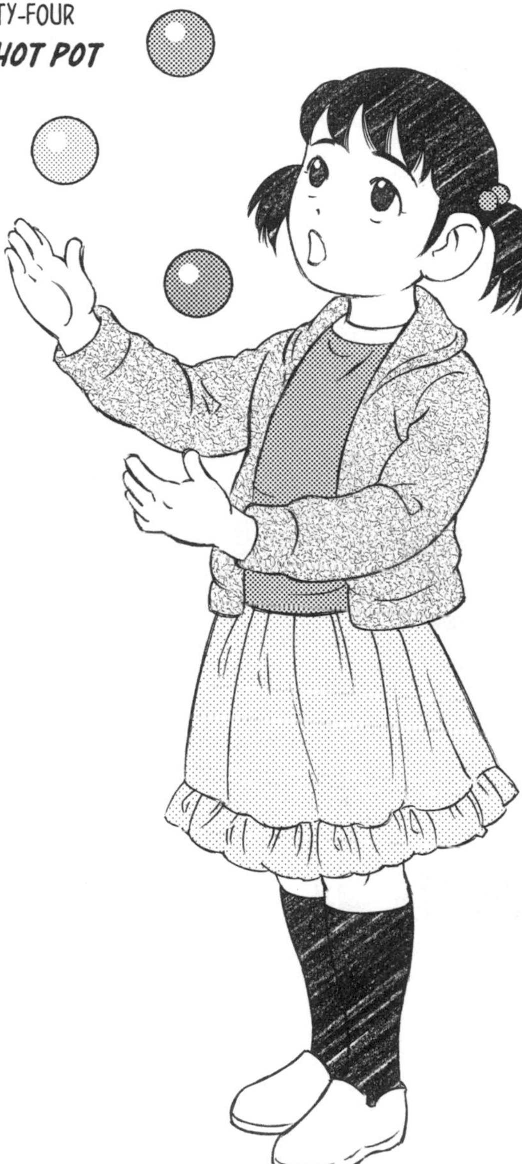

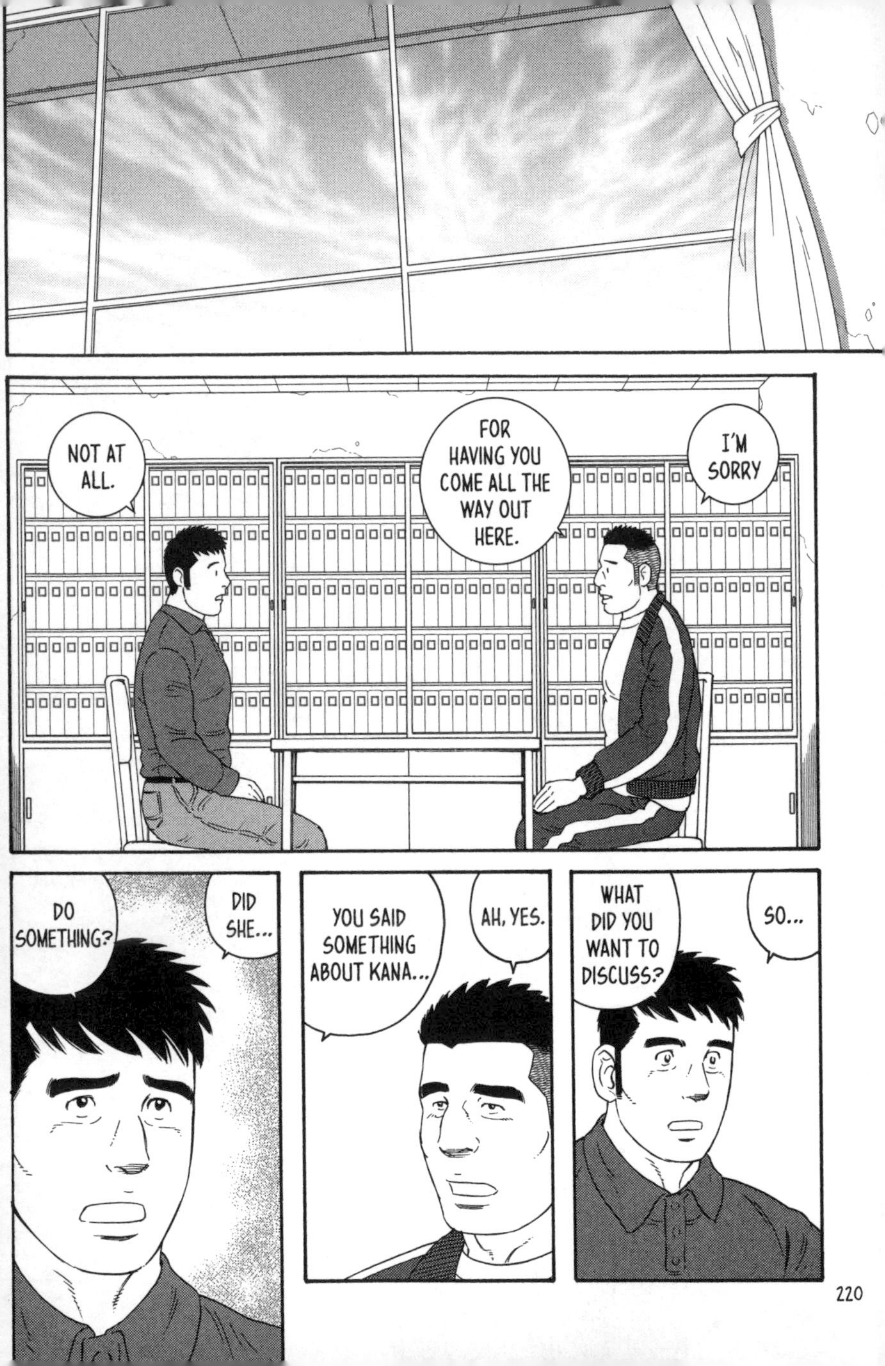
I'M SORRY
FOR HAVING YOU COME ALL THE WAY OUT HERE.
NOT AT ALL.
SO...
WHAT DID YOU WANT TO DISCUSS?
AH, YES.
YOU SAID SOMETHING ABOUT KANA...
DID SHE...
DO SOMETHING?

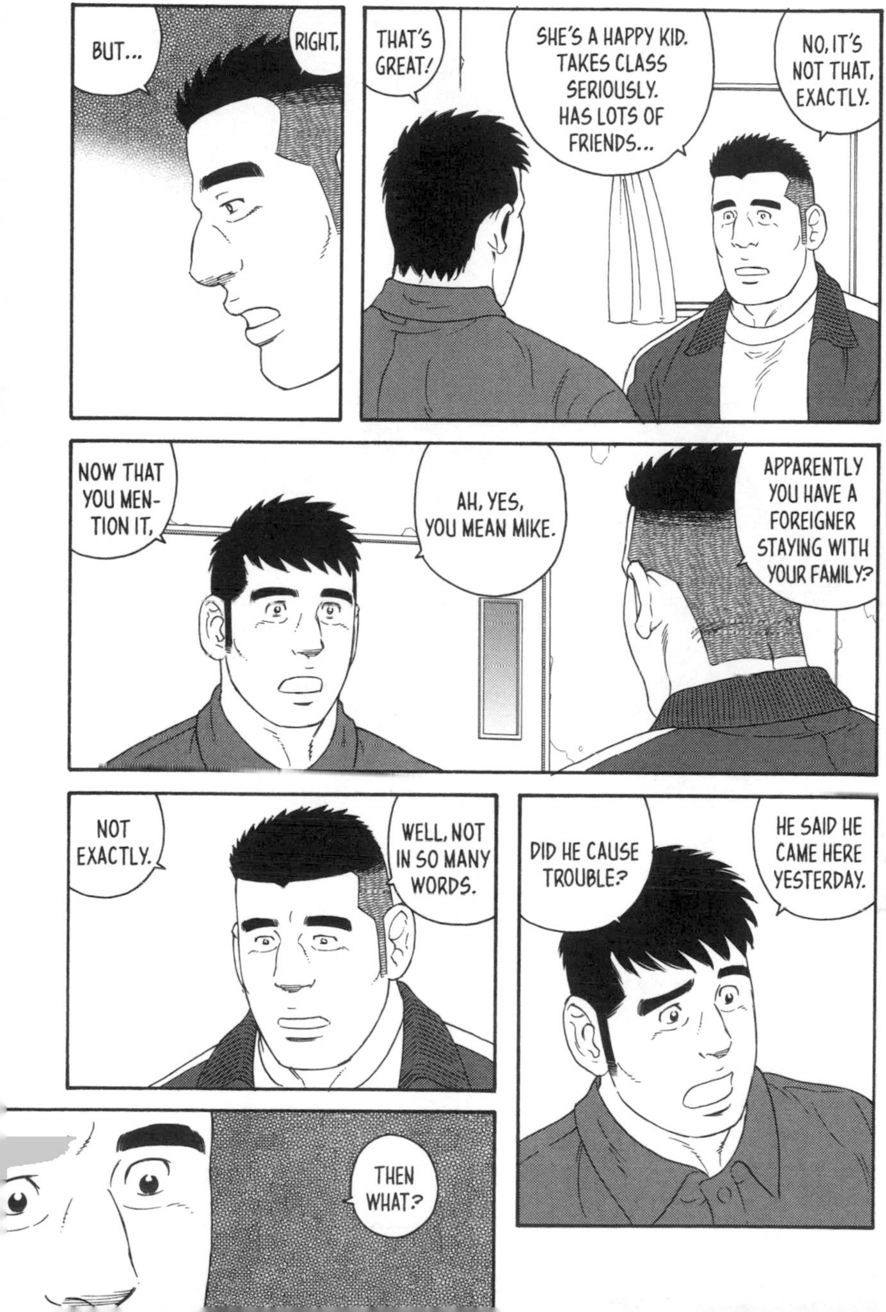
NO, IT'S NOT THAT, EXACTLY.
SHE'S A HAPPY KID. TAKES CLASS SERIOUSLY. HAS LOTS OF FRIENDS...
THAT'S GREAT!
RIGHT,
BUT...
APPARENTLY YOU HAVE A FOREIGNER STAYING WITH YOUR FAMILY?
AH, YES, YOU MEAN MIKE.
NOW THAT YOU MEN-TION IT,
HE SAID HE CAME HERE YESTERDAY.
DID HE CAUSE TROUBLE?
WELL, NOT IN SO MANY WORDS.
NOT EXACTLY.
THEN WHAT?

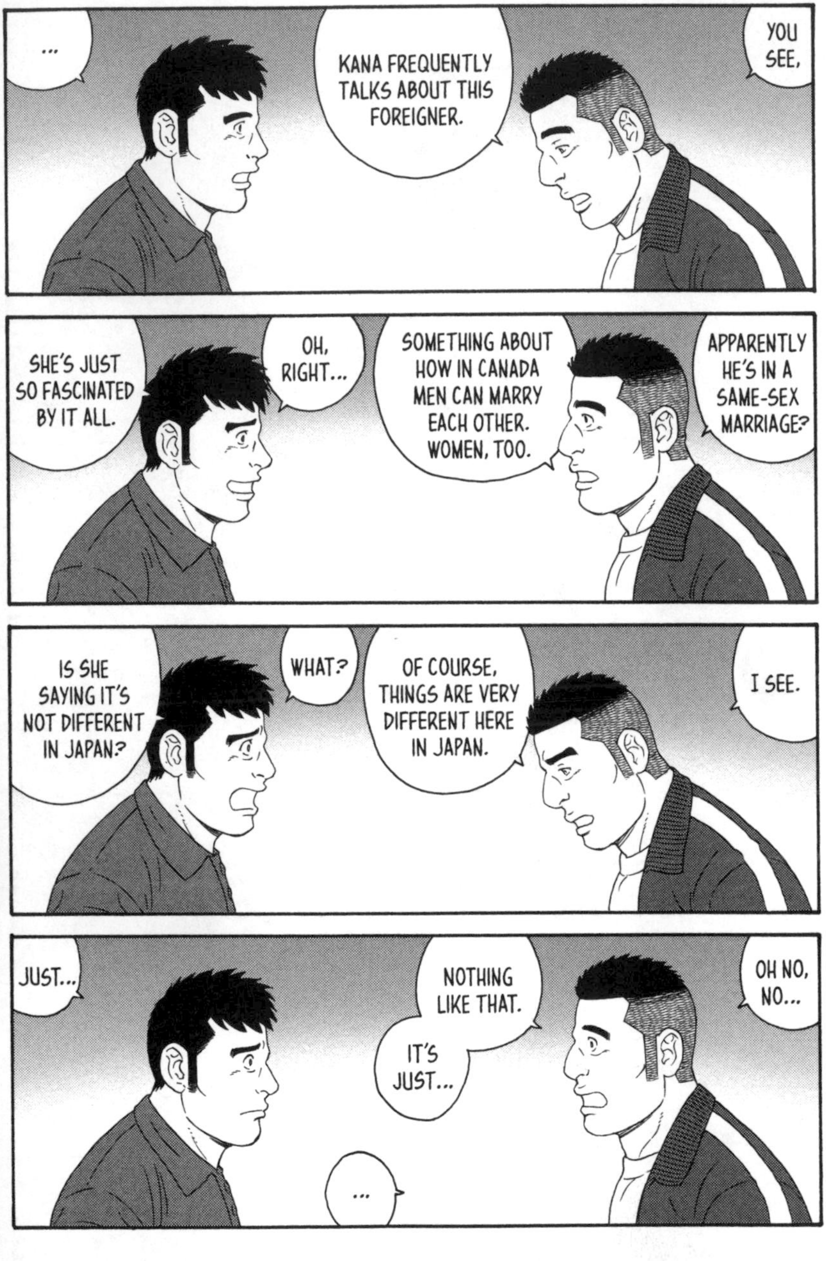
YOU SEE,
KANA FREQUENTLY TALKS ABOUT THIS FOREIGNER.
...
APPARENTLY HE'S IN A SAME-SEX MARRIAGE?
SOMETHING ABOUT HOW IN CANADA MEN CAN MARRY EACH OTHER. WOMEN, TOO.
OH, RIGHT...
SHE'S JUST SO FASCINATED BY IT ALL.
I SEE.
OF COURSE, THINGS ARE VERY DIFFERENT HERE IN JAPAN.
WHAT?
IS SHE SAYING IT'S NOT DIFFERENT IN JAPAN?
OH NO, NO...
NOTHING LIKE THAT.
IT'S JUST...
JUST...
...

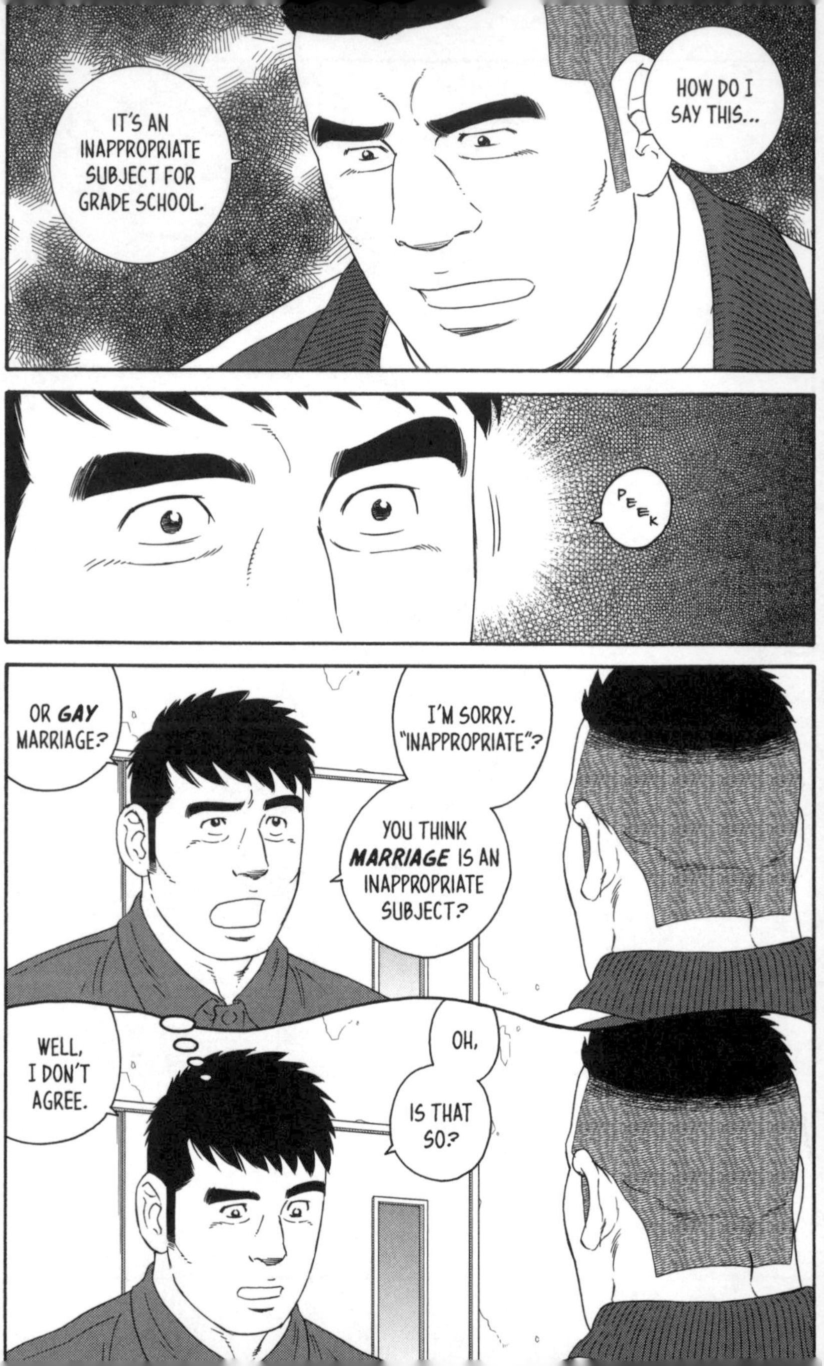
HOW DO I SAY THIS...
IT'S AN INAPPROPRIATE SUBJECT FOR GRADE SCHOOL.
PEEK
I'M SORRY. "INAPPROPRIATE"?
YOU THINK **MARRIAGE** IS AN INAPPROPRIATE SUBJECT?
OR **GAY** MARRIAGE?
OH,
IS THAT SO?
WELL, I DON'T AGREE.

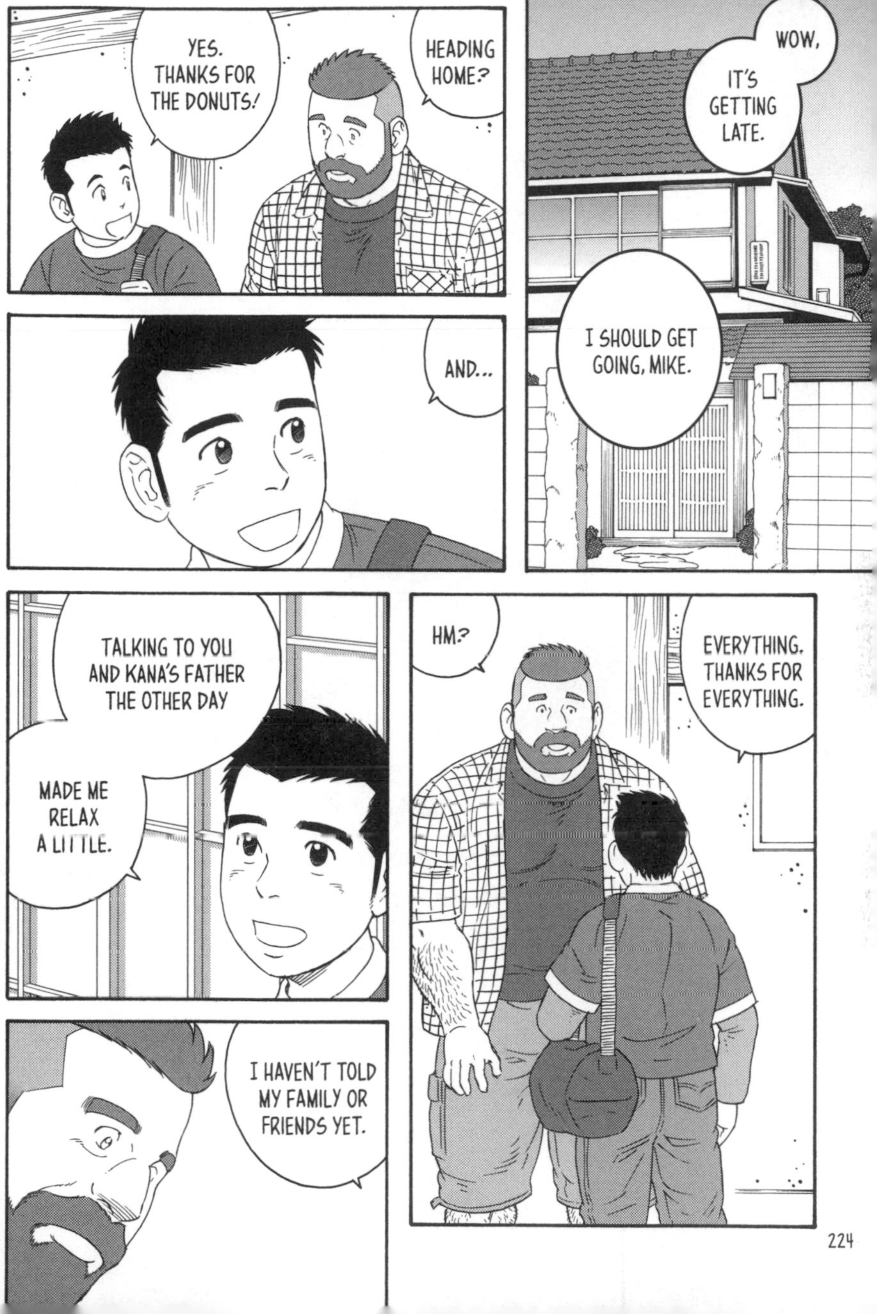
WOW,
IT'S GETTING LATE.
I SHOULD GET GOING, MIKE.
HEADING HOME?
YES. THANKS FOR THE DONUTS!
AND...
TALKING TO YOU AND KANA'S FATHER THE OTHER DAY
MADE ME RELAX A LITTLE.
I HAVEN'T TOLD MY FAMILY OR FRIENDS YET.
HM?
EVERYTHING. THANKS FOR EVERYTHING.

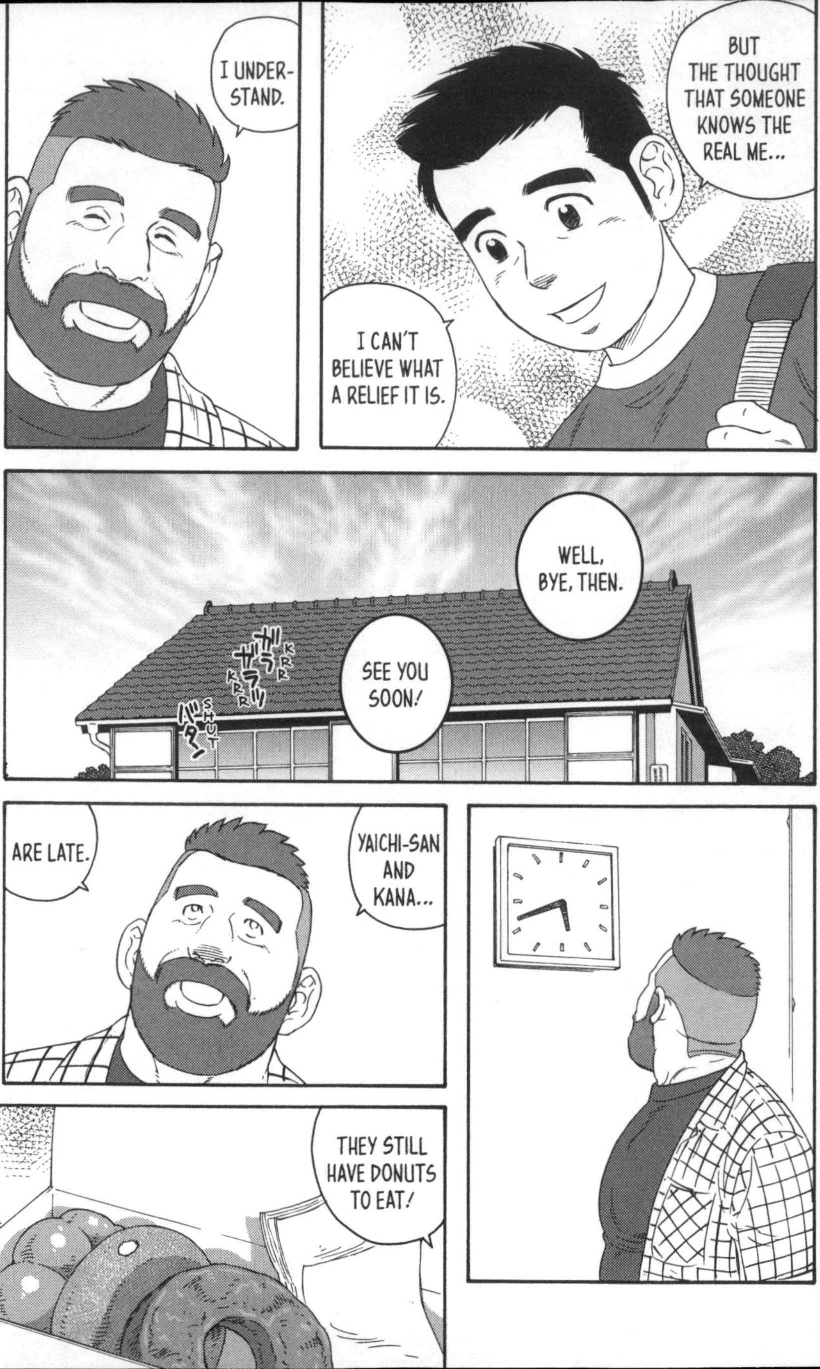
BUT THE THOUGHT THAT SOMEONE KNOWS THE REAL ME...
I CAN'T BELIEVE WHAT A RELIEF IT IS.
I UNDER-STAND.
WELL, BYE, THEN.
SEE YOU SOON!
ガラ KRR
ガラッ KRR
バタン SHUT
YAICHI-SAN AND KANA...
ARE LATE.
THEY STILL HAVE DONUTS TO EAT!

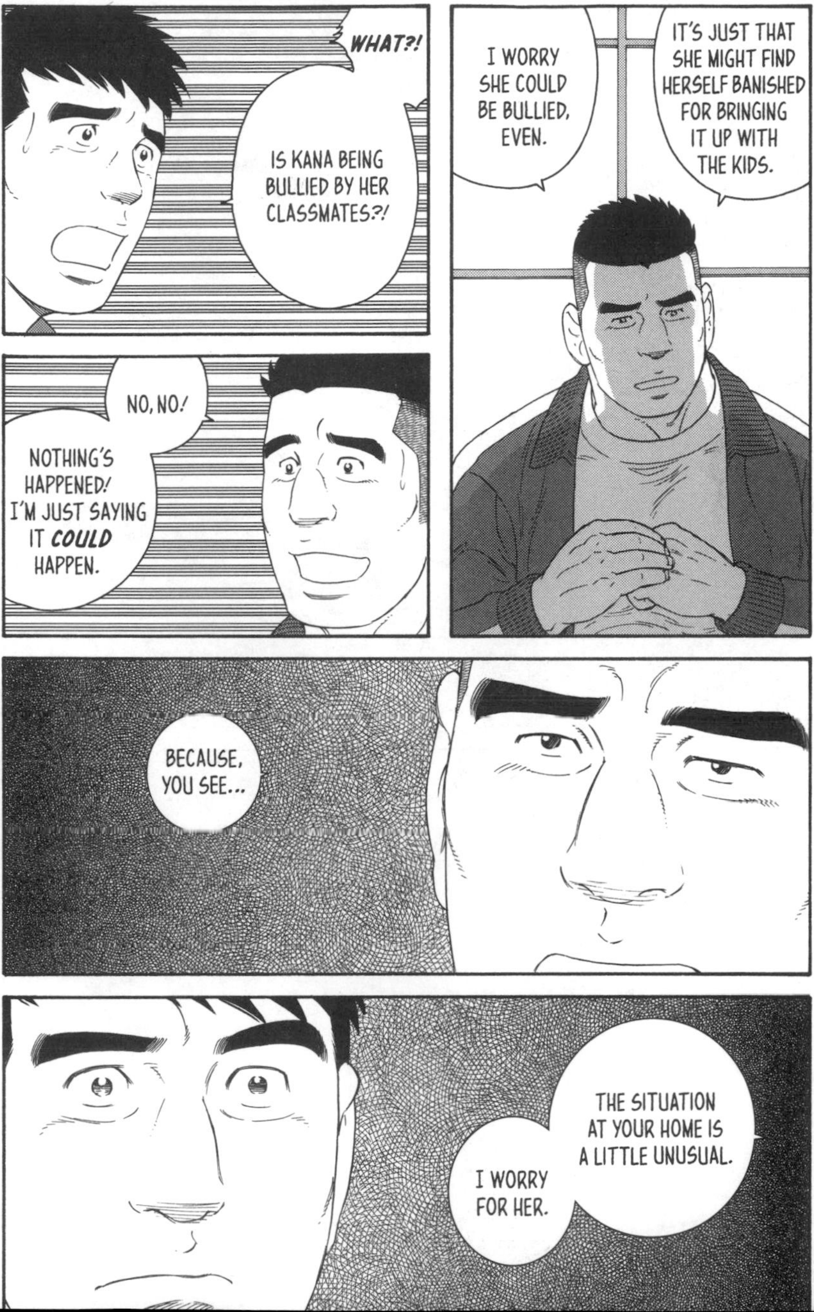
IT'S JUST THAT SHE MIGHT FIND HERSELF BANISHED FOR BRINGING IT UP WITH THE KIDS.
I WORRY SHE COULD BE BULLIED, EVEN.
WHAT?!
IS KANA BEING BULLIED BY HER CLASSMATES?!
NO, NO!
NOTHING'S HAPPENED! I'M JUST SAYING IT *COULD* HAPPEN.
BECAUSE, YOU SEE...
THE SITUATION AT YOUR HOME IS A LITTLE UNUSUAL.
I WORRY FOR HER.

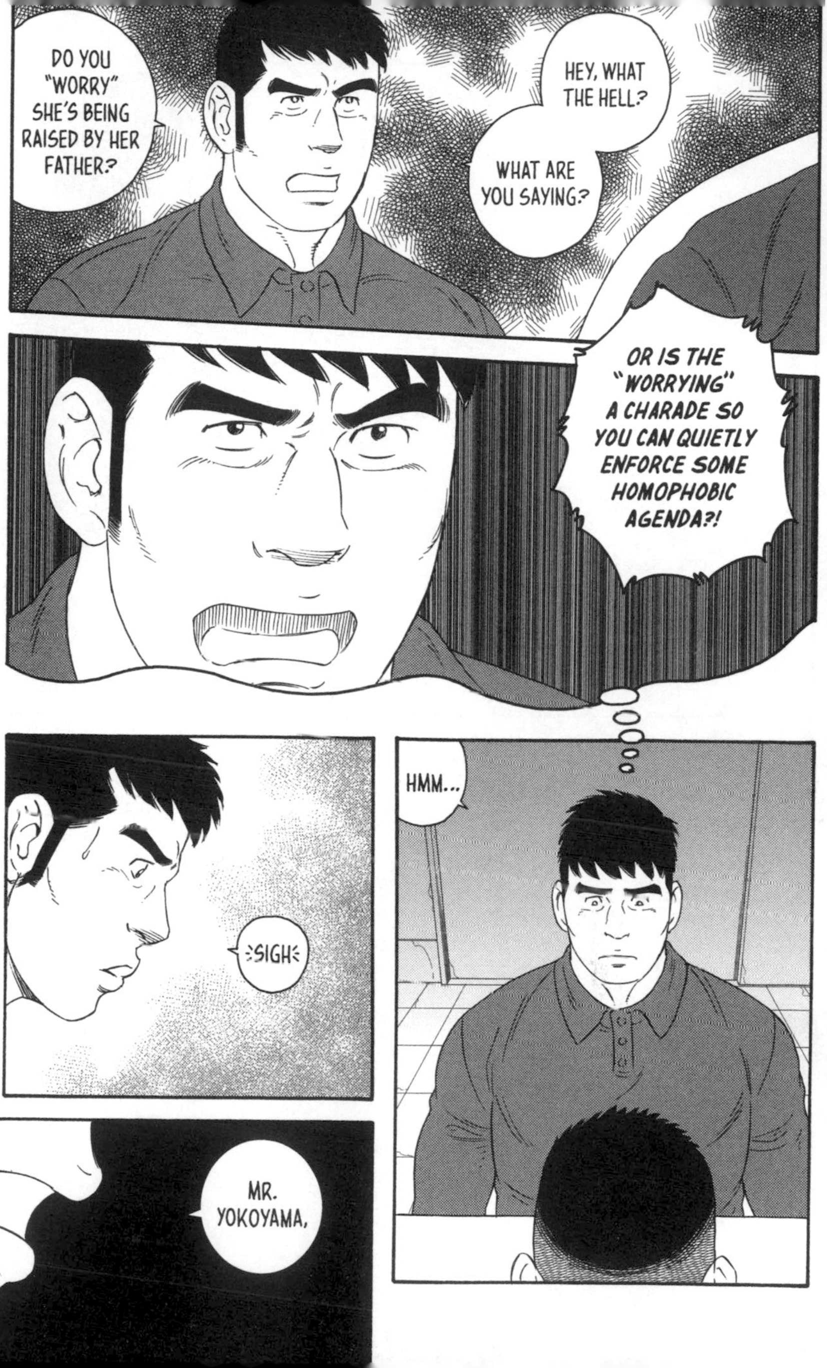
HEY, WHAT THE HELL?
WHAT ARE YOU SAYING?
DO YOU "WORRY" SHE'S BEING RAISED BY HER FATHER?
OR IS THE "WORRYING" A CHARADE SO YOU CAN QUIETLY ENFORCE SOME HOMOPHOBIC AGENDA?!
HMM...
SIGH
MR. YOKOYAMA,

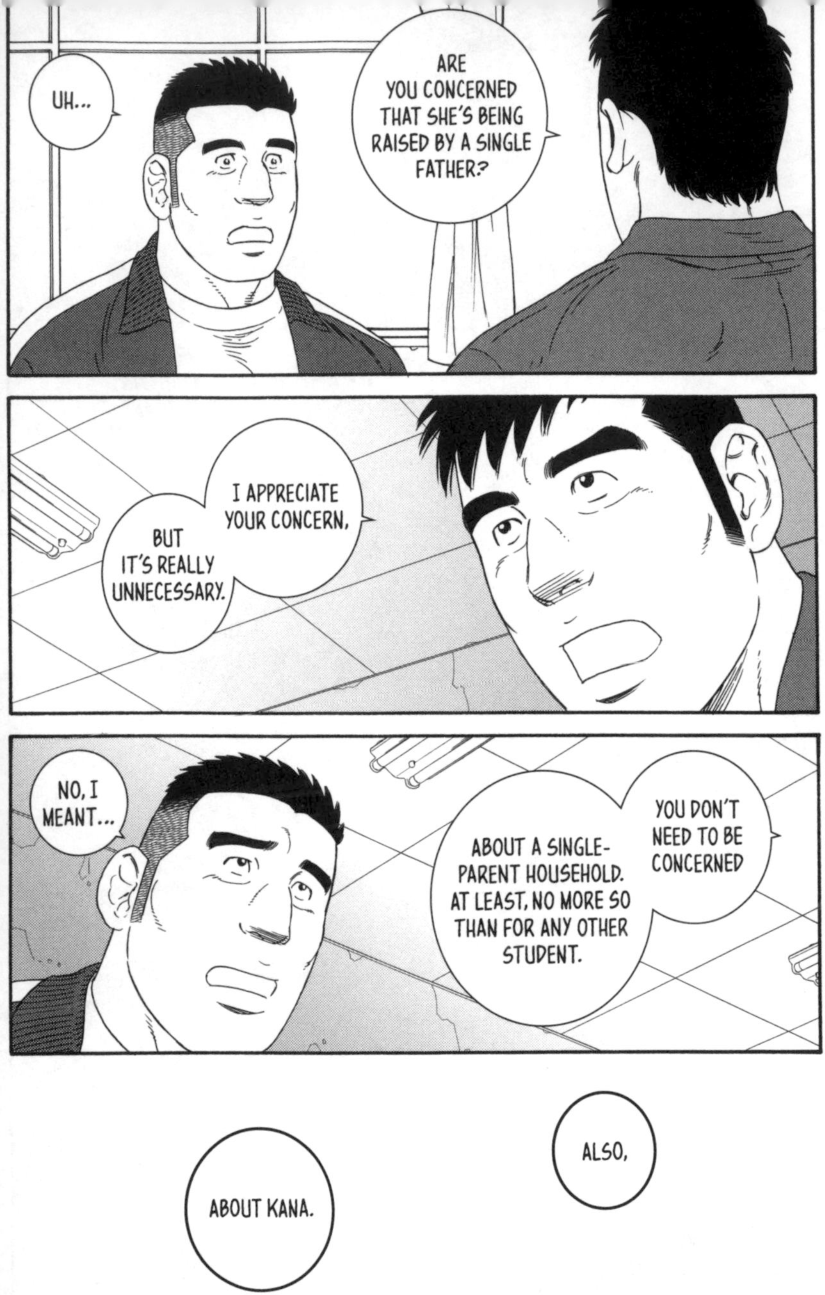
ARE YOU CONCERNED THAT SHE'S BEING RAISED BY A SINGLE FATHER?
UH...
I APPRECIATE YOUR CONCERN,
BUT IT'S REALLY UNNECESSARY.
YOU DON'T NEED TO BE CONCERNED
ABOUT A SINGLE-PARENT HOUSEHOLD. AT LEAST, NO MORE SO THAN FOR ANY OTHER STUDENT.
NO, I MEANT...
ALSO,
ABOUT KANA.

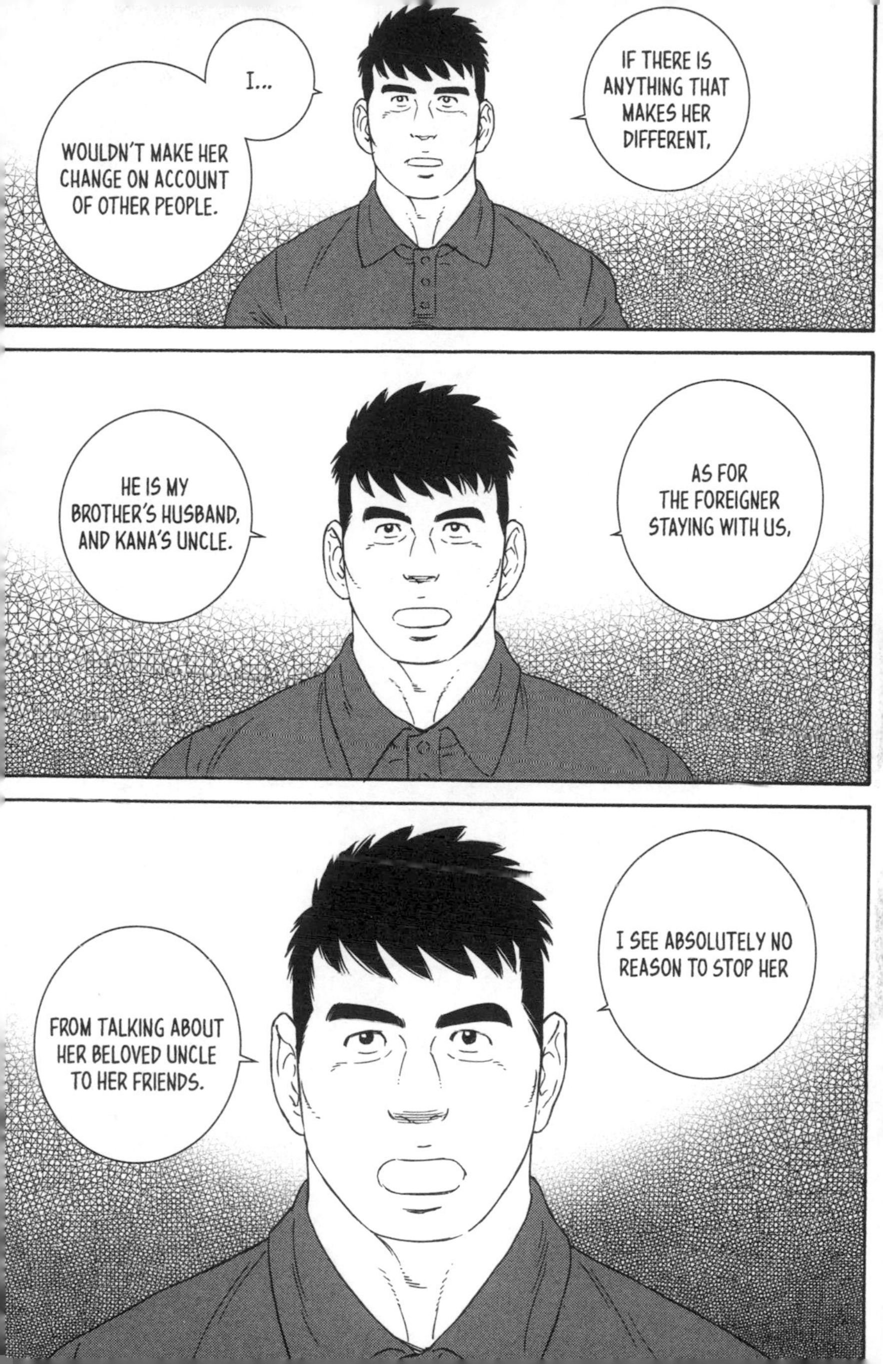
IF THERE IS ANYTHING THAT MAKES HER DIFFERENT,
I...
WOULDN'T MAKE HER CHANGE ON ACCOUNT OF OTHER PEOPLE.
AS FOR THE FOREIGNER STAYING WITH US,
HE IS MY BROTHER'S HUSBAND, AND KANA'S UNCLE.
I SEE ABSOLUTELY NO REASON TO STOP HER
FROM TALKING ABOUT HER BELOVED UNCLE TO HER FRIENDS.

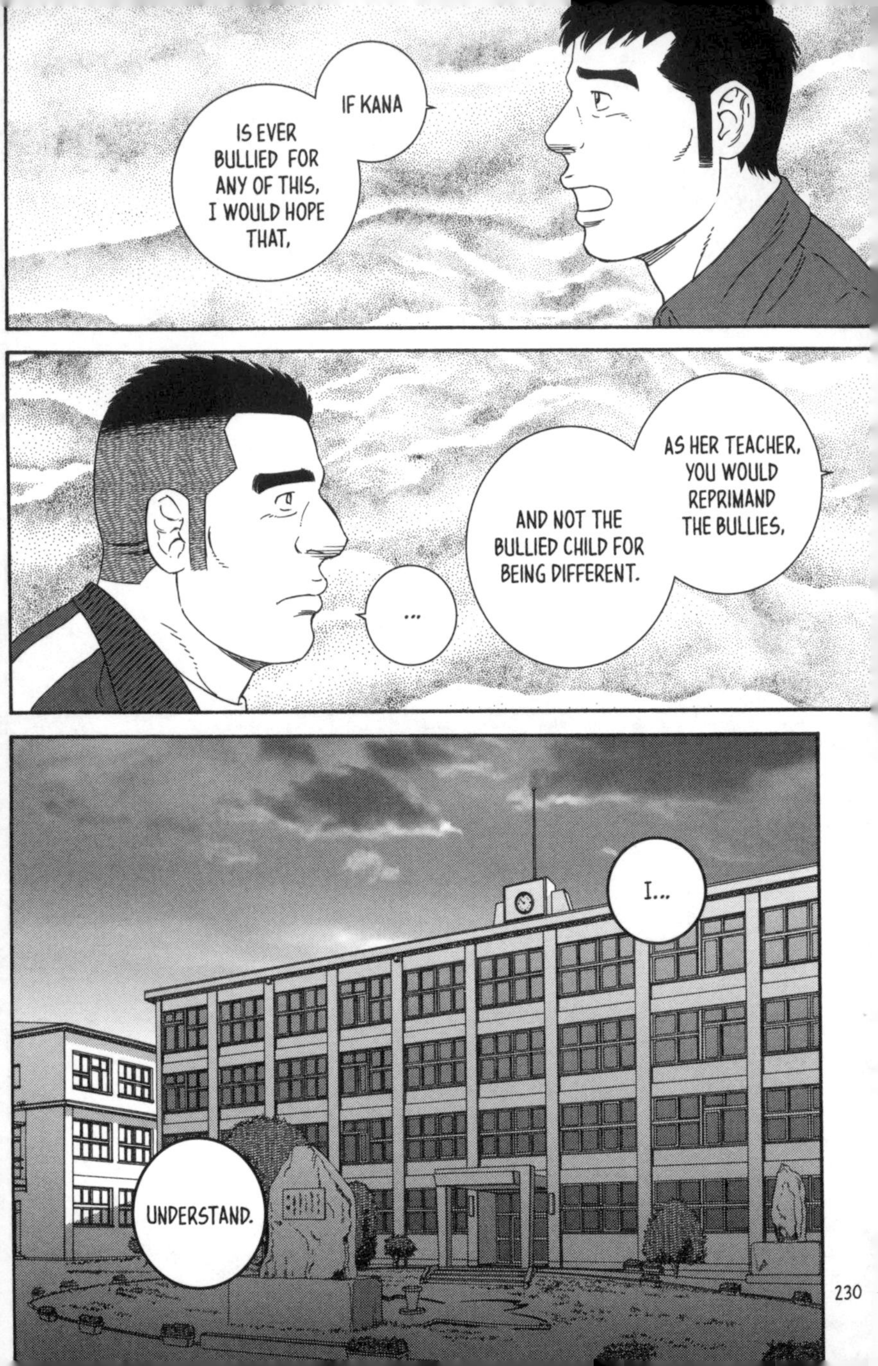
IF KANA
IS EVER BULLIED FOR ANY OF THIS, I WOULD HOPE THAT,
AS HER TEACHER, YOU WOULD REPRIMAND THE BULLIES,
AND NOT THE BULLIED CHILD FOR BEING DIFFERENT.
...
I...
UNDERSTAND.

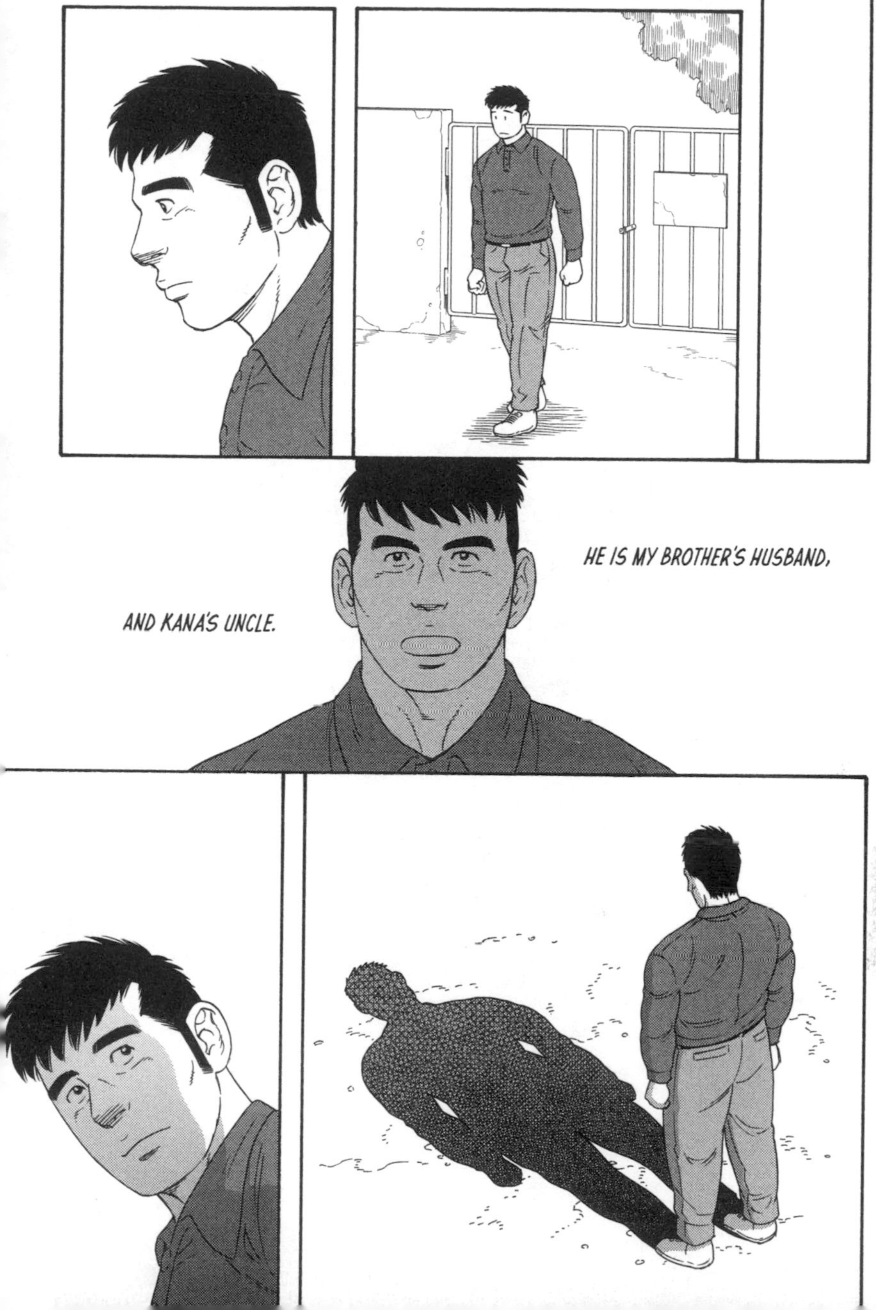
HE IS MY BROTHER'S HUSBAND,
AND KANA'S UNCLE.

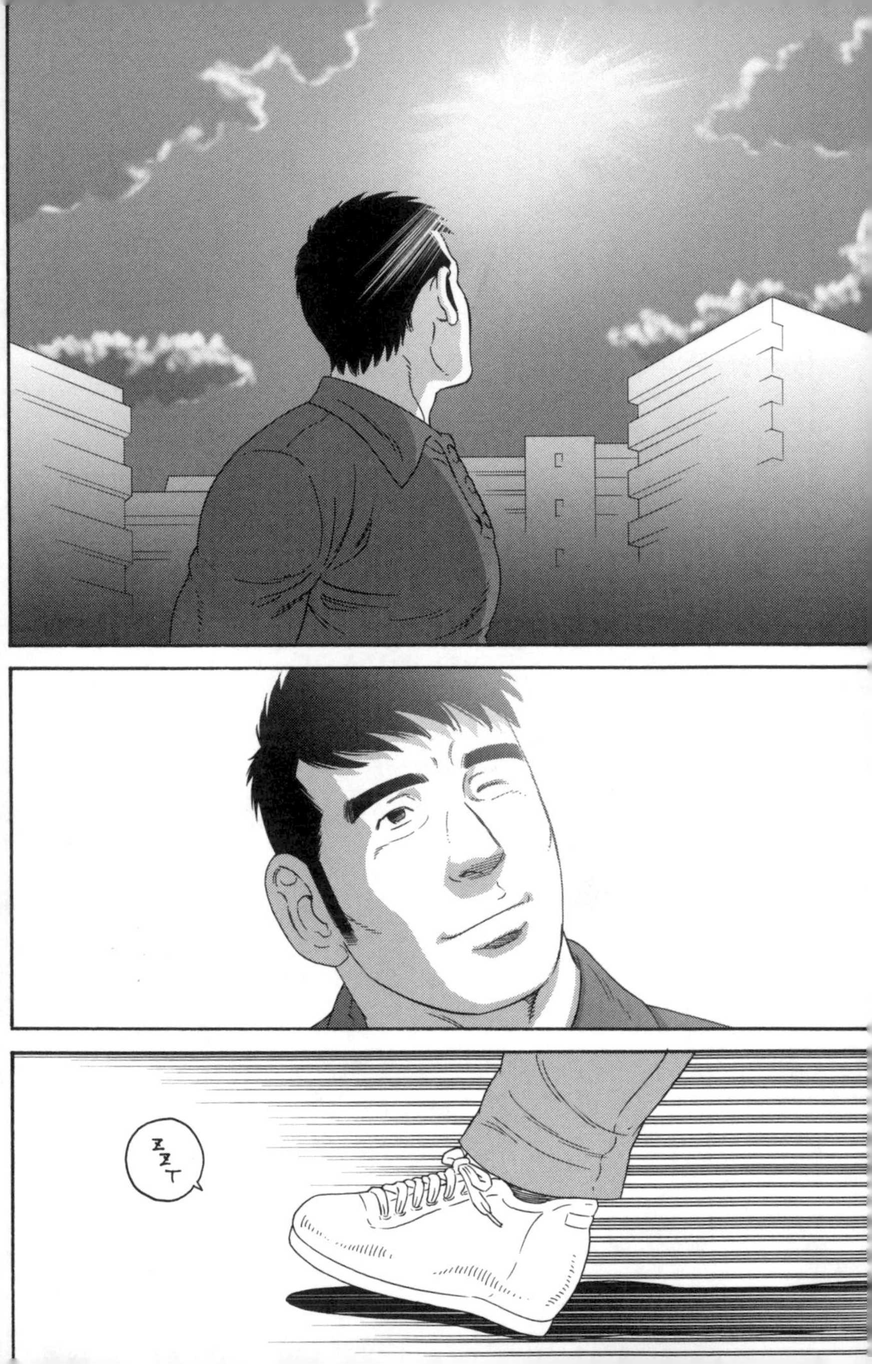
ZZT

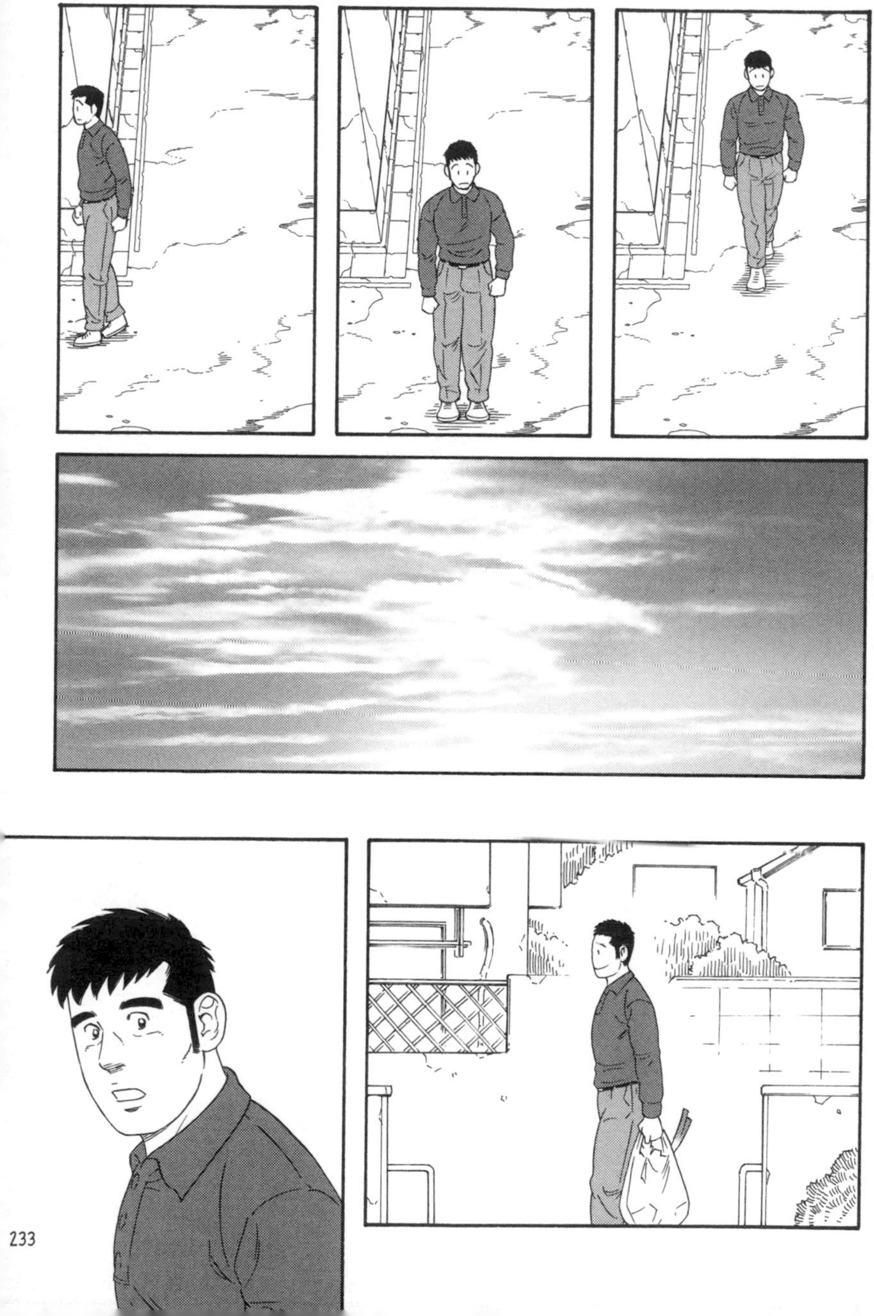

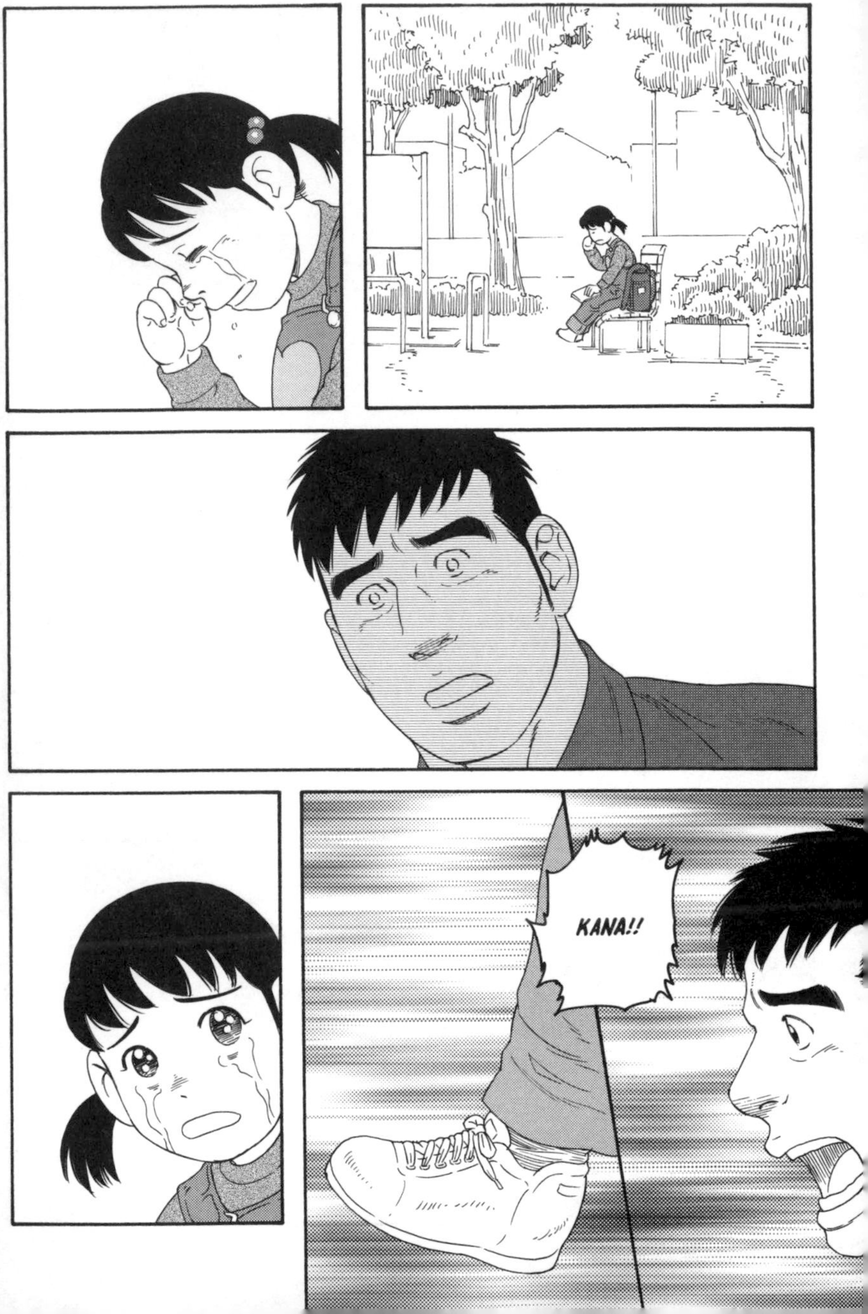
KANA!!

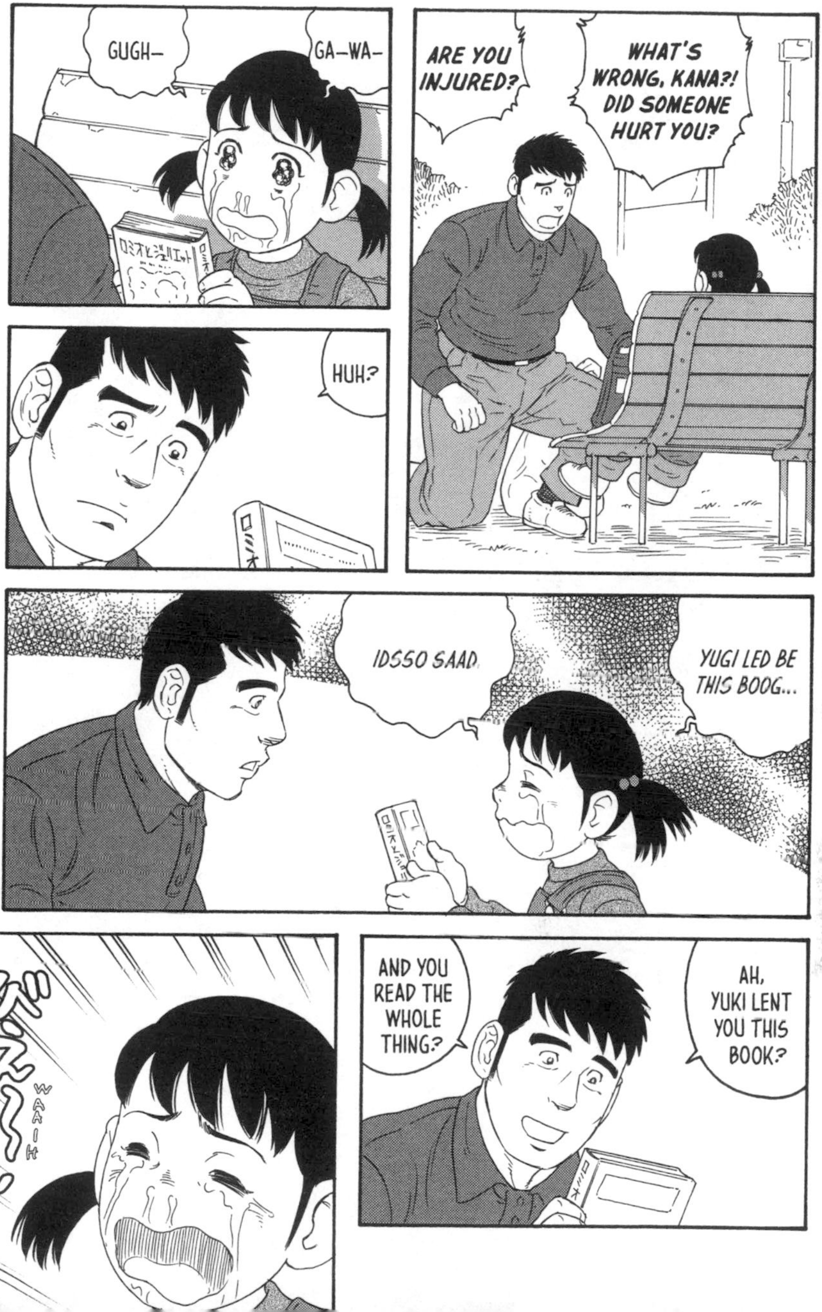
WHAT'S WRONG, KANA?! DID SOMEONE HURT YOU?
ARE YOU INJURED?
GA-WA-
GUGH-
ロミオとジュリエット
HUH?
YUGI LED BE THIS BOOG...
IDSSO SAAD.
AH, YUKI LENT YOU THIS BOOK?
AND YOU READ THE WHOLE THING?
びえ〜〜ん
WAAAH

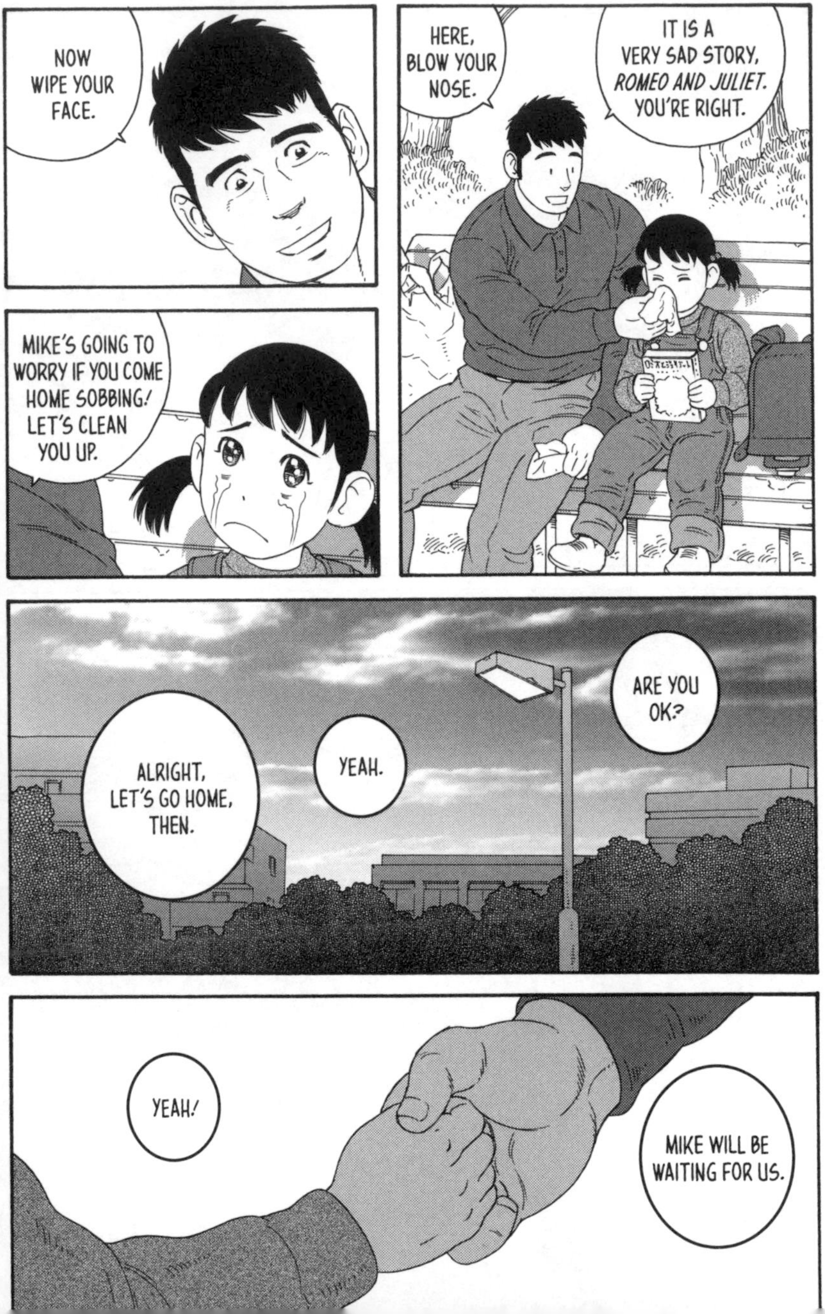
IT IS A VERY SAD STORY, *ROMEO AND JULIET.* YOU'RE RIGHT.
HERE, BLOW YOUR NOSE.
NOW WIPE YOUR FACE.
MIKE'S GOING TO WORRY IF YOU COME HOME SOBBING! LET'S CLEAN YOU UP.
ARE YOU OK?
YEAH.
ALRIGHT, LET'S GO HOME, THEN.
MIKE WILL BE WAITING FOR US.
YEAH!

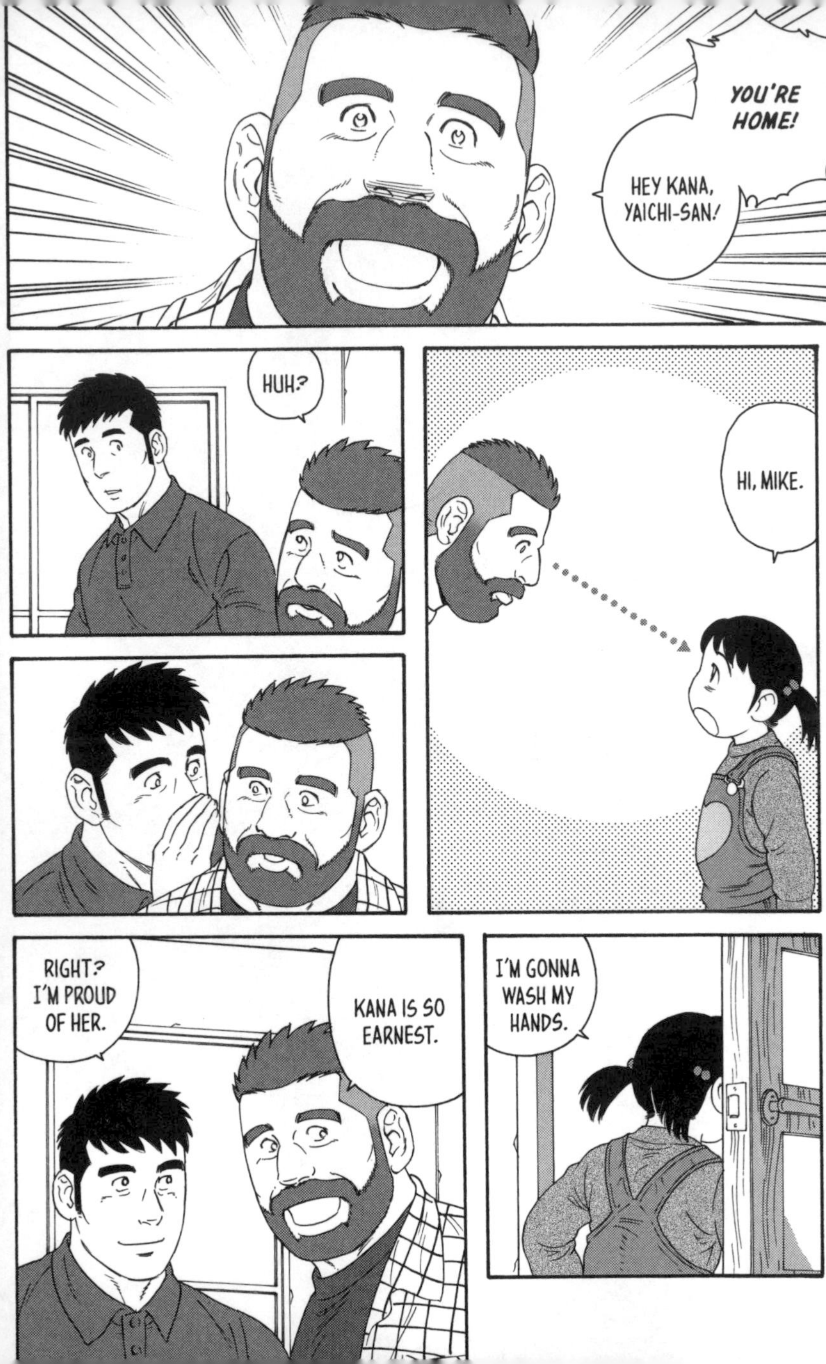
YOU'RE HOME!
HEY KANA, YAICHI-SAN!
HI, MIKE.
HUH?
I'M GONNA WASH MY HANDS.
KANA IS SO EARNEST.
RIGHT? I'M PROUD OF HER.

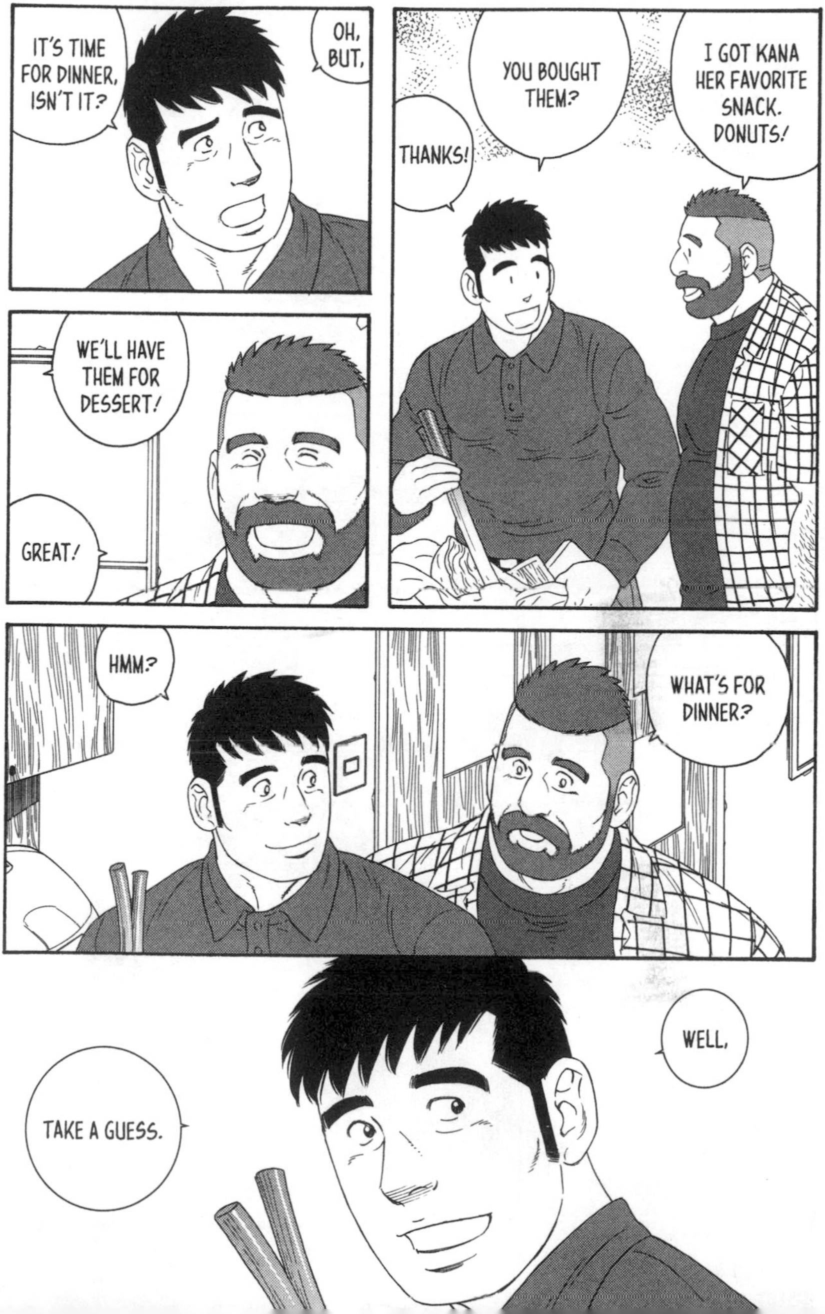
I GOT KANA HER FAVORITE SNACK. DONUTS!
YOU BOUGHT THEM?
THANKS!
OH, BUT,
IT'S TIME FOR DINNER, ISN'T IT?
WE'LL HAVE THEM FOR DESSERT!
GREAT!
WHAT'S FOR DINNER?
HMM?
WELL,
TAKE A GUESS.

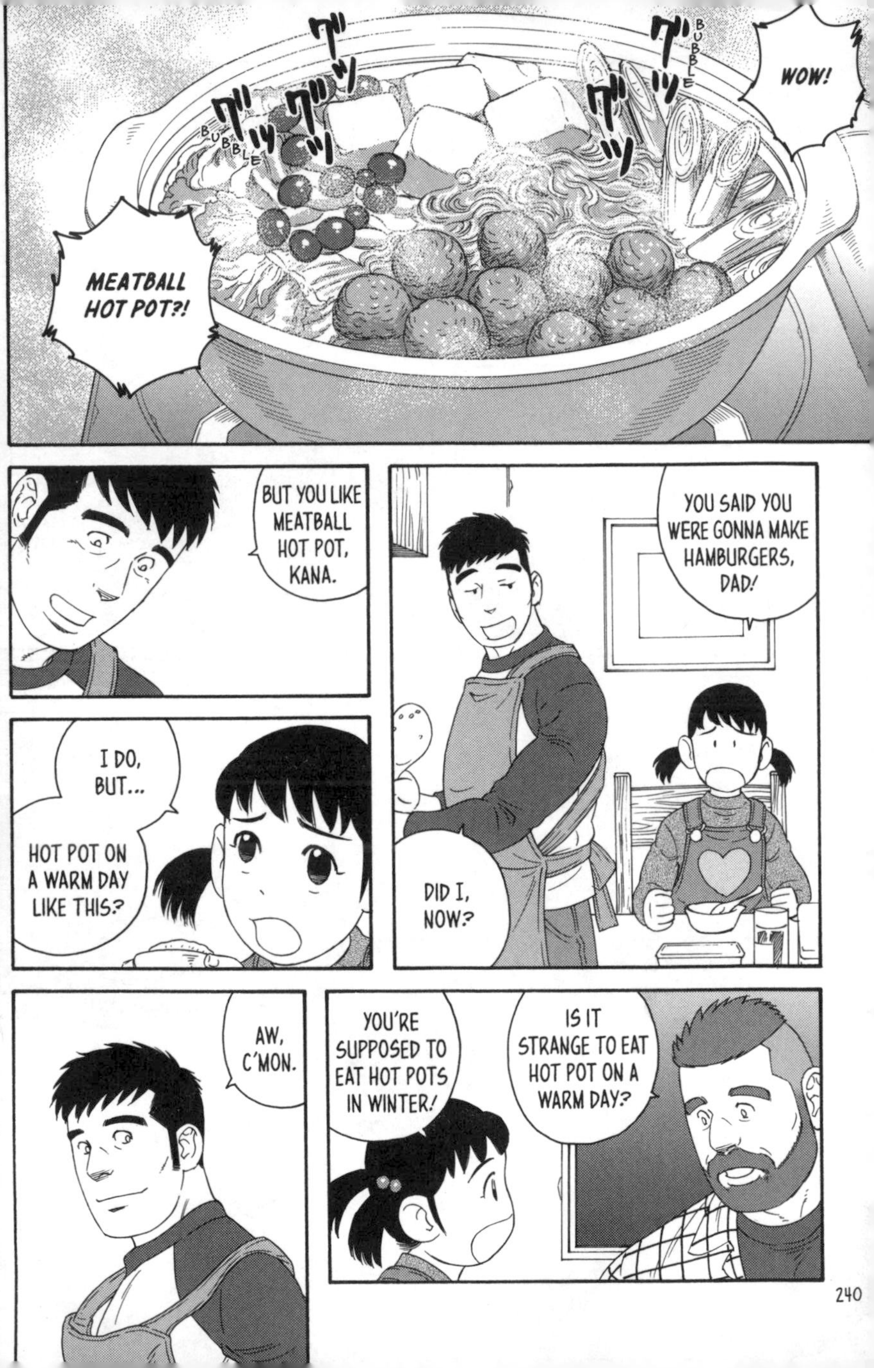
WOW!
BUBBLE
BUBBLE
MEATBALL HOT POT?!
YOU SAID YOU WERE GONNA MAKE HAMBURGERS, DAD!
DID I, NOW?
BUT YOU LIKE MEATBALL HOT POT, KANA.
I DO, BUT...
HOT POT ON A WARM DAY LIKE THIS?
IS IT STRANGE TO EAT HOT POT ON A WARM DAY?
YOU'RE SUPPOSED TO EAT HOT POTS IN WINTER!
AW, C'MON.

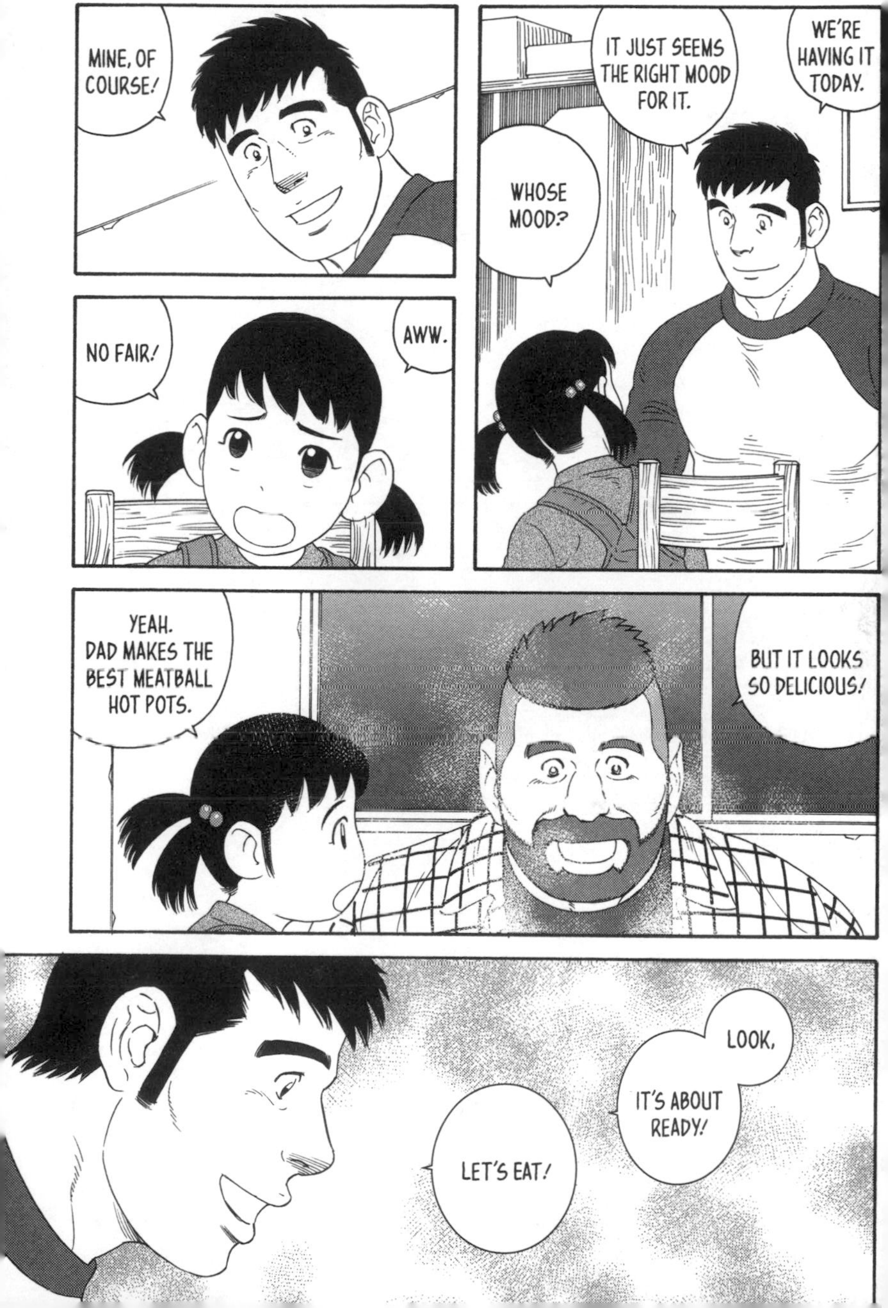
WE'RE HAVING IT TODAY.
IT JUST SEEMS THE RIGHT MOOD FOR IT.
WHOSE MOOD?
MINE, OF COURSE!
AWW.
NO FAIR!
BUT IT LOOKS SO DELICIOUS!
YEAH. DAD MAKES THE BEST MEATBALL HOT POTS.
LOOK,
IT'S ABOUT READY!
LET'S EAT!

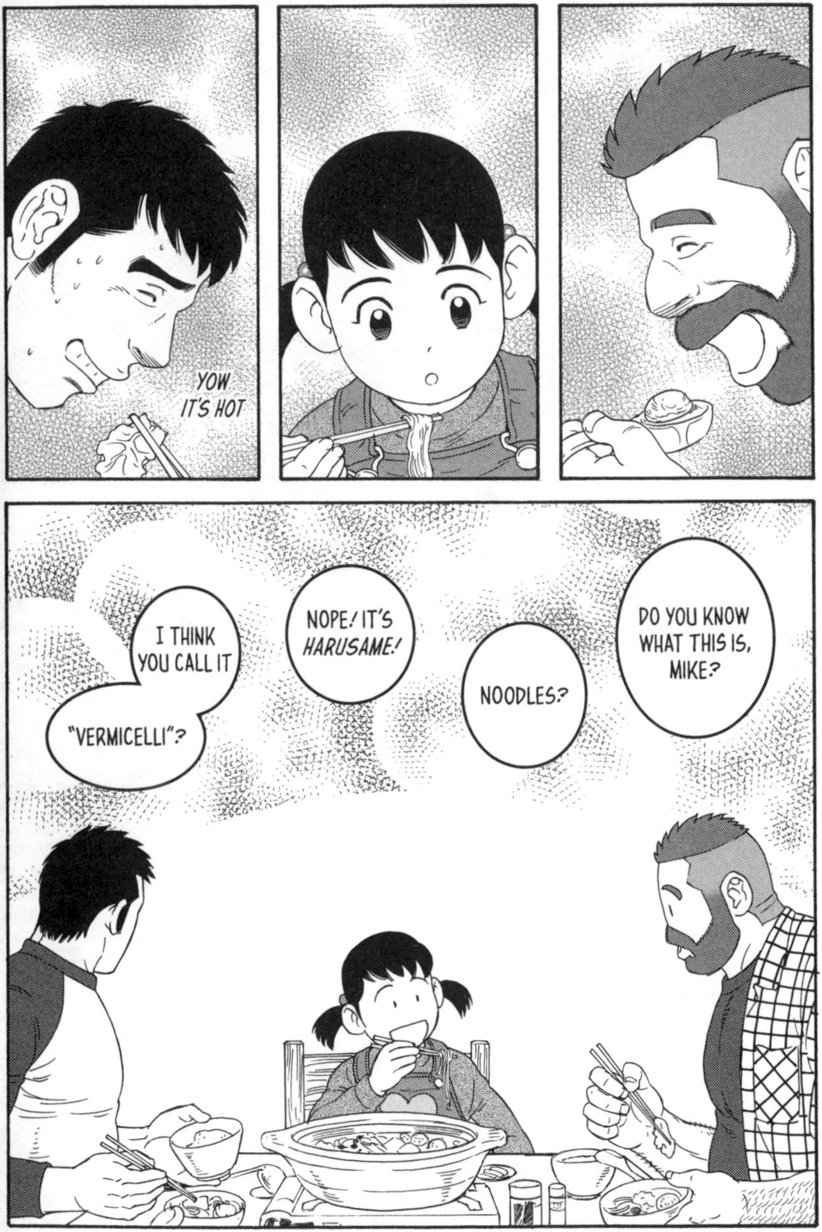
YOW IT'S HOT
DO YOU KNOW WHAT THIS IS, MIKE?
NOODLES?
NOPE! IT'S *HARUSAME!*
I THINK YOU CALL IT "VERMICELLI"?

CHAPTER TWENTY-FIVE
PICTURES

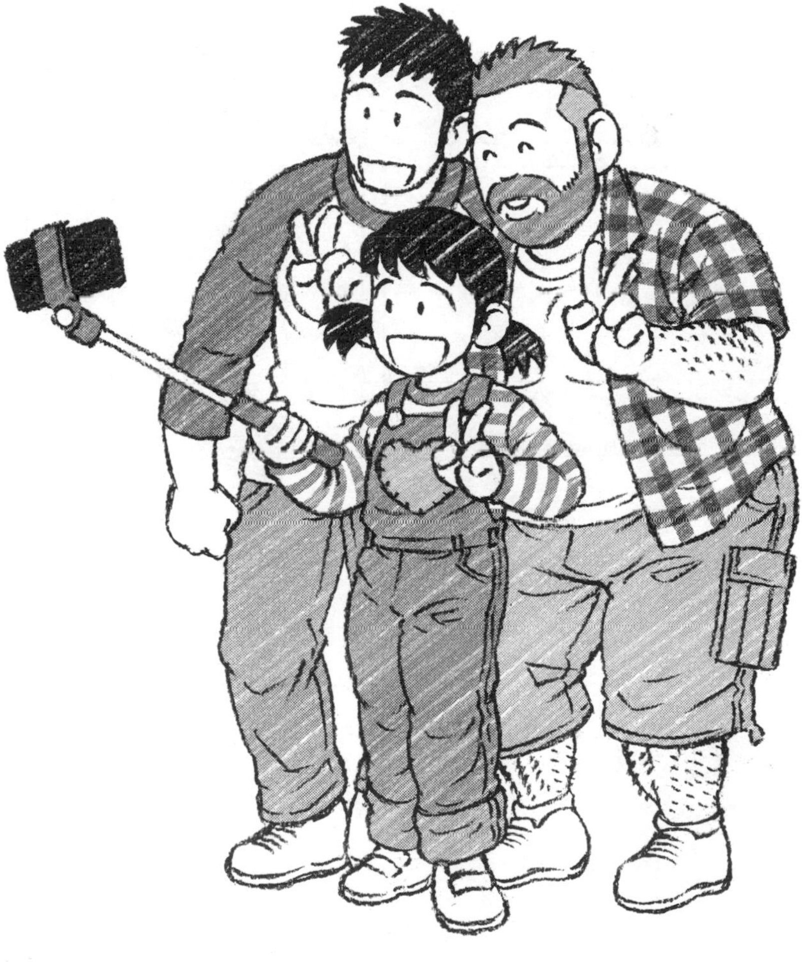

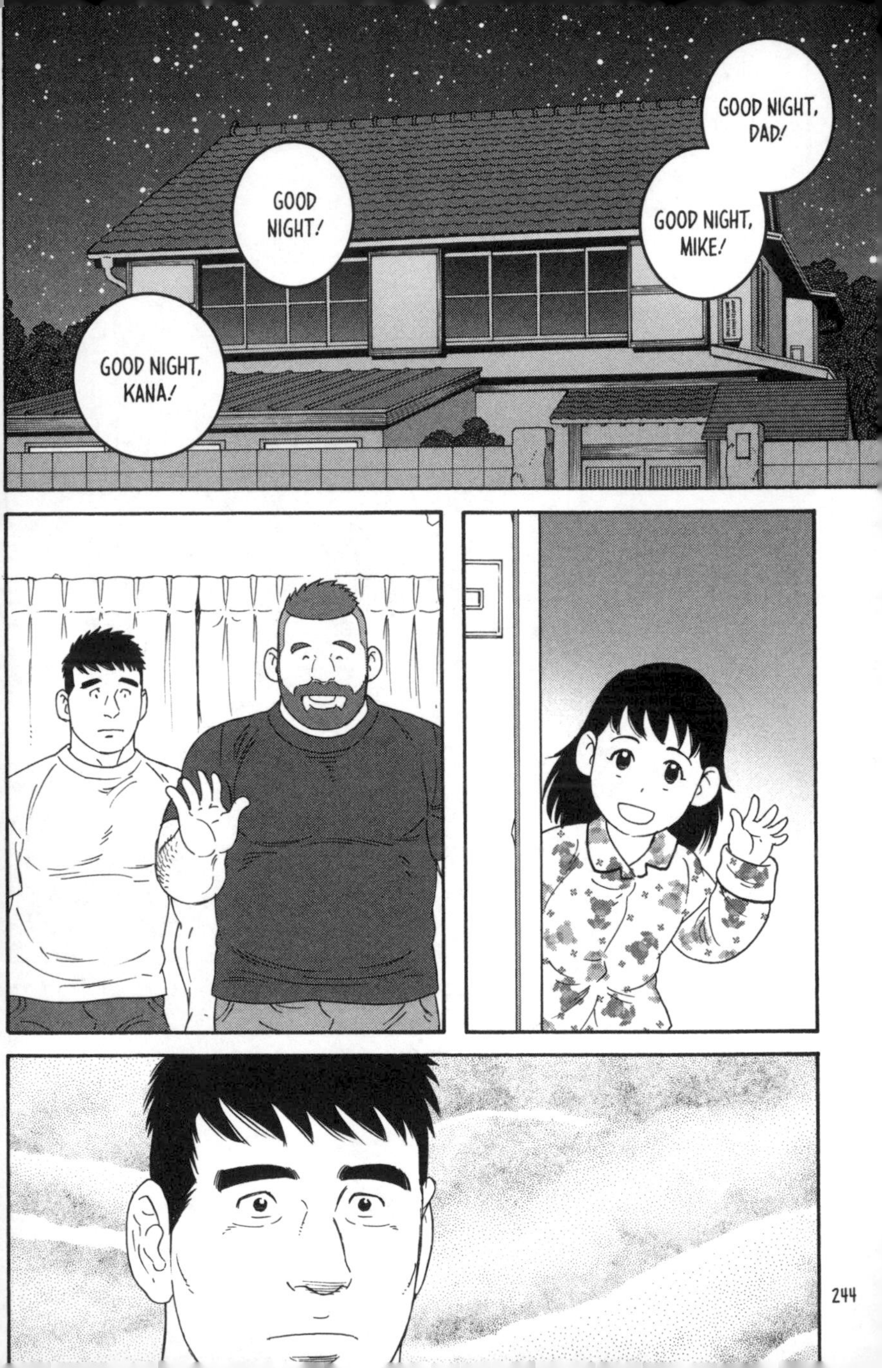
GOOD NIGHT, DAD!
GOOD NIGHT, MIKE!
GOOD NIGHT!
GOOD NIGHT, KANA!

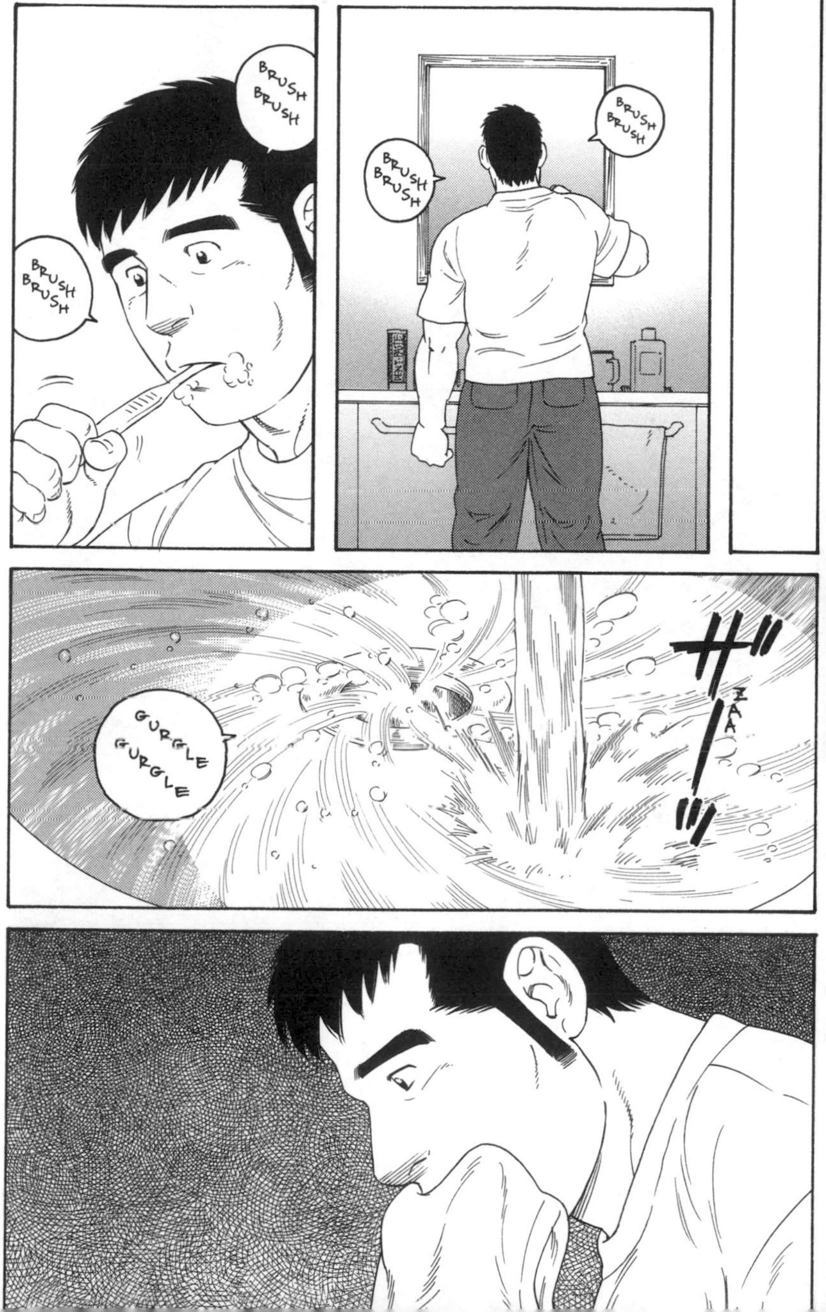
BRUSH BRUSH
BRUSH BRUSH
BRUSH BRUSH
BRUSH BRUSH
ZAA
GURGLE GURGLE

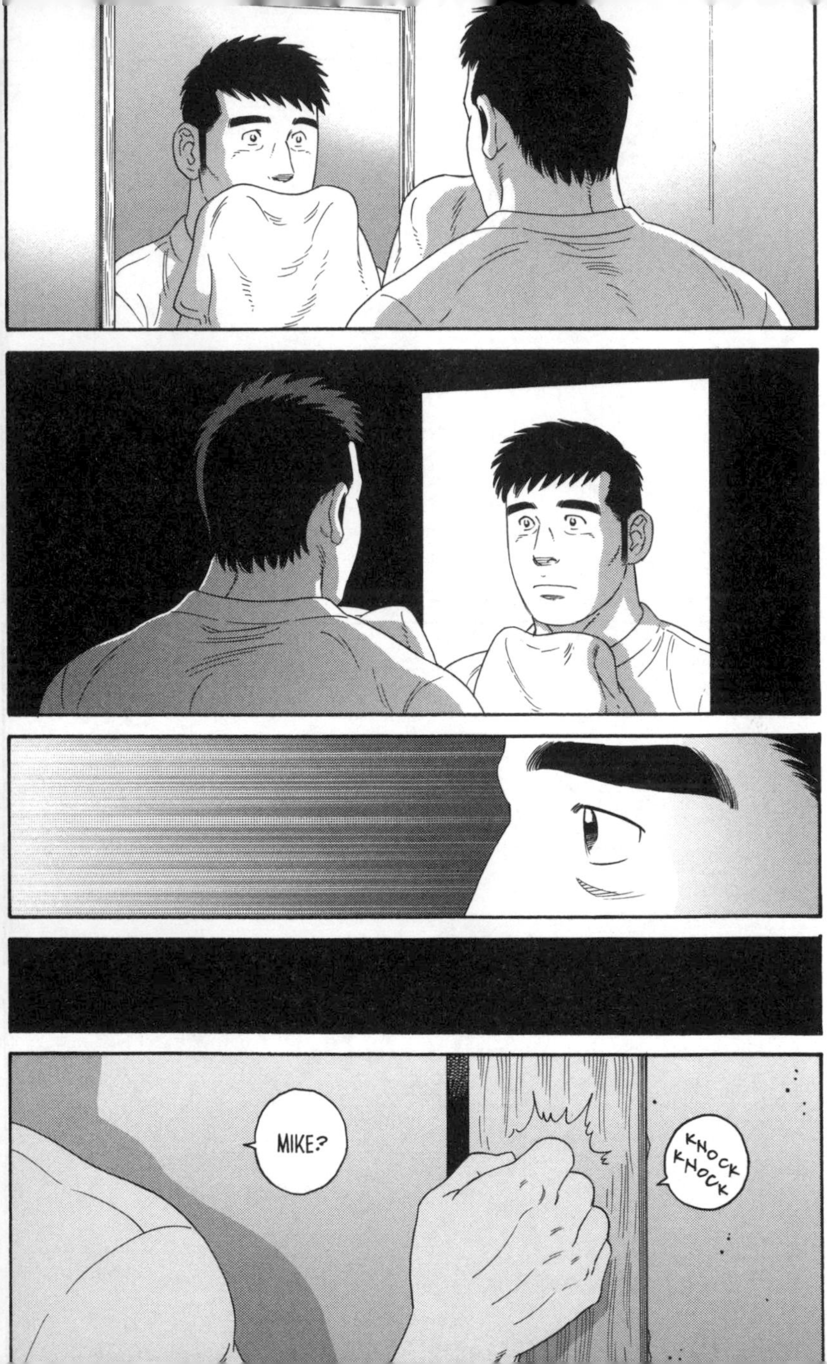
KNOCK KNOCK
MIKE?

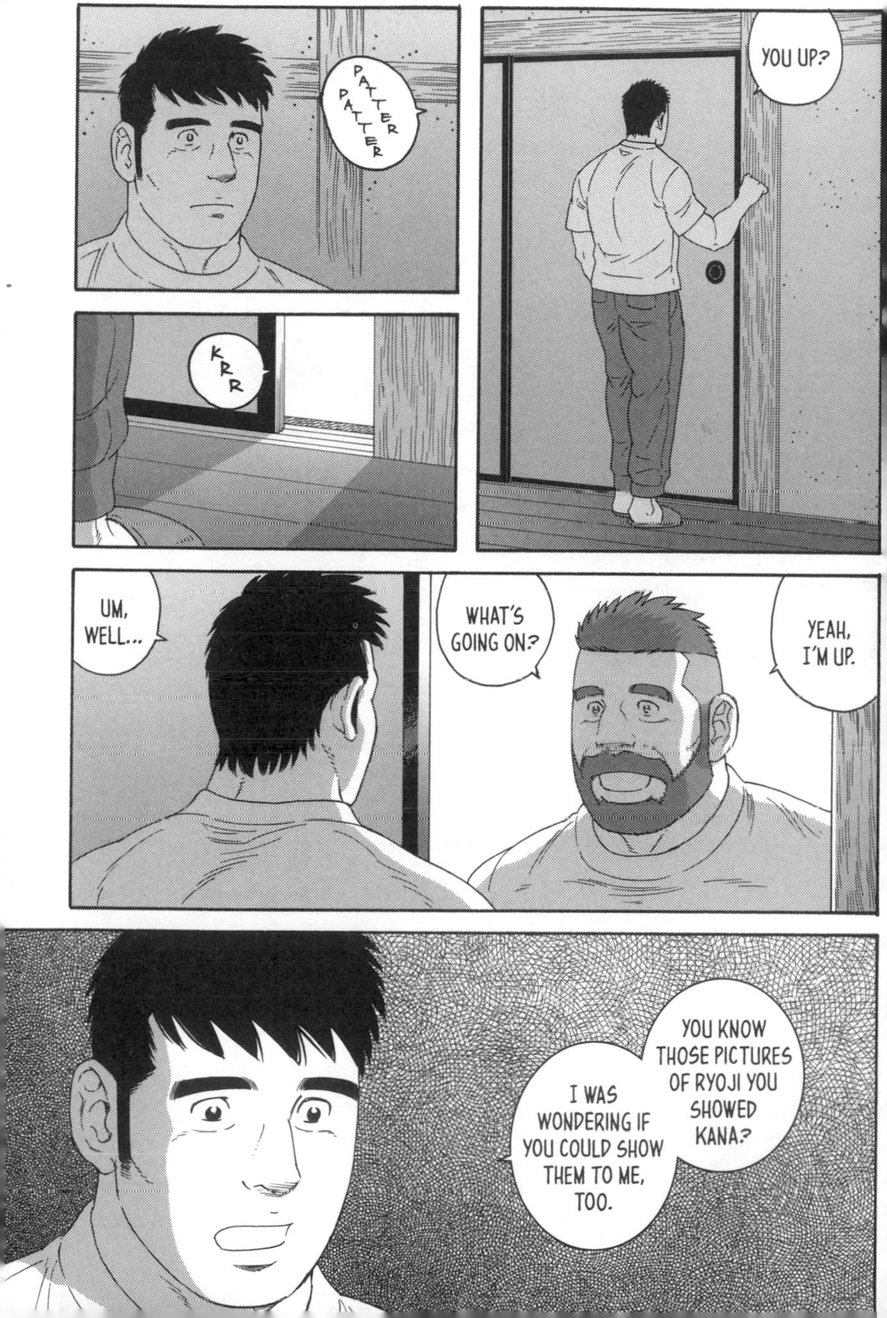
YOU UP?
PATTER PATTER
KRR
YEAH, I'M UP.
WHAT'S GOING ON?
UM, WELL...
YOU KNOW THOSE PICTURES OF RYOJI YOU SHOWED KANA?
I WAS WONDERING IF YOU COULD SHOW THEM TO ME, TOO.

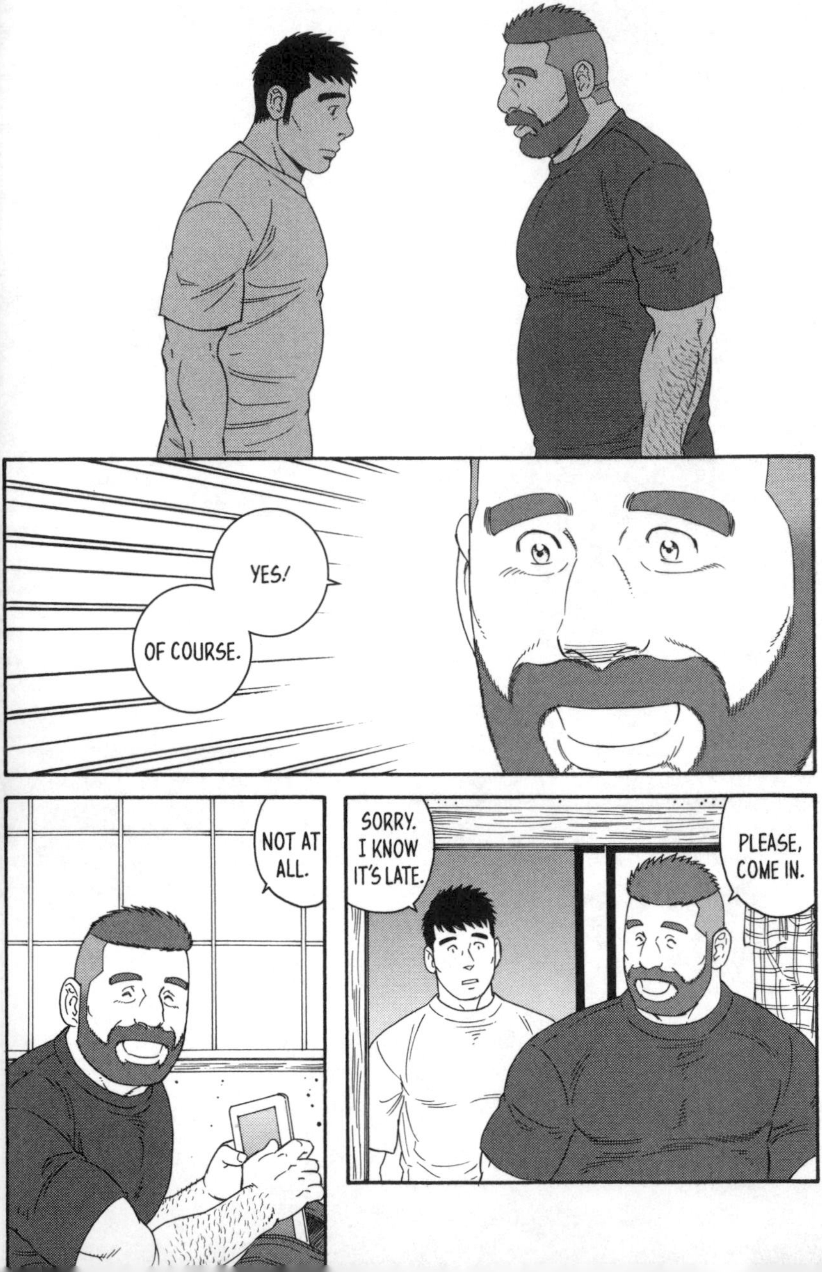
YES!
OF COURSE.
PLEASE, COME IN.
SORRY. I KNOW IT'S LATE.
NOT AT ALL.

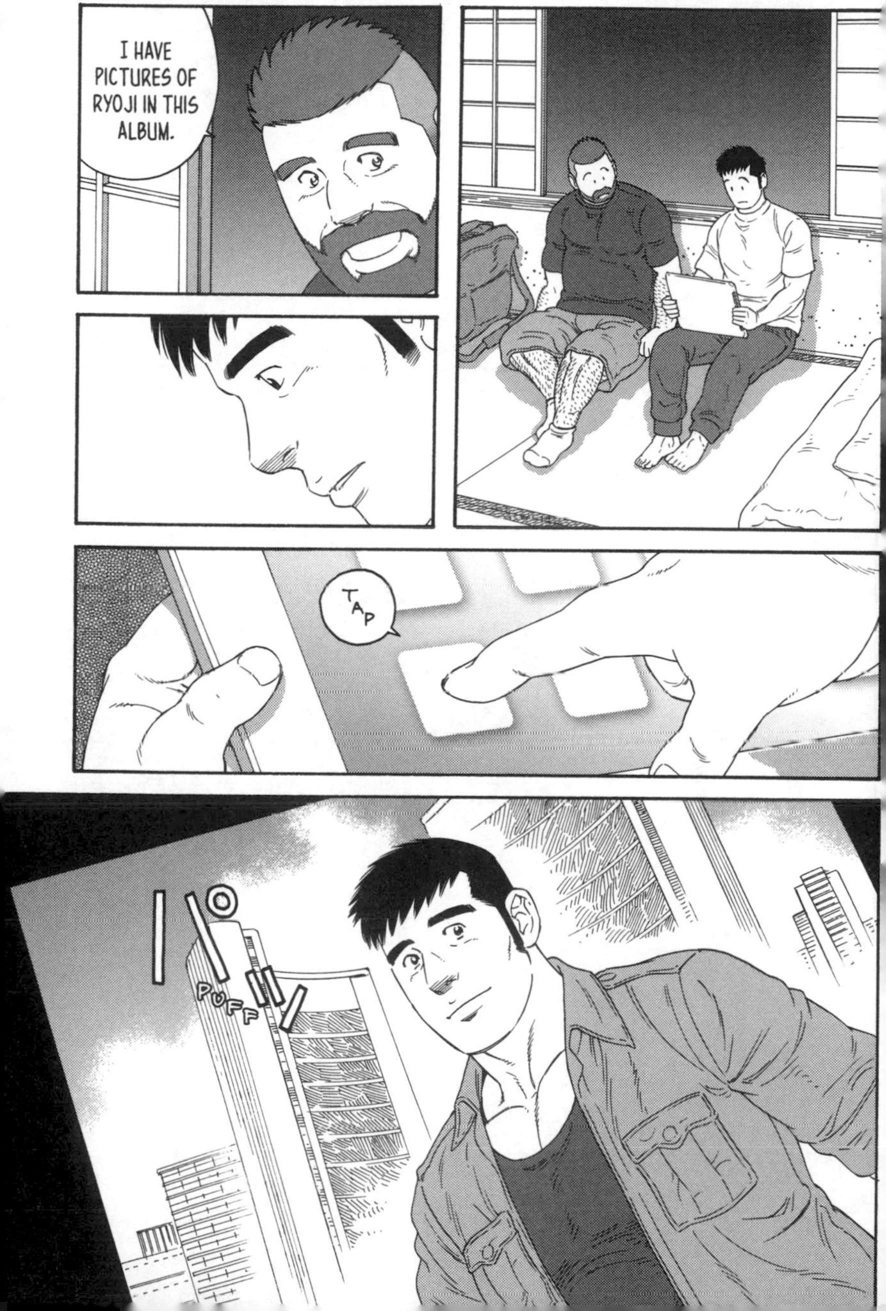
I HAVE PICTURES OF RYOJI IN THIS ALBUM.
TAP
PUFF

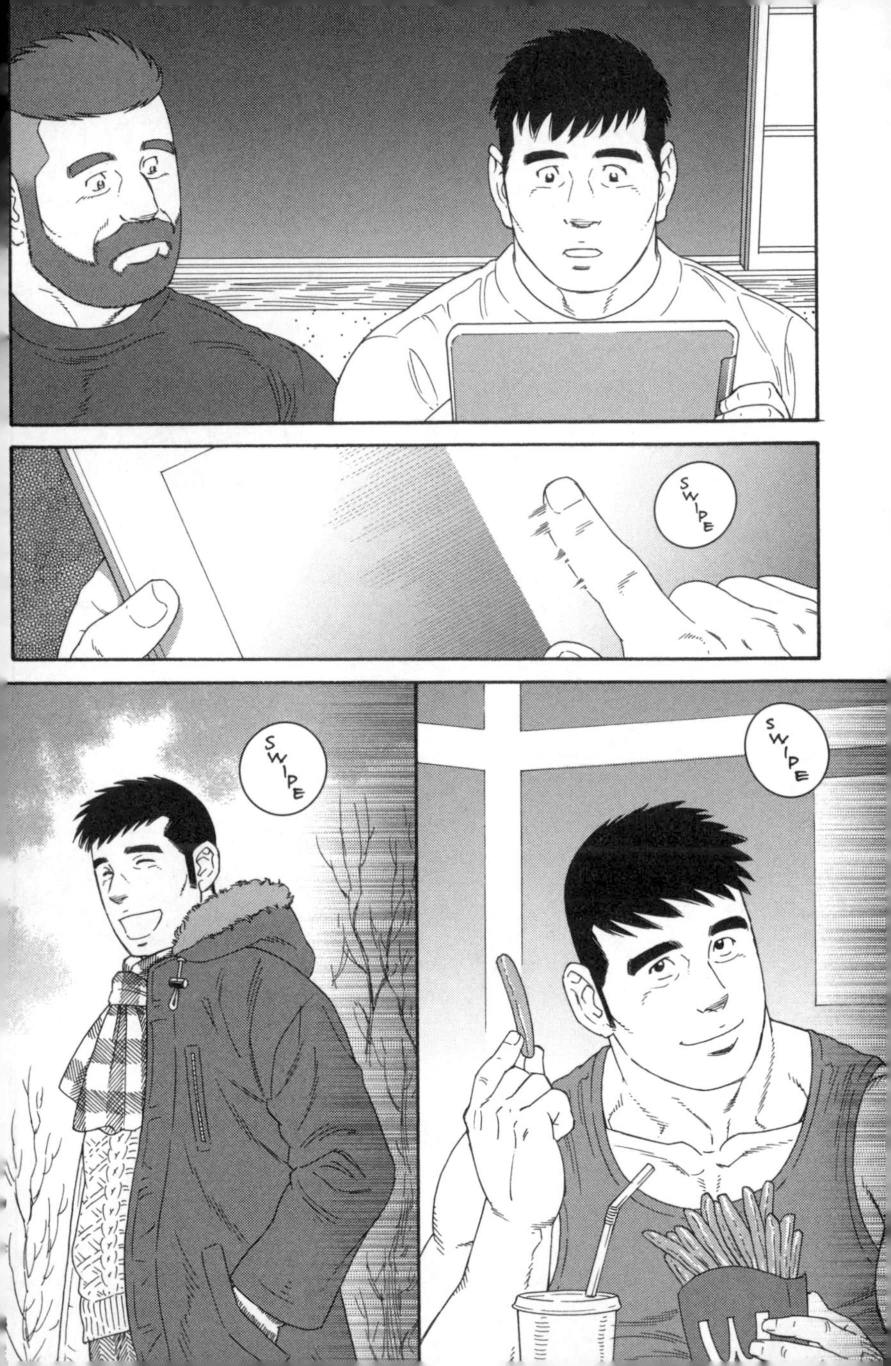
SWIPE
SWIPE
SWIPE

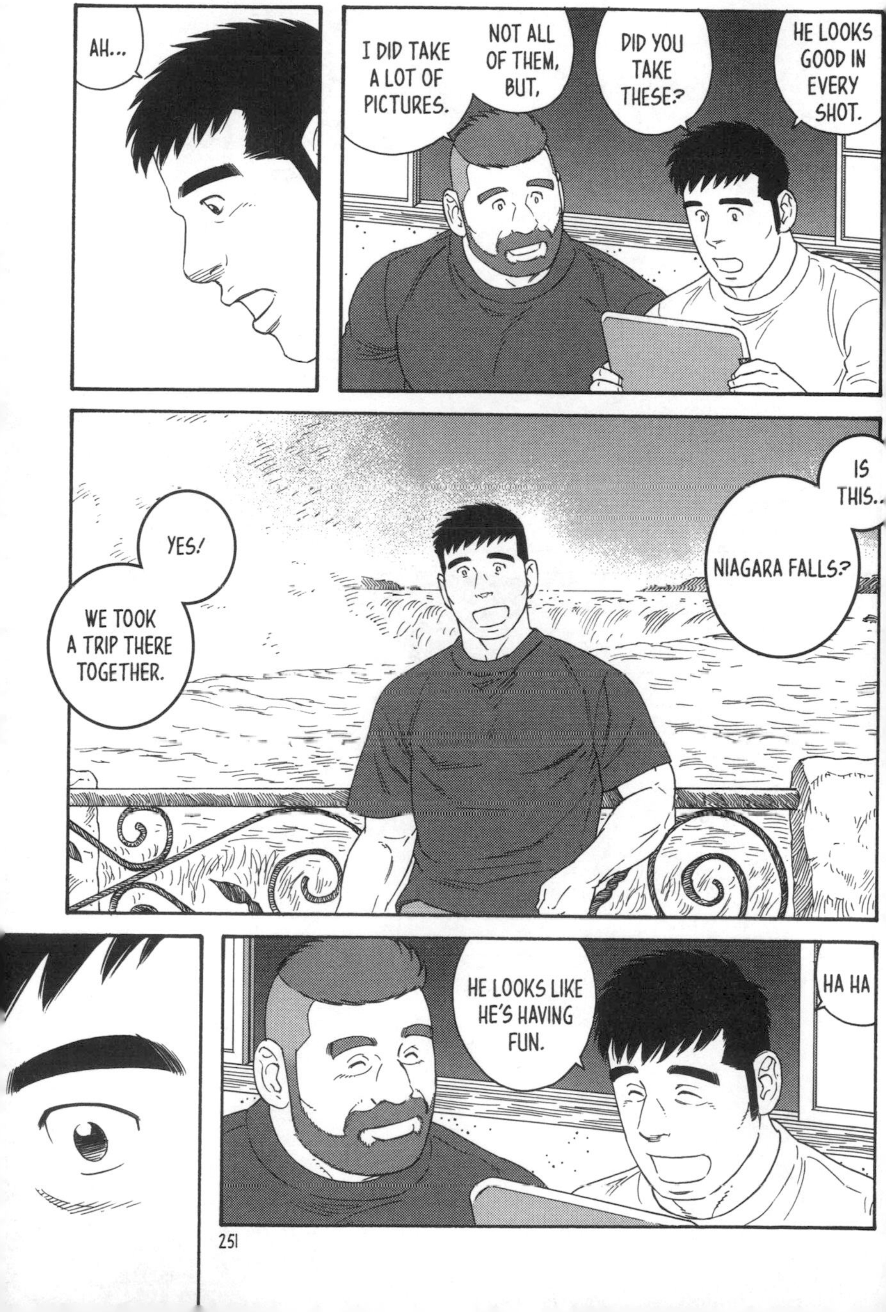
HE LOOKS GOOD IN EVERY SHOT.
DID YOU TAKE THESE?
NOT ALL OF THEM, BUT,
I DID TAKE A LOT OF PICTURES.
AH...
IS THIS..
NIAGARA FALLS?
YES!
WE TOOK A TRIP THERE TOGETHER.
HA HA
HE LOOKS LIKE HE'S HAVING FUN.

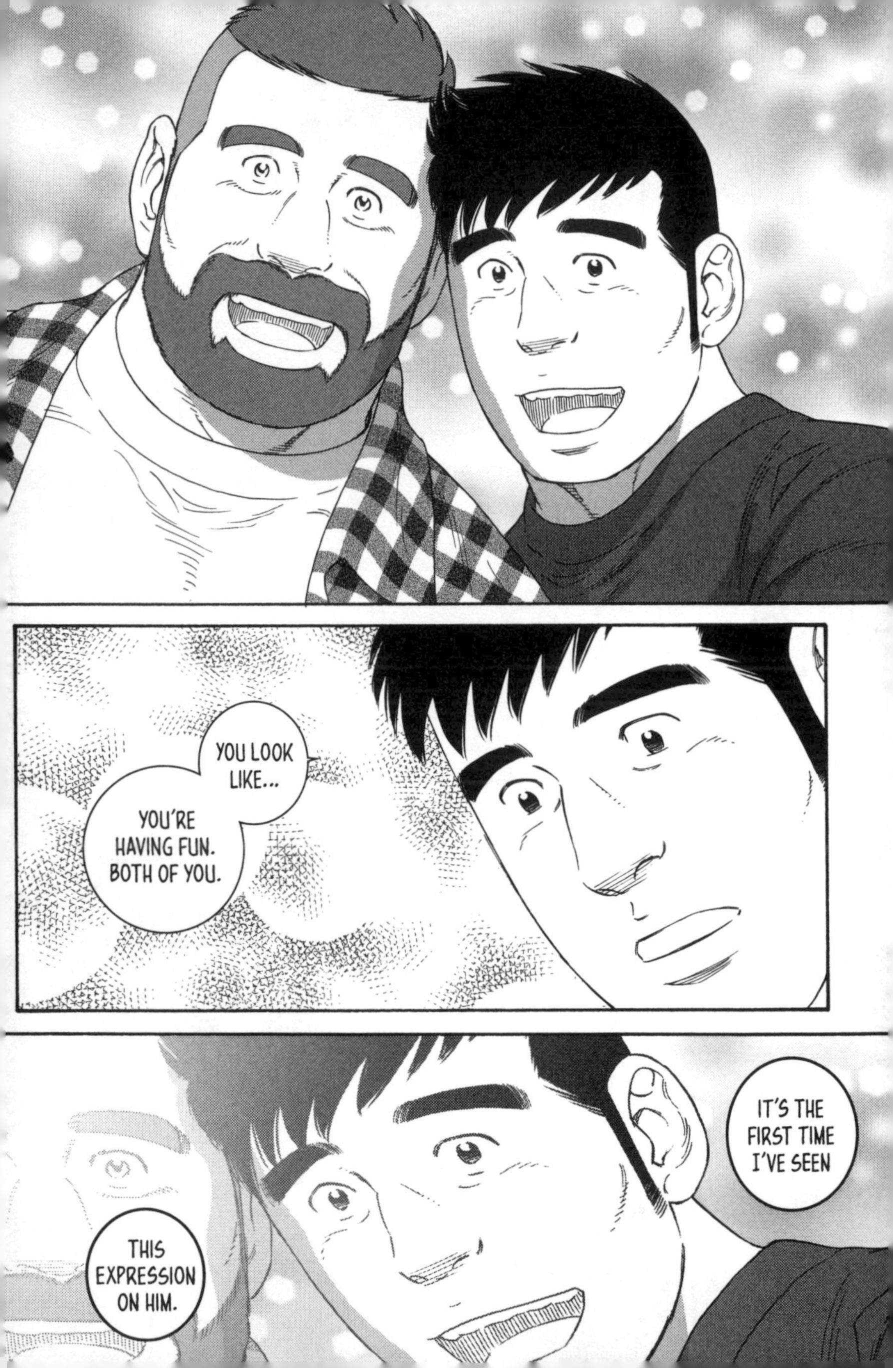
YOU LOOK LIKE...
YOU'RE HAVING FUN. BOTH OF YOU.
IT'S THE FIRST TIME I'VE SEEN
THIS EXPRESSION ON HIM.

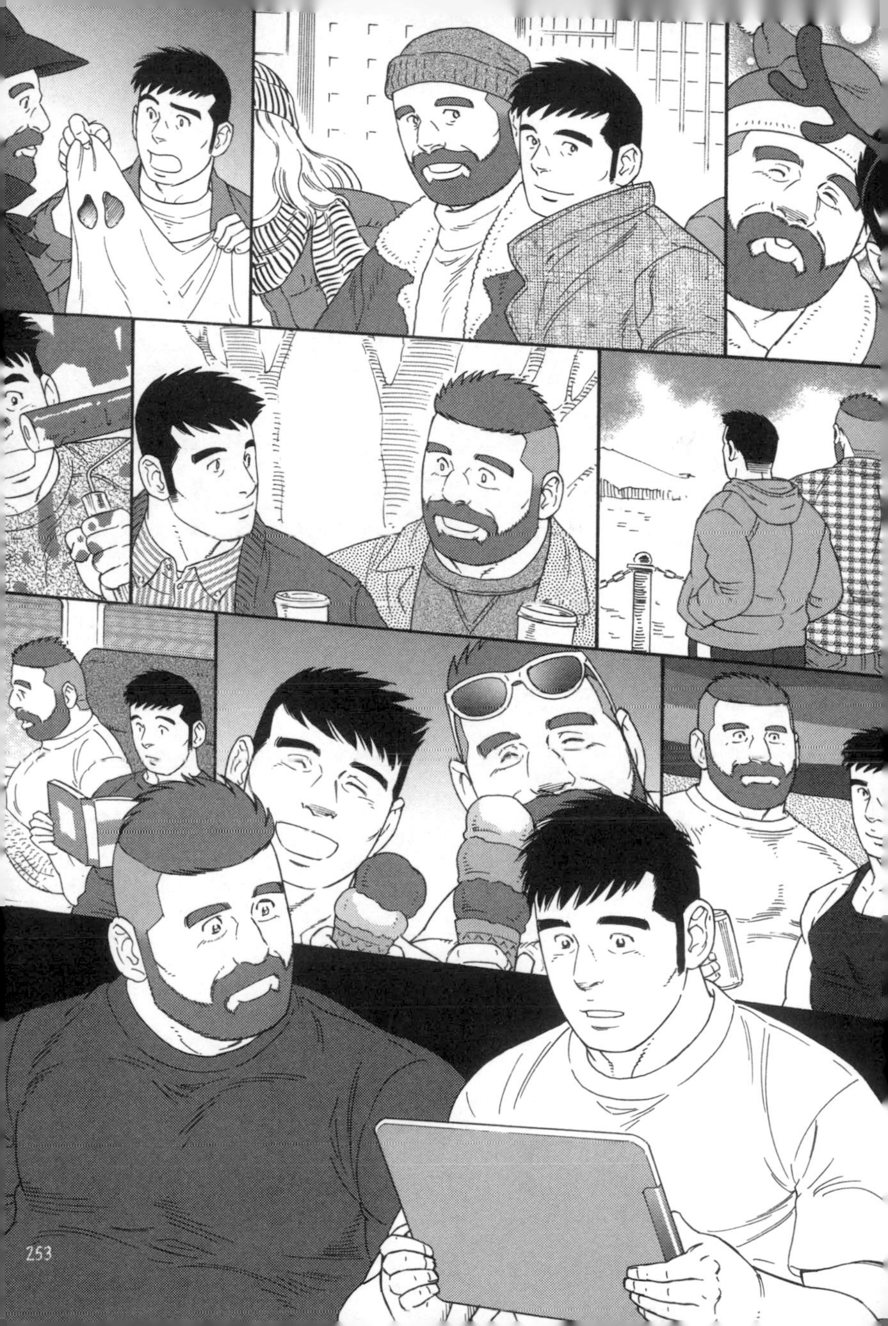

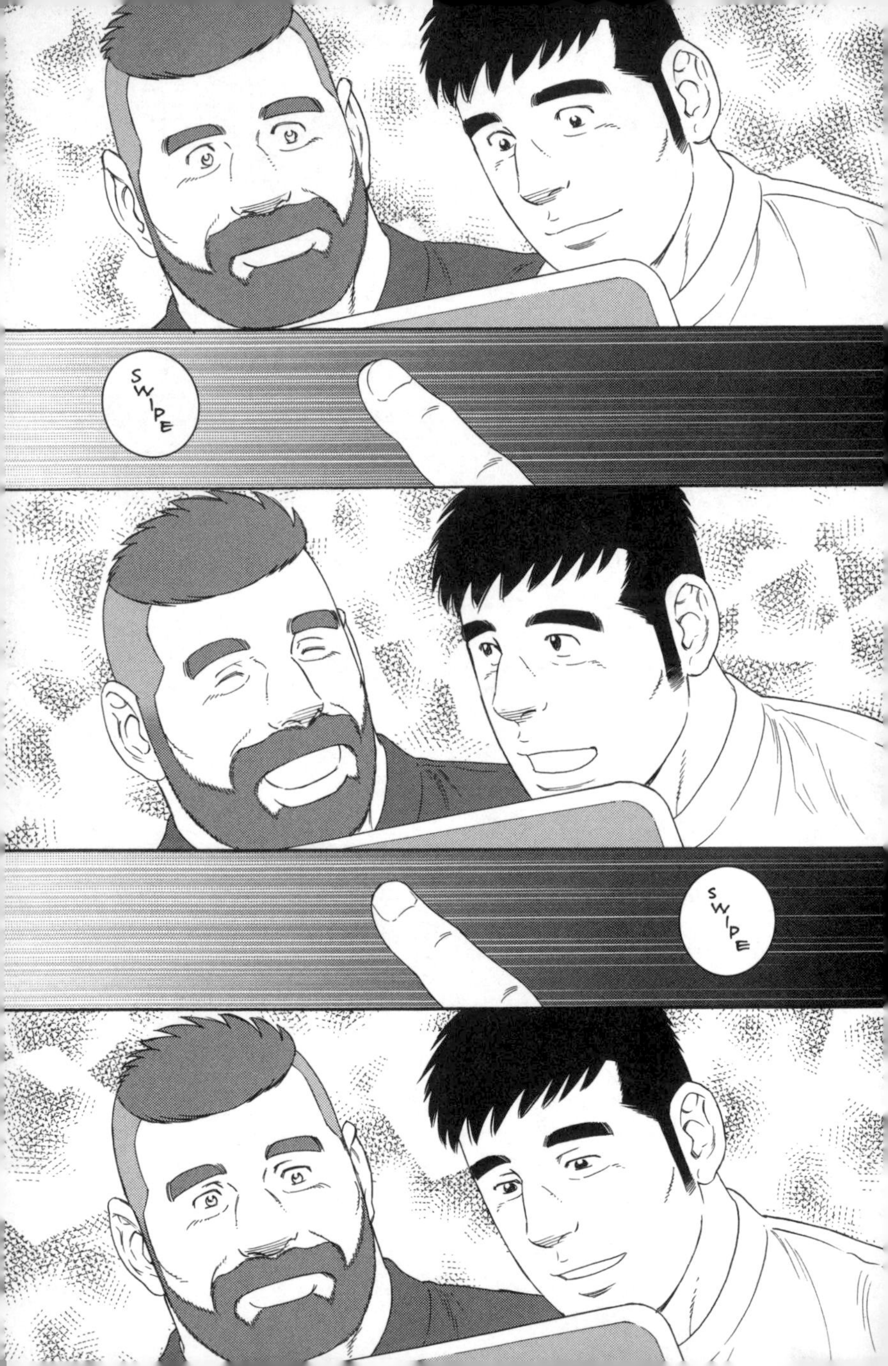
SWIPE
SWIPE

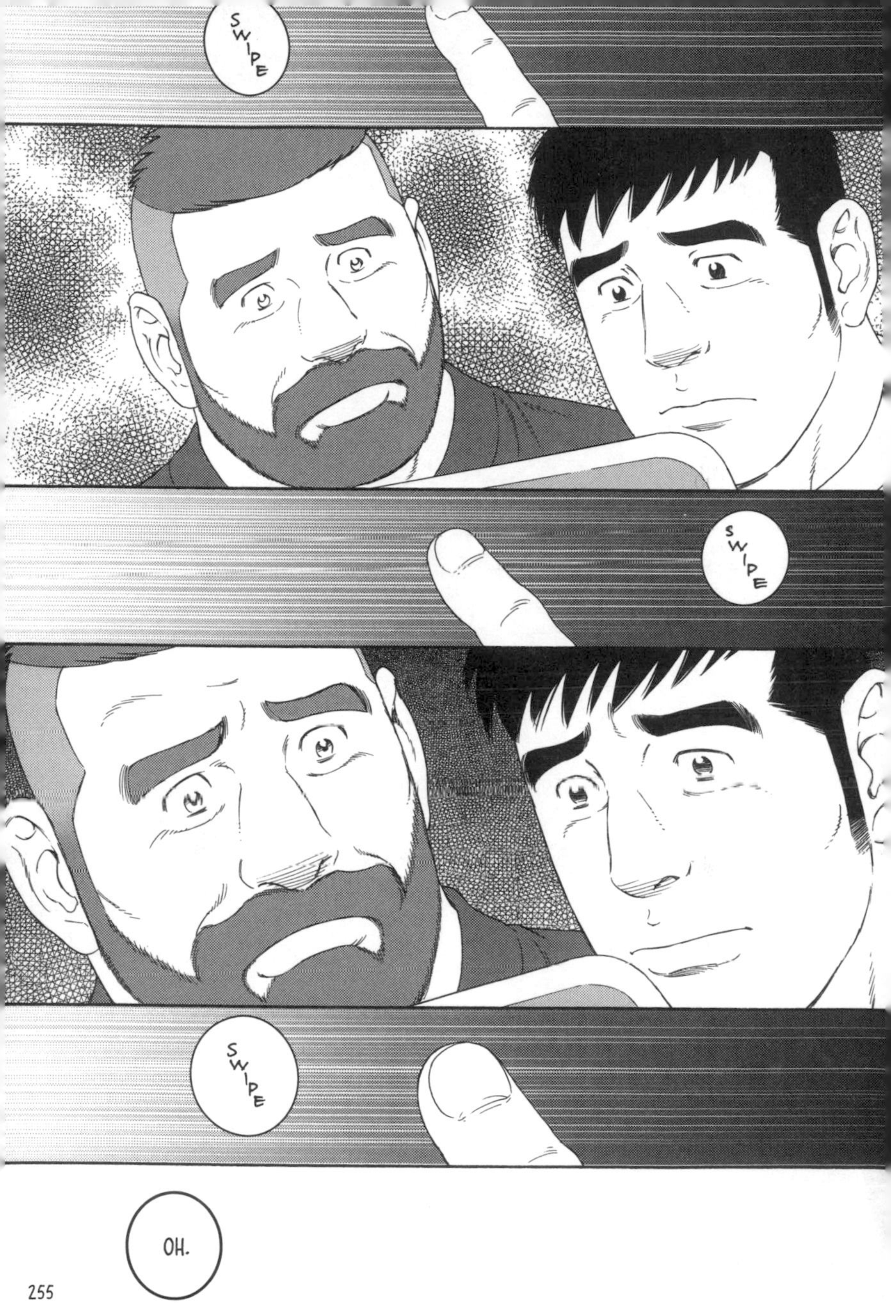
SWIPE
SWIPE
SWIPE
OH.

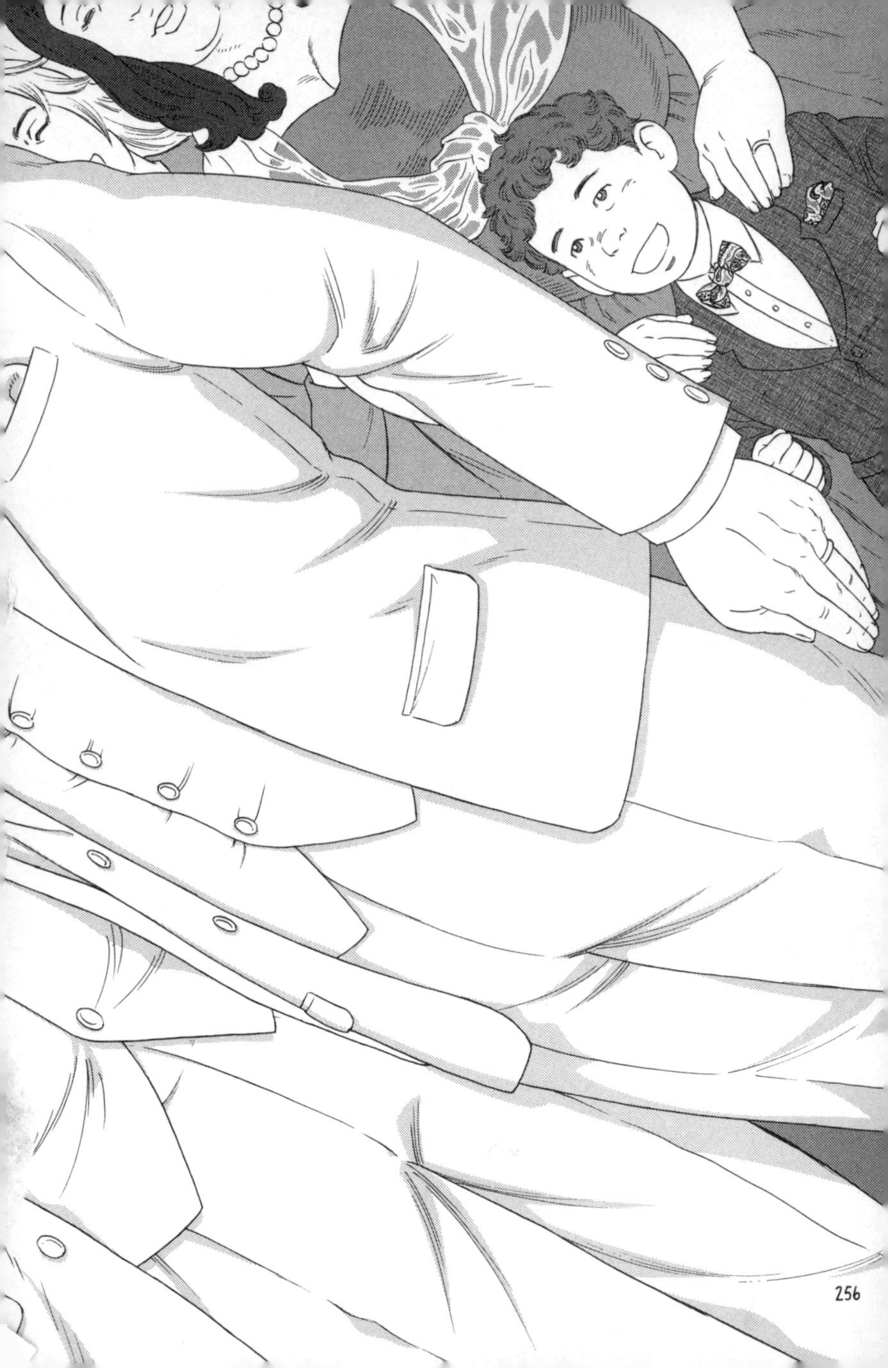

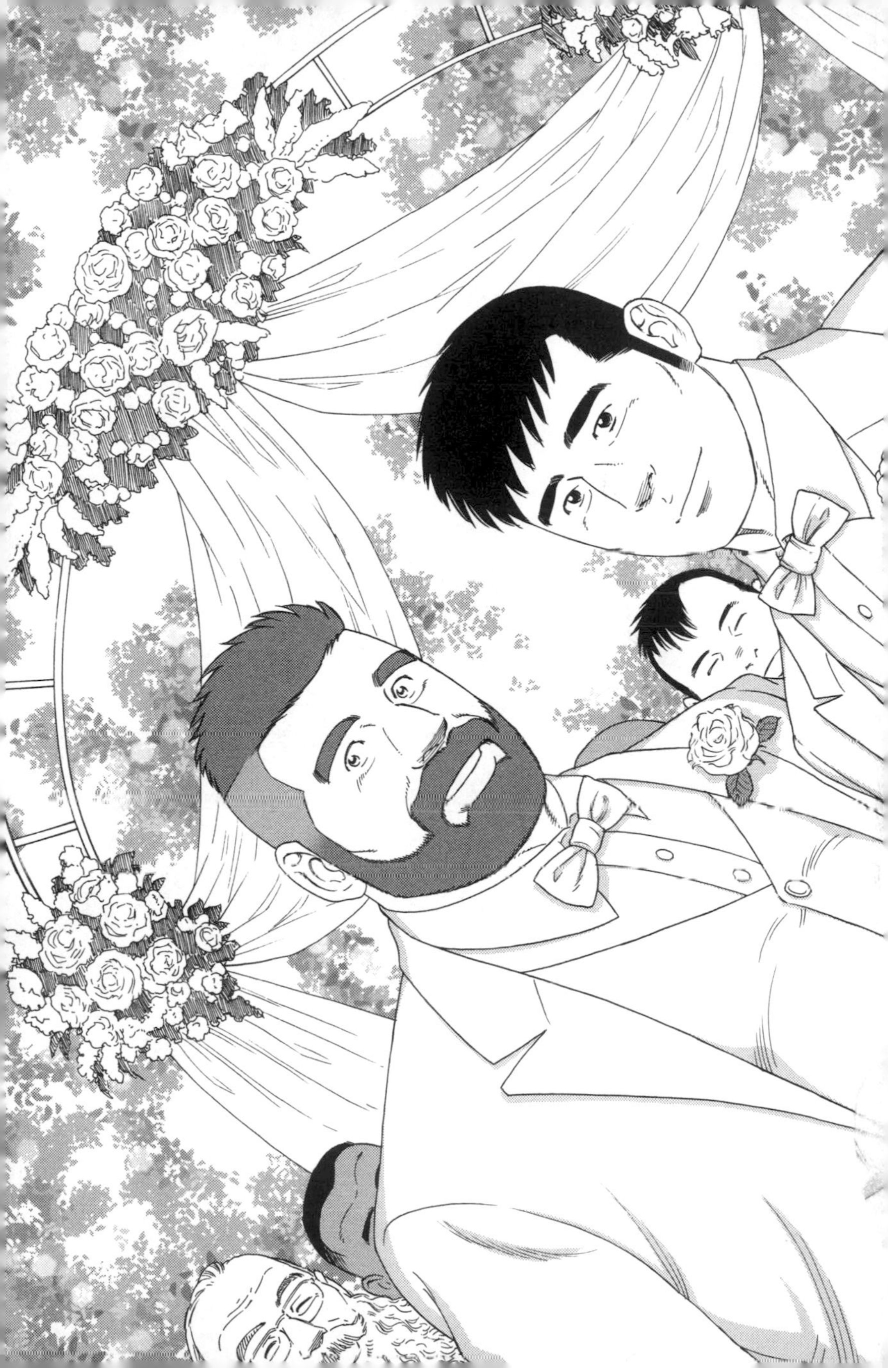

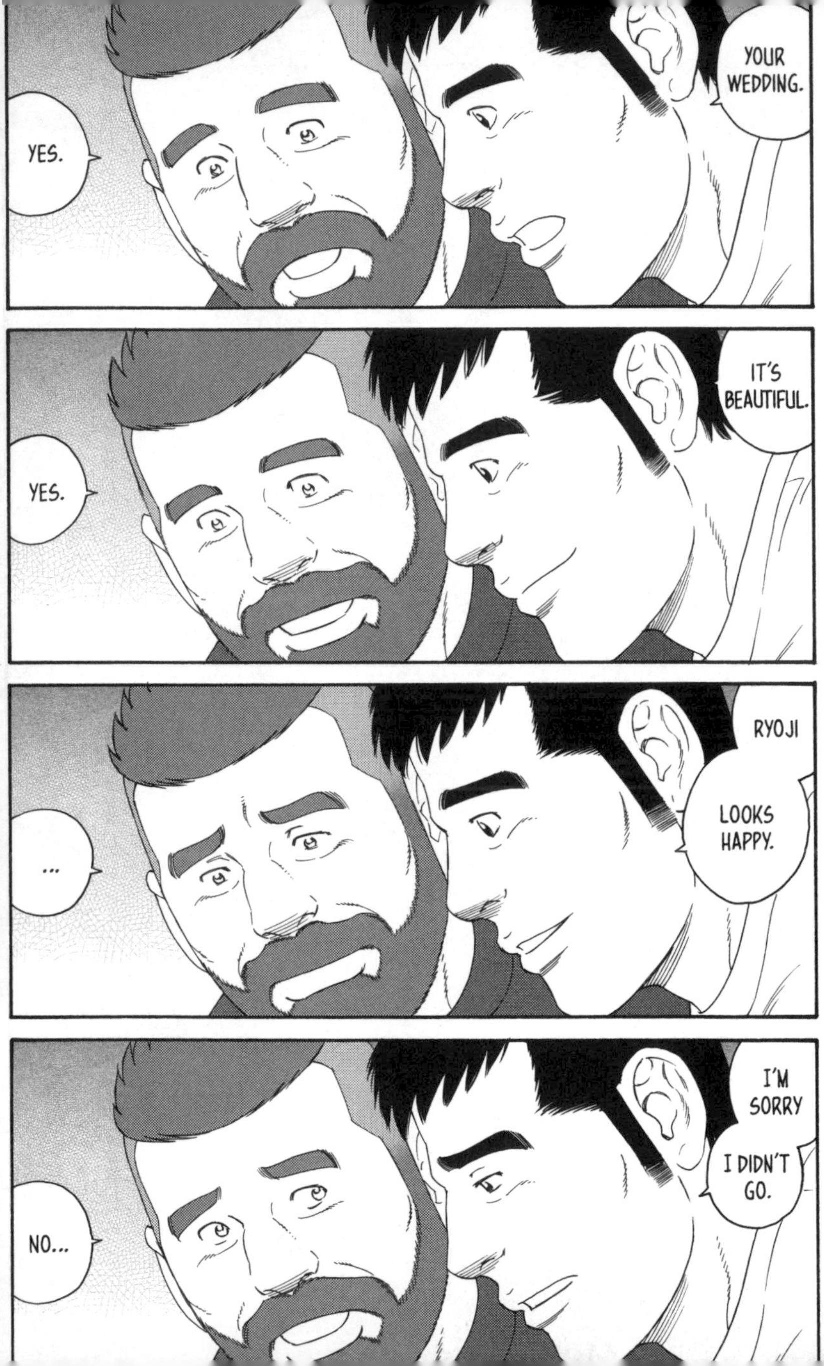
YOUR WEDDING.
YES.
IT'S BEAUTIFUL.
YES.
RYOJI
LOOKS HAPPY.
...
I'M SORRY
I DIDN'T GO.
NO...

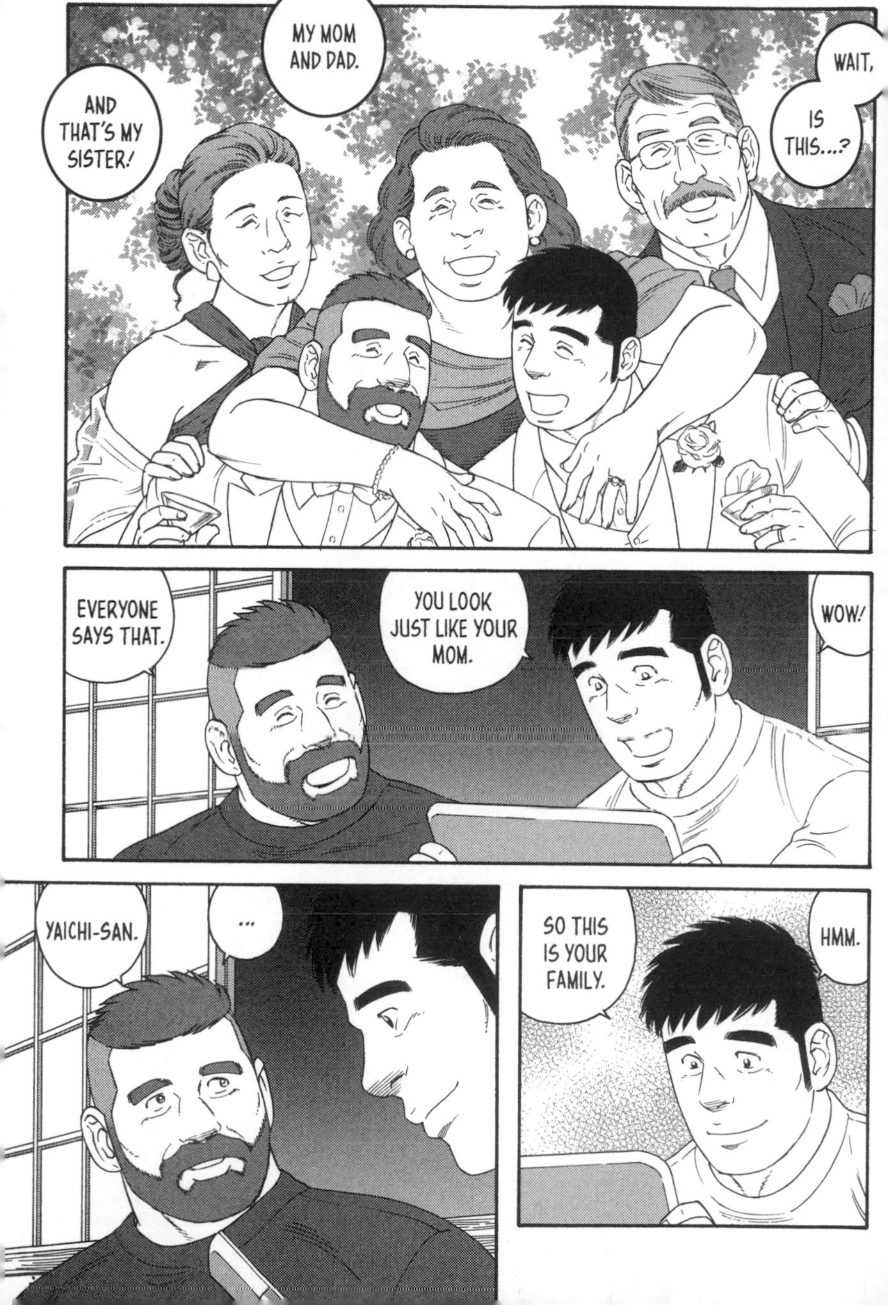
WAIT,
IS THIS...?
MY MOM AND DAD.
AND THAT'S MY SISTER!
WOW!
YOU LOOK JUST LIKE YOUR MOM.
EVERYONE SAYS THAT.
HMM.
SO THIS IS YOUR FAMILY.
...
YAICHI-SAN.

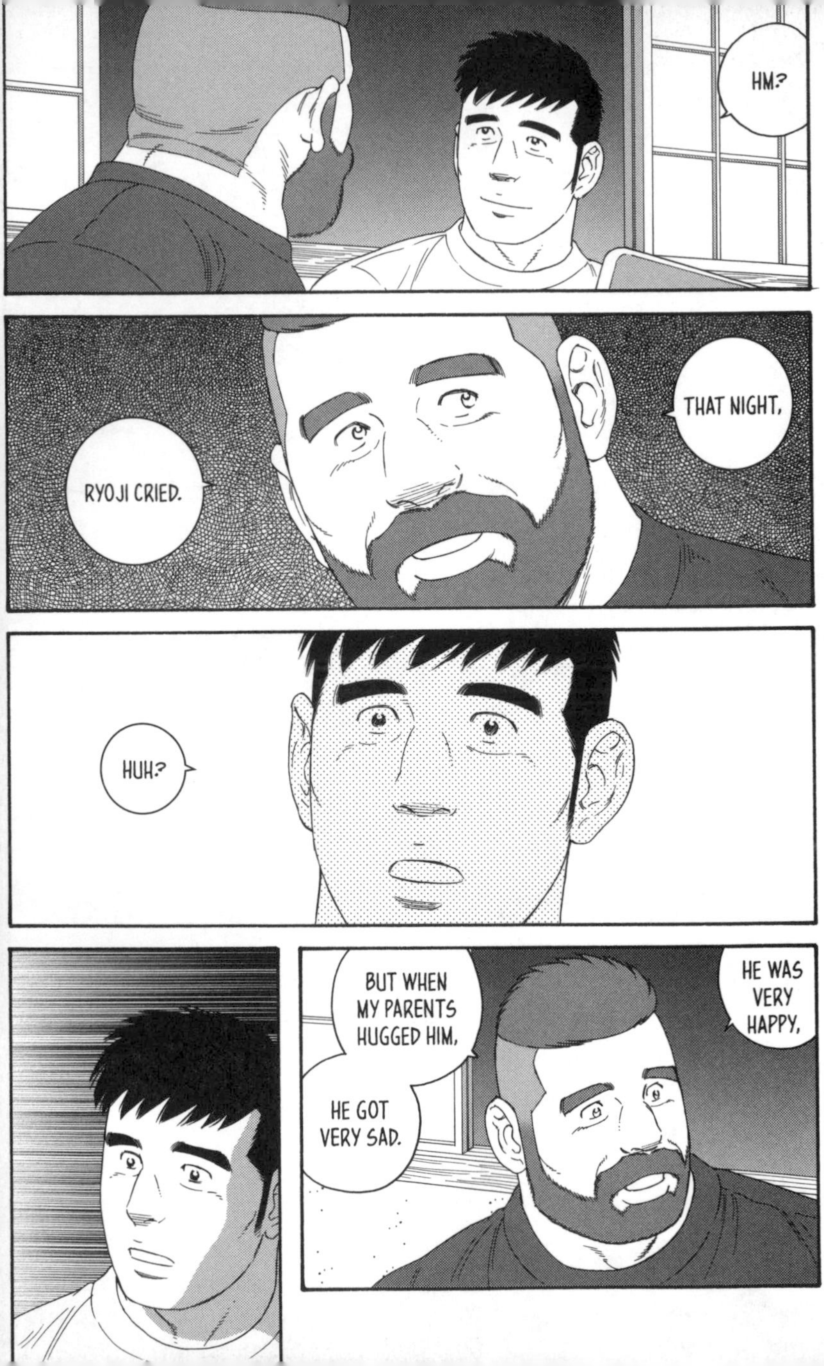
HM?
THAT NIGHT,
RYOJI CRIED.
HUH?
HE WAS VERY HAPPY,
BUT WHEN MY PARENTS HUGGED HIM,
HE GOT VERY SAD.

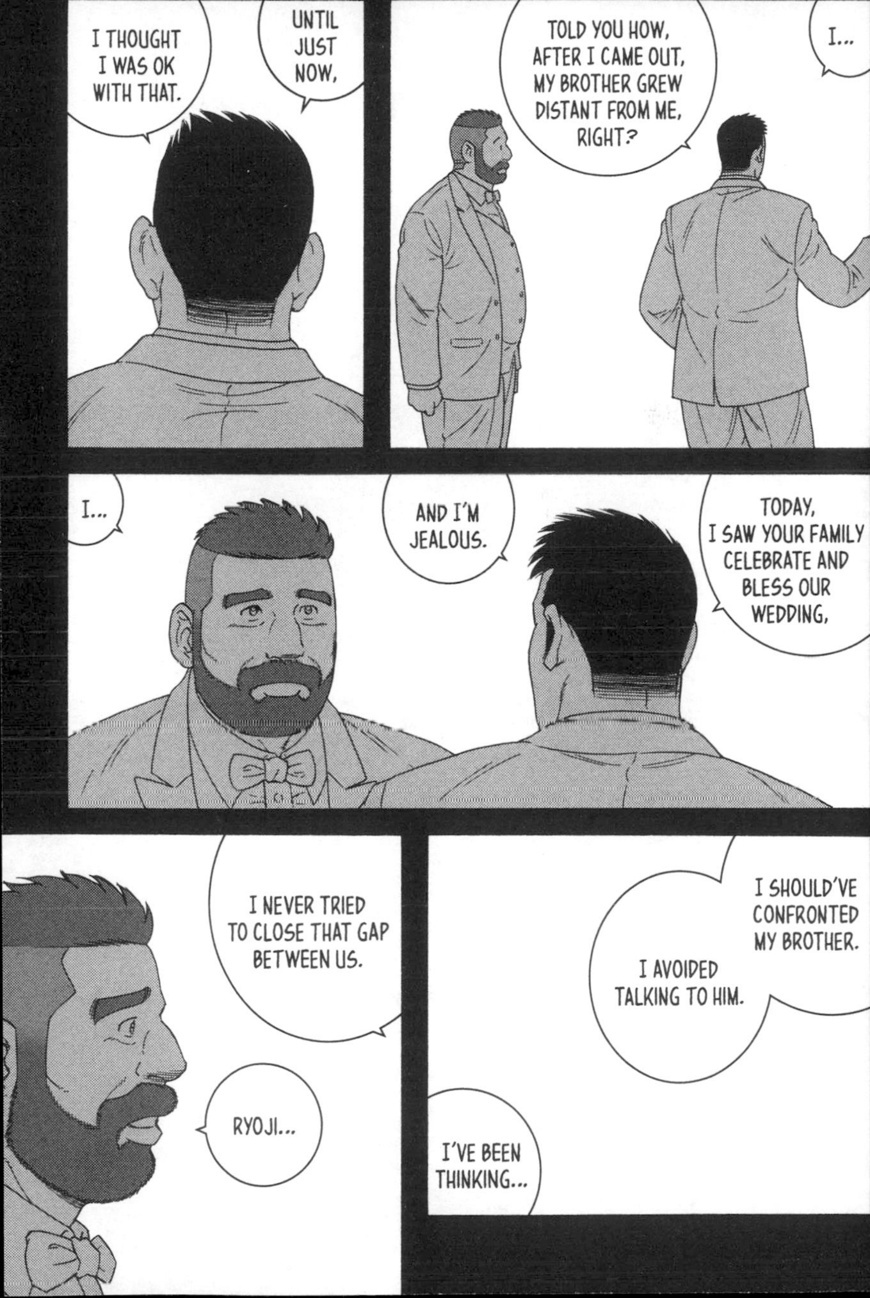
I...
TOLD YOU HOW, AFTER I CAME OUT, MY BROTHER GREW DISTANT FROM ME, RIGHT?
UNTIL JUST NOW,
I THOUGHT I WAS OK WITH THAT.
TODAY, I SAW YOUR FAMILY CELEBRATE AND BLESS OUR WEDDING,
AND I'M JEALOUS.
I...
I SHOULD'VE CONFRONTED MY BROTHER.
I AVOIDED TALKING TO HIM.
I'VE BEEN THINKING...
I NEVER TRIED TO CLOSE THAT GAP BETWEEN US.
RYOJI...

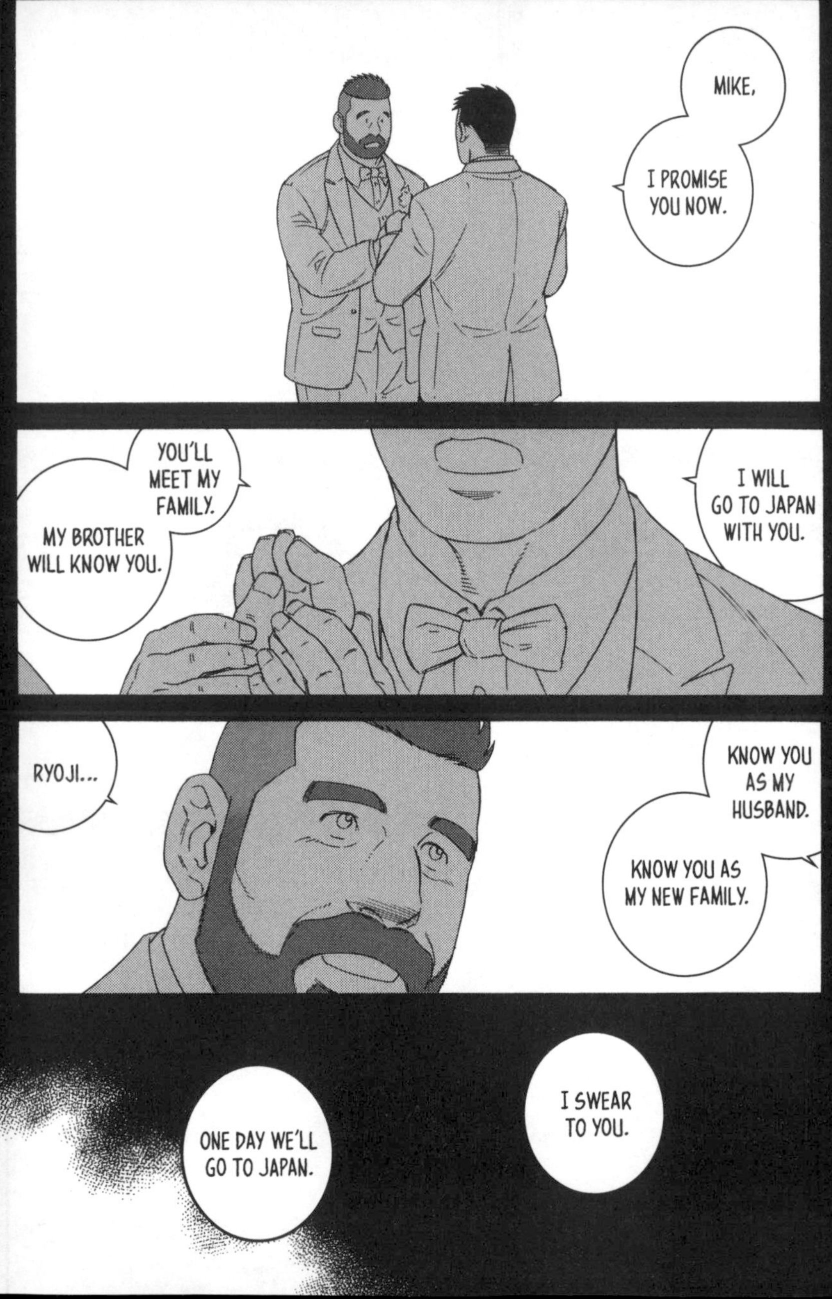
MIKE,
I PROMISE YOU NOW.
I WILL GO TO JAPAN WITH YOU.
YOU'LL MEET MY FAMILY.
MY BROTHER WILL KNOW YOU.
KNOW YOU AS MY HUSBAND.
KNOW YOU AS MY NEW FAMILY.
RYOJI...
I SWEAR TO YOU.
ONE DAY WE'LL GO TO JAPAN.

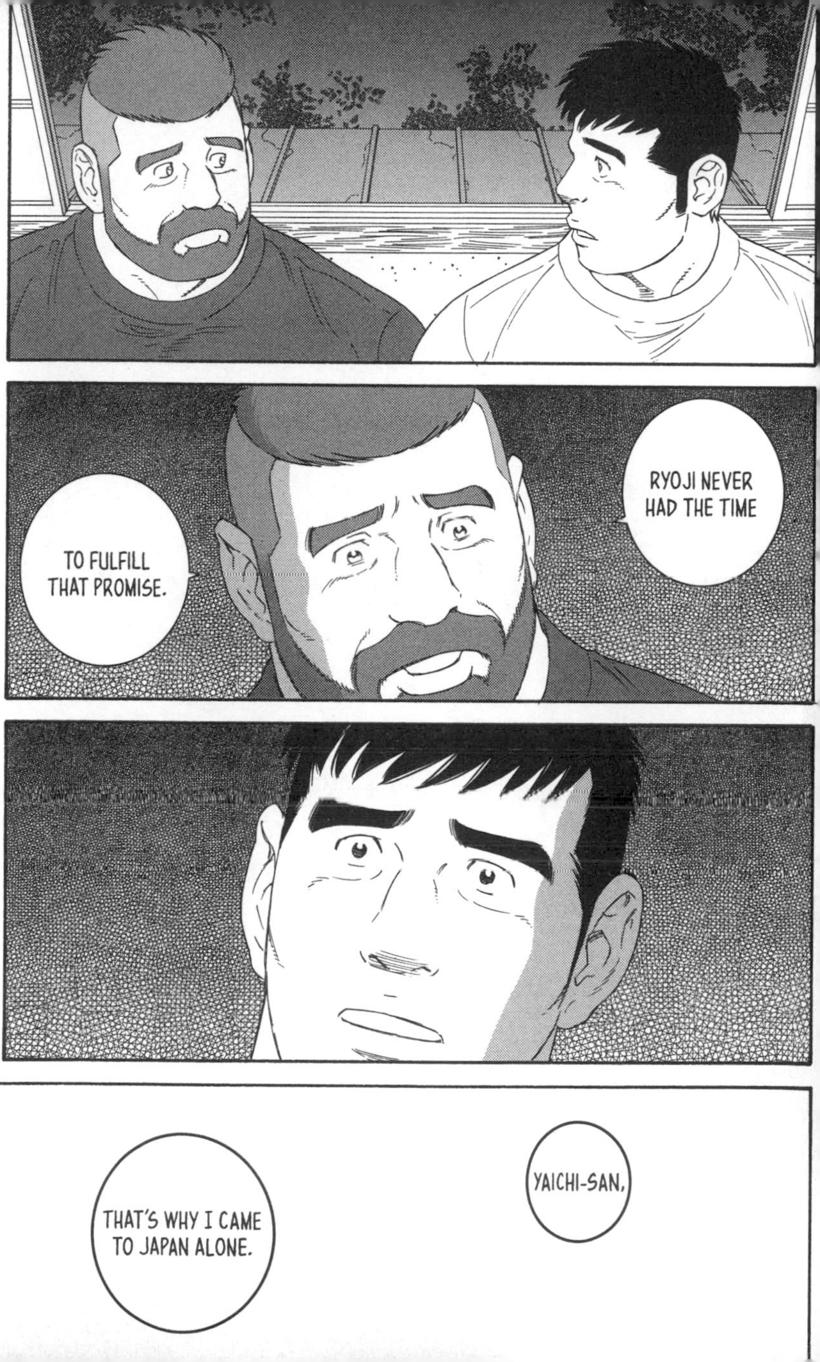
RYOJI NEVER HAD THE TIME
TO FULFILL THAT PROMISE.
YAICHI-SAN,
THAT'S WHY I CAME TO JAPAN ALONE.

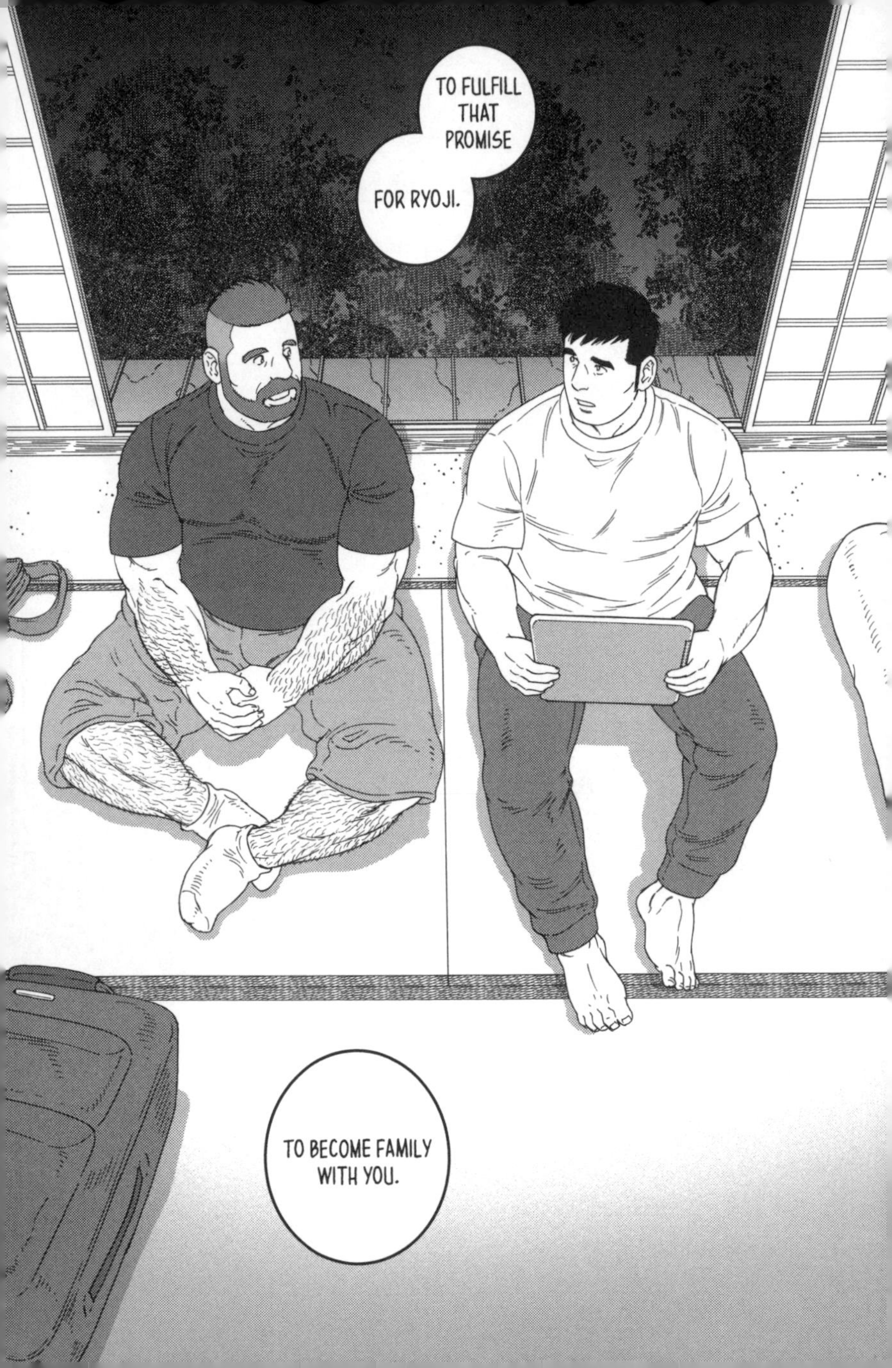
TO FULFILL THAT PROMISE
FOR RYOJI.
TO BECOME FAMILY WITH YOU.

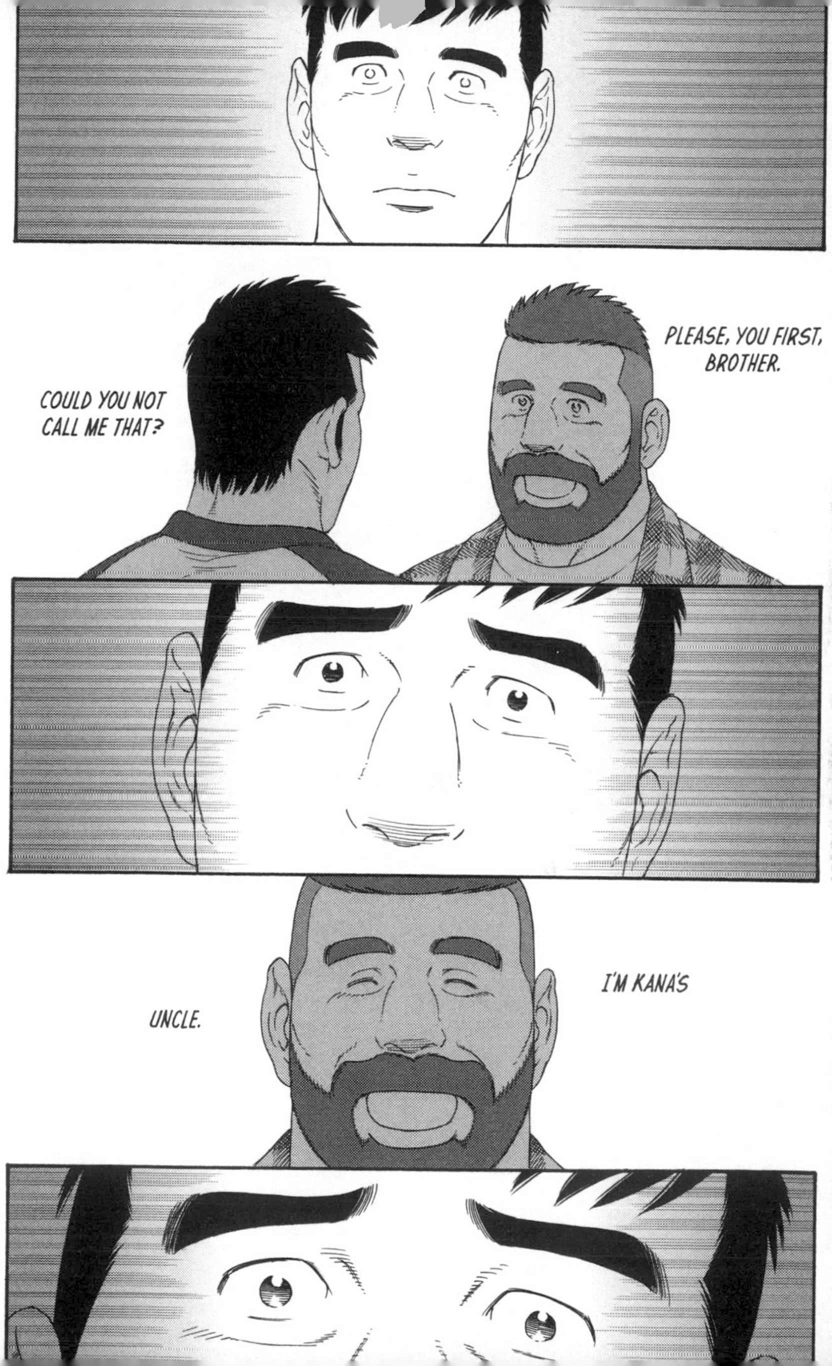
PLEASE, YOU FIRST, BROTHER.
COULD YOU NOT CALL ME THAT?
I'M KANA'S
UNCLE.

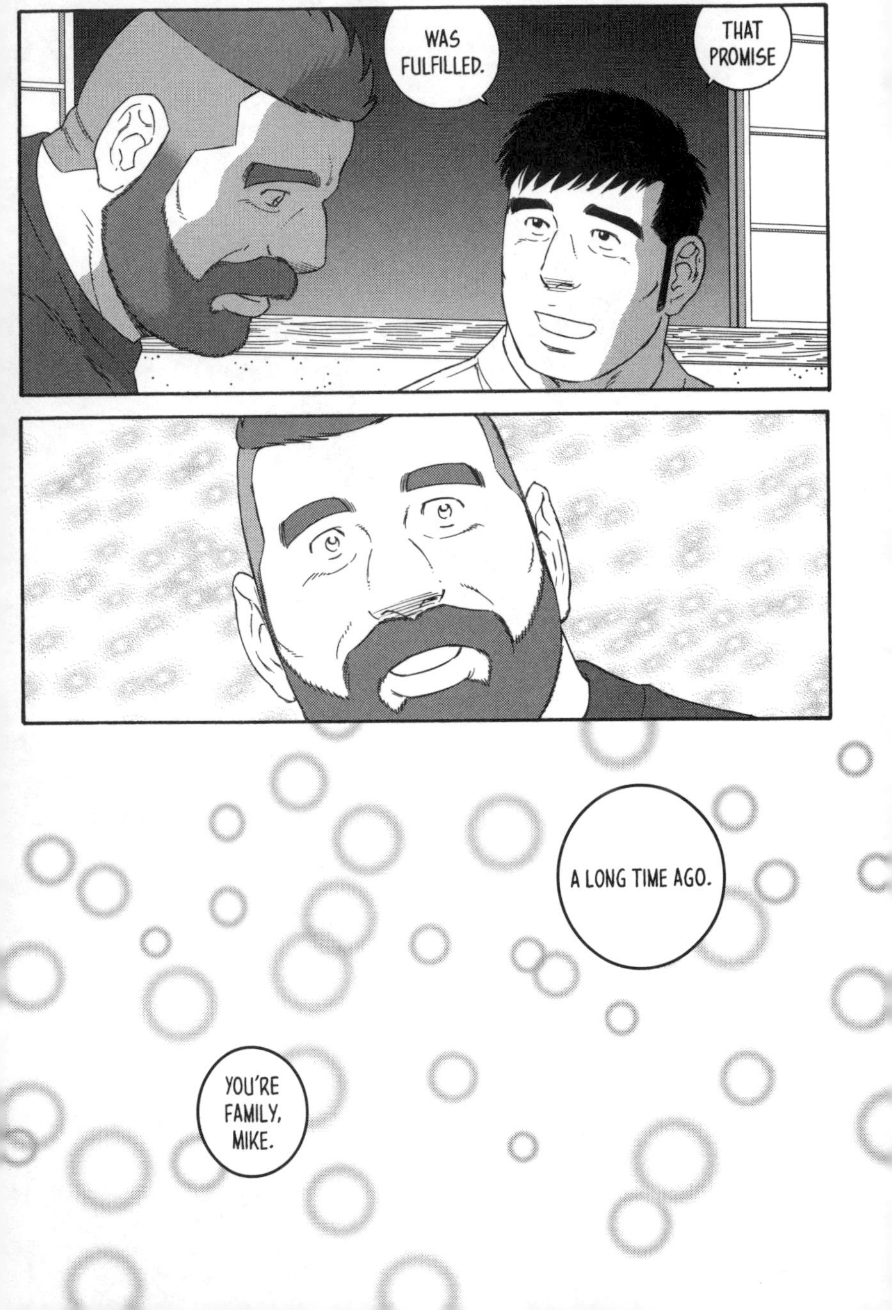
THAT PROMISE
WAS FULFILLED.
A LONG TIME AGO.
YOU'RE FAMILY, MIKE.

CHAPTER TWENTY-SIX
VISITING GRAVES

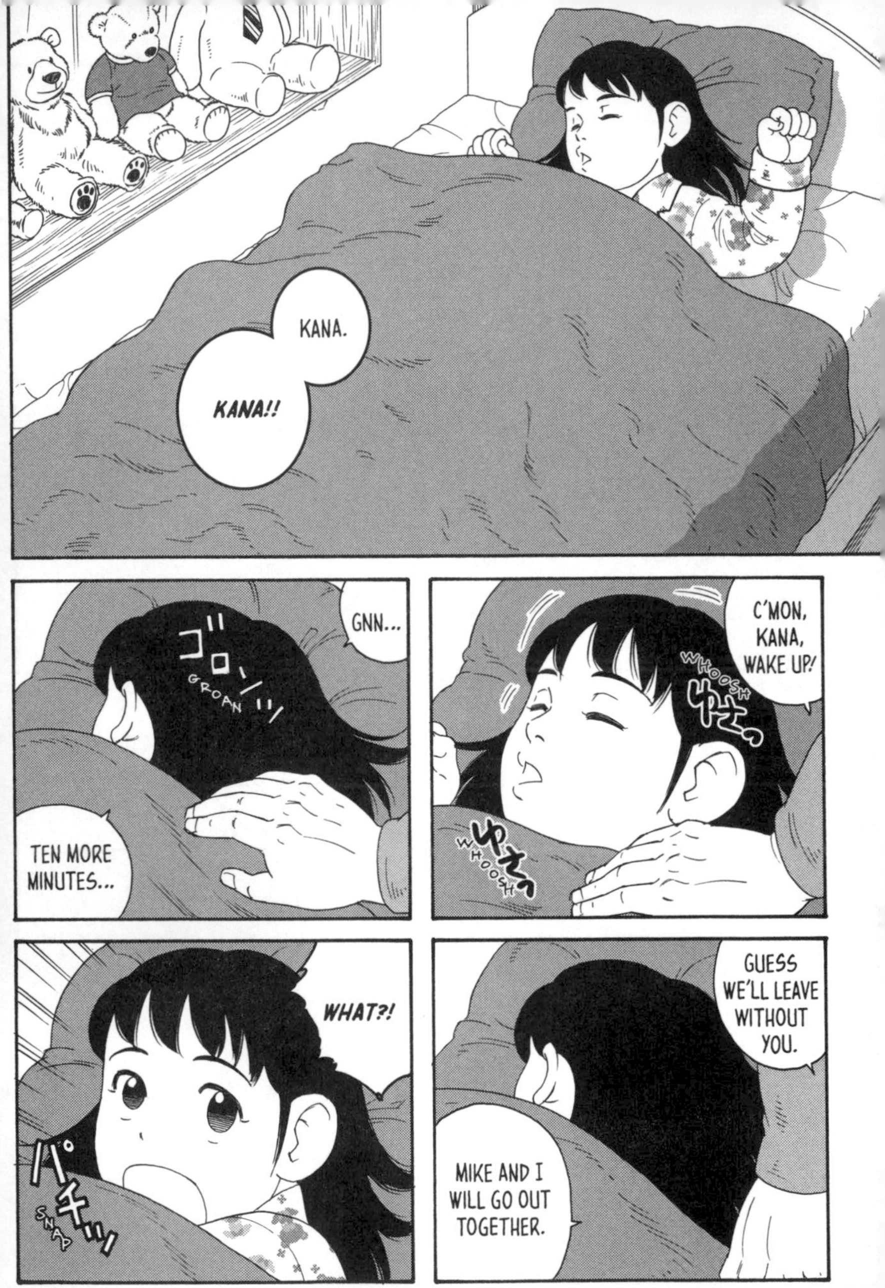

KANA.
KANA!!
C'MON, KANA, WAKE UP!
WHOOSH
WHOOSH
GNN...
GROAN
TEN MORE MINUTES...
GUESS WE'LL LEAVE WITHOUT YOU.
MIKE AND I WILL GO OUT TOGETHER.
WHAT?!
SNAP

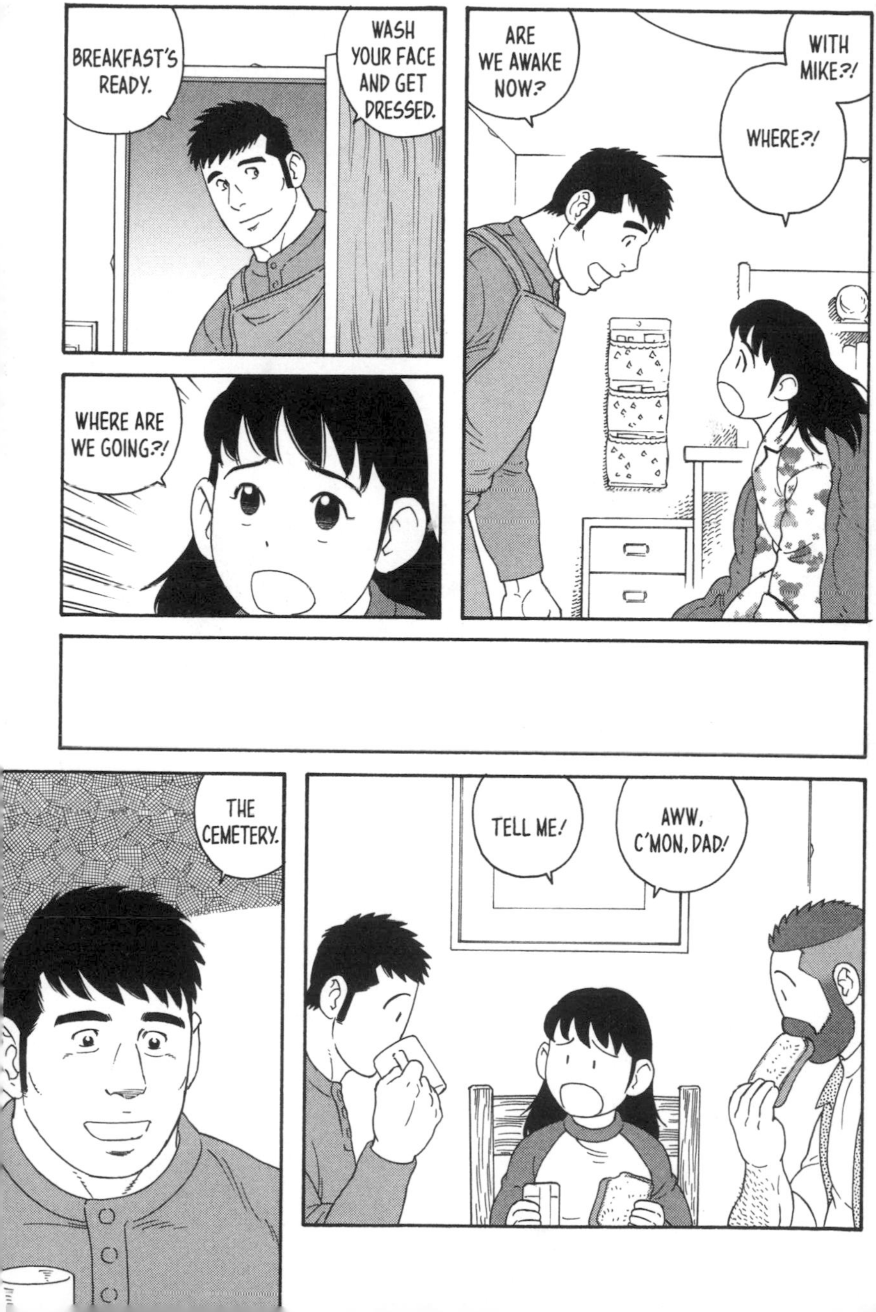
WITH MIKE?!
WHERE?!
ARE WE AWAKE NOW?
WASH YOUR FACE AND GET DRESSED.
BREAKFAST'S READY.
WHERE ARE WE GOING?!
AWW, C'MON, DAD!
TELL ME!
THE CEMETERY.

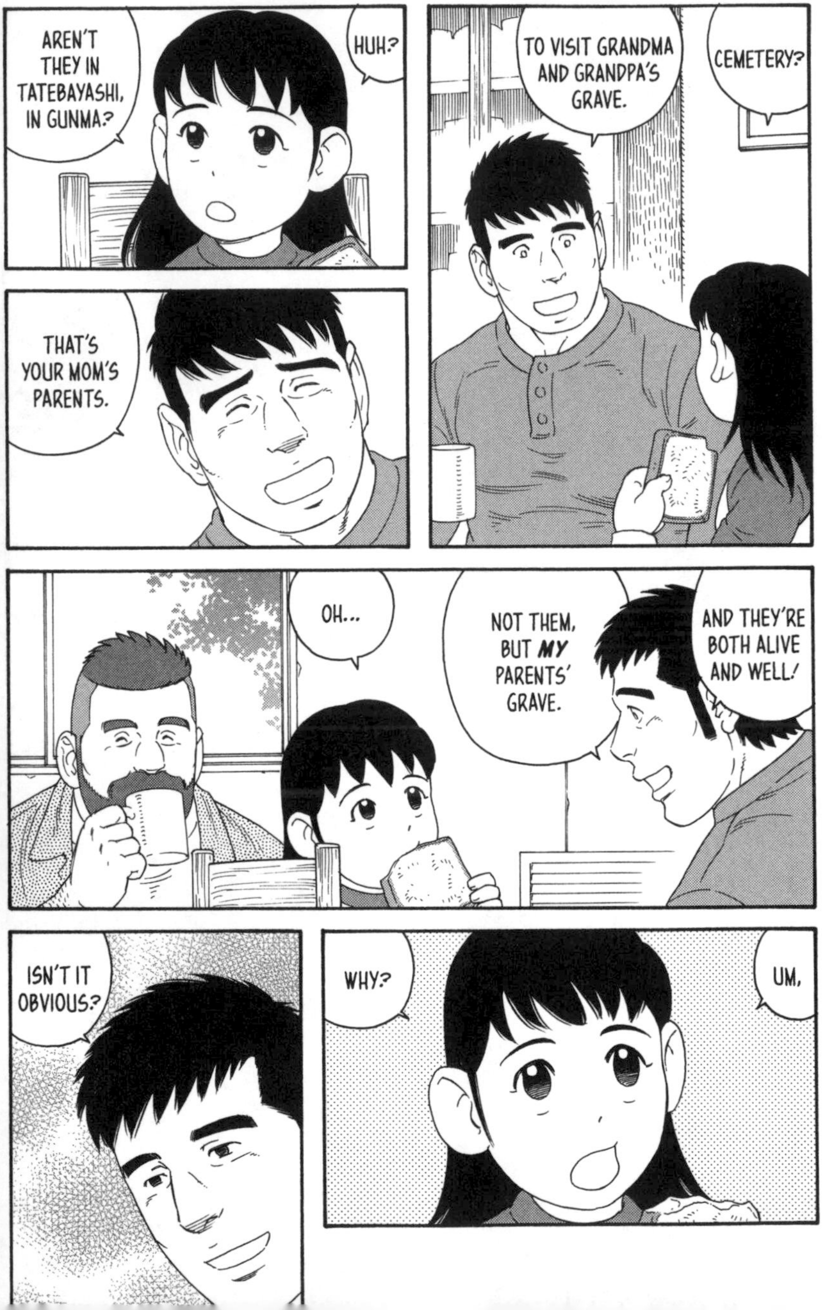
CEMETERY?
TO VISIT GRANDMA AND GRANDPA'S GRAVE.
HUH?
AREN'T THEY IN TATEBAYASHI, IN GUNMA?
THAT'S YOUR MOM'S PARENTS.
AND THEY'RE BOTH ALIVE AND WELL!
NOT THEM, BUT ***MY*** PARENTS' GRAVE.
OH...
UM,
WHY?
ISN'T IT OBVIOUS?

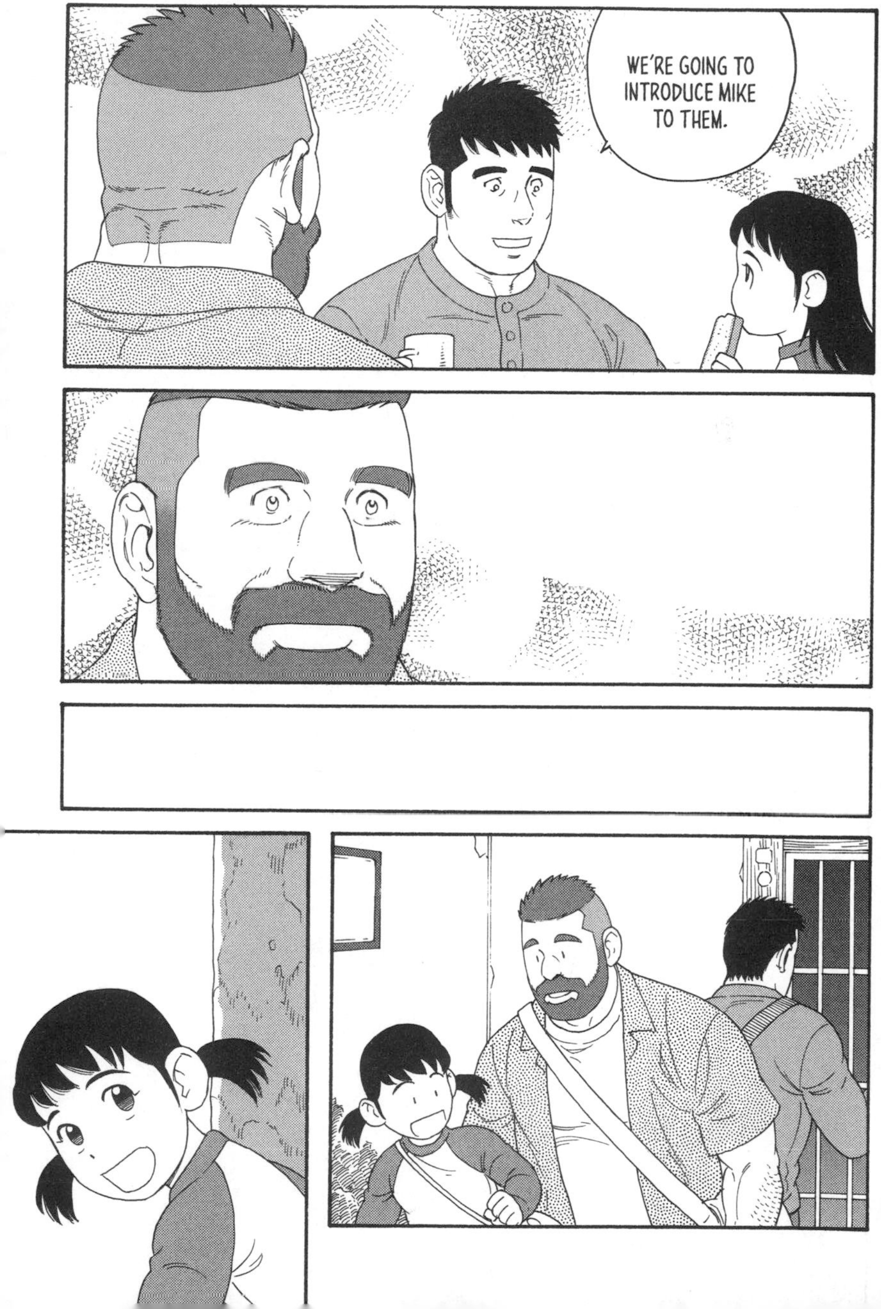
WE'RE GOING TO INTRODUCE MIKE TO THEM.

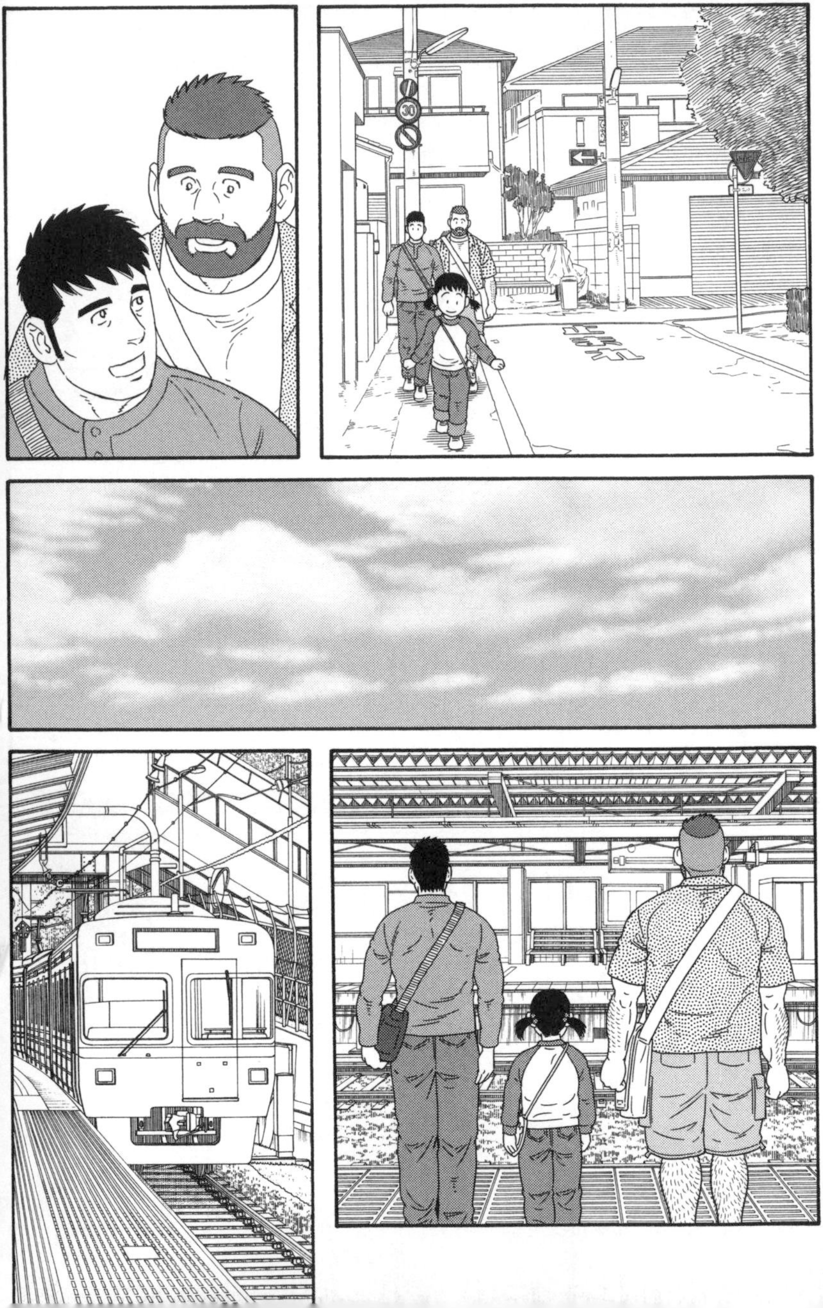
30

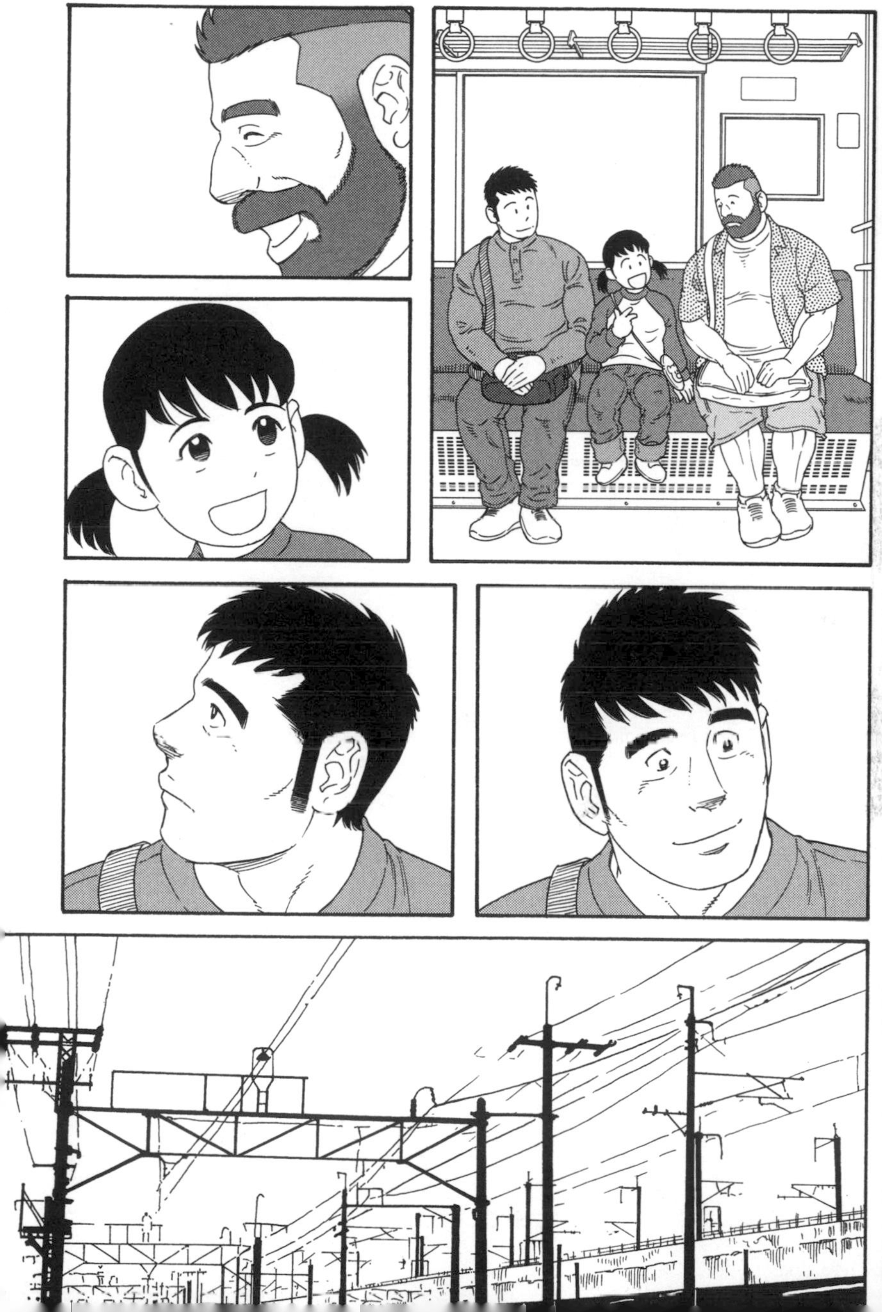

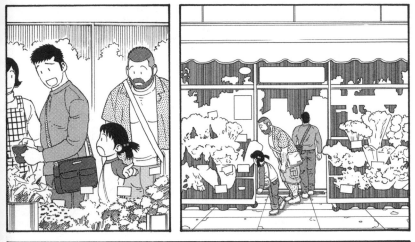

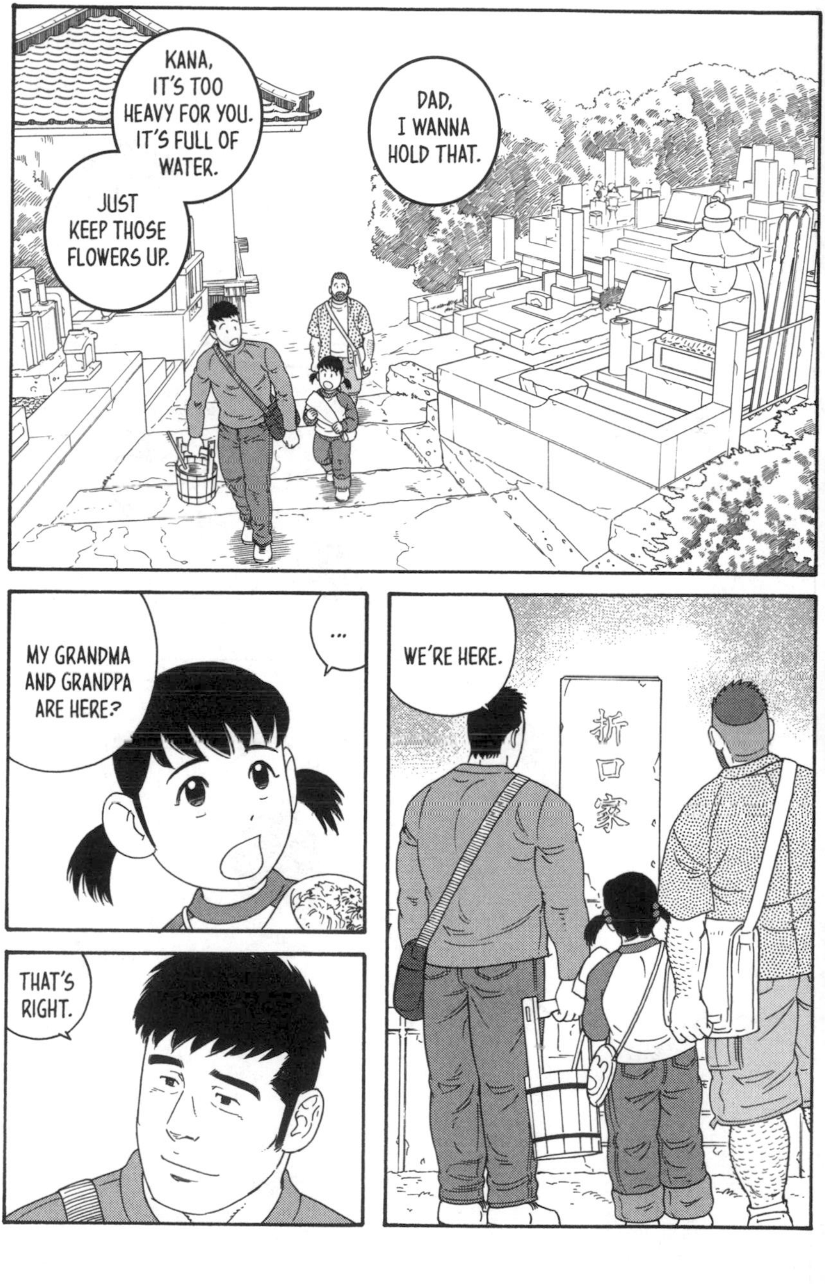
DAD, I WANNA HOLD THAT.
KANA, IT'S TOO HEAVY FOR YOU. IT'S FULL OF WATER.
JUST KEEP THOSE FLOWERS UP.
WE'RE HERE.
折口家
...
MY GRANDMA AND GRANDPA ARE HERE?
THAT'S RIGHT.

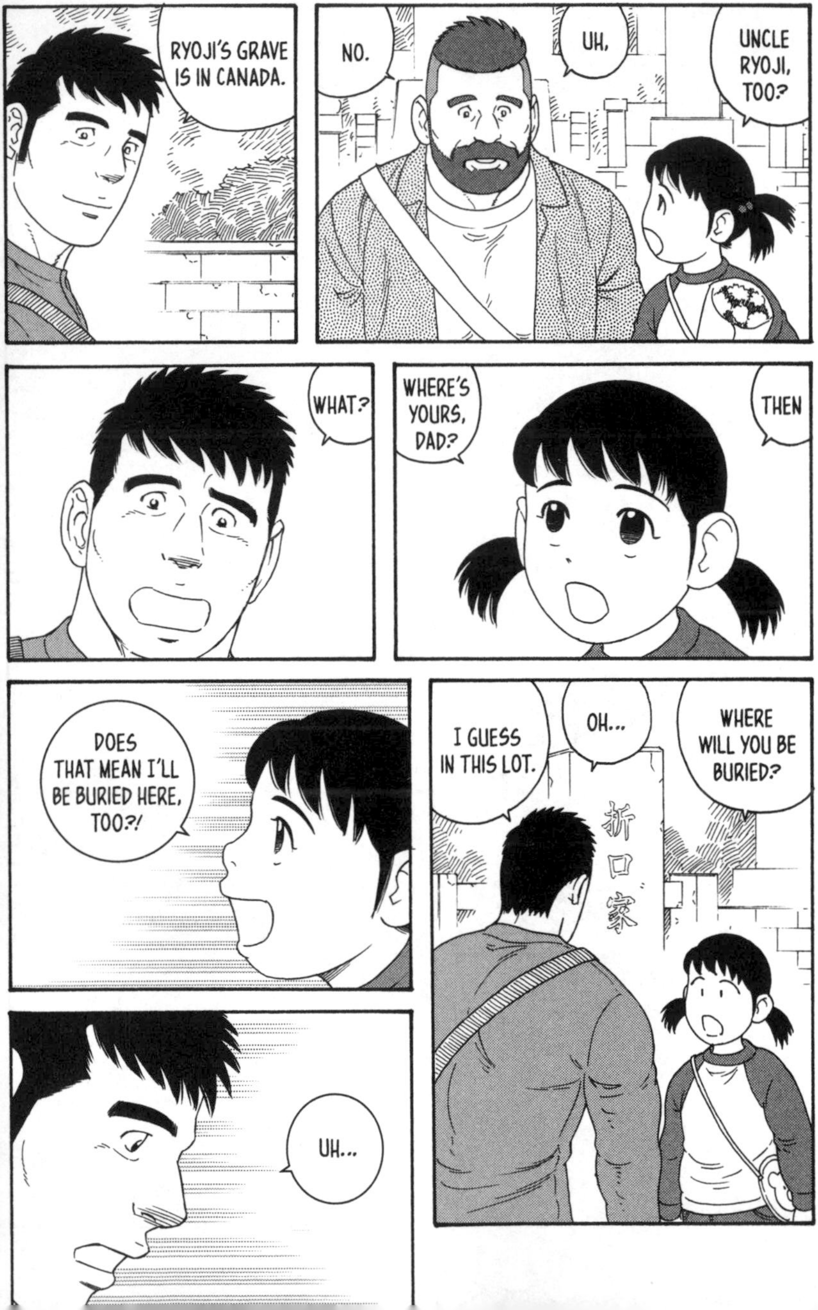
UNCLE RYOJI, TOO?
UH,
NO.
RYOJI'S GRAVE IS IN CANADA.
THEN
WHERE'S YOURS, DAD?
WHAT?
WHERE WILL YOU BE BURIED?
OH...
I GUESS IN THIS LOT.
折口家
DOES THAT MEAN I'LL BE BURIED HERE, TOO?!
UH...

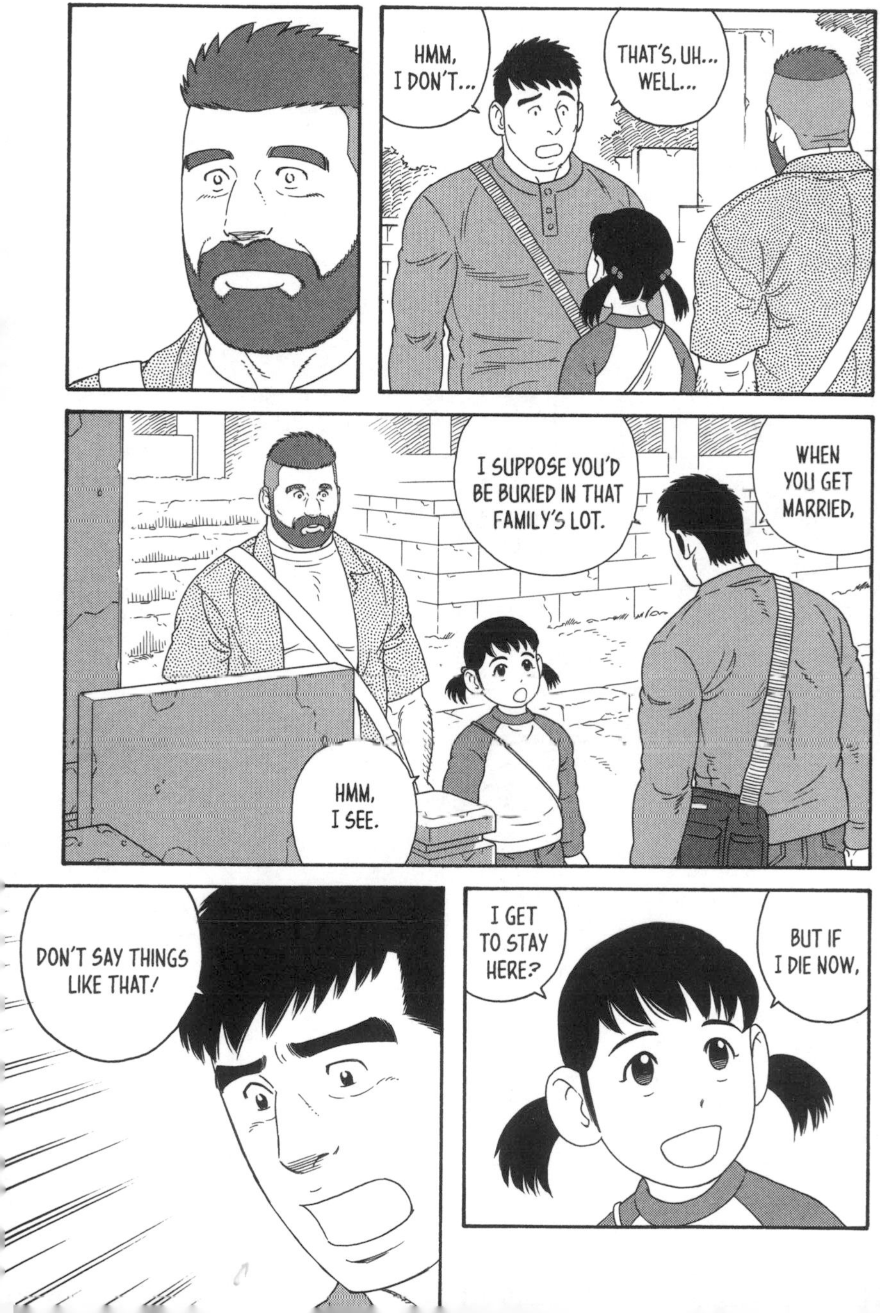
THAT'S, UH... WELL...
HMM, I DON'T...
WHEN YOU GET MARRIED,
I SUPPOSE YOU'D BE BURIED IN THAT FAMILY'S LOT.
HMM, I SEE.
BUT IF I DIE NOW,
I GET TO STAY HERE?
DON'T SAY THINGS LIKE THAT!

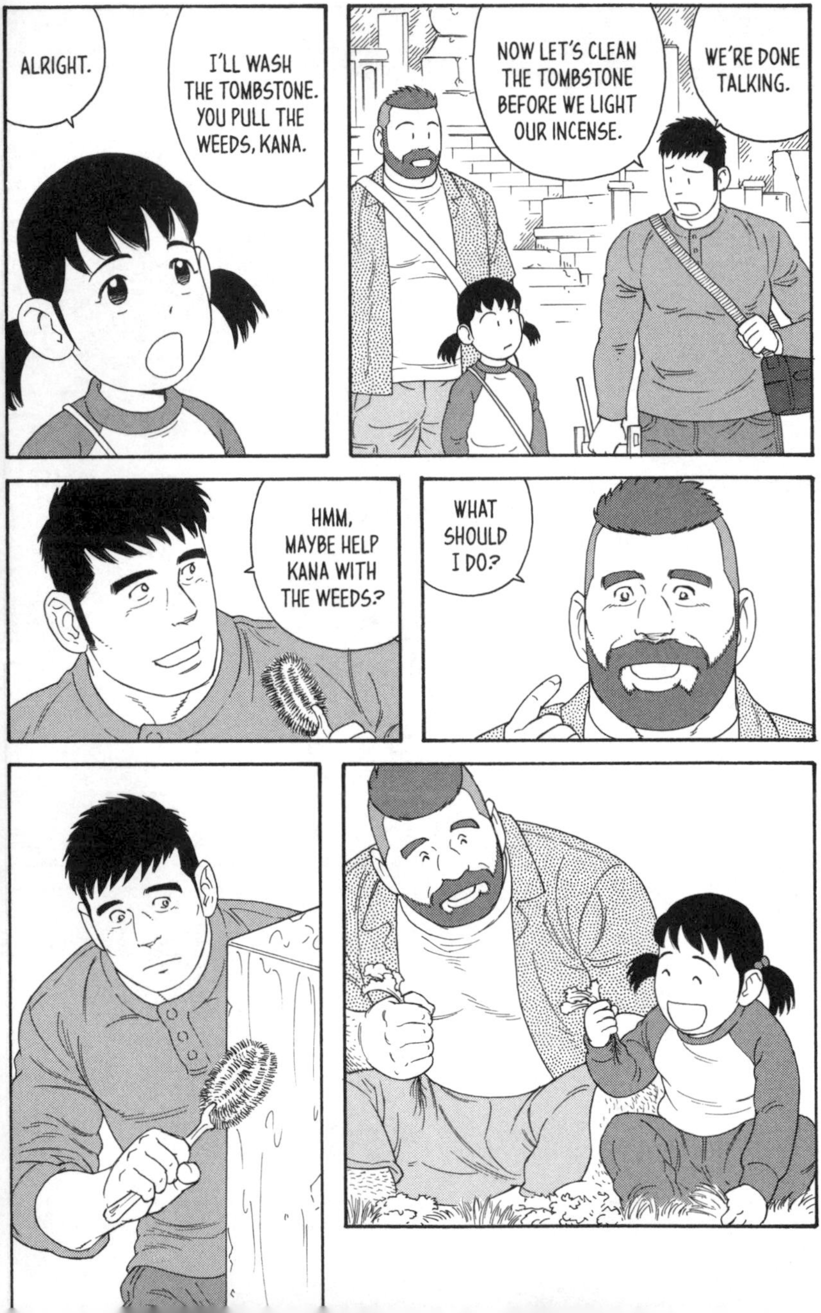
WE'RE DONE TALKING.
NOW LET'S CLEAN THE TOMBSTONE BEFORE WE LIGHT OUR INCENSE.
I'LL WASH THE TOMBSTONE. YOU PULL THE WEEDS, KANA.
ALRIGHT.
WHAT SHOULD I DO?
HMM, MAYBE HELP KANA WITH THE WEEDS?

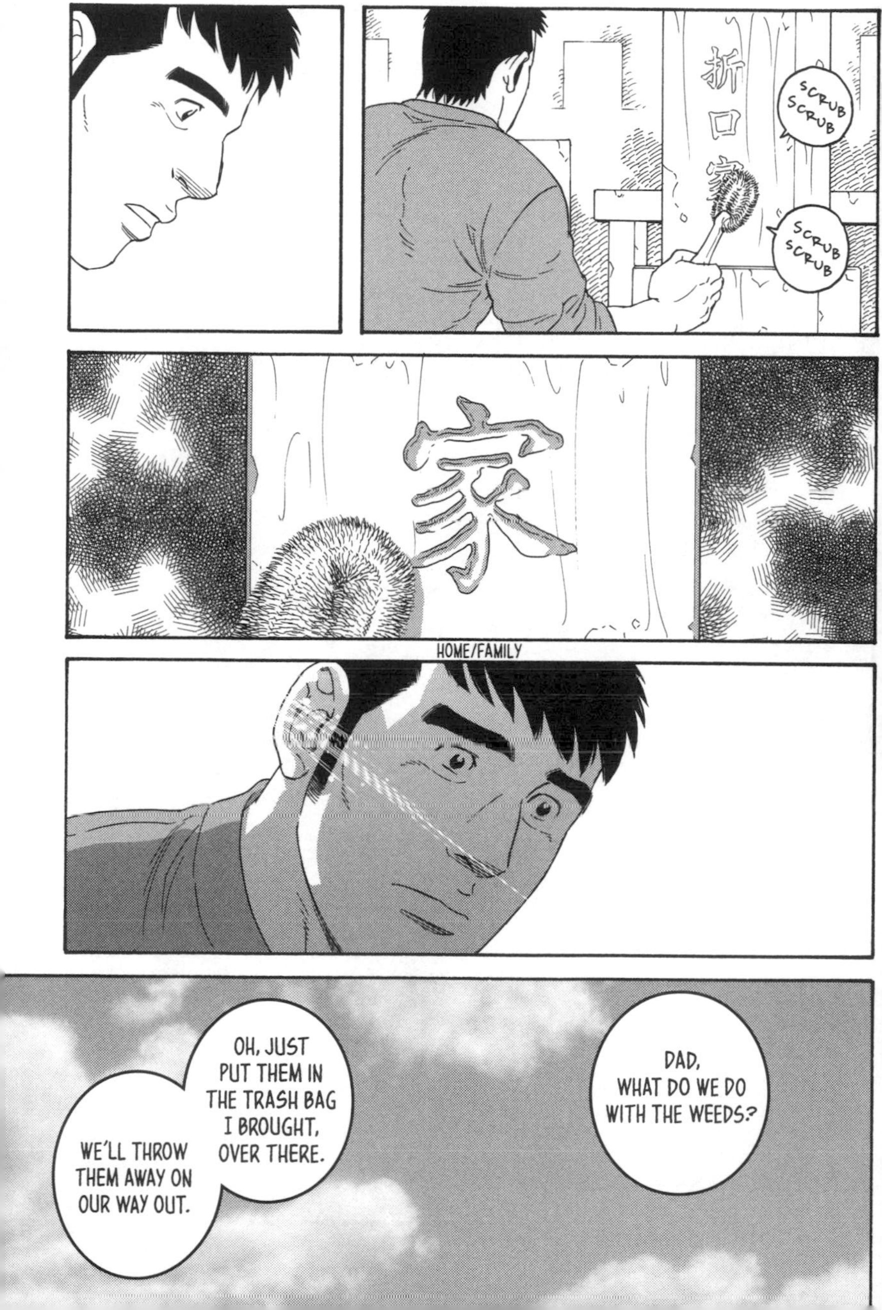
SCRUB SCRUB
SCRUB SCRUB
家
HOME/FAMILY
DAD, WHAT DO WE DO WITH THE WEEDS?
OH, JUST PUT THEM IN THE TRASH BAG I BROUGHT, OVER THERE.
WE'LL THROW THEM AWAY ON OUR WAY OUT.

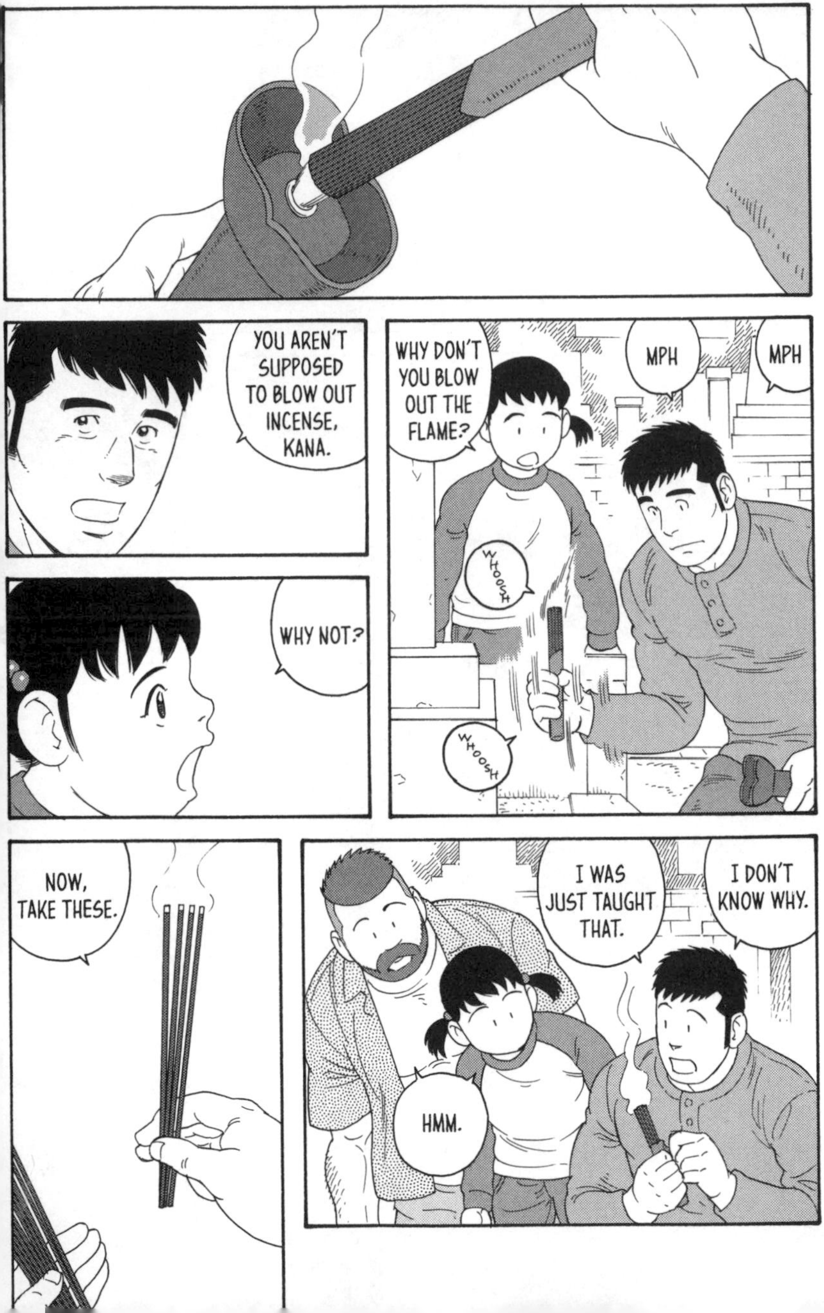
MPH
MPH
WHY DON'T YOU BLOW OUT THE FLAME?
WHOOSH
WHOOSH
YOU AREN'T SUPPOSED TO BLOW OUT INCENSE, KANA.
WHY NOT?
I DON'T KNOW WHY.
I WAS JUST TAUGHT THAT.
HMM.
NOW, TAKE THESE.

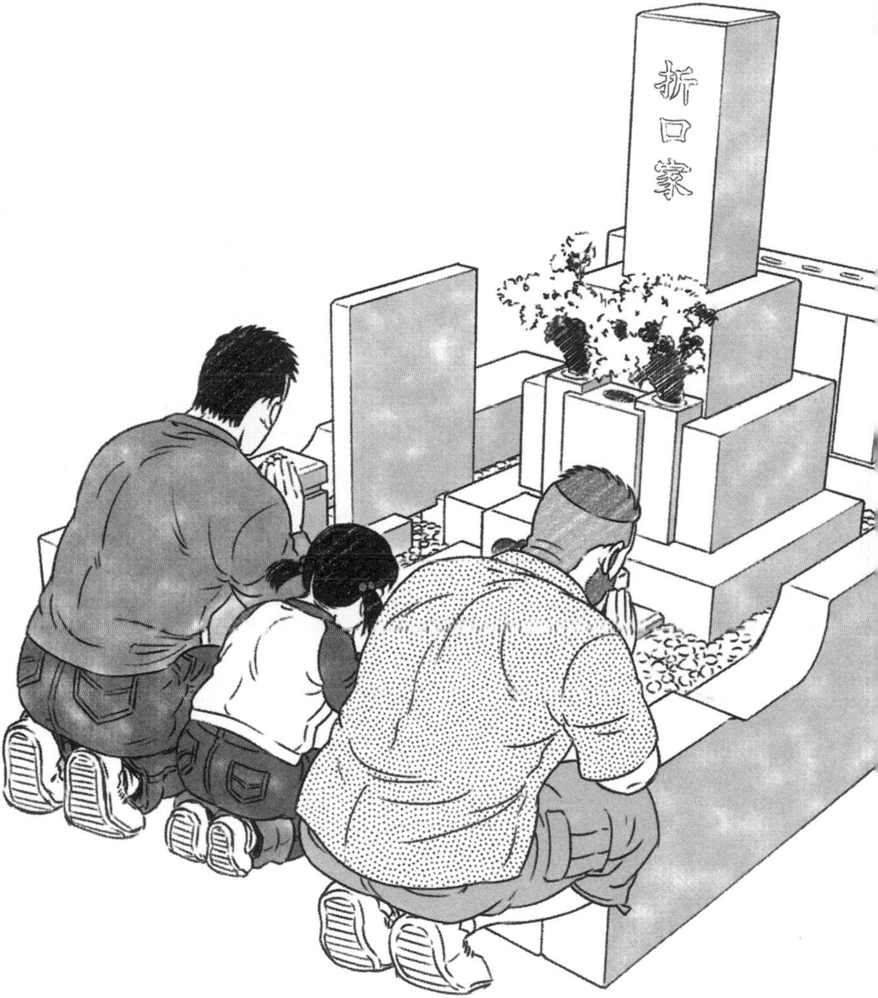
折口家

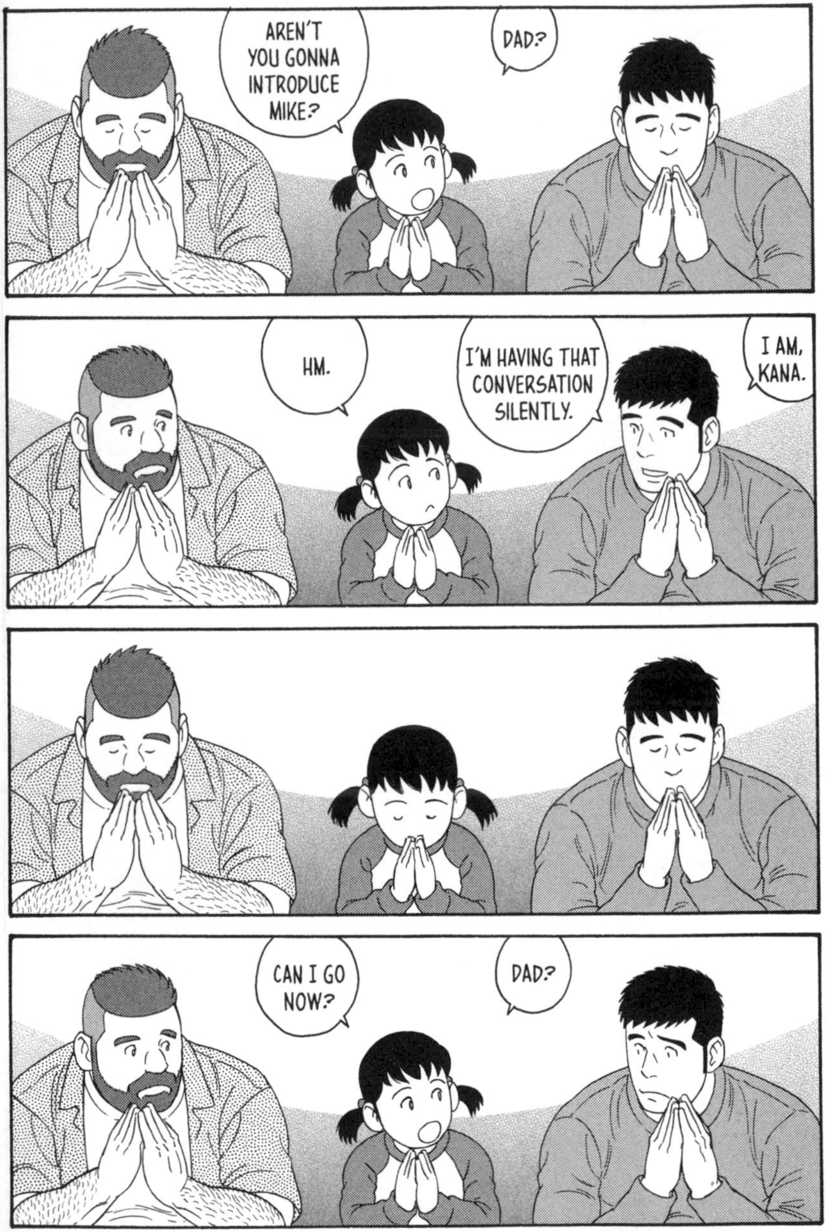
DAD?
AREN'T YOU GONNA INTRODUCE MIKE?
I AM, KANA.
I'M HAVING THAT CONVERSATION SILENTLY.
HM.
DAD?
CAN I GO NOW?

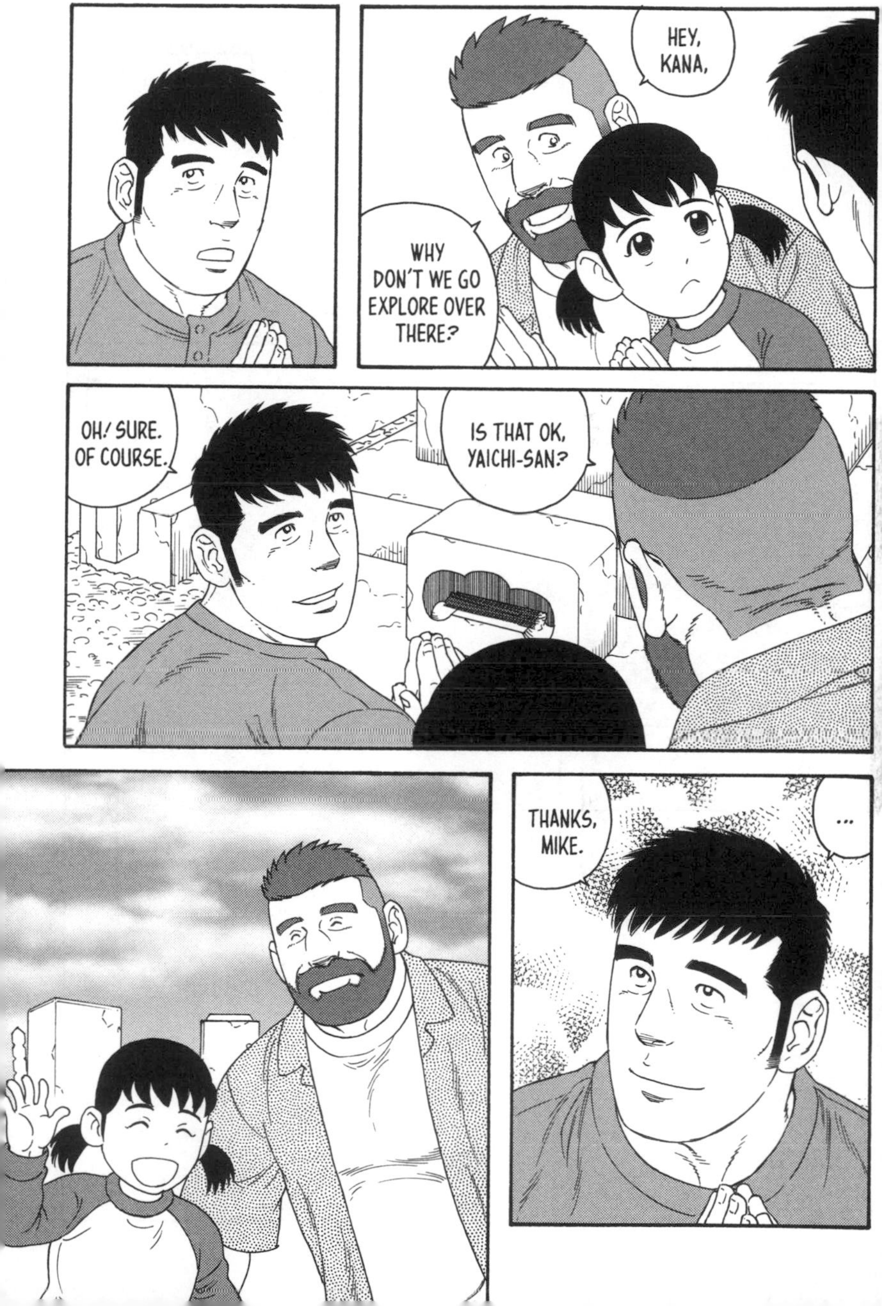
HEY, KANA,
WHY DON'T WE GO EXPLORE OVER THERE?
IS THAT OK, YAICHI-SAN?
OH! SURE. OF COURSE.
...
THANKS, MIKE.

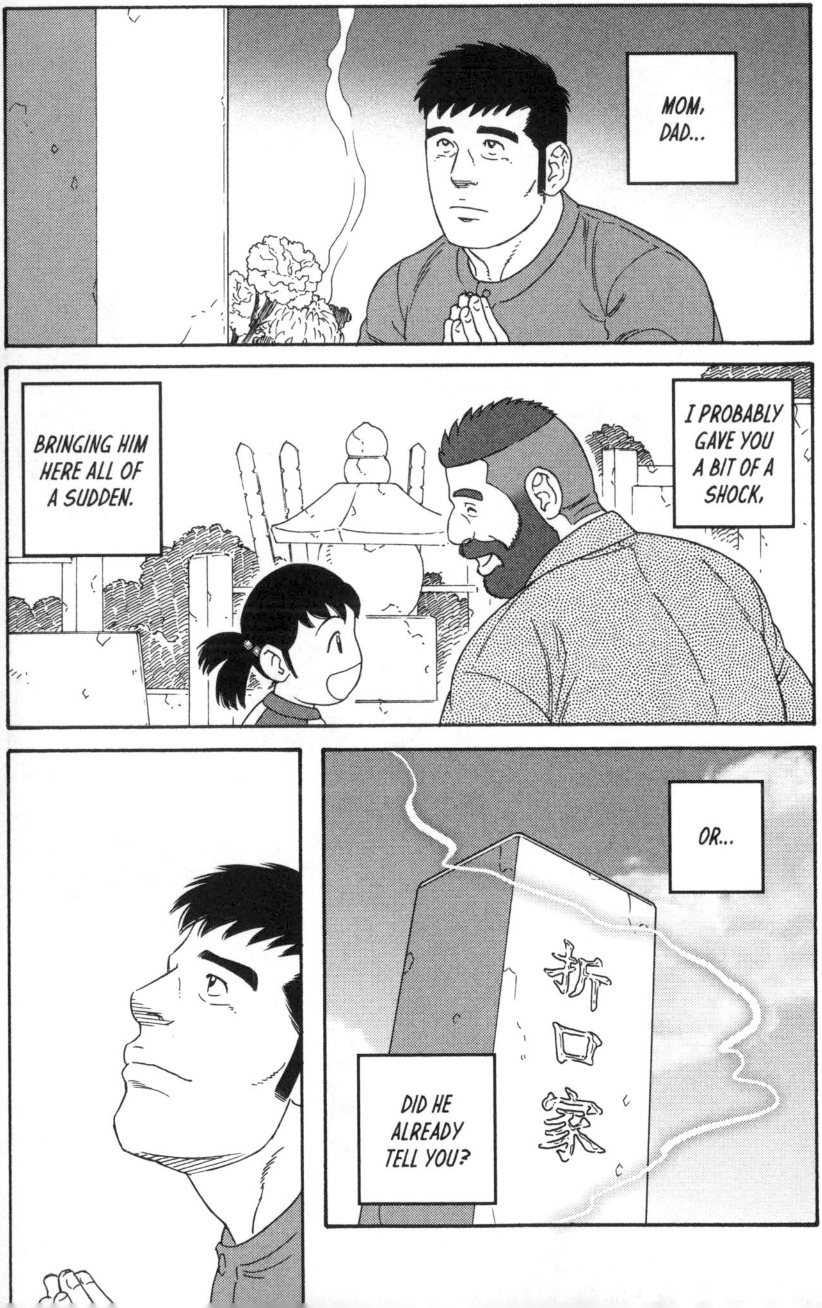
MOM, DAD...
I PROBABLY GAVE YOU A BIT OF A SHOCK,
BRINGING HIM HERE ALL OF A SUDDEN.
OR...
折口家
DID HE ALREADY TELL YOU?

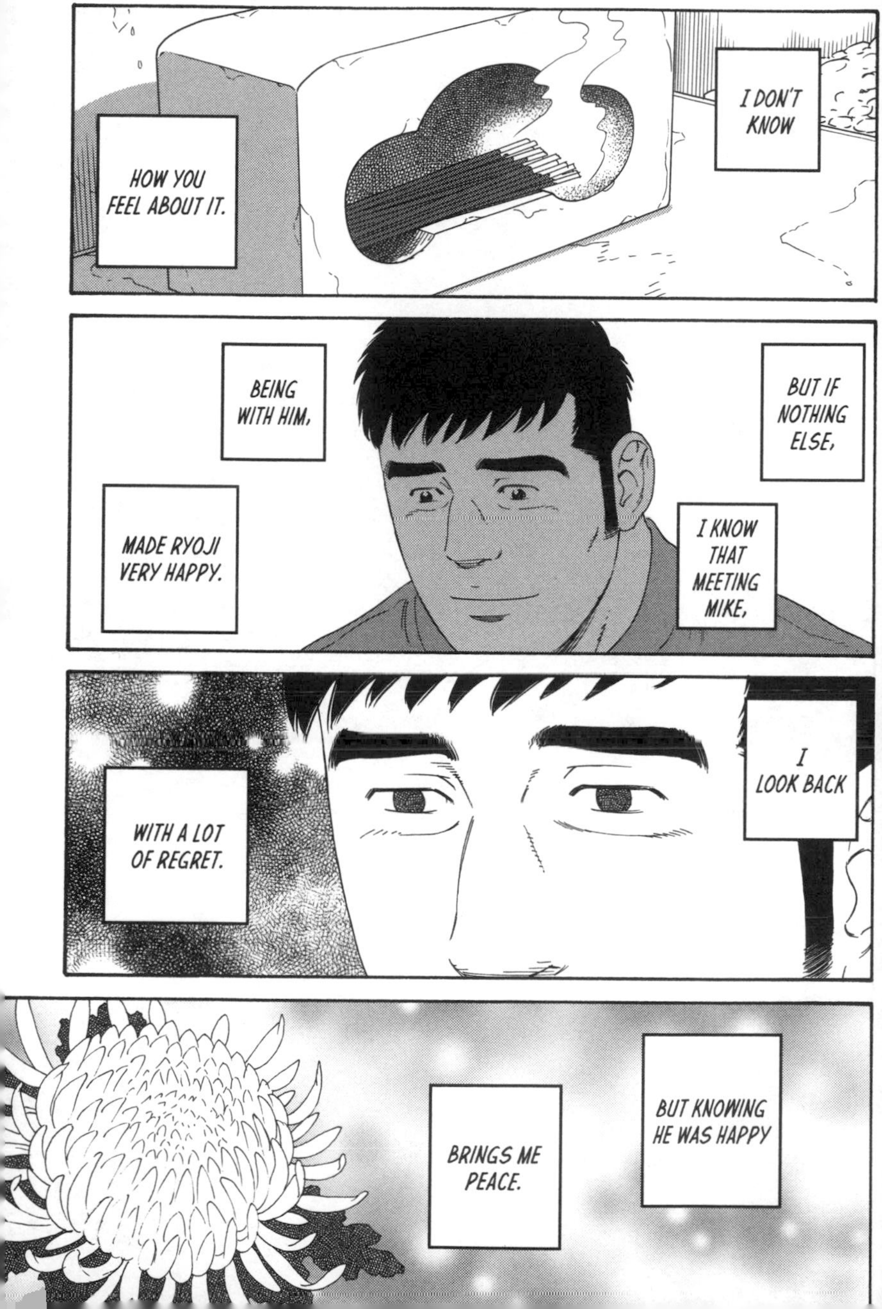
I DON'T KNOW
HOW YOU FEEL ABOUT IT.
BUT IF NOTHING ELSE,
I KNOW THAT MEETING MIKE,
BEING WITH HIM,
MADE RYOJI VERY HAPPY.
I LOOK BACK
WITH A LOT OF REGRET.
BUT KNOWING HE WAS HAPPY
BRINGS ME PEACE.

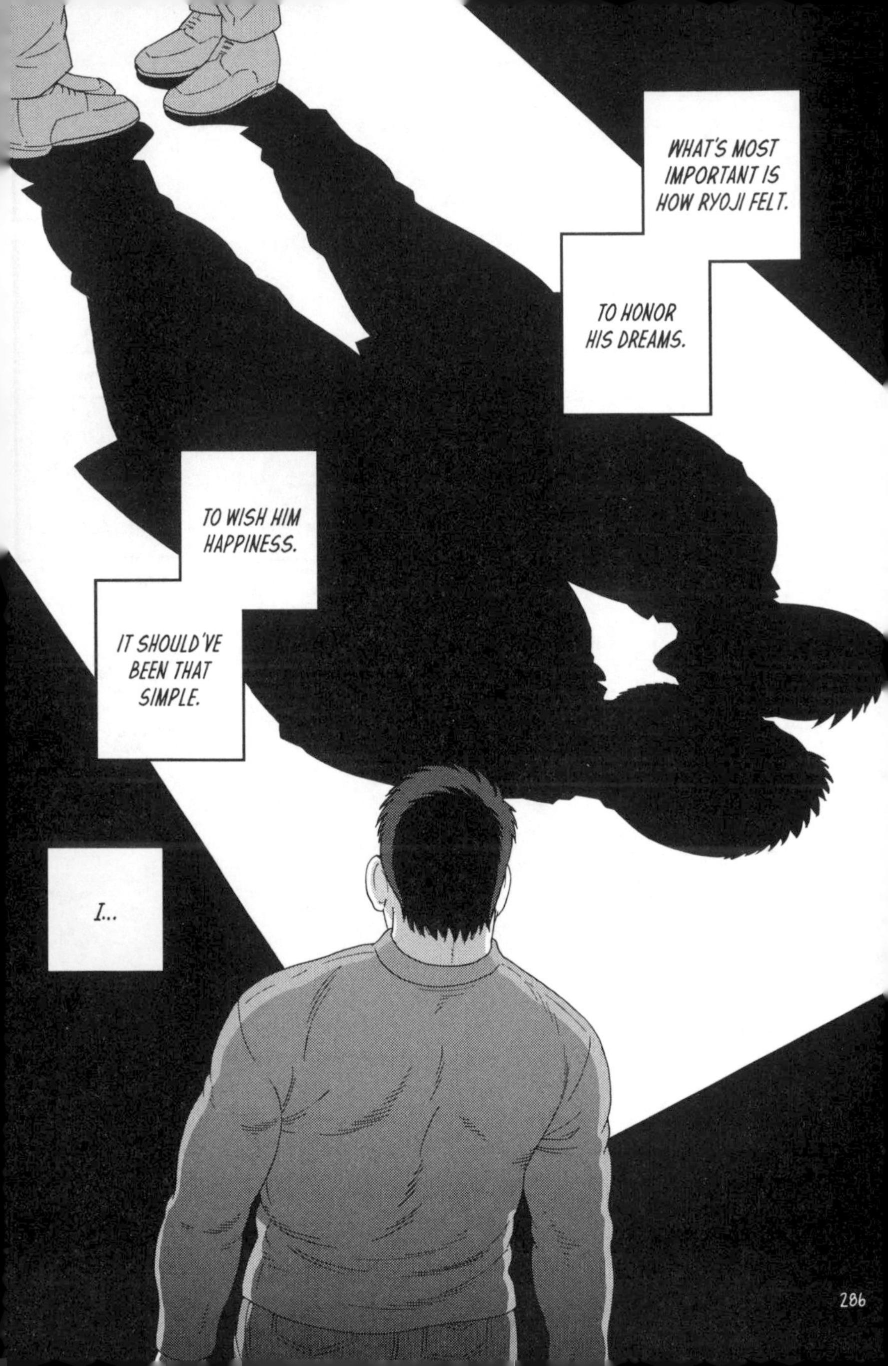
WHAT'S MOST IMPORTANT IS HOW RYOJI FELT.
TO HONOR HIS DREAMS.
TO WISH HIM HAPPINESS.
IT SHOULD'VE BEEN THAT SIMPLE.
I...

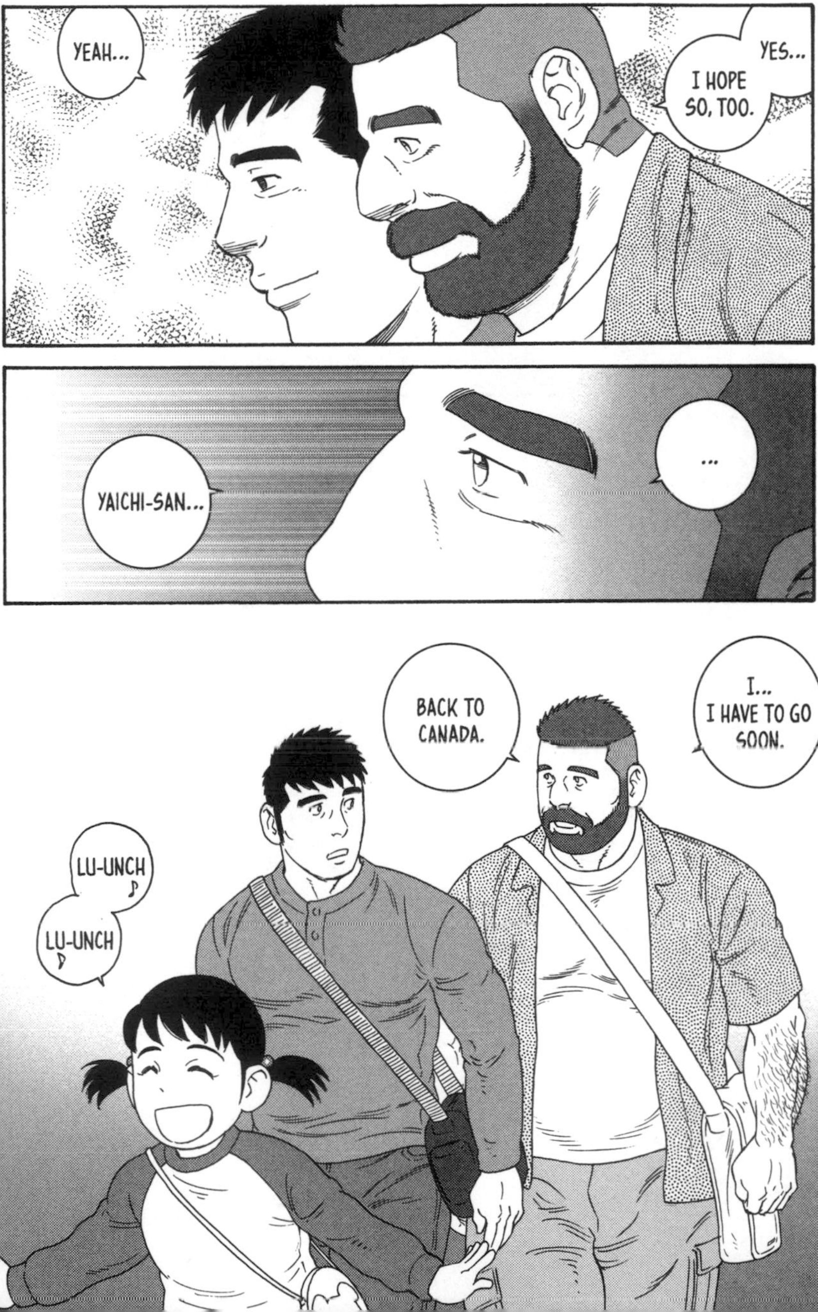
YES... I HOPE SO, TOO.
YEAH...
...
YAICHI-SAN...
I... I HAVE TO GO SOON.
BACK TO CANADA.
LU-UNCH ♪
LU-UNCH ♪

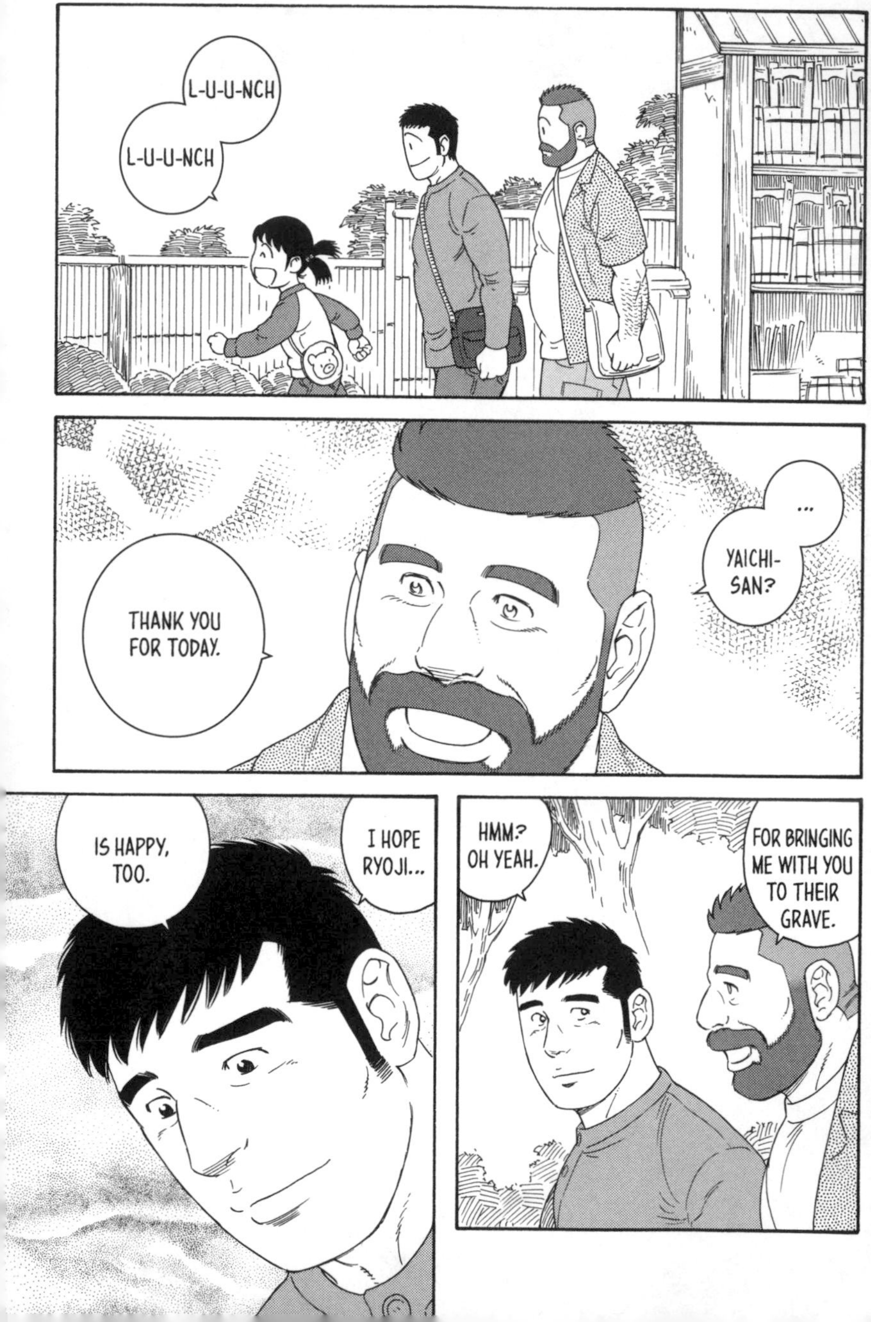
L-U-U-NCH
L-U-U-NCH
...
YAICHI-SAN?
THANK YOU FOR TODAY.
FOR BRINGING ME WITH YOU TO THEIR GRAVE.
HMM? OH YEAH.
I HOPE RYOJI...
IS HAPPY, TOO.

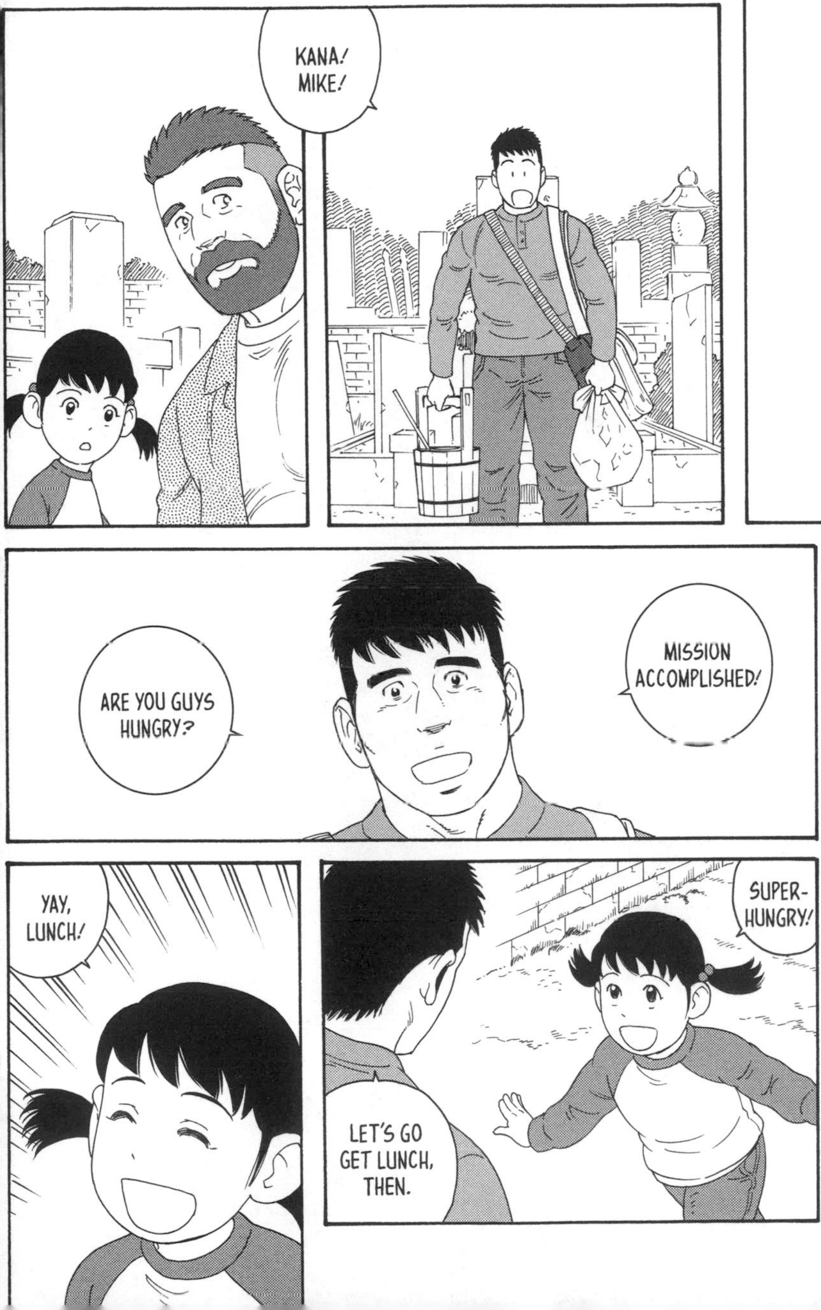
KANA! MIKE!
MISSION ACCOMPLISHED!
ARE YOU GUYS HUNGRY?
SUPER-HUNGRY!
LET'S GO GET LUNCH, THEN.
YAY, LUNCH!

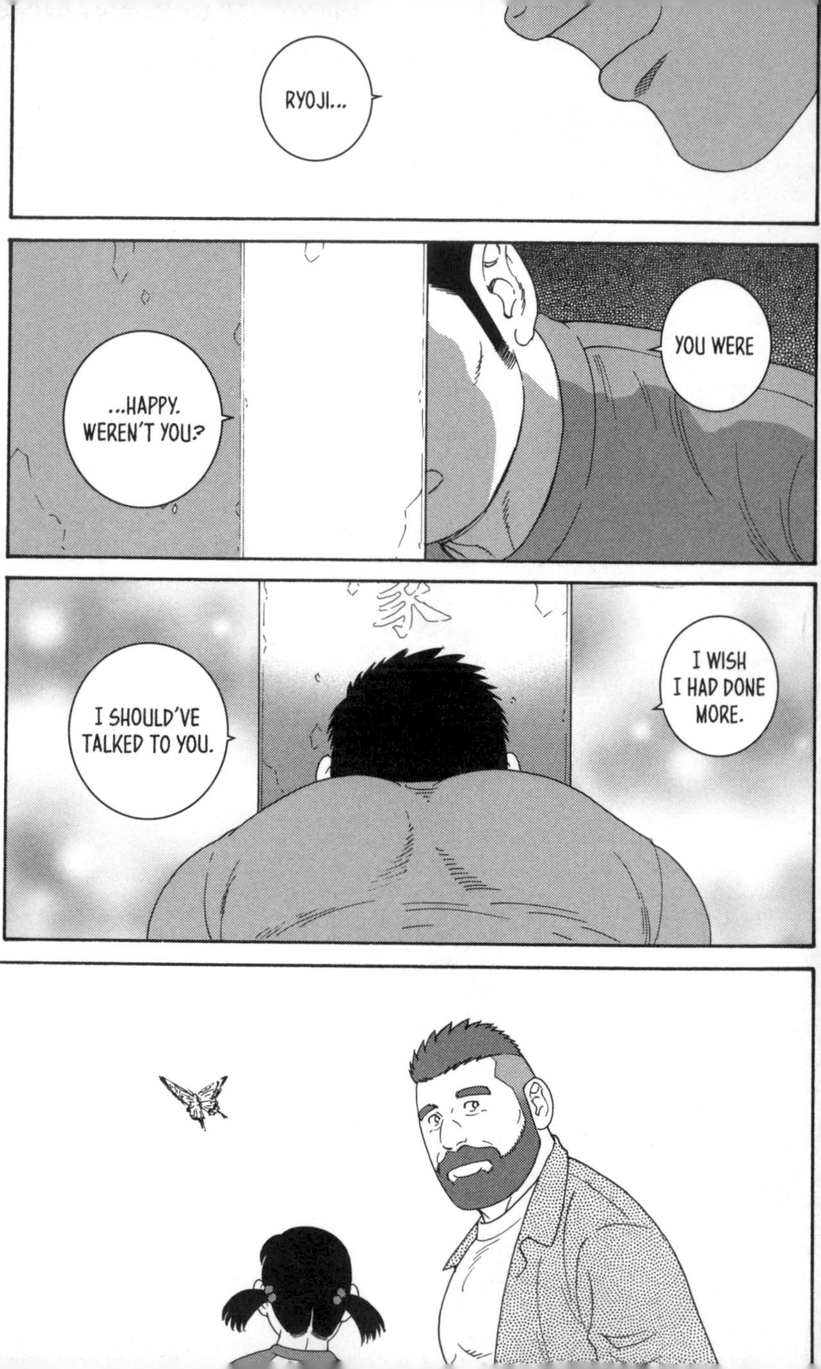
RYOJI...
YOU WERE
...HAPPY. WEREN'T YOU?
I WISH I HAD DONE MORE.
I SHOULD'VE TALKED TO YOU.

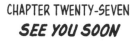

CHAPTER TWENTY-SEVEN
SEE YOU SOON

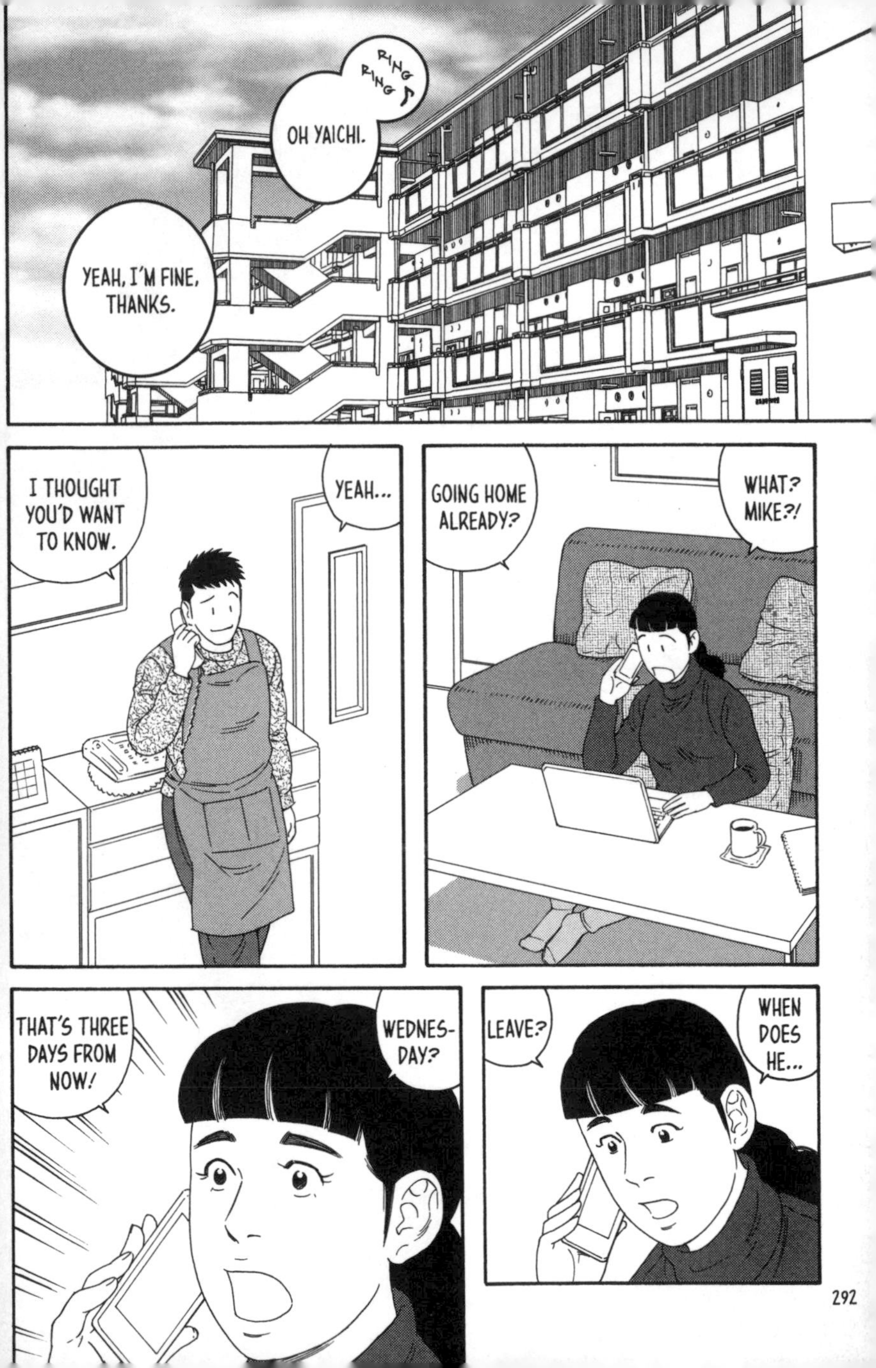
RING RING
OH YAICHI.
YEAH, I'M FINE, THANKS.
WHAT? MIKE?!
GOING HOME ALREADY?
YEAH...
I THOUGHT YOU'D WANT TO KNOW.
WHEN DOES HE...
LEAVE?
WEDNES-DAY?
THAT'S THREE DAYS FROM NOW!

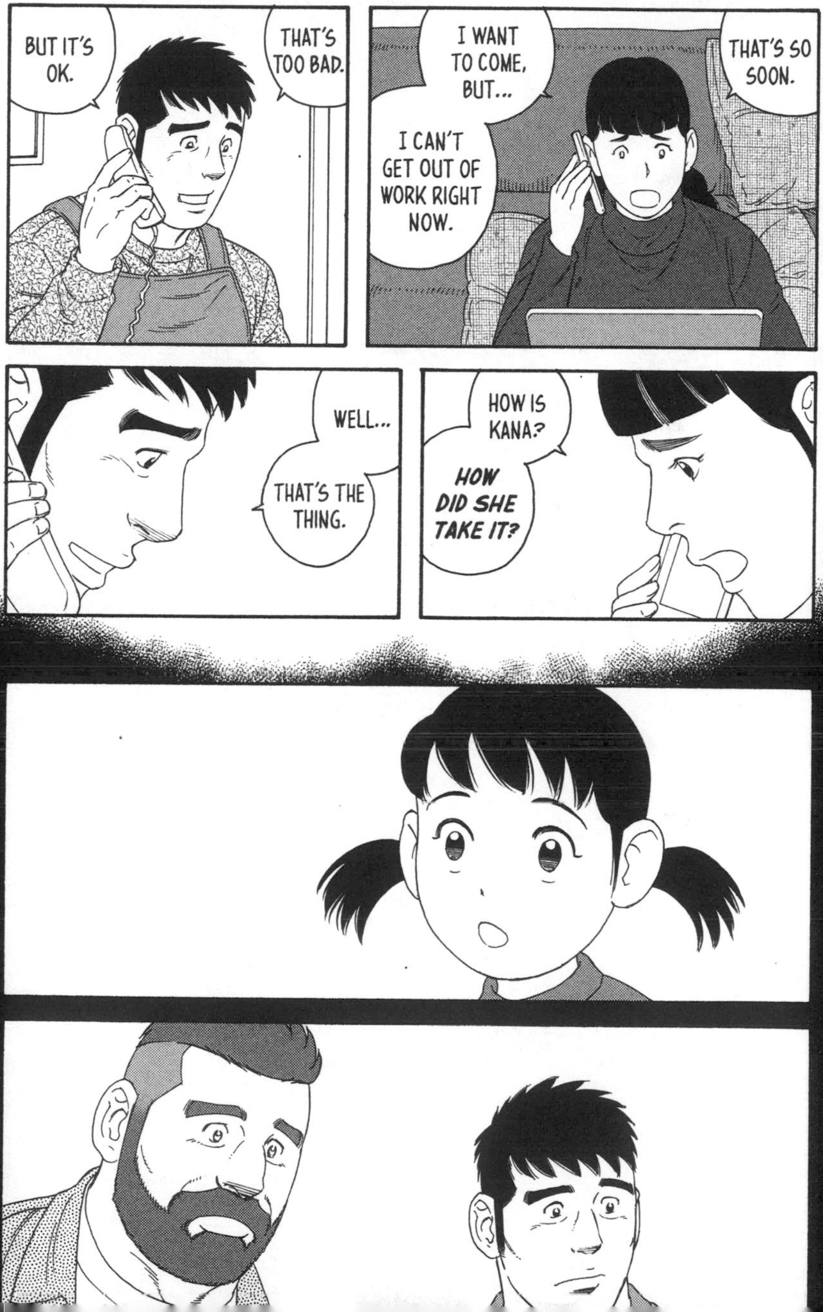
THAT'S SO SOON.
I WANT TO COME, BUT...
I CAN'T GET OUT OF WORK RIGHT NOW.
THAT'S TOO BAD.
BUT IT'S OK.
HOW IS KANA?
HOW DID SHE TAKE IT?
WELL...
THAT'S THE THING.

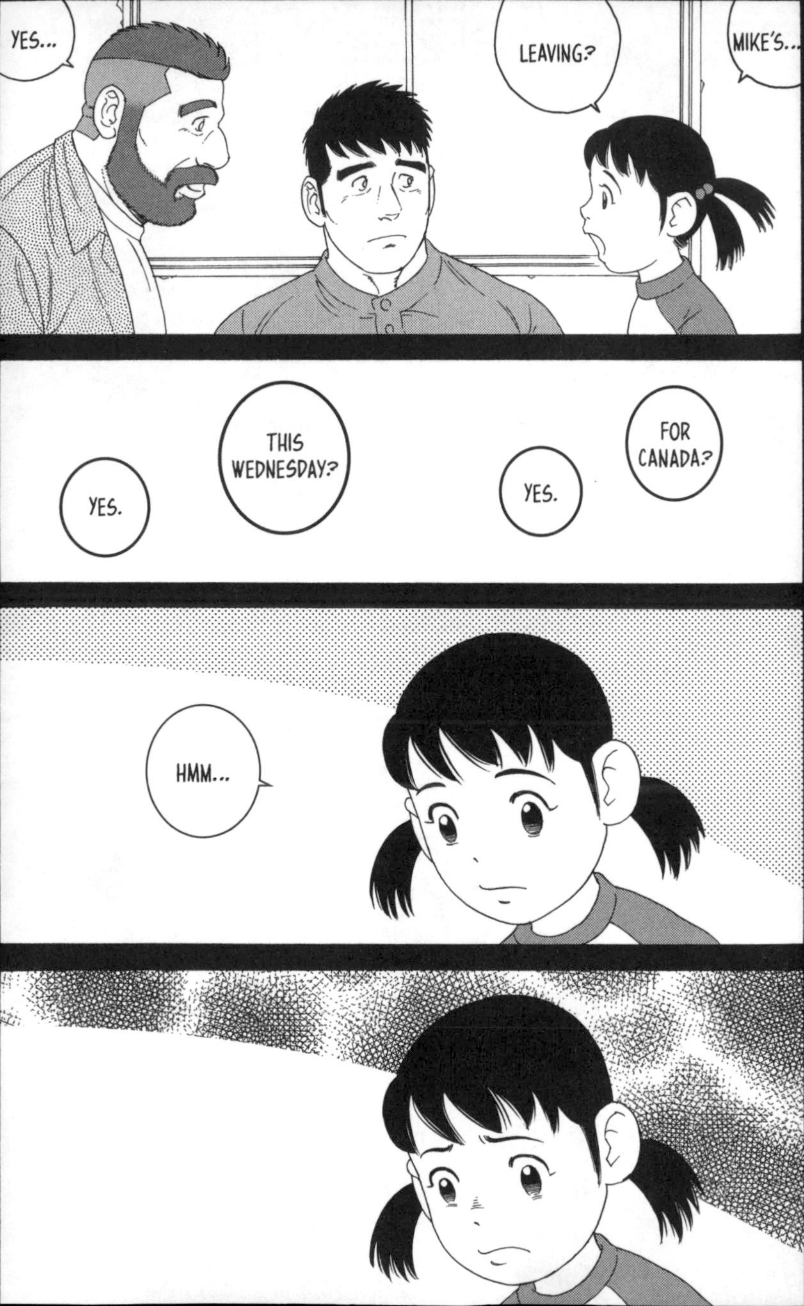
MIKE'S...
LEAVING?
YES...
FOR CANADA?
YES.
THIS WEDNESDAY?
YES.
HMM...

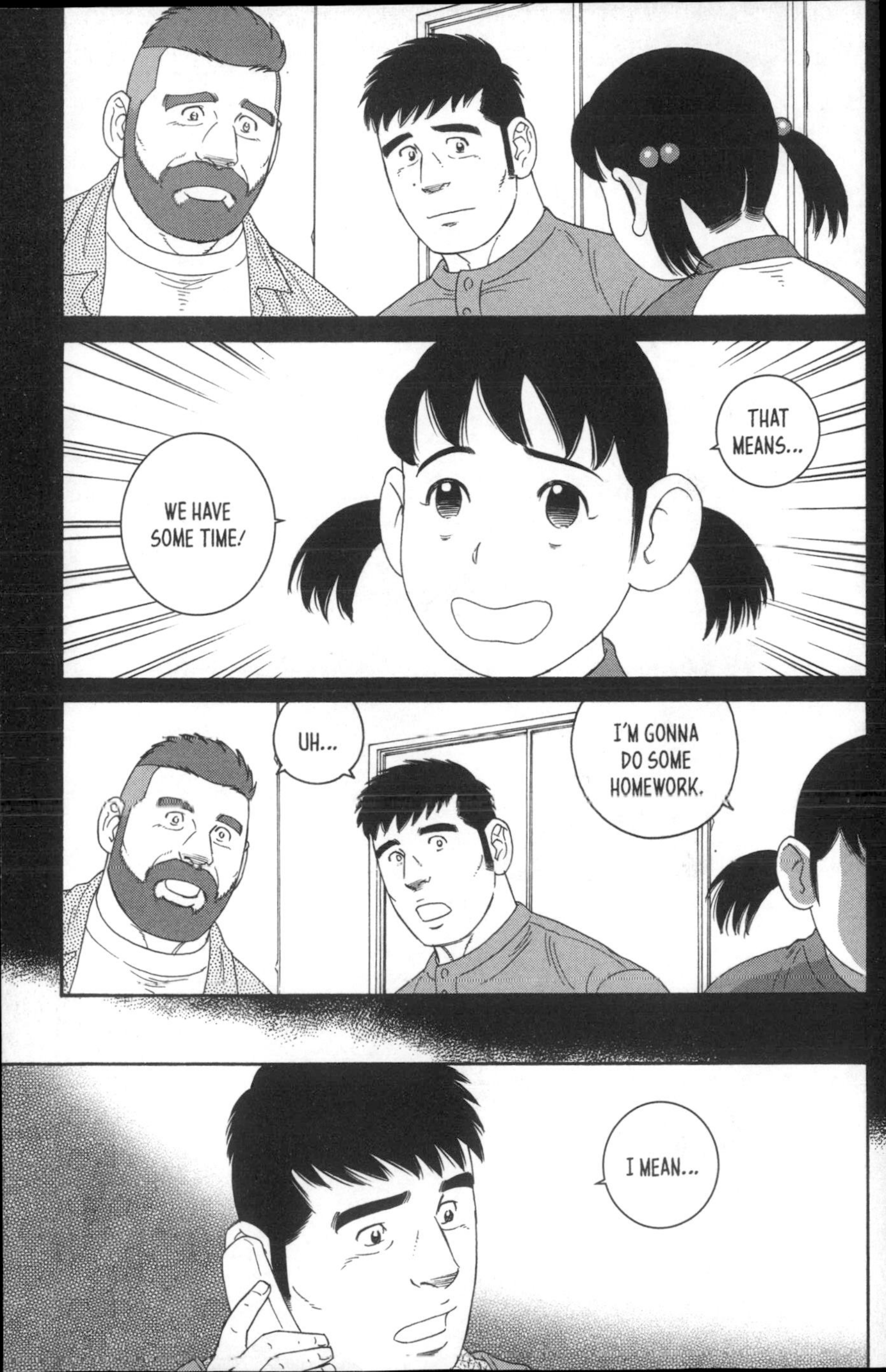
THAT MEANS...
WE HAVE SOME TIME!
I'M GONNA DO SOME HOMEWORK.
UH...
I MEAN...

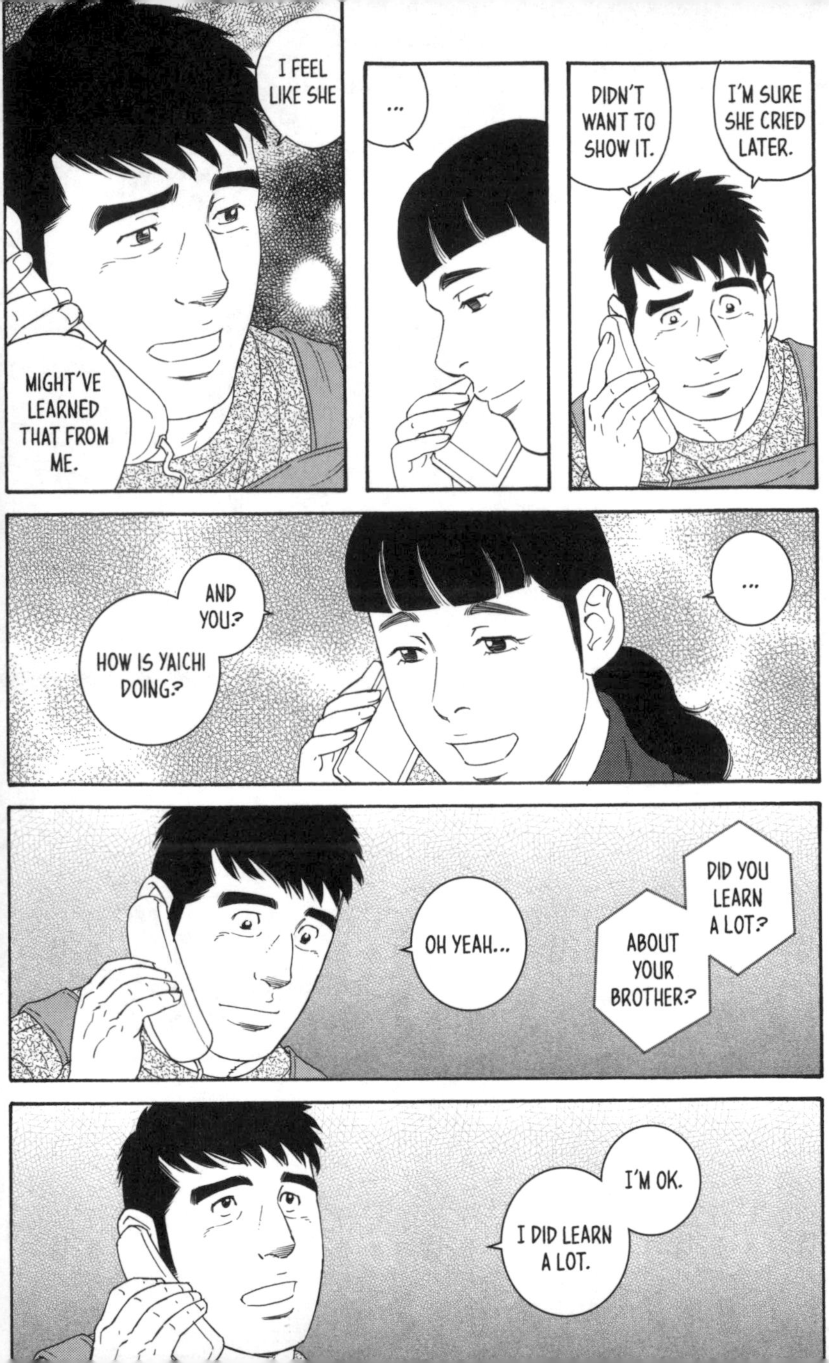
I'M SURE SHE CRIED LATER.
DIDN'T WANT TO SHOW IT.
...
I FEEL LIKE SHE
MIGHT'VE LEARNED THAT FROM ME.
...
AND YOU?
HOW IS YAICHI DOING?
DID YOU LEARN A LOT?
ABOUT YOUR BROTHER?
OH YEAH...
I'M OK.
I DID LEARN A LOT.

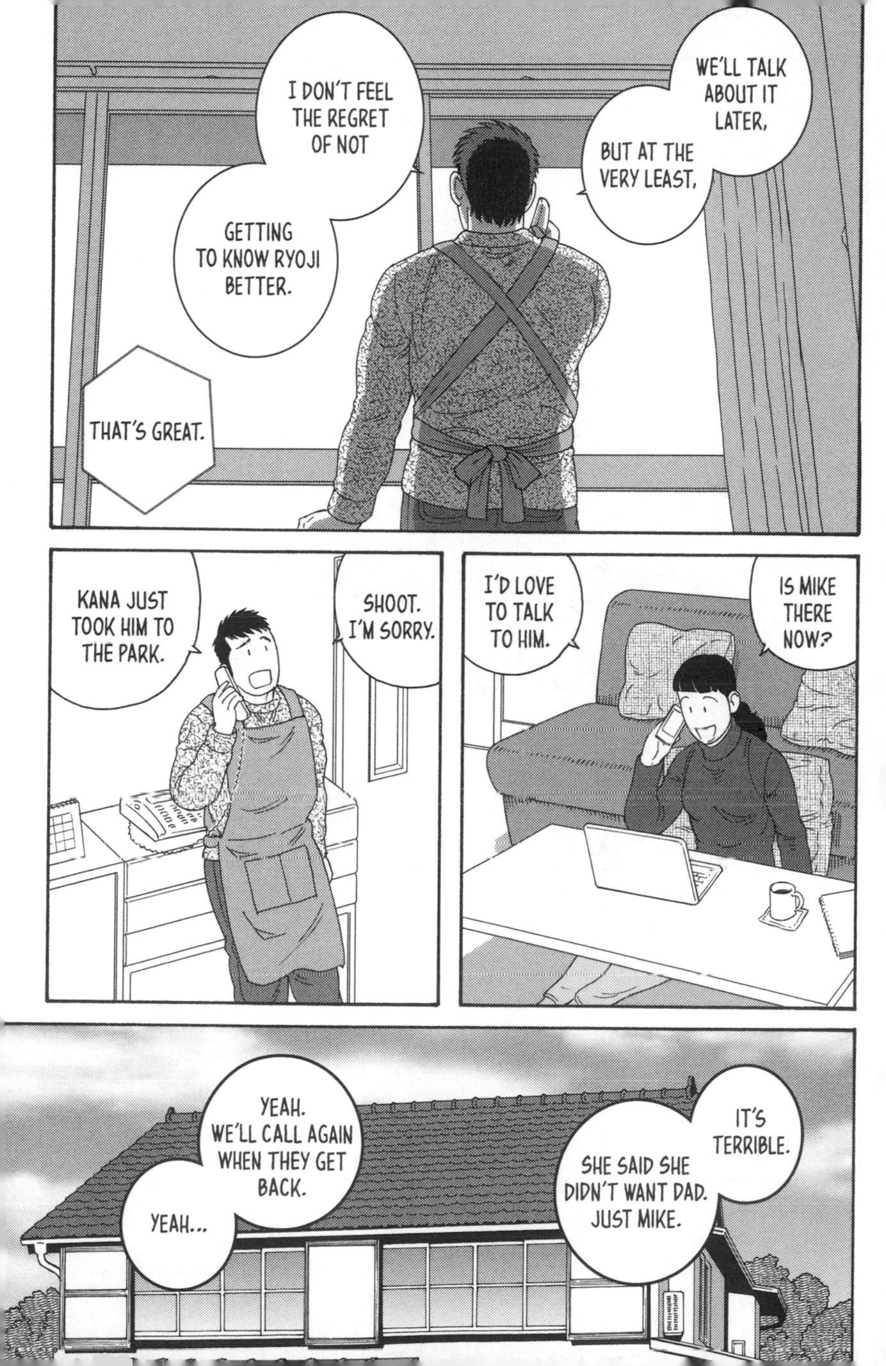
WE'LL TALK ABOUT IT LATER,
BUT AT THE VERY LEAST,
I DON'T FEEL THE REGRET OF NOT
GETTING TO KNOW RYOJI BETTER.
THAT'S GREAT.
IS MIKE THERE NOW?
I'D LOVE TO TALK TO HIM.
SHOOT. I'M SORRY.
KANA JUST TOOK HIM TO THE PARK.
IT'S TERRIBLE.
SHE SAID SHE DIDN'T WANT DAD. JUST MIKE.
YEAH. WE'LL CALL AGAIN WHEN THEY GET BACK.
YEAH...

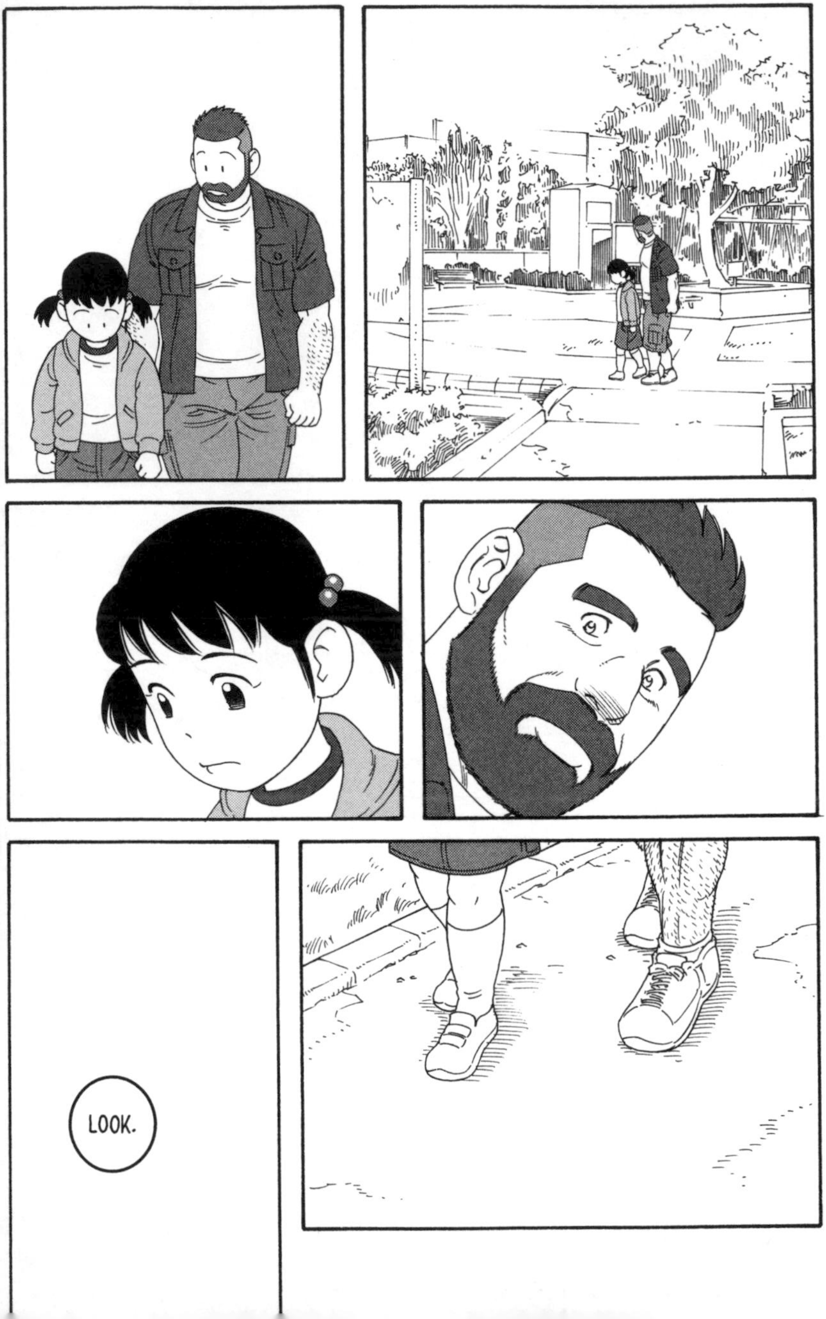
LOOK.

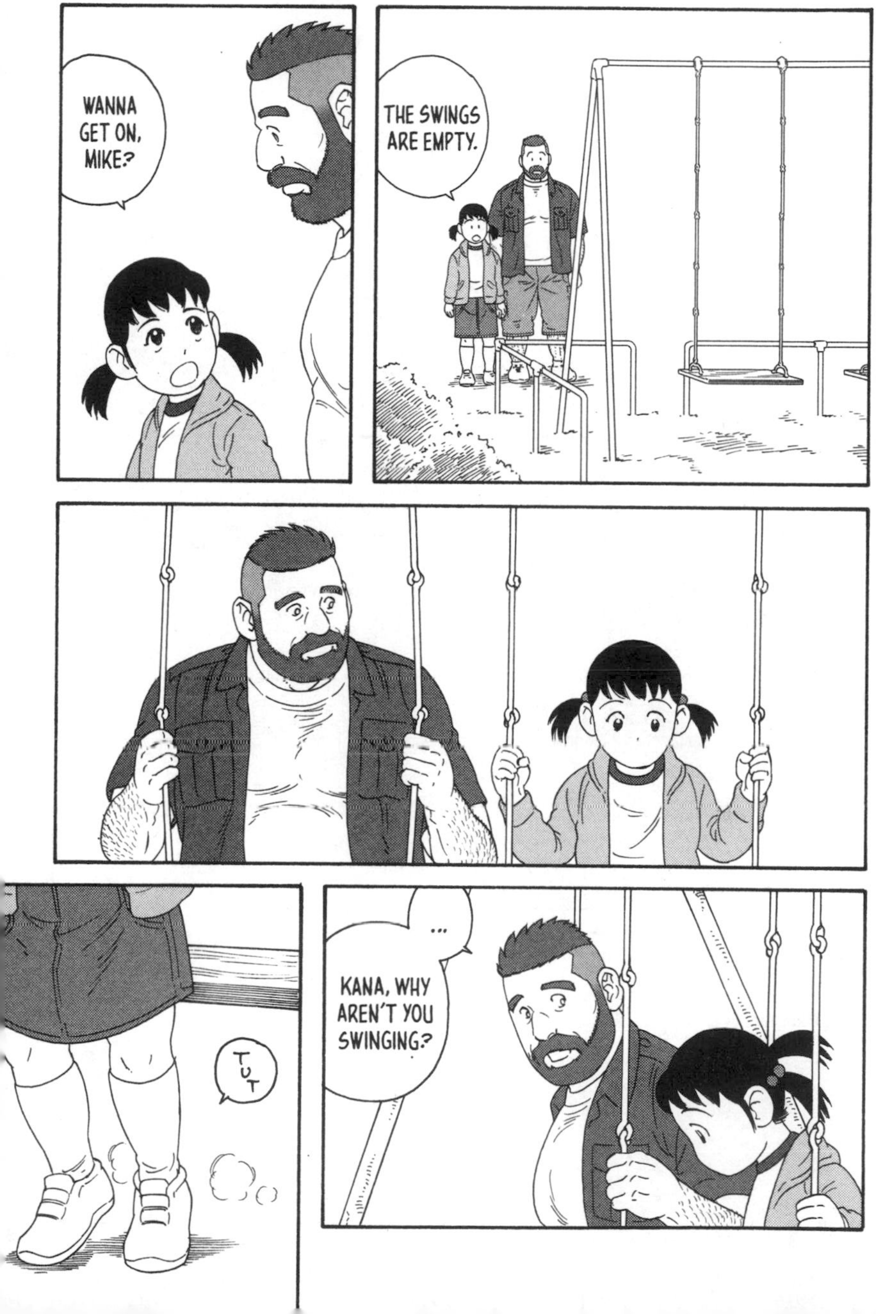
THE SWINGS ARE EMPTY.
WANNA GET ON, MIKE?
...
KANA, WHY AREN'T YOU SWINGING?
TUT

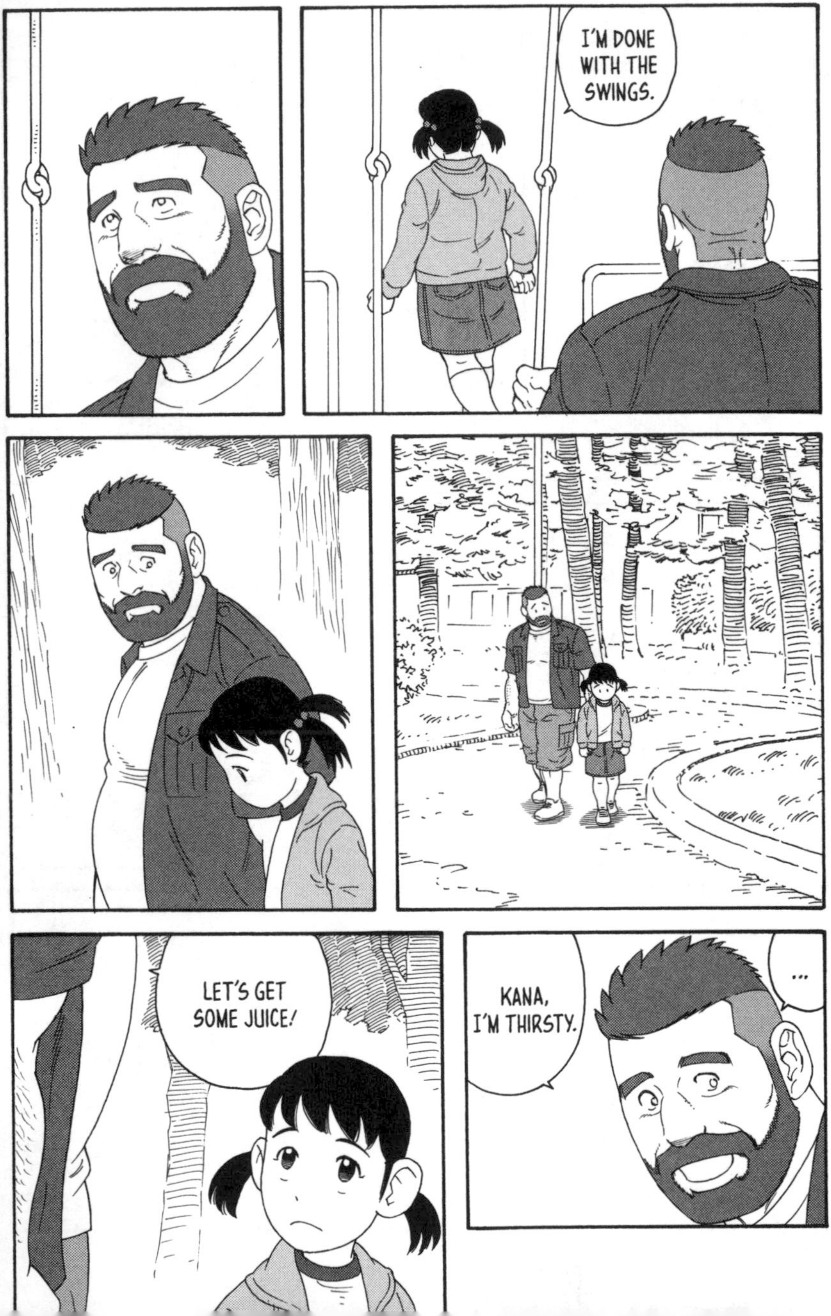
I'M DONE WITH THE SWINGS.
...
KANA, I'M THIRSTY.
LET'S GET SOME JUICE!

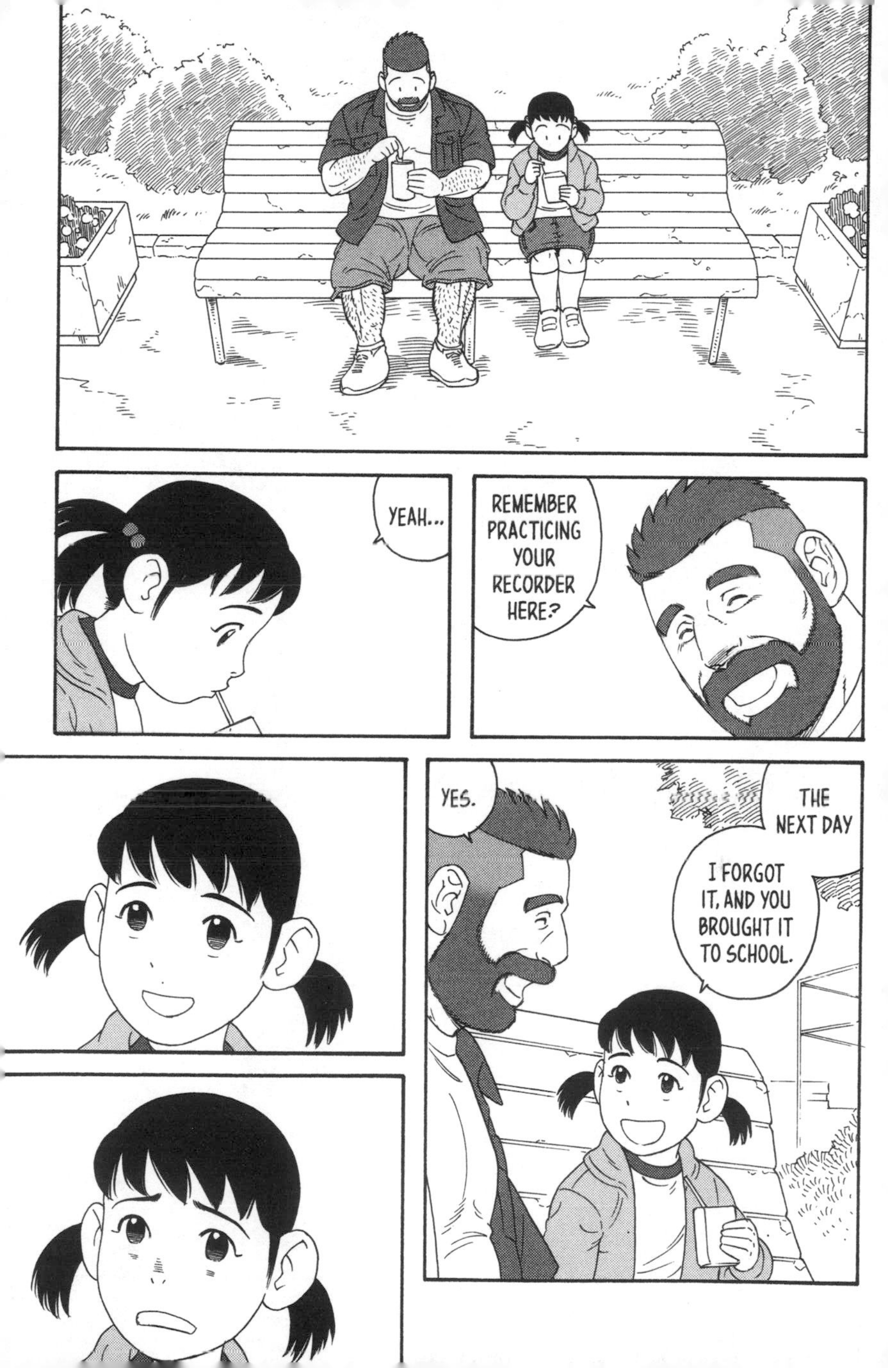
REMEMBER PRACTICING YOUR RECORDER HERE?
YEAH...
THE NEXT DAY
I FORGOT IT, AND YOU BROUGHT IT TO SCHOOL.
YES.

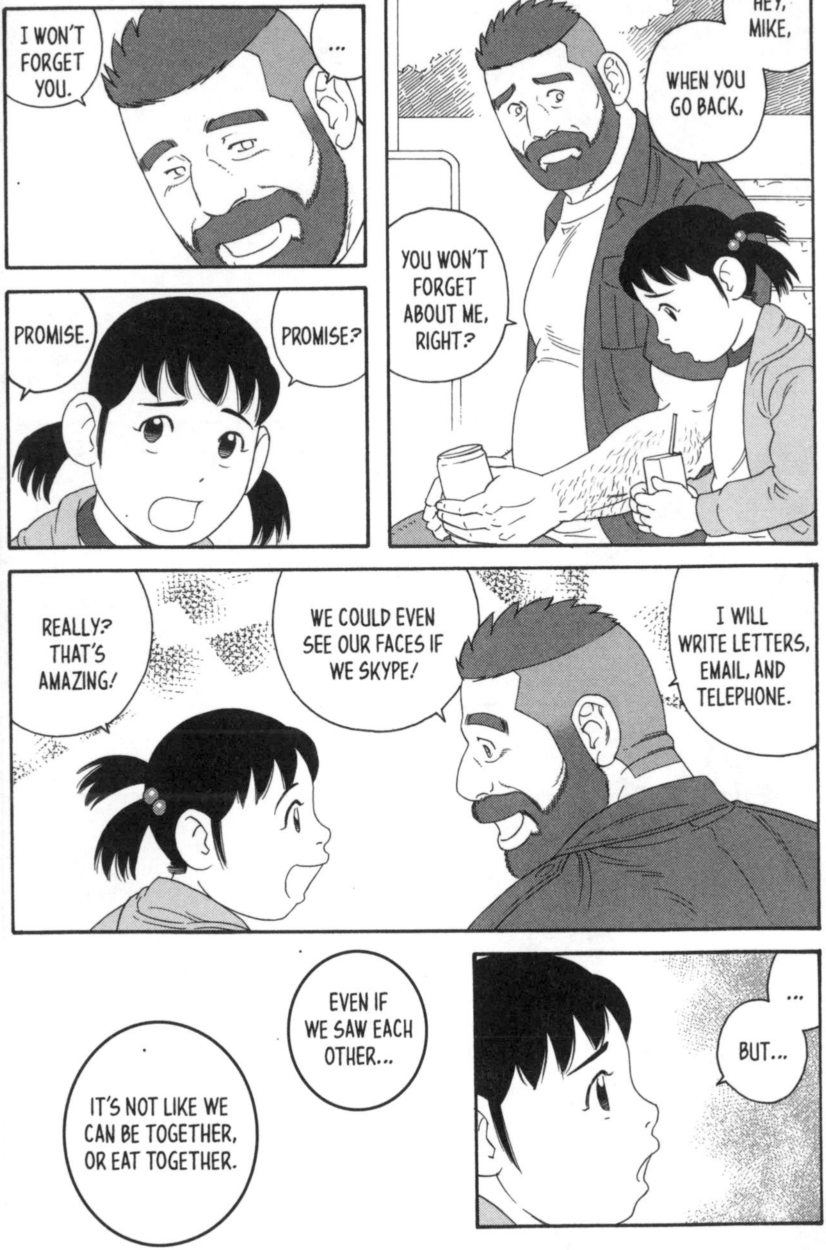
HEY, MIKE,
WHEN YOU GO BACK,
YOU WON'T FORGET ABOUT ME, RIGHT?
...
I WON'T FORGET YOU.
PROMISE?
PROMISE.
I WILL WRITE LETTERS, EMAIL, AND TELEPHONE.
WE COULD EVEN SEE OUR FACES IF WE SKYPE!
REALLY? THAT'S AMAZING!
...
BUT...
EVEN IF WE SAW EACH OTHER...
IT'S NOT LIKE WE CAN BE TOGETHER, OR EAT TOGETHER.

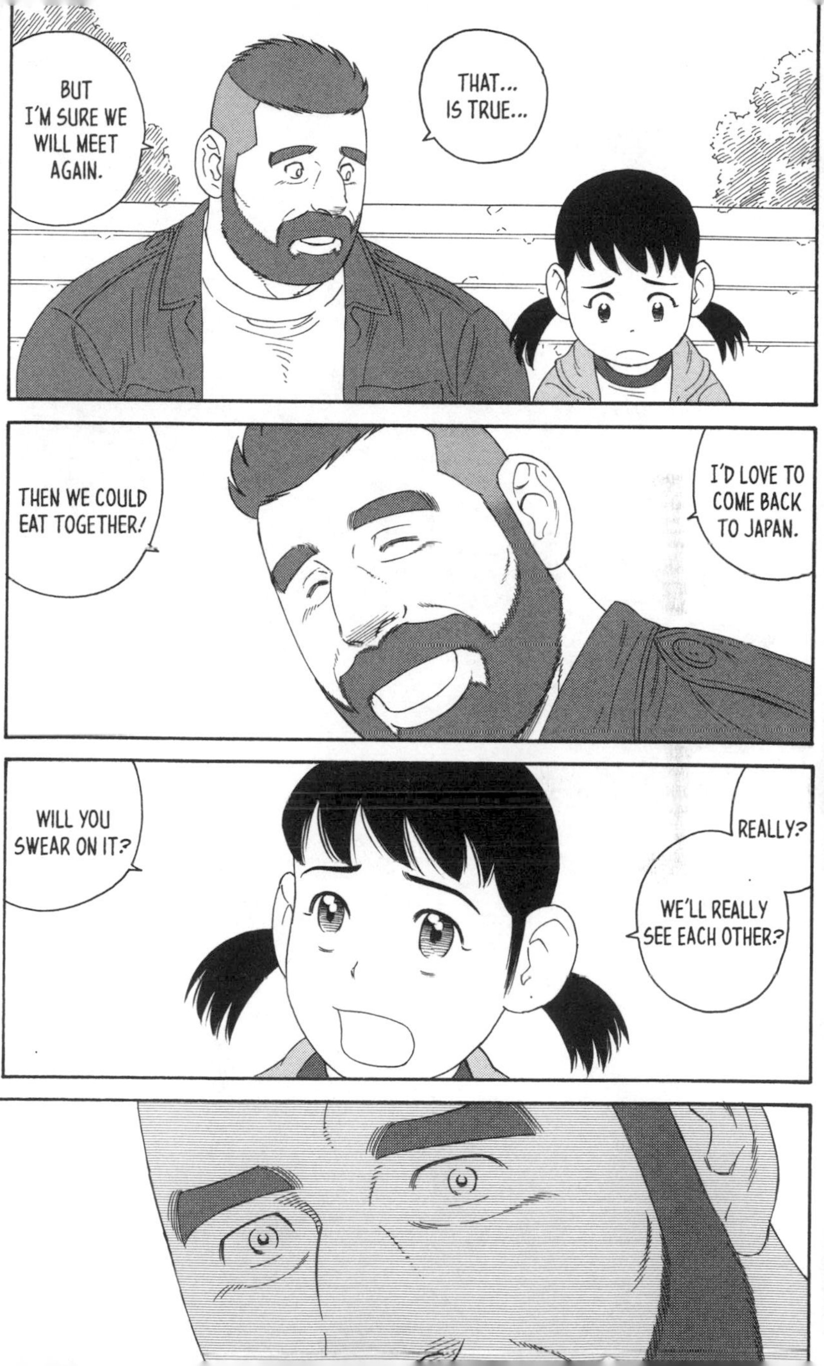
THAT... IS TRUE...
BUT I'M SURE WE WILL MEET AGAIN.
I'D LOVE TO COME BACK TO JAPAN.
THEN WE COULD EAT TOGETHER!
REALLY?
WE'LL REALLY SEE EACH OTHER?
WILL YOU SWEAR ON IT?

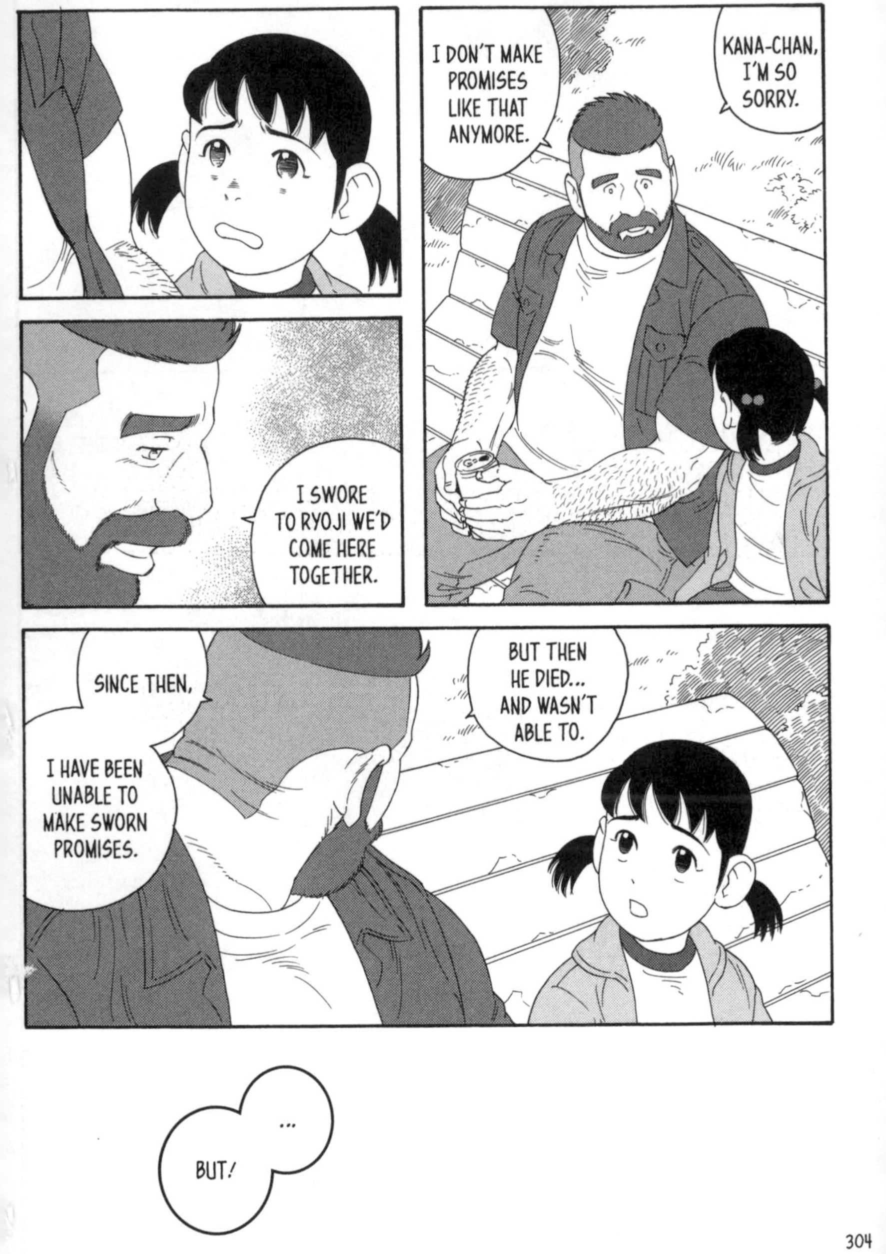
KANA-CHAN, I'M SO SORRY.
I DON'T MAKE PROMISES LIKE THAT ANYMORE.
I SWORE TO RYOJI WE'D COME HERE TOGETHER.
BUT THEN HE DIED... AND WASN'T ABLE TO.
SINCE THEN,
I HAVE BEEN UNABLE TO MAKE SWORN PROMISES.
...
BUT!

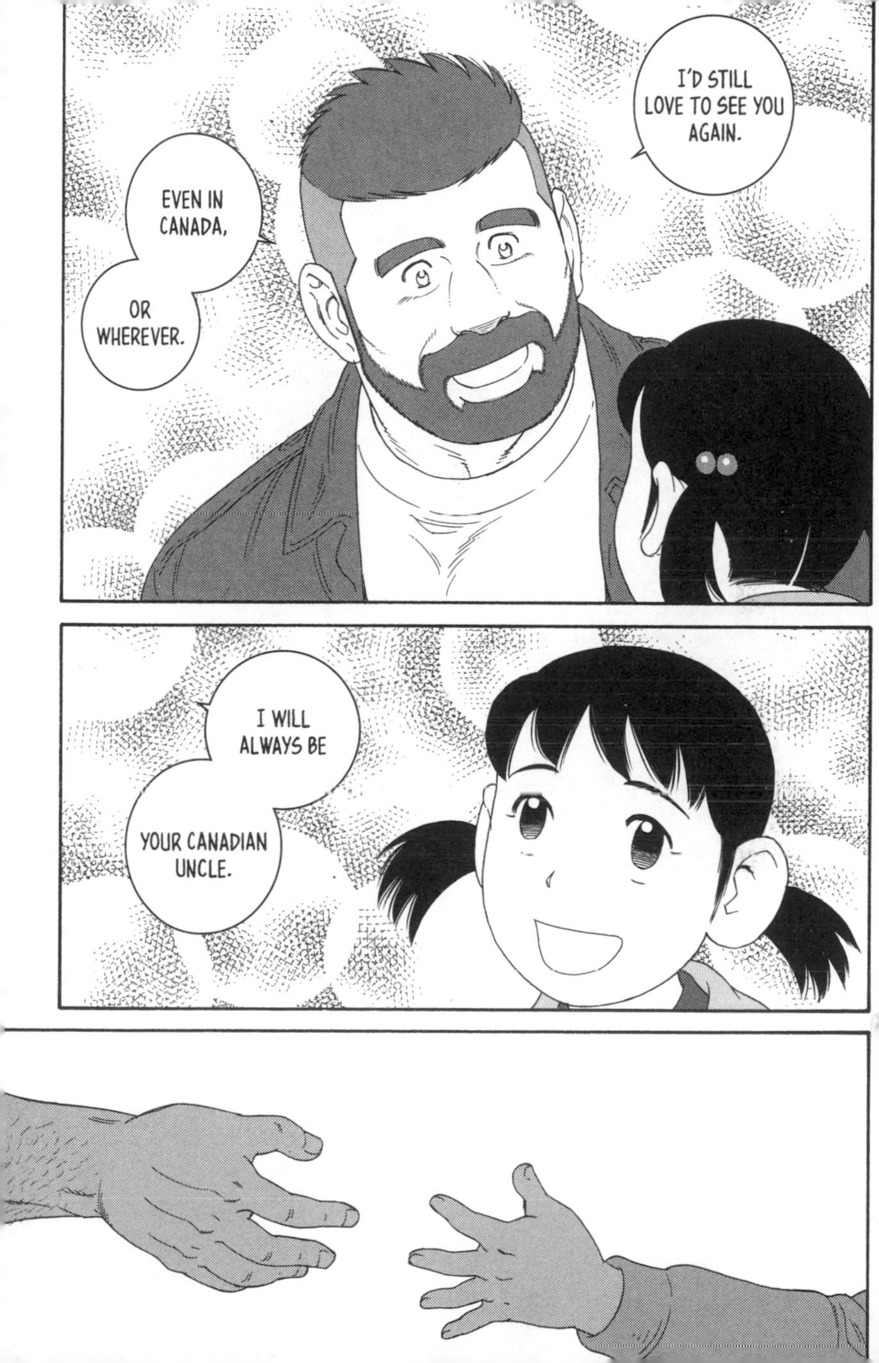
I'D STILL LOVE TO SEE YOU AGAIN.
EVEN IN CANADA,
OR WHEREVER.
I WILL ALWAYS BE
YOUR CANADIAN UNCLE.

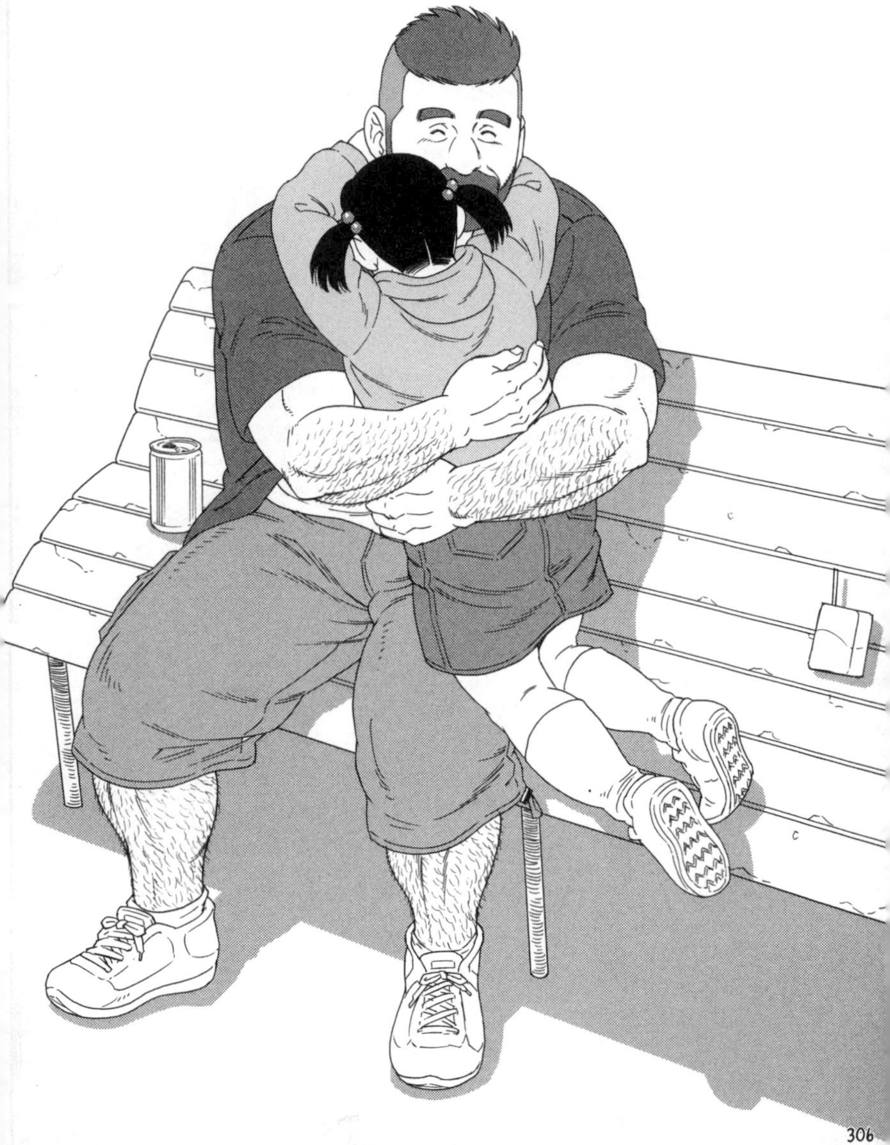

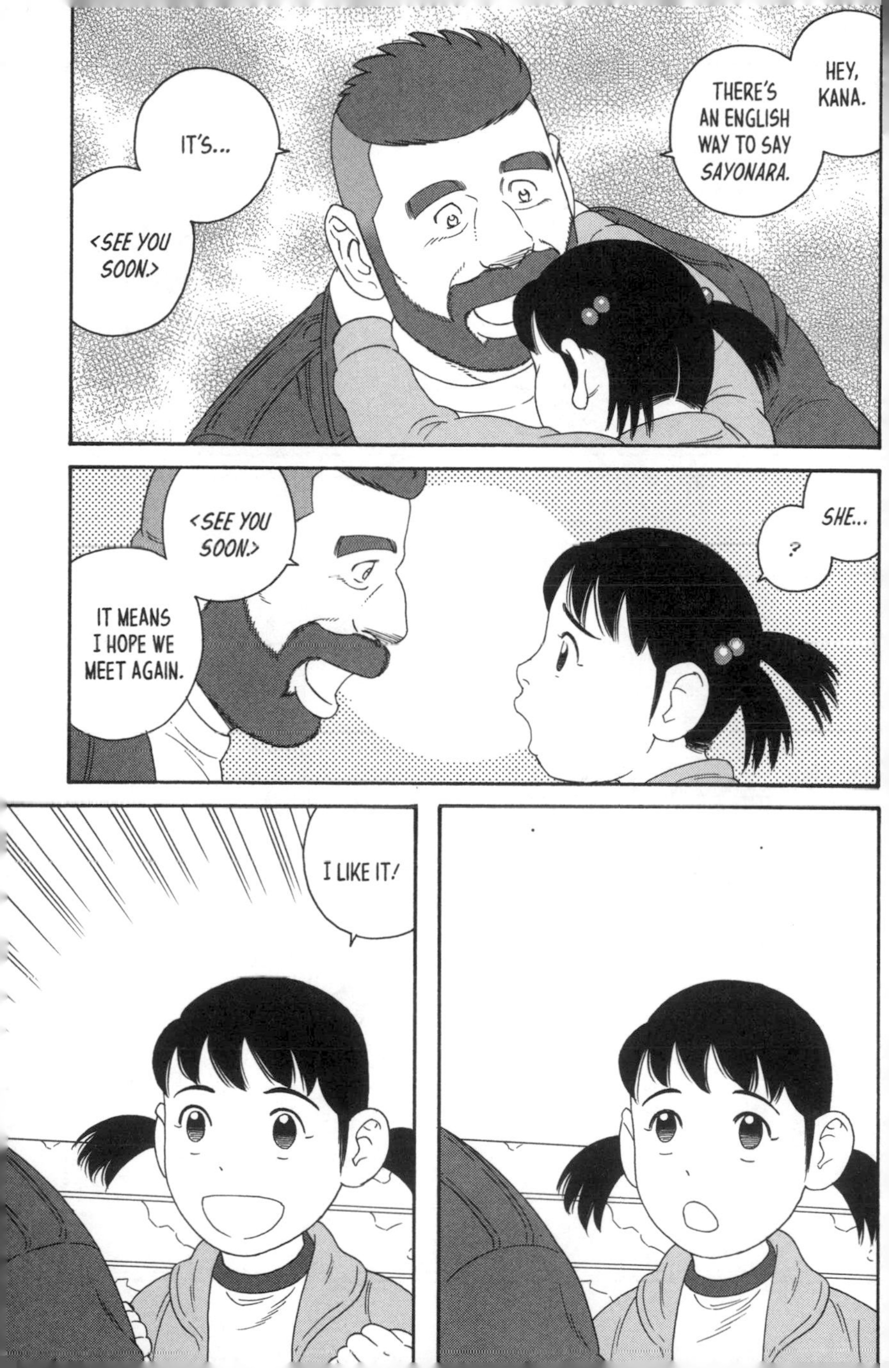

HEY, KANA.
THERE'S AN ENGLISH WAY TO SAY *SAYONARA*.
IT'S...
<SEE YOU SOON.>
SHE...
?
<SEE YOU SOON.>
IT MEANS I HOPE WE MEET AGAIN.
I LIKE IT!

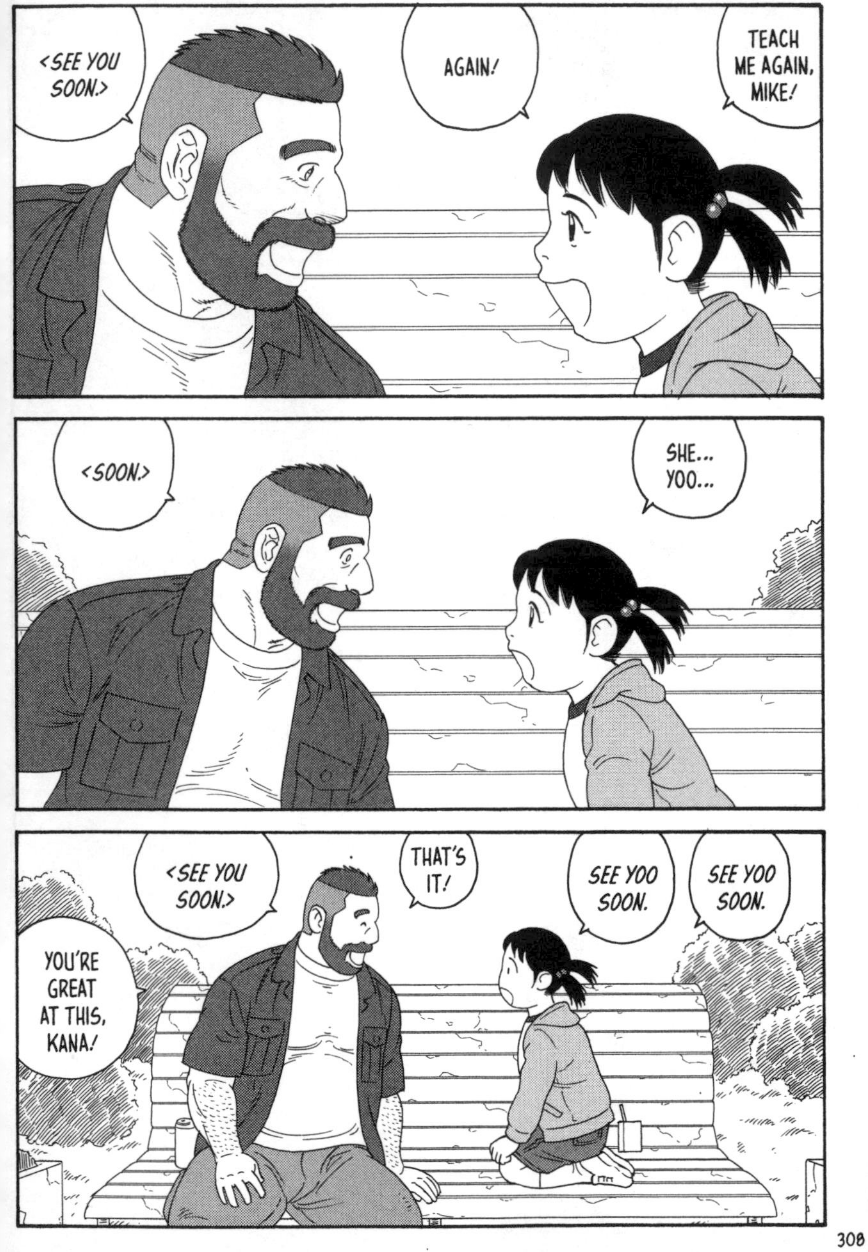
TEACH ME AGAIN, MIKE!
AGAIN!
<SEE YOU SOON.>
SHE... YOO...
<SOON.>
SEE YOO SOON.
SEE YOO SOON.
THAT'S IT!
<SEE YOU SOON.>
YOU'RE GREAT AT THIS, KANA!

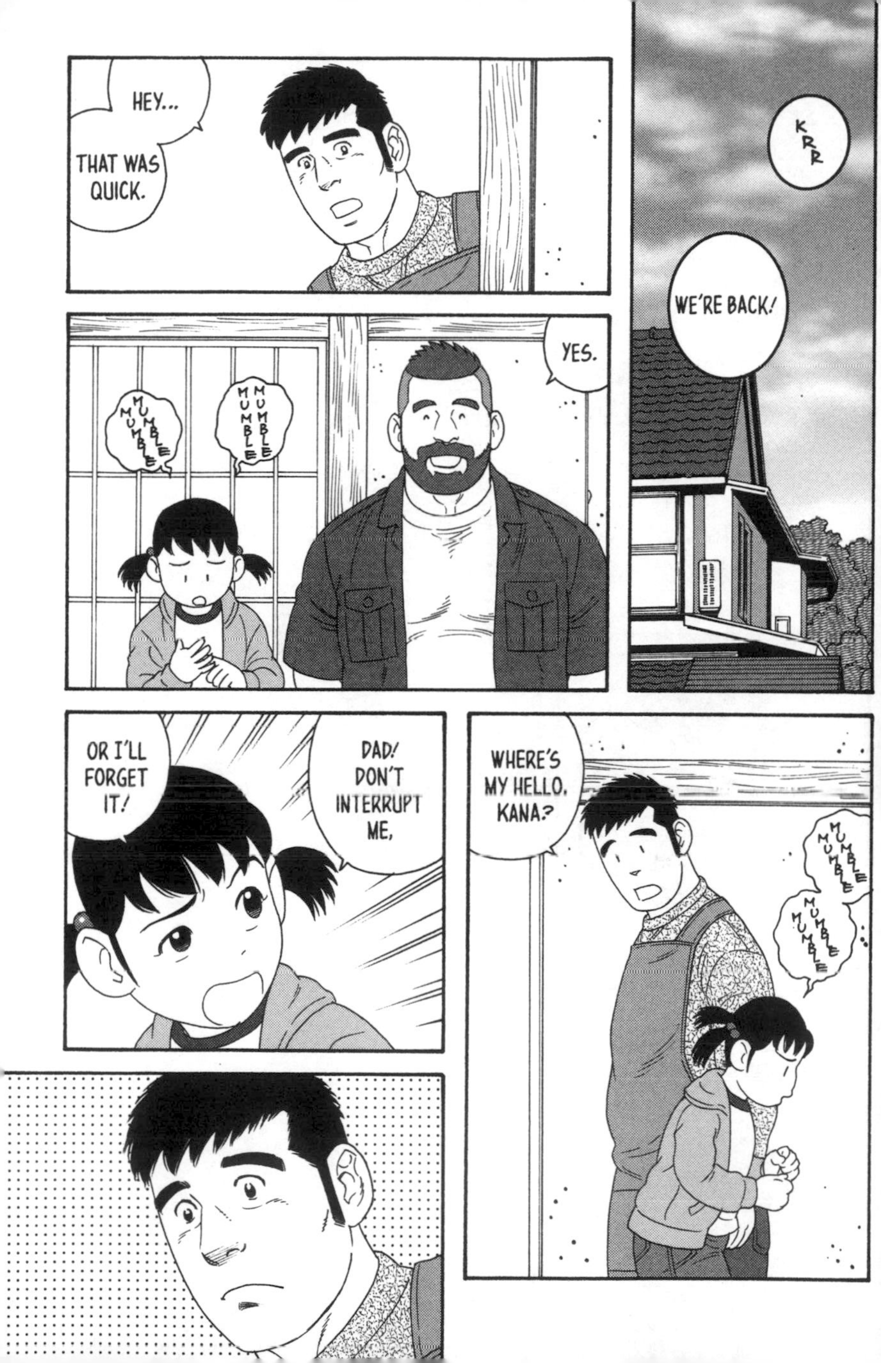
KRR
WE'RE BACK!
HEY...
THAT WAS QUICK.
YES.
MUMBLE MUMBLE
MUMBLE MUMBLE
WHERE'S MY HELLO, KANA?
MUMBLE MUMBLE
MUMBLE MUMBLE
DAD! DON'T INTERRUPT ME,
OR I'LL FORGET IT!

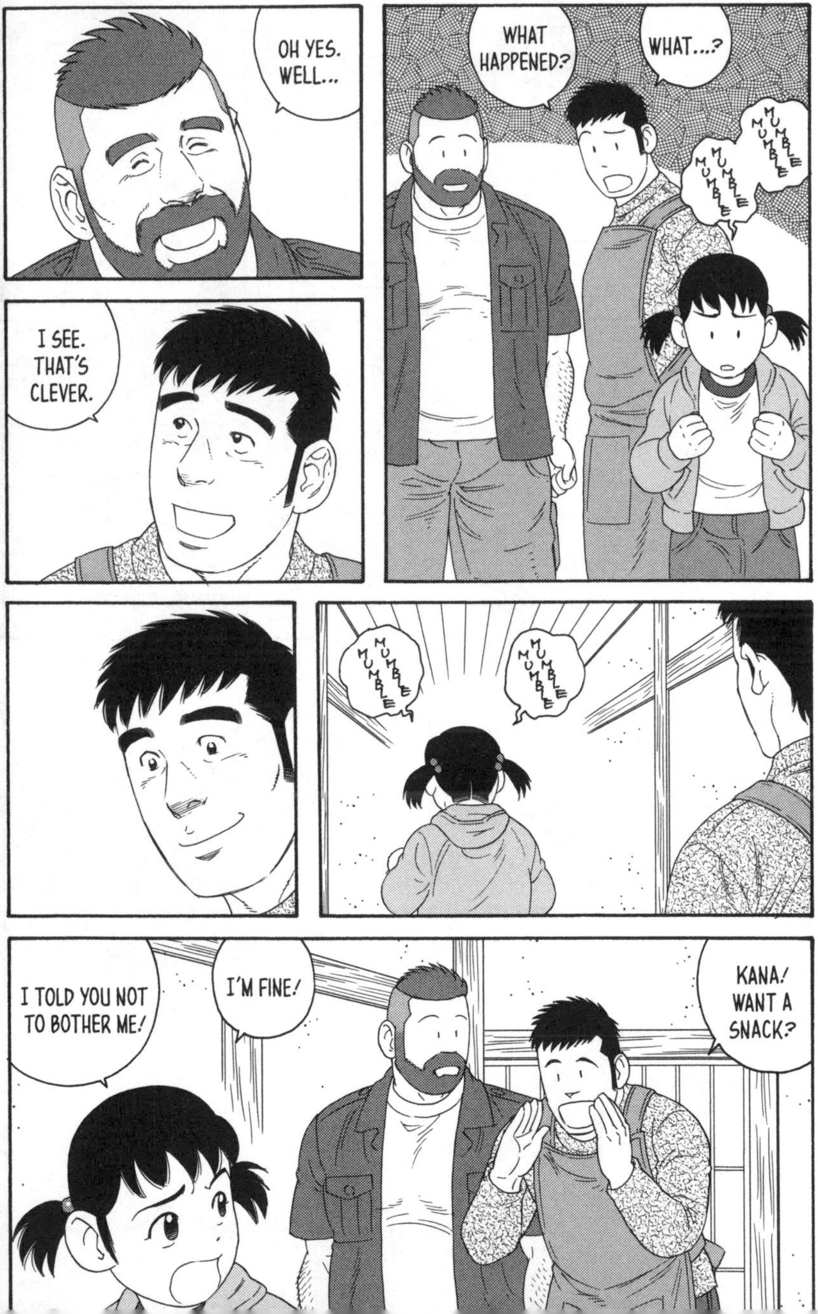
WHAT...?
WHAT HAPPENED?
MUMBLE MUMBLE
MUMBLE MUMBLE
OH YES. WELL...
I SEE. THAT'S CLEVER.
MUMBLE MUMBLE
MUMBLE MUMBLE
KANA! WANT A SNACK?
I'M FINE!
I TOLD YOU NOT TO BOTHER ME!

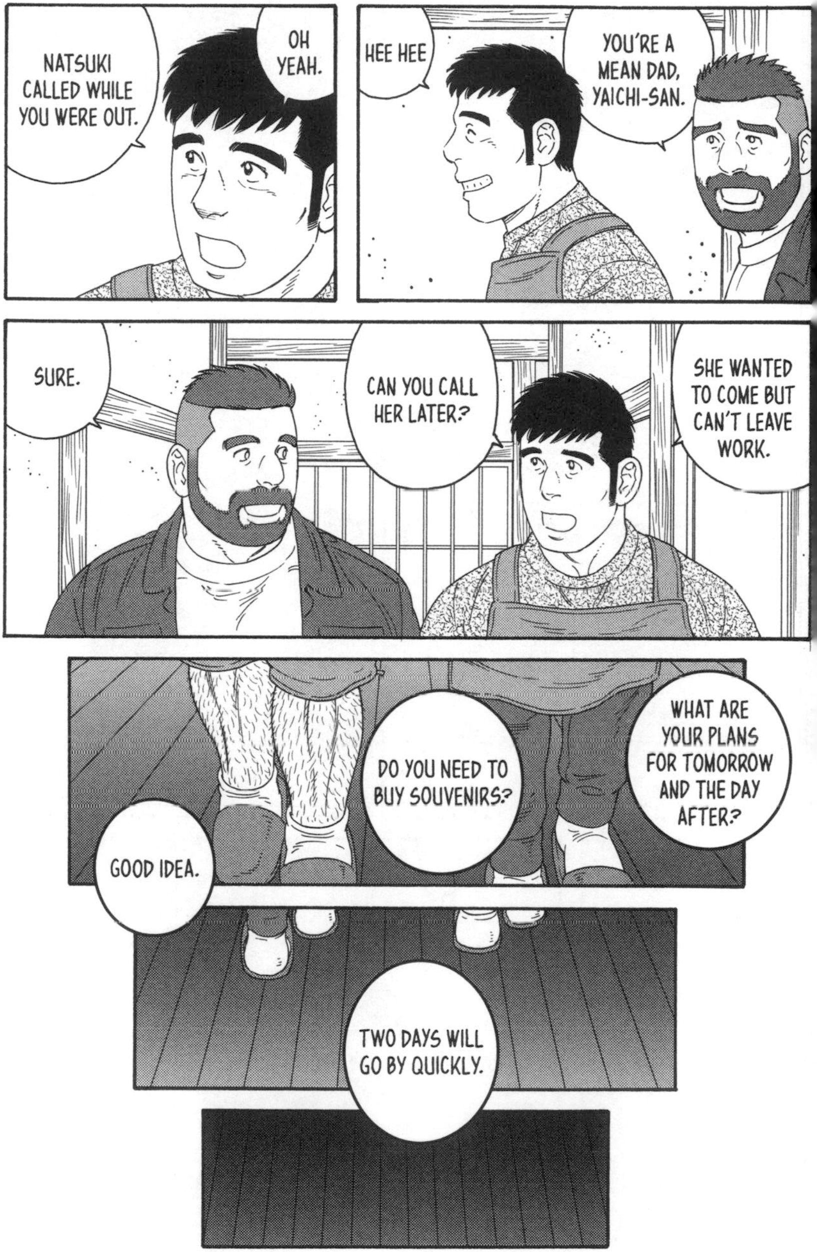
YOU'RE A MEAN DAD, YAICHI-SAN.
HEE HEE
OH YEAH.
NATSUKI CALLED WHILE YOU WERE OUT.
SHE WANTED TO COME BUT CAN'T LEAVE WORK.
CAN YOU CALL HER LATER?
SURE.
WHAT ARE YOUR PLANS FOR TOMORROW AND THE DAY AFTER?
DO YOU NEED TO BUY SOUVENIRS?
GOOD IDEA.
TWO DAYS WILL GO BY QUICKLY.

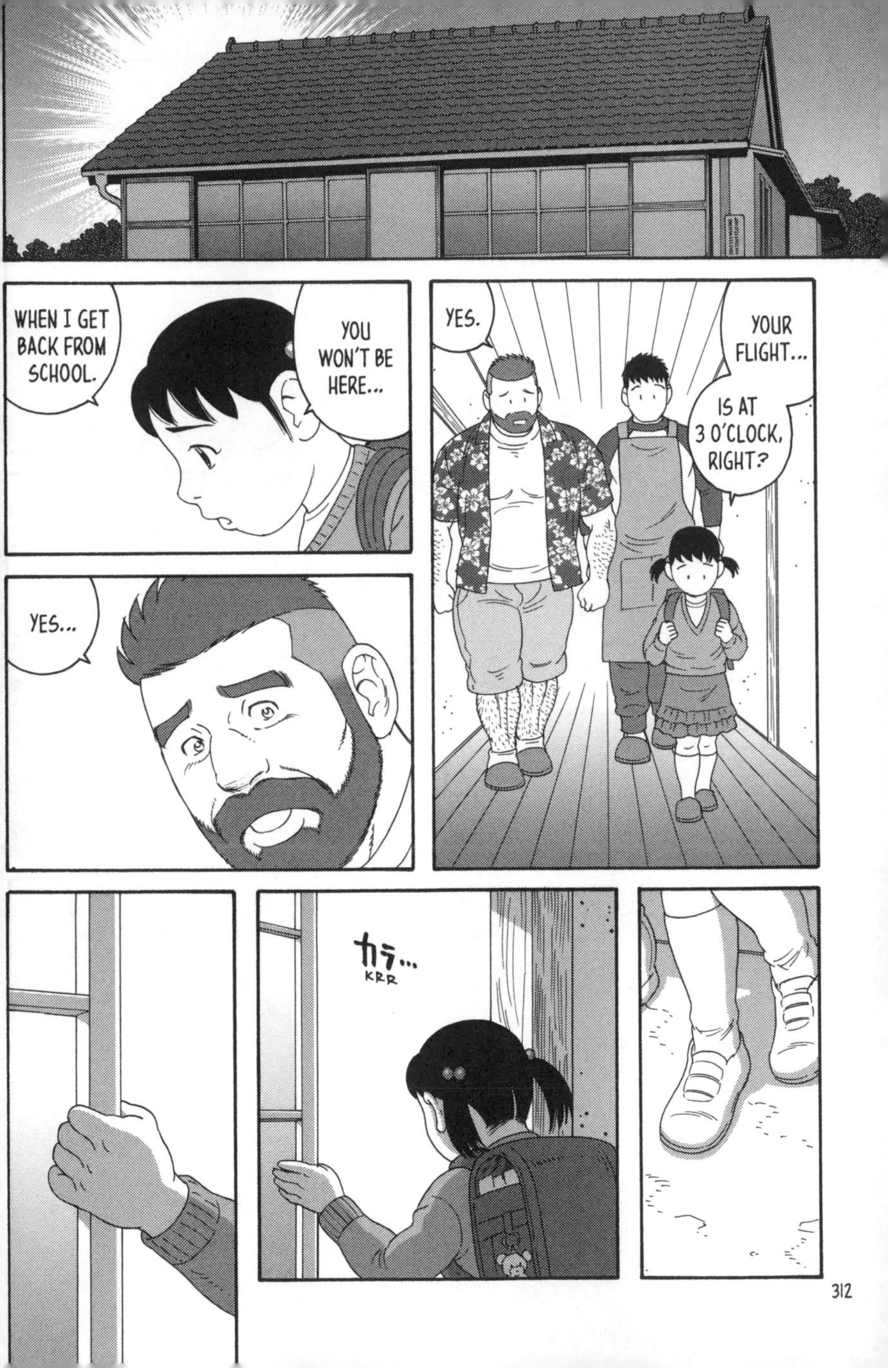
YOUR FLIGHT...
IS AT 3 O'CLOCK, RIGHT?
YES.
YOU WON'T BE HERE...
WHEN I GET BACK FROM SCHOOL.
YES...
カラ...
KRR

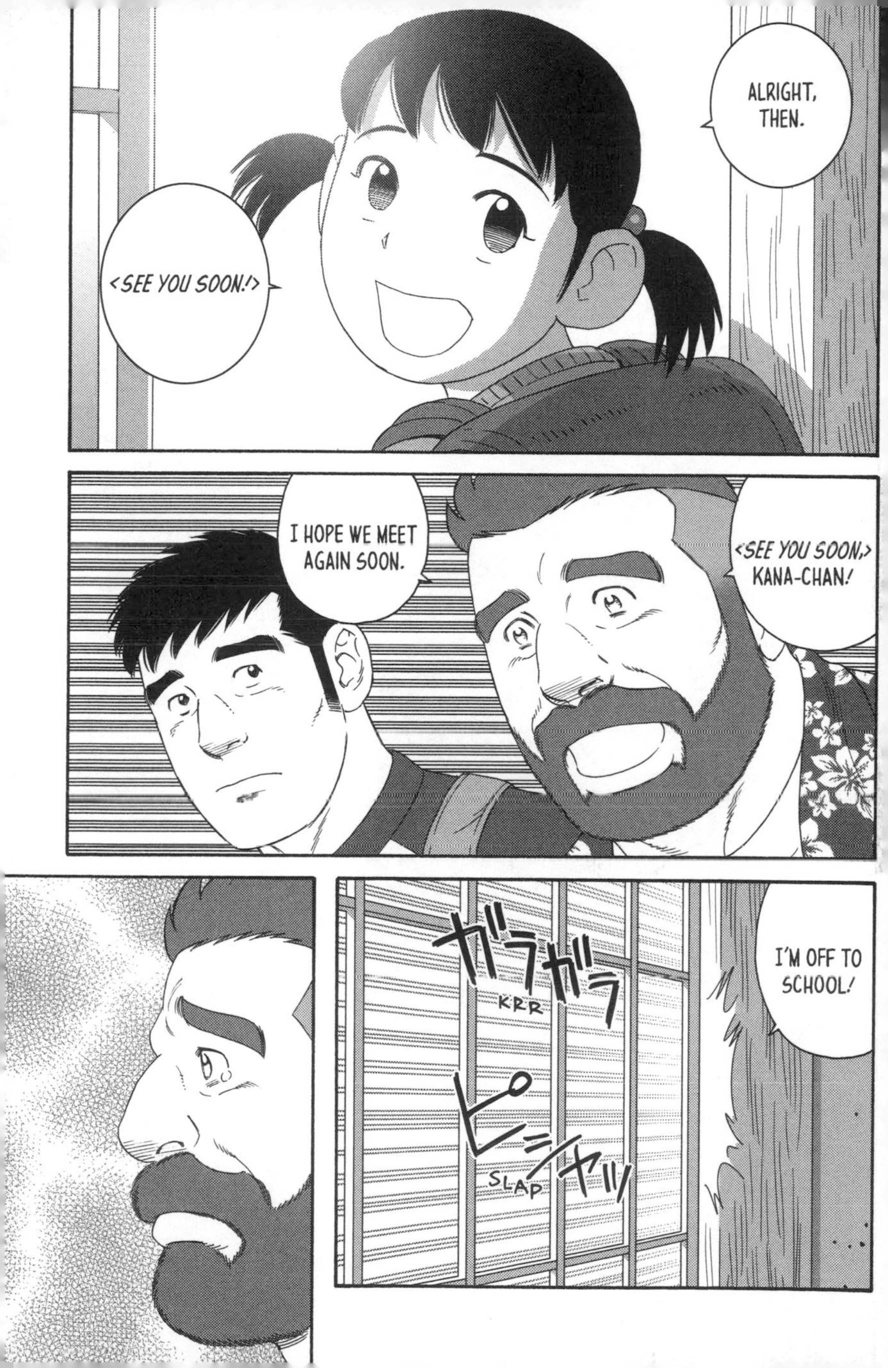
ALRIGHT, THEN.
<SEE YOU SOON!>
<SEE YOU SOON,> KANA-CHAN!
I HOPE WE MEET AGAIN SOON.
I'M OFF TO SCHOOL!
ガラガラ
KRR
ピシャッ
SLAP

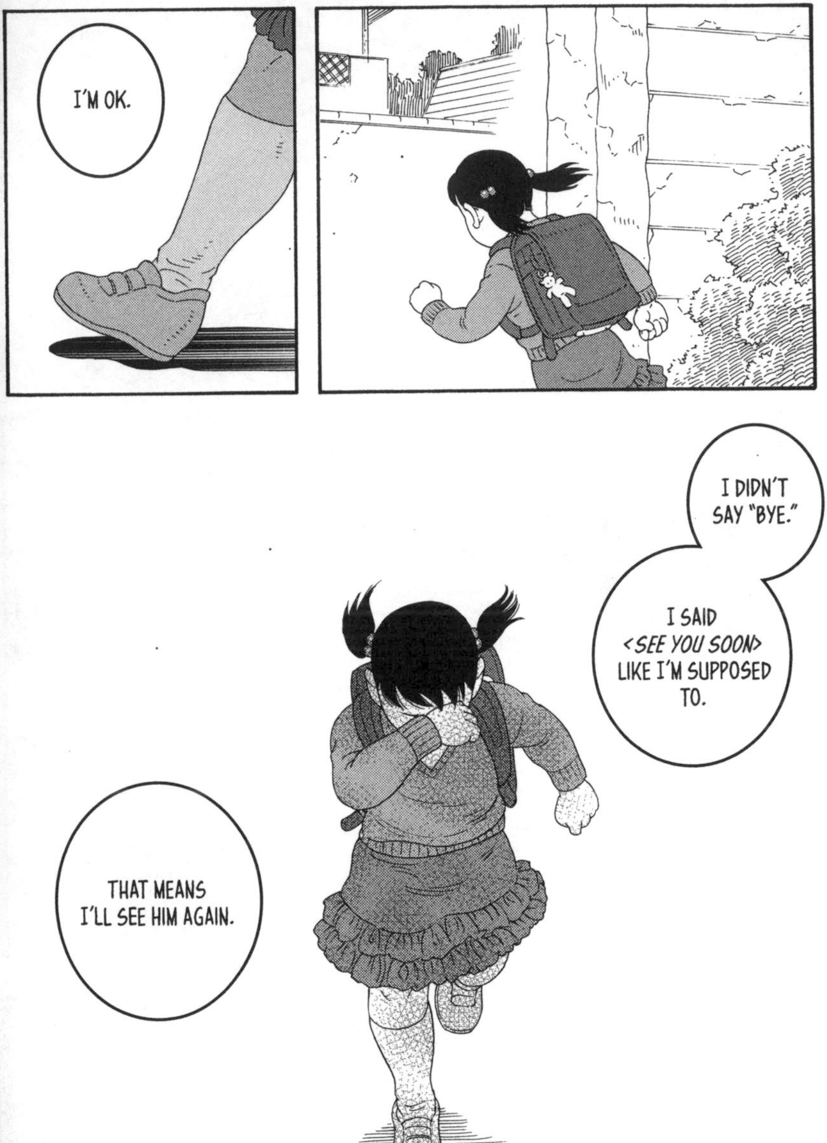
I'M OK.
I DIDN'T SAY "BYE."
I SAID <SEE YOU SOON> LIKE I'M SUPPOSED TO.
THAT MEANS I'LL SEE HIM AGAIN.

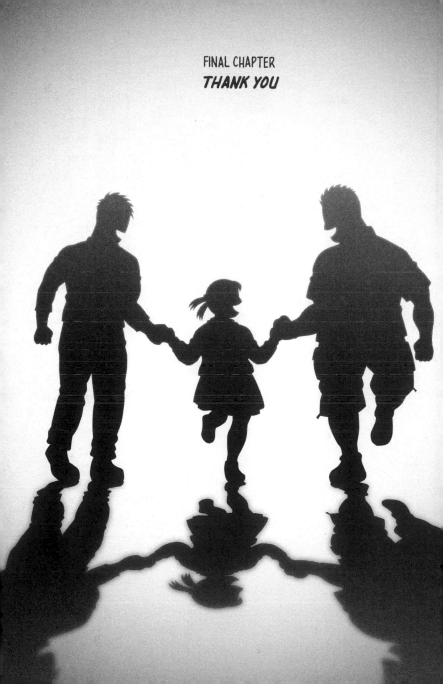

FINAL CHAPTER

THANK YOU

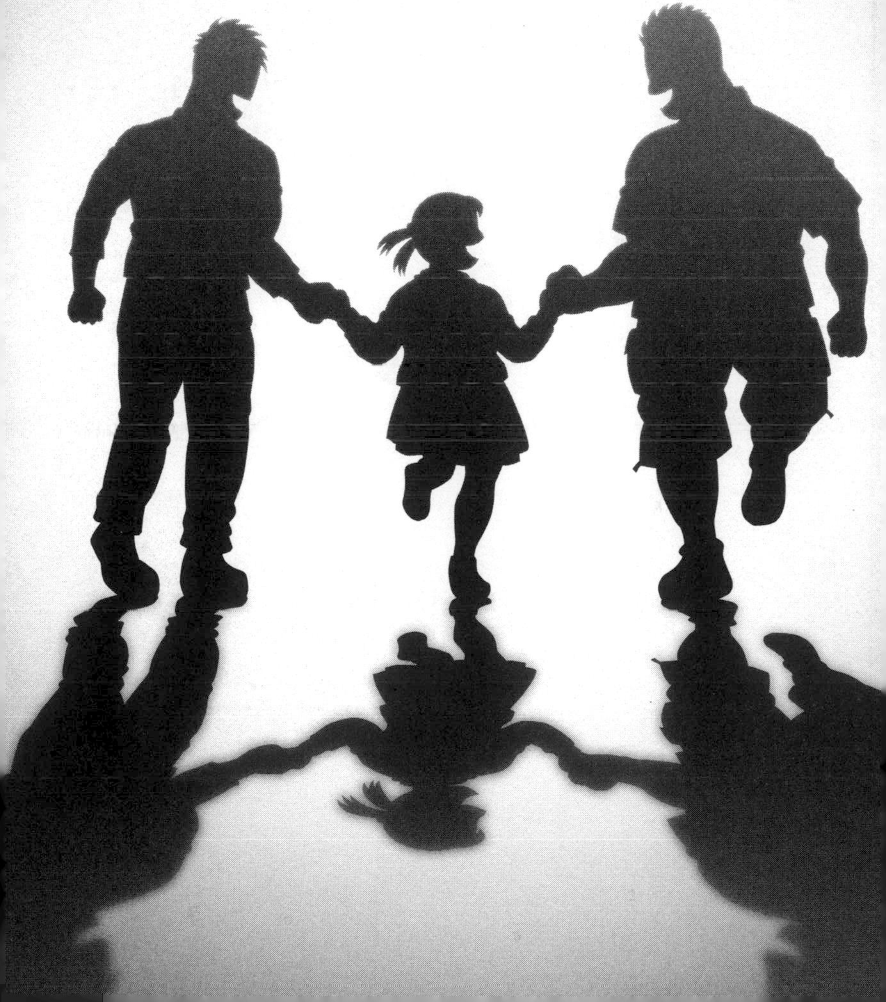

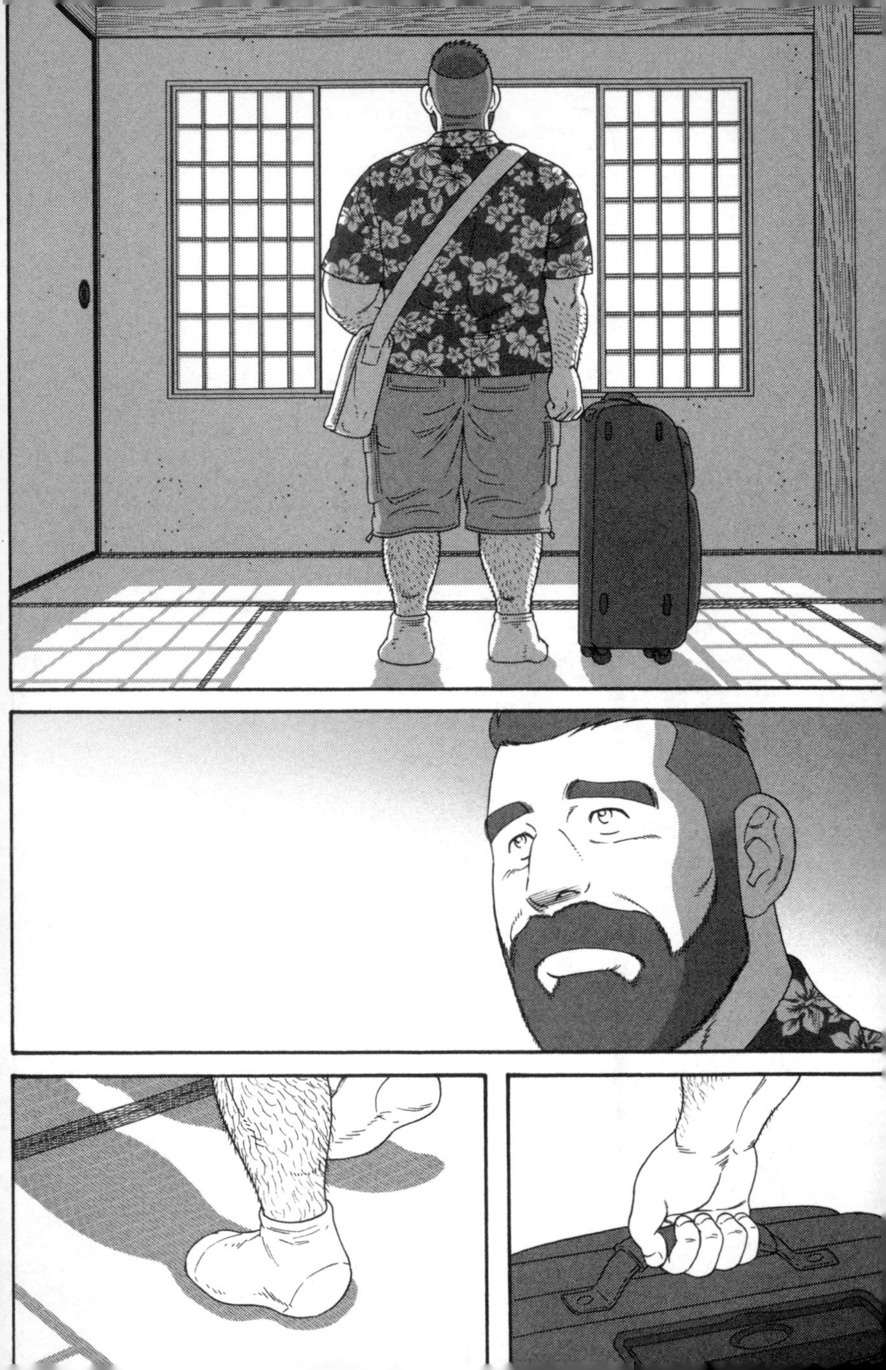

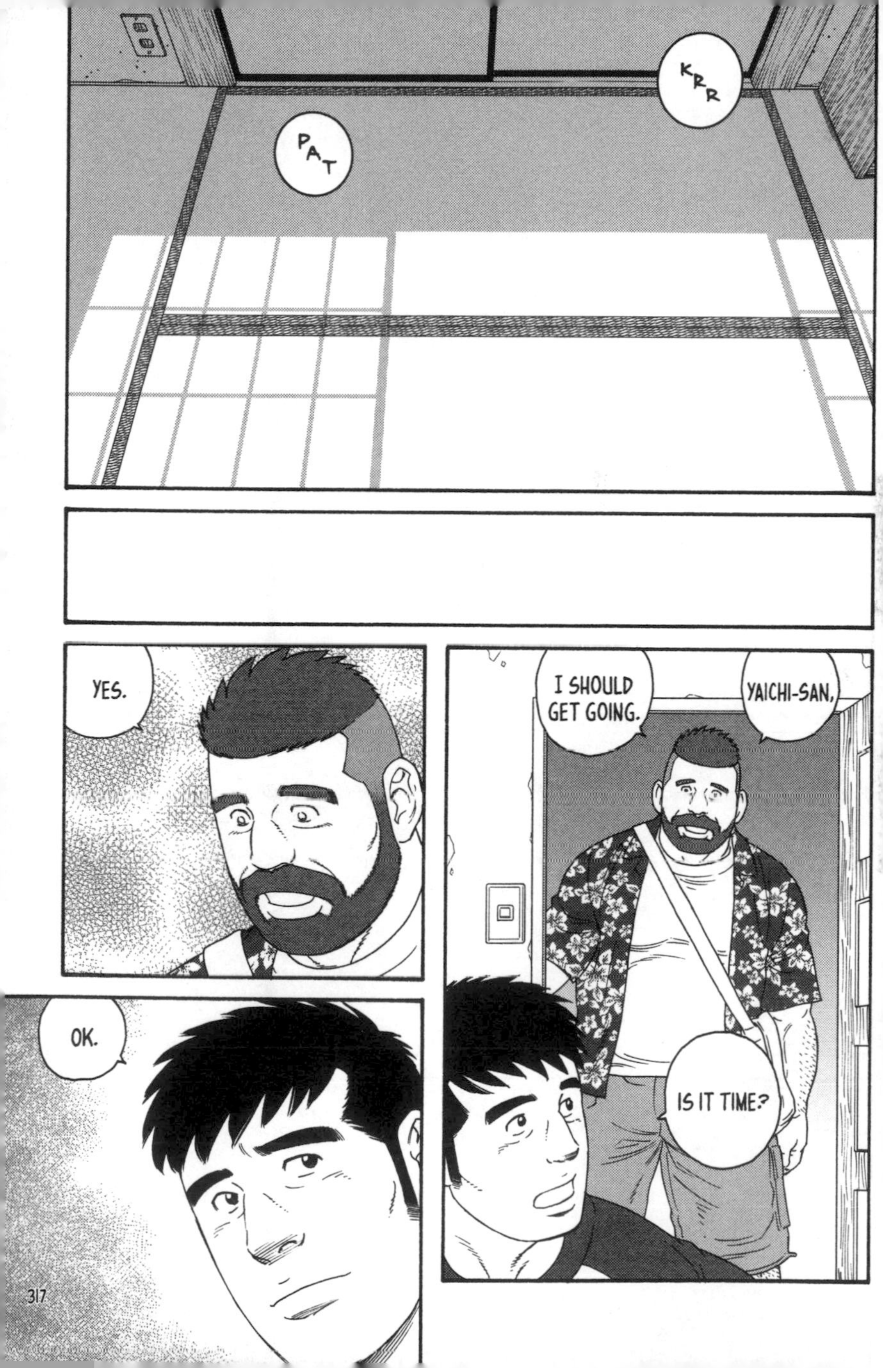
KRR
PAT
YAICHI-SAN,
I SHOULD GET GOING.
IS IT TIME?
YES.
OK.

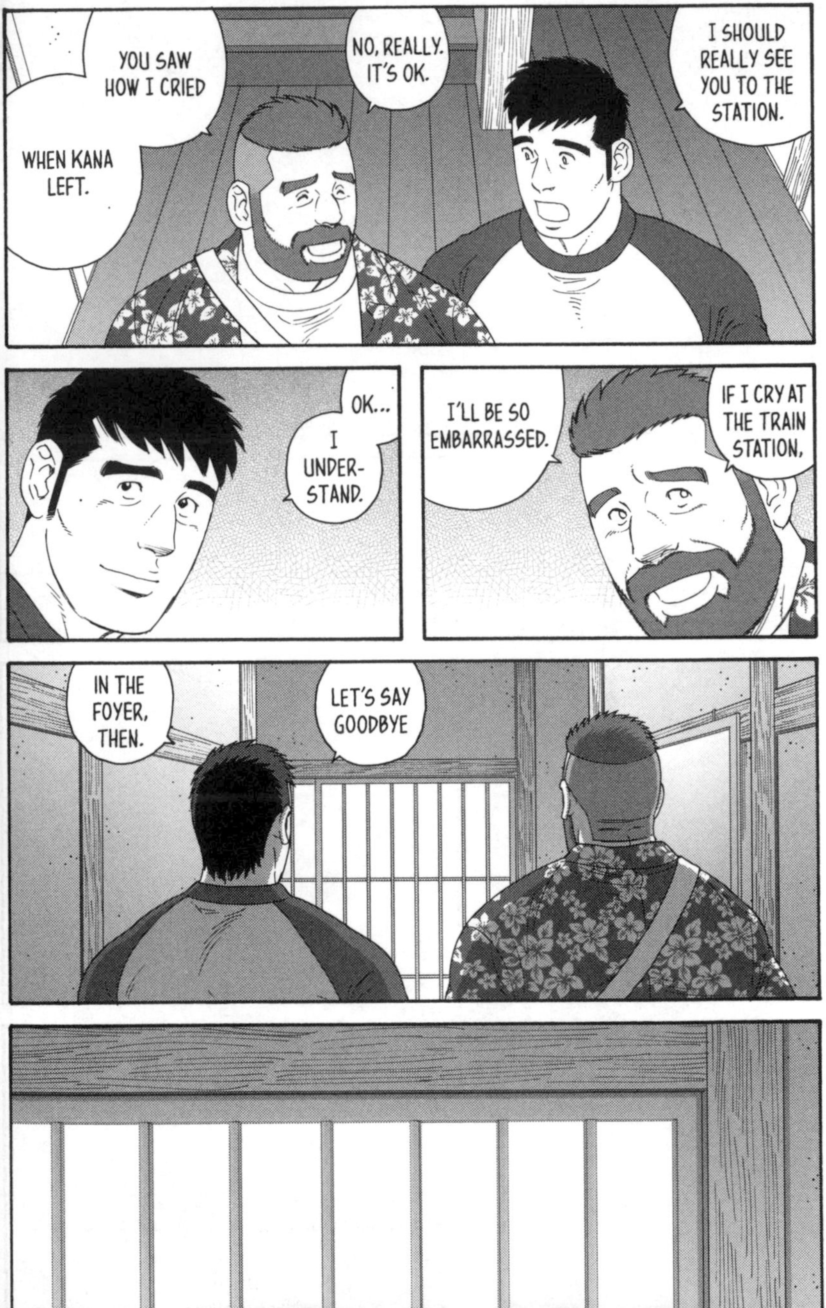
I SHOULD REALLY SEE YOU TO THE STATION.
NO, REALLY. IT'S OK.
YOU SAW HOW I CRIED
WHEN KANA LEFT.
IF I CRY AT THE TRAIN STATION,
I'LL BE SO EMBARRASSED.
OK...
I UNDER-STAND.
LET'S SAY GOODBYE
IN THE FOYER, THEN.

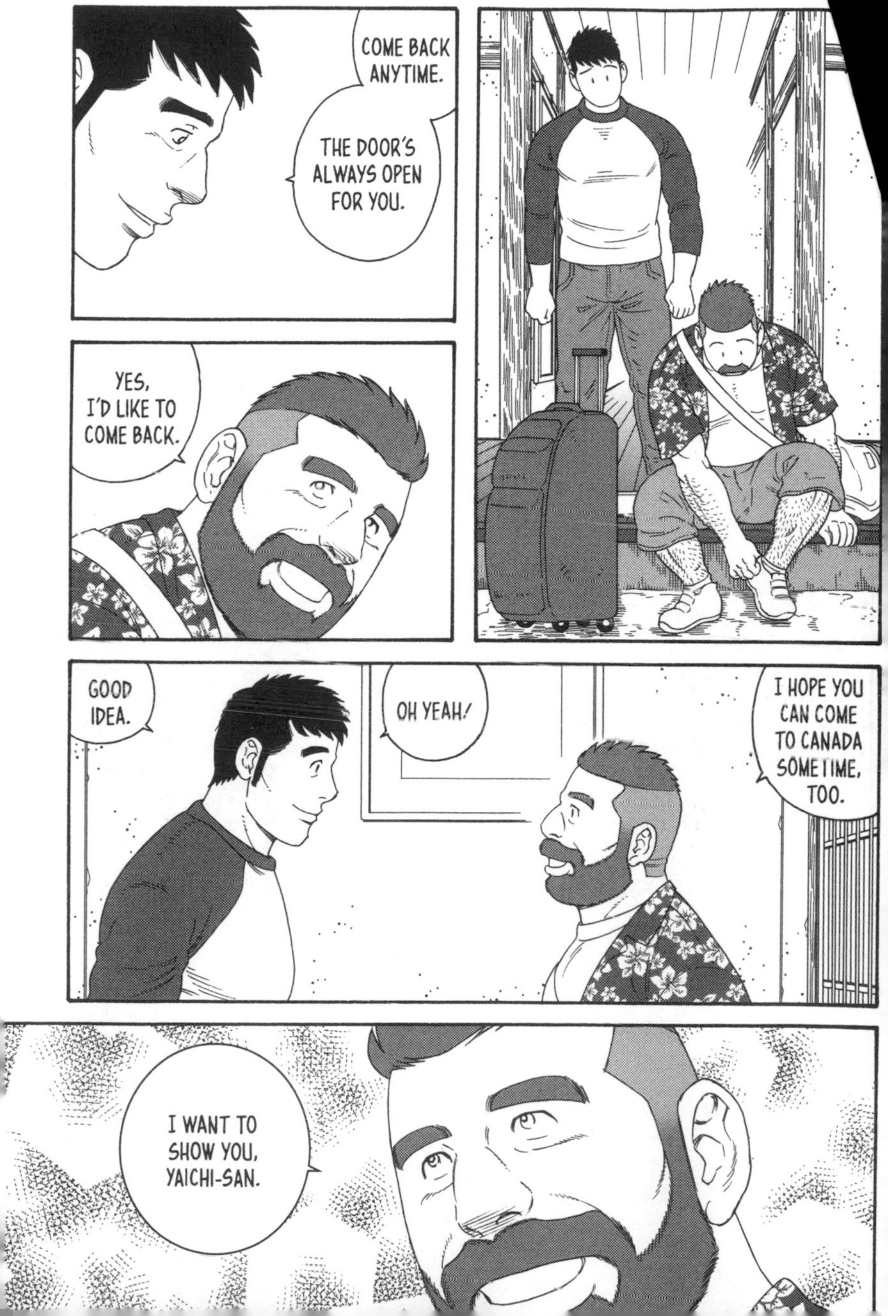
COME BACK ANYTIME.
THE DOOR'S ALWAYS OPEN FOR YOU.
YES, I'D LIKE TO COME BACK.
I HOPE YOU CAN COME TO CANADA SOMETIME, TOO.
OH YEAH!
GOOD IDEA.
I WANT TO SHOW YOU, YAICHI-SAN.

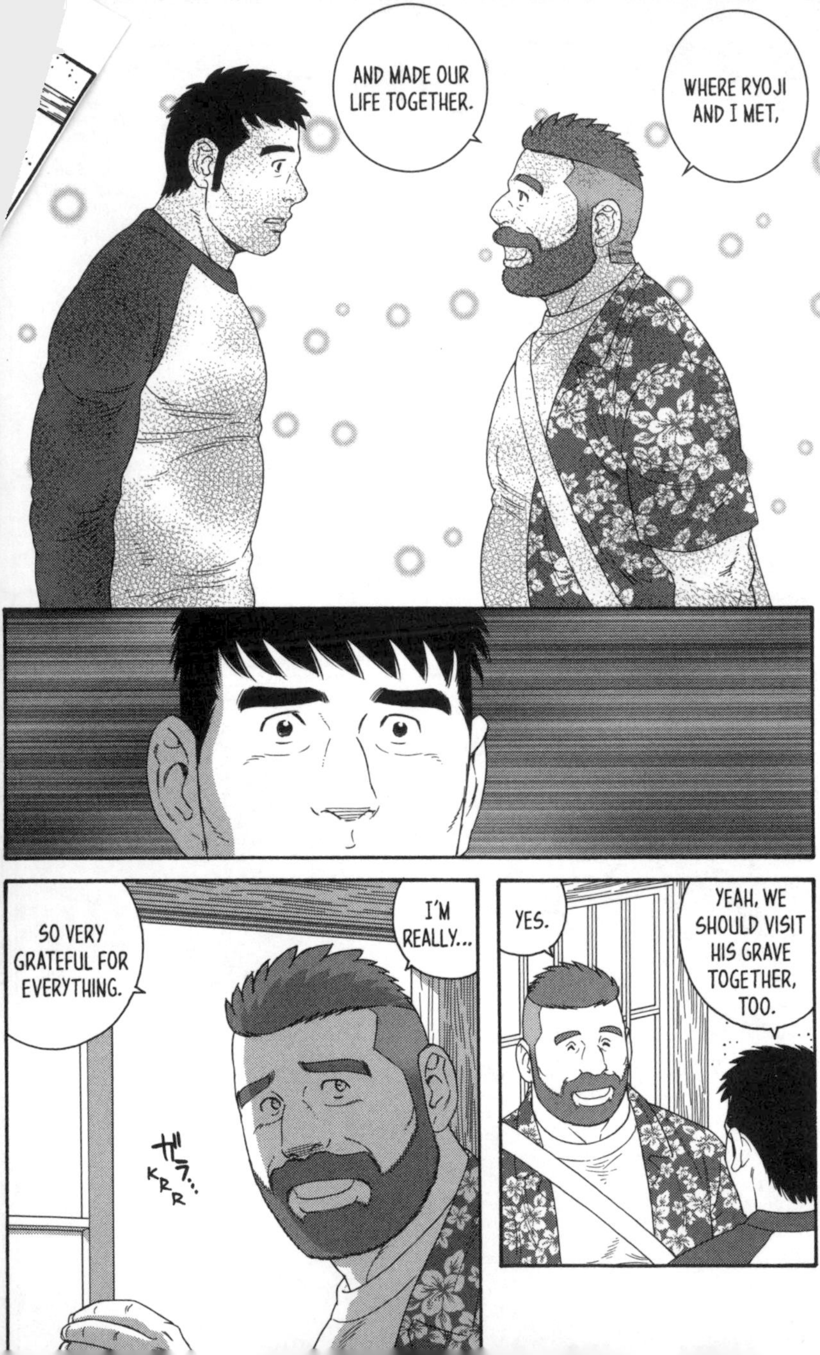
WHERE RYOJI AND I MET,
AND MADE OUR LIFE TOGETHER.
YEAH, WE SHOULD VISIT HIS GRAVE TOGETHER, TOO.
YES.
I'M REALLY...
SO VERY GRATEFUL FOR EVERYTHING.
ガラ…
KRR

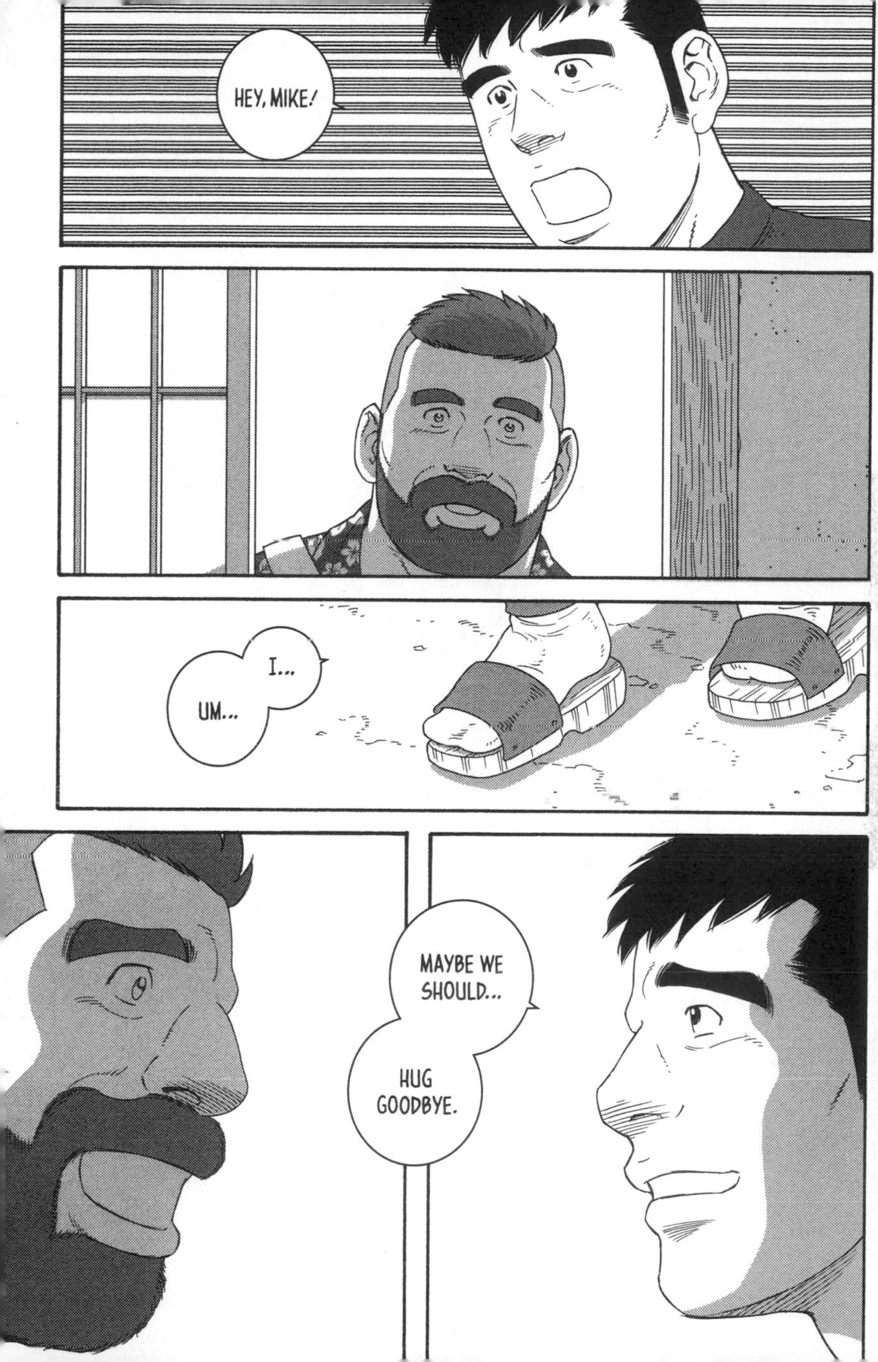
HEY, MIKE!
I...
UM...
MAYBE WE SHOULD...
HUG GOODBYE.

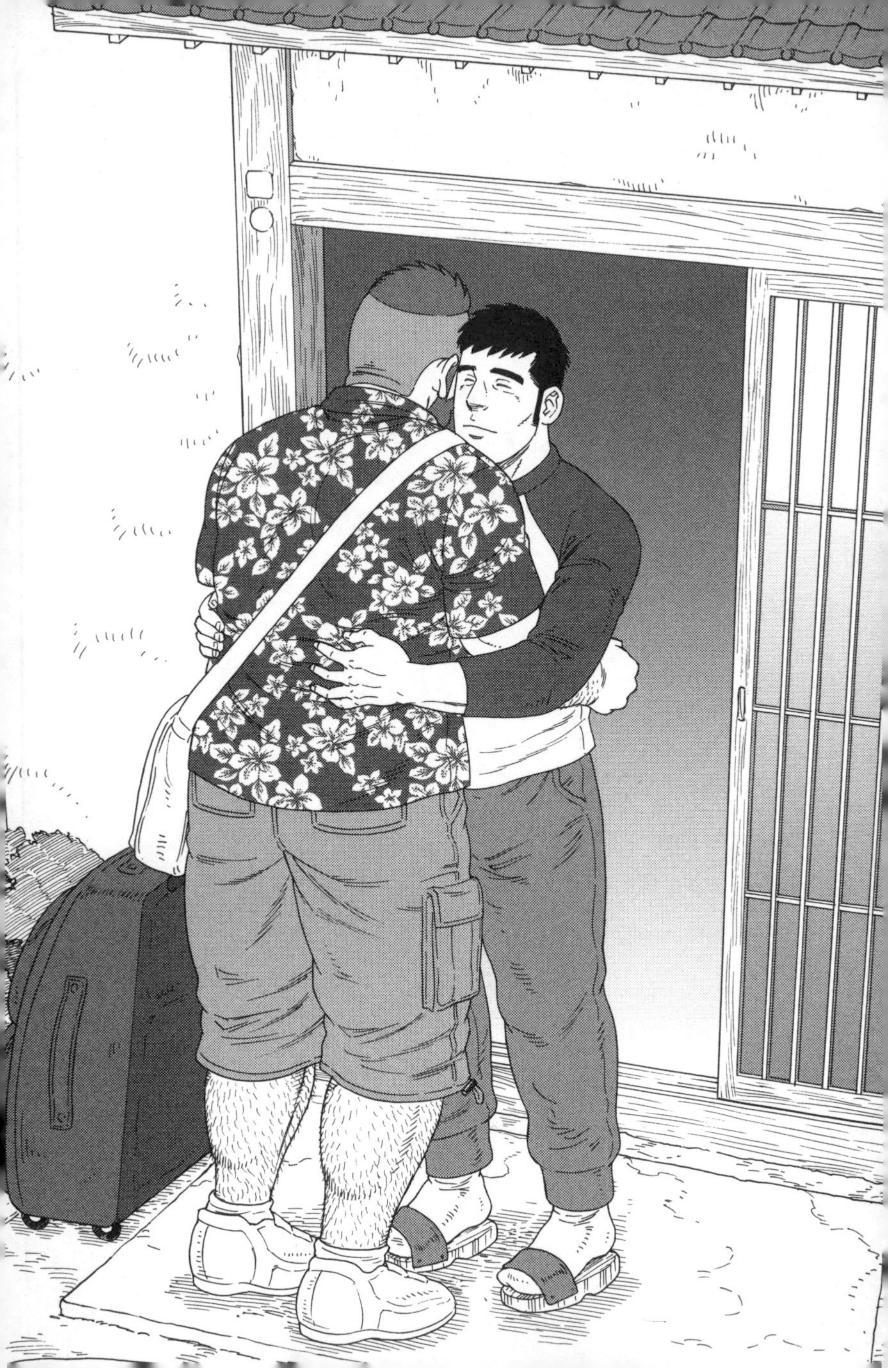

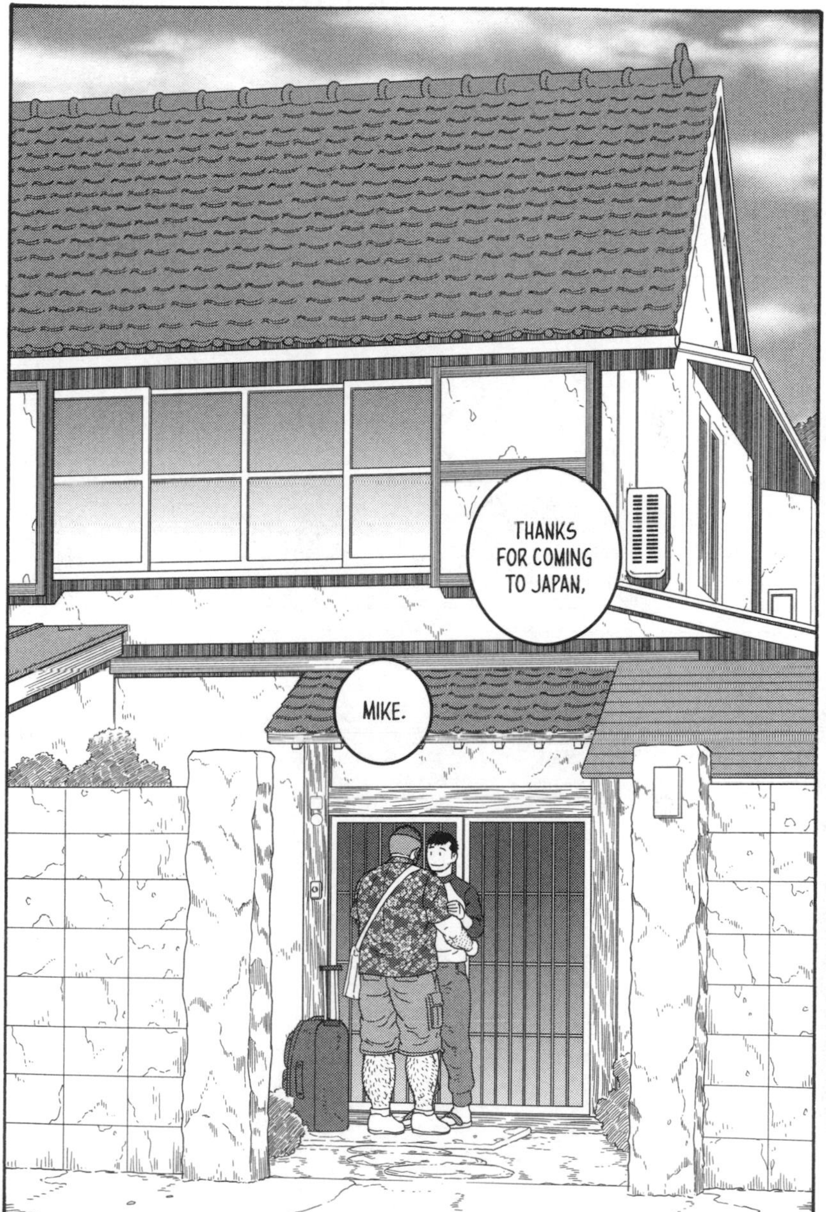
THANKS FOR COMING TO JAPAN,
MIKE.

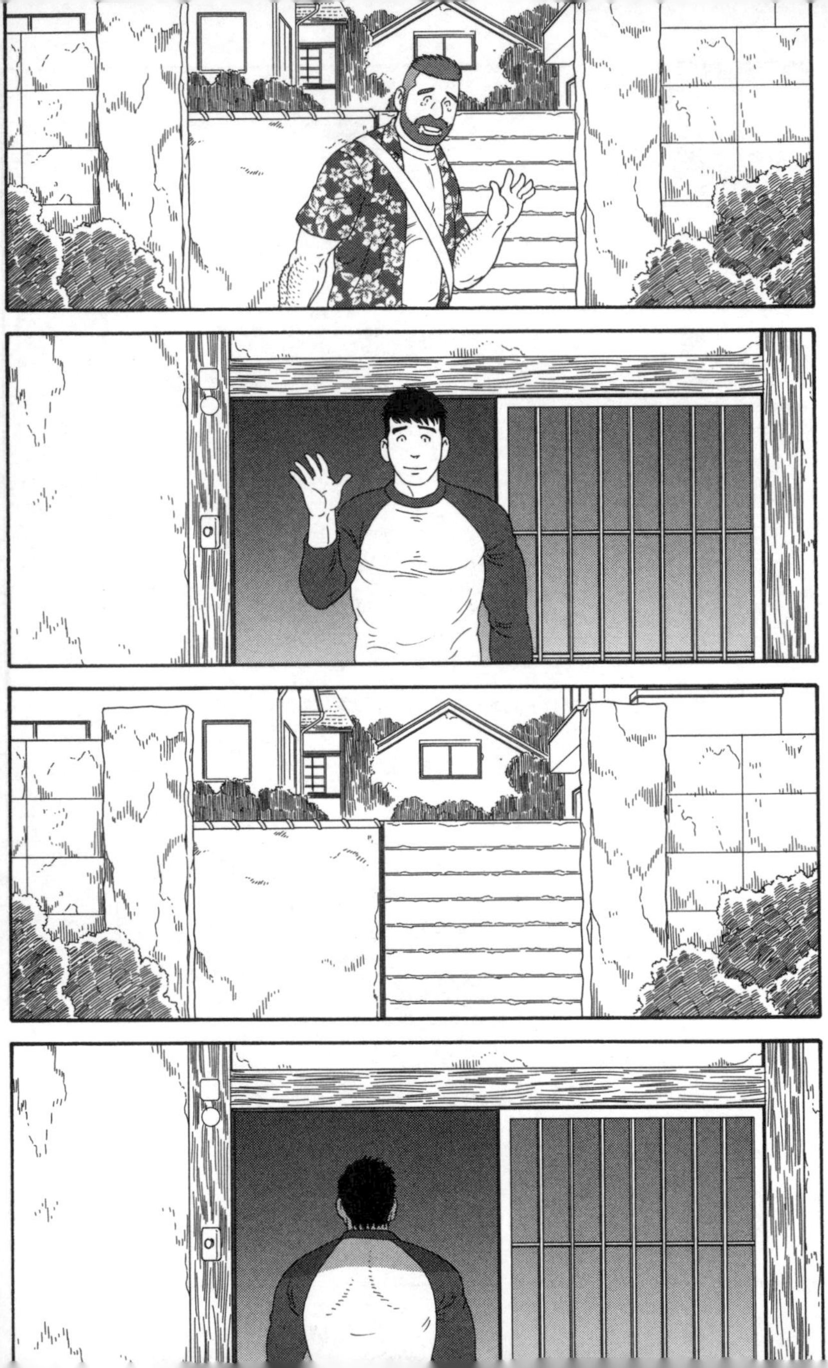

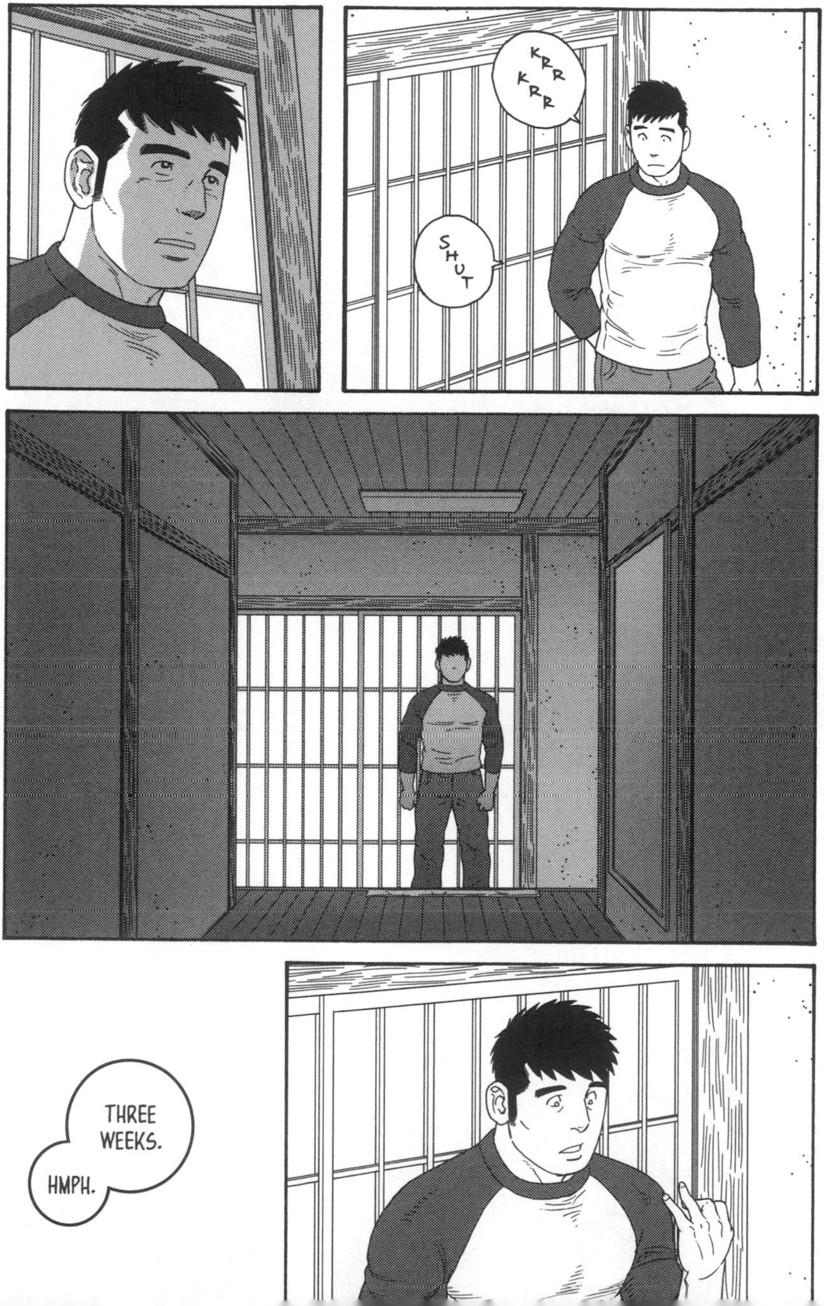
KRR KRR
SHUT
THREE WEEKS.
HMPH.

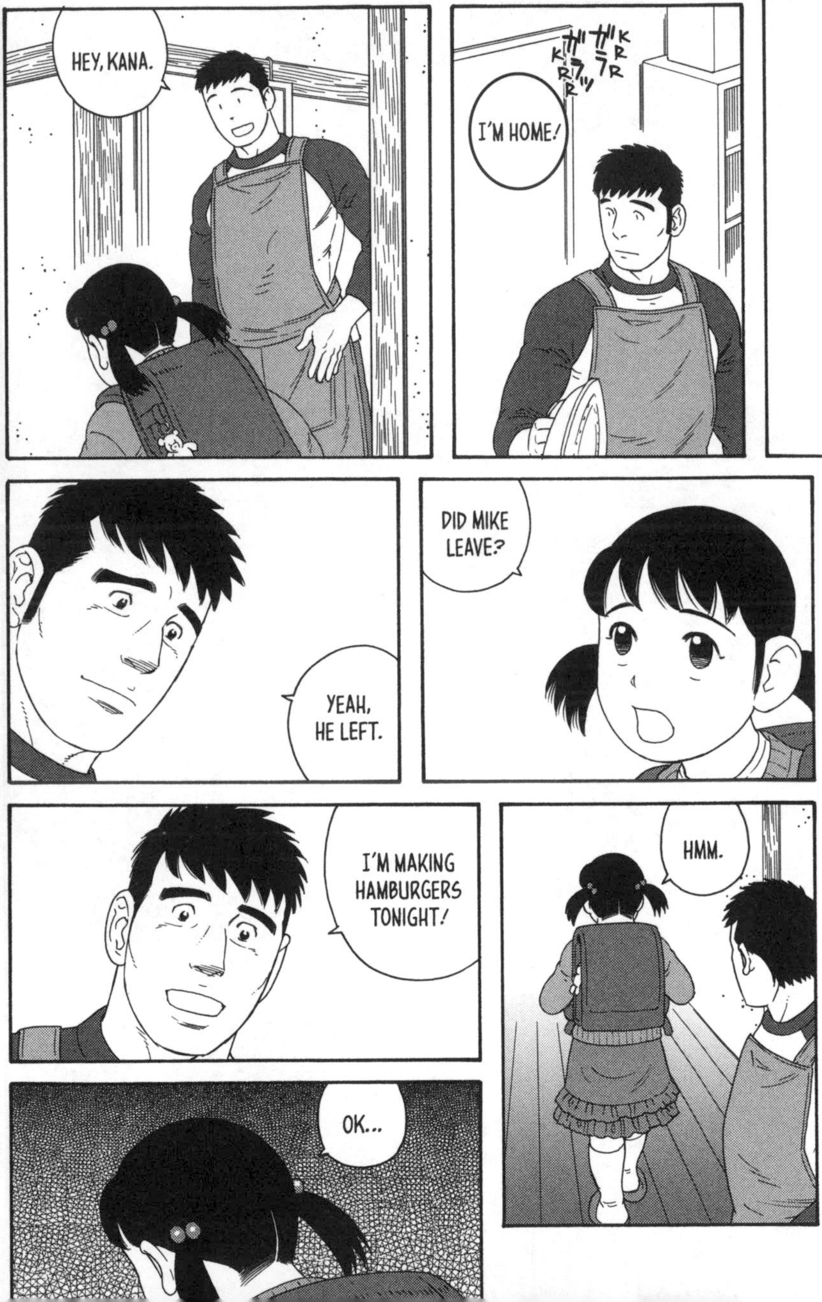
ガラ KRR
ガラッ KRR
I'M HOME!
HEY, KANA.
DID MIKE LEAVE?
YEAH, HE LEFT.
HMM.
I'M MAKING HAMBURGERS TONIGHT!
OK...

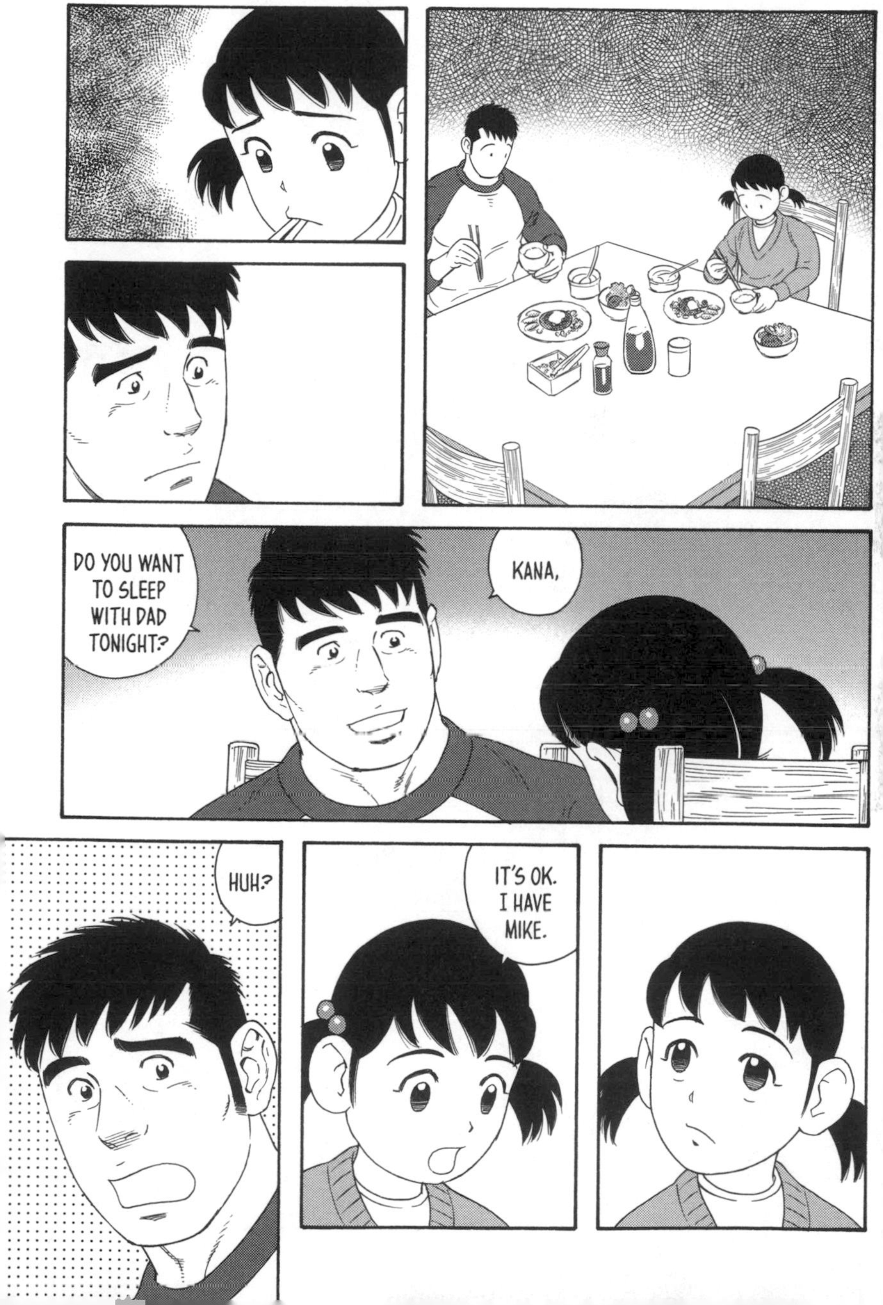
KANA,
DO YOU WANT TO SLEEP WITH DAD TONIGHT?
IT'S OK. I HAVE MIKE.
HUH?

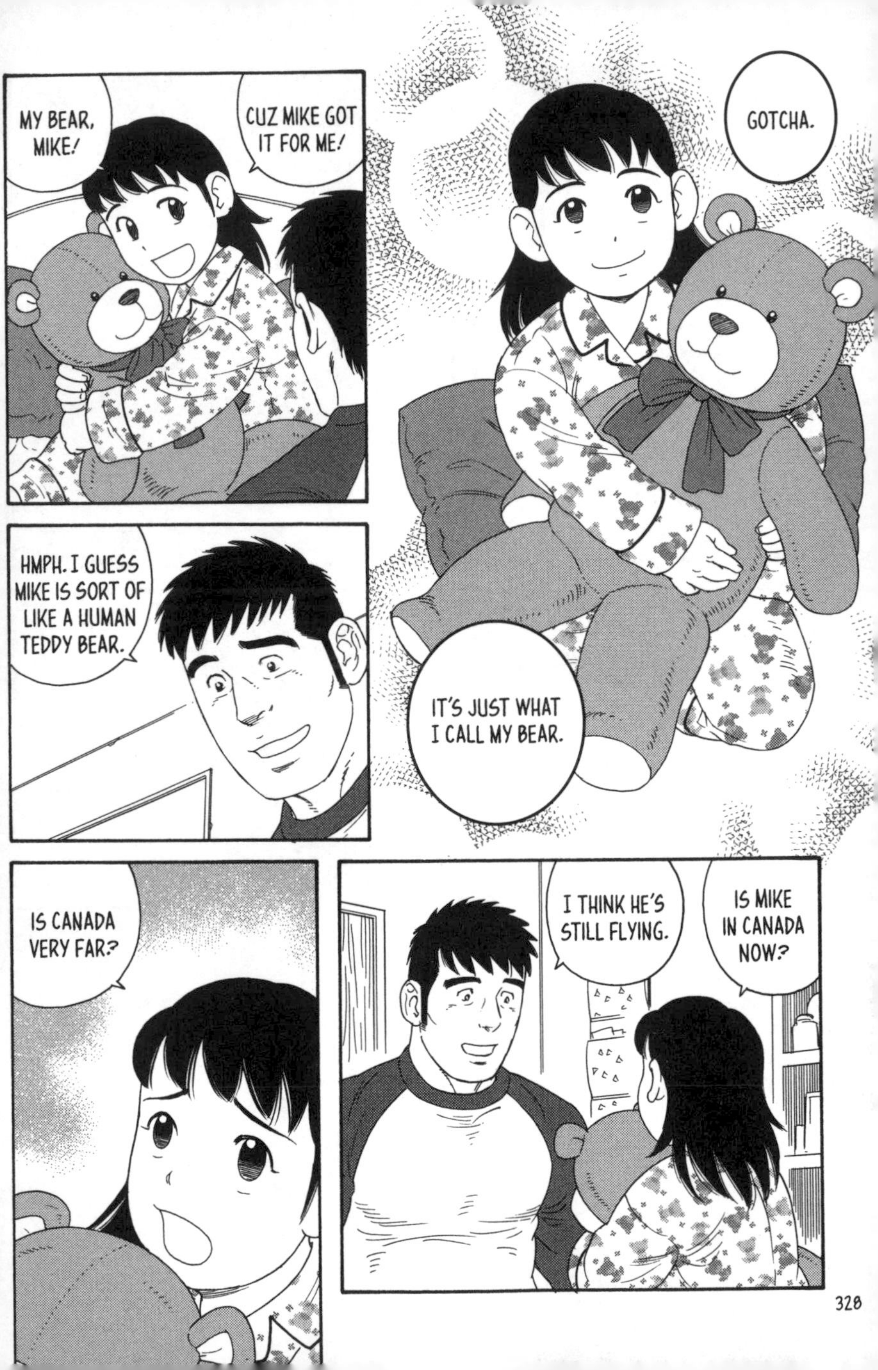
GOTCHA.
IT'S JUST WHAT I CALL MY BEAR.
CUZ MIKE GOT IT FOR ME!
MY BEAR, MIKE!
HMPH. I GUESS MIKE IS SORT OF LIKE A HUMAN TEDDY BEAR.
IS MIKE IN CANADA NOW?
I THINK HE'S STILL FLYING.
IS CANADA VERY FAR?

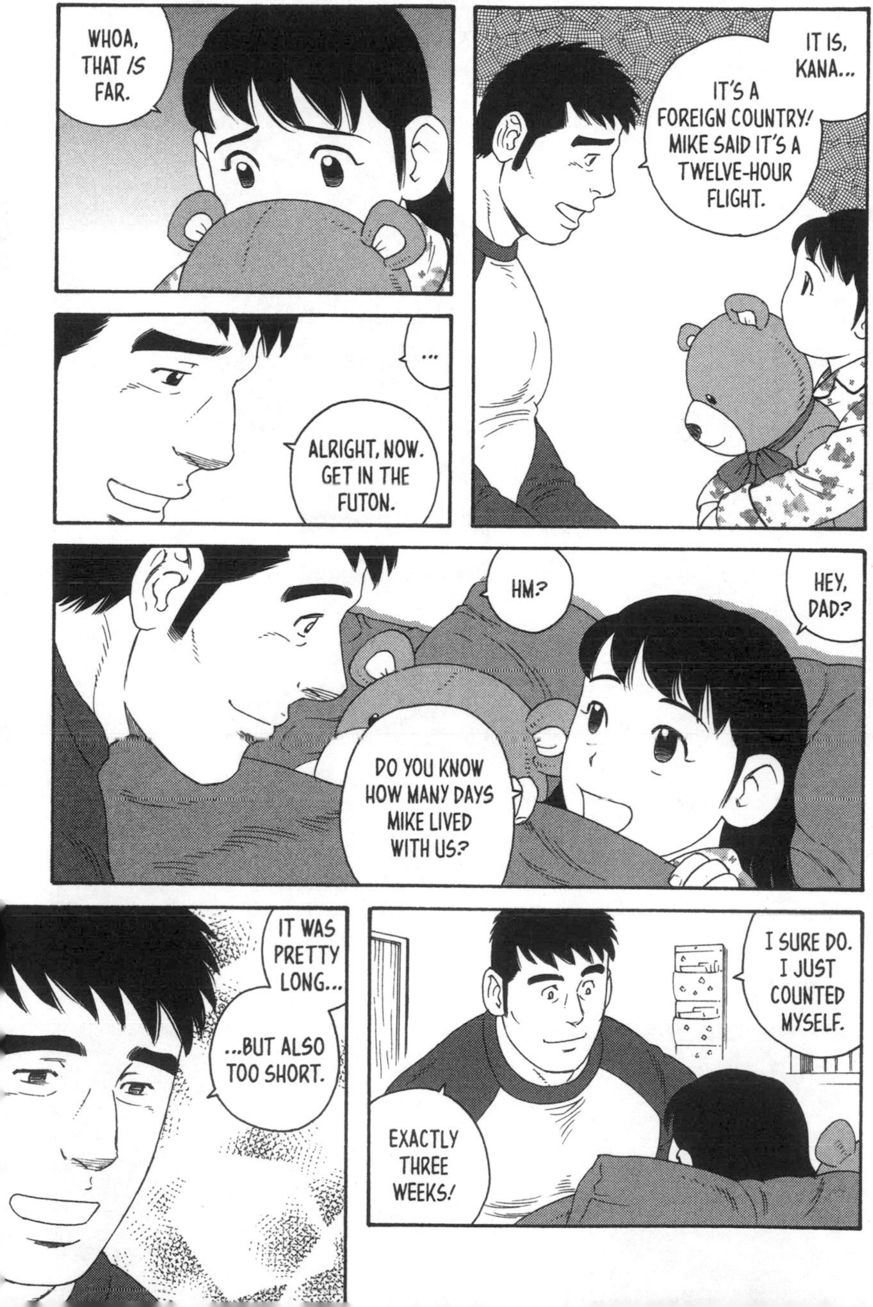
IT IS, KANA...
IT'S A FOREIGN COUNTRY! MIKE SAID IT'S A TWELVE-HOUR FLIGHT.
WHOA, THAT IS FAR.
...
ALRIGHT, NOW. GET IN THE FUTON.
HEY, DAD?
HM?
DO YOU KNOW HOW MANY DAYS MIKE LIVED WITH US?
I SURE DO. I JUST COUNTED MYSELF.
EXACTLY THREE WEEKS!
IT WAS PRETTY LONG...
...BUT ALSO TOO SHORT.

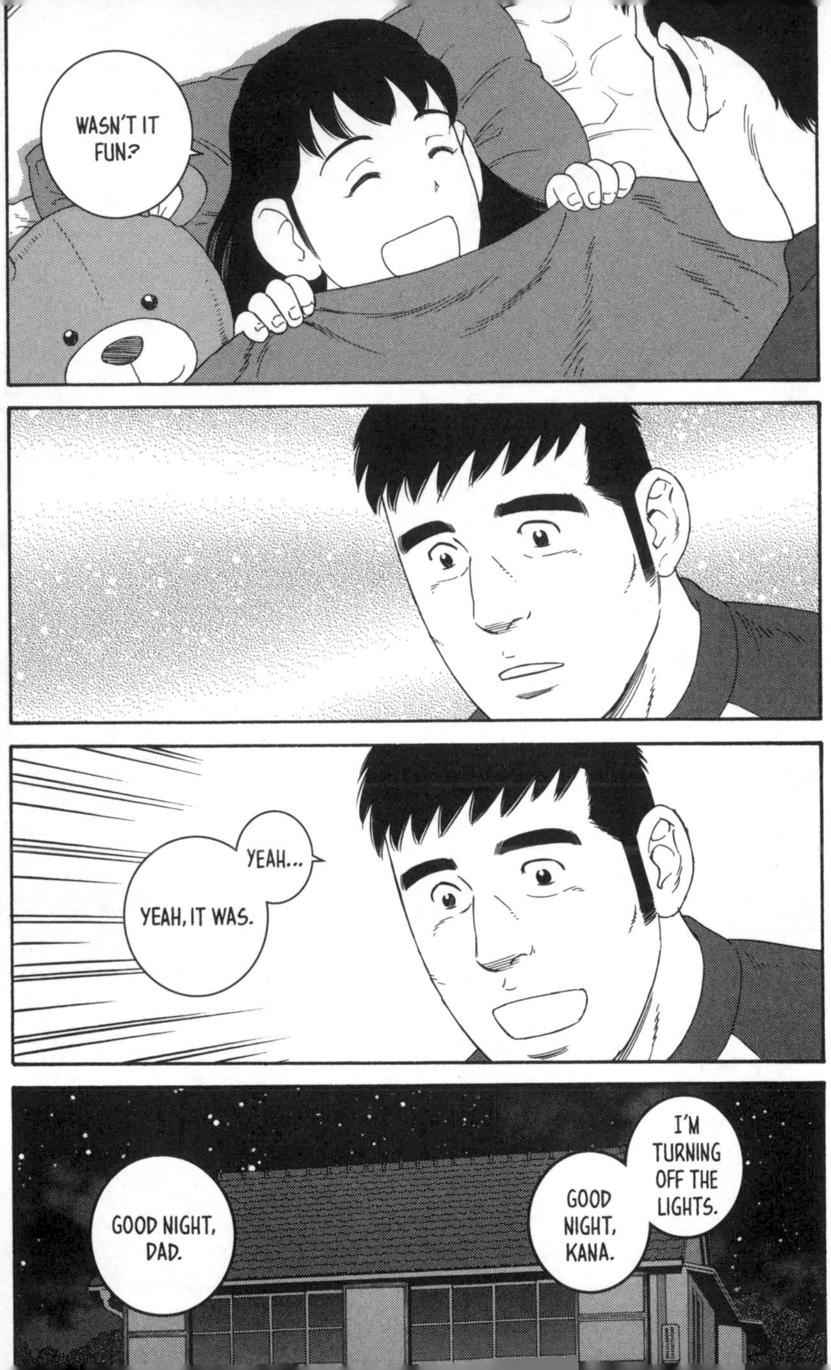
WASN'T IT FUN?
YEAH...
YEAH, IT WAS.
I'M TURNING OFF THE LIGHTS.
GOOD NIGHT, KANA.
GOOD NIGHT, DAD.

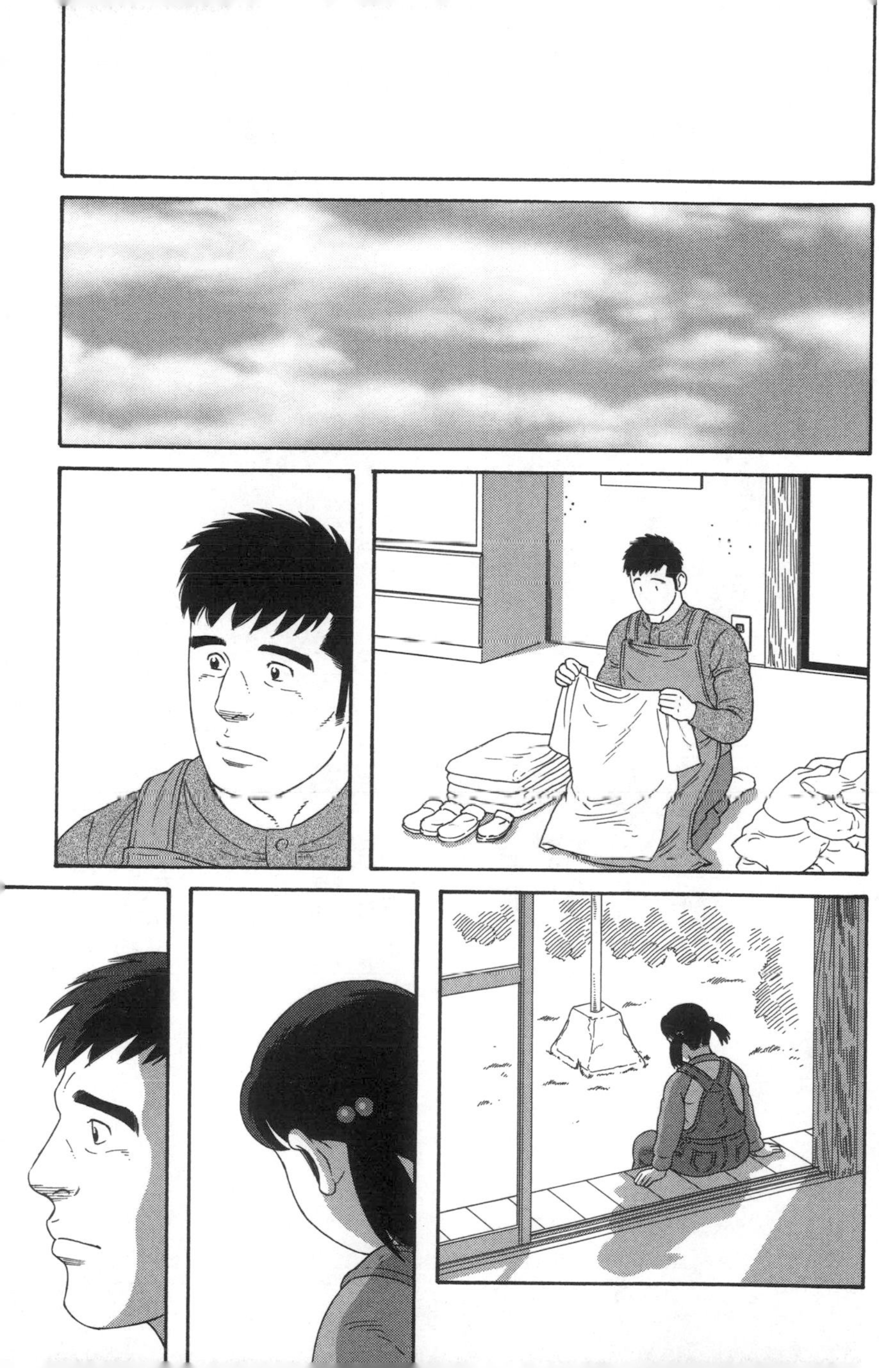

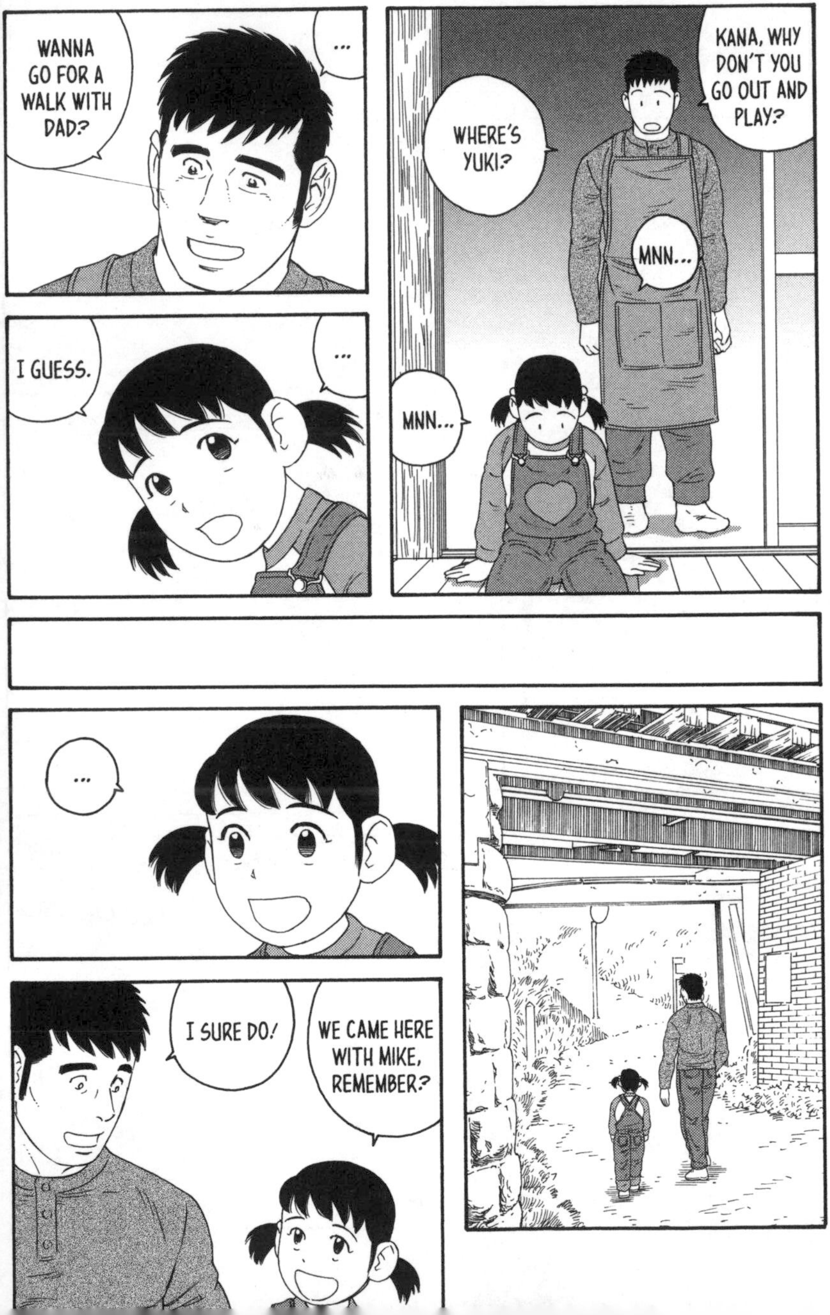
KANA, WHY DON'T YOU GO OUT AND PLAY?
WHERE'S YUKI?
MNN...
MNN...
...
WANNA GO FOR A WALK WITH DAD?
...
I GUESS.
...
WE CAME HERE WITH MIKE, REMEMBER?
I SURE DO!

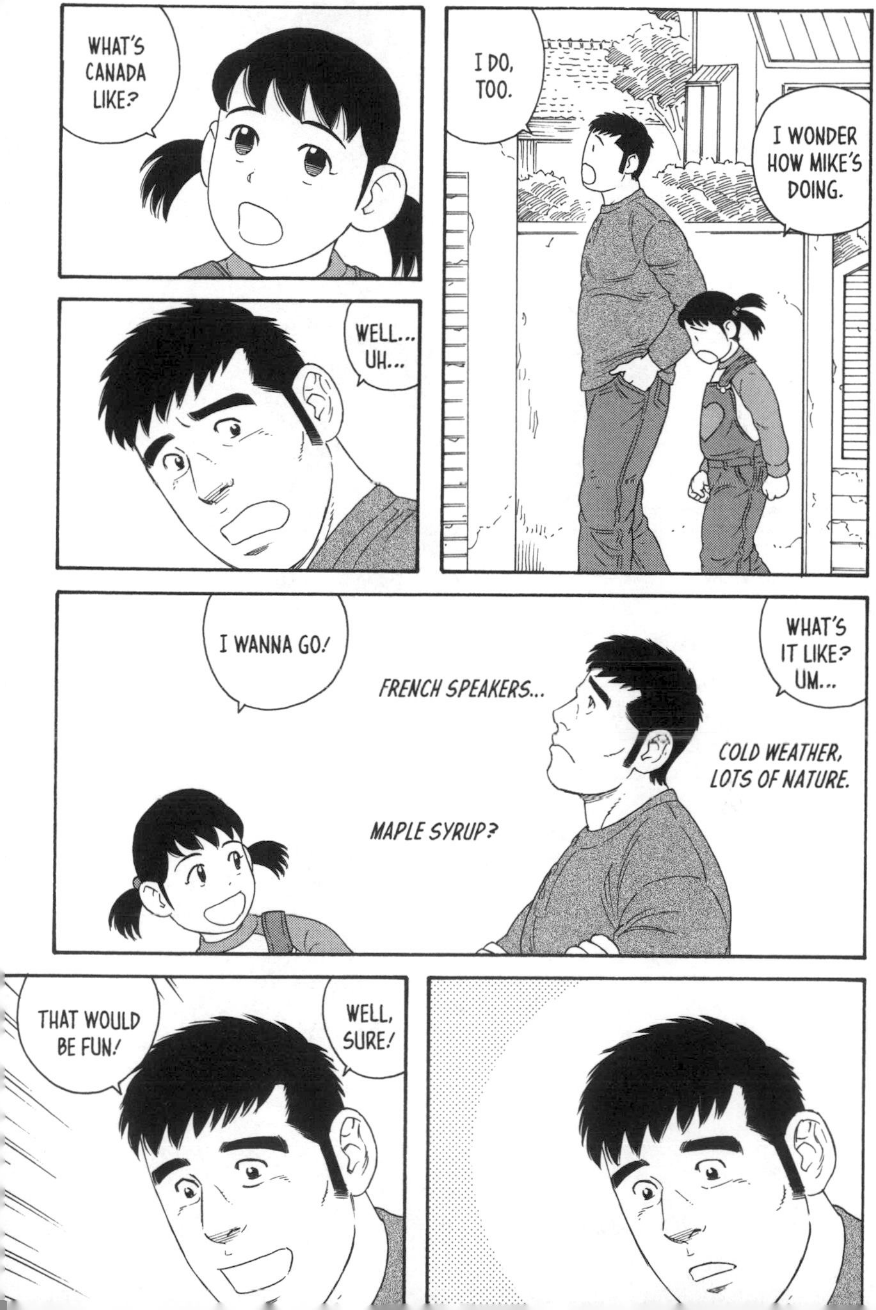
I WONDER HOW MIKE'S DOING.
I DO, TOO.
WHAT'S CANADA LIKE?
WELL... UH...
WHAT'S IT LIKE? UM...
FRENCH SPEAKERS...
COLD WEATHER, LOTS OF NATURE.
MAPLE SYRUP?
I WANNA GO!
WELL, SURE!
THAT WOULD BE FUN!

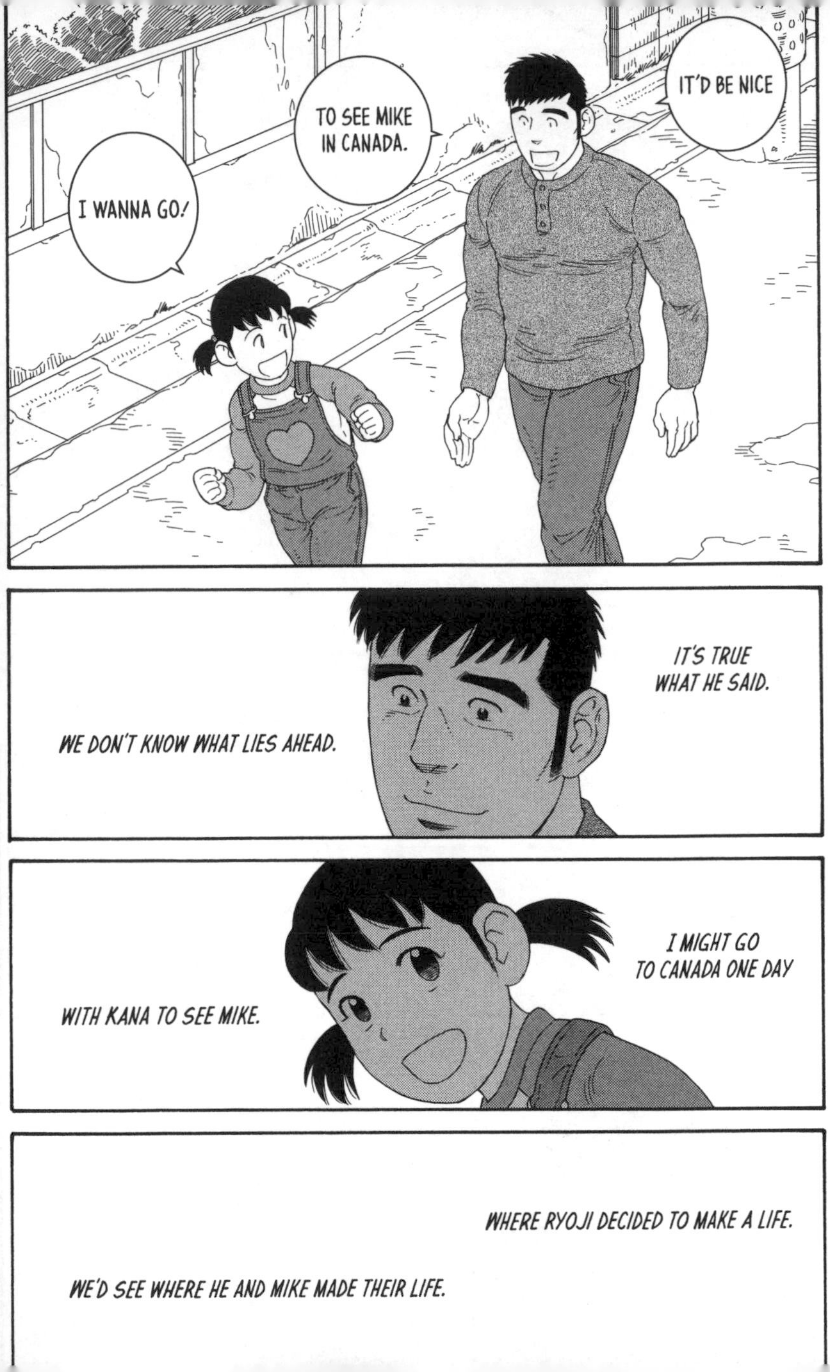

IT'D BE NICE
TO SEE MIKE IN CANADA.
I WANNA GO!
IT'S TRUE WHAT HE SAID.
WE DON'T KNOW WHAT LIES AHEAD.
I MIGHT GO TO CANADA ONE DAY
WITH KANA TO SEE MIKE.
WHERE RYOJI DECIDED TO MAKE A LIFE.
WE'D SEE WHERE HE AND MIKE MADE THEIR LIFE.

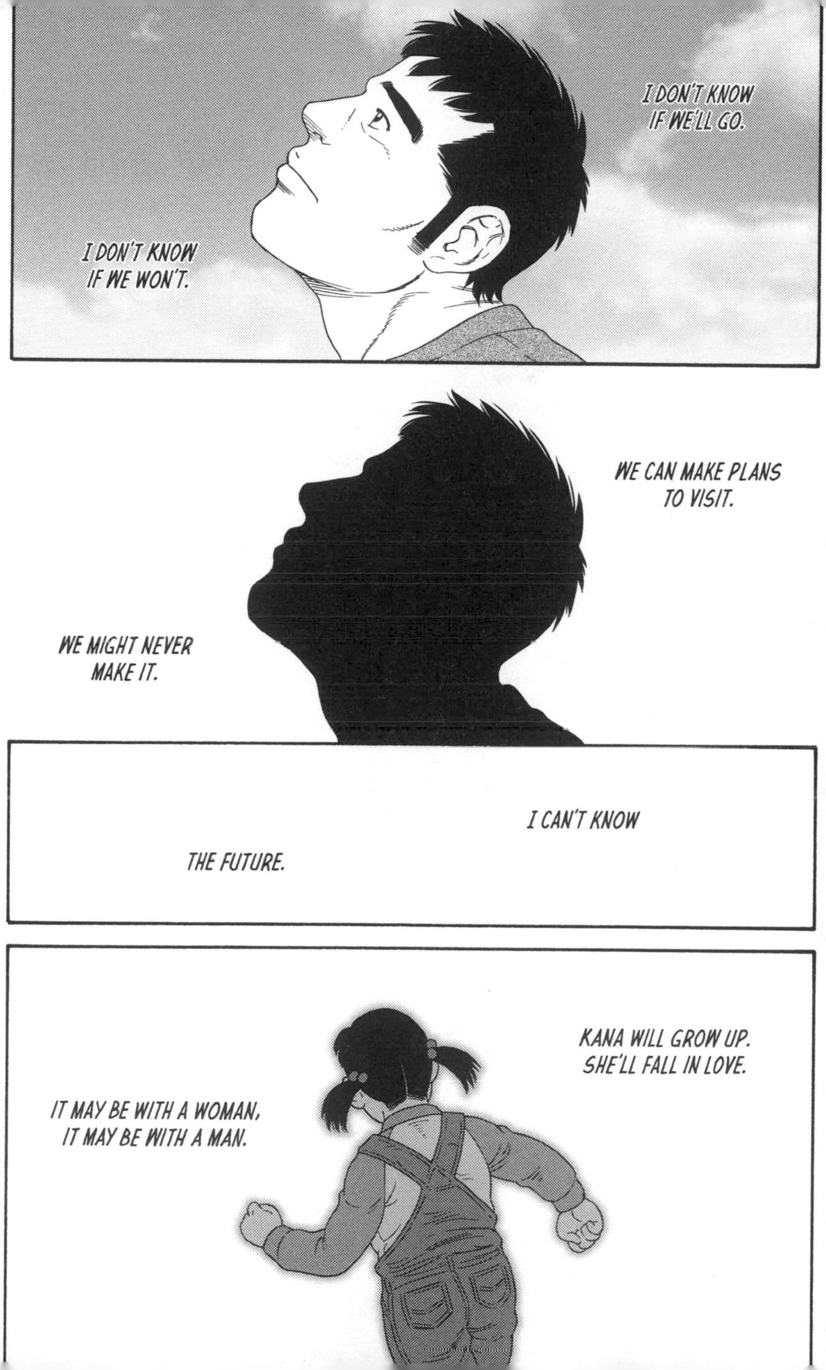
I DON'T KNOW IF WE'LL GO.
I DON'T KNOW IF WE WON'T.
WE CAN MAKE PLANS TO VISIT.
WE MIGHT NEVER MAKE IT.
I CAN'T KNOW
THE FUTURE.
KANA WILL GROW UP. SHE'LL FALL IN LOVE.
IT MAY BE WITH A WOMAN, IT MAY BE WITH A MAN.

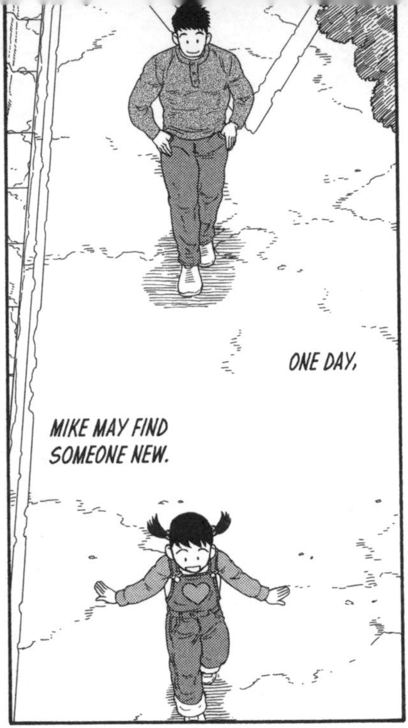
ONE DAY,
MIKE MAY FIND SOMEONE NEW.

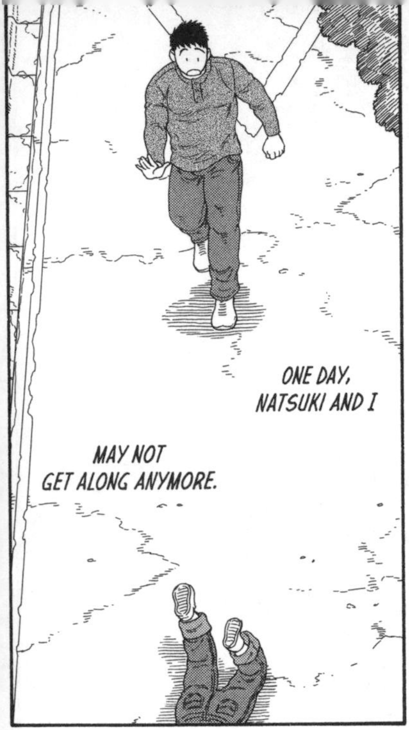
ONE DAY, NATSUKI AND I
MAY NOT GET ALONG ANYMORE.

NO ONE CAN KNOW FOR CERTAIN

WHAT'S AHEAD.

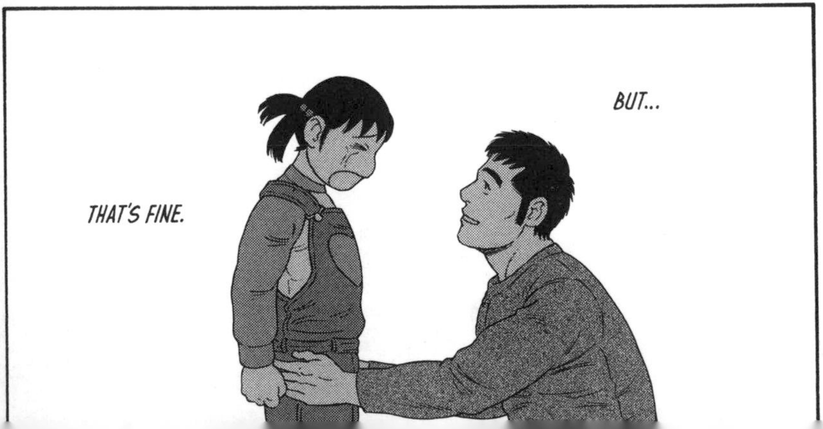
BUT...
THAT'S FINE.

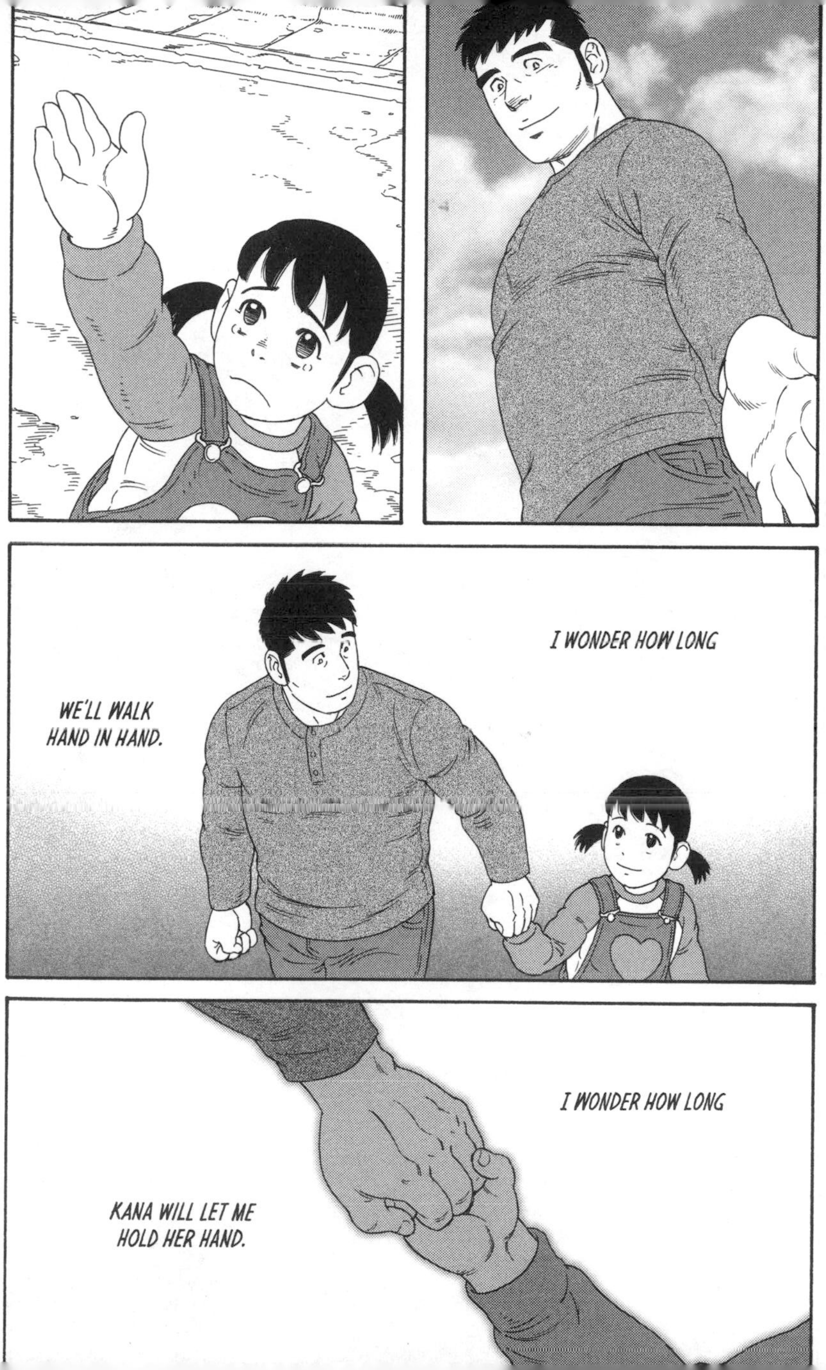
I WONDER HOW LONG
WE'LL WALK HAND IN HAND.
I WONDER HOW LONG
KANA WILL LET ME HOLD HER HAND.

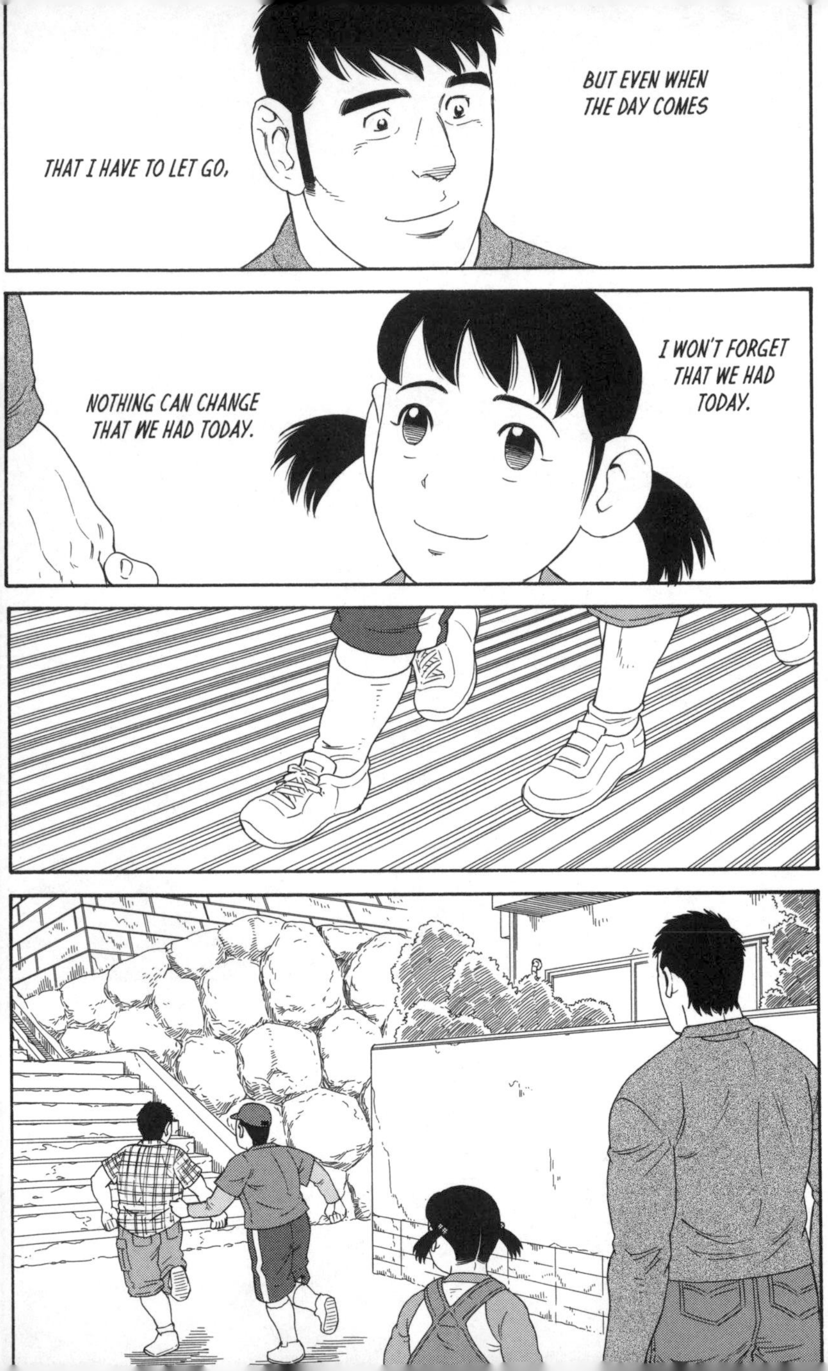
BUT EVEN WHEN THE DAY COMES
THAT I HAVE TO LET GO,
I WON'T FORGET THAT WE HAD TODAY.
NOTHING CAN CHANGE THAT WE HAD TODAY.

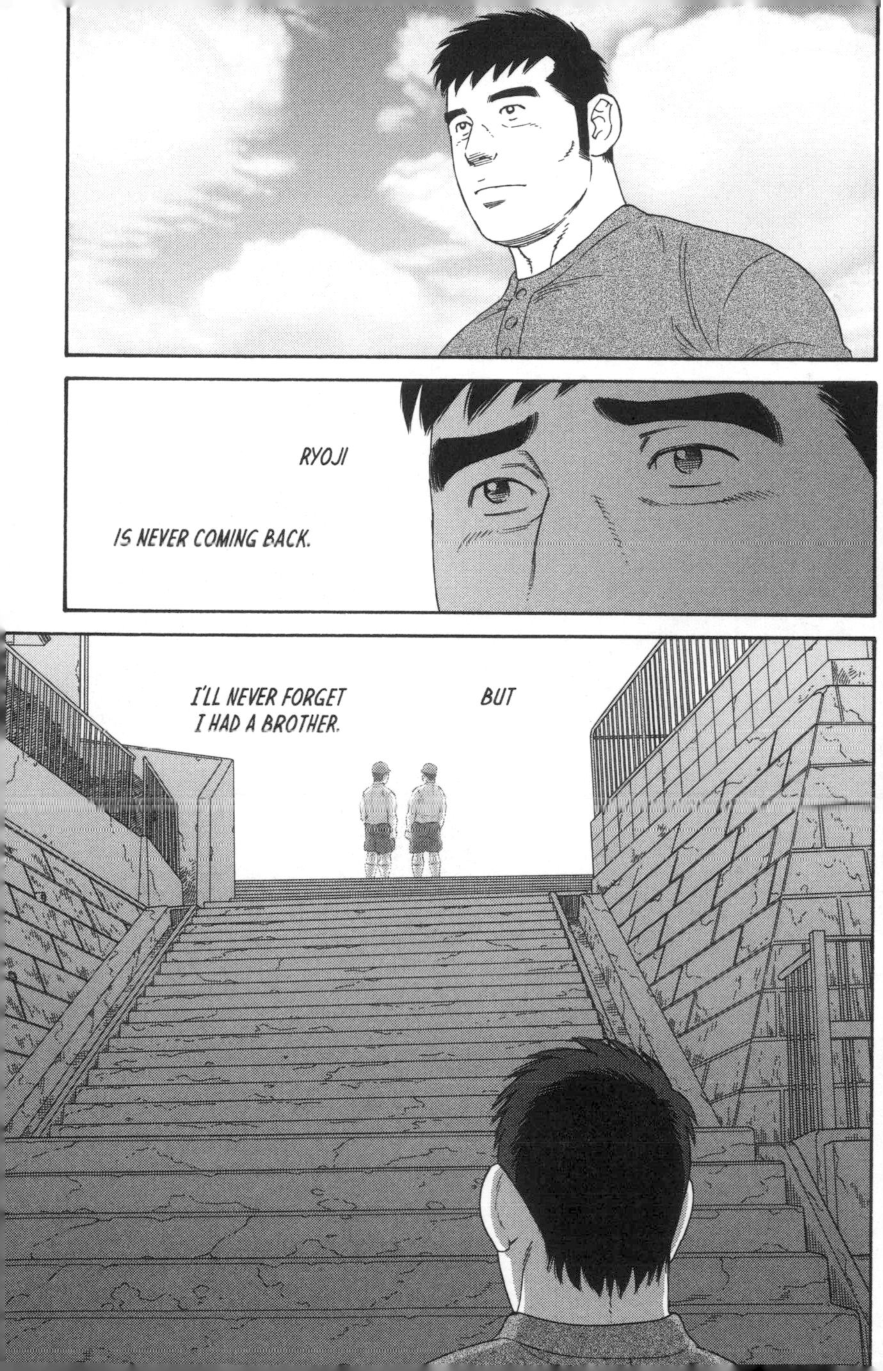
RYOJI
IS NEVER COMING BACK.
BUT
I'LL NEVER FORGET
I HAD A BROTHER.

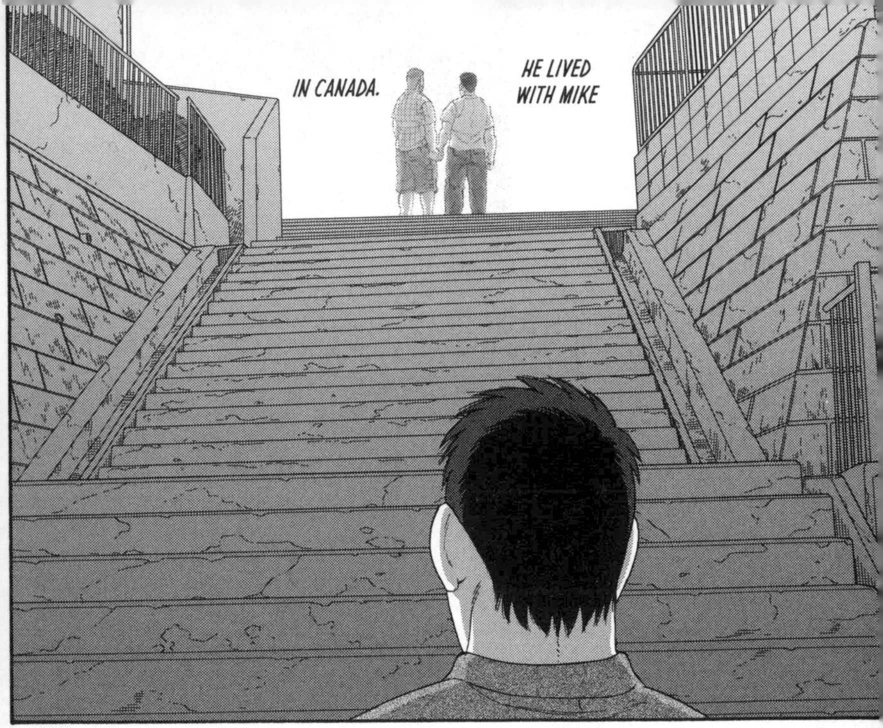
HE LIVED WITH MIKE
IN CANADA.

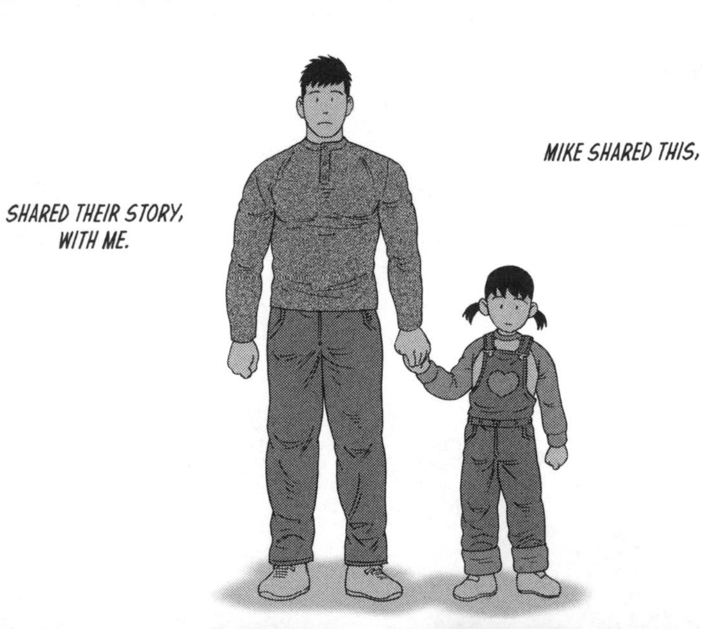
MIKE SHARED THIS,
SHARED THEIR STORY, WITH ME.

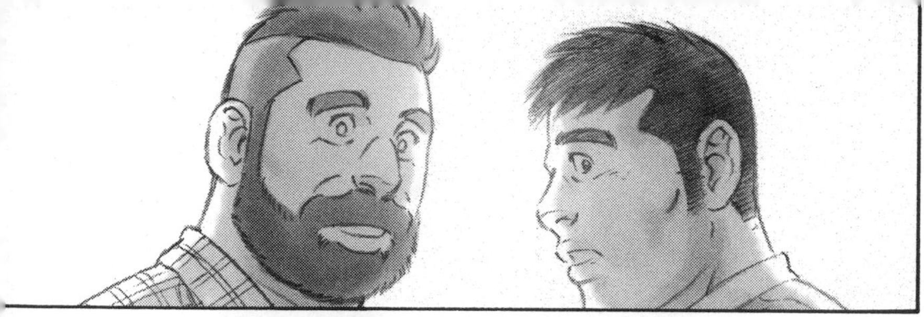

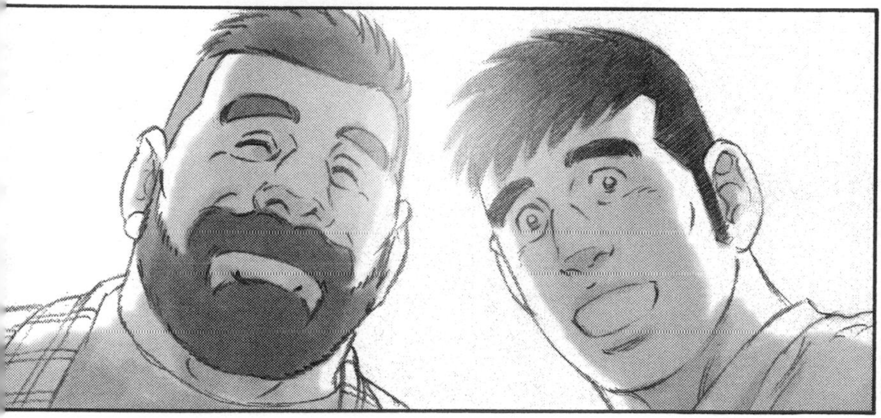

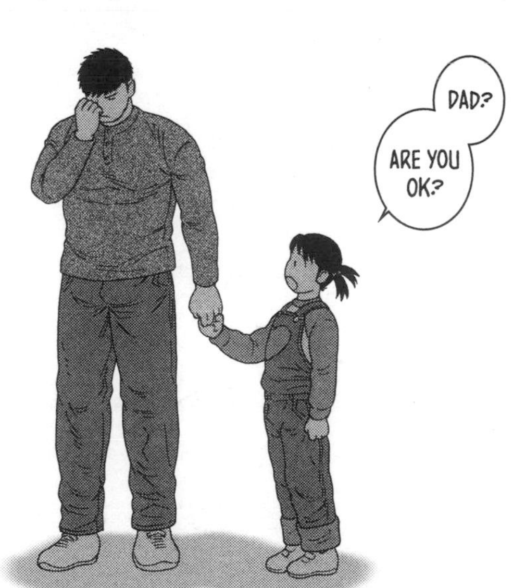
DAD?
ARE YOU OK?

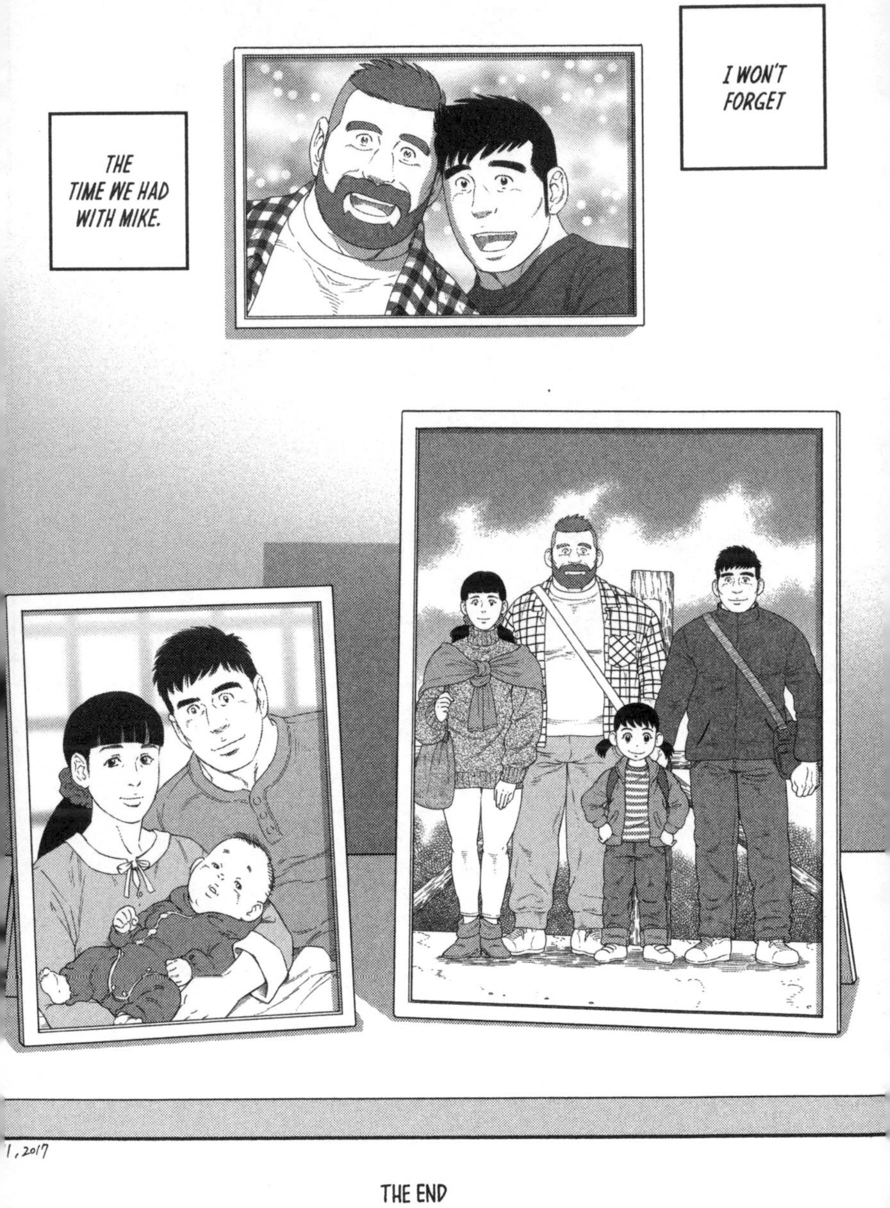
I WON'T FORGET
THE TIME WE HAD WITH MIKE.

1, 2017

THE END

PENCILS

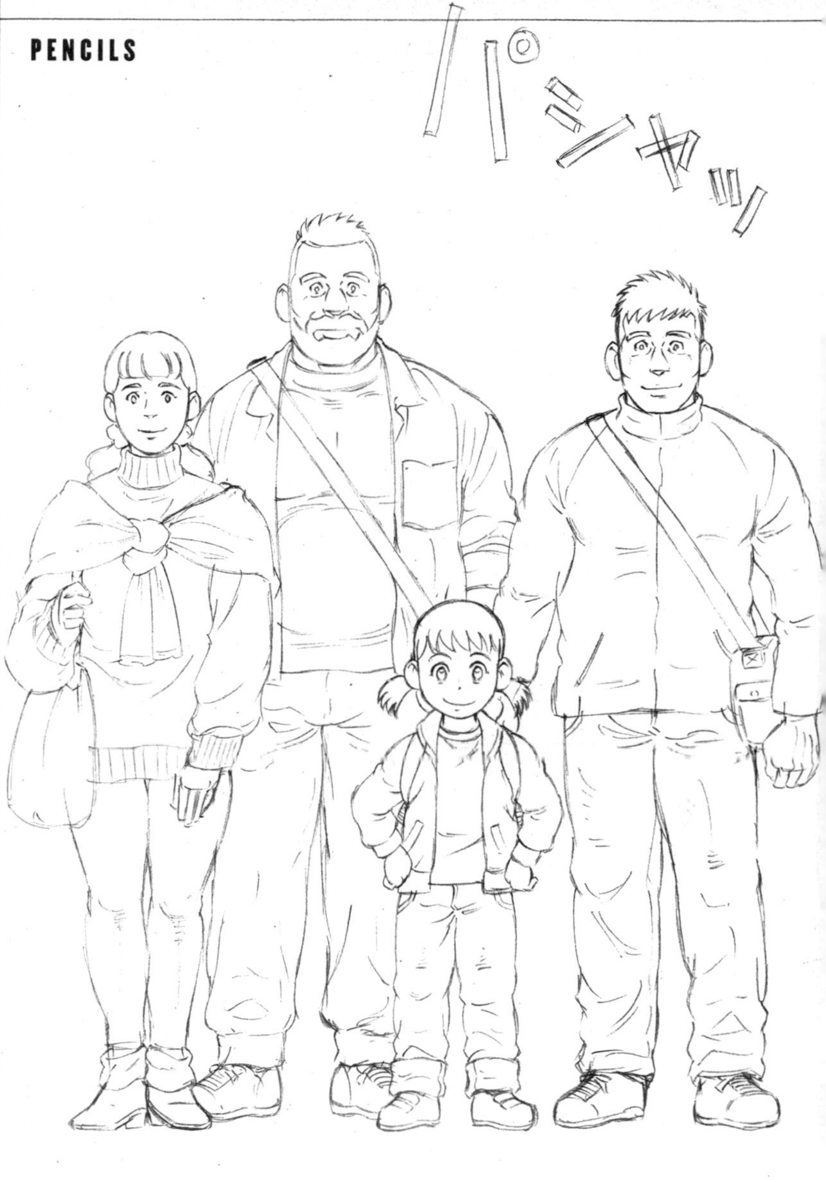
パシャッ

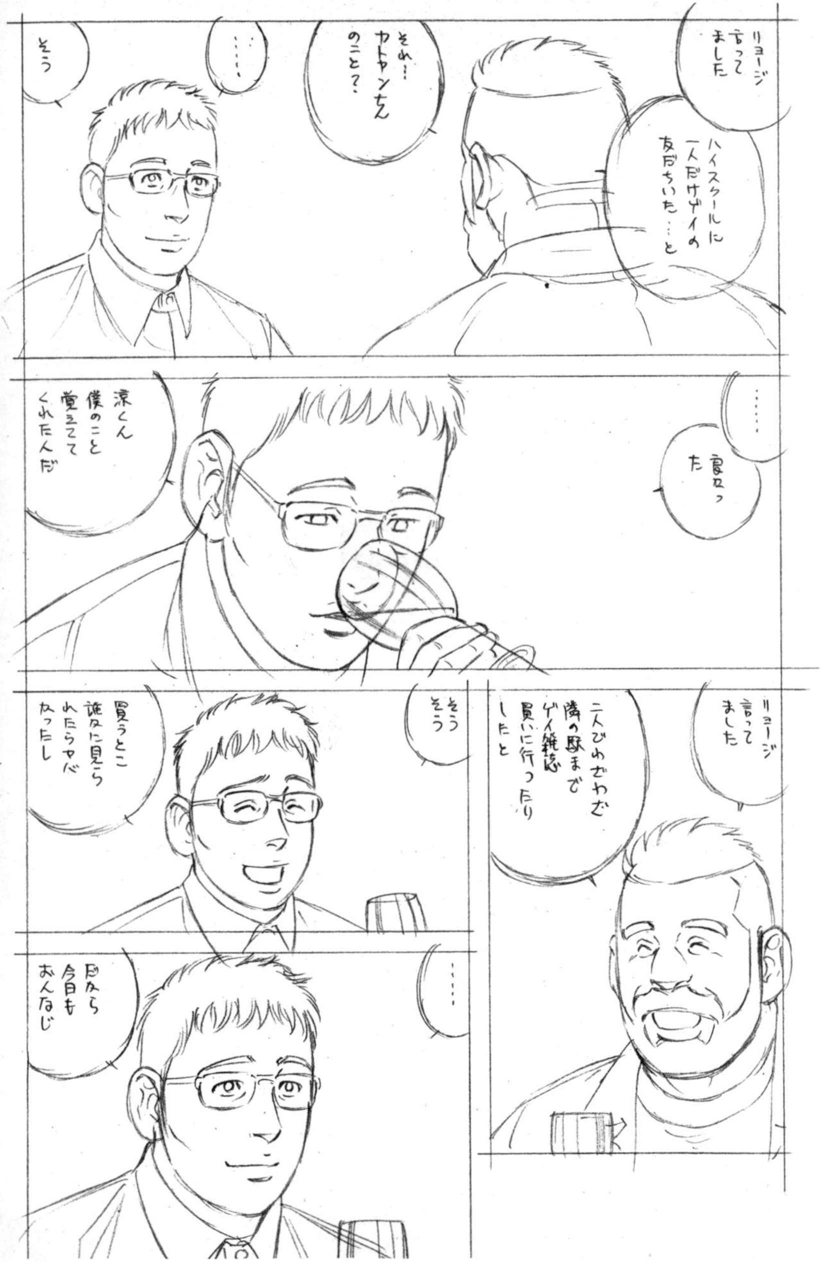
リョージ言ってました
ハイスクールに一人だけゲイの友だちいた…と
それ…カトちゃんのこと？
……
そう
……
良かった
涼くん僕のこと覚えててくれたんだ
リョージ言ってました
二人でわざわざ隣の駅までゲイ雑誌買いに行ったりしたと
そうそう
買うとこ誰かに見られたらヤバかったし
……
だから今日もおんなじ

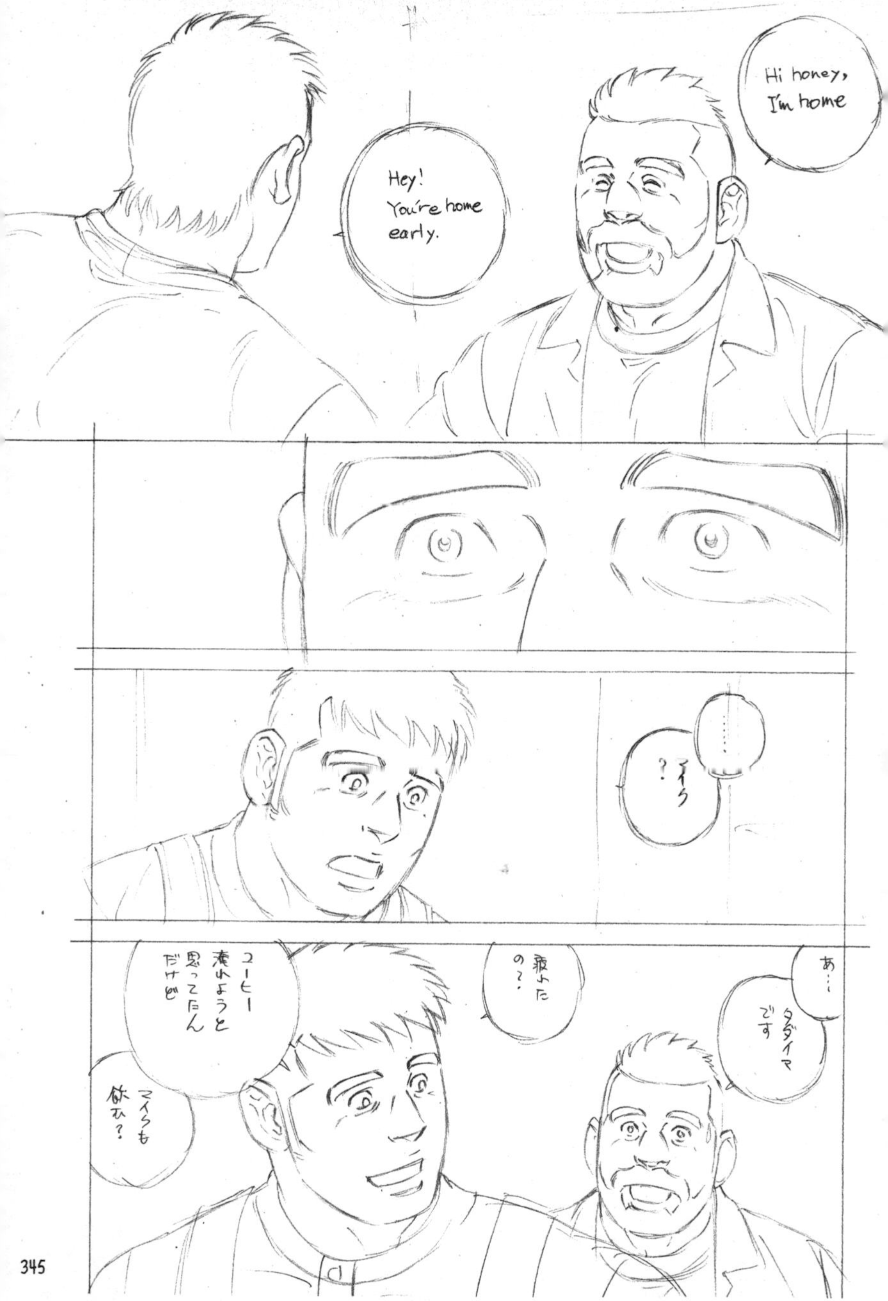
Hi honey, I'm home
Hey! You're home early.
……
マイク？
あ…
タダイマです
疲れたの？
コーヒー淹れようと思ってたんだけど
マイクも飲む？

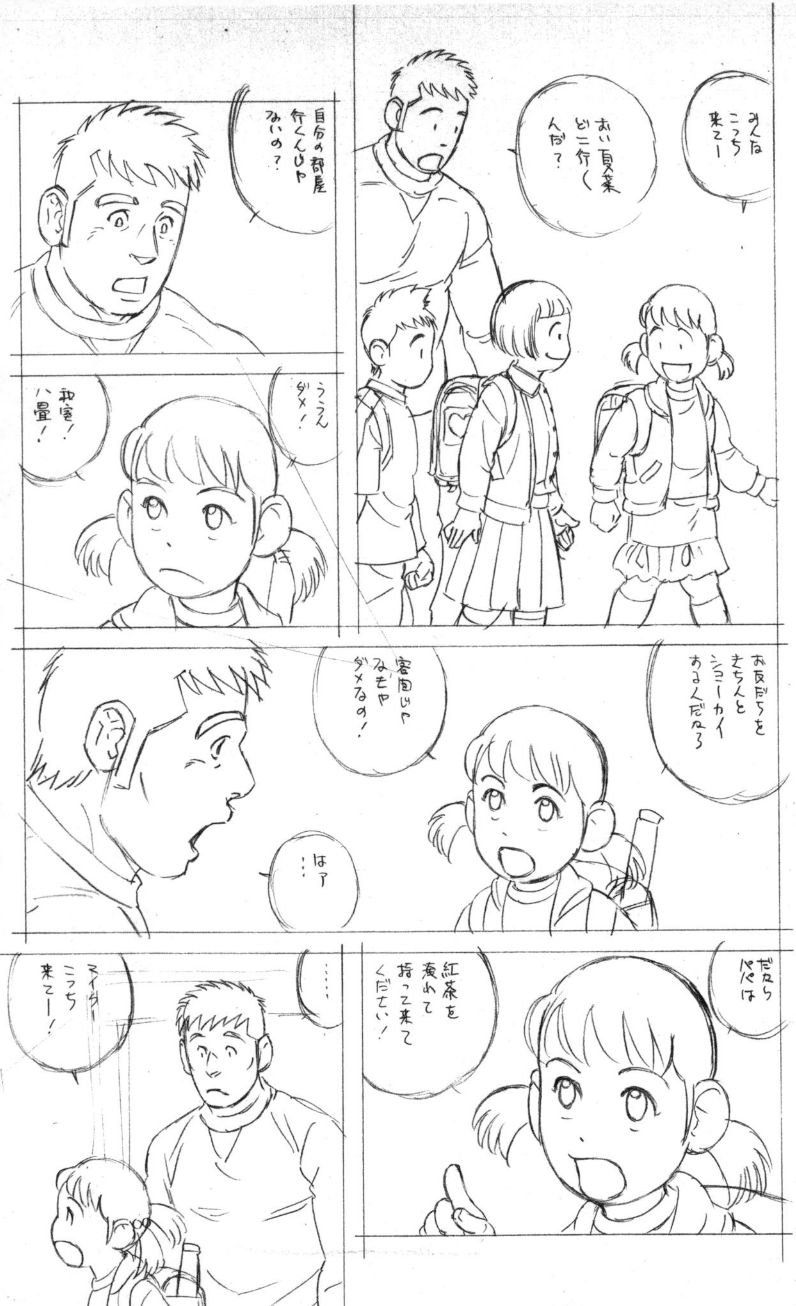
みんなこっち来てー
おい夏菜どこ行くんだ?
自分の部屋行くんじゃないの?
ううんダメ!
和室!八畳!
お友だちをきちんとショーカイするんだろ
客間じゃなきゃダメなの!
はァ…
だからパパは
紅茶を淹れて持って来てください!
……
マイターこっち来てー!

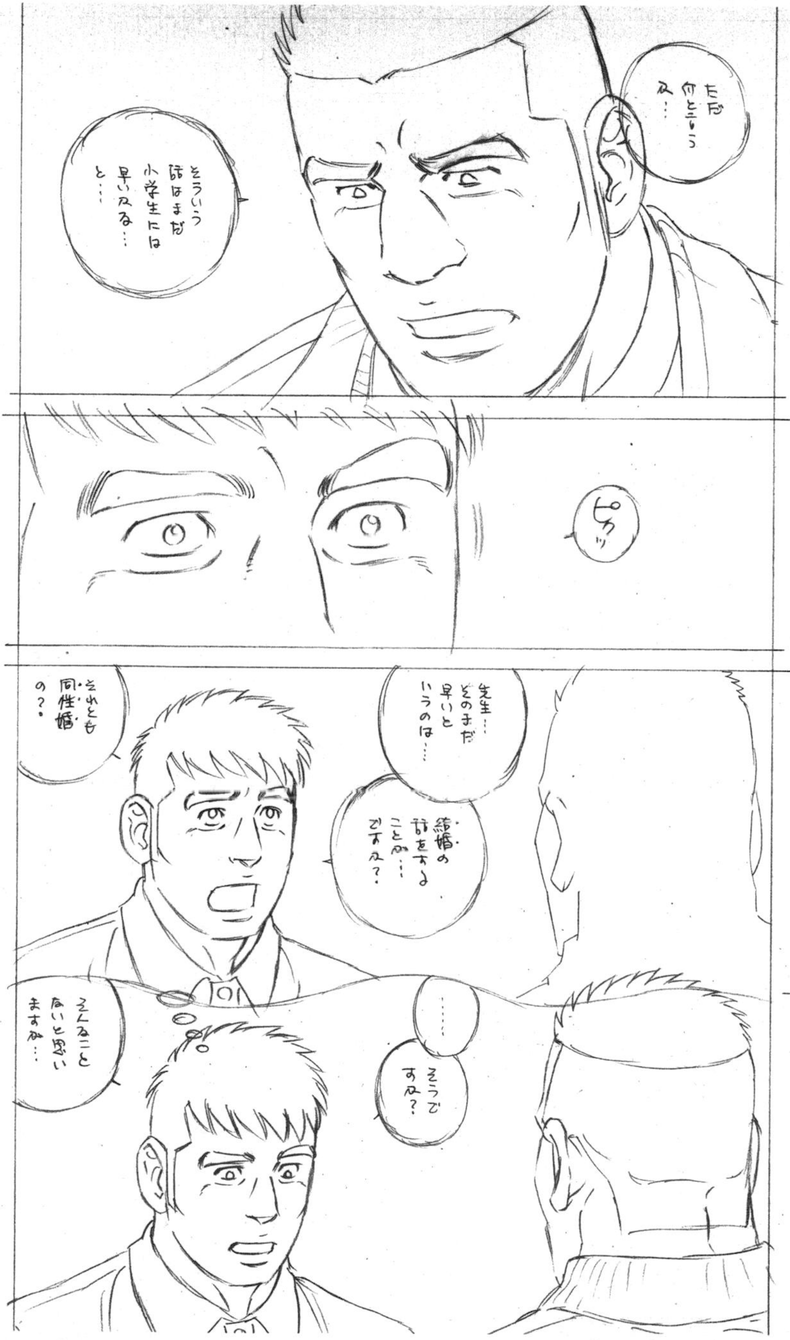
ただ何と言うか…
そういう話はまだ小学生には早いかなと…
ピクッ
先生…そのまだ早いというのは…
結婚の話をすることがですか？
それとも同性婚の？
……
そうですか？
そんなことないと思いますが…

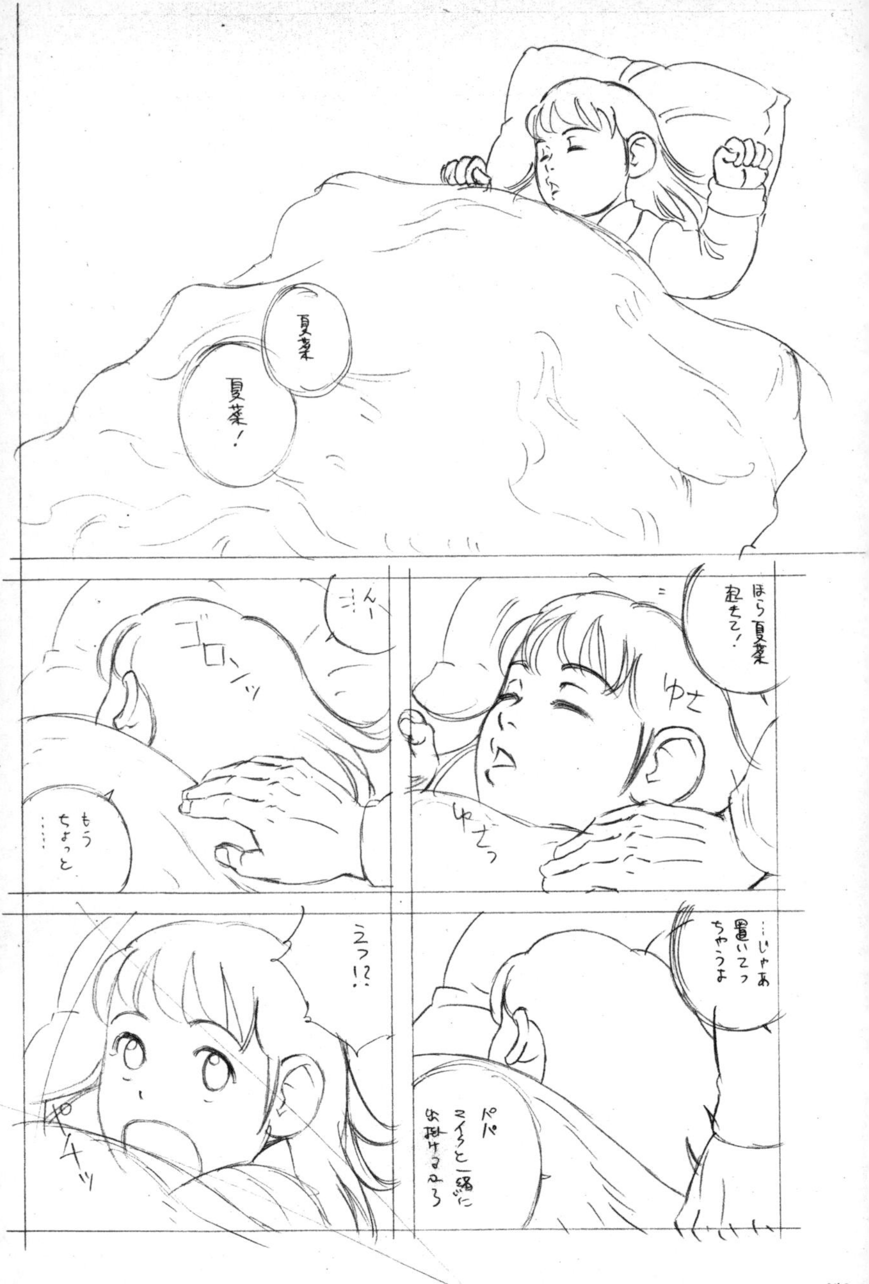
夏菜
夏菜！
ほら夏菜 起きて！
ゆさ
ゆさっ
ん～
ゴロンッ
もう ちょっと……
…じゃあ 置いてっちゃうよ
パパ ミイ子と一緒に 出掛けるぞ
えっ!?
パチッ

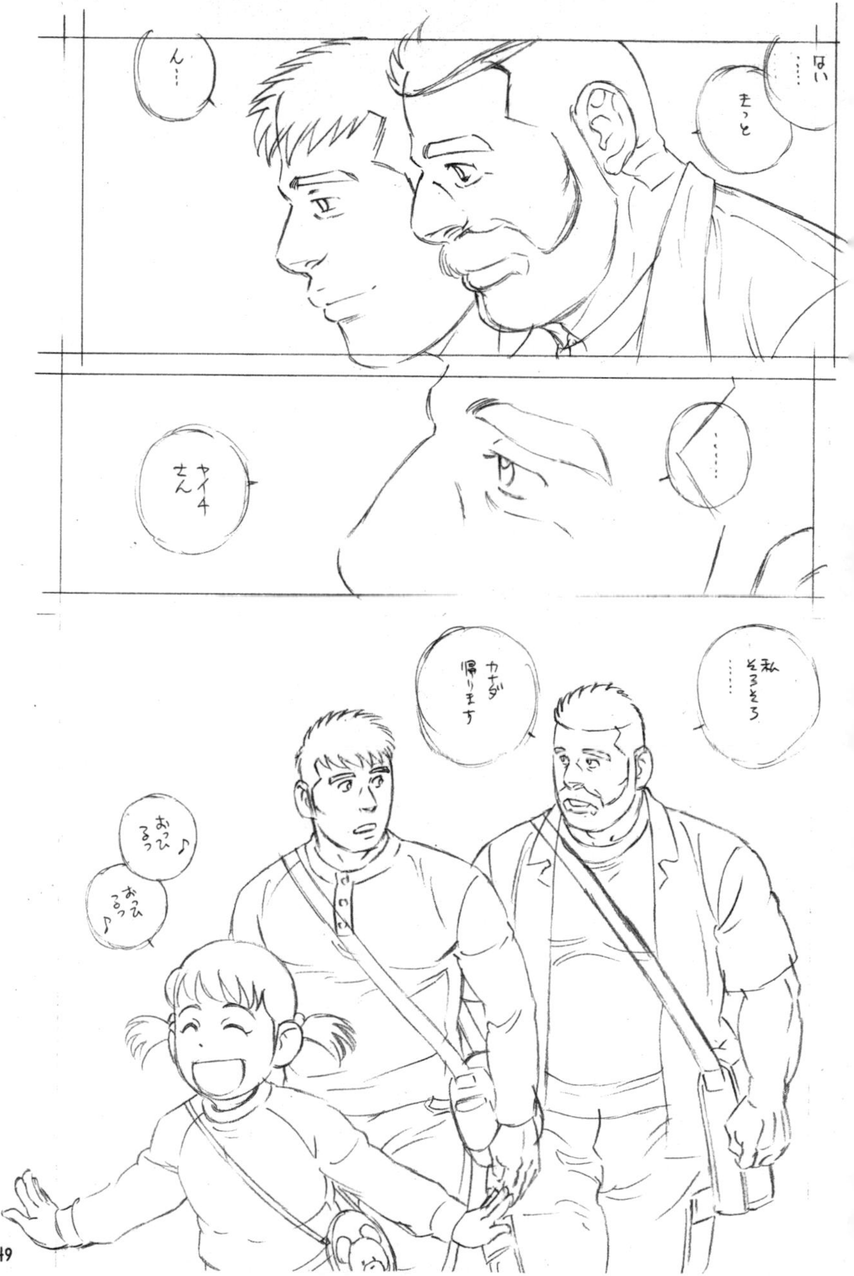

はい……
きっと
ん…
……
ヤイチさん
私そろそろ……
カナダ帰ります
おっひるっ♪
おっひるっ♪

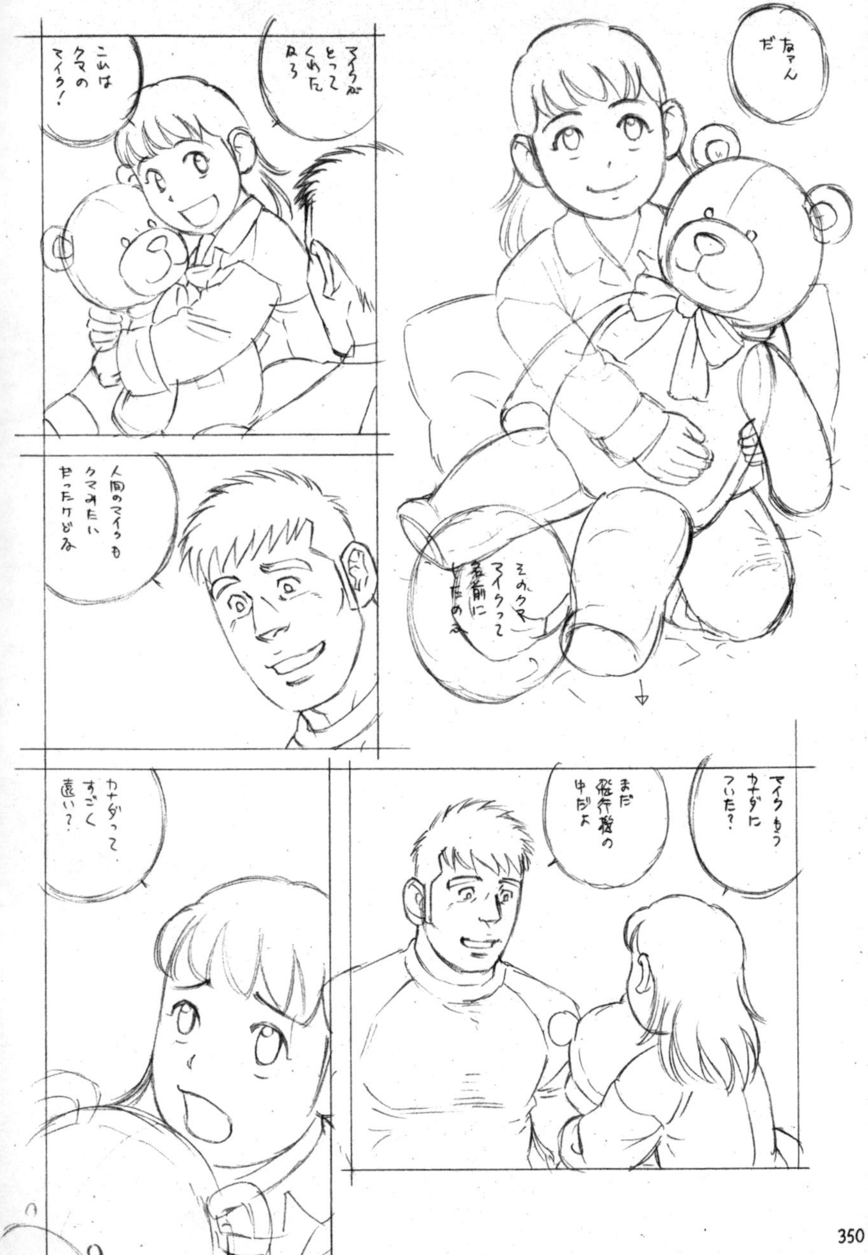
なァんだ
そのクママイクって名前にしたのね
マイクがとってくれたねろ
これはクマのマイク！
人間のマイクもクマみたいだったケどな
マイクもうカナダについた？
まだ飛行機の中だよ
カナダってすごく遠い？

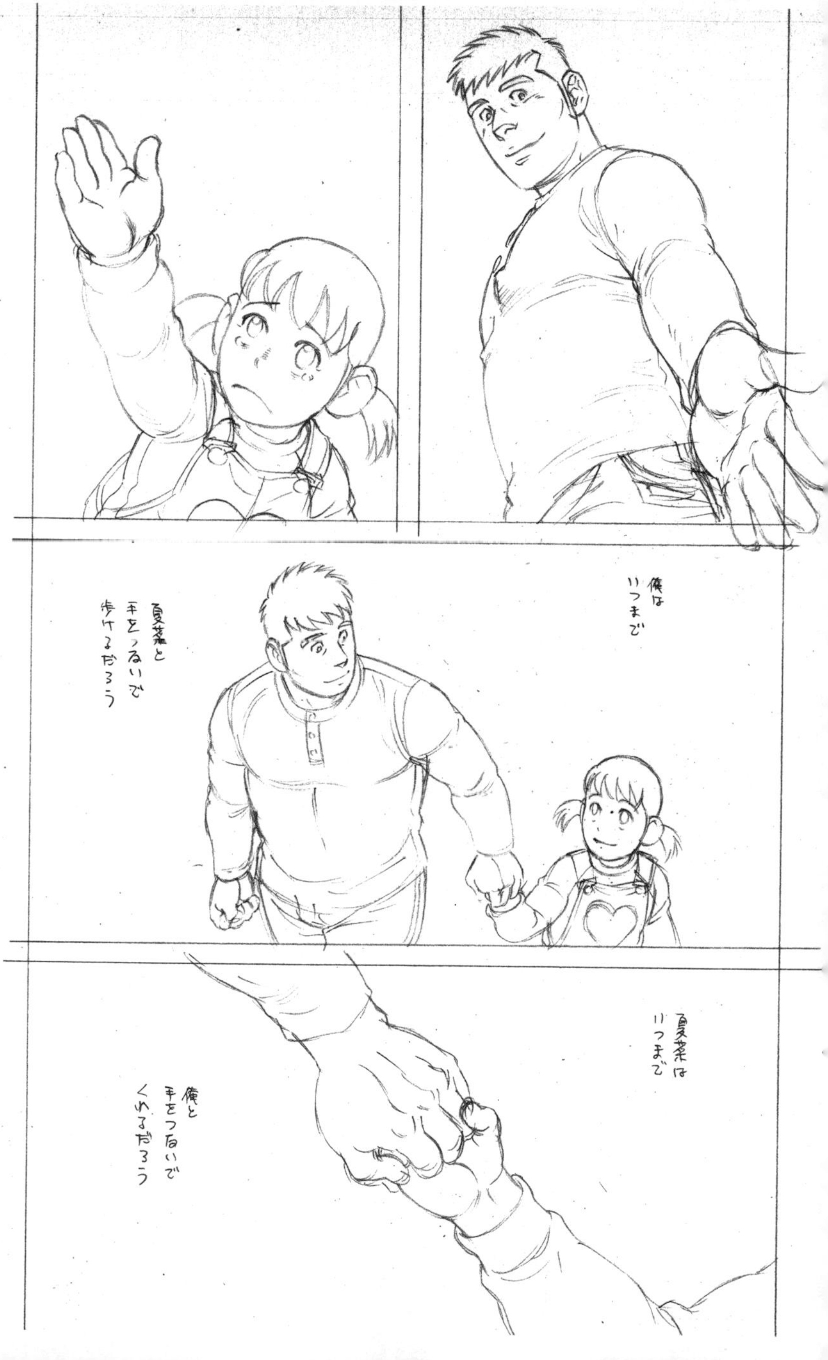
俺は
いつまで
夏菜と
手をつないで
歩けるだろう
夏菜は
いつまで
俺と
手をつないで
くれるだろう

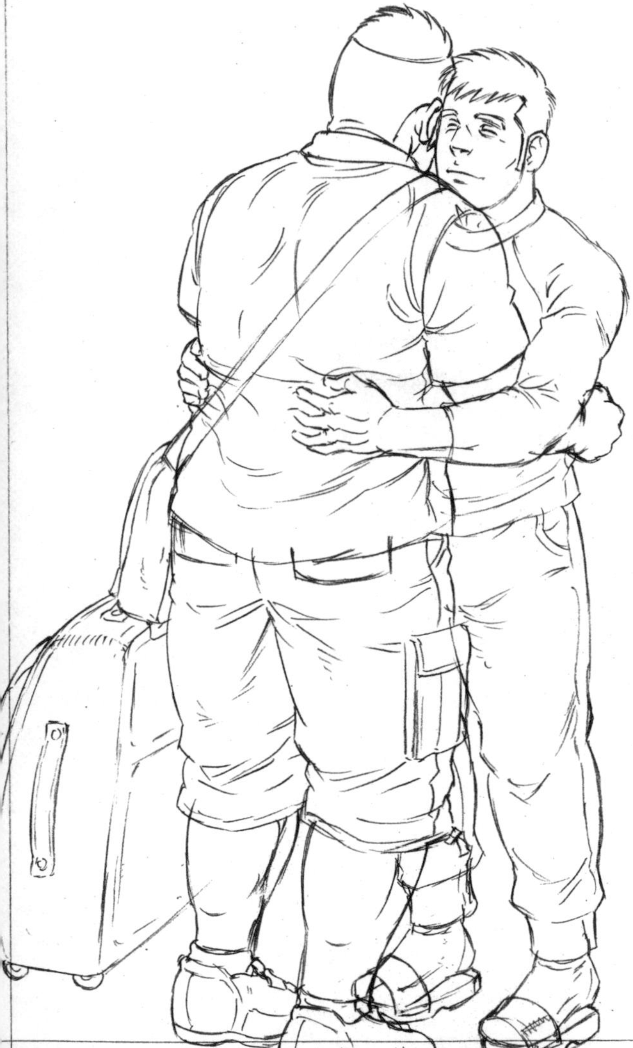

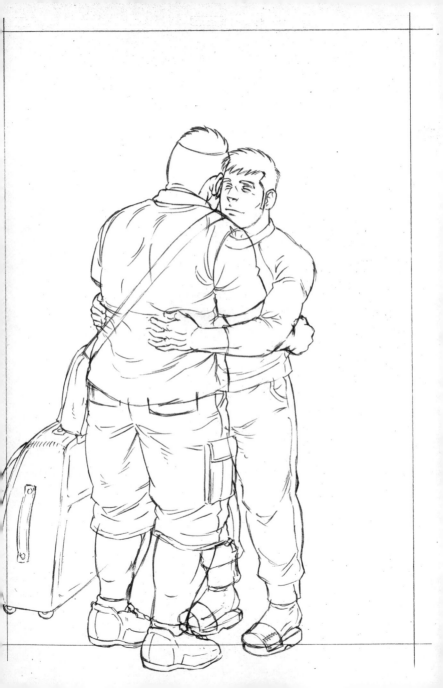

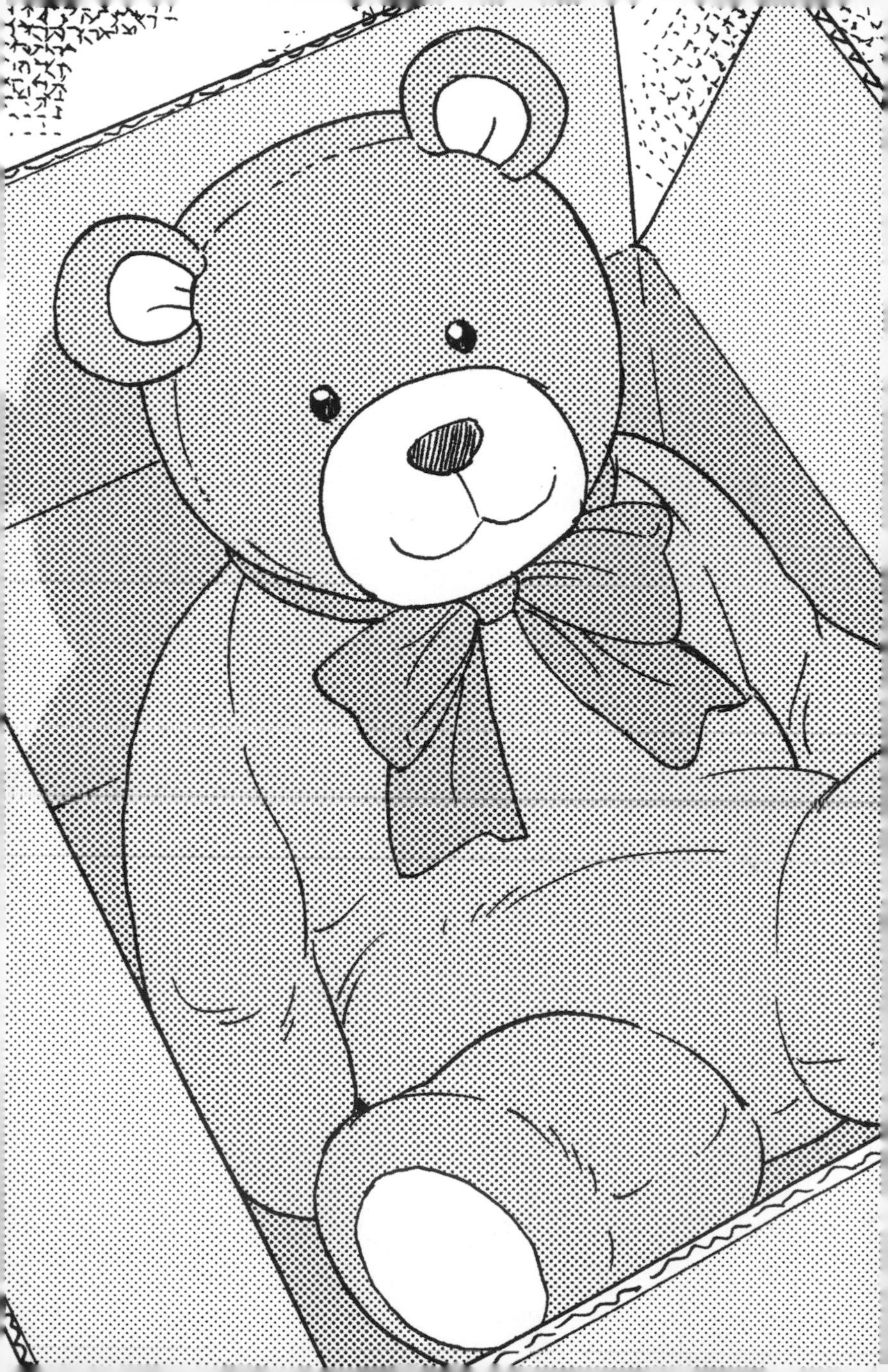

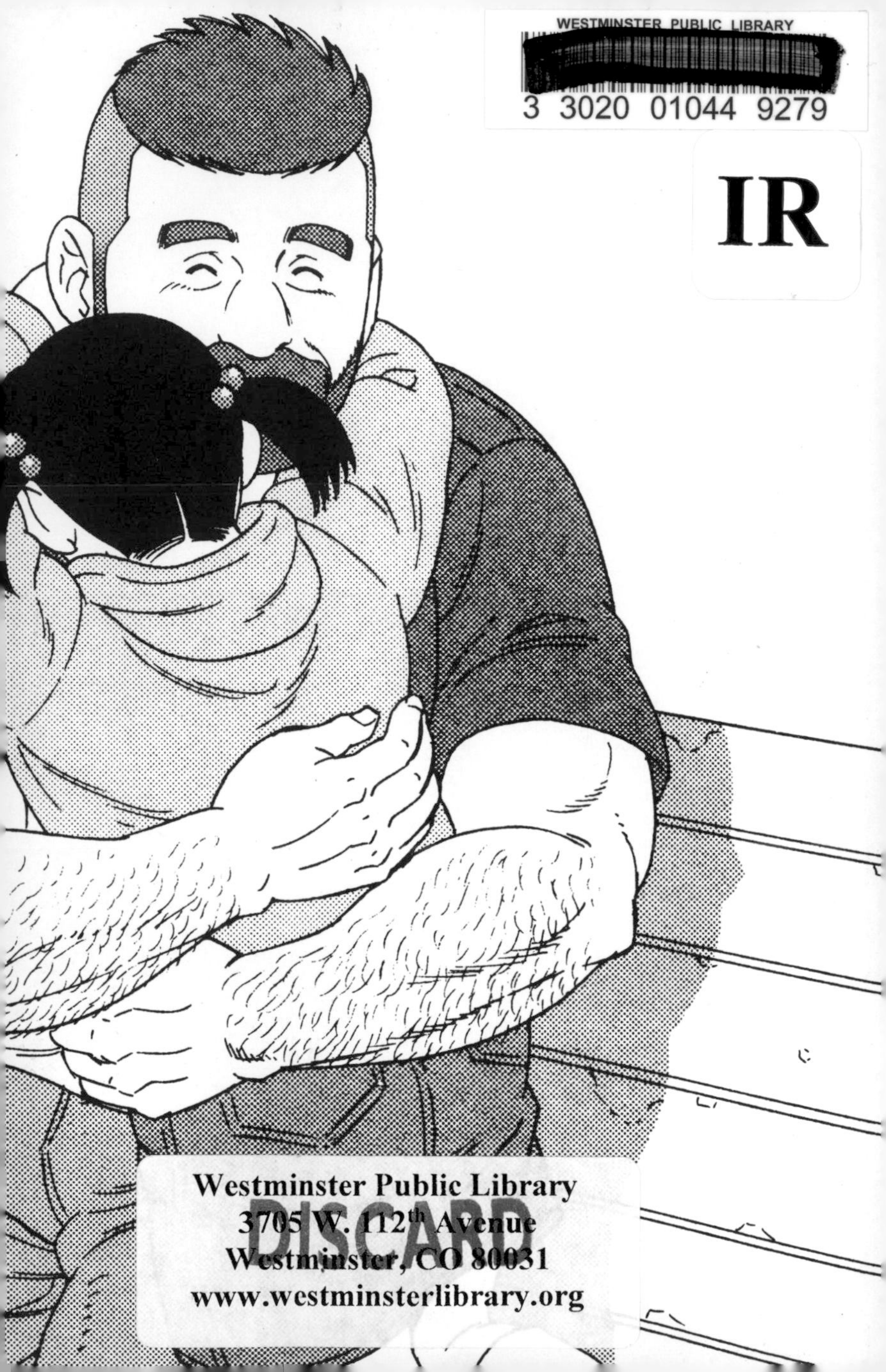